THIRD EDITION
INTERNATIONAL POLITICS on the World Stage

I count myself in nothing else so happy
As in a soul remembering my good friends.

Shakespeare, *King Richard II*

DEDICATED TO LINDA, JOHN, ADAM, AND EMILY BANTELL BY UNCLE JOHN

John T. Rourke, Ph.D., is a professor of political science at The University of Connecticut. He is the author of *Congress and the Presidency in U.S. Foreign Policymaking* (Westview, 1985), *Making Foreign Policy: United States, Soviet Union, China* (Brooks/Cole, 1990), the editor of *Taking Sides: Clashing Views on Controversial Issues in World Politics,* Third Edition (Dushkin Publishing Group, 1991), and the author of numerous articles and papers. He enjoys teaching introductory classes, and he does so each semester at the university's Storrs and Hartford campuses. His regard for the students has molded his approach of conveying scholarship in a language and within a frame of reference that undergraduates can appreciate. Rourke believes, as the theme of this book reflects, that politics affect us all, and we can affect politics. Rourke practices what he propounds; he is involved in the university's internship program, advises one of its political

clubs, has served as a staff member of Connecticut's legislature, and has been involved in political campaigns on the local, state, and national levels.

THIRD EDITION

INTERNATIONAL POLITICS
on the World Stage

JOHN T. ROURKE

University of Connecticut

DPG

The Dushkin Publishing Group, Inc.

Printed in the United States of America

Library of Congress Catalog Card Number: 91-70273

International Standard Book Number (ISBN) 0-87967-923-9

Third Edition, First Printing

The Dushkin Publishing Group, Inc., Sluice Dock, Guilford, Connecticut 06437

PREFACE

When Dean Acheson wrote his autobiography, he called it *Present at the Creation*. His title refers to the genesis of the cold war and the Western alliance system during his service in the State Department. The bipolar world that Acheson and others, East and West, helped mold has passed. Now it is our turn to be present at the creation, this time of a post–cold war world. Such moments of birth present rare opportunities to begin—almost—anew; but beginnings are also times of uncertainty and peril.

This Edition: Changes and Organization   As a result of this text's view that our lives are inescapably affected by world politics, *International Politics on the World Stage*, Third Edition, stresses the impact that world events and international interdependence have on your students' lives. In addition to highlighting the effect that the world has on them, this approach includes pointing out to students the connection between the events of current history and the theories of international politics that have been conceived and refined by political scientists.

When I wrote the second edition I expanded the depth of coverage considerably and did some organizational adjustments based on reactions to the first edition. Future editions, I thought to myself, would be a lot easier. Wrong! This edition proved to be a major challenge and effort. You will see that there is an emphasis on being current without being journalistic. The end of the cold war, the reunification of Germany, the economic and political travails of the Soviet Union, the Middle East conflict of 1990–91, the treaty limiting conventional forces in Europe, the emerging START treaty, and other recent events are all extensively detailed. It is also important to be as current as possible with the massive amounts of changing data that details economic performance and capacity, weapons levels and transfers, and other statistical aspects of world politics. I have used original sources for my data when possible so that students will have the most recent information available.

Additional Chapter   The breathtaking changes we all have witnessed have prompted several changes in this edition beyond extensive updating. Perhaps the most obvious is that there is an extra chapter. I have added chapter 19 on the biosphere, its social and ecological issues, and the progress on them through international cooperation. As a reflection of the changes we are witnessing in world politics, this edition also contains more discussion of international political economy. Most significantly here, there is now an entire chapter, 18, devoted to the issues of and progress toward international and regional economic cooperation (with a particular emphasis on the European Community).

Other Chapters Have Changed Conceptually or in Emphasis Chapter 9 on power, for one, conceptually reorganizes its discussion along functional lines instead of the earlier tangible/intangible dichotomy. As an example of changed emphasis, chapter 10 on the use of force happily reduces its discussion of theater-level nuclear war; unhappily, it has become necessary to increase its analysis of chemical warfare. Chapter 5 has more on the impact of domestic forces on Soviet foreign policy; chapter 6 increases the discussion of the national divisions within the U.S.S.R.; and chapter 7 includes expanded sections on the strong ebb of communism and the less certain flow of democracy in the Soviet Union and elsewhere.

Recent Intellectual Debates This edition also includes new or expanded discussions of some of the provocative ideas that have stirred the intellectual community in recent years. Among others these include Francis Fukuyama's thesis that democracy is becoming the accepted norm of governance, the renewed controversy over whether democracies are more peaceful than authoritarian forms of government, John Mearsheimer's view that the end of the cold war may bring chaos and danger to Central Europe, the continuing debate on Paul Kennedy's theory about declining U.S. power, the argument of many scholars that noncoercive power is on the ascent and coercive power is on the wane, and the assertion by a few scholars that war is about to be a thing of the past, at least among the major powers.

Data and Graphics Many new tables, figures, photographs, maps, and other graphics have been added to emphasize, expand, and give visual life to ideas. Also, significant revisions have been made to both the instructor's manual and to the extensive test-bank that is available from the publisher in both printed and computerized versions. These are further explained in the paragraph on Supplements on page viii, along with the new Student Atlas of World Politics.

Research, Citations, Bibliography, and Suggested Readings One of the aims of this text is to bring together a representative sampling of the latest research in international relations. Scholarly articles, so often ignored in survey texts, are particularly emphasized. This research is documented by extensive references using the "in-text" APA style and by a significant bibliography. In addition to recognizing my intellectual debt to a host of scholars, the references and bibliography also serve as a suggested reading list for students, as explained to them in the "To the Students" section of this preface. As such, references are often meant to serve as a suggested reading and do not necessarily mean that the cited author(s) propounded what is being said at the point of reference.

Using this approach to references and further readings, instead of the end-of-chapter placement, gives inquisitive students an immediate suggestion for additional reading.

Organization   Someday someone will invent a modular, snap-together text that instructors can rearrange so that it will follow their own concepts and syllabus in exact order. Unfortunately, that day has not yet arrived. For those instructors whose organizations differ from mine, care has been given to the table of contents and to the index in order to facilitate integrating the text with your syllabus. You will find, for example, that:

>   **Economics** is discussed in chapter 1 (how it affects students), 9 (as a basis of power), 13 and 14 (developed and less developed countries), and 18 (cooperation).

>   **Arms and force** are addressed in all or parts of chapters 1, 9, 10, 11, and 17.

>   **Moral and humanitarian issues** are taken up extensively in chapters 7, 16, and 19 and also form an important part of the discussions of national interest, force, penetration, and economic challenges in, respectively, chapters 8, 10, 11, and 18.

Despite the substantial changes I have made in this edition, the basic organization of the text continues to reflect my view of world politics. The more I study the subject, the more I am impressed with the idea that the world is a primitive political society. As such, it is a political system that is marked by little organization, by frequent violence, and by a limited sense of global responsibility. It is a world of conflict. But there is also a world of cooperation, a countertheme, based on a still-limited desire among states and their people to cooperate globally as they begin to realize that their fates are inextricably entwined with one another and with the political, economic, social, and environmental future of our planet.

The Parts   Part I, which includes chapters 1 through 5, discusses how to study international politics. Students will read in chapter 1 that there are realists and idealists and will, I hope, be prompted to think about where they, their professors, and others with whom they may discuss politics stand on the realist-idealist scale. Although I take a realist approach, I find myself less sure of my own wisdom on this point as time goes by. In fact, I have become convinced that substantial changes have to be made in the way international politics is conducted. Perhaps "realism with a nagging idealist conscience" would be an apt description of this text's orientation.

Part I also addresses levels of analysis. As students will soon discover, academics disagree about the proper focus of study. Three levels (system, individual, and state) are presented here. The text primarily utilizes state-level analysis (how countries make foreign policy) as discussed in chapter 5, but, here again, my views have evolved and changed since the first edition. The more I learn, the more I have become impressed with the role of system-level analysis (how the nature of the world system influences politics); there are two full chapters on this subject. Chapter 2 outlines the evolution of the world political system, and chapter 3 discusses system-level theory. Both of these chapters pay particular attention to the profound system change that is now occurring. Since it is unwise to ignore the human factor in international politics, that level is explored in chapter 4.

Part II, which includes chapters 6, 7, and 8, deals with some of the motivating factors that affect foreign policy-making including nationalism; ideas, ideology, and morality; and national interest.

Part III, consisting of chapters 9 through 14, examines the way the world drama is played out. In this part, I discuss power, force, penetration and intervention, diplomacy, the economics of the developed countries, and the economics of the less developed countries. Here is a "world full of sound and fury."

Part IV, including chapters 15 through 19, introduces some new issues and also reexamines some of the subjects discussed earlier, but this time from the perspective of cooperation. The chapters on international organization, international law, disarmament and arms control, economic cooperation, and social and environmental cooperation detail some of the problems we and our world face and the ways we are beginning to cooperate in an attempt to solve them.

Supplements   There are several supplements that have been created to assist both instructors and students in the use of this text. The instructor's resource guide, *Teaching and Testing from International Politics on the World Stage,* outlines and discusses the text's objectives, contains several analytical exercises, and gives several other teaching supports. In addition, there are approximately 1,900 multiple-choice and essay questions organized by chapter and degree of difficulty. These examination questions are also available on EZ-TEST computer disc. For the students, and new to this edition, there is the *Student Atlas of World Politics.* This innovative supplement contains 14 full-color world maps that illustrate key geopolitical concepts and relationships. It is available at no cost with copies of the text purchased from the publisher.

To the Student

The world, familiar to us and unknown.

Shakespeare, *Henry V*

Remembering Chris Geoffrey   June 2, 1989, was a Friday. Chris Geoffrey died that day. Chris's death is memorialized near what remains of the Berlin Wall. There are many other markers there. They are dedicated to the people who were killed while trying to escape over, under, and through the Wall to West Berlin. The first markers are for those gunned down in 1961 just after the Wall was built. Chris's memorial is the last.

I was in Berlin just a little over a year after Chris was killed. July 1, 1990, was the day of German economic union. It was also the first day that there were no more guards at the Wall. You could travel freely in either direction, and along with crowds of Germans I had the exhilarating experience of taking an elevated tram over the wall, past the now-empty machine-gun towers, and into East Berlin. The tram was crowded; I had to stand. I did not think I was nervous, but when we arrived at the first stop in East Berlin there was a welt on my hand from holding the overhead strap too tightly.

Each year for the past few years the National Football League has held a preseason exhibition game or two in Europe. One was scheduled for West Berlin to be played in August 1990 between the Los Angeles Rams and the Kansas City Chiefs. When I got off the tram at the first station in East Berlin there was already a poster up advertising the game. Chris had died on June 2, 1989, trying to beat the Wall. Just 393 days later Chris could have caught the tram in the other direction, gone over to West Berlin, and bought a ticket to the Rams-Chiefs game.

This story about Chris, the Wall, and the NFL is about two things. One of these is the amazing changes that have occurred in the past two years. I would love to say that as a brilliant political prognosticator I foresaw the sudden end of the cold war. But I did not. Neither did anyone else. Thus this book is both an analytical epitaph to the bipolar confrontation that, among other tragedies, ended Chris Geoffrey's life, and a glimpse at what can be seen of the future, post–cold war world.

The second important message that Chris's story contains is that world politics is about people. Sometimes people are victims. Chris was. People are also players on the world stage. Chris was that too, and the deaths that occurred at the Wall and the demands of the East Germans for freedom and a unified German people helped end the cold war.

The strong point of view of this text is that we all are both affected by and can affect world politics. Just like Chris.

The text that follows is my attempt to introduce you to the complex and compelling study of international politics. Prefaces are often given scant attention, but they can be a valuable learning tool for you. They let you in on the author's conceptions, his or her mental pictures, of a text. What is the author's approach? What are the author's orientations and biases? Does the text have one or more basic themes? How is the text organized? In this preface I have addressed these issues. I hope you'll read it.

In writing this text I have tried to use straightforward prose and have assumed that students who take this course know little about international politics. To help you further, I have included an outline at the beginning of each chapter. Before you read the chapter, pay attention to its outline. It is axiomatic that if you know where you are going, you will find it a lot easier to get there! Additionally, I have written a numbered summary at the end of each chapter to help you quickly review the scope of the chapter. This, of course, is no substitute for carefully studying the chapter.

There are many figures, tables, maps, and photographs in this book. Pay close attention to them. You will find that they graphically represent many of the ideas presented in the text and will help you understand them. But if you really want to know all about something, you will have to read a lot more than just this book and to involve yourself in more than just the course for which it has been assigned. To make it easier for you to do this I have chosen an "in-text" reference system that gives you citations as you read. Thus (Nye, 1990:18) refers to page 18 of the book or article written by (in this case, Professor Joseph) Nye in 1990, which is listed alphabetically in the references and bibliography. I have also noted studies that helped me think about and organize various topics and those which might be informative to you. I encourage you to utilize the references and bibliography to advance your knowledge beyond the boundaries of this text. You will find a list of the abbreviations that I have used throughout the book on page xxxi. Explanations for terms set in **boldface** will be found in the Glossary at the end of the text.

Some note should be made of this book's title, *International Politics on the World Stage,* and the Shakespearean quotations that begin each chapter and are used from time to time to highlight a point. The idea behind this motif is to convey some of the sweep and complexity of the world drama. No one who has ever read William Shakespeare can dismiss his masterpieces as easily understood or inconsequential. The events on the world stage are similar—complex, full of drama, sometimes hopeful, often tragic, and always riveting. But you, the reader, would be mistaken to assume that the play analogy means that, as a member of the audience, you can be content to sit back and watch the plot unfold. Quite to the contrary, part of what makes the world drama so compelling is that the audience is seated on stage and is part of, as well as witness to, the action that is unfolding. And that is one reason why I have also quoted more recent world players. Shakespeare's plays are of the past; the world drama is ongoing. Furthermore, as in an improvisational play, you in the audience can become involved, and, given the consequences of a potentially tragic rather than happy ending, you ought to become involved. If there is anything this text proposes, it is that each of us is intimately affected by international politics and that we all have a responsibility and an ability to become shapers of the script. As we shall see, our play has alternative scripts, and what the next scene brings depends in part on us.

I am sincerely interested in getting feedback from the faculty members and students who use this text. My pretensions to perfection have long since been dashed, and your recommendations for additions, deletions, and changes in future editions will be appreciated and seriously considered. People do write me, and I write or call them back! You are encouraged to join this correspondence by writing to me in care of The Dushkin Publishing Group, Inc., Sluice Dock, Guilford, Connecticut, 06437. This book, just like the world, can be made better, but its improvement depends heavily on whether or not you are concerned enough to think and act.

John T. Rourke

ACKNOWLEDGMENTS

A difficult task is to keep this acknowledgment of those who have contributed down to a reasonable length. There are many who have played an important part, and my debt to each of them is great. I have tried to make adjustments wherever possible. Some contributors have pointed out specific concerns about matters of fact or interpretation, and a number of corrections were made. On a larger scale, the increased coverage of economics and the chapter on the biosphere are responses in part to suggestions. Ralph Carter at Texas Christian University, Robert B. Charlick at Cleveland State University, Dennis R. Gordon at Santa Clara University, Zho Keyean at Dalhousie University, Stephen Manning at Wittenberg University, Miroslav Nincic at University of California/Davis, Robert A. Poirier at Northern Arizona University, Denis Snook at Oregon State University, and Thomas Zant at Forest Park Community College all supplied helpful suggestions. Two of my colleagues at the University of Connecticut, Elizabeth Crump Hanson and J. Garry Clifford, have used my text in their classes, and their running commentary on matters of theory, fact, and students' reactions have been invaluable. From a somewhat different perspective, James A. Turner, Jr., who teaches at Rampart High School and uses this text in his advanced class on contemporary world affairs, has provided ideas and information that have made the third edition better than the second. I also owe a debt to each author listed in the bibliography of this and the previous editions. The work these scholars have done on specific subjects are the intellectual building blocks that are a significant part of the final structure of this, or any, worthwhile introductory textbook. This text is also evolutionary, and I want to continue to express my appreciation to all those who read and commented on the previous editions. Additionally, I also want to thank the colleagues who have taken the time at International Studies Association meetings or other conferences to give me the benefit of their views. I have even, on occasion, taken off my name tag and helped staff the Dushkin booth at professional meetings. The comments I have received in this anonymity have been sometimes encouraging, sometimes humbling, but always helpful.

Best of all, I have received many good suggestions from students. My own students have had to both read the text and listen to me, and their often obviously candid comments have helped the generations of students who will follow. My favorite was a sophomore who did not do well on his first exam and came to my office to lay blame at the door of the confounded textbook. As we talked, he made some interesting observations. It was also clear he had not connected the author's name on the front of the book with his professor. Boy, was he surprised when it finally dawned on him that he was grumping about the book to its author! Another interesting view was provided by

Professor Chand Wije at Kent State University. He uses the text as a supplement to his political geography course and had students write a review. He sent one of the papers (with the student author anonymous) to me. After some initial kind words, the student spent several pages pointing out improvements that could be made. Professor Wije gave the student an A; so would have I. One of the frustrations about writing an introductory text is that it has to encapsulate in a few sentences or paragraphs what might legitimately merit an entire book. If the student at Kent were to read the text again, though, he or she might find some of the paper's suggestions have been taken. I also received letters from students Nicole A. Stein at State University of New York at Binghamton and Lynn Verhuilla at Indiana University of Pennsylvania with both kind words and suggestions. Thanks!

I owe special thanks to Mark Denham of the University of Toledo, John Allen of the University of Connecticut, and Dale Greenawald of the Social Science Education Consortium, Inc., in Boulder, Colorado. Professor Denham shouldered the task of revising and updating the test item file for this edition and carried it off with great success. My colleague in Storrs, John Allen, was both the source of inspiration for and the creator of the new *Student Atlas of World Politics* that accompanies this edition. Dale Greenawald's analytical exercises in the instructor's guide, *Teaching and Testing with World Politics,* continue to be an outstanding feature of the learning package.

Then there is the staff of The Dushkin Publishing Group. They have encouraged me and supported me. I remain fortunate to have the very experienced and very talented John Holland as my editor. John has been ably assisted by Robert Mill. Bob has an amazing eye for detail, a keen sense of what is and what is not readable prose, and an adept diplomatic touch to convince me his corrections are necessary and proper. Diane Barker's proofreading added to the process of ensuring accuracy. I also want to thank the DPG typesetters headed by Libra Ann Cusack.

One of the things I like best about this edition is the excellent illustrations it contains. Pamela Carley Petersen has taken the lead in assembling photographs and editorial cartoons that bring powerful visual life to the concepts I express in words. Charles Vitelli not only performed the difficult, but crucial, task of arranging text and illustrations, he drew the original cartoons in this book. He took my raw mental images and turned them into wonderful representations of the issues being discussed in the text. In the same area, Whit Vye did an extraordinary job with the exacting art of creating the text's many tables and figures. To Harry Rinehart I owe a debt of gratitude for designing this edition.

I would also like to thank my publisher, Rick Connelly, president of The Dushkin Publishing Group, for his support in providing the resources that make this the most attractive and well-illustrated book on the market in its field.

Finally, anyone who has written will recognize that it is an intensely personal, as well as professional, experience. I am fortunate to have people around me who understand when I am seemingly glued to my word processor for long periods of time and who sometimes insist I shut my computer off. My son and friend John Michael helps me endure the ups and downs of the New York Giants and UConn athletic teams, shares the frustrations of fishing, and occasionally tries to interpret MTV for me. Susan and Jon Zimmerman are good and caring friends, and I owe them much, of which they know. Claudia Jane Elliott is a soulmate of many years who, like Halley's Comet, brightens the sky during her far-too-infrequent passes through my universe. Fortunately for me, 1990 was a C. J. year. Some of my favorite people in this world are the Bantell family: Linda, John, Adam, and Emily. Through good times and through not-so-good periods they have been among the best of all things: good friends. I dedicate this edition to the Bantells as a symbol of my appreciation and of my affection for them.

To all of you:

I can no other answer make but thanks, thanks, and ever thanks.

Shakespeare, *Twelfth Night*

CONTENTS IN BRIEF

CONTENTS

3 System-Level Analysis   57

4 Individual-Level Analysis   83

National Interests and Orientations   197

PART III   The Instruments of International Politics   220

Power   223

10   Force   255

11   Penetration and Intervention   295

14   Economics: The South   395

LIST OF ILLUSTRATIONS

ABBREVIATIONS

The following abbreviations are used in the text for frequently cited sources:

AID	Agency for International Development (U.S.)
BG	Boston Globe
BW	Business Week
CMEA	Council of Mutual Economic Assistance
CR	Congressional Record
CSM	Christian Science Monitor
FAO	Food and Agricultural Organization (UN)
HC	Hartford Courant
LAT	Los Angeles Times
NYT	New York Times
OECD	Organization for Economic Cooperation and Development
SIPRI	Stockholm International Peace Research Institute
WP	Washington Post
WSJ	Wall Street Journal

You may refer to this list for abbreviations that are used in the text:

ABM	Anti-Ballistic Missile (treaty)
ACDA	Arms Control Disarmament Agency
ALCM	Air-Launched Cruise Missile
ASEAN	Association of Southeast Asian Nations
ASW	Antisubmarine Warfare
BIS	Bank for International Settlements
BMD	Ballistic Missile Defense
C³I	Command, Control, Communication, and Intelligence
CAP	Common Agricultural Policy
CEP	Circular Error Probability
CFCs	Chlorofluorocarbons
CFE	Conventional Forces in Europe (treaty)
CIA	Central Intelligence Agency (U.S.)
CITES	Convention on the International Trade in Endangered Species
CMP	Cruise Missile Platform
COCOM	Coordinating Committee for Multilateral Export Controls
COMINT	Communication Intelligence
CSCE	Conference for Security and Cooperation in Europe
CTB	Comprehensive Test Ban
CW	Chemical Warfare
EBRDEE	European Bank for Reconstruction and Development in Eastern Europe

EC	Economic Community	**IFAD**	International Fund for Agricultural Development
ECOSOC	Economic and Social Council (UN)		
ECOWA	Economic Community of West Africa	**IFC**	International Finance Corporation
		IGO	Intergovernmental Organization
ECSC	European Coal and Steel Community	**IMF**	International Monetary Fund
ELINT	Electronic Intelligence	**INF**	Intermediate-range Nuclear Forces (treaty)
EMP	Electromagnetic Pulse		
ERP	European Recovery Plan (Marshall Plan)	**KGB**	Komitet Gosudarstvennoi Bezopasnosti (U.S.S.R.)
EURATOM	European Atomic Energy Community	**LDC**	Less Developed Country
FAEs	Fuel-Air Explosives	**LOI**	Launch on Impact
FAO	Food and Agricultural Organization (UN)	**LOW**	Launch on Warning
		LUA	Launch Under Attack
GATT	General Agreement on Tariffs and Trade	**MAD**	Mutual Assured Destruction
		MNC	Multinational Corporation
GCD	General and Complete Disarmament	**MTCR**	Missile Technology Control Regime
GDP	Gross Domestic Product	**NATO**	North Atlantic Treaty Organization
GNP	Gross National Product	**NBC**	Nuclear-Biological-Chemical (war)
GRU	Chief Intelligence Directorate of the General Staff (U.S.S.R.)	**NCA**	National Command Authority
		NGO	Nongovernmental Organization
HUMINT	Human Intelligence	**NIC**	Newly Industrializing Country
IAEA	International Atomic Energy Agency	**NIEO**	New International Economic Order
IBRD	International Bank for Reconstruction and Development	**NPT**	Non-Proliferation Treaty
		NSA	National Security Agency
ICBM	Intercontinental Ballistic Missile	**NSC**	National Security Council
IDA	International Development Association	**NTBs**	Nontariff Barriers

NTM	National Technical Means
NUT	Nuclear Utilization Theory
OAS	Organization of American States
OAU	Organization of African Unity
OECD	Organization for Economic Cooperation and Development
OPEC	Organization of Petroleum Exporting Countries
OSI	On-Site Inspection
OTA	Office of Technology Assessment
PCIJ	Permanent Court of International Justice (UN)
PLA	People's Liberation Army (China)
PLO	Palestine Liberation Organization
SDI	Strategic Defense Initiative
SDRs	Special Drawing Rights
SEA	Single European Act
SEATO	Southeast Asia Treaty Organization
SIGINT	Signal Intelligence
SIOP	Strategic Integrated Operational Plan
SLBM	Sea-Launched Ballistic Missile
SLV	Space-Launch Vehicle
SOP	Standard Operating Procedures
SRAM	Short-Range Attack Missile
SSBN	Ballistic Missile Submarine
START	Strategic Arms Reduction Talks

UNCTAD	UN Conference on Trade and Development
UNDP	UN Development Program
UNEP	UN Environmental Program
UNESCO	UN Educational, Scientific, and Cultural Organization
UNFPA	UN International Planned Parenthood Federation
UNICEF	UN International Children's Emergency Fund
UNITA	National Union for the Total Independence of Angola
VAT	Value-Added Tax
WFC	World Food Council
WHO	World Health Organization
WTO	Warsaw Treaty Organization

Countries of the World

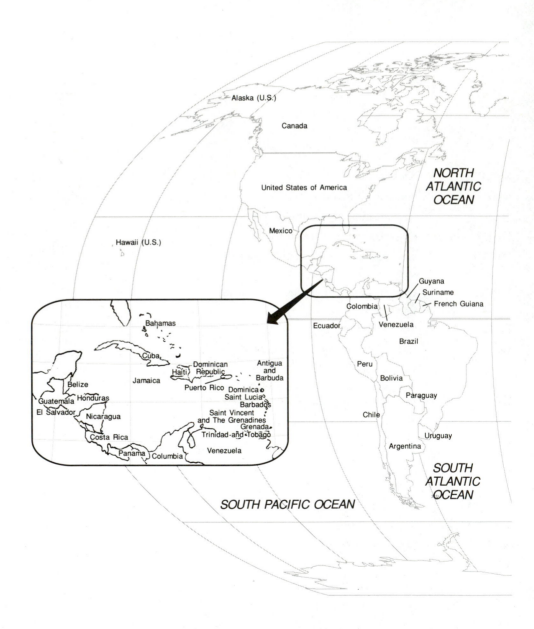

Many political boundaries are in dispute. Later in the text you will read about some of these controversies.

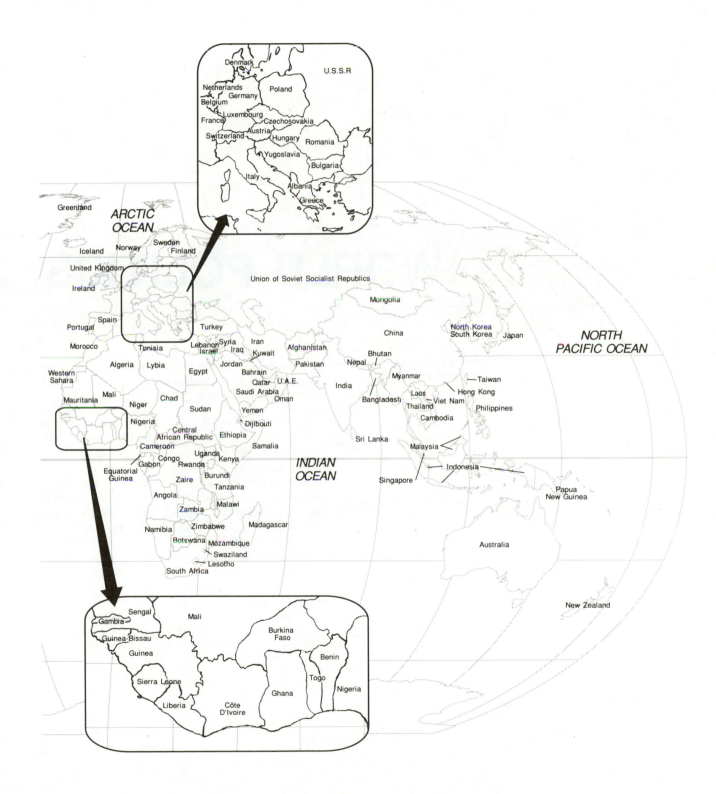

PART I

WORLD POLITICS:

This book is about world politics. It is a subject that fascinates many scholars, political practitioners, journalists, and thinking citizens. The course of international events is also, as we shall see, closely involved with the quality, perhaps even the continuance, of your life. As President John F. Kennedy once put it, "Domestic policy can only defeat us, foreign policy can kill us" (Schlesinger, 1967:395).

With that caveat in mind, this book sets out to explore the forces that shape our political and, to a degree, our physical, cultural, and economic world. This text is organized according to two fundamental and countervailing characteristics of world politics. One is the world divided, competitive, and conflictive. This is the prevailing trait, and the first three parts of the book—which examine the study of international politics in general, the forces that motivate policy, and the instruments used to carry out foreign policy— deal primarily with this competitive side of international politics. The second characteristic of world politics is,

2

YOU AND OTHERS

or ought to be, cooperation, and thus in the last part of the book I focus on the progress toward greater international accord and the need for even more intense and extensive cooperation. Each of these four parts is outlined briefly in the preface.

This part examines the impact of world politics on you and explains how you and others can study international relations. Chapter 1 deals with the interrelationship between you and the world. I try to make the point in this chapter that the world affects you and that you can affect the world. Chapter 1 also introduces the fundamental dimensions of world politics and then goes on to discuss some of the basic orientations, such as realism and idealism, from which you may approach the practice of international politics.

Chapters 2 through 5 take up what is called the "level-of-analysis problem." The question is: what do we study? Some scholars would say, study the international system. Others would say, study how countries make foreign policy. Still others would say, study how

individuals affect world politics. But the best answer is to study all three.

Chapters 2 and 3 deal with the international system. What are the major world forces that shape politics? Chapter 2 sketches the growth and events in the international system over the last six centuries; it pays particular attention to recent startling changes in Europe and the U.S.S.R. Then chapter 3 lays out the basic theory of systems analysis. Chapter 4 addresses the role of individual decisionmakers and, more generically, the impact of humans as psychological, sociological, and ethological species.

The last chapter in Part I examines the primary actor on the world stage, the state or country. The focus there is on how countries establish goals, how they decide on policies to accomplish those goals, and how they implement those decisions. As we shall see, the actual process is a good deal less rational than we would like it to be.

3

An honest tale speeds best being plainly told.

Shakespeare, *Richard III*

Our knowledge is a little island in a great ocean of nonknowledge.

Isaac Bashevis Singer

THE STUDY OF WORLD POLITICS

All the world's a stage," William Shakespeare wrote in the second act of *As You Like It*, "and all the men and women merely players." The Bard of Avon was a wise political commentator as well as a literary great. Shakespeare's lines are used here because they help convey the drama of world politics. The characters are different, of course, the United States, China, and the Soviet Union replacing those of Shakespeare's time and imagination. Beyond that, though, there is a remarkable parallel between international relations and the master's plays. Both are cosmic and complex. The characters are sometimes heroic and at other times petty. The action is always dramatic and often tragic. As with any good play, the audience was drawn into the action at The Globe, the theater where Shakespeare staged his works. Similarly, in the global theater of international politics, we are drawn in. Indeed, we are seated on the stage, no matter how remote the action may seem or how much we may want to ignore it. Like it or not, we and the world are stuck with each other. The progress of the play, even if it continues its long run or closes early, is something we will all enjoy—or endure.

Another quotation from Shakespeare—this time from *Macbeth*—is also worth thinking about here. A despairing Macbeth tells us that life "struts and frets his hour upon the stage" in a tale "full of sound and fury." Again the playwright hits the mark! The history and current state of world politics do not make for a peaceful scene. The view of this text is basically one of a world divided. The world drama has a cast of national actors at odds with one another. Although the actors, or countries, are often at peace, and although there are even elements of charity and humanity that can at times be found in them, they are also full of ambition, self-serving righteousness, and greed. It is a rare day when at least some of the actor states are not in open conflict. And even when they are not threatening one another, they are forever calculating what is good for themselves and then defining those ends in terms of universal justice and the common good of all humankind.

The Importance of Studying World Politics

The last line from Macbeth's soliloquy is where this text and Shakespeare part company. The Bard pronounces the action of life as "signifying nothing." That thought has a gloomy and fatalistic appeal. It allows us to ignore our responsibility. "What the hell," we can say. "What can I do?" That approach may be easy, but it is also self-defeating.

In general, this text does not try to tell you what to think. That would be neither appropriate nor successful. But one message *is* stressed here: the play is important and deserves our careful attention. We are not merely observers. We are inevitably actors because we are on the stage along with everybody else. What is more, the script is not set. It is an improvisational play with lots of room for ad-libbing, interpretation, and even changing the story line. Of course, most of us are bit players, many merely walk-ons with no lines, but we can speak up if we wish and join the action if we try. Capturing center stage is difficult, and even the great have not been able to hold it for long, but we can all play a part.

Well, you might say, if it is so hard to become a star, why bother? A bit player like me won't be missed. Besides, why should I even care? International politics is full of names and places I can't pronounce, which are far away, and which don't really affect me anyway. So why should I care?

The answer is that international politics does matter. It plays an important role in your life, and you should be concerned. To begin to see why, let's take a look at one leader who had the "it's far away, why bother" attitude.

The Danger and Futility of Ignoring World Politics

It was 1938 in Europe, and it was the last chance to stop Adolf Hitler. The Nazi Führer and his Third Reich threatened Czechoslovakia. But there was hope: the Czechoslovakians were well armed and were determined to remain free. Germany had not yet reached its full war potential. If only a major ally could be found to stand by Czechoslovakia and deter or defeat the Germans! Ah, the sad "might have beens" of history! Germany was not deterred and was not defeated until seven years later at the cost of tens of millions of lives.

The decision whether or not to help the Czechoslovakians largely rested on the shoulders of British prime minister Neville Chamberlain. But Chamberlain would not help. Czechoslovakia, he told his countrymen, was "a faraway country about which we know little." Britons agreed. It did seem far away, and if Hitler subjugated the Czechoslovakians, well, that was a pity, but it did not really matter to Great Britain. Within two years, as Luftwaffe bombs fell on London, Chamberlain's thesis was disproved. Little or large, far or near, Czechoslovakia did matter.[1]

In some ways we haven't learned much since 1938. Studies today show that North Americans know very little about the places, people, or politics of the world. Like Czechoslovakia,[2] there are many faraway countries about which we know little.

A National Geographic study released in late 1989 asked young people (18–24) in 10 countries (Canada, France, Italy, Japan, Mexico, the Soviet Union, Sweden, the United Kingdom, the United States, and West Germany) to identify 16 geographic spots on an unlabeled world map. These locations included 13 countries (the 10 countries in

---

1. For a recent revisionist review of appeasement, see Richardson (1988).
2. In 1990 the name of the country was changed to the Czech and Slovak Federal Republic.

The 1989 study sponsored by the National Geographic Society found that many people, especially young Americans, had a poor sense of geography. The 16 spots respondents were asked to identify were: Canada, Egypt, France, Italy, Japan, Mexico, the Republic of South Africa, the Soviet Union, Sweden, the United Kingdom (Great Britain), the United States, Vietnam, West Germany, Central America, the Pacific Ocean, and the Persian Gulf. Can you locate them on this map? Give it a try, then check your answers against a world map.

which the survey was conducted plus Egypt, Vietnam, and the Republic of South Africa), 1 region (Central America) and 2 bodies of water (the Pacific Ocean and the Persian Gulf). American young adults finished dead last with an average of 6.9 (43 percent) correct answers. Soviets in this age group gave an average of 9.3 correct answers, tying them for fourth with Italians and Canadians. Swedes, West Germans, and the Japanese finished in the top three spots. Among Americans, 68 percent could not find Vietnam, the scene of a long and costly American intervention only two decades ago. Only a little more than half could find Central America, less than half could locate Japan, and between 25 and 30 percent could not find West Germany or the Soviet Union. Indeed, 14 percent could not even find the United States. Interestingly, that was similar to Soviet young adults, 14 percent of whom also could not locate their country.

Another survey released in June 1990 by the Times Mirror Center for the People and the Press found that for adults under age 30 the ability to answer questions about current news events and people was the lowest since analysts had begun testing "news knowledge" in the early 1940s. In significant drops from earlier studies, a scant 24 percent said they had read a newspaper the previous day, and only 41 percent said they watched television news the previous day.

World Politics and Your Pocketbook

Chamberlain was wrong in 1938, and his views would be even less appropriate today. None of us is isolated from the impact of world politics. One way we are all affected is economically. The general impact of international economics on domestic societies expands as world industrial and financial structures become increasingly intertwined. Trade wins and loses jobs, and we are dependent on foreign sources for vital resources. Inflation is tied into foreign affairs, as is the domestic allocation of our own resources. The ties between national and international affairs are so close that one observer has coined a new word—**intermestic**—to symbolize the merger of *inter*national and do*mestic* concerns (Maning, 1979).

International Trade and Resource Factors

The interrelationship between *jobs and trade* is one way that international relations affects you. Exports to other countries create jobs. In the United States a total of 4 million Americans owe their jobs to exports. It is not coincidental that Connecticut, which has one of the lowest unemployment rates in the nation, is also the state with the highest percentage of its jobs (6 percent) related to exports. By 1990, in a sagging U.S. economy, analysts estimated that exports were accounting for one-half of the country's economic growth.

Foreign trade can also reduce jobs. During the 1980s the United States ran a massive trade deficit that peaked at $159.2 billion in 1987. By 1990, that figure had eased to a mid-year annualized projection of a better, but still unhealthy, $92.2 billion. Some industries have been particularly hard hit by import competition. There are only half the textile jobs there were a quarter century ago, primary metals processing employment declined by a third between 1980 and 1988, and in the same period 80,000 machinery-making jobs vanished.

International relations also affects you economically because your country probably depends on other countries for a variety of *natural resources*. Some types of resource dependency, such as dependency on oil, are obvious. The reliance of Japan, Western Europe, and the United States on foreign energy suppliers makes a faraway and until recently a little-known country like Kuwait vitally important. In 1989, for instance, Kuwait exported 711,750,000 barrels (a barrel equals 42 gallons) of oil, and it possesses 9.3 percent of the world's petroleum reserves. In August 1990 Kuwait's key role and the importance of oil became obvious in the wake of Iraq's invasion of the country.

Other import dependencies are less obvious. Take cobalt, for example. Cobalt, a mineral used to make high-strength alloys, is important to the defense and commerce of the United States. Cobalt is used in aircraft engines, and if the supply of this vital mineral were cut off, the United States would find it much more difficult and expensive to manufacture military and commercial jet engines. That would adversely affect both national defense and the employment of tens of thousands of aircraft workers. The problem is that the United States currently produces almost no cobalt. Zaire and Zambia, on the other hand, produce approximately 73 percent of the world's total. In 1989 these two countries supplied 52 percent of all U.S. cobalt imports. What do you know of Zaire and Zambia, two other faraway, little-known countries of great importance?

International Monetary Factors

The comparative value of national currencies, or *monetary exchange rates*, also has a significant impact on your economic well-being. Between 1981 and 1985 the value of the American dollar increased 69 percent against the value of other major world currencies. That meant that imported products became relatively cheaper in the United States. It also helped spur the spiraling trade deficit. Then a decline in international confidence in the

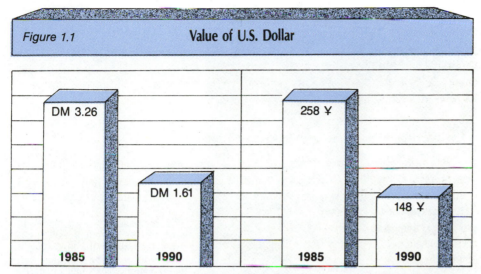

Figure 1.1 **Value of U.S. Dollar**

DM 3.26

258 ¥

DM 1.61

148 ¥

1985 1990 1985 1990

By mid-1990 the U.S. dollar was worth less than half its value in 1985 as compared to the West German mark and had declined almost as much against the Japanese yen.

economic soundness of the United States, combined with U.S. efforts to reduce the trade deficit, began to drive the value of the dollar down. At the beginning of 1985 each dollar was worth 258 Japanese yen; by mid-1990 the exchange rate stood at 148 yen to the dollar. During the same period, the value of the dollar against the West German deutsche mark declined from $1 = DM3.26 to $1 = DM1.61. Overall, between 1985 and 1988, the value of the dollar against major currencies dropped about 50 percent and has been relatively stable since then. This "weakening" of the dollar helped reduce the trade deficit, but it also meant higher prices for many goods that Americans needed or wanted to import. The price of a basic Toyota Tercel rose 50 percent from $5,348 to $7,580 from 1985 to 1988. In addition to foreign cars, other products rose in price, including textiles and electronic equipment. The overall price of imported goods jumped 14.8 percent in 1987 alone. This helped fuel an increase in the U.S. annualized inflation rate that by mid-1990 was over 6 percent in contrast to just 1.9 percent in 1986.

Monetary exchange rates and the flow of trade are not the only causes of inflation. Budget policy also contributes for good or ill. For more than two decades the United States has been spending more money than it collects in taxes and other revenues. The result has been astronomical budget deficits (a projected $169 billion for fiscal year 1990), with an accumulated national debt over $3 trillion. These deficits cause inflation because the government is forced to borrow money to make up the spending-revenue gap. In a classic supply and demand relationship, the more the government needs to borrow (demand) of the money available (supply) to purchase U.S. government securities, the higher the interest rate the government must give to attract funds. What does this mean to you? Among other things, if you, like most Americans, hope to own your own home someday, then what you will pay in mortgage interest and the income you need to qualify for a loan will increase as the interest rate on treasury notes and other indices of the "cost of money" go up. For example, on a $100,000 mortgage (modest by today's standards) for 30 years, an increase of only 1 percent will increase your payments by $897 a year. Furthermore, since investment capital flows to the most attractive world investment, international sources of money and interest rates in other countries affect U.S. interest rates. About a third of all U.S. securities are held by foreign

The expression "having money to burn" meant something very different to Germans in the 1920s than it means to us today. Germany suffered astronomical inflation partly caused by international factors. Money became so worthless that Germans burned it to keep warm, as is this woman who is stoking her stove with German marks.

lenders, and in mid-1990 an upturn of over 1 percent in West German and Japanese interest rates pushed U.S. rates higher also.

At approximately 6 percent, the 1990 U.S. inflation rate is just beginning to reach worrisome levels, and what can happen is illustrated by Argentina, Germany, and Hungary. Argentina represents the worst example of current hyperinflation: between 1973 and 1984, Argentina had an annual inflation rate of 180.8 percent, more than 24 times the U.S. rate (7.4 percent) for the same period. Inflation became so bad that Argentina began to print 1-million-unit currency notes. Instead of being worth a fortune, the million-peso bill was worth only $89, enough to buy a decent radio—if one could have been found in the nearly empty shops. The government introduced a new currency unit, the austral, in 1986 to stabilize the currency. It failed. It initially traded on par (1:1) with the U.S. dollar, but by January 1990 it had plummeted to 1,650:1. The inflation rate for the month of December 1989 alone was 40 percent, raising the 1989 inflation rate to 4,923 percent.

Soaring inflation is not just a problem for Argentina but is spread throughout Latin America. Other countries, such as Brazil and Mexico, also have high inflation, and these countries owe U.S. banks and others hundreds of billions of dollars. Inflation is making it increasingly difficult for them to repay their international loans; if they were to default it would further traumatize the U.S. banking industry.

The inflation problems of Argentina pale, however, when compared with what happened to Germany in the 1920s. Under demands by the Allies to pay reparations after World War I, the German economy fell apart. In August 1923 the German mark had soared to 4,600,000 to each U.S. dollar. By December of that year the figure stood at 4,200,000,000 marks to each dollar, for a monthly inflation rate of over 150 percent. After World War II the Hungarian unit of currency (the pengo), which had equaled 3.38 dollars in 1939, soared to a rate of 500,000,000,000,000,000,000 (500 million trillion) to one. Bank notes of 100 million pengos were printed, and a haircut in Budapest cost

TABLE 1.1

Comparative Defense Expenditures, 1988

Country	Total ($ U.S. Billions)	As % of Budget	As % of GNP	Per Capita ($ U.S.)
United States	296.20	28.0	6.5	1215
Soviet Union*	303.00	45.9	12.3	1067
China*	20.66	20.4	4.4	19
Canada	8.84	9.4	2.2	342
Mexico	0.73	2.3	0.5	9
Nigeria	1.80	2.7	0.8	2
Japan	24.32	6.5	1.0	199
India	9.63	16.9	3.9	12
Israel	5.54	24.7	16.6	1311
Sweden	4.43	6.7	2.9	529

*Estimating Soviet and Chinese defense expenditures is very controversial. U.S. government estimates tend to be higher than other sources and much higher than Soviet and Chinese official figures.

Data source: U.S. ACDA (1989).

800 trillion pengos. Could that happen to you? It is hard to believe it could, but the Germans and Hungarians did not think it could happen to them, either. It did, however, and it was caused in part by international economics.

Domestic Versus Defense Spending

Your government's *distribution of economic resources* is yet another way that world politics affects you economically. The more of a country's wealth that is devoted to military spending, the less is available for private use and for domestic government spending. Table 1.1 compares 10 countries by a number of defense spending criteria. As you can see, some countries like the Soviet Union and the United States devote huge sums to defense. Others like Israel have high expenditures compared to their GNP or on a per capita basis. Some countries spend relatively little on defense. Mexico devotes only $1/2$ of 1 percent of its GNP to defense, and Nigeria spends only $2 per capita.

One question that political scientists study is whether there is a direct (and inverse) correlation between defense and social spending. That is, whether declines in defense spending will mean increases in domestic spending, and vice versa. The answer is that there is no universal and consistent relationship between spending on guns and spending on butter (Snider & Berringer, 1990; Mintz, 1989; Harris, Kelly, & Pranowo, 1988). This means that the much-ballyhooed idea of a post–cold war "peace dividend" that will funnel the money taken from reduced defense expenditures into domestic programs is far from certain. It may happen, but the saved funds may also be used to reduce the deficit or to fend off tax increases.

Still, given finite budget resources, it is illogical not to recognize that there is some relationship between international and domestic spending. The Reagan administration's priorities meant rapidly increasing defense expenditures and spending about $2 trillion on the military during Reagan's eight years. At the same time, spending on colleges,

One way that international politics affects you is that your government has to make budget choices between defense and domestic spending. A B-2 bomber has a projected cost of $850 million if 75 are built. Each bomber weighs 70 tons. If you balance the cost and weight of a B-2 bomber versus the mid-July 1990 value of gold ($362 troy ounce), the B-2 bomber will cost more than if it were made from pure gold. The cost of just one of these warplanes would finance almost any U.S. university for a year or could provide complete scholarships to an expensive private college (at about $20,000) for a year to 42,500 college students.

which intimately affects you, the reader, increased relatively slowly and did not keep up with the escalating cost of college expenses, as you can see in the box opposite.

Does this mean that reduced defense spending is all good news? Not really. The bad news, in addition to the peace dividend uncertainty, is that many national economies, industries, and workers have become heavily dependent on defense spending. The process of conversion from defense to nondefense production is highly complex, but suffice it to say here that factories that produce tanks cannot quickly be retooled to turn out sports cars, and engineers who are skilled at planning high-tech weapons will, for a while, be less adept at the intricacies of refrigerator design. It is easy not to feel sympathetic for the institutional defense industry, but that is composed, in part, of 4.3 million defense workers in the United States. There are also a million civilian employees of the Department of Defense and about 2 million uniformed personnel. Given current projections, most will be unaffected by defense cuts, but perhaps 1.1 million defense industry workers and a quarter to a third of the defense department's civilian and uniformed personnel could lose their jobs in the next 5 years. Using the economic standard that each job directly affects an average of 3 people, some 6 or 7 million Americans may suffer adversely from the defense cutback.[3]

In sum, each of you is probably more individually involved with international economics than you think. You or someone in your family may have a job that has been created by exports or is threatened by imports. Defense spending creates other jobs, but it may cut budget allocations for college scholarships or other domestic programs. International economics affects the price of many of our cars and the cost of the gasoline to run them. On an even more personal level, it would be worthwhile to survey your personal belongings. How many are foreign-made? Sony televisions, Panasonic radios, sweaters from China, European or Japanese cars, Italian shoes, and a host of other

3. The conversion of military production to domestic production is the subject of the entire issue of *Bulletin of Peace Proposals* (1988:19:1), guest-edited by Lloyd L. Dumas.

Defense Dollars and College Dollars

One way to see the relationship between you as a college student and world affairs and national budget priorities is to compare U.S. spending on defense and higher education. Defense spending increased 122.6 percent during the Reagan administration; spending on higher education increased only 47.8 percent while the higher education index jumped 65.3 percent. In 1989, the federal government spent more than $30 on defense for every dollar it spent on higher education. During these years defense spending increased from 22.68 to 26.24 percent of the federal budget; college spending decreased from 1.17 to 0.84 percent of the budget.

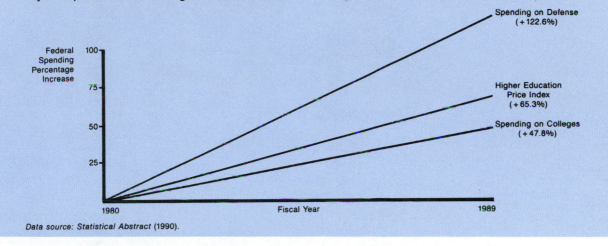

Data source: *Statistical Abstract* (1990).

foreign-manufactured items are likely to make up our individual inventories. International politics and economics, then, are really no farther away than our designer jeans— American-worn, French-named, and Hong Kong–manufactured.

World Politics and Your Life

International politics can affect far more than your pocketbook. It can determine the quality and even the existence of your life.

The Environment

The growth of the world's population and its pressure on resources threaten to change the quality of life as we know it. It took 10,000 years for the world to reach its current 5 billion people. Projections are tricky, but it is reasonable to expect that by the year 2000 the world population will reach 6.3 billion. Within a century, at current rates, the population will have exploded to 18 billion people, a 300 percent increase (see Figure 1.2 on page 15).[4]

4. This book cites many projections by experts who use historic and current data to arrive at them. The reader should be aware, however, that very few projections approach certainty. Most are subject to dramatic change, especially through alterations in human behavior. Birth control, for example, could dramatically reduce the birth rate. Indeed, it is unlikely that the earth could support 18 billion people. Mass starvation and, perhaps, war would act as a brutal limit on the upward population spiral.

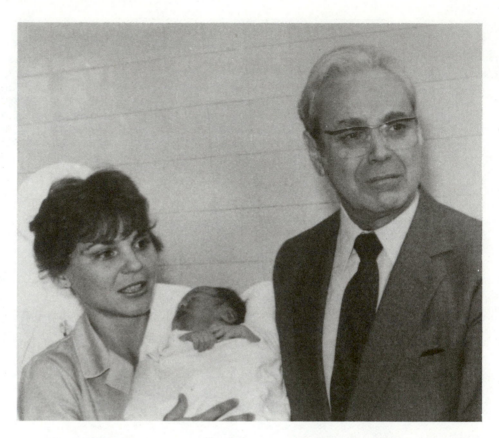

Matej Gaspar, pictured here with a nurse and UN secretary-general Javier Pérez de Cuéllar, was born in Zagreb, Yugoslavia, on July 11, 1987. What makes baby Matej exceptional is that he was selected by the UN to symbolize the birth that brought the world population to 5 billion. This is over a 300 percent population growth in this century alone.

Americans will not be immune to this avalanche of humanity. The burning of fossil fuels to warm and propel this mass is raising the world carbon dioxide level, which many scientists claim is warming the atmosphere and threatening to melt icecaps and flood low-lying areas of the world. Such cities as Boston, New York, New Orleans, and Los Angeles could be affected. The chemicals we spew into the air cause disease and attack the earth's atmosphere, which helps shield the earth from deadly ultraviolet rays.

How do the depletion of the ozone layer and the lagging international effort to control it affect you? Think about being at the beach last summer. Nice, wasn't it? But while there, you were at considerable and rapidly increasing risk of developing skin cancer, the deadliest form of which is melanoma. In 1935, 1 in 1,500 Americans developed melanoma; today 1 in 120 does; by the end of the decade it may be 1 in 90. Since it often takes 20 years for melanoma to develop, the risk to today's youth is uncertain, but it is surely very high.

Fresh water supplies are also polluted and, in many areas, are insufficient to meet the exploding mass of humanity shown in Figure 1.2. Finally, the pressure on fossil fuel resources has led to the rapid construction of nuclear power plants. As of 1989, some 429 were in operation, and another 105 were under construction. In 1986 one in operation at Chernobyl in the Soviet Ukraine exploded. Dozens of people were killed by radiation poisoning and 40,000 were evacuated. The cleanup cost is estimated at $3 to $5 billion, and the future genetic damage is frightening to contemplate.

These ramifications are not the ravings of an ivory-tower academic: they are ongoing realities. A 1980 report submitted to the U.S. president by the State Department and the Council on Environmental Quality warned that in the near future the world would be "more crowded, more polluted, less stable ecologically, and more vulnerable

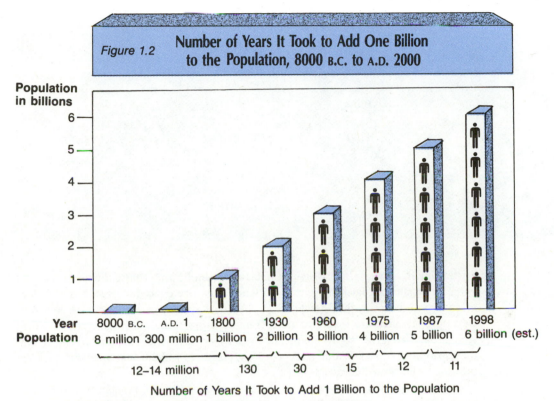

Figure 1.2 Number of Years It Took to Add One Billion to the Population, 8000 B.C. to A.D. 2000

Population in billions

Number of Years It Took to Add 1 Billion to the Population

Year	8000 B.C.	A.D. 1	1800	1930	1960	1975	1987	1998
Population	8 million	300 million	1 billion	2 billion	3 billion	4 billion	5 billion	6 billion (est.)

12–14 million   130   30   15   12   11

Data sources: Preston (1990); World Resources Institute and International Institute for Environmental Development (1986).

The world population is growing at an alarming rate. In July 1987 it passed 5 billion and in 1990 reached 5.3 billion. At current rates, we will add another billion people by the end of the century. This means that the world population is growing at a rate of 2,739,726 per day, 1,903 a minute, 30 a second.

to disruption than the world we live in now." Among other possibilities, the report warned that the search for fuel alone could result in destruction of 40 percent of the world's remaining forests and extinction of 20 percent of the globe's plants and animals.

War

Plants and animals are not the only things facing extinction. Humans may also wind up on the endangered species list. International politics now has the potential of extinguishing most or all of the human race. Until recent times most people killed in wars were soldiers. Increasingly in the twentieth century, civilian casualties have risen and civilians have become a direct target of military operations. During World War II nearly as many civilians as soldiers were killed. In the next—nuclear—war, civilian casualties will far outnumber military deaths. The National Security Council has estimated that a nuclear exchange between the United States and the Soviet Union would kill a minimum of 140 million Americans and 113 million Soviets.

Nuclear war has happened only once, when the United States dropped two atomic weapons on Japan in 1945. The fact that 45 years have passed without a recurrence may be partly luck as well as policy, and the odds of avoiding nuclear war are declining. In 1944 there were no nuclearly armed countries. Now there are six: the United States, the

Ages of U.S. Marines Killed in Vietnam

Age	Deaths	
18–22	12,436	It is the young who die in wars. College-age youth made up 84% of the Marine Corps dead in Vietnam.
23–27	1,590	
28–32	385	
33–37	242	
38–42	84	
43–47	25	
47 +	11	*Data source:* Lock (1985).

Soviet Union, France, Great Britain, China, and India.[5] Furthermore, Pakistan is on the verge of acquiring a nuclear weapon, virtually everyone concedes Israel has a nuclear arsenal, and there are persistent rumors that the Republic of South Africa does too. Beyond that, there are several nations (ranging from Brazil, through Iraq, to North Korea) that have given signs of pursuing the nuclear option and another two dozen with the capability to do so. Within a few decades, countries with nuclear weapons could be the rule rather than the exception.

An individual's involvement in war can also occur in circumstances less cataclysmic than atomic warfare. Many countries, including Germany, the Soviet Union, and China, have a draft to staff their military services. The United States abandoned the draft in the early 1970s, but there is pressure to resume involuntary service, and draft registration is now required of all military-age males.

In the future, the shrinking pool of military-age Americans could mean that if the military must be expanded from its projected post–cold war lows, then the draft would have to be reinstituted to meet needs. Currently, all 18- to 23-year-old males must register, but changing sex role attitudes combined with the declining pool might mean that women would also be included. How would you feel about women being drafted and serving and dying in combat units? It's not farfetched. During the 1989 U.S. invasion of Panama, Army captain Linda Bray, 29, led a platoon into combat against a Panamanian Defense Force position. As Sergeant First Class Georgiana Cleverly put it, "The American public doesn't realize that there are these women soldiers who already put funny little things on and wear helmets and carry rifles and go out and do all these sorts of things you see G. I. Joe doing on television" (*NYT,* 1/25/90:1A). Don't be surprised then if you, male or female, someday find yourself directly involved in world politics by way of the draft and an all-expenses-paid government trip to some exotic corner of the world with Captain Bray and First Sergeant Cleverly as your bosses. You can try to ignore world politics, but it may not ignore you.

World politics, then, does count. We are all involved economically and environmentally. Further, it can threaten our very lives. Wars have continued and will continue to happen. Young men—and probably young women—have been and will be drafted. Some will die—perhaps you. In the worst possible circumstance, nuclear war, it will not make much difference whether you were drafted or not.

5. India exploded a nuclear device in 1974 but claims that it was only a test device and that it has not manufactured any actual weapons.

Changing sex role attitudes and military personnel needs might mean that women will someday be drafted and serve in combat units. Army captain Linda Bray, shown here, led an assault on a Panamanian Defense Force position during the 1989 invasion of that country. U.S. Representative Patricia Schroeder has introduced legislation in Congress authorizing women to serve regularly in combat forces, and a 1989 poll found that 70 percent of all Americans thought women should be allowed to so serve if they wanted to (*NYT,* 1/25/90:1A). Do you agree? How about requiring women (as men are) to serve in combat even if they *don't* want to?

Can We Make a Difference?

The next logical questions are: What can I do? Can I make a difference? Fortunately, we can make a difference. It is true that we cannot all be president or secretary of state, but we can take action and we can make our views known. There are things we can do!

There are a variety of possible personal statements and actions on international politics. Students have often been important agents of political change (Altbach, 1989). The sum of millions of individual actions, ranging from veterans burning draft cards, through massive demonstrations in front of the White House, to students protesting and even dying on our campuses, helped end American involvement in Vietnam.

Fortunately, not all individual actions need to involve martyrdom or other forms of violence. Letter-writing campaigns protesting economic concessions to the Soviet Union unless it grants freedom for its Baltic republics, lawsuits to force the U.S. government to invoke economic sanctions against Japan because of its continued whaling, and demonstrations to encourage colleges to sell their investments in companies that do business in South Africa are all statements of concern and commitment. Best of all, they sometimes succeed, and the world is improved as a result of the efforts of you and others.

Even saving money can help! One way individual Americans can help ease their trade deficit is by being a little more frugal. Figure 1.3 compares the 7 major industrial countries (the Group of Seven, G-7) according to their respective savings rates and their economic growth. GNP growth is based on many factors, but note that the four countries (France, Italy, Japan, West Germany) with the highest savings rates are also the four with the highest economic growth rates, while the three countries (Canada, the United Kingdom, the United States) with the lowest savings rates also lag behind the others in

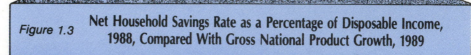

Figure 1.3 Net Household Savings Rate as a Percentage of Disposable Income, 1988, Compared With Gross National Product Growth, 1989

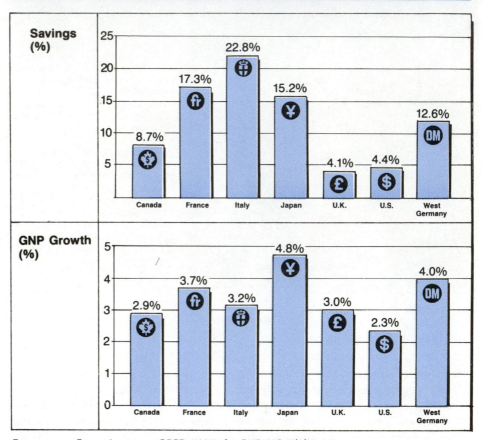

Data sources: For savings rates, OECD (1989); for GNP, *HC* (7/6/90:A7).

One reason for the huge U.S. trade deficit is that Americans save less of their money than the citizens of most other industrialized countries. This means Americans buy great quantities of imported goods.

GNP growth. The U.S. savings rate fell to a 42-year low of 3.2 percent in 1987 and since has improved somewhat to an annualized projection of 5.6 percent for 1990. That still substantially lags behind the most economically expansive countries, however. Canada's rate has dropped from a relatively healthy 12.1 percent in 1985 to 8.7 percent in 1989; during the same period the Canadian GNP growth rate also declined from 7.8 to 2.9 percent.

Individuals can also work within democratic societies to influence foreign policy. The simplest way is by voting in elections. Presidential candidates George H. W. Bush and Michael S. Dukakis differed on a variety of issues in 1988, as shown in Table 1.2 on the following page. The election of George Bush means that strong economic sanctions on South Africa and China will be more strongly opposed by the Administration. It also means that in spite of the end of the cold war some weapons systems like a ballistic

International politics not only affects you, but you can affect it. There were a number of issues related to national defense and foreign policy that divided Republican George Bush and Democrat Michael Dukakis in the 1988 presidential contest. Those who took the time to try to understand these issues and who voted for president had an impact on international politics.

missile defense and a B-2 bomber will be more vigorously sought than they would have been if Michael Dukakis had been elected.

Direct voting on international questions is also possible in some countries. In recent years, the citizens of Spain voted to join NATO, and the Swiss decided not to join the United Nations. The people of the United Kingdom chose to join the European Community; the voters of Greenland rejected a similar option. Finally, expressing your opinion orally, or in writing, or even having your opinion sampled in a poll, can have an impact. Public opinion polls are widely published in the United States and elsewhere, and political leaders keep a weather eye on public attitudes. Even the Soviets and Chinese have recently taken up limited polling.

The point is that you count by voting, protesting, donating, or even by having your thoughts recorded in a political poll. Few individual actions are dramatic, and by themselves few significantly change world politics, but the sum of many smaller actions can and does make a difference. Do not consider politics a spectator sport. It is more important than that. Treat politics as a participant—even a contact—sport.

How to Study World Politics

"Well, OK," you may say, "international politics is important and it affects me. I should know something about it, but where do I start?" Ah, I am glad you asked!

The first thing you should do, if you have not already, is to go back and read the preface and the discussion on pages v–xi. These sections will tell you how I have structured this text and will help you understand what follows.

TABLE 1.2

1988 Presidential Candidates' Views on Foreign Policy

Issue	Candidate and Position	
	Bush	*Dukakis*
Send arms to Contras	favored	opposed
Strategic Defense Initiative	build and deploy	severely limit
More trade restrictions	no	yes
Increase sanctions against South Africa	no	yes
Level of defense spending as percentage of budget	maintain	reduce
Build mobile missiles	yes	no

The Themes of World Politics

The next things to consider are the major themes of world politics: Conflict or Cooperation, the Axes of World Division, the Changing Nature of Power, and Reality modified by Perception. Each of these will be explained briefly in the following paragraphs and will be dealt with extensively throughout the rest of the book.

Conflict or cooperation is the first major theme. The world has traditionally been divided and conflictive. The political map is divided into more than 180 sovereign, self-interested states. Here wars are fought, states maneuver for economic advantage, and diplomacy usually strives to gain political influence. Thus, conflict will be the main focus of Parts II and III.

Countering that main theme is cooperation. Global cooperation rather than national competition is still a secondary process in the world, but it is growing. We will explore this hopeful trend in Part IV. Concepts such as international law and organization are still in their infancy compared with domestic law and organization, but they do exist and have expanded their scope. Further, given the realities of declining resources and a mushrooming population as well as the reality of our military ability to destroy ourselves, it is probable that international cooperation must continue to expand if the world is not to face economic, ecological, and/or nuclear catastrophe.

The *axes of world division* are another dimension of world politics and are a symptom of a divided, often conflictive, international system. One of these axes, the **East-West Axis**, denotes a dramatic focus of tension that existed from the end of World War II in 1945 until very recently. This axis involved the struggle, especially on political-military issues, between the United States and its allies (the West) and the Soviet Union and its supporters (the East). The axis was a good deal less important for economic, social, and environmental matters. Indeed, it is possible to characterize a substantial part of the post–1945 era as a bipolar struggle (a term we will explore in chapters 2 and 3) between these two superpowers.

Now the bipolarity of the earlier postwar period has broken down almost completely. The United States is in relative decline, and the Soviet Union is in a crisis of economic, nationalistic, and social unrest. Some analysts believe that the U.S.S.R. could plunge into civil war or nationalist disintegration. Other countries such as Japan, China, and Germany have developed new strength and in some areas, particularly economic strength, may themselves be emerging superpowers. Furthermore, a number of pressures have persuaded Washington and Moscow to defuse substantially their hostility. Some of the details of this change are discussed in the next chapter, but here we can note that economic and political changes in the Soviet Union have caused it to reduce its defense spending, give up control of Eastern Europe, and seek to ease conflict with the West in many Third World areas. These and other accommodative moves are aimed in part at creating an international climate in which Western technology, investment, and perhaps even foreign aid will flow into the Soviet Union, allowing it to rejuvenate itself economically. The U.S. budget deficit and other economic difficulties have encouraged Washington to respond to the Soviet shift by beginning to reduce U.S. military power. Also, these shifts are a part of the changed international system, in which the bipolar blocs dissolved, and the former subordinate allies of both superpowers began to follow independent foreign policies. In some cases these countries became economic and even political rivals of their erstwhile allies, the superpowers.

Germany is the most powerful symbol of these changes. Until 1990 there were two Germanys, East and West. Now there is one Germany. Until recently the Berlin Wall was guarded by automatic machine gun towers, now it is being chipped into innumerable souvenirs and carted away by tourists. A few years ago the two Germanys were politically subordinate to their respective superpowers. Now Germany has seized its own destiny, has (with the superpowers largely as spectators) reunited, and looms as a formidable competitor of both the United States and the Soviet Union. Optimism about the final dissipation of the East-West axis should, however, be tempered by two realities. One is that even given the relatively moderate policies of President Mikhail S. Gorbachev and the responsiveness of the United States, substantial differences remain. The two superpowers often define their respective national interests in ways that conflict. Each country also possesses a potentially world-destroying arsenal of nuclear and conventional weaponry, and they still face each other, if at a greater distance, in Western Europe. There *is* a significant lessening of hostility, even limited cooperation, but it would be a flight of fancy to imagine that the two superpowers have achieved general accord.

Déjà vu (the feeling you have seen it before) ought to suggest a second note of caution. United States–Soviet hostility, from the 1917 Communist Revolution through the 1930s, was reversed when the two became allies against the Nazi threat during World War II. For Americans and Britons, the glowering dictator Josef Stalin became "Uncle Joe." After the war, relations again froze in what became known as the cold war. In the late 1950s, relations briefly warmed a bit. Soviet leader Nikita Khrushchev visited the United States. As someone who expressed a desire to visit Disneyland, he didn't seem so bad. The thaw was called Peaceful Co-existence. By 1960 diplomatic temperatures plummeted again, and the cold war resumed. The 1970s reversed the downward trend, and President Richard M. Nixon and General Secretary Leonid I. Brezhnev achieved a more balanced relationship, often called Détente. The Soviet invasion of Afghanistan in 1979, Soviet pressures on Poland in 1980, and the coming to office of the stridently anticommunist Ronald W. Reagan in 1981 re-formed the bipolar icecap. It took seven years for it to begin to melt. The point is that tensions have eased before.

Peaceful Co-existence and Détente proved transitory. Whether the yet-unnamed period of current cooperation, the "Gorby phenomenon," will persist or whether it too will pass remains to be seen. Skeptics are particularly prone to warn that the Soviet Union is not seeking true accommodation, but rather a "breathing spell" in which to

The North-South Axis is one of the important lines that divide the world. The people in the industrialized countries of the North are mostly comfortable, even relatively wealthy. This little girl, who typifies many of the people of the South, lives in a sorely impoverished world, struggling amid the garbage heaps of urban Bogotá, Colombia. She and her family survive by searching for things they might be able to sell or use. This sort of existence has long been the case for people in the South.

restructure and revitalize its economy so that it can reemerge as an even more formidable foe of the West.[6]

During the last three decades a new geographic axis of tension has developed. It is often called the **North-South Axis**. We will examine this dimension carefully in chapters 14 and 18, but it is well to introduce the division here. The North symbolizes the wealthy, industrially developed countries, which lie mainly in the Northern Hemisphere. By contrast, the South represents the **less developed countries (LDCs)**, the majority of which are near or in the Southern Hemisphere. Of course, the economic circumstances of countries are not truly polar, and instead form a scale ranging from general opulence (the United States) to unbelievable poverty (Bangladesh). There are also some countries of the South that have begun to industrialize and whose standards of living have risen rapidly. These countries are called **newly industrializing countries (NICs)**. In general, though, there is a tremendous economic gap between the few people in the few countries of the North and the many people in the many countries of the South. As Figure 1.4 (p. 24) shows, by economic, educational, or health measures, the countries of the North and the countries of the South live in virtually different worlds. The North is largely a

---

6. A great deal has been written expounding this skeptical view. One important piece, "To the Stalin Mausoleum," was written by the anonymous "Z"; see p. 44 for an analysis of the "X" article that outlined what became known as the anticommunist containment policy. In addition to Z (1989), see Ausland (1989), Hahn (1990), and Kass (1989).

place of reasonable economic security, literacy, and adequate health care. By contrast, the lives of the people of the South are marked by poverty, illiteracy, rampant disease, and early death.

The gap between the rich and poor countries is not new. What has changed is the awareness in the LDCs of their relative poverty. These countries are no longer willing to accept a world system in which wealth is so unevenly distributed. They want a new, more equitable system, a New International Economic Order (NIEO), and to that end they are increasingly pressing the developed countries to share their wealth and to alter their self-serving economic policies. To date, the North has done relatively little to meet these demands, and tensions between countries on the two ends of the economic scale have begun to build. So far the strain on North-South relations is moderate, but it may reach crisis proportions as populations expand, resources decline, and the South's military capability (especially nuclear) increases.

Along with the themes of conflict or cooperation and the axes of world division, a third strand that is important throughout this text is the *changing nature of power.* When we think of national power it is common to consider military power first. Certainly military forces remain an important component of a country's power, but most analysts agree that the utility of military force is declining. Analysts also generally concur that economic power is becoming more significant as part of a country's overall power equation. Given worldwide television and other advances in modern communications, a country's ability to project itself well, to win friends and admirers, and to set an example also have increased in importance as a power factor.

The changing relative importance of military and general economic power is complex and is discussed further in several chapters, especially chapters 9 and 10. We can say here, though, that growing economic interdependence, changes in international norms (values) about the legitimacy of using force, and other factors are sometimes restraining countries from taking military action in cases where they might have used force a decade or so ago. In contrast to the efficacy of military forces, economic power has increased in importance. One reason is that the extraordinarily high cost of modern military technology means that a country must have a powerful economic foundation to afford a strong military. Indeed, economic capability is even central to creating sophisticated military technology. Additionally, economic interdependence means that the supply of products any country uses, the value of its currency, its interest rates, its inflation rate, and a host of other vital economic indices are significantly dependent on the relative strength of that country and other countries.

A fourth theme of this text is based on the fact that the political world is one of *reality modified by perception.* There is a world that is, and there is a world as we see it. Often those two worlds are dramatically different. Sometimes reality is indisputable or inescapable in world politics. When Soviet T-72 tanks rumbled into Afghanistan in 1979, the anticommunist forces there and observers throughout the world could not mistake what was happening. Similarly, China's 1.1 billion people, Saudi Arabia's vast oil resources, and France's nuclear weapons are all real and their existence is acknowledged by everyone. To a degree, each of these realities affects international relations.

Often, however, world politics is based on perception rather than reality. We will discuss perception more in chapter 4, but two quick points about the phenomenon can be made here.

The first point is that *perceptions often distort reality.* Consider Vietnam, for example, and its founding father, Ho Chi Minh. Ho, who took up the cause of Vietnamese independence as early as 1919, saw himself as the George Washington of Vietnam. Others, including most of the people of Vietnam, also saw Ho as a revered

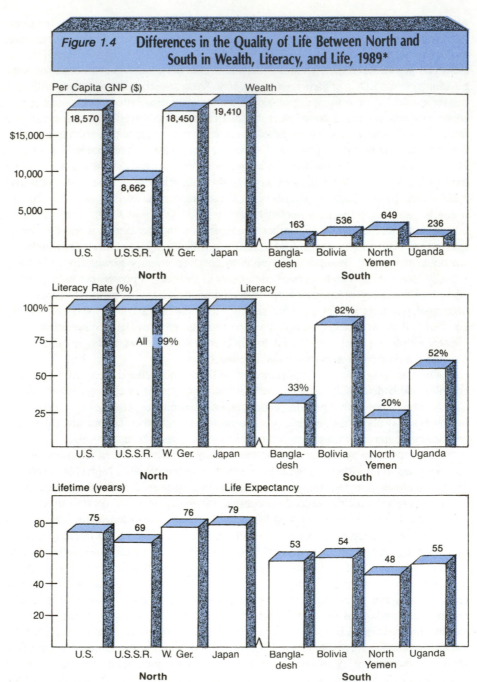

Figure 1.4   Differences in the Quality of Life Between North and South in Wealth, Literacy, and Life, 1989*

*Statistics are for 1989 or the latest figures available.
Data sources: Statistical Abstract (1990); *World Almanac* (1990).

The difference between the lives of people in the North and those in the South is shown here in terms of wealth, literacy, and life expectancy. By these, or many other standards, the people of the South are severely disadvantaged compared to those who live in the North.

nationalist leader struggling to free and unify his country. Americans, however, perceived Ho primarily as a communist. That meant U.S. policymakers thought that Ho's attempts to free Vietnam from French colonial rule in the 1950s and his attempt as the leader of North Vietnam after 1954 to unify his country by toppling the pro-Western government in South Vietnam were part of the worldwide communist movement that threatened the "free world." President Lyndon B. Johnson, for one, did not care much about Vietnam as such. Indeed, he considered it "a raggedy-ass fourth-rate country." But Johnson also believed that if "we don't stop the Reds in South Vietnam, tomorrow they will be in Hawaii, and next they will be in San Francisco" (Paterson, Clifford, & Hagan, 1983:554). From the perspective and perceptions of the 1990s, that seems to most people to be unlikely. Given the perceptions of the early 1960s, Johnson's view was widely accepted.

The second point is that often *action is based on perception*, whether the image is accurate or not. Whatever the truth was about Ho, the American perception of Ho as an international communist menace (at least a partial distortion) led to a massive U.S. military intervention in Vietnam in an ultimately futile attempt to stop Ho.

International politics is thus more than a matter of objective facts. It is a study of subjective judgments based on images of oneself and other international actors. It is something of an Alice in Wonderland tale in which what is important often is not what is but rather what we imagine it to be.

Approaches to the Study of World Politics

Another thing to know about the study of world politics is that orientations toward the subject differ among scholars and political leaders. These orientations can be divided into four broad groups: realist, idealist, scientific, and economic. It should be noted, parenthetically, that this four-category grouping paints many subtle ideas with a broad brush. Like most categories used herein, these four are best understood as a teaching device, and if you read further in the extensive theoretical literature, you will find other perspectives that are rich and diverse (Nye, 1988; Dougherty & Pfaltzgraff, 1990).

One word of caution before we begin evaluating the various approaches: Do not get fooled by the connotations of the names of the various approaches. "Realist" and "idealist" are particularly misleading, although they are used here because they are the common names for their schools of thought in international relations theory. The "realist" approach does not, however, mean that those who follow it see things as they "really" are. Nor, as Kober (1990) points out, are the "idealists" a bunch of fuzzy-headed dreamers. Indeed (and ignoring some nuances) realists can also be termed traditionalists, balance-of-power theorists, *realpolitik* advocates, or power theorists. Idealists are sometimes called liberal internationalists, global/world order theorists, or utopians. As you will see, perhaps a better tag for realists would be "pessimists," and, conversely, "optimists" is probably a more enlightening, if not more precise, label for idealists. The point is not to prejudge books by covers or theories by labels.

The Realist Approach

As a theory of international politics and standard for its conduct, realism extends far back in history. Over 2,000 years ago, Kautilya, minister of the first Maurya emperor of India, wrote, "The possession of power . . . in a greater degree makes a king superior to another; in a lesser degree, inferior; and in an equal degree, equal. Hence a king shall always endeavor to augment his own power" (Bernholz, 1985:17). This view, that world politics is a contest for power, has continued to dominate the thinking of most of the decisionmakers who practice international affairs.

During most of the post–World War II period to 1970, realist theory was also the main theme of academic international relations theory (Smith, 1986). In an early example of realist writings, Frederick Schuman (1969:271) characterized world politics as a process in which each country "necessarily seeks safety by relying on its own power and [views] with alarm the power of its neighbors." Probably the most influential realist theorist of recent times has been Hans Morgenthau (1973), who has defined politics as a "struggle for power." Morgenthau, like most realists, argues that human nature and societies are both imperfect and imperfectible. Therefore conflict is an inherent danger. Given this reality, decisionmakers should structure their policies and define national interest in terms of power. They should follow policies designed to maximize their power and should avoid policies that overstep the limits of their power.

Realists, then, whether they base their orientations on scholarly study or on the intuition and observation of political leaders, share a number of assumptions on how world politics operates. These include:

1. Countries often have conflicting interests.
2. Differing interests can lead to war or other forms of conflict.
3. A country's power is crucial in determining the outcome of conflict and also determines its influence over other countries.
4. Politics, then, is aimed at increasing power, keeping power, or demonstrating power.

This view of the world carries with it important dictates about how to carry on foreign policy. For realists, it implies not only that international relations are based on power politics but that diplomats should follow the dictates of power or else they invite disaster. Typifying this view, realist President George Bush said while helping his wife Barbara christen the $3.5 billion aircraft carrier USS *George Washington* that although "today is not a time of war," the world had not entered "an era of perpetual peace." The 100,000-ton, 1,092-foot-long, 4.5-acre-flight-deck carrier was therefore necessary, the president reasoned, as "an indipensable element in the American arsenal: projecting power, preserving the peace" *(HC,* 6/16/90:A10).

As a corollary, most realists do not believe that the basic drive for power in human politics can be changed significantly. They are pessimists about human nature. Many realists would trace their intellectual heritage to such political philosophers as Thomas Hobbes (1588–1679). In his most famous work, *Leviathan*, Hobbes argues that "if any two men desire the same thing, which nevertheless they cannot both enjoy, they become enemies and . . . endeavor to destroy or subdue one another." Given that reality, Hobbes goes on to reason that it is natural for man "to master the persons of all men he can, . . . til he sees no other power great enough to endanger him." Therefore, "men live without other security than what their own strength . . . shall furnish."

Does this mean, as some charge, that realists are warmongers? Absolutely not. They desire peace but believe that peace can be achieved only through strength. Realists also believe, however, that political leaders can avoid war by not pursuing goals they do not have the power to achieve. It is necessary, therefore, to understand the goals and the power of your opponents, thereby not underestimating their abilities or threatening their vital interests.

Based on these views, realists advocate a relatively pragmatic approach to world politics, sometimes called *realpolitik*. This orientation argues that countries should practice balance-of-power politics. This concept will be further discussed in chapter 3, but here we can say that balance-of-power politics argues that diplomats should strive to achieve an equilibrium of power in the world in order to prevent any other country or coalition of countries from dominating the system. This can be done through a variety of methods including building up your own strength, allying yourself with others, or dividing your opponents.

Before leaving realist theory, some mention should be made of a recent offshoot, dubbed *neorealism*. This subtheory attempts to adjust classical realism with the realities of modern international relations. Specifically, neorealists hold that the structure of the international system (which we will study in chapters 2 and 3) affects policy. Thus they are also sometimes called structural realists. They believe, for example, that the anarchical nature of the political system (not just the urge to power) is responsible for arms races as self-reliant, and otherwise unprotected, countries seek security. Some neorealists also hold that the increasing economic interdependence of the world is decreasing the utility of military force and increasing economic strength as the primary power factor determining any country's success or failure in pursuing its national interest (Dougherty & Pfaltzgraff, 1990:119).

The Idealist Approach

Some students and practitioners of world politics reject the idea that international affairs should or must be played according to the dictates of power politics. Those who hold this belief are called **idealists**. They differ from realists in a number of ways. First, idealists do not believe that acquiring, preserving, and applying power is the essence of international relations. Instead, idealists argue that foreign policy should be formulated according to more cooperative and ethical standards. More than any other recent American president, Jimmy Carter was an idealist in his approach to international politics. Speaking at the White House on the 30th anniversary of the Universal Declaration of Human Rights in 1978, Carter declared himself:

> proud that our nation stands for more than military might or political might. . . . Our pursuit of human rights is part of a broad effort to use our great power and our tremendous influence in the service of creating a better world in which human beings can live in peace, in freedom, and with their basic needs met. Human rights is the soul of our foreign policy. (Carter, 1979:2)

Carter himself admitted that "seldom do circumstances permit me . . . to take actions that are wholly satisfactory," but he tried. Carter's realization that ideals could not always be fully applied also indicates that idealists are not fuzzy-minded. In fairness, it should also be added here that realists do not dismiss human rights or the desirability of acting morally. It is just that they agree with former U.S. secretary of state George P. Shultz that "we Americans have had to accept that our passionate commitment to moral principles could not be a substitute for sound foreign policy in a world of hard realities and complex choices." The problem, according to the secretary, is that "our moral impulse, noble as it might be, could lead either to futile and perhaps dangerous global crusades, on the one hand, or to escapism and isolationism, equally dangerous, on the other" (Shultz, 1985:247).

Most political leaders follow the realist approach to international relations. One exception was President Jimmy Carter, shown here. Carter followed an idealist approach, especially early in his presidency. He especially believed that the promotion of human rights should be a high priority goal of U.S. foreign policy.

Idealists also dismiss the charge of some realists that pursuing ethical policy works against the national interest. Carter's secretary of state, Cyrus Vance, called it a "dangerous illusion" and "nonsense" to hold that "pursuing values such as human rights . . . is incompatible with pursuing U.S. national interests." To the contrary, Vance argued, "Our own freedom, and that of our allies, could never be secure in a world where freedom was threatened everywhere else" (Vance, 1986:11).

A third way that idealists differ from realists is that the former believe that the world must seek a new system of order. The current world system is based primarily on sovereign countries that define, promote, and defend their own interests. There is no effective central authority in the world political system to regulate the relations among countries. This contrasts with domestic political systems, which have governments to regulate relations among their citizens. Idealists have never been comfortable with a world system based on sovereignty, but they now argue that it is imperative to find new paths to cooperation. According to the idealists, the spread of nuclear weapons, increasing economic interdependence among countries, declining world resources, the daunting gap between rich and poor, and the mounting damage we are doing to our ecosphere mean that humans must learn to cooperate more fully or we are in grave danger of suffering a catastrophe of unparalleled proportions.

Finally, in contrast to realists, idealists are prone to believe that humans and their countries are capable of achieving more cooperative, less conflictive relations. In this sense, they might trace their intellectual lineage to political philosophers such as Jean-Jacques Rousseau (1712–78). Humans joined together in civil societies, Rousseau argued in his famous *The Social Contract*, because they "reached the point at which the obstacles [to bettering their existence were] greater than the resources at the disposal of each individual." Having come to that point, Rousseau went on (and today's idealists would heartily agree), people realized "the primitive condition can then subsist no longer; and the human race would perish unless it changed its manner of existence."[7] Like Rousseau, modern idealists tend to be optimistic about human nature. They believe that people joined together in civil societies to better their existence, and idealists are confident that people can join together to build a cooperative and peaceful global society.

The Scientific Approach

The **scientific school** of political science is interested in recurring patterns and causal relations of international behavior. Those who follow this approach, also called the behavioralist approach, often use quantitative methods to arrive at and prove hypotheses that will explain both why certain events have occurred and under what circumstances they might occur again. They also often use cross-cultural analyses to test whether similar or divergent causal patterns occur between different political systems as well as over time. Scholars of all of the orientations discussed here use quantitative methods, but behavioralists are especially likely to do so.

A traditional belief in international relations is that domestic conflict (an **independent variable**) might lead to external conflict (a **dependent variable**) as a country's leaders try to divert the focus of conflict to an external enemy. By doing so, the domestic leaders would encourage national unity and also help maintain their regime in power. The work of a number of behavioralist political scientists has generally shown that assumption to be wrong. Rudolph Rummel (1963), for one, analyzed the levels of internal and external conflict in 77 countries during the mid-1950s and found little relation between the two variables. That does not mean that domestic unrest will not be followed by international aggressiveness. Indeed, other studies using behavioralist techniques have shown that in some cases domestic conflict is followed by international tension. But the connection (causal relation) between the two circumstances is less certain than we once assumed (Hoole & Huang, 1989; Levy, 1988; James, 1987).

Like realists, behavioralists have little interest in advocating fundamental changes in the world system. Where they differ is that realists accept what is and often advocate that politicians should also accept and operate within the framework of power politics. Behavioralists, from their "value-free" or "scientific" perspective, are more disinterested in the good or ill of world politics. They tend to operate from a value-free posture, neither condoning nor condemning what is. They only describe what is and why and try to predict what will be. This value-free approach has been the source of some criticism of behavioralism by those who contend that the problems and stakes of the world are too great to be studied dispassionately. Behavioralists have also been criticized for studying only what is quantifiable and ignoring less quantifiable subjects. Finally, behavioralists have sometimes been disparaged for being more concerned with what is the best statistical formula to study a problem than with the resolution of that issue.

The Economic Approach

A fourth approach to the study of world politics is the **economic orientation**. Political scientists and politicians who operate from this perspective believe that economic forces

---

7. Rousseau probably would have objected to the idea of a world political system. He believed that effective societies were limited in size. As he argued, "in every body politic there is a maximum strength which it cannot exceed and which it only loses by increasing in size. Every extension of the social ties means its relaxation; and, generally speaking, a small State is stronger in proportion than a great one" (*The Social Contract*, 1762).

and conditions play the primary role in international relations. Some analysts in this general group are classic Marxists. They study political structure and process from the perspective of the control and distribution of economic resources. They contend that a historically inevitable series of economic pressures and counterpressures (dialectical materialism) will, and should, lead to the destruction of capitalism and the triumph of communism. Marxists believe that international conflict results from the imperialist aggression of capitalist countries in their drive (1) to amass wealth and (2) to avoid their own inevitable collapse by destroying the communist wave of the future. It should be clearly understood that being a Marxist does not mean you are pro-Soviet. Indeed, many Marxists condemn the Soviet Union for its internal repression and its own form of imperialism.

There is also a wide-ranging school of *political economy* that extends far beyond Marxism. One group, sometimes called the neo-Marxist, radical, or *dependencia* school, argues that the industrialized countries in collusion with oppressive elites in the Third World conduct policy in a way to keep the less developed countries economically and politically dependent (Galtung, 1971; Magdoff, 1978). Another illustrative group, sometimes called "mercantilist" scholars (Blake & Walters, 1987:9), maintains that world political relations are heavily influenced by the competition among countries for resources, wealth, and thus power (Krasner, 1978).

What to Study: Levels of Analysis

Another major division among analytical approaches used by political scientists has to do with the level of focus. The essential question here is "what do we study?" One approach by political scientists has been to divide their foci of study into **levels of analysis**. These refer to levels of the factors that affect international politics. One early study suggested two general levels of analysis. Other political scientists have refined and expanded that concept to include many more levels of analysis, but for our analysis here we will adopt a middle ground by discussing three levels of analysis.[8]

1. **System-level analysis**—a world view.
2. **State-level analysis**—a view in which the concern is with the characteristics of an individual country and the impact of those traits on the country's behavior.
3. **Individual-level analysis**—a view in which the focus is on people, and which can be further subdivided into three categories:
   a. the *humans-as-individuals approach*, the study of the attributes and views of individual decisionmakers,
   b. the *humans-in-organizations approach*, which focuses on how decisions are affected by the dynamics of group behavior, and
   c. the *nature-of-humankind approach*, with its concern with biological and psychological explanations of the behavior of the human species.

8. For example, a five-level approach is shown in chapter 5 of James N. Rosenau's *The Scientific Study of Foreign Policy* (1971). The approach used herein resembles the approach used in the classic work by Kenneth N. Waltz, *Man, the State, and War* (1959), in which Waltz uses three "images" to examine the causes of war.

Focus on one level of analysis does not mean exclusion of the others. Indeed, it would be best to think of the levels as occurring along a scale from the general (system level analysis) to the specific (individual-level analysis). It is possible to focus on one level and yet still use elements of the others. In the following four chapters, we will extensively examine the implications of each of these levels. Chapters 2 and 3 take up system-level analysis, including the evolution of the world system and theory about how systems operate. Then chapter 4 discusses individual-level analysis, followed by chapter 5 on state-level analysis.

Chapter Summary

1. This book's primary message is captured by Shake-speare's line, "All the world's a stage, and all the men and women merely players." This means we are all part of the world drama and are affected by it. It also means that we should try to play a role in determining the course of the dramatic events that affect our lives.

2. Economics is one way we are all affected. The word "intermestic" has been coined to symbolize the merging of *inter*national and d*omestic* concerns, especially in the area of economics. Countries and their citizens have become increasingly interdependent.

3. Economically, trade both creates and causes the loss of jobs. Trade also supplies vital resources, such as oil.

4. Exchange rates between different currencies affect the prices we pay for imported goods, the general rate of inflation, and our country's international trade balance.

5. Our country's role in the world also affects decisions about the allocation of budget funds. Some countries spend a great deal on military functions. Other countries spend relatively little on the military and devote almost all of their budget resources to domestic spending.

6. Your biological life is also affected by world politics. You may be called on to serve in the military. Whether or not you are, war can kill you. International cooperation is needed to reverse, or at least stem, environmental degradation.

7. There are many things any one of us can do, individually or in cooperation with others, to play a part in shaping the future of our world. Think, vote, protest, support, write letters, join organizations, make speeches, run for office—do something!

8. This book's study of world politics focuses on several major themes. They are Conflict or Cooperation, the Axes of World Division, the Changing Nature of Power, and Reality Modified by Perception.

9. Conflict or Cooperation addresses the dual nature of the world: one which is characterized by division, self-interest, and struggle, and the other which is marked by attempts to find new ways to cooperate politically, economically, and socially.

10. The Axes of World Division bifurcate global relations into an East-West axis, the declining cold war confrontation, and a newer North-South axis denoting the differing economic circumstances of, and tensions between, the North's industrialized countries and the South's less developed countries.

11. The Changing Nature of Power involves the decrease in use of military power and the concurrent increase of other dimensions of national power, especially economic capacity and communications technology.

12. Reality Modified by Perception stresses the fact that there is a world as it really is and a world as we perceive it, and the two are often dramatically different. Furthermore, since we act on our perceptions, what we perceive is very important.

13. There are several approaches to understanding and conducting world politics. Realists view the world as a struggle for power. Idealists argue that foreign policy should be formulated according to more cooperative and ethical standards. The scientific approach studies politics from a value-free (non-normative) perspective, often using quantitative means. The economic approach operates from the belief that economic forces and conditions play a primary role in international relations.

14. There are three levels of analysis from which world politics can be studied. They are system-level analysis, state-level analysis, and individual-level analysis. Each of these levels is discussed in detail in the next several chapters.

I am amazed, methinks, and lose my way among the thorns and dangers of the world.

Shakespeare, *King John*

I think there is a danger that history will make a judgment that these were the days when the tide began to run out for the United States.

John F. Kennedy, 1960

I really don't [know] . . . what will happen to the U.S.S.R. Our future will depend on the present; where we end up will depend on how we come through this extremely critical passage that we're making right now. . . .

Mikhail S. Gorbachev, 1990

CHAPTER 2

EVOLUTION OF THE WORLD POLITICAL SYSTEM

This chapter has two purposes. The first is to establish a historical foundation on which we can build our discussion of the conduct of international relations. To this end the following pages give a brief historical narrative in order to emphasize the themes and events you will encounter repeatedly in this book. Of course this chapter cannot fully detail six centuries of history, so you might consider reviewing a text in world history to explore further the events discussed in the following chapters. This would increase your understanding of both history and political science.

This chapter's second goal is to sketch the evolution of the current—albeit rapidly changing—world political system, since it is important to understand the characteristics of the current global order and how they came into being. Thus this chapter is closely related to the next chapter on **system-level analysis**. A system is a concept that defines the global political environment in terms of (1) who the major actors are; (2) the distribution of power among the actors; (3) the level and scope of interactions among the actors; (4) norms of behavior; and (5) the nonhuman factors (technology, resources, ecology) that have an impact on the actors. As we shall see, the nature of the current world political system has a great deal to do with the course of international politics. The next chapter will have much to say about systems theory. To help you understand the theory you should know the history; to understand the history it would be helpful if you had a grasp of the theory. So it might be a good idea to return to this chapter a second time after you have digested the next chapter.

The Evolving World System: Major Themes

Several themes stand out in the history and the nature of the current world political system. The first theme involves the evolution of the **actors**. In about the fifteenth century, the most significant international actor, the *state* (or country), began to evolve.

During most of the five centuries that the state-based system has existed the most powerful states were in Europe. Thus a great deal of the operation of today's world system is based on the European tradition. But today the Eurocentric nature of the system has changed. As a result of two devastating world wars, the European states (except the Soviet Union) declined in power. Non-European states, like the United States, Japan, and China, have become central actors. Furthermore, in the last several decades dozens of new countries, primarily in Africa and Asia, have come into being.

One important thing to note about states is that they are *sovereign*. This means that a state recognizes no authority higher than itself. Structurally, this means that the international political system is generally organized horizontally, in contrast to domestic political systems. They are organized vertically to a significant degree, that is, with a hierarchy of powers, with units subordinate to a higher level of authority.

The world political system is more than that, though. In addition to states, other actors have existed and played roles in world affairs, and they continue to do so. International organizations have roles to play. They have increased in number and importance, and, with international regimes, international law, and similar phenomena, are in the forefront of the struggle for order in the political arena.

A second important theme involves the *distribution of power among the actors*. Often this trait is analyzed in terms of the number of *poles of power*. Most of the five centuries discussed in this chapter were characterized by a European-based **multipolar system**. This is also sometimes referred to as a "balance-of-power" system, a term we will discuss in the next chapter. The point for now, though, is that political power was distributed among a number of poles, that is, countries or alliances. Late nineteenth-century Europe, for example, included Great Britain, France, Germany, Austria-Hungary, and Russia among its great powers. A few other countries, such as Italy, stood just below the rank of great power.

After the destruction caused by World War I and World War II, a new distribution of power emerged. The United States and the Soviet Union dominated the world and amassed most of its political power. This distribution of power is called a **bipolar system** or the East-West Axis. Finally, in the last two decades, the dominance of the two superpowers has lessened and the intensity of their rivalry ebbed. These changes have ended the bipolar system. We will speculate on the future distribution of power toward the end of this chapter and in the next one. Suffice it to say here, there is no consensus among political scientists about the future evolution of the world system.

A third theme identified in this chapter and the next is the *level and scope of interaction*. A striking change in the international system is the rapid increase of the level at which countries are interacting and cooperating and the even faster spread of the scope of issues on which they are cooperating. Voluntarily or not, countries have lost considerable freedom of action as the level of interaction increases, and they are also cooperating on subjects ranging from regulating ozone-depleting chlorofluorocarbon production to coordinating the value of their currencies.

The *norms of behavior* that help regulate and characterize any political system are a fourth theme in our discussion. Behavior in virtually all political systems is governed by a mix of coercion and voluntary compliance. Norms, or values, are what determine voluntary compliance. The values about using force as a policy tool, for example, are changing, and war has lost much of its legitimacy. Unpunished mistreatment of some or all of one's citizens under the guise of sovereignty has also lost considerable legitimacy.

The final theme involves the impact of *nonhuman* factors such as technology and resources. Nuclear power is one technological factor that helped structure the bipolar system and the pattern of interaction. At first the exclusive possession of nuclear weapons and then the massive buildup of them played a role in defining the United States and the Soviet Union as the bipolar superpowers.

A combination of technology and resource factors has also vastly increased the importance of economics in the international political system. A country's productive capacity, its resources, and the extent of its trade have always played an important part. In the last three centuries, though, the industrial revolution, the subsequent need for natural resources, and the uneven distribution across the globe of such resources vastly expanded the impact of economic considerations on world politics. Today power is increasingly defined in terms of economics. There is also increased *economic interdependence* among countries, a trend which some argue will enhance the prospects for peace. Yet there is also increased pressure to compete for scarce resources. That competition will probably increase in the future, and it could be the source of substantial conflict. Finally, there is increased conflict over the uneven distribution of global wealth. The industrialized countries of the North have much. The less developed countries of the South have relatively little. But they are now demanding what they see as their fair share of the wealth. Therein lies the division of the world into the North-South Axis.

Evolution of the World System

As noted, you can trace the evolution of the current world political system to the fifteenth century. It was at this time that modern states, the current dominant international actors, began to be formed. Their creation involved two contradictory trends—one of disintegration, the other of coalescence—that transfigured the system that had existed for the preceding millennium.

The Origins of the National State: Universal Authority and Feudal Organization Decline

After the collapse of Rome in 476, secular political power in the West became fragmented; only occasionally did a powerful centralizing force such as Charlemagne, who ruled the Frankish empire from 768 to 814, arise. It was Christianity as interpreted by the Catholic Church and led by the pope that served as the integrating force of Western civilization during the Middle Ages. Even kings were theoretically (and often substantially) subordinate to the pope. Indeed it was Pope Leo III who crowned Charlemagne "Emperor of the Romans" in Rome on Christmas Day in 800. Charlemagne's empire did not last much beyond his death, but the idea of a new Christian-Roman universal state was re-created in the tenth century when Otto I was crowned head of what became known as the Holy Roman Empire.

By the twelfth century there were tears in this fabric of universalism and feudalism. Advances in military technology, such as the increasing use of gunpowder, meant that the limited realms of feudal lords no longer provided security (Herz, 1959). Economic activity expanded, and the new manufacturing and commerce needed larger political units to operate efficiently. Furthermore, improved communications and transportation made people more aware of and cooperative with their ethnic kin in other areas (Deutsch, 1979:17). Religious political authority began to decline as the authority of kings grew, and in some countries, such as France, England, and Spain, monarchs slowly succeeded in subduing local feudal and ecclesiastical power centers and incorporating them into their kingdoms.

Evolution of the World Political System

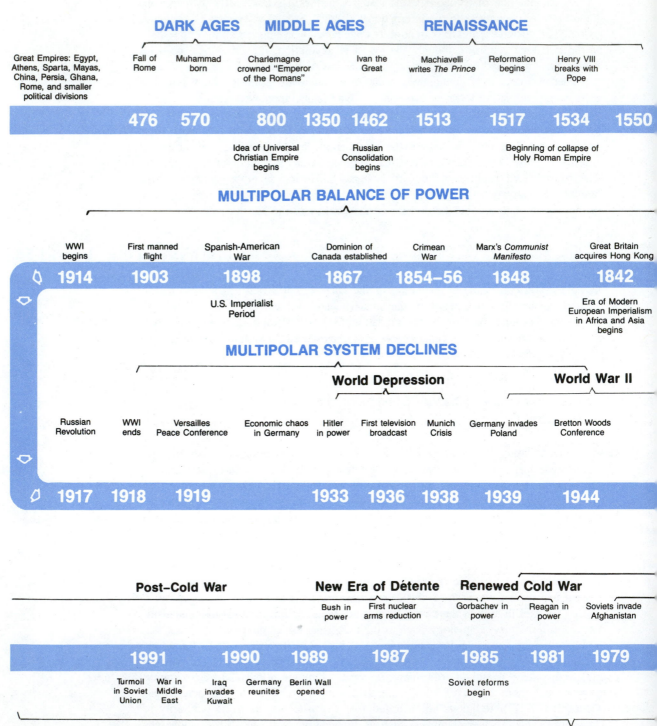

DARK AGES   **MIDDLE AGES**   **RENAISSANCE**

| Great Empires: Egypt, Athens, Sparta, Mayas, China, Persia, Ghana, Rome, and smaller political divisions | Fall of Rome | Muhammad born | Charlemagne crowned "Emperor of the Romans" | | Ivan the Great | Machiavelli writes *The Prince* | Reformation begins | Henry VIII breaks with Pope | |
| 476 | 570 | 800 | 1350 | 1462 | 1513 | 1517 | 1534 | 1550 |

Idea of Universal Christian Empire begins   Russian Consolidation begins   Beginning of collapse of Holy Roman Empire

MULTIPOLAR BALANCE OF POWER

| WWI begins | First manned flight | Spanish-American War | Dominion of Canada established | Crimean War | Marx's *Communist Manifesto* | Great Britain acquires Hong Kong |
| 1914 | 1903 | 1898 | 1867 | 1854–56 | 1848 | 1842 |

U.S. Imperialist Period   Era of Modern European Imperialism in Africa and Asia begins

MULTIPOLAR SYSTEM DECLINES

World Depression   **World War II**

| Russian Revolution | WWI ends | Versailles Peace Conference | Economic chaos in Germany | Hitler in power | First television broadcast | Munich Crisis | Germany invades Poland | Bretton Woods Conference |
| 1917 | 1918 | 1919 | 1933 | 1936 | 1938 | 1939 | 1944 |

Post–Cold War   **New Era of Détente**   **Renewed Cold War**

| | | | Bush in power | First nuclear arms reduction | Gorbachev in power | Reagan in power | Soviets invade Afghanistan |
| 1991 | 1990 | 1989 | 1987 | 1985 | 1981 | 1979 |

Turmoil in Soviet Union   War in Middle East   Iraq invades Kuwait   Germany reunites   Berlin Wall opened   Soviet reforms begin

NEW INTERNATIONAL SYSTEM EMERGING

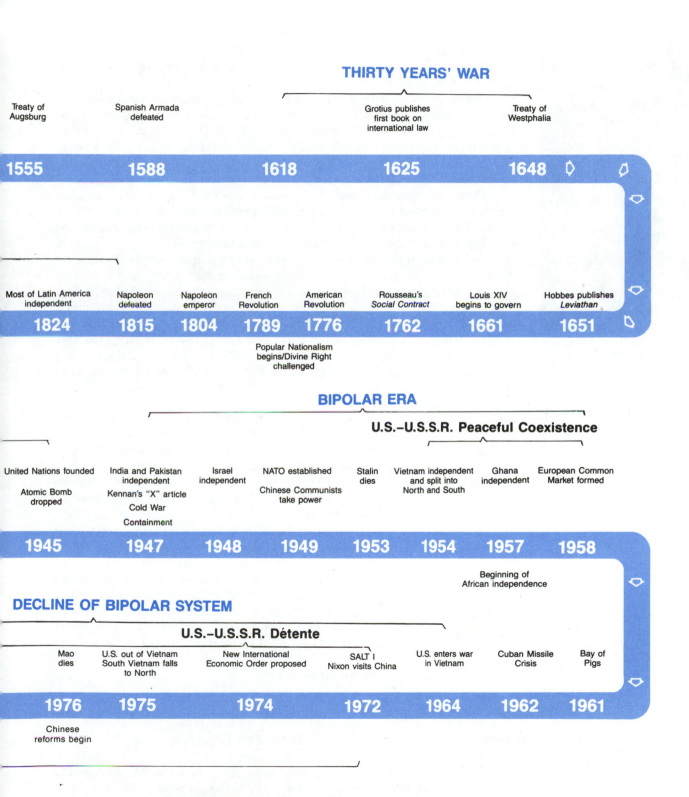

THIRTY YEARS' WAR

| Treaty of Augsburg | Spanish Armada defeated | | Grotius publishes first book on international law | Treaty of Westphalia |

1555 **1588** **1618** **1625** **1648**

| Most of Latin America independent | Napoleon defeated | Napoleon emperor | French Revolution | American Revolution | Rousseau's *Social Contract* | Louis XIV begins to govern | Hobbes publishes *Leviathan* |

1824 **1815** **1804** **1789** **1776** **1762** **1661** **1651**

Popular Nationalism begins/Divine Right challenged

BIPOLAR ERA

U.S.–U.S.S.R. Peaceful Coexistence

United Nations founded	India and Pakistan independent	Israel independent	NATO established	Stalin dies	Vietnam independent and split into North and South	Ghana independent	European Common Market formed
Atomic Bomb dropped	Kennan's "X" article		Chinese Communists take power				
	Cold War						
	Containment						

1945 **1947** **1948** **1949** **1953** **1954** **1957** **1958**

Beginning of African independence

DECLINE OF BIPOLAR SYSTEM

U.S.–U.S.S.R. Détente

| Mao dies | U.S. out of Vietnam South Vietnam falls to North | New International Economic Order proposed | SALT I Nixon visits China | U.S. enters war in Vietnam | Cuban Missile Crisis | Bay of Pigs |

1976 **1975** **1974** **1972** **1964** **1962** **1961**

Chinese reforms begin

In 1534 King Henry VIII of England rejected the religious and political authority of the pope and the Roman Catholic Church. This separation of spiritual and temporal authority was an important part of the origins of national sovereignty, national identity, and the current nation-state system.

The decline of papal authority and the increase in royal power were reinforced by the Renaissance (about 1350–1550), which was a period of cultural and intellectual rebirth and reform. Educated people looked back to the classical Hellenic and Roman cultures as models and developed a concept of personal freedom that ran counter to the authority of the Church.

One significant outcome of this secular movement was the Protestant Reformation. Renaissance thinking was one of the factors that led Martin Luther to reject the Church as the necessary intermediary between people and God. In 1517 Luther protested that the common people could have an individual relationship with God. Within a few decades, nearly a quarter of the people of Western Europe came to agree with him and became Protestants.

These two trends, the growth of kingdoms and the breakdown of central religious dominance, combined to give rise to the modern **nation-state**. This concept means a political unit (1) that is sovereign (i.e., it does not recognize a higher political authority) and (2) whose inhabitants identify politically with it and support it. As you will see in chapter 6 on nationalism, there are many gaps between this ideal concept and reality, but the national state did begin to form in rough outline at this juncture.

The first great secular break with the Catholic Church occurred in England, where King Henry VIII (1509–47) rejected the authority of the Church and established a national Protestant religion. The Reformation also touched off a political-religious struggle on the continent of Europe that lasted for almost a century and a half. The issue was religious freedom, but there were also heavy political consequences. The details of the struggle between the imperial and Catholic Holy Roman Empire and the nationalist and Protestant ethnic groups is fascinating, if beyond our scope here. It caused a century of warfare. When the warfare was ended with the Treaty of Westphalia (1648), central political power in Europe was over. The Holy Roman Empire had splintered into two rival Catholic monarchies (Austria and Spain), a number of Protestant entities (such as Holland and many German states) gained independence or autonomy, and other countries, such as Catholic France and Protestant England, were more secure in their independence. Thus, 1648 marked the end of two centuries of political gestation and the birth of the age of the modern national state and a world political system based on sovereign states as the primary political actors.

During the next several centuries the genesis of national states continued as economic and social interaction grew, and monarchs such as Louis XIV of France (1643–1715), Frederick II (1740–86) of Prussia, and Peter the Great (1682–1725) of Russia expanded and consolidated their domains. In the development of the modern national state, however, one key element was yet to come. Missing was the concept that the state is an embodiment of the nation (the people), not a possession of the king ruling by "divine right." Symbolic of this God-given, personal dominion of kings, France's Louis XIV could proclaim: "*L'etat, c'est moi*" (I am the state). Perhaps so, but a future French king, Louis XVI, would lose his head in 1793 over this presumption, and the people would claim the state for themselves.

Nationalism, Imperialism, and the Multipolar Balance-of-Power System: The Eighteenth and Nineteenth Centuries

The late 1700s and early 1800s were years of major change for the world. The American (1776) and French (1789) revolutions were part of a thought process that changed the entire philosophy about the proper relationships between those who governed and those

The French Revolution of 1789 was a key event in the growth of democratic nationalism, which embodies the idea that the state is a possession of the people rather than of the king. Therefore all political authority resides with the people. Here Eugène Delacroix's classic painting *Liberty Leading the People* symbolizes the overthrow of the French monarchy by the French nation.

who were governed. *Democracies* were established on the principle that political power rests with the people rather than with the monarch. This view also changed and expanded the concept of *nationalism* to include mass identification with and participation in the affairs of the state (country). One symbol of this change was that Napoleonic France was the first country to have a true military draft and to raise an army a million strong.

From its beginnings in America and, particularly, in France, democratic nationalism spread throughout Europe. Within just a little more than a century, monarchs (especially powerful ones) became the exception rather than the rule. The first two decades of the twentieth century marked the real end of monarchial government, with the collapse of the dynastic reigns in China, Germany, Austria-Hungary, Russia, the Ottoman Empire, and other smaller states. This growth of nationalism is discussed further in chapter 6.

The 1800s were a time of rapidly increasing *industrialization*, mainly in Europe and the United States. The era illustrates the role of such *nonhuman* factors as industrial technology and the resulting need for greater supplies of natural resources. This technology-resource combination had a number of impacts. One was a shift in the power of states, as those, such as Germany, that most rapidly industrialized grew in power. A second result of industrialization (and associated technological advances) was that the European powers gained strength compared with nonindustrialized Asia and Africa. Closely related to this disparity in development was the fact that the industrial countries needed to find resources and markets to fuel and fund their capitalist expansion. Economic expansion needed colonies. Many industrialized countries also coveted colonies as a matter of prestige. The result was an era of Euro-American *imperialism* that subjected the peoples of Africa and Asia to white domination. The fate of Africa is

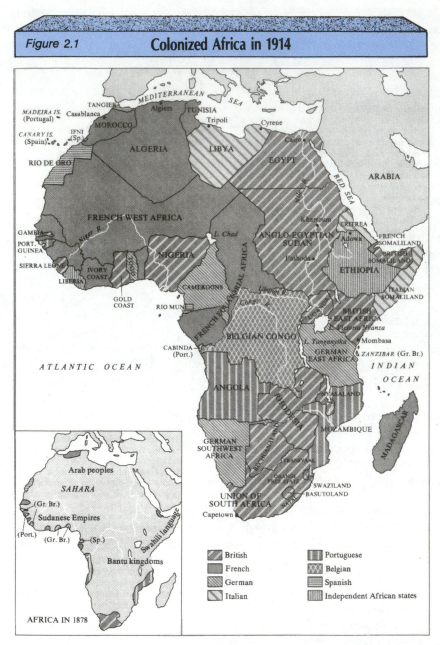

Figure 2.1   **Colonized Africa in 1914**

Source: Marvin Perry, Myra Chase, James R. Jacob, Margaret C. Jacob, and Theodore H. Von Laue, *Western Civilization: Ideas, Politics, and Society,* Third Edition. Copyright 1989 by Houghton Mifflin Company. Used with permission.

The industrialization of Europe and North America was one factor that caused a period of imperial expansion in the late 1800s and early 1900s. This map and its inset show that Africa in 1878 (inset) was largely controlled by its indigenous peoples and that by 1914 (larger map), Africa had been divided into numerous colonies by the European powers. Within another seven decades, virtually all of the colonies regained their independence.

graphically displayed in Figure 2.1. China, it should be noted, was never technically colonized, but after the 1840s that proud culture was divided into spheres of influence among the Western powers, and China lost substantial territories to Great Britain (Hong Kong), Japan (Taiwan/Formosa), and Russia (about 1 million square miles in Central Asia and Pacific Siberia).

The United States also joined in the scramble for colonial possessions overseas. Pacific territories such as Hawaii and Samoa were acquired by the United States in the 1890s, and victory in the Spanish-American War (1898) added Guam, Puerto Rico, and the Philippines. Additionally, during the next several decades, U.S. domination over many of the Caribbean and Central American countries became so strong that their true independence was in doubt.

The imperialist subjugation of Asians, Africans, and others by Europeans and Americans set the stage for what later became the North-South Axis. Indeed, in the overlapping currents of history, the anticolonial movement had begun. An earlier imperial era that had brought European control to the Western Hemisphere began to crumble rapidly. In 1804 Haiti won its independence from France, and by 1824 all of Spain's colonies in Central and South America as well as Portugal's colony of Brazil had thrown off colonial rule. The North-South Axis had begun to form.

The international political relations among the major European powers during the period extending from the Treaty of Westphalia in 1648 into the mid-twentieth century can be characterized as a *multipolar balance-of-power system*. It was multipolar in the sense that political affairs were dominated by numerous major powers. For example, in the century that extended from the final defeat of Napoleon (1815) to the outbreak of World War I (1914) the powers were Great Britain, France, Prussia/Germany, Austria-Hungary, Russia, and to a lesser extent Italy and the Ottoman Empire/Turkey. Also beginning at the end of the 1800s, other powers, in particular the United States, Japan, and then much later China, began to play important roles.

The balance-of-power system obtaining between 1648 and 1945 was a time of shifting alliances designed to prevent any single power or combination of powers from dominating the European continent and, by extension, the world. This antidomination instinct, according to one scholar, underlies the basic "law of behavior of states in a balance of power system," a rule that dictates that countries

> join alliances against the strongest member or against a potentially hegemonic alliance . . . to prevent domination. Once the threatening country has been defeated, do not weaken it so much that it cannot join you later as an ally to prevent another country from gaining ascendant power. (Bernholz, 1985:35)

The antidomination, balancing mechanism successfully prevented any single power or coalition from controlling Europe and perhaps the world for three centuries, and its specific operation between 1800 and 1945 can be seen in Table 2.1 on the following page.

The Multipolar European Balance-of-Power System Totters: The Early Twentieth Century

World changes usually evolve rather than occur suddenly, but by the beginning of the 1900s things were moving quickly. Democracy was rapidly undermining dynastic monarchism, and while in 1900 there were still czars and kaisers, they would be gone in less than two decades. *Nationalism* was similarly eroding the foundations of empires.

TABLE 2.1

Operation of the Multipolar
Balance-of-Power System, 1800–1945

Threatening Power(s)	Year(s)	Antidomination Coalition	Outcome
France	1800–15	Great Britain, Prussia, Austria, Russia	Defeat of Napoleon
Russia	1856	Great Britain, France, Turkey	Defeat of Russia in Crimean War
Germany, Austria-Hungary, Turkey	1914–18	Great Britain, France, Russia, United States	Defeat of Germany and allies in World War I
Germany, Italy, Japan	1939–45	Great Britain, France, Soviet Union, United States	Defeat of Axis powers in World War II

World War I was a pivotal point. Two major empires (the Austro-Hungarian and Ottoman) were among the losers. There had been a great deal of nationalist/independence feeling among their ethnic subjects, and that sentiment was further encouraged by President Woodrow Wilson's call in his Fourteen Points for "self-determination," or the right to self-rule by national groups. The result was the (re)establishment of countries such as Poland, Czechoslovakia, and Yugoslavia. Other countries like Syria, Jordan, Lebanon, and Palestine/Israel came under the mandate (control) of the League of Nations and finally became independent after World War II. As we will see in our recounting of that postwar period, the drive to national self-determination truly exploded in the second half of the twentieth century.

It is possible to argue that the *balance of power* that governed European relations had generally kept the peace during the 1800s, but it broke down in the tragedies of World War I and World War II. The reasons were many and are still subject to dispute. We can say, however, that the European system changed from being one that was fluid and permitted shifting alliances and pragmatic cooperation to a system dominated by two increasingly rigid and hostile alliances. In 1914 one side included Germany, Austria-Hungary, and Turkey. The other consisted of France, Russia, and Great Britain. After the defeat of the Central Powers (principally Germany), there was an attempt to reestablish a balance-of-power system. After initially severe treatment in the 1920s under the provisions of the Treaty of Versailles, Germany was allowed to rebuild its strength in the 1930s.

Events in Russia were in part responsible for the lack of dismay at German revitalization. In 1917 the overthrow of the czar and the coming to power of the Bolsheviks in 1918 under Lenin had evoked a strong negative reaction in the West. There were some halfhearted attempts by the Western European powers and the United States to overthrow the Bolsheviks, and the Soviets were generally treated as outcasts. Thus, a strong Germany was seen by some as a bulwark against the "Red menace."

Great Britain had an additional **realpolitik** reason for turning a blind eye to the growth of German power. As an island, Great Britain had long followed the principle of preventing any single country from dominating all of continental Europe and becoming a threat. With Germany prostrate after World War I, the British were concerned that France or the Soviet Union would achieve dominance and threaten them. Therefore they tried to balance power by acquiescing to German rearmament and diplomatic demands to modify the World War I peace treaties. It was, for the British, a near-fatal mistake.

Another cause of Germany's unimpeded restrengthening was the timorousness that World War I had instilled in Britain and France. Each had lost almost an entire generation of young men, and as Hitler came to power (1933) and rearmed his country, they vacillated over taking action. The *Munich Conference* (1938) became synonymous with this lack of will when Great Britain and France gave way to Hitler's demands for the annexation of part of Czechoslovakia. British prime minister Neville Chamberlain and other leaders agreed to the dismemberment of Czechoslovakia in false hope that an *appeasement policy* toward Germany would maintain the peace.

During the first 40 years of the twentieth century there was an expansion of the world community. Some states established their independence; other existing states, especially Japan and the United States, that had previously been on the periphery of European-dominated diplomacy gradually began to play a more significant role. Many other non-European countries joined world diplomacy through membership in the League of Nations. The point is that international relations still focused on Europe during the first four decades of the 1900s, but a shift was under way. The North-South Axis continued to form.

Fundamental Changes in the World System: The Years Since World War II

World War II was a human tragedy of unequaled proportions. It also marked major changes in the nature and operation of the world political system. One is the shift in the power structure (poles) of the system. First, in 1945 the three-century-old multipolar system ended and a new bipolar system took its place. The antagonistic poles were grouped around the United States and the Soviet Union in an East-West Axis. This system is now in eclipse, and a key concern is the nature of the system that will follow. A second unsettling change in the world political system was occasioned by the nuclear age. The possession of atomic weapons by major powers changed forever the interactions between them.

A third change in the international system was the rapid advance in travel and, even more importantly, communications. This has made international interaction and cooperation more possible. It has also increased and sharpened the images of the world, thereby affecting attitudes. The televised ravages of the Vietnam War, for instance, helped turn U.S. public opinion against it. More recently, the changes in the Soviet Union, Eastern Europe, and elsewhere have occurred, in part, because of the growing inability of leaders to prevent their citizens from seeing and desiring the material wealth and democratic freedoms of the West.

Fourth, economic factors played a stronger part in world politics. National power became increasingly a function of a country's economic strength, rather than its military forces alone. Trade and, as a result, monetary relations also expanded rapidly, and the world entered an era of growing economic interdependence. A fifth change was evidenced by a widening gap between the wealth of the North and South causing increased tension along the North-South Axis.

A sixth related change involved the number and types of system actors. More

The overthrow of the czarist government in Russia in March 1917 was applauded widely in the West. When the Bolsheviks, as the early communists were called, came to power in November of that year, the specter of communism alarmed many Europeans and Americans. This early cartoon (1920) depicts the frightening image of Soviet communism common in the West at the time.

national actors, as states, came into existence in the South as the colonial empires collapsed. Also, a host of new international organizations and other types of transnational actors were established and now play a large role in the conduct of international relations. States remain the principal actors, but they now share the stage with others. Each of these six changes will be reviewed in more detail.

Shifts in the Polar Structure of the System

One series of shifts in the system involved the actors and, indeed, the polar structure of the system itself. World War II finally destroyed the multipolar structure that had been teetering since early in the century. It was replaced by a bipolar system dominated by the Soviet Union and the United States. By the early 1970s that system, in turn, was beginning to weaken, and in the late 1980s it disintegrated with astounding speed. There is, in its place, a new system emerging, one whose structure and operation are not yet clear.

The Rise and Decline of the Bipolar System   The ravages of World War II devastated most of the existing major actors, and they fell from the first rank of world politics. In their place, the United States emerged as a military and economic *superpower*. The Soviet Union, though incredibly damaged, emerged as the United States' chief rival. It could not match the United States economically, and for two decades or more the United States maintained a strong nuclear lead, but the Soviets possessed a huge conventional force that threatened Western Europe and an ideology that seemed to press American interests around the globe. The East-West Axis was established.

The exact causes of the confrontation, termed the *cold war*, are complex and controversial. It is safe to say, however, that varying economic and political interests and the power vacuum created by the collapse of the old balance-of-power system led to a new *bipolar system* in which a great deal of world politics was centered on the confrontation between the two superpowers.

The American reaction to the perceived world Soviet/communist threat was the doctrine of *containment* (see box below). Applying lessons learned by analogy from

Containment

More than any single source, the intellectual origins of the containment doctrine can be traced to George Kennan, a U.S. State Department official. In July 1947 Kennan published an article in the establishment journal *Foreign Affairs* entitled "The Sources of Soviet Conduct." It was anonymous, attributed only to "X." "Mechanistic Soviet power," Kennan wrote, "moves inexorably along a prescribed path, like a persistent toy automobile wound up and headed in a given direction, stopping only when it meets some unanswerable force." The West's response to this threat, he opined, should be "the adroit and vigilant application of counterforce at a series of constantly shifting geographical and political points, corresponding to the shifts and maneuvers of Soviet policy," thereby confronting the Soviets "at every point where they show signs of encroaching upon the interests of a peaceful and stable world."*

*In fairness, it should be noted that Kennan has subsequently and repeatedly claimed that he has been misinterpreted. He maintains that he did not wish to emphasize military counterforce, and instead favored moral, economic, and political opposition to Soviet expansionism.

Munich's appeasement, the United States defined containment as trying to counter Soviet/communist expansionism wherever it threatened. A later, related theory, the *domino theory*, supposed that if communism conquered one country, then its neighbor would fall, then another, and another, just like a row of dominoes standing on end, until the chain reaction led to America's doorstep. Based on these strategic assumptions, the United States moved from a prewar norm of isolationism to a postwar *globalism*, opposing the Soviet Union (and later Communist China) diplomatically and militarily around the world. The United States sponsored a number of regional alliances, the most important of which was the North Atlantic Treaty Organization (NATO, established 1949), which consisted of the United States, Canada, and most Western European countries. The Soviets responded in 1955 with the Warsaw Treaty Organization (WTO, Warsaw Pact), an alliance between the Soviet Union and its client states in Eastern Europe. Both sides also vied for power in the developing Third World, and both Soviet and American arms and money flowed to various governments and rebel groups in the ongoing communist-anticommunist contest.

There was also a series of more direct confrontations between Soviet and American power. The most serious of these, and the closest the world has ever come to nuclear war, occurred in Cuba in October 1962. In the aftermath, President John F. Kennedy estimated the chances of nuclear war had been between one-in-three and even. *The Cuban missile crisis* erupted when the Soviets tried to station medium-range nuclear missiles in Cuba and the Kennedy administration resolved to force the missiles out. In the end, because the United States possessed a vast nuclear superiority and because it handled the crisis with some skill, the Soviet missiles were withdrawn. In the longer term, however, the crisis led to a major increase in Soviet military strength. The Kremlin was determined never again to be so humiliated. The Soviets began a massive nuclear armament program that soon brought them to parity with the United States.

The containment doctrine also led to America's involvement in *Vietnam*. After World War II, the Vietnamese, led by nationalist/communist Ho Chi Minh, struggled for independence against the French. In 1954 Ho achieved victory, but the country was divided between his forces in the north and a pro-Western government in the south. Unification elections were supposed to occur soon, but the South resisted, and they did not. The struggle resumed in the early 1960s, and the United States, fearing a communist victory, intervened on behalf of the South. As the United States increasingly became involved, so did its prestige, and the American goal shifted from preventing a communist victory to avoiding a defeat that would damage American prestige and credibility.

The war, though popular at first, soon became a domestic trauma for America as the violence and casualties mounted on all sides. The depth of the American domestic opposition to the war was tragically underlined by the death in 1970 of four students at Kent State University during antiwar clashes between demonstrators and Ohio National Guardsmen. War-weariness finally led to the complete disengagement of the United States, and within a short time the South fell (1975) to the North.

Vietnam led to a number of important changes in American attitudes about international relations. One was the reassessment of the need to fight communism everywhere. To some degree, and in direct contrast to the "lesson of Munich," the "lesson of Vietnam" that some drew was that the United States should fight nowhere, and in the 1970s America severely constrained its military power.

Second, and related to wider developments, the United States saw more clearly that the world was no longer bipolar. Some aspects of bipolarism certainly remained, especially in the military sphere. In many other ways, though, the alliance systems around the two poles began to fragment. Additionally, other actors who were not associated with either pole gained a greater role in world politics. The communist "camp" fragmented, with China becoming more of an antagonist to than an ally of the Soviet Union. On the Western side, Japan and Western Europe both recovered economically and increasingly followed foreign policies that sometimes diverged from those of the United States. Perceiving the realities of a changing balance of power, President Nixon and his secretary of state, Henry Kissinger, moved to better relations with the Soviet Union and China with a policy of *détente*.

The End of the Bipolar System   During the 1970s and most of the 1980s, relations between the United States and both the Soviet Union and China had upswings and downswings, especially with the Soviets during the first Reagan administration, but overall they continued to improve. Then in 1985 things began to change more rapidly, especially U.S.–Soviet relations.

Before beginning this brief survey of the events between 1985 and the present, it is important to encourage you to read further about them. They are not merely historical, they are historic . . . even breathtaking. The limits of space in this text necessarily mean that the discussion here can be only a short review of the recent high drama that has so sweepingly changed the world stage, but they should not be underestimated.

A second caveat is that given the rapid and remarkable changes that are under way, it is fully possible that some of what you read here may be dated by the time you read it, perhaps only six months from now. It is impossible to find a serious analysis that predicted how fast changes would occur, and trying to depict what is occurring in a way that will remain accurate is, in the words of one frustrated analyst, "like trying to paint a moving train" (*NYT,* 1/16/90:A20).

Mikhail S. Gorbachev, who in 1985 was named as general secretary (head) of the Soviet Communist Party, is both a cause and a symptom of the recent changes. He is a cause of change because he represents a new type of Soviet leader, both younger and less tied to ideology than his predecessors. He is a symptom of change because he was elected by an inner circle that had begun to recognize that economically and socially the Soviet Union was in serious trouble. The old-guard party elite was willing to accept the relatively young Gorbachev in the hope he would provide new ideas to rejuvenate the Soviet Union. Neither they, nor Gorbachev, one suspects, realized how remarkable his changes would be.

To accomplish his goals, Gorbachev believed he needed to end the stranglehold that the incredibly inefficient centralized planning bureaucracy had on the Soviet economy and to introduce at least some level of free market incentives to evaluate and motivate both managers and workers. As part of this process, Gorbachev also came to realize that he had to diminish the political role played by the Politburo and other Communist party organizations and to increase the role of the less ideologically bound government. Among other moves, Gorbachev promoted constitutional changes that increased the power of the formerly symbolic Soviet presidency. He, himself, was elected to that office in 1989 by the national legislature. The Russian word *perestroika,* which means restructuring, symbolizes these complex changes. Gorbachev also instituted a policy dubbed *glasnost* (openness) to increase the volume and accuracy of information available to Soviet citizens. At least in significant part, glasnost was designed to expose the ineptitude of the burdensome bureaucracy and build grassroots support for perestroika.

Perestroika and glasnost would not alone be enough, Gorbachev realized. The Soviet economy also needed a massive infusion of development capital (money) and technology to expand and modernize. That required better relations with the West. As Gorbachev told British prime minister Margaret Thatcher, "We [Soviets] need a lasting peace to concentrate on the development of our society and to proceed to improve the life of the Soviet people" (Rourke, 1990:40).

A lessening of cold war tensions was vital to Soviet economic rejuvenation for two reasons. First, it would allow Gorbachev to reduce the share of the Soviet budget (almost 50 percent in 1985) allocated to military spending and to redirect Soviet technological skills to domestic purposes. To that end, he announced in December 1988 a unilateral reduction of Soviet forces by 500,000 troops, and he has sought and sometimes achieved agreements to further restrain or reduce conventional and nuclear forces. Second, better relations with the West would mean increases in the development capital and technology from those countries. Increased trade on better terms, foreign investment in the Soviet economy, loans, and credits were and are Gorbachev's goals.

To accomplish his goals, Gorbachev launched a "peace offensive" that was a combination of skilled public diplomacy (see chapter 12) and action. He withdrew Soviet forces from Afghanistan, cooperated with the United States to ease tensions in southern Africa, Central America, and elsewhere, and announced an end to the earlier Soviet contention (the Brezhnev Doctrine) that it could intervene in socialist East European countries to protect their governments from "bourgeoisie counterrevolutions." Instead, Gorbachev was willing to let Eastern Europeans follow their own domestic policies. It was the "Frank Sinatra Doctrine," joked Soviet spokesman Gennadi I. Gerasimov, "they'll do it their way" (Komisar, 1990:8). Accompanying this policy, the Soviets also began to reduce their economic subsidies to their client states in Eastern Europe and elsewhere, thereby saving further billions of budget dollars.

The West responded slowly, albeit steadily, to these changes because it reasonably took time to comprehend and accept the marked shift in Soviet policy and because some of the West's leaders, especially President Reagan and Prime Minister Thatcher, were particularly leery of the Soviets. But progress was achieved, including the signing of the 1987 Intermediate-range Nuclear Forces Treaty, the first reduction of nuclear weapons. By the end of his term, even Reagan was willing to admit, "Gorbachev is a different kind of fellow than those previous [Soviet] leaders. We can get along. We can cooperate in this world" (Rourke, 1990:268).

The easing of cold war tensions also served to loosen the ties within the West. A combination of rising economic rivalry and a declining sense of threat from a common enemy left the now economically recovered and politically confident Europeans and Japanese more willing to follow their own foreign policy agenda rather than to give way to U.S. leadership. Thus, Western solidarity, while not nearly as fragmented as the former Soviet bloc, was also in serious disrepair by the late 1980s.

From 1985 through 1988 the changes in the world political atmosphere changed at what seemed a rapid pace, but those years pale with what happened beginning in 1989. In the Soviet Union, the revolution from the top initiated by Gorbachev threatened to escape his control. The pent-up frustrations of Soviet citizens were released in an explosion of criticism that, in a time of glasnost, was aired widely and that, in turn, engendered further dissent. Also, the promise of perestroika for a better life remained unfulfilled; indeed, economic circumstances declined and anxieties increased. Finally, the lessening of political controls sparked resurgent independence/autonomy demands by Lithuanians, Azerbaijanis, and most of the other national groups in the U.S.S.R. (see chapter 6). The result was that by 1990 the Soviet Union was in critical political and economic trouble, and some analysts were warning that the country could disintegrate or career into civil war. Gorbachev remained in power through a combination of his

The reunification of Germany is perhaps the most dramatic single symbol of the end of the cold war. The recreation of *ein Deutschland,* one Germany, after 45 years of division occurred at the stroke of midnight, October 3, 1990. At that moment, the Germans, shown here at the Brandenburg Gate in the heart of Berlin, erupted into a tumultuous celebration.

amazing political and economic dexterity and the lack of a credible alternative leader or policy, but his long-term political survival is, at the time of this writing, in serious doubt.

The enervation of the Soviet economic and political system also allowed nationalist forces in Eastern Europe to make a bid to break away from Moscow's orbit without fear of Soviet intervention. Popular protests led to free elections, and by mid-1990 Poland, Czechoslovakia, and Hungary all had noncommunist governments, and substantial reforms had taken place in Romania and Bulgaria. Soviet troops were leaving Czechoslovakia and Hungary, and the Soviet-led alliance, the Warsaw Treaty Organization, was all but defunct.

More than anywhere else, however, Germany—East, West, and finally, Germany—was the most dramatic focus of change. If describing these general events is akin to painting a moving train, then, in the words of former CIA director Richard Helms, the events in Germany were "a kind of runaway freight train that nobody . . . seems able to contain" (*HC*, 3/4/90:A19). Beginning in late July 1989, an increasing number of East Germans sought refuge and eventual transit to West Germany by flooding into West German embassies in Budapest and Prague. The Czechoslovakians and Hungarians, themselves in the process of reforming, began to allow East Germans to transit through to the West, and the hemorrhage of East Germans to the West that the Berlin Wall had been constructed in 1961 to stop began anew. Attempts by East Germany to stem the tide sparked increasingly large demonstrations in the country that culminated in a pro-democracy, anti–Berlin Wall march by 500,000 in East Berlin in early November. The hard-line government of the ailing Erich Honecker had already been replaced in mid-October, and the moribund communist government announced on November 9 that exit visas would be immediately granted to all citizens allowing them to cross the border if they wished without special permission. With that seemingly innocuous announcement,

Truth Is Stranger Than Fiction

One of the fascinations (and frustrations) of being a political scientist is the ability of the world to do the totally unexpected. In the wonderful "truth is stranger than fiction" realm, consider this: For several decades the horror of Western Europe was an image of Soviet troops inside NATO. Now it's happened! Not by invasion, but by incorporation. Since the former East German *Landers* (states) joined West Germany, they and all Germany are now part of NATO. But since the Soviet troops stationed in East Germany (to protect it, they said, from NATO) remain there, Soviet troops are now stationed inside NATO. Furthermore, and this is the best twist of all, because East Germany had subsidized the Soviet troops, and because the new Germany has assumed East Germany's former obligations, then not only are Soviet troops inside of NATO, but Germany is paying to maintain them there!

the Berlin Wall ceased to be a barrier. That night hundreds of thousands of East and West Berliners partied around and atop the wall celebrating the political death of the hated symbol of division. Within days what once had been synonymous with oppression was literally vanishing, being chipped into pieces and carted away by local citizens and tourists.

The breaching of the wall accelerated another momentous event, the reunification of Germany. Within a few weeks, the East German government had ceased to function as more than a caretaker to keep processes functioning during the rapid drive toward unification. On July 1, 1990, the West German currency became legal tender throughout all Germany, and in October East Germany technically dissolved itself, and its constituent parts (*Landers*) were admitted to the now-single German state. What had once seemed possible only in the dim future, if at all, had come about in less than one year.

The Emergence of a New Polar Structure. For all the excitement of the events centering on Central Europe and the collapse of the bipolar structure, an equally fascinating and even more important matter is the shape of the world to come. There are a few who maintain that the world is (and should be) moving toward a system in which national sovereignty breaks down or is severely weakened and in which there are greater controls exercised by a *supranational* international organization (see chapter 3, p. 59). At its extreme, this could be a world government, and the system would be **unipolar**. Such a system has its attractions as well as its drawbacks, and it is discussed further in Part IV; for the immediate future there is "a negligible probability of [its] being realized" (Bernholz, 1985:210). Equally improbable is another variation of a unipolar system, a *universal empire*, in which one of the two current superpowers (or a new superpower, say, China) achieves world **hegemony**.

Another possibility is a **tripolar system** with the United States, the Soviet Union, and China at its three pivot points. It can be argued that Japan and Germany are only economic powers, and Western Europe does not have the political unity to qualify as a superpower. It is also possible to envision that China will develop into a true superpower. Former president Richard Nixon (1980:126), for example, estimates that China "could become the most powerful nation on earth during the twenty-first century." If anything near that happens, and if the United States and the Soviet Union maintain their superpower status, then it may be that a tripolar system will develop.

The United States and the Soviet Union have rapidly moved from bitter enemies to wary accord, even friendly cooperation. Soviet president Mikhail Gorbachev and U.S. president George Bush met five times in Bush's first two years as president-elect and president, and the two are proud of their leadership in bringing the cold war to an end. That pride was evident in the cartoon shown here. Gorbachev presented it to Bush at their September 1990 summit meeting in Helsinki, Finland, and it depicts the two victorious presidents having knocked out an opponent, in the foreground, labeled Cold War in Russian.

The most likely possibility for a polar structure, though, is a renewed multipolar system. The United States, the Soviet Union, China, Japan, and Germany are five probable poles. A few other countries, most notably India, might join that group. It also might be that a mixed system of regional/national poles will develop. Europe, in the form of the European Community,* might be a pole. There is already a free trade agreement between the United States and Canada. Mexico is negotiating to make that a trilateral group, and President Bush has called for a hemispheric free trade area. It is possible, then, that North America or even the Western Hemisphere could become another regional pole.

*The technically correct name is the European Communities, because the EC is an amalgam of the European Economic Community, the European Steel and Coal Community, and the European Atomic Energy Community. The singular Community, instead of Communities, will be used in this book because it is most frequently used, because the plural confuses the important fact that in discussing the EC one is discussing a singular entity, and because the singular verb with Communities (as in "the Communities is" instead of "are") is a stylistic nightmare.

There are yet other possibilities beyond these, and they are discussed further in the next chapter. What you will find there is that the polar structure of the system helps determine the system's pattern of interactions, that is, how the system works. Therefore, the evolving polar structure, whatever it is, will importantly affect your future.

The Advent of a Nuclear World

Whatever the progress toward nuclear arms control, the world system was forever altered by the atomic flash over Hiroshima on August 6, 1945. Atomic weapons not only brought total self-destruction within the range of human possibilities, they changed power relationships. They virtually divided the world into two classes of powers—the two superpowers, who had the vast majority of all the nuclear weapons, and the others. The probable result of a nuclear war is so cataclysmic that a major focus of the current political system is avoiding Armageddon. One result is that the nuclear superpowers have avoided war directly with one another. Another is that nuclear arms talks have become an ongoing process. The decades of arms talks have brought some, but limited, success. The 1963 Test Ban Treaty and the 1972 SALT I treaty brought some restraints but no reductions. The 1979 SALT II treaty was never ratified because of the decline in relations, but was tacitly followed by both superpowers for years. Finally, the 1987 INF Treaty eliminated a small class of missiles. It was a small step numerically, a huge advance psychologically. Now, there is a strong possibility of a significant reduction of U.S. and Soviet strategic weapons through the START negotiations between Washington and Moscow.

Rapid International Travel and Communications

Another and more salutary impact of technology on international politics is the result of the vastly improved forms of international travel and communications. This has an impact on the leader-to-leader level and the people-to-people basis. Among leaders, communications and even face-to-face meetings have become more common. Summit diplomacy has its pitfalls (see chapter 12), but the ability of leaders to see other leaders and their countries in human terms is likely to ease the stereotypical misperceptions that are one cause of suspicion and tension. Early in their times of leadership, Presidents Reagan and Gorbachev had negative images of one another and their countries. To Reagan, the Soviet Union was the "evil empire," and, he groused, "somebody said the second most stupid thing in the world that a man could say was that he could understand the Russians. I've often wondered what was first." For his part, Gorbachev said of Reagan, "Sometimes when you stand face-to-face with someone, you cannot see his face," and he was convinced Reagan "couldn't make peace if he wanted to. He's a prisoner of the military-industrial complex." Four years and several summits later things had changed. "There is good chemistry between us," Reagan observed of his interaction with Gorbachev. "I think progress has been made by us. I think that through this succession of summits there is a much better understanding." And so there was (Rourke, 1990:268–69).

The advances in communications have also affected the views of the general public, and with the increase of the democratization of foreign policy-making, international politics is changed. Less than a century ago, an American diplomat referred to the Spanish-American War as a "splendid little war." No war, with its death and pain, has ever been splendid, but modern communications is bringing that home to people. Vietnam, it has been said, was the first war fought on television, and the nightly images

Rapid communications are dramatically changing international relations in many ways. One is by rapidly and widely conveying strong images that evoke powerful emotions about the events in and conditions of the world. One example was the February 11, 1990, release of black South African leader Nelson Mandela, shown here with his wife Winnie in his first moments as a free man after being held 28 years in a South African prison for his political activities.

of the fighting and suffering helped turn American opinion against the war. Some complain that it weakened American willpower, and columnist George Will grumped that if television had existed during the American Civil War the North would have sued for peace, the Union would have been lost, and slavery would still exist. Whether he was right or not on that, he clearly recognized the power of the telecast image.

More recent images have also had galvanic effect: a lone Chinese student defying a tank column in Beijing's Tiananmen Square; South Africa's Nelson Mandela striding away from 28 years of imprisonment; cheering Berliners atop the Wall; Contra rebels driving a wooden stake through the heart of a pinioned peasant in Nicaragua; drug cartel gunmen assassinating a presidential candidate in Colombia; emaciated children in Ethiopia. All of these were powerful images that both reflect the drama of world events and promote further change.

The Growth of Economic Interdependence

World War II also signaled major shifts in world economics, both in trade and in monetary relations. The level of world trade had been gradually rising for several centuries, but after the war it greatly accelerated. In addition to nonpolitical technological and economic factors, trade was encouraged by the belief that trade barriers had contributed to the economic collapse (world depression) that preceded and (some argued) helped cause World War II. As a result, and in its own interest, the United States led moves to remove tariffs and other trade restrictions. The General Agreement on Tariffs and Trade (GATT) organization was a primary focus of that activity. One result of increased trade, as well as other factors, is increasing *economic interdependence*: almost all countries have economies that rely on foreign markets and sources of supply. The free trade philosophy still dominates Western thinking, although in recent years there has been restrengthened pressure to practice more "protectionism."

Monetary relations were also considerably revamped at the end of the war, primarily at a conference (1944) at Bretton Woods, New Hampshire. The resulting monetary arrangements, known as the Bretton Woods system, were based on the gold standard and the strength of the American dollar. That system lasted until the early 1970s, when a number of factors, including the weakening of the dollar and the unwillingness of the United States to sell gold at a fixed (and no longer realistic) rate, brought the world to a new system of currencies that generally "float"—that is, are exchanged on the basis of supply and demand conditions. The Bretton Woods structure also included the International Monetary Fund (IMF), which was designed to help stabilize currency exchange rates by loaning countries money to meet international currency demands, thereby keeping the supply and demand stable. The IMF continues to play a vital role in monetary relations. Most remarkably, there is the European Economic Community, which is scheduled to attain nearly complete economic cooperation among most Western European countries by 1992.

Not all trends have been positive, however. Economic relations have become increasingly troublesome in the 1970s and 1980s. Trade and monetary tensions exist among the **trilateral countries** (United States, Western Europe, Japan), with U.S./ Japanese relations particularly troubled by the imbalance (in Japan's favor) of trade between the two. Monetary relations are also unsteady on a number of fronts. In recent years, the most serious problem has related to the massive loans made to the less developed countries (LDCs) and the difficulty those countries (especially in Latin America) are having meeting principal and interest payment schedules. On a broader scale, economic relations and international politics are increasingly concerned with the wide gap between the relatively wealthy industrialized states and the poorer LDCs.

Economic Disparity Between North and South

A basic world economic reality is that the substantial majority of people and countries are poor. These countries are designated the *South*. By contrast, world wealth is concentrated in a few industrialized countries (the *North*). The North-South Axis was introduced in chapter 1. Although some of the South's absolute economic (and related social) conditions are slightly improving, the gap between the North and South is widening. Increasingly, the poor countries are making demands that a *New International Economic Order* (NIEO) be established based on a greater sharing of wealth and the end of trade and monetary policies that favor the North. The response of the North has been limited to date, and the question of Third World development and North/South relations will remain a perplexing and contentious aspect of international relations for years to come.

Expansion of the World Nation-State System

The Third World has also played a pivotal role in the expansion of the world's nation-state system. The colonial empires established by the imperial Western powers collapsed after World War II, and in the ensuing years over 100 new countries have gained independence (nearly tripling the previous number). Almost all these new countries are part of the Third World. Nationalism, once thought on the decline, has been reinvigorated, and the perspectives and demands of these countries have considerably changed the focus and tone of world political and economic debate.

Two scholars, Hedley Bull and Adam Watson (1982:425), have observed that between 1500 and 1900, the international "scene was transformed by the expansion of the Europeans over the rest of the globe." Further, "a cardinal rule" of the system was that the European states "had come to conceive [of] themselves as forming an exclusive club enjoying rights superior to those of other political communities."

In the last half-century, the long-standing history of European (and American) power and privilege has been dramatically altered. The Third World countries are becoming more of a force in world politics. Many support extensive changes in the international system, and a few, like Libya, take radical action that, for better or worse, commands the attention of the developed countries. A few other Third World countries, like Saudi Arabia, have achieved substantial wealth and influence. Other countries, such as India, Brazil, and Nigeria, have become regional powers.

Third World countries have joined together in such movements and organizations as the Nonaligned Movement and the Group of 77 in order to promote their causes. They have also gained considerable sway in other international organizations. Third World countries now command a majority in the United Nations General Assembly, and they dominate some of the UN's other agencies and bodies. This had led to regular defeats for the West in UN voting and the threatened—and actual—withdrawal by some industrialized countries from UN organizations.

This expansion of the international system, the lessening of Euro-American influence, and the growth of Afro-Asian-Latin influence have had a profound impact. As Bull and Watson (1982:428–29) put it, the Third World countries:

> accelerated the pace of decolonization or national liberation, and brought about a new . . . climate in world affairs in which colonial rule . . . [and] . . . rule by settler minorities, came to be regarded as illegitimate. They found a new target in neocolonialism, the domination of . . . weak countries by indirect means. They upheld the equality of races, especially in relation to the white supremacist governments of southern Africa. They formulated demands for economic justice between rich and poor nations . . . [and advocated] cultural liberation, the repudiation not merely of the political and economic, but the intellectual or spiritual suzerainty of the West. They propagated a Third World ideology or world view . . . that served to explain the history of relations between European and non-European people in terms acceptable to themselves.

Development of Increased International Cooperation

While discord has continued to be a persistent theme of international relations, the period after World War II has also been notable for renewed attempts to further international cooperation. The United Nations, founded in 1945 as a successor to the League of Nations, has made contributions in peacekeeping and economic and social betterment. Its role, however, has been limited by the resistance of all countries to compromising their own interests for the common good. In addition to the UN, a wide array of *transnational* governmental and private organizations has been established that work to better the world's economic and social conditions. Many of these organizations also try to find solutions to the many environmental and resource problems that increasingly beset the world. The concept of international law has also made progress, although international law remains a primitive system. The system-level actors are introduced in the next chapter, and they are extensively discussed in Part IV.

Chapter Summary

1. This chapter has two primary goals. One is to establish a reference framework from which the historical examples used to illustrate the theoretical points made in this book can be understood in context. The second goal is to sketch the evolution of the current world political system.

2. Several themes stand out in the history and the current nature of the world system. One is that its main actors are states (countries) that are sovereign (answer to no higher authority).

3. A second theme is that the system has evolved through several polar configurations, that is, patterns of the distribution of power among the major actors. Systems that have different numbers of poles operate differently. Multipolar, bipolar, and tripolar systems are especially important to recent history, current events, and perhaps future world politics.

4. The way that any polar system operates is also affected by other factors such as technology and the distribution of natural resources, its norms, and its level and scope of interaction.

5. The current world system began to develop in about the fifteenth century when modern states began to form.

6. Before that time the world system was characterized both by claims to universal authority and by feudal organization.

7. Many factors, including military technology, improved communications, the growth of economic productivity and trade, and new intellectual views combined to end the old universal-feudal system and to give rise to the state system.

8. Scholars tend to view the Treaty of Westphalia (1648), more than any other event, as demarcating the change between the old and new system.

9. The American (1776) and French (1789) revolutions symbolize a process that changed the entire philosophy about the proper relation between rulers and citizens in states. Slowly, democracy—the idea that political power rests with the people—began to take hold.

10. Also, nationalism began to grow rapidly. Nationalism involves the people's identification with and participation in the affairs of the state. It is denoted by the concept of the nation-state.

11. In the later 1800s there was also a burst of imperialism that led to the colonial subjugation of large parts of Africa and Asia.

12. The three centuries between 1648 and 1945 were characterized by a multipolar balance-of-power system in Europe. The relatively realpolitik, fluid attempts of countries to maintain an equilibrium of power and thus keep the system operating in rough balance were evident during these centuries.

13. That system began to totter after World War I, and it collapsed after World War II. Non-European powers, including the United States, Japan, and China, increasingly became a factor in world politics.

14. A bipolar system emerged in place of the collapsed multipolar system. The United States and the Soviet Union were at the ends of the East-West Axis. The system was rigid and hostile. Containment of the Soviet Union was a key concept of U.S. foreign policy during the cold war era.

15. The bipolar system gradually declined as other countries have achieved more importance, as transnational actors have become more important, as the expense of continuing confrontation has strained American and Soviet budget resources, and as the relative power of the two superpowers has declined.

16. Then from 1985 through 1990 the bipolar system rapidly disintegrated amid Soviet turmoil, German reunification, East European freedom, and other dramatic changes.

17. A significant question is: what will follow the bipolar system? The most likely possibility is some form of new multipolar system.

18. Whatever the exact configuration of the new system, it will be influenced by several fundamental changes since World War II. One is the advent of the nuclear age. A second is the increase in travel and communications technology. Third is international economic interdependency. Fourth is the economic and social disparity between North and South. Fifth is the rise in power and international influence of states outside Europe and North America. Sixth are the still elementary but rapidly rising incidents and patterns of international cooperation.

Mad world! Mad kings! Mad composition!

Shakespeare, *King John*

Power moves the world for good or ill, and no nation will give up its power.

Richard Nixon

CHAPTER 3

SYSTEM-LEVEL ANALYSIS

The discussion in chapter 1 of how to study international politics deals in its final section with what is called levels of analysis. The issue is what to study: people as individuals or a species (individual-level analysis); how countries make foreign policy (state-level analysis); or the nature of the world (system-level analysis). The best answer is to study all three levels. The last chapter began this study through a brief historical survey of the evolution of the current world system. This chapter will continue this process by examining system-level analysis (often shortened to systems analysis) as a theory.

Understanding International Systems

Political scientists who take the system-level analysis approach essentially adopt a "top down" approach to studying world politics. Their primary focus is the external events and world political environment that determine the pattern of interaction in any given system. Systems analysts believe that any system operates in predictable ways—that there are behavioral tendencies that the actor countries usually follow. An imperfect analogy might be a solar system.[1] In such a system, the planets and other celestial bodies move in remarkably regular and predictable patterns, which are determined by such factors as the size and gravitational pull of the sun and the size and distance of a planet from the center of the solar system. It can also be noted that a system can even have subsystems. A planet, for example, may have a number of moons that revolve around it, while the entire subsystem revolves around the sun.

If we follow this analogy, systems analysts can be thought of as political astronomers. What they focus on is determining the nature (size, shape, spatial relations

1. The idea of a solar-system analogy is borrowed from Kaplan (1979).

between bodies, etc.) of the system and its subsystems. Even more important, systems analysts are interested in the interactive patterns within the system. How does it work? What are the relations between bodies? When and why do they collide or travel safely on? What can be predicted about future movements?

It should be noted that the astronomy analogy has its limitations in explaining systems analysis. Most political systems analysts do not see the international system always operating in an unchanging and regular manner like the solar system. Instead they believe that the configuration of a system creates certain rules and likelihoods of international behavior, but they should be thought of as pressures or tendencies rather than laws.

Having defined system-level analysis, our next task is to explore in detail the nature and operation of international systems. To do this, we will first look at the characteristics of various international systems. Then we will discuss how the world changes from one international system to another. How world politics works within the context of differing international systems will be our third major concern. This will be followed by a special look at balance-of-power theory, and, finally, there will be an evaluation of system-level analysis as an approach to understanding world politics.

System Characteristics

A solar system has a variety of identifiable characteristics. It is a certain size and has existed for a finite period. The types and numbers of celestial bodies (suns, planets, moons, asteroids, comets) can also be described. The size of the bodies, their distances from one another, their relative movement, and a number of other relational characteristics are also important.

Similarly, political systems analysts are concerned with the characteristics of international systems and subsystems. Political scientists have not yet developed an agreed-on list of factors, but the most common possibilities include the following: system-level actors, number of poles, distribution of power assets, norms of behavior, geographic characteristics, and scope and level of interaction.

System-Level Actors

An initial question to ask about a system is, Who are the actors? What organizations operate in the system, and what impact do they have on the course of international relations? We can answer these questions by dividing actors into three general categories: national actors, supranational actors, and transnational actors.

National Actors For approximately five centuries, states (countries) have been the most important actors in the international system. The nature and operation of states will be dealt with extensively in chapters 5 and 6, but we can briefly define them here. A state is a territorially based political organization that claims and is generally accorded sovereignty. Sovereignty means independence and at least theoretical equality with other states (see chapter 2, p. 34).

Since the Treaty of Westphalia (1648), the most important characteristic of the international system has been that it is dominated by a large number of self-interested states that do not routinely obey any higher political authority. There are no powerful centralizing organizations in the system. These factors cause the largely anarchical nature of the world system. The preponderant role of states does not mean, however, that they are the only system actors or that the system is without any centralizing forces.

Supranational Actors   One centralizing force in the international system is supranational organizations. Their distinguishing characteristics are that (1) they have individual countries as members and (2) *theoretically*, at least, some aspects of the organization's authority transcends that of its individual members. Many view supranational organizations as a "higher," more desirable form of international order than the current system of independent states. At the ultimate, some theorists envision a United States of the World. In other words, a supranational organization is one in which the whole is greater than the sum of its parts, an organization to which countries surrender all or part of their sovereignty, and an organization to which member states are at least somewhat subordinate. There are several types of supranational organizations. These are discussed in depth in chapter 15, but in brief, they are the following:

• General-Purpose, Universal Organizations.   The United Nations is the only existing general-purpose worldwide organization that, in theory, has some supranational characteristics. Not all countries are members, but the vast majority are. The UN also has a life and authority beyond the wishes of its individual members, and in theory, member states are bound to follow UN policy in many areas. As we will see in chapter 15, however, there is a substantial gap between the ideal and reality.

• Regional Organizations.   A wide variety of regional organizations exist today. As their name implies, they are multipurpose (military, economic, social, and political) organizations centered in a given region of the world. The Organization of American States, the Organization of African Unity, the Arab League, the Association of Southeast Asian Nations, and the European Community are major regional organizations.

• Alliances.   Defensive associations that stress military cooperation are also a limited form of supranational organization. The key is that there are at least some aspects of transcendency. Member nations are expected to come to the aid of the collective and thus have, in theory, surrendered a part of their independence. The North Atlantic Treaty Organization is an example of a multinational military alliance that has a coordinating organizational structure. It should be noted that not all alliances constitute supranational organizations. The United States–Japan Security Treaty, for example, is a bilateral treaty and has neither the multinational nor the organizational aspects necessary to warrant the name *supranational*.

The virtual collapse of the Warsaw Treaty Organization (WTO) and the resulting uncertainty about the future role, or even existence, of the North Atlantic Treaty Organization (NATO) have increased interest in the formation and impact of alliances. For NATO a critical question is, Can there be an alliance without an enemy? The answer is yes, because alliances can be based on a desire to dominate, on common attributes or good feelings without specific goals, or on a geostrategic desire to have access to another country's political or economic resources, as well as on a defensive reaction to threat (Wise, 1990; Siveron & Starr, 1990). This relates to the issue of impact, whether alliances help preserve peace or promote war. So far, the answer is unclear, and alliances have had varying impacts at different times in history (Oren, 1990; Singer & Small, 1968; Siverson & Sullivan, 1984).

• Regimes.   A **regime** is a collective noun defined (Keohane & Nye, 1977:19) as a "network of rules, norms and procedures that regularize behavior and control its effects" in an area of international concern such as the use of the oceans or the environment (Hahn & Richards, 1989). Another element of a regime is "expectations" of behavior (Krasner, 1982). Regimes, therefore, consist of rules of international law; treaties; international organizations; patterns of compliant behavior by states and other actors; as well as expectations of the international actors and the people of the world that, collectively, regulate an area of international concern (Zacher, 1990; Young, 1989). Some elements of the oceans regime are given in Table 3.1. The growth of international regulatory regimes is often opposed by many national interests, especially when a regime's rules threaten to reduce the wealth or power of a country's interest groups. They, in turn, bring pressure on their governments to ignore regime rules or to frustrate rule-making, and they may be the focus of international struggle (Haggard & Simmons, 1987; Keeley, 1990). The United States, for instance, has refused to sign the Law of the Sea Treaty, in part because of the objection of U.S. mining interests that are afraid international regulation will reduce their ability to mine the seabed.

Transnational Actors   **Transnational organizations** constitute a third category of actors in the international system. There are both **intergovernmental organizations** (IGOs) and **nongovernmental organizations** (NGOs) that qualify as transnational actors insofar as they share three identifying characteristics: (1) They are organized, usually with identified leaders and a bureaucratic structure. (2) They are specialized, performing a limited number of defined tasks or functions. This functional perspective distinguishes transnational IGOs from multifunctional, supranational IGOs. (3) They operate across international boundaries and have an orientation or allegiance that is, at least in part, not bound to the views or interests of any individual state.

The number of both IGOs and NGOs has grown tremendously during the twentieth century. In 1900 there were 30 IGOs and 69 NGOs. By 1980 the number of IGOs had grown almost ten-fold to 292, and the 69 NGOs expanded almost 36 times over to 2,427. Furthermore, the influence and range of activities of transnational actors are growing as their numbers increase and as technological advances allow them to move and communicate more effectively across political boundaries (Armstrong, 1989).

• Intergovernmental Organizations.   IGOs perform a wide variety of functional, or nonpolitical, tasks in the world today (Finkelstein, 1990). Many are *economic* in nature.

TABLE 3.1

Regime for Oceans and Seas[1]

International Laws and Norms	Treaties	International Organizations	Expectations and Action
Freedom of Navigation Maritime Rules of the Road Conservation of Fisheries Conservation and Sharing of Seabed Natural Resources Prevent Pollution	Law of the Sea Treaty[2] Convention on Fishing and Conservation Convention on the Continental Shelf Anti-dumping Convention	International Court of Justice deciding cases International Seabed Authority International Whaling Commission International Maritime Organization	National laws to prevent pollution Pressure on Japan to obey whaling quotas National courts enforce rules of the road

[1]The laws, treaties, organizations, and expectations listed here are but a few of the many examples that could be cited.
[2]The Law of the Sea Treaty has not been fully ratified by this date, and its Seabed Authority has yet to form. They are listed as examples of the progress of regimes.

This table represents a single regime for the regulation of oceans and seas which are of substantial international concern.

One example, the International Monetary Fund (IMF), has 85 member countries and functions to keep world currencies stable. Other transnational organizations concentrate on *social* functions. The Food and Agricultural Organization (FAO), with 147 members, is an example. Not only is the number of IGOs increasing, but they are involved in an ever-increasing range of activities, as can be seen in Table 3.2 on the next page.

• Nongovernmental Organizations.   The number of private organizations that operate internationally has grown phenomenally in the recent past. Like IGOs, they are involved in a wide spectrum of activities. Almost any classification scheme would omit some of the nearly 2,500 NGOs, but a few of the more significant categories can be noted.

One type of NGO consists of *religious organizations* that are widespread and active in world politics. The World Evangelical Alliance, founded in 1846, is an early example of a Protestant NGO. It is worth noting here that Terry Waite, an envoy of another Protestant NGO, the Anglican Church, to the Lebanese has been held hostage (at the time of writing) since 1987. The Roman Catholic Church is by far the largest and most influential of current religion-based NGOs. The Vatican itself is, of course, a state, and the pope is a secular as well as a spiritual leader. The political influence of Roman Catholicism, however, extends far beyond the Vatican itself. The pope and other Church officials, for example, were active in the crisis in Poland in the 1980s. Polish patriotism and the Church have been closely linked since the baptism in A.D. 966 of the country's first ruler, Prince Mieszko I. Some analysts have identified the visit of the first Polish pope, John Paul II, to his homeland in 1979 as one of the sparks that ignited Polish nationalism, which led, in part, to the Solidarity labor movement and resistance to the Soviet-supported communist government. During the crisis in Poland in the 1980s, the Church was deeply involved as a supporter of Solidarity and as a mediator between Solidarity and the government. Many years ago when a subordinate cautioned Josef Stalin about risking the displeasure of the Church, the communist leader was supposed to have dismissed the Church's influence with the sarcastic question "How many [army]

TABLE 3.2

Sample Intergovernmental Organizations

Organization	Members (1989)	Headquarters	Nationality of Chief Officer (1989)
Intergovernmental Civil Aviation Organization	161	Montreal	Indian
International Atomic Energy Agency	113	Vienna	Swedish
International Telegraphic Union	167	Geneva	Australian
International Criminal Police Organization (INTERPOL)	147	Paris	British
International Fund for Agricultural Development	146	Rome	Algerian
World Health Organization	166	Geneva	Japanese
International Monetary Fund	166	Washington	French

Intergovernmental organizations perform a wide variety of functional, or nonpolitical, tasks in the world today whether they concern themselves with catching criminals, regulating civil aviation, or promoting health.

The historic Vatican meeting shown here between President Mikhail Gorbachev and Pope John Paul II in the Vatican was the first between a Soviet leader and a Catholic pontiff. The U.S.S.R. until 1990 was officially an atheist state. This December 1989 meeting reflected the Soviets' changing attitudes toward religion and their recognition that the pope has a powerful political as well as religious voice.

divisions does the pope have?'' The Soviet and Polish communists found out that the pope may have few divisions, but his legions are many. Perhaps the best recognition of the strength of the Catholic Church was recently given by one of Stalin's successors, Mikhail Gorbachev. In December 1989 he became the first Soviet leader to set foot in the Vatican. The atheist president's political pilgrimage to the pope's presence had overtones of the journey to Canossa made in 1077 by Holy Roman emperor Henry IV to seek the pardon of Pope Gregory VII. Unlike Henry, Gorbachev was not forced to wait three days in the snow. Nevertheless, the fact that Gorbachev addressed John Paul II as ''Your Holiness,'' agreed to allow freedom of religion in the Soviet Union, established diplomatic relations with the Vatican, and invited the pope to visit the Soviet Union meant that Gorbachev had made significant concessions to the spiritual power of the pope and his legions.

NGOs also take the form of *transnational business organizations*. The expansion of international commerce has brought with it the rise of huge multinational corporations (MNCs), or companies with affiliates in more than one country. The role of MNCs is discussed in detail in chapter 14, but suffice it to say that the economic power of these corporate giants gives them a substantial role in international affairs. Some idea of the economic power of the MNCs can be gained from comparing their gross corporate product (GCP, sales) to the gross national product (GNP) of various countries (Fig. 3.1). The biggest 1989 MNC, General Motors, had a GCP of $127.0 billion that was (compared to national GNPs) about equal to Austria's ($126.7 billion), almost twice Turkey's ($65.3 billion), more than three times the Philippines' ($34.5 billion),

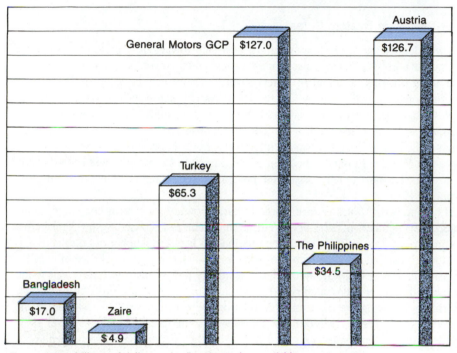

Figure 3.1 **General Motors' Gross Corporate Product Related to Gross National Product of Selected Countries, 1989***

*Figures are in billions of dollars and reflect latest data available.

Data sources: Fortune (7/30/89); *Statistical Abstract* (1990); World Bank (1989).

Transnational business organizations are one category of NGOs. Some idea of the enormous economic power of multinational corporations can be illustrated by comparing General Motors' gross corporate product to the gross national product of some countries.

approximately 7.5 times greater than Bangladesh's ($17.0 billion), and nearly 26 times Zaire's GNP ($4.9 billion).

International banks are another form of MNC. Banks play significant roles in such areas as monetary exchange rates and international lending to governments for development projects. One measure of banks' economic strength worth pondering is their assets. In 1989 the world's largest bank, Japan's Dai-Ichi Kangyo Bank, controlled assets of $413.2 billion, making it bigger by some standards than the largest industrial MNC. In fact, if just the top six multinational banks (all Japanese) combined their assets ($2.3 trillion), they would about equal the combined GNPs of France ($967 billion) and West Germany—before reunification with East Germany—($1.103 trillion). There is a "golden rule" of politics that says, "He who has the gold gets to make the rules," and the MNCs have plenty of gold.[2]

Also playing an increasingly important role in world affairs are transnational

2. The five other Japanese banks and their assets in billions are Sumitomo Bank ($407.2), Fuji Bank ($397.6), Mitsubishi Bank ($380.9), Samwa Bank ($373.4), and Industrial Bank of Japan ($292.2). The largest U.S. bank (9th in the world) is Citicorp Bank ($230.6). No Canadian bank is in the world's top 50 banks (*Fortune,* 7/30/90:328).

movements. Forces like communism, Islam, Zionism, feminism, and humanitarianism all project their message and their call for action across national borders. Some have one or more organizations affiliated with their cause; others do not, but they are nonetheless actors on the world stage.

Number of System Poles

Once we identify the actors in a system, a next step toward describing that system is denoting the number of major poles of more or less equal power. A system pole can be a single actor (usually a country). Alternatively, a pole can be a vertical structure consisting of a powerful country and the less powerful states in its orbit, such as the former bloc of the Soviet Union and its Eastern European allies. Finally, a pole may be a horizontal structure made up of a number of countries, no one of which is powerful enough to be a pole alone but which collectively merit this description. Some analysts project that Western Europe in the form of the European Community will soon develop into just such a horizontally organized pole after its economic integration in 1992 (Bernholz, 1985).

The number of poles is an important characteristic of a system because systems with different numbers of poles operate differently. This is discussed further later in this chapter, but one illustration of this is the relationship between number of poles and war. One study found that a system with two poles (bipolar) has a medium chance of war. By contrast a three-pole (tripolar) system has a relatively low propensity toward war, while systems with four or more countries (multipolar) have the highest probability of war, with five poles being the most unstable (Ostrom & Aldrich, 1978). If we add in the contention of Bernholz (1985:69) that unipolar systems are relatively peaceful, it is possible to draw the diagram in Figure 3.2 showing the relationship between the number of poles and the system's propensity for war.[3]

Distribution of Power Assets

Power assets are the components of national power that help determine any country's strength. They include military strength, industrial capacity, natural resources, technological sophistication, and population, among other things. These power assets will be more fully discussed in chapter 9. The distribution of power assets is important in two ways. First, it defines which actors constitute a pole and which do not. Second, the fact that assets are not distributed evenly across the system creates pressures within the system. The fact that industrial capacity is located in the North, while vast natural resources are located in the South, led in part to the imperialism of the nineteenth century and the neoimperialism (indirect domination and exploitation) of the twentieth century.

United States and Western European intervention in the Persian Gulf war between Iran and Iraq in the mid-1980s and their sharp reaction to Iraq's 1990 invasion of Kuwait and its threat to Saudi Arabia and other oil states in the region can also be partly

---

3. Fig. 3.2 on the facing page is meant to be only illustrative of the type of theorizing that scholars do about the relationship between polarity and warfare. Other scholars have found differing relationships between a system's number of poles and its propensity toward instability. In a recent article, Thompson (1986) said that unipolar configurations were the least violent and multipolar configurations were the most violent. But he found that while bipolar configurations were on average relatively stable, at times they could be as destabilizing as a multipolar system. Some question the impact of poles at all (Bueno de Mesquita & Lalman, 1988). For a general discussion see Dougherty & Pfaltzgraff (1990:159–62) and Brown (1987:72).

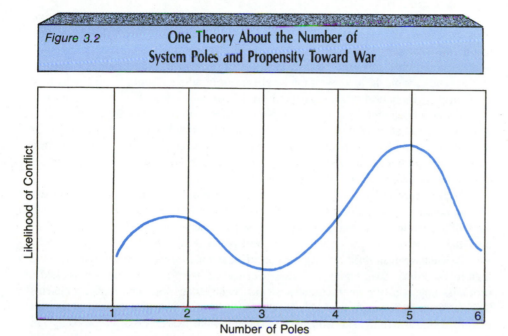

Figure 3.2   **One Theory About the Number of System Poles and Propensity Toward War**

Likelihood of Conflict (vertical axis)

Number of Poles (horizontal axis, marked 1 through 6)

A pole can be a single country, a powerful country and its satellites, or a combination of less powerful countries. Although there is scholarly disagreement about polar-war relationships, it has been suggested that a system with two poles has a medium chance of going to war, three poles have a lesser chance, and four poles or more have the highest chance of going to war. This graph is meant to be suggestive. The vertical axis is not quantified and no specific measurements are implied.

explained by the distribution of resources. The industrialized countries consume much more oil than they produce. Turmoil in the Gulf threatens needed supplies. Therefore, there was heavy pressure on the United States and others to uphold the right of free passage of the oil through the Gulf and to avoid domination of the region by any hostile power.[4] Surely, the Reagan and Bush administrations made decisions to intervene in the region, but a system-level analyst would point out that they had little choice. Even President Jimmy Carter, the least bellicose of recent U.S. presidents, announced that the United States would use all means to keep the Gulf open. In this case, then, the U.S. commitment to keep the oil flowing was somewhat akin to deciding to give a mugger your money when he is pointing a gun at you. Handing over your wallet is not really a decision, in the sense of there being reasonable options. Rather it is a reaction that is caused by system realities and necessities.

Norms of Behavior

A fourth set of characteristics that you should explore to understand any political system are its norms of behavior (Miller, 1990). Political systems, unlike computer or robotic systems, are not electromechanical automatons. Instead, they are social systems

---

4. The United States does not itself import large quantities of oil from the Gulf region. Western Europe and Japan do, however, and the United States, being the successor of Great Britain as the major naval power and the general leader of the noncommunist industrialized countries, felt compelled to take action to maintain the important concept of free navigation and the flow of oil to its industrial partners.

composed, at base, of humans (J. Thompson, 1990; Muncaster & Zinnes, 1990; Morrow, 1988). For various psychological and social reasons, humans develop values that define what they judge to be ethical and moral. Humans also tend to construct social systems based on regularized patterns of behavior because of their pragmatic need to interact and to avoid the anxiety of random behavior of others. Think, for example, how your local sociopolitical system, say your school, would work if there were no norms. Students might pelt professors who were poor lecturers, professors might shoot students who did not pay attention, people would drive their cars on lawns and sidewalks, your possessions would not be safe in the dorm—without values and behavior regularities, life would be dangerous and unpredictable. In general, though, life is both safe and your and others' behavior is predictable because of norms.

The international legal system also has norms based on values and the pragmatic need to interact. To a significant degree, these are reflected in international law, although we will see in chapter 16 that international law has a higher voluntary component than does the domestic law that governs your local political system.

As we have mentioned briefly, two important system norms are sovereignty and the legitimacy of war. Sovereignty for states over the last four or five centuries has had a profound impact on the international system. Countries answer to no higher authority. This means that they are responsible for their own protection, a prime cause of the fact that all countries are armed. You, in your local system by contrast, are probably not carrying a gun because you are not sovereign, are answerable to the law, and are also protected by the law and its enforcement agencies. The quasi-anarchial nature of the international political system has also tended to legitimize war, not just for self-protection, but also to accomplish national interest. Only a brief moment ago in history bellicose phrases such as German chancellor Otto von Bismarck's "blood and iron" or U.S. president Theodore Roosevelt's "speak softly and carry a big stick" were both considered laudable expressions and were accurate portrayals of public policy. Compare these statements to the norms of your own domestic political system. If you use force, except in self-defense, you are apt to go to jail.

Sovereignty also means that countries are free to regulate their own internal affairs. This policy is positive in an enlightened regime; it is destructive in a repressive regime. To contrast this policy again with a domestic political system, parents are not totally free to govern their children. Instead, they must send them to school, they may not physically or sexually abuse them, and they must otherwise reasonably provide for and protect their children. Indeed, in 1990 a couple was convicted for refusing on religious grounds to provide medical care for their critically ill child. The couple prayed, the child died, and the couple was found guilty of a felony.

The norms of the international political system change, as do human values and behavior patterns, over time. These changes affect the way a system works. Sovereignty, for example, is being eroded. Countries are also not as free as they once were to govern themselves internally. The norms of democracy and human rights are on the rise. International pressure, among other things, persuaded the Soviets to allow greater Jewish emigration, forced South Africa to ease apartheid, and helped convince the Sandinista government in Nicaragua to hold internationally observed elections. Also, international violence is considered less legitimate. Wars still occur, but they are being perceived as less legitimate, and are more widely condemned in principle. There are seedlings of international security cooperation in the peacekeeping forces in the United Nations and of international adjudication in the decisions of the International Court of Justice. These changing norms mean that even if the world again becomes multipolar, it will not operate in exactly the same way as the nineteenth-century multipolar system

International pressures, including economic sanctions and near-universal condemnation, have helped bring about an easing of apartheid in South Africa. One change was the 1990 repeal of the Separate Amenities Act of 1953 that mandated racially segregated restrooms and other public facilities. Here, a black South African enters a formerly whites-only restroom. Just the day before, "whites only," in both English and Afrikaans, had been painted out. "Here" means "men" in Afrikaans.

operated. In chapter 5 we will discuss, for instance, the theory that democratic countries are unlikely to go to war with one another. If that is true, the rising norm of democracy could mean a more peaceful international system in the future, no matter what its polar characteristics are.

Geographic Characteristics

A fifth determinant of an international system is the geographic characteristics of its actors. System-level analysts are interested in such factors as location, size, and topography of the various actors. Technology may have reduced, but it has not eliminated, the importance of these factors. The fact that two of our three major actors, the Soviet Union and China, border on each other and that the United States borders on neither is important. Among other things, the Soviet Union or China could directly invade the other's territory. The two countries also have significant border disputes. World politics would be considerably different if, let us say, the Soviet army were stationed on the Rio Grande.

Scope and Level of Interaction

A sixth characteristics of any political system is the number and variety (scope) of areas in which the actors interact and the frequency and intensity (level) of those interactions. In the last century and even in the first half of this century, the scope and level of international interaction were very limited compared to today. This important phenomenon has been touched on in several places already, including the discussion in the last chapter of the impact of modern telecommunications and travel, and the comments earlier in this chapter on the rapidly rising number of IGOs and NGOs.

It is absolute nonsense, for instance, to talk about any country being able to "go it alone" in "splendid isolation." Even for a powerful country like the United States, a "fortress America" policy is impossible. Given current energy sources, a United States without foreign oil, to pick one obvious illustration, would be an America stopped. This economic intertwining, the mutual reliance of national economies, is termed interdependence, and some theorists argue that large-scale, extended war is becoming difficult or impossible between economically interdependent countries. Many hope, for example, that a restrengthened Europe will remain peaceful within the European Community (EC) rather than reverting to the strife that led to two world wars. Societies are also much less culturally isolated than they used to be, and some systems analysts believe that increased intercultural contact between countries through modern travel and communications has decreased the chances of war.

Factors That Cause Systems to Change

If we think about solar systems again, we will see that they are both stable and changing. The system we live in has existed for untold millennia and will probably remain pretty much the same for eons more. Thus it is relatively stable. But solar systems, ours included, are also dynamic. Usually these changes are evolutionary. Suns, for example, have a life cycle. They are born, expand, then gradually cool and die out. As that happens, over the ages, the system will slowly change.

Sometimes, though, the change can be revolutionary. A sun can explode, throwing the system into mayhem. It is also possible that "domestic" events on one of the planets could radically change the system. If, for example, the earth went on a binge of nuclear self-destruction, the cumulative effect of massive detonations might be to throw so much dust, dirt, and debris into the atmosphere that the Sun's warming rays would be largely blocked out and the Earth's temperature would plummet, causing a "nuclear winter" fatal to humans, animals, and plant life.

International systems also change, usually slowly but sometimes more rapidly. There are, for instance, a number of theories of long-term cycles associated with shifts in the international system. Immanuel Wallerstein (1976) theorizes that the world system is divided between a core (the industrialized countries, today) and a periphery (the Third World). He is also concerned with the rise and decline of hegemonic (dominant) powers within the core. Wallerstein believes that hegemonic power and center-periphery relations are mostly based on economics and the changes therein determine the nature of the international system. His theory is part of the economic approach to international political analysis discussed in chapter 1, and it will be further discussed, especially in chapter 14. It may be, for example, that the future empowerment of current periphery countries (such as China or India) could create a new core and end the dominance (imperialism/*dependencia*) of the Third World (South) by the current industrialized core (North).

Another well-known theory of system change is associated with political scientist George Modelski (1987), who has developed the concept of "long cycles" in world politics. Modelski and others (W. Thompson, 1988, 1990; Rosecrance, 1987) believe that long cycles occur over approximately 100 years and are demarcated by systems, or "hegemonic," wars. A war that shatters the existing system creates a new hegemonic power that politically, militarily, and economically dominates the world. Eventually, changes in the nature of the system erode the position of the hegemonic power, others arise, struggles ensue, the old hegemon falls, and a new cycle begins.

Other political scientists dispute the validity of such grand theories of cyclical systems change, but all agree that the international system does change and that the shifts are important (Nye, 1990). Therefore, in the rest of this section we will look at a few of the factors that cause systems to change. This will be followed by a section discussing the transitional phase between systems and a section that outlines the way that different systems work.

Power Changes and Prophecy

One of the things system-level analysts would like to be able to do accurately is observe changes in power and to predict how this will affect the configuration of the system. The discussions below of unipolar, tripolar, and polyarchal systems are just such speculation. Is it possible to predict? Perhaps. Consider the following observations of two nineteenth-century observers who lived in the Eurocentric multipolar system and who predicted the U.S.–Soviet bipolar system.

Europe has had its day. . . . The future of the world lies between these two great nations [Russia and America]. One day they will collide, and then we will see struggles the like of which no one has ever dreamed of.

Charles-Augustin Sainte-Beuve, 1847

There are today two great peoples which, starting out from different points of departure, advance toward the same goal—Americans and Russians. . . . Each of them will one day hold in its hands the destinies of half of mankind.

Alexis de Tocqueville, 1835

Changes in the Number or Power of the Major Actors

Because a system is defined in part by its number of poles (countries or blocs of relatively equal power), changes in the number of major actors or their power can significantly alter the nature of the system. The decline or loss of power suffered by the major world actors—Great Britain, Germany, France, and Japan—as a result of World War II changed the existing multipolar system to a bipolar (U.S.–U.S.S.R.) system.

More recently, the bipolar system has largely broken down, and a new system has begun to form whose shape and operation is not yet clear. One of the two superpowers, the United States, is in *relative decline* compared to several rising powers, and the Soviet Union is experiencing serious political turmoil and is, at least temporarily, in a state of political semi-eclipse. There are several possibilities for new polar actors. First, poised, or at least with the potential, to become true global, single-state actors are Japan, Germany, China, and India. Other countries such as Brazil and Nigeria have longer-term potential. Second, some of the major actors, or poles, in the future may be regional associations. Europe in the form of the EC is increasingly integrated economically, and it is extensively cooperating politically. In August 1990, for instance, the EC imposed an oil embargo and other economic sanctions on Iraq in retaliation for its invasion of Kuwait. The United States and Canada already have a free trade association. Mexico is negotiating to join them, and President Bush has proposed a hemispheric free trade group. The Western Hemisphere's political cooperation will come more slowly than its economic cooperation, but as in Europe, a regional pole could develop. Other groups such as the Association of Southeast Asian Nations (ASEAN) and the Organization of African Unity (OAU) are also potential foundations for regional poles or blocs in the future. Third, there are also some who urge greater powers for the United Nations, and it is even conceivable that the UN could become a major actor. Fourth, NATO and the WTO, the bipolar alliances, have lost their focus and may not survive, and they may be replaced by new yet unpredictable alliance systems that are coherent enough to constitute polar actors. What is certain is that the number of major actors is expanding. What is uncertain and fascinating is the exact cast of major actors that will dominate international politics in the future and the pattern of interaction that will develop among them.

Major actor changes are not always crucial, however, and sometimes actors can rise or fall without significantly changing the basic nature of the system. This is particularly true for a multipolar system. In the European multipolar system that extended roughly from 1648 to 1945, there were shifts in the country-actors over time. Spain and Sweden were early major powers. They declined to secondary status over time, but they were replaced by other rising powers, such as Prussia (later Germany). In this case, the number of major powers remained above four, and, therefore, the system continued to operate by the rules of a multipolar system (for rules, see How Systems Work, p. 74).

Changes in Technology

Changes in technology can alter systems. The development of nuclear weapons plus the ability to unleash them anywhere in the world via missile in a matter of minutes dramatically changed the system from what it had been in the 1930s. Systems analysts would say, for instance, that the United States did not abandon its isolationist stance and become an active internationalist actor after World War II by choice. Rather, the system, including the nuclear missile age, compelled the United States to extend its activities to maintain itself. It could no longer confidently hide behind oceans. The peaceful use of nuclear energy may also change the system. In the future, the development of nuclear power and other alternatives to fossil fuels as energy sources will have a profound impact on the world system if countries become energy–self-sufficient and decrease their interdependency with the rest of the world. If this comes to pass, for example, the Middle East and the Persian Gulf regions will become much less a focus of interest for the industrialized states. In an energy-independent world, the U.S. interventions in the Persian Gulf war and the 1990 Middle East crisis might not have occurred.

In the case of nuclear weapons, technology may have also shifted the rules by which a system operates. Three earlier bipolar systems that pitted Athens against Sparta, Macedonia against Persia, and Rome against Carthage in ancient times were marked by warfare between the two "superpowers" and the eventual defeat of one by the other. In recent times, another bipolar system occurred, but it did not result in the military death struggle that characterized the earlier bipolar systems. The technology-based nuclear devastation that each superpower can wreak on the other has worked to keep the two powers from directly attacking one another. Each is heavily armed, each has used its military, and each supports surrogates (North or South Vietnam; Israel or Syria) who fight one another, but the superpowers have not waged war directly on each other. Technology has made the outcome predictable.

Communications and transportation technology, as noted earlier, is also strongly impacting the system. It is, among other things, eroding sovereignty. The technology of industrialization is also instrumental in creating economic interdependence.

Domestic Factors

The international system often affects or even controls the actions of states, but the policy decisions made by countries can also change the system. Most commonly, national policies and conditions within a country have an impact on its power or its reputation for power. The Soviet Union provides the most dramatic example of the impact of domestic factors on foreign policy and, in turn, on the international system. The crisis that the Soviet Union is experiencing has seriously eroded its international power. To shift economic resources away from the national security sphere and toward domestic revitalization, President Gorbachev has cut military spending and troop and equipment levels, sought new arms control agreements, withdrawn from Afghanistan,

The impact of domestic factors on the foreign policy of a major country, and therefore on the international system, is dramatically evident in the Soviet Union. Extreme economic difficulties have been one factor that has caused the Soviets to seek accommodation with the West and to reduce military expenditures. These Red Army soldiers, who might once have been arrayed against NATO, were instead harvesting carrots near Novgorod in the fall of 1990 in an attempt to stave off food shortages during the coming Soviet winter.

allowed Eastern Europe to escape from Soviet domination, reduced Moscow's support of such (former) client states as Nicaragua, Vietnam, and Cuba, and taken a wide variety of other actions designed to ease national security spending and increase economic help from the West. These changes in Soviet policy and the international perceptions of Soviet power and intentions have brought a speedy end to what had been a more evolutionary decline of the bipolar system.

System changes can also occur because of "crazy states" (Dror, 1973). Internal pressures can cause a country to act "abnormally," to break the norms of the system. This, in turn, can upset and even transform the system. The failure of the balance-of-power system that existed between World Wars I and II can be partly attributed to Adolf Hitler, who was anything but a rational statesman. The system was also changed by acute pacifism in Great Britain, which, in part, prevented that country from acting to keep the system in balance by restraining Germany. In more recent years, Iran, with its seizure of the American Embassy and its gruesome war with Iraq, is an example of a state whose acts did not follow system norms. Ideology can also be an important factor.

Transitions Between Systems

A subject of special current concern is the course of international politics during periods of transitions between systems. Many scholars believe that systems are highly unstable and violence-prone during times of shifts in the power of the major actors. Robert Gilpin (1981:209), for example, argues that "hegemonic war historically has been the basic mechanism of systemic change in world politics." According to Gilpin, wars occur when the hegemonic (dominant) position of one power is challenged by an emerging power and subsequent research has supported this view (Doran, 1989; Wayman, 1989).

Times of power-transition are dangerous because there may be a gap between real and perceived power because of rapid fluctuation, and misperception may lead to errors. This misperception occurs because countries sometimes see themselves and others in terms of what their power was rather than accurately grasping the new realities. Further,

TABLE 3.3

Power Fluctuations, 1900–1975
(Higher numbers equal greater power)

	Germany[1]	Great Britain	Russia/ U.S.S.R.	France	United States[2]	Austria-Hungary	Italy	Japan	China
1900	14	11	8	4	21	3	1	2	0
1910	14	8	4	4	26	4	1	2	0
1920	8	11	1	3	39	-	1	2	0
1930	9	8	6	5	31	-	1	2	0
1939	13	8	11	4	27	-	2	4	5
1947	0	6	9	1	53	-	0	0	1
1955	4	4	15	2	41	-	?	2	7
1975	2	2	24	2	22	-	?	5	7

[1]For 1955 and 1975, Germany is West Germany.
[2]Beckman calculates both power and "projectable power" for the United States. For the United States, projectable power figures are 1900 (4), 1910 (5), 1920 (8), and 1939 (5). Projectable power is power divided by days needed to project the power, and the low number reflects the low level of U.S. military preparedness.

Data source: Beckman (1984).

rising countries may try to assert themselves, and declining countries may also assert themselves, either to attempt to recapture their former glory or to fend off the rising state.

Each of these possibilities can be seen in the events that led to World War I and World War II as the multipolar system underwent momentous power shifts in the last half of the nineteenth century and the first half of the twentieth century. Peter Beckman (1984) has made some interesting calculations of power that are shown in Table 3.3. Beckman does not calculate power in the nineteenth century, but if he had, he would have found that the United States and Germany had risen rapidly and that Austria-Hungary had declined markedly. By the beginning of the twentieth century the newly united and powerful Germany was ready to challenge the previously dominant states, primarily Great Britain, for ascendancy. By contrast, Austria-Hungary had faded to a shadow of its former glory as the Holy Roman Empire, and it had become aggressive in a futile attempt to prevent its demise as a great power. For opposite reasons, then, Germany and Austria-Hungary joined in common cause, but they were ultimately defeated. The years between the end of World War I and World War II show even greater fluctuation. Germany and the Soviet Union rose rapidly, and Japan doubled its power, while Great Britain declined and U.S. "projectable" power also ebbed.

Adding to the instability was the gap between the ability of the United States to project its power and its real power. The United States kept its military forces very small, leading Beckman to calculate U.S. "projectable power" at only 5 in 1910 and 1939. This small force caused a misperception during World War I that clearly led to German action against U.S. shipping that, in turn, precipitated America's entry into the war. The gap also probably emboldened both Japan and Germany prior to World War II. The result was the second hegemonic war of the century and the destruction of the multipolar system.

Finally, Beckman's power calculations show the rise and decline of the bipolar system. In 1947, U.S. power was transcendent, but a closer bipolar equilibrium came

Because of its long tradition against having a large standing army the United States kept its military forces and its supplies of arms very small. Many analysts argue this left the country ill-prepared for war and also encouraged recklessness in its enemies. Here, for lack of real weapons, new soldiers train with broomsticks as substitutes for unavailable rifles during World War I.

into being over the next two decades as Soviet power grew to nearly equal that of the United States. Toward the end of this era, other powers began to rise, and if Beckman's formula were applied to countries today, the European countries (especially Germany), Japan, and China would have even higher numbers.

Thus, the world is in a period of system transition, and times of transition have proven perilous in the past. The power calculations and "rules of the game" that governed the bipolar system are now largely irrelevant, and those that will characterize the newly forming system are not clear. One analyst recently predicted, "We may . . . wake up one day lamenting the loss of the order that the Cold War gave to the anarchy of [the new system] of international relations" (Mearsheimer, 1990a:35). Doran (1989:398) has similarly observed that we may be entering a time with the "system confronting the trauma of critical systems transformation," and, even more alarmingly, Goldstein (1988:357) suggests that the decline of U.S. hegemony and the resulting systems shift "seems to increase the danger of hegemonic war."

This discussion of the instability of systems transitions is meant to dispel some of the popular press's euphoria that has accompanied the end of the cold war. Certainly no one will miss the Soviet-American nuclear confrontations, but it is naive to assume that the lions and lambs are necessarily about to lie down together in world peace. History provides a less sanguine image, one of young lions attacking reigning kings of the political jungle in an attempt to dethrone them.

Should we be pessimistic, then? Are we doomed to another hegemonic struggle? The answer is no. Fatalism is as inappropriate as untutored euphoria. In the first place, systems characteristics such as weapons and communications technology, norms, and economic interdependence also determine international behavior along with actor changes and polar configurations. And these characteristics are different than at any time in history and may allow a peaceful transition. Furthermore, as one analyst argued, "At best, the various schematizations of hegemony and war are only suggestive. They do not prove a reliable basis for . . . evaluating the risk of world war as we enter the twenty-first century" (Nye, 1990:192). And even those who do find instability during changes are apt to concede that their findings are only "probabilistic, and thus leave ample room for national strategists to manipulate events" (Wayman, 1989:17). Knowledge, caution, and careful management, then, are needed as we enter a new era, one with great potential for both great good and ill.

How Systems Work

One of the things that makes systems analysis an exciting approach for some political scientists is the idea that various kinds of systems work in different and somewhat predictable ways. If, for instance, bipolar systems have one set of rules and multipolar systems have another set of rules, then analysts can explain and predict at least some actions and reactions according to which system exists at the time.

Insofar as this predictive ability is valid, the ability to understand how systems work is very important for policymakers as well as scholars. Let us suppose that the world is moving from a bipolar to a multipolar system. Systems analysis could first warn us to be especially careful during the current power-transition period. As noted earlier, that is a particularly unstable time. Second, if we understand the dynamics of a multipolar system, it will be possible to adopt policies that safely manage the transition in order to promote stability.

One way to begin to understand system rules is to analyze how past systems have operated and to hypothesize about how future systems might function using one characteristic, polarity, as our organizing principle. One of the originators of systems theory, Morton Kaplan (1969), identified six different systems.[5] We can use two of these that have existed historically, a multipolar and a bipolar system, to illustrate each's rules of operation. Additionally, unipolar, tripolar, and polyarchal systems will be added to the mix to illustrate future possibilities.

Multipolar Systems

To recap the concept of a multipolar system, it is one in which there are four or more major powers, much like the 1648–1945 system. It is a relatively fluid and competitive system in which the countries involved form shifting alliances. All are interested in their own benefit and are primarily responsible for their own protection. Since too much strength for any one actor or even any one alliance would threaten all the other actors, there is a tendency to form counteralliances and to try to win allies away from the predominant coalition. This type of system is sometimes characterized as a balance-of-power system. The rules of the game for each actor are:

1. Increase power, but do so by negotiations rather than by fighting.
2. Fight rather than fail to increase power.
3. If fighting, stop short of destabilizing the system by destroying another major actor.
4. Oppose any actor or alliance that threatens to upset the balance by becoming preponderant (Christensen & Snyder, 1990).
5. Restrain revolutionary actors who do not subscribe to the system and do not play by the rules of the game.
6. Permit defeated major actors to maintain their status or, if a major actor is eliminated, find a new actor to take its place in order to maintain the potential for balance in the system.

5. Kaplan's original six were "balance of power," "loose bipolar," "tight bipolar," "universal," "hierarchical," and "unit veto." In the following discussion, "multipolar" is equivalent to "balance of power." This latter term is the source of much confusion and is addressed later in this chapter. Additionally, "bipolar" is used to denote Kaplan's loose bipolar system. The subsequent discussion of a unipolar system bears some resemblance to Kaplan's hierarchical system. And the polyarchal system is somewhat akin to his universal system.

Bipolar Systems

This system is characterized by two roughly equal coalitions of actors. There may be other important actors, but they are neutral and do not threaten, either singly or in alliance, the two predominant blocs. This configuration closely resembles the system that existed after World War II and featured the United States and its allies against the Soviet Union and its allies. The rules of the game are:

1. Try to eliminate the other bloc.
2. Fight if necessary to eliminate the other bloc, but only if the risks are acceptable.
3. Increase power relative to the other bloc.
4. Fight to avoid elimination or subordination by the other bloc.
5. Attempt to bring new members into your bloc. Attempt to prevent other members from joining the rival bloc.
6. Nonbloc members act as mediators to reduce the danger of war between the blocs.

Unipolar Systems

A third type of system would have just one dominant power. Most domestic political systems are unipolar. There are two ways that a unipolar international system might come about. One would be if one country was able to gain dominance over all others and establish a universal empire. This has never really happened, although in ancient times there were examples where one power conquered all the civilized societies near it. The Roman and Chinese Empires at their height are the best examples. There were certainly other civilized states in the world, but they did not border on the universal power and were only dimly known to it (Bernholz, 1985:70).

Another path to a unipolar system would be through some form of world government. In this system the single major power would be a world organization, such as a much-strengthened United Nations. There might well be subordinate actors, such as the current states, and they might even have a level of autonomy, but they would be governed by the central power on matters that affect the system or the other subordinate actors. You might note, as an aside, that this model of an international system bears some resemblance to the U.S. domestic structure and its federal-state relationships.

The exact rules would depend on which model of unipolar system took place and on the degree of autonomy of subordinate units, but in rough approximation, the rules might be:

1. Standards of conduct that affect the system and more than one actor would be determined by the central power.
2. Disputes between subordinate units would be mediated or arbitrated by the central power.
3. Subordinate units that violate the standards of conduct established by the central power would be punished by the central power.
4. The central power would act to dominate or even monopolize military and economic instruments.
5. Attempts by subordinate units to achieve independence would be suppressed by the central unit.
6. The central power would gradually attempt to lessen or eliminate the autonomy of subordinate units.

Tripolar/Strategic-Triangle Systems

Yet another possible polar configuration is a tripolar system. This has no exact historical example, but the current strategic-triangle system among the United States, the Soviet Union, and China gives us both some sense of how a tripolar system would work and some inkling that such a system might come into being (Segal, 1989; Nelsen, 1989).

By its nature, a triangular system can have four possible alignments. They are provocatively described as (1) a "*ménage à trois*," in which all three actors are friendly; (2) a "romantic triangle," in which one actor is friendly with the other two, but those two are hostile toward each other; (3) a "marriage," in which two of the actors are friendly, and both are hostile toward the third actor; and (4) a "unit-veto" triangle, in which all three actors are mutually hostile (Dittmer, 1987:34).

The ideal position for any country is to be the pivot player in the romantic triangle, that is, to be the country with good relations with both other countries who, in turn, are hostile toward one another. In this position, the other two need you, and you can gain concessions for your continued friendship. The least favorable position is to be the odd man out in the marriage triangle, where the other two players are friendly, and both are hostile toward you. Dittmer goes on to postulate that the rules of play in a triangular relationship are:

1. Each player will, maximally, try to have good relations with both other players or, minimally, try to avoid having hostile relations with both other players.
2. Each player will try to prevent close cooperation between the other two players.

One curiosity of recent U.S. foreign policy is that two of the most anticommunist presidents, Nixon and Reagan, also moved to better relations with China. How do you explain this inconsistency, the anticommunist zealots opening America's door in friendship to the Chinese Communists? A system-level analyst would say that the strategic triangle left the U.S. presidents little choice. Given China's growing strength and the stresses in U.S.–Soviet relations, they could not afford to have similar hostility with China, thereby risking being odd man out. So, whatever their personal antipathies toward communism, system realities pressured them to maintain good relations with at least one of the two communist giants.

Polyarchal Systems

A common feature of most of the polar systems is the assumption that states are the primary, if not the only, actors. One exception would be the world government model discussed as a variant of the unipolar configuration. It may well be, though, that such state-centric assumptions are faulty. Some scholars argue that states are under increasing disintegrative pressure, and that the future world system may look very different structurally than it does today. There are pressures for both greater (international) and more localized (intranational) political organizations. On the one hand, there are a burgeoning number of international organizations; expanding international legal norms; important transnational ideas such as democracy, human rights, and environmentalism; multinational corporations and banks; increased economic interdependence; and, in general, new importance for international regimes. All of these factors are working to create a world system based on international structures and norms. Working in the other direction, toward more micropolitical, intranational structures, such as multitudinous separatist movements of ethnic/national groups demanding autonomy or even independence, as is evident in the Soviet Union.

Here President and Mrs. Reagan are pictured with Deng Xiaoping, China's senior leader, in Beijing in April, 1984. Many people find it ironic that the archconservative Reagans wound up holding hands with the chief Chinese Communist. The logic of the strategic-triangle system, however, pressured the president to befriend China or risk the simultaneous hostility of both China and the Soviet Union that would have made the United States odd man out.

Some scholars believe the world's complex interdependence will result in a system of greater order (Koehane & Nye, 1977). Hedley Bull is less optimistic and has argued that the world is returning to something like the medieval system that prevailed before the Treaty of Westphalia (1648) and the rise of national states (Bull, 1977; Bull & Watson, 1982).

Seyom Brown straddles these views, contending that the future world system will be a "polyarchy" or a polyarchal system. He defines this as:

> a situation of many communities, spheres of influence, hegemonic imperiums, interdependencies, trans-state loyalties—some of which overlap, some of which are concentric, some of which are substantially incongruent—that exhibits no clearly dominant axis of alignment and antagonism and has no central steering group or agency. (1988:242)

Brown does not specify rules for his polyarchal system, but he does foresee two possible variants: Polyarchy I and Polyarchy II. The first somewhat parallels Bull's new medievalism, that is, according to Brown (1988:245), a polyarchy "in which nation-states, subnational groups, and transnational special interests and communities are all vying for the support and loyalty of individuals." Such a system, Brown speculates (p. 260), "could turn into anarchy, where raw power is the principal social arbiter."

Polyarchy II, somewhat like Nye and Keohane's view, would be one in which "international and transnational webs of political accountability, many of them global in scope," dominate (Brown, 1988:263). Since more and more of the issues addressed by politics are transnational in scope, Brown argues that this model would tend toward greater international integration and cooperation and a more peaceful world.

Which will evolve? Brown can only tell us that the future "has not been predetermined." Rather, "which of the variants does emerge will depend on the choices and commitments made by politically influential groups in the years ahead" (1988:243).

Balance of Power

Any discussion of how international systems operate must also address the concept of balance of power. An initial problem, though, is that scholars have used the term with many different connotations. These include, among others, whether or not there is an equilibrium (balance); what the power distribution is even if it is not balanced (imbalance); attempts to achieve a balance (balancing); or a multipolar, balance-of-power system (Wight, 1987b; Simowitz, 1983:3). Analysts also disagree about whether achieving or trying to achieve an equilibrium works for peace or conflict, whether or not equilibrium is the rule or exception, and whether the concept of balance of power has any relevance to today's world.

Given these complexities and disagreements, the puzzle will not be solved here. We can, however, look at the assumptions of balance-of-power theory and their impact on world politics. Fundamentally, realists who believe in the efficacy of balance-of-power theory assume that:

1. There is a possibility, and perhaps a natural tendency, for some states to seek regional or even global hegemony.
2. Other states will seek to prevent hegemony by strengthening themselves or entering antihegemonic alliances with other threatened states.
3. A balance of power, therefore, is desirable because it (a) preserves the independence of countries and (b) creates an equilibrium that promotes order and peace.

Balance-of-power concepts have strongly influenced foreign policy in the recent past. The policies of the Nixon administration within the strategic triangle were heavily influenced by these concepts. Nixon (1978:340) believes in "the importance of isolating and influencing the factors affecting worldwide balances of power," and his secretary of state, Henry Kissinger, has written (1979:55, 70) that "there can be no peace without equilibrium" and finding "this balance is the perpetual task of statesmen." The other two triangle powers also practice balance of power. Good Sino-American relations were part of what urged Mikhail Gorbachev to end the decades-long Sino-Soviet split, and in May 1989 he became the first Soviet leader to visit China in 30 years (Gregor, 1990). He was successful, but in a small but important gesture of mutual Sino-American reassurance and balancing, on the very day of Gorbachev's visit to Shanghai the USS *Blue Ridge* made a port call to Shanghai at China's invitation. It was the first American warship to visit that city in four decades.

The breakdown of the bipolar system and the tentative emergence of some new form of the multipolar or polyarchal system has brought forth new ramifications of balance-of-power policies with new complexities and new partners that reaffirm the old saying that "politics makes strange bedfellows" (Clark, 1989; Niou, Ordeshook, & Rose, 1989). In Europe, for example, the decline of the Soviet Union and the reunification and strengthening of Germany have resurrected concerns about German power in Europe. Virtually everyone, including eventually even the Soviets, agreed that Germany should remain in NATO. In part this was not to strengthen the alliance, but to restrain Germany—to avert a new chorus of *Deutschland über Alles* (Germany Above

All), the feared anthem of an earlier, aggressive fatherland. A quip made by British diplomat Lord Ismay in the 1950s that NATO was established in Europe to "keep the Russians out, the Americans in, and the Germans down" is being quoted anew (Lind, 1990:38). For the Polish foreign minister, keeping Germany in NATO is necessary to "avoid a situation where Germany tries to become a power or a superpower on the European stage" (*NYT,* 2/15/90:A18). The Poles even acted cautiously on the question of Soviet troop withdrawals from their country. Poland would prefer no foreign troops on its soil, but Prime Minister Tadeusz Mazowiecki explained, "we have to evaluate this situation realistically from the prospect of the Germany problem" (*HC,* 2/18/90:A6).

Indeed, balance-of-power considerations have led to Western concern about the future of the Soviet Union as a power. Keep in mind that in a bipolar system one rule is to try to destroy the other power, and for years Moscow and Washington were mortal enemies. In a multipolar system, by contrast, a rule is not to destroy other major actors lest the system be unbalanced. That is one explanation of why the Bush administration and other Western governments have not tried to take advantage of Soviet turmoil. They are afraid that a Soviet collapse would accelerate the already rapid rise of Germany's relative power. This concern also helps explain the West's lack of serious pressure on Moscow over issues like Lithuanian independence, and the West's willingness to extend economic benefits, perhaps even overt foreign aid, to the Soviet Union.

The changing structure of the international system has additionally engendered some strange Pacific region permutations that would have been unthinkable not long ago (Gregor, 1990; Segal, 1990). The United States is beginning to view Japan as a rising opponent and China as a possible ally. This has added something of a Sino-Japanese-American Pacific triangle to U.S. concerns about China's role in the Sino-Soviet-American strategic triangle. As President Bush put it, defending his forgiving posture toward Beijing less than a year after the Tiananmen Square massacre, "I want to retain contacts [with China] because, as you look around the world. . . . Take a look at Japan. Take a look at a lot of countries in the Pacific. China is a key player" (*CSM,* 2/29/90:19). Furthermore, this view of a rising Japanese threat is shared by some Southeast Asian and Pacific countries. During a 1990 meeting of Asian diplomats, Malaysian foreign minister Abu Hassan Osmar brought up the delicate subject of qualms about Japan's growing power. While many share that concern, saying so publicly was still "like dragging a dead cat across the stage and plunking it down square in the middle of the conference table," according to the Australian foreign minister (*WP* 8/19/90:A18). Thus, by the logic of balance-of-power politics, former enemies are sometimes embraced, and friends fall under suspicion.

Whatever the past wisdom of operating according to the principles of balance-of-power politics, scholars disagree about whether or not it should be a guideline for the future. Hedley Bull (1977:117) argues that although the world has changed a great deal since the classic balance-of-power era of the 1800s, the concept remains valid because (1) the general balance "serves to prevent the system of states from being transformed by conquest into a universal empire"; (2) regional balances "serve to protect the independence of states in particular areas from absorption or domination by a locally preponderant power"; and (3) both the general and local balances of power "help provide the conditions in which other institutions on which international order depends are able to operate."

Others disagree (for example, Hoffmann, 1986). Among the counterarguments is the fact that many of the earlier balance-of-power conditions, such as cultural heterogeneity and a multipolar system, no longer exist. Even more fundamentally, critics (who are often idealists) charge that balance-of-power politics is inevitably power politics, and in the nuclear age the pursuit of power may lead to ultimate destruction. The critics are correct about the power basis of balance-of-power politics. As Nixon (1978:340) put it, he and Kissinger agreed "that whatever else a foreign policy might be, it must be strong to be credible—and it must be credible to be successful." This is a classic debate, then, between realists and idealists, whether they be academics or practitioners.

System-Level Analysis: An Evaluation

Obviously the nature of the international system plays a strong role in determining the direction of world affairs. Some political scientists emphasize state-level analysis. Others prefer individual-level analysis, but few would ignore the role of the system.

States, like people, exist in an environment that helps to determine their actions. We have free will, but we exercise it with restraint. Formal law and social norms affect us. We learn to eat with utensils, despite the fact that fingers would often be handier, and we refrain from hitting others when we get mad at them. System needs also affect us. We go to work even on nice days instead of fishing because we need money, and in our system employment is the most common way for us to obtain economic necessities. The degree to which the system affects us, however, depends greatly on many circumstances. The norms of a subsystem, like our families, may be more important than the norms of our communities. If you hit the lottery, your need to show up at work may decline dramatically! It is also true that you or I may occasionally ignore pressures to conform, and decide to go fishing or stay home and read a novel. There are even eccentrics, who regularly contravene the norms. They usually suffer for their oddities, but a few persist and survive.

Similarly, countries have free will, but they are often restrained in their actions by the norms and realities of the system in which they exist. The current changing system

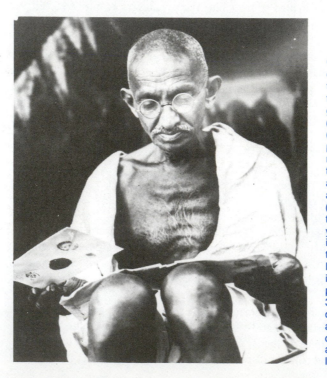

Countries, movements, and, occasionally, individuals can alter the international political system. One such movement was guided by Mohandas K. Gandhi (1869–1948), called Mahatma (great-souled) by the Indian people. A British-trained attorney, he returned to India in 1915 to work for independence. He adopted a life of simple spirituality and advocated *satyagraha* (passive resistance) as the path to end British rule. After 32 years, many of which were spent in British jails, he led his people to independence in 1947. This helped spur other demands for independence among colonized people which, over the following 30 years, led to the virtual end of colonies. Ironically, Gandhi was assassinated by a Hindu fanatic during one of his prayer vigils against violence perpetrated on India's Muslim minority.

has pushed some capitalist countries apart and some capitalist and communist countries together. Recently system economic realities virtually compelled the industrial powers to intervene in the Persian Gulf region to keep oil flowing and avoid its domination by any single country. Like individuals, though, states are far from automatons controlled by the invisible forces of the international system. The impact of the system on a country's policy will vary according to the specific issues and circumstances involved. It may also be that a state decides to ignore the rules or change them. Revolutionary movements, be they communist, religious, or for some other cause, often do this. Often the system suppresses them, but sometimes they have succeeded in changing the system—as have the movements of Lenin, Gandhi, Mao, and the Ayatollah Ruhollah Khomeini.

Chapter Summary

1. System-level analysis is an approach to the study of world politics that argues that factors external to countries and the world political environment combine to determine the pattern of interaction among countries and other transnational actors. Countries are often compelled to take certain courses of action by the realities of the world in which they exist.

2. Many factors determine the nature of any given system. Systemic factors include its actors, the number of poles, the distribution of power assets, norms, geography, and scope and level of interaction.

3. Supranational actors and transnational actors operate in a system along with national actors (states).

4. The number of poles in a system influences the way it operates. Bipolar systems work differently, for instance, than multipolar systems.

5. The distribution of power assets (resources, such as oil) also influences the operation of a system. International clashes in the Middle East over the distribution of oil from that region are an example.

6. Norms are the values that help determine patterns of behavior.

7. The geographic relationships of major actors also influence how a system operates. The fact that the Soviet Union and China share a border, while the United States is geographically isolated, is a current illustration.

8. The scope and level of international interaction involves the breadth of issues involved in world politics and the intensity of interaction over them.

9. Systems change as a result of many factors, including changes in the number or power of the major actors, changes in technology, and changes in domestic circumstances within states.

10. Times of transition from one system to another are often unstable. We are in a transitional period.

11. Historically, scholars have investigated and hypothesized about the operation of multipolar, bipolar, unipolar, tripolar (or strategic-triangle), and polyarchal systems.

12. Any discussion of how international systems operate must also address the concept of balance of power. Scholars disagree about how to define this term and about whether or not the concept has any application to the study and conduct of current and future world politics.

13. The view of this book is that system-level analysis is a valid approach to the study of world politics. However, it must be used in conjunction with other approaches in order to understand world politics fully.

There is history in all men's lives.

Shakespeare, *Henry IV*, Part II

It is human nature that rules the world, not governments and regimes.

Svetlana Alliluyeva (Stalin)

INDIVIDUAL-LEVEL ANALYSIS

This chapter will take up the analysis of humans as actors on the world stage. This focus lies at the opposite end of the scale from the macroscopic, system-level analysis approach to studying world politics that we reviewed in the last two chapters. The fundamental question here is, "What role do humans play in world politics?"

Individual-Level Analysis: Three Approaches

We can begin to address this question by delineating three approaches to individual-level analysis. One, the "nature-of-humankind" approach, examines the fundamental human characteristics that affect world politics. A second approach is labeled "humans-in-organizations." It studies how people act in organizational settings such as policy-making groups. Third, the "humans-as-individuals" approach explores the motivations, perceptions, and impact on world events of specific humans, both leaders and private citizens.

The Nature-of-Humankind Approach

One of the pivotal questions for social and behavioral scientists is whether human attitudes and behavior are totally the product of cultural environment or whether people are born with certain genetically determined tendencies. For many years the main thrust of scholarly opinion was that people were born almost totally "empty vessels," and that they were shaped by the circumstances of their upbringing. More recently, genetic research and other studies of human behavior have modified this belief. Certainly, no one claims that human behavior is basically instinctual, but there is no longer general agreement that people are born a tabula rasa (blank slate).

Studying the nature of humankind can focus on either psychological or biological factors.

Psychological Factors

Psychological theories can be used to explain human behavior. Here the focus is the common psychological traits of humans, not the psychological makeup of an individual. Sigmund Freud theorized that individuals are torn between two instincts, *Eros* (the life instinct) and *Thanatos* (the death instinct). Death is attractive because it brings release from anxiety. Humans resolve the tension between Eros and Thanatos through *displaced aggression*. That is, some people vent their destructive instincts on others rather than on themselves.

More recent psychological studies have focused on *frustration-aggression theory* as a source of international conflictual behavior. Theorists have contended that aggression can take many forms, including being aimed directly at the source of frustration, being redirected to a scapegoat, or even turned on oneself (suicide).

Frustration-driven behavior can be amassed and projected through national aggressive behavior. It is possible to argue, for example, that the rise of Adolf Hitler and German aggression in World War II can be attributed to mass frustration. The end of World War I, the defeat of Germany in November 1918, came as a shock to many Germans. Russia had earlier surrendered to Germany, and when the German collapse on the western front came, the battle lines were still in France. There were underlying reasons for Germany's defeat, but they were not apparent. Defeat was followed by humiliation at the hand of the victorious allies and the Treaty of Versailles in 1919, which forced the Germans to admit war guilt and left them heavily indebted, occupied, disarmed, and diplomatically isolated. The 1920s brought economic chaos in Europe, and the beginning of the 1930s saw the worldwide Great Depression. Germans were frustrated and angry. Hitler seized on these emotions. Germany had not lost the war, he told the masses, it had been betrayed by Jewish and Bolshevik conspirators, the "enemies of November" who had ruined Germany's economy and capability of carrying on the war. Reject the humiliating Versailles Treaty, Hitler told the Germans, rearm and reclaim your proud heritage. There are only two choices, he proclaimed in *Mein Kampf*, "Germany will be either a world power or it will not be at all." The frustrated German people believed, and rallied behind the prophecy—a prophecy that Hitler helped Germany ironically fulfill.

Biological Factors

It is also possible to explain human behavior by biological theories. *Biopolitics* is concerned with the relation between humans' physical and political nature. One subdivision of this approach, ethology, argues that animal, including human, behavior is, at least to some degree, based on innate genetic characteristics. Ethology studies animal behavior and attempts to draw parallels with human behavior. Ethologists such as Konrad Lorenz (*On Aggression*, 1969), Desmond Morris (*The Naked Ape*, 1967, *The Human Zoo*, 1963), and Robert Ardrey (*The Territorial Imperative*, 1961, *African Genesis*, 1966) have raised provocative questions about the genetic basis of aggressiveness and other forms of human international behavior. Ardrey, for example, contends that "territoriality—the drive to gain, maintain, and defend the exclusive right to a piece of property—is an animal instinct" and that "if man is a part of the natural world, then he possesses as do all other species a genetic . . . territorial drive as one ancient animal foundation for that human conduct known as war" (1963:12–14).

Researchers have found that, in addition to conflict over food and sex, animals will fight to gain or maintain territory, will protect their young and group, will try to expel strange members of their species with whom they come into contact, will protect objects toward which they are possessive, will fight rather than be deprived of status, and will become more aggressive as they earn rewards through repeated success.

Thus far there is no consensus among social and behavioral scientists on the role of biopolitics. One recent study, for example, argued that there are forces that "predispose genetically related individuals to band together in groups, oriented for conflict" (Shaw & Wong, 1987:5). This statement was criticized, however, on the grounds that "[It] does not contribute to our understanding of war, and merely repeats some of the most mechanistic and ill-supported ideas of sociobiology" (Goldstein, 1987:33). Yet another idea is that power-seeking is a particularly male sexual impulse. Consider Napoleon's claim that "power is my mistress," or Henry Kissinger's confession that "power is a great aphrodisiac" (*NYT*, 1/19/71). Are such characterizations rhetorical flourishes, or are they deep-seated revelations? It is important here to treat this line of inquiry as serious scholarship rather than titillation. There is, for example, some important (and controversial) work being done on the sexual content of defense thinking and planning (Cohen, 1987; Klein, 1987). These studies explore an approach represented, for example, by Helen Caldicott's provocative book *Missile Envy*, in which she argues that phallic worship is a significant motivating force behind the nuclear buildup. Such studies describe the language of "thrust-to-weight ratios," "vertical erector-launchers," and "soft-defense penetration" that is rife in defense literature. Prudence proscribes a detailed account of the prurient imagery, but it is a challenging consideration.

At the individual level of analysis, the question of whether or not sex of an individual makes a difference in political attitudes and actions, and whether any gender differences are purely a matter of socialization, or whether some are inherent is just beginning to be studied. Because there have been few female international leaders, it is difficult to make comparisons with their male counterparts. But certainly aggressiveness and tough leadership have not been lacking in England's Elizabeth I, Russia's Catherine the Great, Israel's Golda Meir, and Great Britain's Margaret Thatcher.

Whatever the exact role of inborn psychological and ethological factors may be, it is important to bear in mind that for the most part human behavior is learned rather than instinctual (Zur, 1987). Learning can modify behavior even if that behavior is partly genetic. The basically peaceful conduct of interpersonal relations in domestic societies is an example. It can also be shown that "triggers," such as frustration, do not always lead to aggressive behavior (Berkowitz, 1978).

Still, nature-of-humankind research and theories cannot be totally dismissed. Ponder, for example, the Falkland Islands War and the venerable British lion's defense of its territory. Male lions mark off their territory by scenting it. Woe betide any other male lion who enters that claimed space! In 1833 the British lion took possession of the Falkland Islands, which lie 250 miles off Argentina's coast. Argentina, which calls the islands the Malvinas, never surrendered its claim to these islands. In 1982 Argentina seized the undefended islands.

The islands themselves have no strategic or economic value for Britain. There are only 1,900 or so inhabitants of British heritage who raise sheep and goats on the windswept, treeless islands that are primarily known as a breeding ground for penguins, seals, and other marine life. Yet the British mounted a military expedition to recapture the islands. That effort succeeded, but at the cost of hundreds of British and Argentine

Some people believe that the urge to acquire power and the conflict that results are particularly male traits and that a world led by women would be a more peaceful place. The example of British prime minister Thatcher would not support that theory. She won more elections and served longer than any British prime minister in this century. She also ordered British forces to war against Argentina in 1982, and one of her last acts as prime minister in November 1990 was to double the number of British troops facing Iraq in the Middle East. Here you can see Thatcher commanding a Challenger tank during a NATO exercise in Germany.

lives; the sinking of a British frigate and an Argentinian cruiser; and a cost of vast sums of money, which Britain could ill afford. The government of British prime minister Margaret Thatcher now maintains a garrison on the islands, which further costs the British millions of pounds annually. Why? It is hard to make sense of it. Political scientists can hypothesize a number of reasons, such as an attempt by Thatcher to build popularity prior to approaching elections (Sanders, Ward, Marsh, & Fletcher, 1987). Still, one has to wonder. It may be that the British lion, now aged and in decline, roared perhaps one last time in an ethological defense of its territory.

Whether we consider the Falkland Islands War or the Gran Chaco War of the 1930s between Bolivia and Paraguay, in which 100,000 people were killed in a dispute over an arid, desolate tract of essentially useless land, our roots in the animal kingdom seem a lot closer than 'we may wish to think. We may console ourselves with the thought that, insofar as we are genetically coded, we are also a species of intellect that can learn to overcome our primordial instincts. Idealists certainly believe we can; realists doubt it.

The Humans-in-Organizations Approach

A second approach within the general individual level of analysis is to examine how people act in organizations. Just as our overall cultural setting influences how we behave, so do the more specific pressures of our positions and the dynamics of group interaction affect how we behave. Two particular concepts, "role" and "group behavior," can be used to discuss the humans-in-organizations approach.

Role Factors

We all play roles. As individuals, it may be that, for example, you and your professor are more alike than you think. Both you and your professor may like sports, enjoy Jack Nicholson movies, eat pepperoni pizzas, make love, and have anxiety attacks. Yet, in class, the roles are well defined and different. You mostly sit, listen, and take notes. The professor talks and evaluates you. You probably wear jeans, sweatshirts, and sneakers to class. Most professors dress up. If male, they wear uncomfortable suitcoats, button their shirts around their necks, and wear vertical pieces of cloth called neckties. If you often cut class, your classmates probably won't mind. If the professor frequently cuts class, you will probably be angry. Why the differences in behavior and expectations? The answer is role.

Decisionmakers play a **role** just like students and professors. Roles are the ways in which leaders act based on what they think others expect of them and what they expect of themselves, not personally, but as leaders. Role additionally involves a leader's views about his or her country's proper place and conduct in the world and the leader's part in meeting those expectations (Walker, 1987). In the next chapter we will see that an individual's views can be affected by loyalty to the bureaucratic institution, such as the military, of which he or she is a member, but role is subtly different. If institutional identification determined role, then everyone in the same position would act the same. This is clearly not true, because individuals come to positions with different ideas of what those positions should be and they interact with people who have varying views of the position's proper role.

Take Harry S. Truman, for example. Almost everyone remembers him as a tough, feisty, confident president. And, indeed, Truman tried to convey that image and came to believe it himself. He even put a sign on his desk that proclaimed, "The Buck Stops Here." Decisive! That's how presidents are supposed to act! Truman knew it and played the role to the hilt.

Was that the "real" Harry Truman? Not exactly. Sometimes he was scared. A U.S. senator recalled that when Truman was sworn in as president, "the tears ran right down [Truman's] cheeks. He kept saying, 'I'm not big enough for this job, I'm not big enough for this job' " (Rourke, 1983:1). But we never saw the self-doubting Truman. Instead, he publicly played the presidential role that he—and we—expected.

The impact of role-playing on foreign policy is important. Sometimes Truman made decisions when he was unsure of himself because presidents do not get to say, "I don't know what to do!" Truman also sometimes overcompensated for his anxieties by being too combative. Just weeks after becoming president, the still-uncertain Truman had to meet with Soviet foreign minister V. M. Molotov. There were problems with the Soviets, but there was still hope for postwar cooperation. Truman thought he ought to be firm, but he overdid it and subjected Molotov to a salty dressing down that left the Soviet gasping. Molotov had never been spoken to like that before—not even by Stalin! Truman gloated: "I gave it to him straight, a straight one-two to the jaw" (Paterson, Clifford, & Hagan, 1983:438). Truman was proving to himself that he was tough enough to be president, but postwar relations with the Soviets were off to a bad start.

British scholar Steven Smith (1985; Hollis & Smith, 1986) has given us another informative look at the impact of roles in his study of the Iranian hostage crisis (1979–81). The views of almost all the principal Washington decisionmakers about whether to try an armed rescue attempt were all partly related to their roles. President Carter saw himself as being responsible for protecting American honor, and that role image was reinforced by some of his advisers. "Your greater responsibility [than protecting the hostages] is to protect the honor and dignity of our country," national security adviser Zbigniew Brzezinski told the president (Glad, 1989:47). Carter agreed, and that eventually persuaded him to do something, even if it imperiled the hostages. Secretary of Defense Harold Brown, CIA Director Stansfield Turner, and Chairman of the Joint Chiefs of Staff David Jones were also, as might be expected, proponents of using force to free the hostages. Presidential press secretary Jody Powell and White

House chief of staff Hamilton Jordan also supported the rescue attempt, but for a different reason. They defined their roles as boosting the president's political popularity, and the rescue of the hostages would have been a political bonus—one that might have even gotten Carter reelected. The only opposition to action came from Secretary of State Cyrus Vance and his deputy secretary, Warren Christopher, who predictably cast themselves in the roles of diplomats instead of warriors. It was role-playing that helped determine the course of action that each of the players advocated.

Group-Behavior Factors

People act differently in organizations than they act alone while playing a role. Behavioral and social scientists have offered complex and extensive theories of group decision-making. For our purposes here, the most important aspect of organizational decision-making is the pressure within groups to *achieve consensus*. One analyst has labeled the process "**groupthink**" and argues the more the "*esprit de corps* among members of a policy-making in-group, the greater is the danger that independent critical thinking will be replaced by groupthink, which is likely to result in irrational and dehumanizing actions directed against out-groups" (Janis, 1983:13).

The urge for consensus affects both group leaders and subordinate group members. Leaders tend to seek consensus behind their policies because they believe that it is important to have a unified front against opponents. Consensus also enhances a politician's self-image as a national leader. Finally, leaders often seek consensus to maintain the loyalty and support of their staffs.

Subordinate group members also strive for consensus. Like leaders, they believe in a united front. They also don't want to be the dissenter, the odd man out or the devil's advocate because it is psychologically uncomfortable. Being a dissenter carries the risk of disapproval by group members or even future exclusion from the group: "Non–Team Players Need Not Enter." That fear of disapproval or banishment is especially strong for subordinate group members in relation to the group leaders.

The drive for consensus has several impacts on policy. Five important ones are (1) incremental decision-making; (2) ignoring or suppressing discordant information and policy options; (3) failure to evaluate policy options fully; (4) suppressing or excluding dissenters; and (5) choosing the least objectionable policy option.

Incremental decision-making. The foreign policy adopted by most countries is the product of a long history and the country's political momentum. Policy is seldom changed radically or quickly. Decisionmakers tend to follow existing policy or to make only marginal changes. This has been called **incremental decision-making** (Lindblom, 1959). As former U.S. national security adviser Zbigniew Brzezinski pointed out, "Foreign policy is like an aircraft carrier. You simply don't send it into a 180-degree turn; at most you move it a few degrees to port or starboard" (Paterson, Clifford, & Hagan, 1983:624).

Ignoring or suppressing discordant information and policy options. When a country has a "policy history," or even if there is no specific existing policy, groupthink tends to favor information and options that fit into current policy patterns and conventional wisdom. When the U.S. troops engaged South Vietnam's ragtag Vietcong communist rebels and elements of the relatively lightly armed North Vietnamese army in Indochina, it was difficult for Americans to believe that the victor of World War II, the great superpower, could not prevail. There was, as Senator William Fulbright (1966) suggested in his book of that title, an *Arrogance of Power*. It was especially hard for Secretary of Defense Robert McNamara, a former president of Ford Motors and early advocate of computer-assisted decision-making, to believe that the mighty Americans could not vanquish the weak Vietnamese. When one "heretical" assistant had the gall to suggest that the United States could not win, McNamara revived the inquisition: "Where is your data? Give me something I can put in the computer. Don't give me your poetry" (Paterson, Clifford, & Hagan, 1983:532). The aide was heard of no more; the war went on.

Failure to evaluate policy options fully. A related groupthink phenomenon is that once a general course of action is decided upon, negative potential impacts of the policy are ignored. This phenomenon was evident in the Iran hostage crisis. Frustrated as they were by deadlocked negotiations, and concerned over the president's political vulnerability, Carter and most of his aides favored a rescue attempt. Once they began to move in that direction, Smith (1984:118–22) observes, "the key decisionmakers simply did not realistically appraise the plan for the rescue mission." Among other things, the White House ignored an initial evaluation by the mission commander that the probability of success was "zero." Nor did they consider a CIA estimate that at least 60 percent of the hostages would be killed, or the report of one observer that a dress rehearsal for the rescue attempt was "the sorriest display of professionalism I've ever seen." Because consideration of operational problems might have brought the policy decision into question, such an evaluation was ignored.

Suppressing or excluding dissenters. Every policymaker who comes to office proclaims that he or she wants to hear all sides, and values the devil's advocate. In practice, few do. As dissent against the war in Vietnam grew, President Johnson's circle of advisers, the "Tuesday lunch group," got progressively smaller as doubters were exiled. Finally, even McNamara, who had grown to appreciate poetry more than in earlier days, was cast out. The defense secretary, Johnson rationalized, had come under such pressure from people "telling him that the war was terrible and immoral . . . [that] he felt he was a murderer. . . . I was afraid he might have a nervous breakdown. I loved him and didn't want to let him go, but he was just short of cracking up, and I felt it'd be damn unfair to force him to stay" (Kearns, 1976:321). Faced with doubts from his senior defense adviser, Johnson changed advisers, not policy.

This pattern was again evidenced by Carter during the hostage crisis. When the time for a final decision on the rescue mission arrived, Carter and his aides moved to avoid dissent by calling a quick National Security Council (NSC) meeting when the raid's chief opponent and one of the NSC's statutory officials, Secretary of State Vance, was out of town (Smith, 1984). The meeting predictably supported Carter's urge to act. "I could feel my heart speed up," presidential chief of staff Jordan recalled, "He's going to do it! He's had enough!" (Glad, 1989:51).

The debate was not quite over, however. An enraged Vance insisted on another NSC meeting to press his case. Perhaps he should have known better; the decision was a *fait accompli,* and he only earned the derision of Carter and others. Just as Lyndon Johnson had treated McNamara, the Carter White House officials wrote Vance off. Jordan remembered that when Vance finished there was an "awkward silence." Vance scanned the room, "his eyes begging for support. I fidgeted, feeling sorry for Cy, who sat there all alone." "A good man who has been traumatized [and made weak] by his Vietnam experience," was Brzezinski's patronizing evaluation. "Vance has been extremely despondent lately," the president even less charitably confided to his diary, and, he later wrote, "deeply troubled and heavily burdened." As it turned out, Vance was right in his evaluation of the raid; it was a disaster. But that made little difference. Within a month Vance was out of office, and Carter was introducing a new secretary of state as a "more statesmanlike figure" (Glad, 1989:50, 51, 56).

Often, it should be noted, it is not necessary for leaders to fire or work around advisers to avoid dissent. The pressures of groupthink tend to make subordinates reluctant to oppose the preferences of their superiors or to suggest alternatives that do not fit the conventional wisdom. The pressure to say yes to a superior is clearly illustrated by one of Lyndon Johnson's advisers who ruefully remembered:

> The President, in due course, would announce his decision and then poll everyone in the room. . . . "Mr. Secretary, do you agree with the decision?" "Yes, Mr. President." "Mr. X, do you agree?" "I agree, Mr. President." During the process I would frequently fall into a Walter Mitty–like fantasy: When my turn came I would rise to my feet slowly, look around the room, and then look directly at the President, and say very quietly and emphatically, "Mr. President, gentlemen, I most definitely do *not* agree." But I was removed from my trance when I heard the President's voice saying, "Mr. Cooper, do you agree?" And out would come a "Yes, Mr. President, I agree." (Baker & Peters, 1979:34–35)

Choosing the least objectionable policy option. Groupthink tends to arrive at the lowest common denominator. It is apt to adopt the policy that is least objectionable, rather than the optimal policy. A closely related concept is satisficing, which means considering options sequentially (rather than concurrently) until you arrive at one that is minimally acceptable (Simon, 1959). At that point you select that option, rather than continuing to search for a maximal choice.

The Cuban missile crisis illustrates this tendency. President Kennedy and his advisers did not decide to blockade Cuba because it was the best thing to do. In reality, the naval action did not directly accomplish what they wanted: to get the missiles out of Cuba. Some advisers wanted to use the military to bomb the missiles or even to invade Cuba. Others wanted to use diplomacy to pressure Moscow or wanted to offer to withdraw U.S. missiles in Turkey in exchange for the withdrawal of Soviet missiles from Cuba. Agreement between the decisionmakers on their various solutions was impossible; they settled on the blockade. It was a compromise, and it bought time, but it was the product of a failure to agree on any of the preferred options.

A review of the decisional inadequacies brought on by groupthink leads to the question, *Do poor decisions result in policy failures?* The answer is yes. Decision-making by groupthink invariably deviates substantially from sensible foreign policy. This was confirmed in a study by three scholars who studied 19 crisis decisions and rated them for evidence of 7 different symptoms of defective decision-making (Herek, Janis, & Huth, 1987, 1989; Welch, 1989). Eight decisions had either zero or 1 symptom and were rated "high quality." Four decisions with 2 or 3 symptoms were rated "medium quality," and 7 decisions with 4 or more symptoms were rated "poor quality." The researchers then asked experts to evaluate the impact of each decision as positive or negative in its effects on U.S. national interest. As Figure 4.1 indicates, there is a distinct relationship between the quality of the decisional process and the effectiveness of the policy adopted.

The Humans-as-Individuals Approach

A third approach under the general heading of individual-level analysis focuses on humans-as-individuals. The humans-as-individuals approach emphasizes the characteristics of political leaders. It makes the assumption that individuals make foreign policy decisions and that different individuals are likely to make different decisions. In its

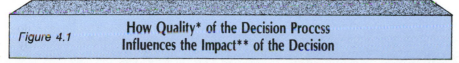

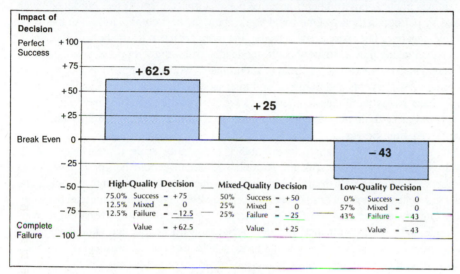

Figure 4.1 — How Quality* of the Decision Process Influences the Impact** of the Decision

* High Quality = Zero or one symptom of defective decision-making.
   Medium Quality = Two or three symptoms of defective decision-making.
   Low Quality = Four or more symptoms of defective decision-making.

** Success = Experts agreed outcome favorable for U.S. interests = +1.
   Mixed = Experts disagreed on whether or not outcome was favorable to U.S. interests = 0.
   Failure = Experts agreed outcome was unfavorable for U.S. interests = −1.

Data source: Herek, Janis, & Huth (1987:217).

The quality of the decision-making process affects the quality of the decisions, as this figure shows. Unfortunately, the dynamics of organizational decision-making often lead to poor decisions. To create this figure, successes were assigned an abstract value of +1, mixed results received a null value of 0 (zero), and failure received a value of −1.

simplest form, this approach includes examining biographies and memoirs as political histories. More recently, the study of decisionmakers has become more sophisticated. Political scientists, psychologists, and others have written "psychobiographies" that explore the motivations of decisionmakers. Scholars are also using increasingly sophisticated methodologies such as content analysis, which analyzes the content of a decisionmaker's statements and writings to understand the basic ways he or she views the world.

This approach is represented in a book by John Stoessinger that argues that "a leader's *personality* is a decisive element in the making of foreign policy. . . . Differences in leaders' personalities thus may make or break a nation's foreign policy. It matters very much, in short, *who* is there at a given moment" (1979:xv). You might ask yourself what the communist revolution would have been like or whether it would have occurred at all if there had not been a V. I. Lenin in Russia or a Mao Zedong in China. Would World War II have occurred if Adolf Hitler had never lived? If John F. Kennedy had lived, would 50,000 Americans have died in Vietnam? The answers to these questions are, of course, unknowable. It is probable, however, that history would have been different (Burke & Greenstein, 1989). Scholars have done innovative studies that focused on factors such as personality attributes. One well-known approach categorizes political personality along an active-passive scale and a positive-negative scale (Barber, 1985). Active presidents are policy innovators; passive presidents are reactors. Positive personalities have egos strong enough to enjoy (or at least equably endure) the contentious political environment; negative personalities are apt to feel burdened, even abused by political criticism. One could argue about the best combination, but the worst is active-negative. The more active a leader, the more criticism he or she will encounter. Rather than taking that in stride though, the leader will assume opponents are enemies and may withdraw into an inner circle of subordinates who are supportive and who give an unreal view of events and domestic and international opinion. Both Lyndon Johnson and Richard Nixon were classic active-negative personalities, and as they came under heavy fire during their presidencies they both developed a bunker mentality until they were forced from power.

Crusaders and pragmatists form another personality scale (Stoessinger, 1979). Woodrow Wilson or, better still, the Ayatollah Khomeini would be good examples of crusaders; and George Bush and Mikhail Gorbachev would score high as pragmatic leaders. Another recent illustrative study (Shepard, 1988) classified American decision-makers in the administrations from 1969 through 1988 along an introversion-extroversion scale and a high dominance–low dominance (toward people and situations) scale. The purpose of this study was to attempt to see whether or not a placement on this scale could predict if an extrovert would be more likely to favor cooperation with the Soviet Union than an introvert. An answer was also sought as to whether a dominant personality would be more likely to favor using military force than a low-dominant personality. The study, in disagreement with an earlier study (Ethridge, 1978), found that extroversion and cooperation were unrelated. It confirmed, however, that earlier study's conclusion that dominant personalities are more likely than others to be aggressive militarily.

Advocates of the biographical approach are primarily interested in the psychohistory of individual leaders. The question is not *what* these persons decided. Rather, the question is *why* they chose certain paths. What are the internal, psychological factors that motivate decisionmakers?

The list of possible psychological factors is long and varies from analyst to analyst. For our discussion, though, we will consider four basic factors from the decisionmaker's point of view:

1. *How I feel*—What is the decisionmaker's physical and mental health?
2. *What I know*—What is the decisionmaker's view of history in general? What have been the experiences of his or her personal history?
3. *What I believe*—What are the individual's ideology, perceptions, and operational code?
4. *What I want*—What factors of ego and ambition affect the individual's decisions?

Mental and Physical Health

The mind and body can be important factors in decision-making. According to Soviet premier Nikita Khrushchev, his predecessor Josef Stalin suffered from severe paranoia. If it is true that "Stalin was a very distrustful man, sickly suspicious," that "everywhere and in everything he saw enemies," and that "Stalin had completely lost consciousness of reality" (Duchacek, 1975:197), then it follows that Soviet policy after World War II

Woodrow Wilson was a very ill man in 1919 when he was negotiating with the Allies at the Versailles Peace Conference in Paris, and with the U.S. Senate over ratification of the peace treaty and U.S. entry into the League of Nations. The condition of his health may have had an important impact on these negotiations. Many of his ideals as expressed in his Fourteen Points were rejected in Paris, and the treaty and League membership were rejected in Washington. Wilson soon suffered a massive stroke, never fully recovered, and died a few years later.

might have been more cooperative with either a mentally healthier Stalin or a different Soviet leader directing foreign policy.

The physical health of Stalin's American contemporary, Franklin Roosevelt, may also have affected Soviet/American relations. When Roosevelt met Stalin at Yalta in February 1945, the president's blood pressure was an astronomical 260/150 and he suffered from chest pains. It has been argued that FDR was too weak to stand up to Stalin. One scholar has written, "By the time of the Yalta Conference, Roosevelt was very seriously ill and unable to deal effectively with complex diplomatic issues to be discussed" (Riccards, 1977:226). Two months later Roosevelt was dead. What might have been if a healthy Roosevelt had gone to Yalta?

Similarly, the settlements at the end of World War I may have been affected by President Wilson's physical health and associated psychological symptoms. Edwin Weinstein traces Wilson's several strokes and other cardiovascular difficulties and suggests his medical problems may have affected Wilson's judgment and caused him to become less willing to compromise. According to Weinstein:

> Diminished emotional control, greater egocentricity, increased suspicion and secrecy, and lapses in judgment and memory are common manifestations of cerebral arteriosclerosis. In Wilson's case, the symptoms seem to have been brought on by a combination of vascular disease and the extraordinary degree of external stress to which he was subjected. (1981:323)

If Weinstein is correct, it helps explain why Wilson was so adamantly opposed to compromising with the Senate on ratification of the Treaty of Versailles. Wilson's obdurateness finally led to the rejection of the treaty by the Senate, the failure of the United States to join the League of Nations, and possibly the absence of a stabilizing U.S. participation in world events during the 1920s and 1930s.

Although not common, drugs or alcohol may also affect a decisionmaker's judgment. Adolf Hitler provides a dramatic example. As the war progressed and German fortunes declined, Hitler's drug intake reached epic proportions, including barbiturates, cardiac stimulants, desoxycorticosterone (for muscle weakness), hormones from both female placentas and from the testes and prostates of young bulls, caffeine, Pervitin (an amphetamine), and Eukodal (a morphine equivalent). Beginning in mid-1944 Hitler also received cocaine treatments four times daily for sinusitis. As an analysis of the impact of such drug use notes, "The precise effects of this pharmaceutical cocktail on Hitler's mental state is difficult to gauge. Suffice it to say, in the jargon of the street, Hitler was simultaneously taking coke and speed" (*HC*, 2/4/90:C4).[1] The use of these drugs would produce a high-low cycle, producing euphoria and delusions of grandeur followed by paranoia and irrational anger. This bizarre pattern closely resembles Hitler's wildly inconsistent moods and decision-making late in the war.

History and Personal Experiences

The past is another factor that helps shape a political leader's approach to world problems. It has been said that generals fight and diplomats try to prevent the last war. That is an oversimplification, but it has an element of truth. Decisionmakers often apply the "lessons" of world history to current situations. As such, according to one scholar, "history is prophecy looking backwards" (Arieli, 1982:69). The "lesson of Munich" is one such history-prophecy that has done much to affect the actions of Western leaders since World War II. The British, in an attempt at **appeasement**, allowed Hitler to annex part of Czechoslovakia. This later became an obvious failure as Germany attacked the rest of Czechoslovakia, then Poland, and finally most of Europe. Munich serves as a symbol of what came to be regarded as a fatal series of concessions to the Germans, Italians, and Japanese that only encouraged aggression and finally led to World War II. The lesson (known as the **Munich syndrome**) drawn by postwar leaders was that you do not compromise with aggression—"Don't give 'em an inch, or they'll take a mile."

During the cold war years western leaders repeatedly applied the lesson of the 1930s. When President Truman was faced with the North's invasion of South Korea, he drew a parallel in history:

> In my generation this was not the first occasion when the strong attacked the weak. I recalled some earlier instances: Manchuria, Ethiopia, Austria. I remembered how each time that the democracies failed to act it had encouraged the aggressors to keep going ahead. Communism was acting in Korea just as Hitler, Mussolini, and the Japanese had acted. . . . If this was allowed to go unchallenged it would mean a third world war, just as similar incidents had brought on a second world war. (May, 1973:32)

Truman decided for war.

In 1956 British prime minister Sir Anthony Eden was faced with a crisis over Egypt's nationalization (seizure) of the Suez Canal. He drew on Munich as a lesson from history:

> Success in a number of adventures in the breaking of agreements in . . . the Rhineland, in Austria, in Czechoslovakia . . . persuaded Hitler . . . that the

---

1. For a fuller discussion of Hitler's drug abuse, see L'Etang (1970).

democracies had not the will to resist. . . . As my colleagues and I surveyed the scene . . . we were determined that the like should not come again. (May, 1973:x)

Eden decided for war.

John Kennedy also remembered Munich, and indeed his senior thesis at Harvard was entitled *Why England Slept* and argued that America could learn profitable lessons from Great Britain's attempt to appease Hitler instead of confronting him in 1938. The president carried that lesson to the Cuban missile crisis, telling Americans:

The 1930s taught us a clear lesson: aggressive conduct, if allowed to go unchecked and unchallenged, ultimately leads to war. (Paterson, Clifford, & Hagan, 1983:530)

Kennedy confronted the Soviet Union at the risk of nuclear war.

In 1964 Lyndon Johnson faced a crisis in Vietnam. As he later remembered:

Everything I knew about history told me that if I got out of Vietnam . . . then I'd be doing exactly what Chamberlain did in World War II. I'd be giving a big fat reward to aggression. . . . And so would begin World War III. (Kearns, 1976:264)

Johnson decided for war.

More than a half-century after Munich, Iraq's president Saddam Hussein ordered his troops into Kuwait and threatened Saudi Arabia. George Bush told the American people:

If history teaches us anything, it is that we must resist aggression or it will destroy our freedoms. Appeasement does not work. As was the case in the 1930s, we see in Saddam Hussein an aggressive dictator threatening his neighbors. (*HC,* 8/9/90:B13)

Bush ordered U.S. military forces to the Middle East to confront Iraq.

Lessons of history often fade as those who remember them become fewer, and it may be that the new generation of leaders who came of political age during the 1960s and early 1970s will be affected by another lesson: Vietnam. That lesson may be just the opposite from the one learned at Munich and just as easy to misinterpret. In fact, the 1980's debate over U.S. policy toward Central America provided an interesting example of countervailing historical lessons. President Reagan, who well remembered Munich, referred to it on more than one occasion and favored confrontation. We must, he cautioned, "be realistic about the nature of the world and our adversaries. . . . Making excuses for bad behavior only encourages bullies and invites aggression. . . . I have spoken of similarities, and the 1980s like the 1930s may be one of those crucial junctions in history that will determine the direction of the future" (U.S. Department of State, 1984).

Many of his domestic critics were younger, from the Vietnam era. Their cry was "no more Vietnams" and when the president intervened or threatened to in El Salvador,

Individuals sometimes play a pivotal role in the course of international politics. One such individual was Mao Zedong. He is shown here as a young revolutionary at about the time he led his communist forces on the Long March (1934–35) into the mountains of China. Within 15 years, he emerged from his stronghold, took control of his country, and established a communist political system that encompassed 20 percent of the world's population. He began a modernization program that may one day bring China to true superpower status.

Lebanon, and elsewhere, there were dire warnings of another Vietnam. The dispatch of the U.S. 82nd Airborne Division in 1988 to Honduras on a "training exercise" (translation: to threaten Nicaragua) brought howls of protest. "There is no reason to have troops down there [in Honduras]. . . . We don't need another Vietnam in Central America," declared Democratic presidential candidate Michael S. Dukakis (*HC*, 3/16/88:A1). For better or worse, the "Vietnam syndrome" affected policy, helping to abort the Reagan administration's attempt to drum up support for a military intervention in El Salvador in the early 1980s. A surprised White House found public and congressional opinion was firmly against action. "The White House did not appreciate how rapidly El Salvador would take off in the minds of the press as a Vietnam," a White House assistant remarked while explaining the Administration's retreat from its call to arms (Paterson, Clifford, & Hagan, 1983:652).

Americans, of course, are not the only people who draw historical analogies. The Soviet psyche was traumatized by the surprise Nazi invasion in June 1941. Twenty million Soviet citizens were killed and much of the country lay in ruins. Although the motivations behind Soviet foreign policy are complex, most scholars agree that the lessons of 1941 made the Soviets particularly defensive. That helps explain their tight grip on Eastern Europe as a buffer zone and their drive to achieve unassailable military strength. It also helps account for their suspicion of attempts to reach peace accords. They remember that the nonaggression pact with Hitler they signed turned out to be a worthless scrap of paper.

There is, however, a new generation of Soviet leaders. Mikhail Gorbachev was just 10 when the Nazi panzer divisions assaulted his country. He lived in a somewhat remote region in the south, and although the Germans occupied the area, they were driven out after only 6 months. There is no evidence that Gorbachev suffered during the war. Indeed, by his own account, it was not until 1950 when he traveled to Moscow to begin his university studies that he saw the war's devastation of his country.

There is little doubt that Gorbachev is a prime example of the impact that an individual can have on international politics (see the box on pages 98–99). An intriguing question that was debated after he came to power was whether Gorbachev and the new generation of Soviet leaders would act differently because they were not affected by the invasion of 1941. Some analysts speculated, for example, that they would be less defensive, would ease their hold on Eastern Europe, and would be willing to reduce their armament levels. Others contended that 1941 instilled the earlier generation with a horror of war that made them very cautious about using Soviet military forces in any way that could lead to war with the Western powers. By contrast, the new, unchastened generation might be willing to take more risks.

Belief Systems

What decisionmakers believe is a third personal element that influences foreign policy. *Ideology* is a key factor here. Ideology, which is discussed extensively in chapter 7, forms a "lens" or "prism" through which we perceive reality. It helps precondition our images of both ourselves and others. As used here ideology is a broader term referring to complex, preexisting images that decisionmakers hold. Try borrowing a pair of glasses from a friend. Look at the world around you. It becomes distorted, the degree of distortion depending on how thick the lenses are. Similarly, ideology acts as a perceptual lens, the degree of distortion related to the strength of the beholder's ideology.

A classic study of the role of belief systems has been done by Ole Holsti. He used content analysis techniques to examine 5,584 statements on the Soviet Union by Secretary of State John Foster Dulles. From these, Holsti was able to construct an *operational code* for Dulles. The study found that Dulles viewed the Soviets through a heavy ideological lens that told him that "the Soviet Union was built on the trinity of atheism, totalitarianism, and communism" (Holsti, 1962:244–52). From this perspective, Dulles saw the communist Soviets as unrelentingly hostile. Even when the Soviets showed a willingness to coexist, to compromise, or to redirect their resources from military to domestic uses, Dulles interpreted their actions as signs of weakness or trickery rather than as good intentions. He was also unable to view Soviet policy from his opponent's perspective. He could see no legitimate Russian national interest, only the evil designs of godless communism. He once compared Soviet foreign policy to that of a hotel burglar who lurked in corridors, indiscriminately trying doors until he found one unlocked.

One of Dulles' successors as secretary of state, Henry Kissinger, had a very different operational code (Starr, 1984). Kissinger's childhood was spent in Germany where he was traumatized by the anti-Semetic hysteria provoked by the Nazis. Later, his early scholarship focused on the order-creating balance-of-power system that prevailed in Europe during the nineteenth century. These experiences led Kissinger to adopt an operational code that carried over into his views and actions as policymaker. His code emphasized (1) maintenance of stability; (2) big-power-balancing to maintain stability; (3) big-power diplomacy to manage peripheral areas and countries; and (4) use of force to preserve balance and stability (defeat revolutionary, unbalancing tendencies), but in a restrained manner and as a supplement to negotiations.

An interesting variation on the general idea of operational codes is what one scholar (Rogers, 1987) calls "crisis bargaining codes." What this means is that decisionmakers have an image of not only the world (belief system) but also of the dynamics of crisis bargaining, including such things as escalation, bluffing, and how war is likely to start. These differ among decisionmakers, and individual crisis bargaining codes influence how different leaders react to and act in a crisis. Richard Nixon believes:

> relations are a lot like poker—stud poker with a hole card. The hole card is all important because without it your opponent—the Soviet leader, for instance,

Mikhail Sergeyevich Gorbachev

Born:
March 2, 1931, in Privolnoye, a farming village (pop.: 3,000) in southern Russia.

Family:
Father Sergi (died 1976). Mother Maria Pantelyevna still lives in Privolnoye on a monthly pension of 39 rubles ($49.30). She is a practicing Russian Orthodox Christian. She complains her son only visits home every few years, but he recently bought her a color TV set. Wife (since 1954) Raisa Maximovna (Titorenko) has a doctorate in philosophy/ideology. They met in a coed dorm at college. Daughter Irina is a physician. Two granddaughters, Ksenia and Anastasia.

Education:
Law degree, Moscow University (1955); agriculture degree (by correspondence), Stavropol Agricultural Institute (1967).

Personal:
Nickname, Misha. Largely untouched by World War II. Worked as a combine operator as a teenager. Earned Red Banner of Labor at age 18.

Experience:
Worked as Communist party youth organizer in college. After graduation served in southern Russia as a party official, especially in agriculture. Appointed to the Party's Central Committee (1971) and its Politburo (1979). Appointed general secretary of the Central Committee (March 1985). Informally, presiding officer of the Politburo. Elected to the symbolic position of president of the Soviet Union (1988) and reelected to a newly empowered presidency (1990).

Won the 1990 Nobel Peace Prize and was named *Time*'s "Man of the Decade" for the 1980s. Also received a big raise in 1990, doubling his annual salary to 48,000 rubles ($77,760) gross, or $44,712 take-home after taxes. Likes cultural events, movies, reading, and walking in the forest, but grumbles that "virtually all my time except for several hours needed to sleep are given to work" (*HC*, 1/15/90:A1). Mikhail Gorbachev reached the pinnacle of Soviet political power in March 1985 when he was chosen as general secretary of the Soviet Communist party. He is the first Soviet general secretary to have been born after the communist revolution (1917), the first who was not politically active during World War II, and the first to have a college degree. Aged 54 when appointed general secretary, he was more than 20 years younger than his predecessor.

What is clearest and most important about Gorbachev is that he has announced his intention to change the Soviet Union dramatically. He declared that he and the party were "guilty before the working class" for the country's economic lag and political paralysis (*NYT*, 11/30/90:A15). Domestically, he called for perestroika ("restructuring" the party and government) and for glasnost ("openness" in government). Gorbachev's principal goal is to rejuvenate the overly centralized Soviet economy. "We cannot remain a major power in world affairs unless we put our domestic house in order," he told the Central Committee (*Time*, 1/4/88:29). As part of this effort, Gorbachev said that the U.S.S.R. needs "a lasting peace to concentrate on the development of our society and to proceed to improve the life of the Soviet people (*Time*, 7/27/87:41).

has perfect knowledge of whether he can beat you. If he knows he will win he will raise you. If he cannot, he will fold and get out of the game. The United States is an open society. We have all but one of our cards face up on the table. Our only covered card is the will, nerve, and unpredictability of the President—his ability to make the enemy think twice about raising the ante. (Rogers, 1987)

That poker image does a lot to help explain why Nixon raised the ante in Vietnam, for example, by mining Haiphong Harbor and unleashing a tremendous "Christmas" bombing offensive, both of which, Nixon believed, helped persuade the North Vietnamese and their Soviet backers to cash in their chips and agree to more serious negotiations. In truth, the terms Nixon got after the bombing were only marginally better than those offered before. Be that as it may, the point is that the president's crisis-

There can be little doubt that Gorbachev has tried to achieve much of what he outlined. He has significantly changed the political structure, downgrading the Party and upgrading the government. He has moved tentatively toward economic reform. Glasnost has increased. Internationally, he has shifted policy dramatically by reducing his military, giving up Soviet control of Eastern Europe, and cooperating extensively with the West.

Still, there are doubts about Gorbachev and the Soviet Union. Fewer analysts than before are skeptical of his motives, but this view still exists. It holds that what Gorbachev is really after is *peredyshka,* a "breathing space," to rejuvenate his country for a new round of struggle. Former French premier Jacques Chirac (1989:14) warns that the West's "chronic aspiration" to see Russia become Europeanized "has been intelligently exploited at regular intervals by rulers of that country. . . . [W]e must bear in mind that Russia has always had two faces—a modern countenance that it exhibits to the West and another, ambiguous one that it presents to itself. . . . [W]e must not lose sight of this cleavage between appearance and reality in the Soviet Union."

The other concern about Gorbachev and the U.S.S.R. relates to his ability to succeed, or even survive, in office and what might follow if he fails. There is certainly strong domestic opposition. The economy has declined and people are angry. One poll found that 57 percent had no confidence in the future, and Gorbachev's Nobel Peace Prize was greeted by derision in Moscow. One woman there suggested he use the prize money ($710,000) to buy Big Macs for hungry Soviet children (*NYT,* 10/16/90:A1). Separatist nationalism is rampant. Entrenched party and bureaucratic officials are threatened and obdurate. Conservative Politburo member Yegor Ligachev has publicly criticized Gorbachev for unleashing "nationalist, separatist and antisocialist forces [that] pose the primary threat, a fatal threat, to . . . the Soviet Union" (*NYT,* 2/9/90:A6).

Will Gorbachev survive, prevail? Richard Nixon thinks so. He has characterized Gorbachev as "either the greatest actor the political world has produced . . . or a man totally in charge with the power and the ability to chart his own course" (*Time,* 7/27/87:39). And scholar Jerry Hough recently wrote an editorial "Why Gorby Is Defying the Pundits' Predictions" to explain why "Mikhail Gorbachev confounded the conventional wisdom [that he was in political trouble] once again" (*WP,* 2/11/90:C1). U.S. defense secretary Dick Cheney predicts, by contrast, that Gorbachev will "ultimately fail; . . . he will not be able to reform the Soviet economy . . . [and] when that happens he's likely to be replaced by somebody who will be far more hostile" (*NYT,* 5/2/90:A1).

And what does Mikhail Sergeyevich (as he would be properly addressed in Russian) think? "I really don't even want to attempt a detailed forecast of what will happen to the U.S.S.R.," he told an interviewer. "Our future will depend on the present; where we end up will depend on how we come through this extremely critical passage that we are making right now as we introduce radical changes in our society, all in the context of world civilization" (*Time,* 6/4/90:34). On that, Mikhail Sergeyevich, we can all agree.

operational code caused his violent reaction and he justified his decision by believing later that it was a major turning point to end the war.

Ego and Ambition

The fourth psychological factor that influences a statesperson's point of view is personal motivation. Here the issue is not what a decisionmaker wants in terms of national interest. The point is what the decisionmaker wants in terms of personal interest. How do policy choices relate to the individual's ego and ambitions?

A leader's self-image and concern about his or her political fortunes often seem to intertwine. John Kennedy's initial reaction to proof that Soviet leader Nikita Khrushchev had placed missiles in Cuba was an intensely personal "He can't do that to *me.*" That sense of ego attack and Kennedy's concern about his political future were among the reasons he decided to risk nuclear war to force the missiles out. "If you hadn't acted, you would have been impeached," the president's younger brother Robert observed just after the crisis. "That's what I think," the senior Kennedy replied (Rourke, 1983:107).[2]

Ego, perhaps the male variety in particular, also sometimes works to make leaders want to appear tough. Lyndon Johnson, who was incredibly insecure under his brash exterior, was bedeviled by the image of becoming "the first American president to lose a war," and so he pressed on in Vietnam. (Burke & Greenstein, 1989:87; Kearns, 1976.) A seemingly more pacifistic Jimmy Carter was also subject to this sort of ego concern. The hostage crisis endangered his reelection chances, and he also wanted to beat the wimp image that dogged his presidency. Revealingly, he later recalled that a top compliment he had received as president was from Colonel Charles Beckwith, a real live Rambo type who headed Delta Force, the commandos who attempted the hostage rescue in Iran. "My men and I," Carter proudly remembers Beckwith telling him, "have decided that our boss [Carter] . . . is as tough as woodpecker lips" (Glad, 1989:53). Nor is this just an American trait. After a meeting with the Soviet leader in Moscow, an impressed U.S. senator Alan Simpson recalls he "told Gorbachev that he was a no-bullshit kind of guy." Absolutely, a puffed-up Gorbachev replied, adding that he knew "how to say that word in 14 different languages" (*Time,* 1/1/90:55).

Ronald Reagan's ego may have worked for both confrontation and conciliation. "Politics is just like show business," he once allowed. "You have a hell of an opening, you coast for a while, and then [you] have a hell of a closing." True to form, Reagan's presidency had one hell of a swashbuckling opening. The Soviets became the cinematic "evil empire," Libyan jets were blasted from the sky, the Marines went adventuring in Lebanon, paratroopers appeared over Grenada. But soon the press reviews turned sour, and Reagan's standing with the audience sagged. Not only that, but a new star, Mikhail Gorbachev, upstaged him. Gorbachev's bold initiatives turned the spotlight away from the "great communicator" and onto himself. Gorbachev's name was now on the marquees of politics and in the headlines of the newspapers. "I don't resent his popularity," Reagan manfully said of the new superstar. "Good Lord, I co-starred with Errol Flynn once" (*Time,* 12/14/87:16). But that sort of magnanimity is not usually the stuff of Hollywood or Washington.

How to have a hell of an ending became the question. "Peace," Nancy Reagan said she whispered in her husband's ear each evening. That would be a grand ending. And so as his run on Pennsylvania Avenue came to an end, Reagan startlingly transfigured his official character. The consummate warrior proclaimed the Soviet Union was no longer an evil empire; he transformed Gorbachev from a Darth Vadar–like persona into a reasonable fellow; Reagan and Gorbachev met so often and amicably they were dubbed the "Ron and Gorby Show." They signed the first (INF) Nuclear Arms Reduction Treaty in history, and pledged to cut strategic nuclear weapons by half. Whether all this was the product of a national statesman or a grasping for historical adulation by an ego facing the last curtain, it was certainly a surprise ending. *Exit, stage right.*

George Bush provides the most recent example of possible ego impact. The new president came to office with a reputation for being overly cautious. When he did not intervene to help an October 1989 attempt to overthrow Panamanian dictator Manuel Noriega, the "wimp factor" became a regular subject of journalistic comment and cartoon caricaturization. In the words of one analyst, the "indecision profoundly frustrated the president and embarrassed the White House; it may have shaped action

---

2. It should be pointed out that domestic politics was just one of the factors that motivated Kennedy. There were also reasonable national security concerns. For a good review with a different view of Kennedy's motives, see Paterson & Brophy (1986).

"Should I use a worm? . . .
I'll tie a fly . . . Hmmm . . .
Maybe a spoon . . .
a nine iron?"

later in the year" when, on December 20, some 24,000 U.S. troops stormed into Panama. It was, the *New York Times* (12/21/89:A1) headlined in a clear image of sexual maturity, "War: Bush's Presidential Rite of Passage." George Bush was a wimp no more.

Perceptions: Recreating the World in Your Mind

The introductory section of chapter 1 included the comment that one of the major themes of world politics is that there are two worlds: one of reality and one of perception. Inasmuch as perceptions strongly affect how individuals act in world politics, this is a good juncture to return to the discussion of perceptions.

The Sources and Nature of Perceptions and Misperceptions

There are several sources of perceptions, and some were touched upon in the earlier discussion of the various factors that shape decisionmakers' points of view. One key source of images is an individual's belief system. If, like George Bush or Margaret Thatcher, you see Iraq's Saddam Hussein as a near-reincarnation of Adolf Hitler, you are apt to react strongly, as they did.

Values are a second source of perceptions. We tend to react favorably to events and individuals who support our values. Conversely, things that contravene our values are perceived negatively. Henry Kissinger, as we have seen, valued stability. Therefore, events or actors that seemed revolutionary, that threatened to destabilize the status quo, were perceived in a negative light by him. Third, perceptions are based on information. Each of us is dependent on others to supply us with information about the world. Accurate information does not ensure we will see the world as it actually is. Indeed, we often reject information that does not fit into our preexisting ideas in a process called *cognitive balancing*. Erroneous information or the lack of information, however, will almost surely lead to misperception. As the next chapter's discussion of bureaucracy shows, presidents, prime ministers, and party chiefs are all too often misled by false, one-sided, or missing information.

The study of perceptions is too extensive to detail here, but it is appropriate to look at some of the most important aspects of the phenomenon. Before proceeding, though, it is important to point out that perceptions often are more than just individual images. Sometimes, most of a nation and its leaders can share similar perceptions. These are based on common cultural values, ideologies, or historical experiences. The anticommunist consensus shared by most Americans from the late 1940s through the late 1960s is one example of a national perception.

The distortions caused by perceptions are in many ways specifically related to individuals and circumstances, but there are common tendencies. Professor Robert Jervis (1968) has suggested a number of general perceptual characteristics found in world politics. Among these are:

1. *There is a tendency to see other countries as more hostile than your own.* A Canadian official has recalled that when Gorbachev visited that country in 1981 they got into an argument about armaments. The Canadian remembers Gorbachev "going on about how the U.S. was the aggressor, how it was making weapons . . . [and how] the U.S. was returning to the [cold war] conditions of the 1950s." When the Canadian minister countered that the Americans saw the Soviets as the heavily armed threat, Gorbachev snapped, "That is erroneous" (*Time*, 1/4/88:30).

   The tendency to perceive others as hostile is particularly strong when there is a lack of knowledge about others. Gorbachev had never been to the United States or dealt extensively with Americans when this conversation occurred. In 1986 Gorbachev told an American visitor that he believed that President Reagan was a prisoner of the military-industrial complex who "couldn't make peace if he wanted to." Within two years, more information and extensive contacts with Americans had softened Gorbachev's image. He signed an arms treaty that he had earlier thought Reagan could not achieve. In meetings with the Soviet leader, former president Nixon "sensed that Gorbachev's attitude toward the President and the First Lady was one of genuine affection. His last words to me as I was leaving his office in the Kremlin were, 'Give my warmest regards to President Reagan and to Lady Nancy' " (*Time*, 11/30/87:18).

2. *We tend to see the behavior of others as more centralized, disciplined, and coordinated than ours.* Both the Americans and the Soviets have been prone to imagine that the other side has a carefully planned, well-executed master strategy to expand its power and influence and to frustrate and defeat its opponents. By contrast, both sides view their own countries as defensive and as responding on a piecemeal basis to the aggressive thrusts of the other side. Former secretary of state Henry Kissinger described U.S.–Soviet relations in terms of this perceptual phenomenon:

   The superpowers often behave like two heavily armed blind men feeling their way around a room, each believing himself in mortal peril from the other whom he assumes to have perfect vision. . . . Each tends to ascribe to the other side a consistency, foresight, and coherence that its own experience belies. Of course, over time even two armed blind men in a room can do enormous damage to each other, not to speak of the room. (1979:1202)

3. *It is hard to believe that the other side is afraid of us.* Not only is each side convinced that it wears the white hats and that the other side wears the black hats, but it is hard to believe that the other side can doubt our sincerity. When we propose a peace plan, how can they reject it? They can't be afraid of us. It must be that they really do not want peace, because if they did, they would accept our plan—the "good guy" plan.

One result of the inability to understand that others perceive our defensive acts as threatening is the arms race. The U.S. plan to build a defense (the Strategic Defense Initiative, SDI) against nuclear missiles provides a good illustration. When President Reagan announced the project to the nation in March 1983, he declared it a way to real safety in a nuclear world; he pledged, "We seek neither military superiority or political advantage. Our only purpose—one all people share—is to search for ways to reduce the dangers of nuclear war."

The Soviets perceive SDI very differently. To them it is a threat. They refer to SDI technology as "nuclear space strike weapons." A few days after Reagan's speech, Soviet general secretary Yuri Andropov characterized SDI as an offensive threat to his country, "a first nuclear strike capability . . . to secure the possibility of . . . rendering [us] unable of dealing a retaliatory strike, [SDI] is a bid to disarm the Soviet Union in the face of the U.S. nuclear threat" (Nogee & Spanier, 1988:180).

Another common perceptual phenomenon is called **mirror image**. This is a tendency for two countries to see each other in similar terms. Mirror images can be either positive or negative. The latter occurs when "two countries involved in a prolonged hostile confrontation develop fixed distorted attitudes of one another that are really quite similar. Each sees itself as virtuous, restrained, and peace-loving, and [each] views its adversary as deceptive, imperialistic, and warlike" (Dougherty & Pfaltzgraff, 1990:221). The effect of the U.S.–Soviet mirror image is to create a degree of reciprocity, or multiple symmetry, in relations. There are variations for different issues, but to some extent, there is a symmetry between the policies of the two countries as well as their attitudes (Dixon, 1986). Consider the two maps on the following pages. One is from a publication entitled *Soviet Power, 1987* published by the U.S. Defense Department, and it shows with menacing arrows the thrust of Soviet aggression outward toward a vulnerable world (Fig. 4.2). The second map is from *Whence the Threat to Peace* published by the U.S.S.R. Defense Ministry, and it shows with menacing arrows the thrust of American aggression inward toward the vulnerable Soviet Union (Fig. 4.3). What is amazing, at least to me, is that the maps are virtually mirror images with only the direction of the arrows and the aggressor and victim reversed. Mirror images can also be positive, and recent polls in the United States and the Soviet Union show both countries with parallel, friendlier images of one another.

The Impact of Perceptions and Misperceptions

The most obvious impact of perceptions on world politics is that they often distort our understanding of events, other actors, and even ourselves. This can cause us to misjudge the actions of others and to fail to understand how our own actions are perceived by others. If this were the only extent of the impact of perceptions, their role would be limited, but it is not. Perceptions affect how we act on the world stage.

Figure 4.2   **Soviet Aggression as Perceived by the United States**

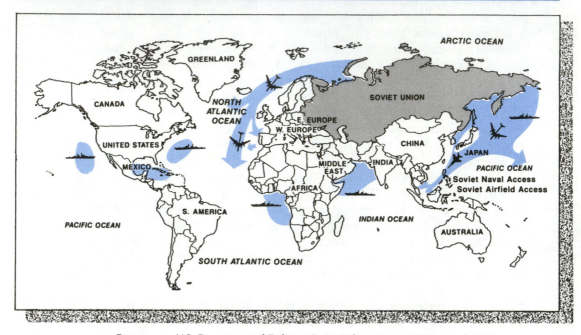

Data source: U.S. Department of Defense, *Soviet Military Power, 1987,* March 1987.

Perceptions play a strong part in the course of international politics. One perceptual phenomenon is the mirror image, which means that countries are apt to see each other in similar terms. These two maps show the mirror image that the Soviet Union and United States long had of one another, except that the U.S. map (above) has aggressive arrows coming out of the U.S.S.R., and the Soviet map (opposite) has equally threatening arrows coming out of the U.S.

The link between perception and world politics is the concept of **operational reality**. Not only is reality distorted by our (mis)perceptions, but we tend to act, or operate, based on those perceptions. The reaction of the Reagan administration to Nicaragua is a good example. Reagan believed that "the Soviet Union underlies all the unrest that is going on." He also believed in the *domino theory* (if one country succumbs, others will sequentially fall): "If [the Soviets] weren't engaged in this game of dominoes, there wouldn't be any hot spots in the world." In Reagan's logic, the United States was the "last domino" (Paterson, Clifford, & Hagan, 1983:652). Add to this Reagan's belief that Daniel Ortega and the Sandinistas turned Nicaragua into a Soviet client state and you can see why the president worried about Nicaragua being "just two days driving time from Harlingen, Texas" and a "mortal threat to the entire New World." Many found it hard to perceive Nicaragua, which is one-fifth the size of Texas and whose population is just slightly larger than Houston's, as a critical threat, but Mr. Reagan did.

The key to the conduct of American policy, though, was the fact that Ronald Reagan was president of the United States, and others were not. Therefore, the operational reality was that U.S. policy operated on the perception of communist threat, and it supplied arms to the Contra rebels, mined Nicaraguan ports, and sent U.S. troops to Central America to intimidate the Sandinistas. The image, then, assumed a sort of reality because it motivated American action.

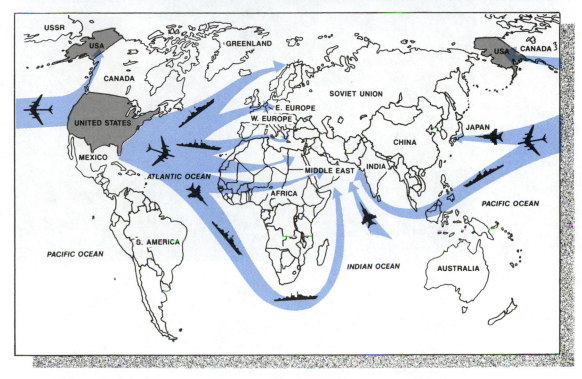

Figure 4.3   **U.S. Aggression as Perceived by the Soviet Union**

Data source: U.S.S.R. Ministry of Defense, *Whence the Threat to Peace* (Moscow: Military Publishing House, 1982).

The Soviet cartographer showed here a slightly different geographic perspective from the American-drawn map in Figure 4.2. The important thing to note, however, is that this map is a virtual mirror image of the map opposite.

Individual Citizens and World Politics

Before leaving our discussion of individual-level analysis it is important to stress that leaders are not the only individuals who can have an impact on world politics. They certainly are in the best position to do so, but remember that world politics not only affects you, but that you can affect it. The common theme to the minibiographies that follow is that each is a private citizen who tried and succeeded in making the world at least a little better place.

Michelle Alexander
American schoolgirl, who when she was 11 years old invented a board game called "Give Peace a Chance." She has played it with world leaders including Soviet president Andrei Gromyko and India's prime minister Rajiv Gandhi. In April 1988 Michelle received the World Children's Day Foundation award and addressed the UN General Assembly.

You do not have to be the president of the United States, the prime minister of Canada, the general secretary of the Soviet Union, or the secretary-general of the United Nations to play a role in international politics. Michelle Alexander, at age 11, invented a game about world peace. If you achieve peace, you win. Michelle is playing the game here with Vice President Ulanhu of China.

Bob Geldof

Irish rock music impresario. Active in famine relief for Africa. Organized the Live Aid rock concert in London in 1985. Geldof's leadership inspired British rock stars singing in a group called Band Aid to record *Feed the World* and American recording artists to join as U.S.A. for Africa in singing Michael Jackson and Lionel Richie's platinum single *We Are the World*. Geldof was knighted by Queen Elizabeth II for his efforts.

Vaclav Havel

Playwright, political dissident, and political prisoner last arrested by the Czechoslovakian communist government on October 27, 1989. Elected president of Czechoslovakia 62 days later in recognition of his leadership in freeing his country from political repression and Soviet domination. Havel told a joint session of the U.S. Congress that Thomas Jefferson was an inspiration, not just for what he said about democracy, but because the author of the Declaration of Independence "backed it up with his life. It was not just his words; it was his deeds as well."

Macha McKay

President of the MATCH International Centre, a Canadian organization that supports projects that help women in the Third World obtain better health care, child-care options, occupational training, and employment.

Jiro Nakayama

Twelve-year-old organizer of a group of kids in Nagano, Japan, who collect old newspapers and aluminum cans to sell to recycling plants. They turn the funds they earn over to the International Children's Rainforest Program. Their efforts have raised $5,000 that purchased and saved 40 acres of forest in Costa Rica.

Desmond Tutu

Moderate leader of the black freedom struggle in South Africa. Anglican archbishop of Cape Town. Arrested several times in his home country, addressed joint session of the U.S. Congress, winner of the Nobel Peace Prize in 1984. Quote: "Despite all that the powers of the world may do, we are going to be free."

Terry Waite

British hostage negotiator who was able to win freedom for several people kidnapped in Lebanon's political and religious strife. Personal aide to the archbishop of Canterbury. Waite was himself kidnapped and remains a hostage.

Wang Weilin

Nineteen-year-old Chinese student who on June 4, 1989, stood alone in front of a tank column in Tienanman Square. His six-minute stand is a classic essay in personal courage. He is feared to have been among the thousands killed in the Beijing square or later executed.

Michael Werikhe

Kenyan auto plant security supervisor who since 1982 has walked thousands of miles across Africa and Europe to dramatize the plight of the black rhino. Sometimes accompanied by Survival, his pet python, he has raised over $1 million for wildlife sanctuaries. The black rhinoceros population is now increasing, though it is still a critically endangered species.

The countries of the world are beginning to cooperate to protect the biosphere. Michael Werikhe is one person who has helped promote environmental awareness. His fund- and consciousness-raising walkathons on behalf of the black rhinoceros, along with the efforts of others, have brought international agreements and national laws aimed at protecting endangered species.

Chapter Summary

1. Individual-level analysis studies international politics by examining the role of humans as actors on the world stage.
2. Individual-level analysis can be conducted from three different perspectives. One is to examine fundamental human characteristics. The second is to study how people act in organizations. The third is to examine the motivations and actions of specific humans.
3. The nature-of-humankind approach examines fundamental human characteristics including psychological and biological factors.
4. The humans-in-organizations approach studies role factors, that is, how people act in certain positions. The approach is also concerned with how groups behave and how the interactions affect decisions.
5. The humans-as-individuals approach explores the factors that determine the perceptions, decisions, and actions of specific leaders. A leader's mental and physical health, understanding of history and personal experiences, belief system, and ego and ambition are all relevant factors.
6. Perceptions are especially important to understanding how leaders react to the world.
7. Perceptions spring from three sources: an individual's belief system, the individual's values, and faulty or misperceived information.
8. How an individual perceives a situation, another individual, or another country is often a distortion of reality.
9. Distorted perceptions are important because leaders act on what they perceive to be rather than on what is objectively true. This phenomenon is called operational reality.
10. Not only national leaders play a role in world politics. There are many who do not hold government positions who also play a part.

An old man, broken with the storms of state,
Is come to lay his weary bones among ye;
Give him a little earth for charity.

Shakespeare, *Henry VIII*

He'll sit right here, and he'll say "do this, do that." And nothing will
happen. Poor Ike, it won't be a bit like the Army. He'll find it very
frustrating.

Harry S. Truman, just before passing the office of president to
Dwight D. Eisenhower.

CHAPTER 5

STATE-LEVEL ANALYSIS

State-level analysis is a third perspective from which to study world politics. This chapter will emphasize both states as international actors and policy-making forces within countries. The discussion of how foreign policy is made by countries will entail discussion of types of political systems, types of situations, types of issues, and subnational actors, including political leaders, bureaucracies, legislatures, political opposition, interest groups, and the people.

The State as an International Actor

The most powerful actors on the world stage today are the states. Indeed, the state is so much the primary form of political organization and the focus of political loyalty that it is hard to imagine a political system based on any other unit. Yet, as we saw in chapter 2, the state system is only a few hundred years old. And other forms of world order are possible based on organizations like those discussed in the section on system-level actors.

The State Defined

A **state**, or country, is a tangible entity. The United States, Canada, the Union of Soviet Socialist Republics, and the People's Republic of China are all states. So are Bahrain, Fiji, and Swaziland. What distinguishes a state, whether large or small, populous or not, is a set of six characteristics.

Sovereignty   The single most important political characteristic of a state is **sovereignty** (see chapter 2, p. 34). This term strongly implies political independence from any higher authority. Sovereignty also includes the idea of legal equality among states.

Independence is the central element of sovereignty. In the history of Western political thought and international law, sovereignty developed as the rulers of Europe broke away from the secular domination of the Holy Roman Empire and the theological authority of the pope after the Middle Ages. Independent states arose that exercised *supreme authority* over their territory and citizens. The basic idea, then, is that a sovereign state is free to order itself internally and to make and enforce domestic law without external interference.

Independence, however, is a relative term. We sometimes object to and try to interfere with another country's treatment of its citizens. South Africa oppresses its black citizens, and many countries have imposed economic sanctions in response to and in an attempt to change the white government's apartheid system. There are also many countries whose freedom to exercise true foreign-policy independence is questionable. Until recently, most of the East European countries found it wise to adhere closely to the Soviet Union's foreign policy line. In that region, Lithuania, Estonia, and Latvia provide another illustrative case. Each lost its independence in the early days of World War II and was incorporated into the Soviet Union as a republic. Technically, however, the United States refused to recognize the legality of their absorption and has continued to recognize them as sovereign states. In the last two years, these Baltic countries/republics have pressed for independence or autonomy. They have not yet achieved their goal, however, and realistically they cannot yet be again accorded the title of "state." The issue has also led to the rather odd debate in the United States over whether Washington should recognize the independence of these Baltic republics when, as a fine technical point, the United States has never terminated the recognition it extended to them 70 years ago.

A somewhat similar example involving the United States exists in the Pacific. There the Federated States of Micronesia and the Republic of the Marshall Islands consider themselves independent, but each has signed a Compact of Free Association giving the United States control over their defense and foreign affairs. These two political entities are also heavily reliant on U.S. financial aid, and are so dependent that their sovereign status is very questionable. Independence, then, is a key element of sovereignty, but not all sovereign states are equally independent, and some governments that claim the status of state are so lacking in independence that they can hardly be recognized as legitimate countries.

Sovereignty also has an element of *equality*. If states recognize no higher authority, then it can be argued that they are all equal. That theoretical principle is given application in the UN's General Assembly, where each member state has one vote. Are all states really equal, though? Compare Vanuatu and China (Table 5.1). It is obvious that in many ways the two states are not equal. That reality is also recognized in the fact that the UN Security Council has five permanent members (the United States, the Soviet Union, China, Great Britain, and France), each of which possesses the veto power. Finally, the question of equality has great practical import. As discussed in chapter 15, the basis of representation is a sensitive question in current international organizations. Attempts to work toward even greater international cooperation and integration must someday deal with how to define *equal* and how to determine voting power.

Territory   A second characteristic of a state is having a territory. It would seem obvious that to exist, a state must have physical boundaries. Most states indeed have recognized

TABLE 5.1

Statistics on Vanuatu and China: Theoretically Sovereign Equals

	Vanuatu	China
Area (sq. mi.)	5,700	3,750,000
Population	160,000	1,070,000,000
GNP ($)	90,000,000	270,000,000,000
Military personnel	0	2,950,000
Vote in UN General Assembly	1	1

Data source: World Almanac (1990).

The possession of territory would seem to be a fundamental characteristic of a state. It may not always be, though. Here Palestine Liberation Organization head Yasser Arafat addresses the United Nations General Assembly in a setting usually reserved for heads of state. Many countries recognize a Palestinian state and maintain that its territory is illegally occupied by Israeli Zionists. As such, the status of Arafat, the PLO, and Palestine is a major international issue.

boundaries, but on closer examination, the question of territory becomes more complex: numerous international disputes exist over border areas; territorial boundaries can expand, contract, or shift dramatically; and it is even possible to have a state without territory. Many states recognize the Palestinians as a sovereign member of their fraternity, yet that nationality is scattered in other countries such as Lebanon and Jordan. Depending on one's view, the Palestinians either have no territory or have been expelled from the territory now occupied by Israel. It is also possible to maintain, as the United States currently does, that the Palestinians are not a state at all.

Population   People are an obvious requirement of any state. The populations of states range from a few thousand to China's one billion, but all states count this characteristic as a minimum requirement.

Diplomatic Recognition   A classic rhetorical question is: If a tree fell in the forest and no one were around to hear it, would it make a sound? The same question governs the issue of statehood and the recognition by others. If a political entity declares its independence, and no other country grants it diplomatic recognition, is it really a state? The answer seems to be no. It would be difficult for any aspirant to statehood to survive for long without recognition. Economic problems resulting from the inability to establish trade relations is just one example of the difficulties that would arise.

How many other countries must grant recognition before statehood is achieved is a more difficult question. When Israel declared its independence in 1948, the United States quickly recognized the country. Was Israel a state at that point? It certainly seems so. By contrast, consider the Republic of Transkei. This enclave within the Republic of South Africa was established in 1976 by the white racist government of that country. The purpose was to settle the racial question in South Africa by segregating that country's black majority into several "independent" territories (the Republics of Bophuthatswana, Venda, Transkei, Ciskei, and others). These noncontiguous "countries" are in areas with no resource base and are economically dependent on South Africa. Even though they have been recognized by South Africa and recognize one another it is doubtful that they can be considered states (see Fig. 5.1 on the following page). Thus, a state cannot be said to exist without diplomatic recognition, but the fact that the South African homelands recognize one another does not make them legitimate states. Kuwait provides an example of a third variation. Even though it was occupied by Iraq in 1990 and restyled an Iraqi province, other countries refused to accept the change. Whatever Iraq's assertion, most countries continue to recognize Kuwait as a legal state.

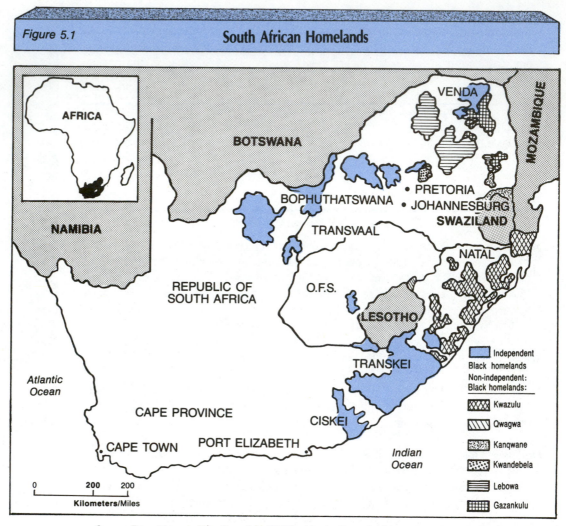

Figure 5.1 — South African Homelands

Source: From Maps on File. Copyright 1988 by Martin Greenwald Associates. Reprinted with permission of Facts on File, Inc., New York.

Internal Organization   It is generally conceded that states must have some level of political and economic structure. Most states have a government, but statehood continues during periods of severe turmoil, even anarchy.

It is even possible for rival governments to claim that they legitimately represent the same state. China is an important example of one country (in theory) and two governments. The Nationalist Chinese on Taiwan and the Communist Chinese on the mainland agree that the mainland and Taiwan are both part of the one China. Each claims to represent that China. Until 1979 the United States recognized the Nationalists. The United States then switched to the Communists but still treats Taiwan as an independent country. The result is a Byzantine and troublesome political tangle.

Internal Loyalty   The final characteristic of a state is internal loyalty. This implies that a state's population has a feeling of positive identification with the state *(patriotism)* and that the population grants the state the authority to make rules and to govern (legitimacy). The fate of East Germany provides a dramatic example. Once Soviet reforms ended Moscow's support for the East German Communist regime, it rapidly collapsed. In the fall of 1989 and winter of 1990 massive rallies toppled one, then another Communist government, each weaker than the one before. In essence, the popular legitimacy of the East German government evaporated. By January 1990 West German chancellor Helmut Kohl could tell 100,000 cheering East Germans that "Unity is within our grasp. We will reach our goal together, facing the future as one." Expressing skepticism the next day in *Izvestia,* Soviet foreign minister Eduard Shevardnadze predicted, "I don't think that unification will happen as quickly as they [the Germans] imagine. . . . At the fastest, it requires several years" (*HC,* 1/21/90:A6). Nine months later East Germany was no more; there was only *ein Deutschland,* one Germany.

State, Nation, and Government Differentiated

It is clear, then, that although an international state is defined by a number of distinct characteristics, those traits are often extremely complex in their application. The deeper you dig, the more complicated the questions become. Two other concepts need to be mentioned here and distinguished from the state. They are **nation** and **government**. These three terms, *state, nation,* and *government,* are often used synonymously, but they are really quite different.

In political science terminology, *nation* is a cultural term. It refers to a group of people who identify with one another politically because of common characteristics such as a common heritage, language, culture, religion, and race. A nation is intangible, a matter of mutual perceptions of cultural kinship, whereas a state is more tangible. Americans are a nation; the United States is a state. Many states and nations do not coincide. Canada, for example, contains both an English-speaking and a French-speaking nation. Chapter 6 discusses the international problems that result from the frequent lack of fit between states and nations, and in chapter 9 we shall see that the interests of the nation are not always the same as the interests of the state.

The term *government* can refer to either the system of government, such as the democratic system in the United States or the communist system in China, or it can refer to the specific regime, such as the Bush administration or the government of China's premier Li Peng and Communist party general secretary Jiang Zemin. In either case, governments are usually much more transient than either states or nations. It is not uncommon for leaders to confuse the interest of their government with that of the state and nation, as we will see in chapter 9. As analysts of international politics, it is important that we remember the distinctions among the three concepts.

Inside the State: The Foreign Policy-making Process

If we continue to dissect the state, we find that it is even more complex than the state/nation/government categorization just discussed. Indeed, the state is sometimes referred to as a "shell" that encapsulates many "subnational" political actors. This complexity is the focus of political scientists who emphasize state-level analysis and who ask the question: How is foreign policy made?

To answer this question, let us begin by looking at a common assumption about foreign policy-making. Many people think of foreign policy in terms of presidents or prime ministers making policy. They decide, and it is done, or so we may think. In

We remember Franklin Delano Roosevelt as a powerful president. Even Roosevelt, however, sometimes had trouble controlling bureaucrats. Despite Roosevelt's jocular pose here on the USS *Houston* with Admiral Claude Bloch, the president was often frustrated with the difficulty of controlling the U.S. Navy and its admirals.

reality, decision-making is much less singular, swift, or sure. To see this, consider for a moment the authority of Franklin Delano Roosevelt and the power of Lilliputians.

FDR was the leader who defeated both the Depression and Hitler, and he has been rated by historians as among the three best American presidents. Obviously, he must have been very much in charge.

If you asked Roosevelt, however, you would get a different perspective. The bureaucracy, for one, restricted his ability to command. FDR despaired of getting the N-A-A-A-V-Y, as he sometimes pronounced it with exasperation, to do anything he wanted. "To change anything in the N-A-A-A-V-Y," the president once moaned, "is like punching a feather bed. You punch it with your right and you punch it with your left until you are finally exhausted, and then you find the damn bed just as you left it before you started punching" (DiClerico, 1979:107).

Sometimes the navy would not even tell the president what it was up to. "When I woke up this morning," FDR groaned on another occasion,

> the first thing I saw was a headline in the *New York Times* to the effect that our Navy was going to spend two billion dollars on a shipbuilding program. Here I am, the Commander-in-Chief of the Navy, having to read about that for the first time in the press. Do you know what I said to that?

> No, Mr. President [the listener replied].

> I said: "Jesus Chr-rist!" (Sherill, 1979:217)

Congress also hemmed Roosevelt in. Its isolationist members hampered his attempts to aid the allies against the Axis powers before Pearl Harbor, and toward the end of the war, Congress threatened to block his dream of a United Nations. Career diplomat Charles Bohlen has recalled how bitterly FDR viewed senators, denouncing them as "a bunch of obstructionists" and declaring that "the only way to do anything in the American government [is] to bypass the Senate" (1973:210).

Public opinion was a third of many restraints on Roosevelt. The British ambassador to Washington reported to London that FDR complained that "his perpetual problem is to steer between . . . (1) the wish of 70% of Americans to keep out of the war and (2) the wish of 70% of Americans to do everything to break Hitler even if it meant war" (Yergin, 1977:45–46).

Roosevelt's evaluation of his own powers, then, was less grandiose than we remember. Indeed, he might have compared himself to Gulliver from Jonathan Swift's classic tale. The shipwrecked Gulliver was washed ashore in Lilliput. Although the Lilliputians were only a few inches high and he was a giant among them, Gulliver awoke to find himself bound by countless tiny ropes. He could have broken any one of them, but he could not free himself from all of them.

The purpose of these stories about Roosevelt and Gulliver is to point out that presidents, prime ministers, and even dictators are not as free as we think they are. They are decisionmakers, but, like Gulliver, they operate within a complex web of governmental and societal restraints that make up the modern state. Our job in this section, then, is to see how the various components of a state affect the choices of individual decisionmakers.

Foreign Policy-making

Foreign policy is formulated by a decision-making *process*. In the end, decisions are made by human beings, but, like Roosevelt, these decisionmakers do not exist in a vacuum. Instead, people make decisions within what one scholar termed a "murderously complex" political environment (Morgan, 1984:159). At best, a single chapter can only begin to introduce foreign policy-making and its many variables, but in order to give you a foundation we can explore four major considerations: types of political systems, types of situations, types of issues, and subnational (domestic) political actors. What we will see is that there is no such thing as *one* foreign policy-making process. To the contrary, there are many foreign policy-making processes, which vary, among other things, according to the nature of the political system in a given country, according to the intensity of the situation (for example, crisis or noncrisis), according to the subject of the decision, and according to the domestic political actors that become involved.

Types of Political Systems

One of the variables that affect the foreign policy process is a country's type of political system. We can surmise, for example, that the foreign policy process in Saudi Arabia, which is ruled by a powerful king and royal family, will be different from the foreign policy process in Canada, which is governed by a prime minister and a freely elected parliament.

Given this assumption, our task is to classify types of political systems (Bebler & Seroka, 1990). One obvious way, advanced by James Rosenau (1966), is to distinguish between "open" (democratic) and "closed" (authoritarian) systems. Rosenau's early work in foreign policy theory has been followed by others who have devised more complex models. One is to classify governments according to *who* can participate and *how much* they can participate (Hermann, 1987), an effort represented in Figure 5.2.

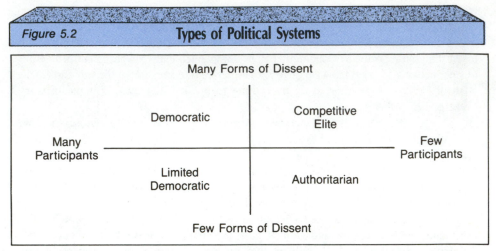

Figure 5.2 — **Types of Political Systems**

Authoritarian: few can participate, and there are minimal rights to oppose policy or compete for power.

Competitive Elite: few can participate, but they have extensive rights to oppose and compete.

Democratic: many can participate, with extensive rights to oppose and compete.

Limited Democratic: many can participate, but only with limited rights to oppose or compete.

Data source: This figure draws on the concepts of Hermann (1987) and Dahl (1971) but uses different terminology for the categories.

The exact way that countries make foreign policy varies according to a number of factors. One is the type of government. This figure shows one way to classify governments; each of the four types of political systems makes foreign policy in a different way.

The "how many participate" dimension relates to how widespread political participation is. In some countries, such as Canada, political participation is extensive, with few adults formally excluded from participating in or criticizing the political process. In other countries, participation is limited to an elite based on political party, economic standing, or some other factor. The "forms of dissent" dimension involves the degree of opposition. In China open disagreement with policy, even among the Communist-party elite, is limited. When in 1989, for example, student-led demonstrations for greater democracy broke out in Beijing's Tiananmen Square and other locations throughout China, the dissenters were suppressed. This included not only the students, but also many high Communist party and government officials that sympathized with them. The head of the party, General Secretary Zhao Ziyang, for one, wanted to deal gently with the demonstrators and at one point even broke into tears trying to convince the Tiananmen Square multitude to disperse. That was the last time Zhao was seen in public as party chief. He was soon driven from power and placed under house arrest by old-guard elements of the party and the government. Then tanks rolled into the square to crush the students politically and literally. Zhao's successor, Jiang Zemin, had no tears for the dead demonstrators. When later asked at a press conference whether the "Tiananmen tragedy" could have been avoided, Jiang stolidly answered, "We do not believe there was any tragedy in Tiananmen Square." Instead, he asserted, the massacre was the "unavoidable" consequence of an attempt to "overthrow the socialist system," and the horrific reports (which included television pictures) by the Western press were like "fairy tales from the *Arabian Nights*" (*Time,* 10/9/89:44).

Many political analysts believe that the type of political system a country has affects the substance of its foreign policy. One theory argues that democracy is becoming the norm, and that since democracies are less bellicose, the world will be more peaceful. Authoritarian systems still persist, however, and the mid-1989 attempt of Chinese students to democratize their country was crushed despite the heroic stand of Wang Weilin before a column of army tanks in Tiananmen Square in Beijing. It is believed that Wang Weilin was among those later executed for their roles in the protests. This photograph of the standoff was taken from an upper-story window of a nearby building.

Once we classify types of regimes, we can examine them to see how they differ in the *process* by which they make foreign policy and how those procedural differences affect the *substance* of the policy they make. In other words, do different types of governments, say democracies and dictatorships, behave differently in foreign affairs? Discussing process, Charles Hermann (1987:4) hypothesizes, for example, that "the more opposition a regime permits, the greater the number and kind of foreign problems that are likely to be influenced by that competition." This means that in democracies, compared to authoritarian systems, more decisions on a wider variety of issues will be affected by more subnational actors.

Moving to the key issue of policy substance, we know that changes in political regimes do lead to changes in foreign policy behavior (Hagan, 1989) and that revolutionary regime changes are often followed by conflict between the new regime and other states (Maoz, 1989). But this does not tell us whether, for instance, democracies and dictatorships vary. This question is both timely and relevant to much of the latest work being done on regime type and policy differences.

Interest in the foreign policy nature of democracies has increased recently because of the democratization of Eastern Europe and countries in many other regions. Indeed, this trend led Francis Fukuyama (1989:3) to speculate that "we may be witnessing . . . the end of mankind's ideological evolution and the universalization of Western liberal democracy as the final form of government." Fukuyama's thesis set off a sharp intellectual debate (Bloom et al., 1989; Huntington, 1989), and it also raises the fascinating and politically important question of whether a truly democratic world would pursue international politics differently than it has in the past (Gasiorowski, 1990; Manicas, 1989).

The philosopher Immanuel Kant argued in *Perpetual Peace* (1795) that the spread of democracy would change the world by eliminating war. This would result, Kant reasoned, because "if the consent of the citizens is required in order to decide that war should be declared . . ., nothing is more natural than they would be very cautious in commencing such a poor game, decreeing for themselves all the calamities of war." Modern scholarship has taken up this question of whether democratic regimes are more peaceful, especially with one another. R. J. Rummel (1989:40), for one, believes that democratic regimes are less violent both externally and internally and that "research establishes that democratic civil liberties and political rights promote nonviolence and lay a path to a warless world." Rummel's view on domestic violence is important because of the possibility that domestic and international violence behaviors are related (Hoole & Huang, 1989). Other scholars are more cautious than Rummel, and have found that democracies are generally no more or less likely than autocracies to be involved in international conflict. But they have also concluded that democracies are more likely to be allies with each other than with authoritarian regimes (Siverson & Emmons, 1990), and that democracies are less likely to fight each other than they are to conflict with nondemocracies (Maoz & Abdolali, 1989). Still other scholars find that while democracies are somewhat less likely to be aggressive, their behavior is strongly influenced by factors such as whether they are prosperous or not, with democracies more likely to fight during times of economic stress (Morgan & Campbell, 1990; Holmes & Elder, 1989). Finally, there are some who contend that the relationship that exists between democracy and peace is tied to a specific set of historical circumstances that may not persist in the future. "The 'democratic zone of peace' argument," Huntington (1989:7) contends, "is valid as far as it goes, but it may not go all that far."

These questions about the relationship between democracy and foreign policy have practical importance beyond their intellectual interest. One policy-relevant issue is whether "too much democracy" is inadvisable in the foreign policy process. Alexis de Tocqueville asserted in *Democracy in America* (1835) that democracies are "decidedly inferior" to more controlled governments in the conduct of foreign relations because "impulse rather than prudence" dominates a democracy. Many current observers agree with de Tocqueville's classic view. One U.S. foreign policy text, for example, argues that "the conduct of foreign policy—whose principal aim is safeguarding the nation's security so that life may be preserved and enjoyed—requires a concentration of executive power" (Spanier & Uslander, 1985:2). This view is highly debatable, however, and concentration of power in the executive, or anywhere else, is dangerous to democracy.

This book takes a very different view. As chapter 1 stresses, international politics affects you, and you can affect it. Furthermore, you should be involved. If, for instance, Immanuel Kant and some modern scholars (Hagan, 1990; Hermann & Hermann, 1989) are correct in their view that broad democratic participation in all policy, foreign and domestic, is likely to result in less bellicose policy, then more democracy is better than less. Furthermore, research does not support the view that centralized decision-making produces better policy. Some of the most ill-conceived U.S. foreign policy decisions were executive-centered. The Johnson administration's intervention in Vietnam, the Carter administration's attempted hostage rescue in Iran, and the Reagan administration's sale of weapons to Iran and illegal use of the proceeds to supply weapons to the Contras in Nicaragua leap to mind as examples that could hardly be described as prudent. Indeed, some research concludes that increased democratization of foreign policy does not lead to its degradation. For example, a recent study of Danish security policy finds that many of the fears "linking increased democratic debate with erratic and fundamental changes in security policy are not borne out." Instead, "despite a clear trend towards increased participation and information, both the content of Danish security policy and the decision-making process have remained stable" (Holm, 1989:196, 179). This issue is further discussed below in the section on public opinion.

A second policy-relevant ramification of the debate over the nature of democratic foreign policy-making relates to how we perceive and interact with other countries. U.S. policy toward the Soviet Union is being influenced by the perception that under Gorbachev's leadership the Soviet Union is becoming more democratic (see box on p. 120). A more democratic Soviet Union seems more like the democratic United States or Canada and, therefore, less threatening. This view, combined with the more cooperative stance of the Soviets, is causing Washington to reduce U.S. defense expenditures, to liberalize trade policy with the Soviets, and to consider extending foreign aid to Moscow. As recently as the spring of 1989 half of all Americans thought the Soviets sought to dominate the world. By May 1990 that figure had fallen to 29 percent. In 1987, only 15 percent of Americans had a favorable view of the Soviet Union; by mid-1990, 41 percent felt positively about the Soviets (*HC*, 5/28/90:A6).

It is also important to ponder why democracies may be less bellicose than autocracies. Kant and many modern scholars (Hagan, 1990) believe that the multiplicity of policy voices that characterize democracy create greater restraints on decisionmakers and lessen the chance of war. A second possibility has to do with political stability and a government's repression of its citizens. Charles Hermann (1987:12), for one, suggests that "regimes that tend to engage in physical suppression of the domestic political opposition are more likely to engage in foreign policy activity that seeks to justify this behavior."[1] The idea here is that troubled governments may try to capitalize on the use of a "foreign devil" or "scapegoat" to rally the support of their citizens. Some suggest, for example, that Argentina's military junta chose to attack the Falklands (Malvinas) in 1982 because the regime, which had murdered countless opponents, was in serious domestic difficulty and hoped by such action to deflect popular discontent away from itself and onto the British. It should be pointed out, though, that while such hypotheses make intuitive sense, numerous studies have produced mixed results. There is certainly some relationship between domestic tension and external aggression, but it is far from automatic that a troubled regime will attempt to survive by picking a fight (Levy, 1988; James, 1987).

Before leaving this discussion about democracies, autocracies, and their respective bellicosity, it is important to note that democracy is not always a force for peace. First, as noted above, democracies are not generally more peaceful, and there are even some scholars who are doubtful about whether democracies are inherently less likely to wage war on one another. Second, under some circumstances, public pressure may push democratic leaders toward war rather than away from it. Jingoistic attitudes in the public and Congress pushed somewhat reluctant U.S. presidents into the War of 1812 and the Spanish-American War, for instance. More recently, concern about public opinion and future elections were partly responsible for John Kennedy's decision to blockade Cuba during the 1962 missile crisis, for Jimmy Carter's decision to launch the Iran hostage rescue attempt in 1980, and for George Bush's order to invade Panama in 1989. At this

---

1. Hermann's (1987) discussion is more limited than the generalization used here. He focuses on the regime's international defense, perhaps only verbal, or its actions and its search for outside assistance in acquiring techniques and technology associated with suppression.

Democracy and the Soviet Union

The widespread perception of democratic reform within the Soviet Union combined with a less confrontational Soviet foreign policy has significantly affected American, Canadian, and other Western public opinion about the Soviet Union. Emotionally, we are apt to view those who hold our values (such as democracy) as friendlier than those who hold antithetical values. There is also the contention by some scholars that democratic countries are unlikely to make war on one another. As a result of these views, the West has substantially relaxed its military and political posture toward the Soviet Union.

Apart from controversy about the validity of scholarly theories about democratic peacefulness, an important question is whether or not the Soviet Union is democratic. Second, to the extent that it has democratized, is that trend likely to continue, stall, or be reversed? The answer to the first question, which queries the current state of Soviet democracy, is a relative matter. There can be little doubt that many of the changes promoted by Mikhail Gorbachev would have left his predecessors in stunned disbelief. They would have been particularly amazed and opposed to the Communist party's February 1990 concession that it "does not claim a monopoly" on political power and "is prepared for a political dialogue and cooperation" with political opponents. There has been an accompanying shift of power away from the Party and toward the reconstituted government. Elections in 1989 to the Soviet national legislature were contested and even saw some leading Communist officials upset in their bids for seats. There is more open criticism of the government; there are public demonstrations against the failing economy; various nationalities have declared their autonomy; and there are numerous other examples of freedom of action that would have been immediately suppressed in the Soviet Union just a few years ago. Thus, by Soviet standards, the country is more democratic than ever before.

By Western standards, however, Soviet democracy is limited. Part of its parliament's seats are reserved for the Party. Furthermore, Gorbachev ruled out direct voting for the Soviet presidency for five years, and, instead, had himself elected to that office by the legislature. Then in March and again in December 1990 the legislature approved constitutional changes that considerably increased the president's (and Gorbachev's) power. These amendments included presidential power to propose legislation, declare martial law, and declare war. In September 1990, Gorbachev was granted emergency powers to institute "presidential rule," that is, to issue decrees to manage the economy or defend public order. The legislature even made it illegal to insult the president. Penalties for impugning the "honor and dignity of the president" range up to six years in jail and a fine of 3,000 rubles (about $5,000 and equal to about a year's salary of the average Soviet industrial worker). The law was no idle threat. Prominent critic Valeria Novodvorskaya was soon arrested for her comments in the August 27, 1990, issue of *Commersant,* a dissident journal, that Gorbachev is "a Hitlerite criminal, hangman-murderer." At last report the case was pending while Novodvorskaya was undergoing psychiatric examination ordered by the Moscow prosecutor.

The second question about Soviet democracy involves its future, which is in doubt for two reasons. One is the fact there there is no democratic tradition in the country's history. The Constituent Assembly, the only democratically elected legislature, was overthrown by the Bolsheviks in 1918 after only one meeting. Even the Soviet people are skeptical. "This country has always been ruled by a dictator of some sort, and now the dictator [Gorbachev] is telling us there will be a democracy," one Moscow bakery worker said. "Perhaps there will be, but most people doubt it," she continued. "Maybe I am to blame, after all, I am not out there demonstrating and demanding change," a man shopping for food agreed. "But after 70 years of Communism, we have been robbed of our belief that we can bring about change." As Sovietologist Stephen Cohen points out, "dictatorships can be born in one night, but durable multiparty democracies take a generation, if not more" (*NYT,* 2/8/90:A11).

The second source of doubt about the future of Soviet democracy stems from the difficult period that lies ahead of the U.S.S.R. The economy is failing, the nationalities are restive, and there is the potential for widespread civil disturbances. Some fear that these pressures will persuade Gorbachev, even if he survives politically, to consolidate power further, to abort democracy, and substitute presidential dominance for Party dominance. The most stunning protest came from Foreign Minister Eduard Shevardnadze. In December 1990 he resigned, declaring "Let this be my protest against the advance of dictatorship." A "surprised" and "hurt" Gorbachev defended his aims in the aftermath of his long-time friend and colleague's resignation: "We're not talking about any dictatorship," Gorbachev protested, "but rather strong central powers, and they shouldn't be confused" (*HC,* 12/21/90:A1). It was a subtle distinction that seemed to be lost on Shevardnadze and other sophisticated observers.

The impact on foreign policy of democracy in the form of public opinion is complex. Considerable public opposition to a U.S. attack to expel Iraq from Kuwait signaled the Bush administration that a military solution to the crisis would be unpopular, yet public opinion also pushed the Administration to act quickly before the declining reservoir of public support vanished. Some people also argued that public protests encouraged the Iraqis to hold out in the hopes that the Americans and others would give way rather than face domestic public opposition to a war.

writing, large U.S. and other forces are engaged with Iraqi troops in the Middle East, and public opinion played a large role in influencing Bush's decision to launch an early attack against Iraq. The president pledged in September 1990 before a joint session of Congress in a speech telecast to the country and later seen around the world that "Iraq will not be permitted to annex Kuwait. That's not a threat, not a boast. That's just the way it's going to be." Perhaps, but the UN's economic embargo would have taken a long time to succeed by itself and it is a widely accepted truth in Washington circles that the American public does not have staying power. "If a stalemate is the best we have six months from now," an administration official worried, " . . .why wouldn't the American people begin to wonder why we're still there [in Saudi Arabia]? The long haul . . . is not exactly favorable to us" (*Time*, 8/27/90:16). The point is that Bush may have rhetorically cornered himself. He pledged to get Iraq out of Kuwait, but his administration doubted the American people could be counted on to endure a long, costly crisis while the economic embargo took its toll on Baghdad. The alternative was a U.S. military strike against Iraq.

Types of Situations

The foreign policy-making process also varies according to the nature of the situation. One type of situation is a *crisis,* which can be defined as a situation in which decisionmakers are surprised by an event, feel threatened, and believe that they only have a short time to make a decision (Hermann, 1986). One characteristic of decisions made during a crisis is that they tend to be made by relatively small groups within the political leadership (Paige, 1972). In this sense, crisis decision-making conforms to the "presidential" image of decision-making.

During a crisis leaders usually strive to make rational decisions (O'Neal, 1988;

Scarborough, 1988), but there are aspects of crisis decision-making that limit the ability of a president making a calculated decision. For one thing, the pressure to act and the limited information available during a crisis mean that decisionmakers rely heavily on preexisting perceptions. Henry Kissinger has described the tension of crisis decision-making well:

> During fast-moving events those at the center of decision are overwhelmed by floods of reports compounded of conjecture, knowledge, hope, and worry. These must then be sieved through [the decisionmakers'] preconceptions. Only rarely does a coherent picture emerge. (1979:627)

What this means is that decisionmakers will respond to a situation according to the images they already have. If leaders perceive another country as aggressive, and that country mobilizes its forces during a tense crisis, the decisionmakers will probably see that act as preparation to attack their country rather than a defensive action aimed at getting ready to repel an attack by them. The onset of World War I, for example, can be traced in part to the series of mobilizations and countermobilizations by Austria-Hungary, Russia, Germany, France, and Great Britain, most of which were arguably defensive, but which resulted in a spiral of hostility based on misperceptions (Holsti, North, & Brody, 1968).

Beyond crisis decisions, various scholars have theorized about a number of types of situational variables. They opine that a decision or a series of decisions involved with **innovative policy** (significant changes in direction) will tend to evoke dissent and to involve a wider array of subnational actors, such as legislatures. By contrast, **consensual policy** (conforming to agreed principles) or **incremental policy** (slight changes) will be more closely confined to the political leadership. This means that dramatic shifts in policy are likely to touch off wider discussion and more dissent than more marginal changes. When the United States went from peacetime isolationism to internationalism after World War II, for instance, there was a great deal of debate and discord. This also occurred in the aftermath of the collapse of the anticommunist consensus as a result of the Vietnam War, when the U.S. Congress became more active than usual in foreign policy as the country tried to find a new consensus. Similarly, China since the mid-1970s and, more recently, the Soviet Union have undergone important leadership changes and shifts in policy direction that, predictably, have sparked much broader dissent on foreign policy than normally seen in those countries (Ziegler, 1988). By contrast, incremental and consensual policy decisions will evoke less dissent and activity. Indeed, many such policies are not made by political leaders at all, but are determined and implemented by bureaucratic actors.

Types of Issues

How foreign policy is decided also varies according to the nature of the **issue areas** involved. This type of analysis rests on the idea that issues that address different subject areas will be decided by different decisionmakers and by different processes (Stewart, Hermann, & Hermann, 1989). One early theory about U.S. politics argues that presidents have much more influence in determining foreign and defense policy than domestic policy (Wildavsky, 1966). There is a great deal of disagreement about the validity of Wildavsky's hypothesis (LeLoup & Shull, 1979; Sigelman, 1979; Carter,

1987), but even those who agree with Wildavsky would concede that the gap has narrowed between foreign and domestic policy success.

One explanation may be that policy may be increasingly *intermestic,* that is, a mix of foreign and domestic policy, as discussed in chapter 1. This may dilute the influence of political leaders because other subnational actors are more active on domestic and intermestic issues (Barilleaux, 1986). Foreign-trade issues are intermestic because they not only involve foreign relations, but they also have an impact on the domestic economy in terms of jobs, prices, and other factors. An issue such as the sale of weapons to Saudi Arabia, even during a crisis such as occurred in August 1990, would also be an intermestic issue in the United States because it would involve groups such as the corporations that will supply the weapons, and Jewish-American interest groups that will be afraid that the weapons might be used against Israel. It may also be that presidential leadership is strongest in pure foreign/defense-policy issues, weaker on mixed (intermestic) issues, and weakest on pure domestic issues (Rourke, 1987a).

The key here is that whatever issue-area classification you use, and there are many other schemes, it is clear that different issues evoke different processes. A pure foreign policy issue, such as whether the United States should support one or another of Cambodia's three rebel groups or the government itself in the long and complex civil war there, is likely to be decided among political leaders in a country's executive branch or whatever political structure is at the apex of its political system. By contrast, foreign policy issues that, for one reason or another, activate subnational actors other than the political leadership because of their impact on economic issues, concern of ethnic groups, electoral considerations, or other factors will tend to lessen the role of the political leadership in the overall decision.

Subnational Political Actors

As noted, the state is not a unitary structure. Even states with the most authoritarian regime are complex political organisms. Furthermore, the bigger a country is from the point of view of its size, population, and its economy, and the longer its political system has persisted, the more complex it is apt to be, and the more likely it is to contain powerful bureaucracies, interest groups, and other **subnational actors**. It is important, therefore, to understand the roles of the various subnational elements in foreign policy-making. I will examine six: political leadership; bureaucracies; legislatures; political opposition; interest groups; and the people.

Political Leadership

The beginning of this chapter compared President Franklin Delano Roosevelt to Gulliver among the Lilliputians to point out that the stereotypic image that presidents make foreign policy by command is far from an accurate picture. This is true, but it can also be said that of the various subnational actors, the **political leadership** (the officials whose tenure is variable and dependent on the political contest for power in their country) is normally the strongest subnational actor in the field of foreign policy. These decision-makers are generally located in the executive branch and are called president, prime minister, premier, chancellor, or perhaps by some royal title. It is also possible for leadership to be located outside any of the leading official positions. In China, Deng Xiaoping is the most influential decisionmaker, even though he heads neither his country's party nor its government. Formal position, then, is usually a key to identifying who is the political leader, but "reputation for power" is an important supplementary factor.

Whatever the specific title or position, most countries' political leaders are invested with important constitutional and legislative *formal powers*. For example, the U.S. president is commander in chief, and the Soviet president has the power to declare war. As such, each possesses the ultimate authority: the release of nuclear weapons. Political leaders often possess important *informal* powers as well as formal ones. Their personal prestige is often immense, and skillful leaders can use their public standing to win political support at home and abroad for their policies.

The predominance of political leaders in foreign policy has many causes: One is that kings traditionally controlled foreign and military affairs long after they began to lose some control of domestic affairs to parliaments; second, there is a widespread feeling that successful foreign policy needs a single, decisive leader. As we will see in the discussion of the role of legislatures below, the rally-to-the-chief phenomenon is particularly evident in times of international tension. Senate foreign relations chairman J. William Fulbright once noted with some dismay, a "legislature which does not hesitate to defeat or override the executive on domestic legislation . . . reverts to a kind of tribal loyalty when war is involved" (Rourke, 1983:304). Third, foreign policy often sparks only limited activity by subnational actors, who instead tend to focus more on the domestic issues that affect them directly. Legislators, for instance, concentrate usually on issues that have an impact on their districts, thereby, in turn, affecting their reelection chances. The growing intermestic nature of issues, however, is encouraging wider subnational-actor participation in foreign policy-making that is traditionally the preroga-tive of political leaders. Fourth, most political leaders have important instrumental and informational advantages over other political actors: Instrumentally, presidents can order the military to act, while Congress, for example, can only debate and legislate. And although presidents may certainly be the victims of imperfect information, as heads of the executive branch they can command much greater information-gathering and analysis resources than any other actor.

Bureaucracies

Every state, large or small, democratic or authoritarian, is heavily influenced by its **bureaucracy**. Although the dividing line between decisionmakers and bureaucrats is often hazy, generally we can say that bureaucrats are career governmental personnel, as distinguished from those who are political appointees or elected officials.

Technically, bureaucrats are subordinate to elected and appointed political officials. In reality, perhaps the most common complaint of political leaders is the difficulty they experience trying to control the vast understructure of their governments. Recent laments about bureaucracy by leaders of some of the world's most powerful countries sound strikingly similar. "One of the hardest things" about being president, Ronald Reagan groaned, "is to know that down there, underneath, is a permanent structure that's resisting everything you're doing." Mikhail Gorbachev experienced the same things, lashing out against a bureaucracy dominated by "conservative sentiments, inertia, [and] a tendency to brush aside everything that does not fit into conventional patterns." And China's Zhao Ziyang could agree that the "unwieldiness of government organs, confusion of their responsibilities, and buck-passing" are "a serious problem in the political life of our party and state" (Rourke, 1990:131). American and Soviet presidents and Chinese general secretaries, then, are not very confident about their ability to manage their supposedly subordinate bureaucracy, and it behooves us to explore this powerful subnational actor.

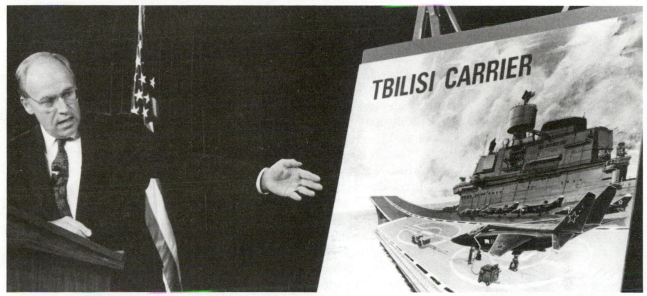

Our discussion of the foreign policy role of bureaucracies will focus on two points. The first is *bureaucratic perspective.* You will see that bureaucracies develop an institutional mentality, have their own set of values and priorities, and often favor and advocate policies based on their organizational view, rather than the national interest. The second is *bureaucratic methods,* or the means by which bureaucracies help to shape and carry out foreign policy.

Bureaucratic perspective heavily influences the policies that government agencies favor. In this picture, U.S. secretary of defense Dick Cheney uses a picture of a new Soviet aircraft carrier to try to convince Congress not to slash the defense budget. It is predictable that Cheney, given his role as defense secretary and the perspective of the Pentagon, would be skeptical about the prognosis for peace in the future and the wisdom of reducing U.S. defense expenditures. All bureaucracies, not just the military, have a particular point of view, and it is important to evaluate any agency's recommendations with the awareness of that bureaucracy's perspective.

Bureaucratic Perspective   Organizations often favor one policy option over other possibilities based on their missions and how a policy will affect them. The views of a country's military establishment on arms control are influenced by the fact that its size, equipment, and budget share will be reduced by any real arms reduction. Changes in Soviet behavior have convinced many in the United States that defense spending should be sharply reduced, but Defense Secretary Richard Cheney is not among those ready to declare a peace dividend. Suspicious that the Soviets are only trying to lull the United States into relaxing its vigil while they restrengthen themselves and fearful of other threats to national security, Cheney has resisted budget cuts. "Would you want a defense secretary who wasn't skeptical?" he asks. Do you want somebody "over there [at the Pentagon] who's euphoric, who comes out leading the cheers saying, 'Nothing to worry about, guys—take down all the forces'?" (*WP,* 4/23/90:4).

It should be added here that while civilian and military defense officials are apt to want to preserve their resources and be cautious about the world political situation, they do not easily fit into the "blow 'em up" military-mind stereotype. In fact, studies have shown that the U.S. military has been somewhat cautious about foreign interventions in the aftermath of its morale-depressing, equipment-draining experience in Vietnam (Petraeus, 1989).

Bureaucratic Methods   An organization's perspective will cause it, consciously or not, to try to shape policy according to its views. Bureaucracies influence policy decisions in several ways. *Filtering information* is one method bureaucracies use to influence policy. Decisionmakers are dependent on their supporting organizations to give them the facts, but what facts they are told depends on what subordinates believe and what they pass on.

A realistic assessment of the situation in South Vietnam, for instance, was made virtually impossible because of information filtering. Earlier, many U.S. diplomats who were stationed in China during its civil war and who had frankly reported the weakness of the U.S.–backed Nationalists and the strength of the Communists were subsequently dismissed or demoted in the frenzy of faultfinding that obsessed Washington. The later result, according to then–U.S. National Security Council staff member James Thompson (1989:593), was that "candid reporting of the strengths of the Viet Cong and the weaknesses of the [U.S.–backed South Vietnamese] Diem government was inhibited by the [diplomats'] memory" of the ill fates of their former colleagues, by the "shadow of the loss of China." Even when a U.S. embassy official was brave enough to attempt to report the truth, it was suppressed "by some higher officials, notably Ambassador [Frederick] Nolting in Saigon, who refused to sign off on such cables [thereby permitting them to be sent to Washington]."

Sometimes, poor information can also be the result of simple ineptitude. The event that precipitated Iran's seizure of the U.S. embassy in Tehran was the admittance of the deposed Shah into the United States for cancer treatment. The White House saw the treatment as a moral imperative; many in Iran considered it a trick to forestall their country's attempt to bring the Shah to justice. The U.S. administration was aware of a potential spasm of reaction in Iran and wanted the Shah sent to Mexico City for treatment. The State Department's medical adviser, however, reported that facilities in Mexico were not adequate and asserted that only hospitalization in the United States would give the Shah a fighting chance. Later studies have shown, however, there was only a cursory check of the treatment available in Mexico and that, as it turns out, the Shah could have been treated there (Glad, 1989). As it also came to pass, the Shah was admitted to the United States, the hostages were seized in Tehran, and he subsequently died of his disease anyway.

At its worst, information filtering occurs because the bureaucrat supplying the information wants to manipulate the decision. Said one former intelligence official of Reagan's CIA director William Casey: "He does not ask us for a review of an issue or a situation. He wants material he can use to persuade his colleagues, justify controversial policy, or expand the Agency's involvement in covert action" (Hastedt, 1987:20).

Recommendations are another source of bureaucratic influence on foreign policy. Bureaucracies are the source of considerable expertise, and they often supply political leaders with analysis that reflects the agency's preferred position. Kissinger has related how bureaucracies sometimes present options:

> The standard bureaucratic device [is] leaving the decision-maker with only one real option, which for easy identification is placed in the middle. The classic case . . . would be to confront the policymaker with the choice of (1) nuclear war, (2) present policy, or (3) surrender. (1979:418)

If you are clever, then—and bureaucracies are—you present a decisionmaker with a series of choices, only one of which is reasonable. It resembles a multiple-choice exam question on which only one answer is correct. "All of the above" or "None of the above" is seldom included.

Implementation is another powerful bureaucratic tool. It is obvious that decision-makers must rely on their subordinates to carry out policy. Discrepancies between what political leaders think they said and what their subordinates actually do can result from misunderstanding; unconscious misinterpretation based on subordinate preferences; or conscious attempts to delay, change, or ignore a decision. One of the most momentous instances of bureaucratic implementation came during the 1962 Cuban missile crisis.

Bureaucrats sometimes operate outside the control of political leaders. Here U.S. Marine Lieutenant Colonel and National Security Council staff member Oliver North testifies before Congress with regard to the scandal known as Irangate or Contragate. North and others sold weapons to Iran in an (unsuccessful) attempt to win the release of U.S. hostages in the Middle East and sent funds derived from the arms sales to Nicaragua to support the Contra rebels there. These actions were not, according to the White House, authorized by President Reagan, and some of them may have violated the law. North was forced to resign from his White House post and was subsequently indicted, but not before damage was done to U.S. foreign policy and prestige. North was subsequently convicted on a few minor charges, but legal maneuvering helped him avoid conviction and jail on the major charges.

The United States was flying U-2 reconnaissance missions over Cuba monitoring Soviet nuclear missile installations and their defending surface-to-air missile (SAM) sites. On October 27, one of the spy-planes was shot down, and the two superpowers reeled closer to nuclear war than at any time before or since the incident. What caused this perilous decision by the highest Soviet leaders? In fact they did not order the shooting at all. It was a case of bureaucratic initiative. In a later analysis, Soviet official Fyodor Burlatsky reported that "Khrushchev had given very strong, very precise orders that Soviet officers should make no provocation, initiate no attack in Cuba" (*NYT*, 10/31/87:A27). Yet it happened anyway. Moscow was as horrified as Washington. As another Soviet official, Sergi Mikoyan, later explained, "We came to the conclusion that it was a human mistake by some small commander who did not want to confess. There was no command to do so from the supreme commanders" (*HC*, 10/14/87:A17).[2] Summing up on the policy/implementation gap, Henry Kissinger has commented: "The outsider believes a presidential order is consistently followed out. Nonsense. I have spent considerable time seeing that it is carried out and in the spirit the president intended" (Halperin, 1974:245).

2. Another study based on the recollections of the participants in the crisis relates that the decision to fire was made by two deputy commanders of Soviet air defense forces who were in Cuba at the time. The study also relates that the Soviet ambassador to Cuba at the time said there was "no direct prohibition" on using SAMs and that the order to fire by the local Soviet generals relied on the standing order of engagement for Soviet forces "to fire on any aircraft that flies overhead in wartime" (Allyn, Blight, & Welch, 1990:165). Whichever explanation is accurate (and they are not mutually exclusive since the commanders may have thought they were not initiating but, rather, being provoked), the point is that the world was moved considerably closer to war by the decision of local commanders. It is also worth noting that, in this second scenario, the Soviet generals interpreted "wartime" very broadly, and they followed standard operating procedure (SOP) even though it might have meant nuclear war.

Legislatures

In all countries, the foreign policy role of legislatures is less than that of executive-branch decisionmakers and bureaucrats. That does not mean that all legislatures are powerless. They are not, but their exact influence varies greatly among countries.

In nondemocratic systems, legislatures generally rubber-stamp the decisions of the executive or, in the case of communist countries, party decisionmakers. China's National People's Congress, for example, does not play a significant role in foreign policy-making.

Even in the more democratic countries, however, legislatures are still inhibited by many factors. One of these is tradition. The executive has historically run foreign policy, especially in time of war or other crisis. Second, there is the axiom that "politics should stop at the water's edge." The belief is that a unified national voice is important to a successful foreign policy. This is particularly true during a crisis, when there is a tendency to "rally around the chief" and to view dissent as bordering on treason. This rally effect is more than issue-specific; it extends to a more general support of presidential foreign policy, at least for a short time (Stoll, 1987). Third, the executive-dominant tradition has led to the executive's normally being given extensive constitutional power over foreign policy. In Great Britain, for example, a declaration of war does not require the consent of Parliament.

Member of Congress Lee Hamilton (1982:113–37) listed some of the other reasons for legislative weakness:

- Diplomacy requires speed; Congress is slow.
- Diplomacy requires negotiation; Congress votes yes or no.
- Diplomacy requires secrecy; Congress leaks.
- Diplomacy requires expertise; Congress has little expertise for foreign affairs compared with the executive.
- Diplomacy requires strong leadership; Congress's leadership is scattered.

None of this means that legislatures do not sometimes play an important role in foreign affairs. Congress was one of the factors that pushed the Nixon administration to get out of Vietnam, and since the war Congress has been more active in foreign affairs than in the past. It is rare for a legislature to reject a leader's foreign policy initiative outright, but it is common for representatives to modify the path of foreign policy. This is especially true when, because of their constituency orientation and their "urge for reelection," legislators become active and influential on issues that have domestic reverberations, including those that involve economics, that spark ethnic-group activity, or that have some electoral implications.

Political Opposition

In every political system, those who are in power face rivals who would replace them, either to change policy or to gain power. In democratic systems, this opposition is legitimate and is organized into political parties. Rival politicians may also exist in the leader's own party. Opposition is less overt and/or less peaceful in nondemocratic systems, but it exists nonetheless.

As one study of political opposition points out, "Just as types of political regimes vary, so do their opponents" (Hermann, 1987:10). One distinction divides opposition between those who merely want to change policy and those who want to gain control of

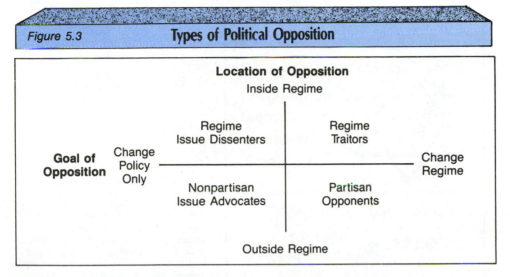

Figure 5.3 — Types of Political Opposition

Location of Opposition
Inside Regime

Regime Issue Dissenters · Regime Traitors

Goal of Opposition — Change Policy Only · Change Regime

Nonpartisan Issue Advocates · Partisan Opponents

Outside Regime

Data source: This figure draws on the concepts of Hermann (1987) but uses different terminology for the categories.

All domestic political systems include those who oppose specific foreign policies and/or the governing regime itself. Such opposition has an impact on foreign policy. Here is shown one way of classifying opposition.

the government. A second division is between those who are located inside and those who are located outside the government (see Fig. 5.3).

Relatively democratic countries like Canada, Great Britain, or France legally allow all four forms of opposition, although critics inside the regime may suffer political consequences, especially when they go public with their opposition. Most opposition, though, is legitimate, and a primary example is organized political parties. In many European countries the number of parties and the range of ideologies and issues on which they are based are greater than in the United States. Many countries have both communist and right-wing parties that favor very different policies. Other parties grow up around specific issues. The "Green" party in Germany focuses in part on nuclear disarmament and environmental issues. In any form, democratic parties serve as a source of criticism and alternative information to executive decisionmakers. Parties also help to contest elections, and as we saw in chapter 1, the outcome of the contest between Democrat Michael Dukakis and Republican George Bush had important foreign and defense policy ramifications.

In more authoritarian governments, like China, where nonpartisan issue advocates and, especially, partisan opponents are not officially allowed, all opposition political activity is difficult to suppress. It is limited, however, and in less democratic regimes the primary pressure for policy change comes from regime dissenters. The Chinese system, for example, is not a dictatorship in the sense of one-person rule. There is evidence of considerable policy disagreement within China's political leadership, and insofar as governing is an ongoing series of discussions and decisions, that leaves a degree of latitude for regime dissenters to try to change policy.

Interest Groups

Interest groups are collections of people who have similar policy views and who try to persuade the government to adopt those views as policy. Here the definition of interest

Interest groups may play an important role in foreign policy-making, especially in more democratic political systems. In the United States, various Jewish groups try to influence U.S. policy toward Israel. These groups also try to influence Israel's foreign policy. The political advertisement pictured here appeared in the *New York Times* (4/22/88:A8) and was aimed at creating support for the political factions in Israel that seek compromise and accommodation with the Arabs.

groups means private organizations. This eliminates bureaucracies from consideration here, although bureaucratic organizations certainly do have interests they pursue.

Traditionally, interest groups were generally considered to be less active and influential on foreign policy than domestic policy issues because foreign policy often had a unifying effect on a country's subnational actors—and because foreign policy only had limited effect on the groups' domestic-oriented concerns. The increasingly intermestic nature of policy is changing that, and interest groups are becoming a more important part of the foreign policy-making process. You can see this by looking at several types of interest groups.

Cultural groups are of one type. Many countries have ethnic, racial, religious, or other cultural groups that have emotional or political ties to another country (Duchacek, Latouche, & Stevenson, 1988). In Lebanon, for instance, some of the terrorist groups are Shi'ite Muslims with ties to Iran. As a country of mostly immigrants, the United States is populated by hyphenate-Americans, and Irish-, Polish-, African-, and other ethnic-Americans influence policy toward their ancestral homes.

Business groups are another prominent form of interest activity. As international trade increases, both sales overseas and competition from other countries are vital matters to many manufacturers, banks, and other companies with international financial interests. They lobby their governments at home for favorable domestic legislation and support for the company when it is having a dispute with a government of a host country in which it is operating (Hansen, 1990).

Workers' groups such as unions and farm associations are yet another type of economic interest group that affects foreign policy. In many countries unions are active on trade issues. They often favor policies that they believe will protect workers and industries threatened by foreign competition. These policies can include contradictory demands for both protection from foreign competition and pressure on other governments to open up their markets.

Issue-specific groups and those concerned broadly with foreign affairs make up another category of interest group. A group of this type is not based on any narrow socioeconomic category, such as ethnicity or economics. Instead it draws its membership from those who have a common policy goal. Antinuclear groups such as SANE/Freeze are active in many countries and have contributed to the pressure on governments to seek arms controls. The orientations of issue-specific groups run the gamut from the very general to the specific. At the general end of the spectrum, the Council on Foreign Relations draws together some 1,500 influential (elite) Americans who hold an internationalist, somewhat liberal point of view. The World Federalists desire a stronger United Nations. On the other end of the ideological scale, the American Security Council (ASC) urges a strong posture against the Soviet Union. One interesting aftermath of the end of the cold war is that groups at both ends of the ideological spectrum have weakened. SANE/Freeze has laid off 25 percent of its staff, and the ASC has lost half its membership.

Transnational interest groups also deserve mention. These are interests that are tied to one country and operate in another. Many foreign interests, for example, operate in the United States. Sometimes they are connected with supportive domestic groups, as in the ties between Israel and various Jewish-American groups. Foreign interests also operate by hiring U.S. public relations firms and retaining the services of influential Americans to lobby on their behalf. Former Senate Foreign Relations Committee chairman William Fulbright lobbied for Saudi Arabian oil interests, former Reagan White House assistant Michael Deaver represented South Korea's Daewoo Industries, and former assistant secretary of state William Walker assisted the interests of Brazil's computer industry. In the strictest sense, transnational lobbies are not subnational actors at all, but rather examples of how one country penetrates another's domestic political system. Whatever their exact classification, though, it is important to remember that transnational lobbies are "conducive to the exercise of limited but concrete influence" by one country on another (Moon, 1988:82).

The People

The last of the subnational actors to consider is the people, the vast majority of citizens in any country that have no direct say in policy-making. To discuss the role of the people, we will look at three factors: the norm of public acceptance of foreign policy leadership, the influence of public opinion on foreign policy, and public opinion and elections.

The Norm of Public Acceptance of Foreign Policy Leadership   The role of public opinion in foreign policy is complex, sometimes contradictory, and difficult to measure. Its role differs greatly among political systems: it is more important in democratic systems and less important in authoritarian systems. There is no system, however, in which public opinion consistently controls policy or in which mass views are totally ignored by leaders. Furthermore, there are variations within types of systems. One illustrative study of public opinion impact on national security policy in four democracies found that public opinion had the greatest impact on policy in the United States with progressively declining influence in West Germany, Japan, then France (Risse-Kappen, 1990).

Politics in general, and international relations in particular, do not consistently command the attention of the average citizen. Insofar as people are concerned with politics, they are normally more concerned with pocketbook domestic issues such as unemployment and taxes and with life-style issues such as abortion. A survey of Americans in 1989, for instance, found only 8 percent thinking some foreign policy issue was the most important problem facing their country. By contrast, 35 percent named one or another economic issue and 34 percent designated a social issue as the most important (Myers, 1989). Another poll asked people in five countries to identify important political issues. Two of the countries, Canada and Uruguay, registered zero concern with international issues. Four percent of Brazilians were worried about the oil crisis, and 5 percent of the British were concerned with immigration issues. Only the Spanish showed a high degree of concern with a foreign policy issue, with 27 percent concerned about that country's entry into the European Common Market (Gallup, 1980).

These figures indicate that most people are not greatly concerned with foreign policy most of the time; they do not indicate that public opinion is unimportant. As Lincoln might have said, some of the people (the attentive public) are interested in foreign policy all the time (and have influence), and almost all the people are interested in foreign policy some of the time. Furthermore, with more countries becoming democratic and with the domestic impact of international affairs becoming more obvious to more people, there is evidence that public interest in and influence on policy is growing (Stählberg, 1987; Tussell, 1988). But in general, the public is normally content to let leaders run foreign policy. In fact, the public regularly shifts its attitudes to favor announced government policy. This pattern is particularly strong in time of crisis. A phenomenon of American foreign policy behavior is that in virtually every crisis the public has rallied behind the government and the president's popularity has soared. This has been true not only in times of success but also in times of failure, such as Reagan's Lebanon policy. A poll in early 1983 found only 30 percent of Americans supporting the president. In October, by contrast, after a terrorist attack killed a large number of marines, a majority of those polled supported the president's use of troops there. It is instructive to consider the similar views of a Nazi leader and an American secretary of state, both of whom recognized the impact of an external crisis on public support. In the words of Hermann Goering: "Voice or no voice, the people can always be brought to do the bidding of the leaders. That is easy. All you have to do is tell them they are being attacked." John Foster Dulles concurred: "The easiest and quickest cure for internal dissension is to portray danger from abroad . . . from one or another of the nation-villains."

In fact, public opinion is not always passive and malleable. At times it can become an important factor in foreign policy formation, as we shall see just below. Furthermore, a number of recent studies have concluded that the public is neither as uninformed nor as quixotic as more skeptical analysts claim. As noted earlier, the Holm (1989:195) study of Danish security policy found "good evidence" that "democratic debate and participation do not necessarily produce erratic foreign policy behavior or fundamental policy change." A related study similarly concluded that American public opinion was generally stable and that "virtually all changes" in Americans' foreign policy preferences in the last 50 years were "reasonable, or sensible" in that they are "understandable in terms of changing circumstances or changing information" (Shapiro & Page, 1988:243). Given this view and the comment on information, it is worth noting that some of the public opinion inconsistency that does exist may stem from lack of information based on government secrecy rather than lack of public interest. The U.S. government reported that for fiscal year 1989 it created 6,796,501 secret documents. These secrets were heavily weighted toward foreign affairs, with the departments of Defense and State and the CIA (along with the Justice Department) creating 99 percent of all classified documents (*HC,* 4/14/90:A1).

The Influence of Public Opinion on Foreign Policy   Many of those who make foreign policy are essentially politicians. Although they are not slaves to public opinion, they keep a weather eye on it. Studies show that the constant barrage of public protest over the war was a factor in ending the U.S. involvement in Vietnam (Small, 1988). Henry Kissinger has explained that the Nixon administration felt the pressure: "The very fabric of the government was falling apart. The Executive Branch was shell-shocked. After all, their children and their friends' children took part in the demonstrations" (1979:514).

Opinion polling is increasing the public's impact on decision-making. It is difficult to prove, but it seems certain that the Reagan administration's disposition in the 1980s to intervene militarily in El Salvador and perhaps in Nicaragua was at least in part forestalled by polls that clearly showed that Americans strongly disapproved of any sort of direct intervention. Polling is more prevalent in open systems, but even the Soviets and the Chinese have begun to conduct some surveys of mass views.

Public Opinion and Elections   National elections are not normally won and lost over foreign policy. One student of French politics, for instance, has suggested that elections in that country are never decided on international issues (Pickles, 1968). Sometimes, though, foreign policy can be very much an issue. Michael Brecher (1972) found that in Israel foreign policy has dominated 40 percent of the national elections. At times very specific issues are involved. Many U.S. voters in the 1968 and 1972 presidential primaries and general elections, for example, cast their vote based on their policy preferences on Vietnam and the candidates' stands on that issue.

Foreign policy concerns can also be part of the general electoral equation. Although they disagree on the degree of impact, several recent studies of U.S. elections concur that at least some voters do pay attention to foreign policy issues in campaigns, that they cast their votes based on those issues and the candidates' positions, and that the number of foreign policy–motivated voters is sometimes significant enough to affect the election (Rattinger, 1990; Aldrich, Sullivan, & Borgida, 1989; Hurwitz & Peffley, 1987a). As a corollary, the electorate's perception of a president's foreign policy competency affects the president's general standing in the public opinion polls (Marra, Ostrom, & Simon, 1989). Foreign policy preferences also help determine voters' party affiliation and electoral behavior in Greece and elsewhere (Dobratz, 1988).

Another important point about the relationship between foreign policy and elections is that whatever the impact found by scholarly studies, politicians believe that foreign policy does play a role on their electoral chances. Decisionmakers therefore react to anticipated electoral consequences. Opposition in the U.S. Congress to the war in Vietnam was partly motivated by the belief, as Democratic Majority Leader Mike Mansfield reported to Lyndon Johnson, that "there is a strong conviction [among senators] that candidates of the Democratic party will be hurt by the war" and that "if the war drags on, the party will suffer badly" (Rourke, 1983:382).

George Bush also believes that foreign policy plays a role in his presidential success and his chances for reelection, and it is possible to argue that his view urged him to take strong action in Panama in 1989 and the Middle East in 1990 and 1991. As he told reporters in a candid moment:

> You work your ass off, get credit for stuff you're barely involved in and none at all for things you've put together behind the scenes. Domestic problems drag you down and nag all the time. You're up in the polls and down and then up again. But sooner or later something major happens abroad that only we [Americans] can do something about. Then you show if you can cut it. If you can't, everything else can be going beautifully and you're probably out of there next time. If you pull it off, a lot else can go wrong and you'll be all

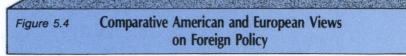

Figure 5.4   **Comparative American and European Views on Foreign Policy**

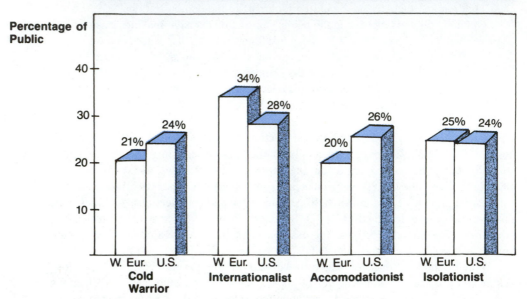

Data sources: Based on statistics from Wittkopf (1987) and Zeigler (1987). The classifications differ somewhat from those of either author. Zeigler measured attitudes toward NATO, but those can be construed as showing general attitudes toward international participation. Some analysts (Chittick & Bilingsley, 1989) argue an even more complex matrix of opinion dimensions is needed to represent attitudes.

right. Because when the people hit the [voting] booth, well, then they think, "Hey, when the chips are down, this guy can defend us and what we stand for, and that's what it's all about." (*Time,* 8/30/90:20)

Public opinion also has a more general impact on policy. The policy opinions of the **mass** (the general public) are strongly influenced by basic attitudes about the proper role of government and by core values about the international community (Hurwitz & Peffley, 1987b). Because of this foundation and the usual lack of mass attention to foreign policy, mass opinion is less flexible than the opinion of policy-making **elites.** Therefore mass opinion tends to anchor policy and prevent it from shifting too rapidly. Public opinion is also more nationalistic than elite opinion. For example, the 1986 Chicago Council on Foreign Relations opinion poll found that 98 percent of all U.S. leaders, compared to only 65 percent of the public, wanted the United States to take an active role in foreign affairs. Forty-three percent of leaders, but 78 percent of the public, believed that protecting jobs of American workers should be a very important foreign goal (Reilly, 1987). Overall, however, there is little consensus within the mass about what the general thrust of policy should be. As Figure 5.4 indicates, mass opinion in both the United States and Western Europe is fairly evenly divided among four major groups: cold warriors (traditional anticommunist view emphasizing military concerns), internationalists (broad participation in world affairs), accommodationists (international economic and social participation, but little military activity), and isolationists.

It is also possible to translate public opinion directly into foreign policy choices. A referendum is a direct public vote on a specific policy question, and there is a still small, but growing, use of this procedure to decide some foreign policy issues in some countries. The United Kingdom, Norway, Denmark, Ireland, and France all used referendums in the 1970s to resolve issues related to membership in the European Economic Community. In 1980, citizens of the province of Quebec decided not to seek autonomy from the rest of Canada. Switzerland decided in 1986 not to join the United Nations, and in 1989 the Swiss decided not to abolish their army by a two-to-one margin. The U.S. Constitution does not provide for holding a binding national referendum. One interesting attempt to change that in the late 1930s was the Ludlow Amendment. It proposed requiring a national vote before going to war in circumstances other than a direct attack on the United States, but it failed to pass Congress.

Chapter Summary

1. States are traditionally the most important political actors. States are political organizations that enjoy at least some degree of sovereignty and have a number of observable characteristics (territory, population, and so on).

2. Foreign policy is formulated by a decision-making process. The exact nature of that process varies, however, according to a number of variables including the type of political system, the type of situation, the type of issue, and the subnational actors involved.

3. States are complex organizations, and their internal, or domestic, dynamics influence their international actions. Internal factors include decisionmakers, bureaucratic organizations, legislatures, political parties and opposition, interest groups, and the public. Each of these influences foreign policy, but the decisionmakers and bureaucratic organizations are consistently (though not always) the strongest factors.

PART II

FORCES THAT

In chapters 1 through 5 we explored our "playbill"—the setting, the actors, and three levels from which we can analyze the world drama. The scenery is diverse. It ranges from the shining beauty of our planet viewed from space to the searing ugliness of a battlefield viewed from its charred earth. The states and the other actors, like the world's population, are many and growing in number. Most play a limited or intermittent role in international politics while a few states dominate the stage. States, like the humans they encompass, can be benevolent. But they are also capable of self-interest and violence. Even when there is peace, the potential for danger is high on the world stage. The actors, again like humans, are evolving. New actors, such as international organizations, emerge and begin to gather strength and upstage others. The leading actors, the states, are themselves changing, as we discussed in chapter 2. Indeed, the entire international environment is changing, and some argue (as we will see in the next chapter) that states have become political dinosaurs, no longer suited to the world in which they exist. There are even those who predict that, like the brontosauruses and tyrannosauruses of prehistoric times, the states will become extinct. Be that as it may, states still roam the earth, and whether they behave like the gentle, fern-munching brontosauruses or like the terrible tyrannosaurus carnivores, they still predominate.

Given this state of affairs, Part II, consisting of chapters 6 through 8, will continue our dramaturgical expedition beyond the protagonists to address the international goals and motives of the actors. Why do countries and others act the way they do? What is it that they want? What is the plot?

Some of that, of course, has been answered in the first five chapters. At a macroanalytical level, international politics occurs within the pressures and restraints of the international system. Countries are sometimes pushed and at other times constrained by the environment in which they exist. At a microanalytical level, policy is partly the product of personal ambitions, perceptions, or other idiosyncrasies. At the intermediate, state level of analysis, political rivalry, interest-group pressure, bureaucratic self-service, and a variety of other domestic factors motivate policy decisions.

In chapters 6, 7, and 8, you will find more causes of international action. The majority of the discussion will focus on factors that cause states to act, but many of the same urges affect other, transnational actors.

The first of these motivations is *nationalism*, and it is examined in chapter 6. More than any other force, nationalism is a symbol of our political identity. Politically, we are Canadians, Chinese, Russians, Peruvians, Nigerians, Turks, or Swedes, for example. The feeling of identification with your country is your feeling of

MOTIVATE POLICY

nationalism. This primary identification is not universal, as we shall see, but most people give their first political loyalty to their country and accept the idea that their country should be defended against outside interference and conquest. Nationalism is not only common in existing countries, but is also common among groups inside an existing state, such as the Palestinians, who seek their own state. In fact, nationalism not only causes friction between countries, it is also the source of conflict within countries, because of the mismatch between groups of people who feel national identity and the states in which they reside. Herein lies perhaps the greatest single driving force in world politics during the last several centuries.

Nationalism, however, is only one type of idea that motivates us. There are other powerful intellectual ideas that drive us, which we will explore in the discussion of *ideas, ideology, and morality* in chapter 7. Our human ability to think abstractly differentiates us from animals, but our abstractions have been the source of both good and evil. The ethics of Judeo-Christian thought teaches us to love our neighbor and to turn the other cheek. Buddhism teaches similar pacifism; the great Hindu, Mohandas Gandhi, instructed that victories are won by suffering rather than violence; and sharing is one of Islam's five pillars. Sometimes we have followed these strictures. But often we have not, and at times, philosophies have been spread by the sword or enforced by the gas chamber. It is debatable whether the pen is mightier than the sword, but it is indisputable that together they form a powerful combination.

We shall see that sometimes ideas are associated with a single state and motivate it. More often, though, ideas are transnational phenomena that cross political boundaries. Chapter 7 spends considerable time examining Islam, for instance, and the powerful role it is playing throughout the Middle East and elsewhere.

Chapter 8 addresses the controversial concept of national interest. Some argue that it does not even exist, and others contend that even if national interest does exist, it should not. Whatever the truth, the concept of national interest is widely used by leaders to justify their actions, and most citizens of most countries accept and even support that standard. Whether we like it or not, the most common standard is to support our own and our country's interest first and only secondarily worry about the needs of others. Thus, we should understand the concept, how it is used, what the issues are, and how we can form our own ideas of what our country's national interest is. Who knows, it may even be, in something of a contradiction of terms, that our national interest is not to have a nation-state at all, to let the brontosaurus, or is it tyrannosaurus, perish so that a new political life-form can emerge and flourish?

I do love
My country's good with a respect more tender,
More holy and profound, than mine own life.

Shakespeare, *Coriolanus*

Every succeeding scientific discovery
makes greater nonsense of old-time
conceptions of sovereignty.

British Prime Minister Sir Anthony Eden

Our aim has been to create genuine
nations from the sprawling artifacts the
colonialists carved out.

Zambian President Kenneth Kaunda

CHAPTER 6

NATIONALISM

liens fascinate us. Not the kinds of aliens immigrations officials worry about, but the kind of aliens that come from other planets. Whether it is Robin Williams playing Mork and standing on his head, or ALF, or the ethereal beings from *Close Encounters of The Third Kind*, our entertainment media are filled with "others." Maybe these others can do more than amuse and occasionally scare us; maybe they can tell us something. For instance, take E.T.—the extraterrestrial being. Now, there was one strange-looking character. He—she?—had a squat body, no legs to speak of, a large shriveled head, saucer eyes, and a telescopic neck. And the color! Yes, E.T. was definitely weird. Not only that, there was a whole spaceship, and presumably a whole planet, full of those characters—all looking alike, waddling along, with their necks going up and down.

Or did they all look alike? Maybe they did to us, but maybe they didn't to one another. Perhaps on their distant planet there were different countries, ethnic groups, and races of E.T.'s. Maybe they had different-length necks, were varied shades of greenish-brown, and squeaked and hummed with different tonal qualities. It's even possible that darker green E.T.'s with longer necks from the country of Urghor felt superior to lighter-shade, short-necked E.T.'s from faraway Sytica across the red Barovian Sea.

We may wonder if E.T. could differentiate among us earthlings. Was he aware that some of those he met were boys and some were girls, that some were black and others white, and that an assortment of ethnic Americans chased him with equal-opportunity abandon? Maybe we all looked pretty much the same to E.T. If he had been on a biological specimen-gathering expedition and had collected a Canadian, a Nigerian, a Peruvian, and a Laotian, he might have thrown three of the four away as unnecessary duplication.

The point of this whimsy is to get us thinking about the world, the human beings who populate it, how different and how similar we are, and how we divide ourselves up perceptually and politically. What we will see is that people tend to see themselves as different. We do not have an image of ourselves as humans; rather, we divide up ethnically into Poles, Irish, Egyptians, Thais, and a host of other "we-groups." It is striking, given how alike humans are, that they are so diverse. There is a strong tendency to organize, or try to organize, politically around that ethnic connection. People overwhelmingly adopt their country as the focus of their political identity. If you think about it, you see yourself politically as a citizen of the United States or perhaps Canada. You might even be willing to fight and die for your country. Would you do the same for your home town? Or the Earth?

This country-level focus is nationalism. As we shall see, national identification is not a given. It has not always been nor, probably, will it always be. Yet, for the time being, it is. Nationalism is a powerful force that has had an important impact on world politics for several centuries and that will probably continue to help shape people's minds and affairs in the foreseeable future. This prospect brings mixed emotions because, like the Roman god Janus, nationalism has two faces. It has been a positive force for political integration and building. It has also brought despair and destruction to the world. It is, in essence, both a uniting and a dividing force in international politics.

Nationalism: A Slippery Concept

One of the things this book tries to do is avoid jargon—the unnecessary use of 50-cent words with specialized meanings. Sometimes, however, it is important to be precise about what a word means so that we will have a common basis of discussion. This is one such place, and we need to define *state, nation, nation-state,* and *nationalism* before their roles and impact can be examined (Snyder, 1990).

As discussed in chapter 5, a *state* is a tangible, objective political entity. It has territory, people, organization, and other observable characteristics. The United States, Angola, and Bolivia are states.

A *nation* is often a far less certain phenomenon. Three factors must exist before a group of people qualifies as a nation. First, the group must share certain *similarities*. Often these are demographic characteristics, such as language, race, or religion, that can be easily identified and quantified. Language, for example, is one of the significant factors that create "we" groups with whom we can communicate and "they" groups with whom we cannot. But the similarities can also include less-measurable aspects, such as a common historical experience, regular social/economic/political interaction and cooperation, and common values. These latter factors allow a demographically diverse people, such as Americans, to come together as a nation. It could be said the American nation is the outcome of McDonald's, CBS, Valley Forge, interstate commerce, the Super Bowl, Michael Jackson, and a host of other factors.

This leads us to a perception, the *feeling of community,* which is the second factor that creates a nation. For all the similarities a group might have, it is not a nation unless it feels like one. Over a century ago, a French scholar defined a nation as "a soul, a spiritual quality" (Renan, 1964:9). What he meant is that those within a group must perceive that they share similarities. Further, these perceived similarities must lead to a feeling of community. This sense of being a "we-group" is, of course, highly subjective, but it can be objectively measured by social scientists through attitudinal surveys.

The third factor necessary for a nation to exist is some level of a *desire to be separate,* especially an urge to be politically independent or at least autonomous. In the United States there are many groups of "hyphenate Americans" (Italian-Americans, African-Americans, Mexican-Americans) that share the first two factors of a nation. They have similarities and a sense of mutual identification. They do not have a separatist

Nationalism tends to make us think of other people as fundamentally different from ourselves. We divide up humans according to racial, ethnic, religious, and other differences; you probably see the people in this picture as very distinct. One has to wonder what E.T. would have made of these people. Maybe that individual from another world would have seen each of these people as basically the same, as humans, which they are.

impulse, however. Thus, they are ethnic or subcultural groups. This is an important distinction, and it separates states that are demographically diverse (the United States) from states that are nationally divided like Cyprus and Sri Lanka. In these countries the minority nationalities refuse to concede the legitimacy of their being governed by the majority nationality (Hall & Ikenberry, 1989).

Sometimes the line between ethnic groups and nations is not so clear, and scholars have spent considerable time discussing classifications and their importance (Symmons-Symonolewicz, 1985; Riggs, 1986). In many countries there are quasi-nationalist groups that either teeter on the edge of having true nationalist (separatist) sentiment or that have some members who are nationalists and others who are not.

Canada is such a country. Nearly 30 percent of Canada's 26 million people are of French heritage. French-Canadians are primarily centered in the province of Quebec, a political subdivision rather like (but politically more independent than) an American state. Quebec is very French, indeed. Eighty-three percent of the province's 6.5 million people speak French; they are Catholic; their culture is French, and if you visited the beautiful city of Quebec, you would imagine yourself transported to an old European city (Duchacek, Latouche, & Stevenson, 1988).

The division between English-heritage and French-heritage Canadians has persisted throughout the country's history, and it continues to cause difficulties. Especially during the 1960s and 1970s, there was an upsurge of Québéçois nationalism led by the separatist *Parti Québéçois*. The movement culminated in a referendum in May 1980 on the question of possible Quebec independence. Separatism was rejected by 59.6 percent of the voters in Quebec, and in 1985 the *Parti Québéçois* was swept from office. Thus the immediate threat of Canada's dissolution was averted (Coleman, 1984).

The issue flared up anew, however, in 1990. Quebec has refused to sign the 1982 revision of the Canadian Constitution. In an attempt to gain Quebec's accession,

National unrest is as close as Canada. The French-heritage province of Quebec has long been restive in its association with the rest of British-heritage Canada. Tensions over the status of Quebec increased after a constitutional compromise, called the Meech Lake Accord, which was designed to recognize Quebec as a "distinct society," failed to be adopted in June 1990. In response, angry protests occurred, including the one pictured here, in which some citizens of Quebec called for their province to declare its independence.

Canada's prime minister Brian Mulroney and all 10 provincial premiers in 1987 signed an amendment to the Constitution that contained, among other things, the "recognition that Quebec constitutes within Canada a distinct society." The agreement became known as the Meech Lake Accord after the lake near Ottawa where it was signed. Adoption of the accord required ratification by the provincial parliaments, and a three-year deadline was established. That time limit expired on June 23, 1990, with the amendment unratified by the provinces of New Brunswick, Newfoundland, and Manitoba. The French-speaking citizens of Quebec, even those opposed to the *Parti Québéçois,* were alienated by what they saw as a rejection of their right to preserve their cultural heritage. "In the name of all Quebeckers, I want to announce my profound disappointment," Quebec's premier Robert Bourassa said. "English Canada must clearly understand that Quebec is today and forever a distinct society, capable," the premier pointedly ended, "of ensuring its own development and its destiny" (*Time,* 7/2/90:30). With almost two-thirds of French-speaking Quebeckers favoring some sort of autonomy even before the failure of the Meech Lake agreement, and—given the warning of a moderate leader like Bourassa and his call for a series of discussions among the people of Quebec beginning in late 1990 aimed at charting Quebec's future relationship to the rest of Canada—it is possible that the province will seek autonomy or even independence from the Canadian federation.

A third phenomenon, the **nation-state**, combines the previous two concepts. A nation-state is, in theory, the natural outgrowth of a nation's desire to have and maintain its own state and to govern itself independently. The nation-state is represented by many symbols such as flags, national anthems, or animals (eagles, bears, dragons). It is the object of patriotic loyalty, and we view it as the highest form of political authority.

In practice, as we shall soon see, the nation-state concept diverges from the ideal in three ways. First, many states contain several nations within their boundaries. Second, many nations overlap one or more international borders. This lack of "fit" between nations and states is often a source of international conflict. Third, as two scholars noted, "Nations and states . . . do not necessarily evolve simultaneously; . . . it is impossible to say, as an inflexible rule, which one come first (Rejai & Enlow, 1979:15; Armstrong, 1982). In Europe, nations generally came together first and only later coalesced into states. In Africa and Asia, by contrast, many states are the result of earlier boundaries drawn by colonial powers and do not contain a single, cohesive nation. Often the people within a former colonial state are of different tribal and ethnic backgrounds and find little to bind them to one another once independence has been achieved and the common enemy (the colonial power) has left. This lack of cohesion often results in civil discord and causes regime instability, and the resulting internal discord often invites outside intervention and, thus, becomes a source of international conflict.

The fourth and final phenomenon, **nationalism** itself, is a coming together of the concepts of state, nation, and nation-state. One scholar (Smith, 1971:20–21) has observed that the "core nationalist doctrine" includes the "far-reaching propositions" that:

1. Humanity is naturally divided into nations.
2. Each nation has its peculiar character.
3. The source of all political power is the nation, the collective whole.
4. For freedom and self-realization, people must identify with a nation.
5. Nations can only be fulfilled by their own states.
6. Loyalty to the nation-state overrides other (political) loyalties.

Nationalism, then, is both a cohesive and a divisive force. It has allowed and continues to allow larger political entities to form where feudal, tribal, and other local loyalties had once existed. But nationalism has also been destructive. It makes us see ourselves as essentially different from (and often superior to) other nationalities, it promotes the idea of self-interested sovereignty, and it blocks the path to a global consciousness and loyalty that some claim to be the wisest course for the future.

Nationalism: Its Rise, Predicted Demise, and Resurgence

As indicated in chapter 2, the evolution of the world political system and the growth of nationalism are intimately intertwined. You would be wise at this juncture to go back and review the interaction between the growth of states and the coalescing of nations and the identification of nations with states. One of the many things that you might note is that nationalism has not always existed as a primary political focus. To the contrary, in the political history of humankind, it is a relatively modern phenomenon. This, by inference, means that nationalism will not necessarily continue to be the primary focus of political identification and organization in the future. Because of the strength of our nationalistic political focus, it is difficult to envision almost any other system of loyalties. But consider this: Only 70 years ago (until the end of World War I) most of the nation-states of central Europe, such as Poland and Czechoslovakia, were all or in part within the realm of the Austro-Hungarian Empire. Only a little earlier than that, there was no Germany or Italy. We often assume countries like these always existed, but they did not. Before the 1860s Germany was a collection of dozens of kingdoms, principalities, and other small entities. Italy was in part controlled by France and Austria and also was subdivided into Sardinia, Lombardy, Parma, Moderna, Tuscany, the Papal States, and the kingdom of the Two Sicilies.

The Rise of Nationalism

The rise of the national state began some five centuries ago and is associated with such events as the Protestant Reformation and the Peace of Westphalia and with such mighty secular monarchs as Henry VIII, Louis XIV, and Peter the Great. That history, which is briefly outlined in chapter 2, does not need recounting here again, but it is worth touching on the story once more at the point of the French Revolution of 1789.

Because of its violence and the dramatic shift from aristocratic privilege to relative "liberty, equality, fraternity," the French Revolution is considered by many scholars to be a landmark in the growth of nationalism. French thinkers such as Rousseau, Voltaire, and Montesquieu were philosophers of popular power, and their ideas spread far beyond France's borders. In 1792 the National Convention proclaimed that "the French nation . . . will treat as enemies every people who, refusing liberty and equality . . . treat with a prince and privileged class" (Snyder, 1977:77). Within a decade, France's legions were forcibly spreading the philosophy of the democratic-national revolution throughout Europe.

The growth of democratic nationalism sometimes occurred through both evolution and revolution. Its growth in England was mostly evolutionary, and by the time of the French Revolution, the power of the English parliament (and people) over the king had been established. Also predating the French Revolution, the Americans had proclaimed their independence in favor of government of, by, and for the people.

From its beginnings in England, France, and the United States, the idea of democratic sovereignty spread around the globe until, by the mid-twentieth century, virtually all of Europe and the Western Hemisphere had been divided into nation-states, and the colonies of Africa and Asia were beginning to demand independence. Nationalism reigned supreme; despite Winston Churchill's bravado statement that he had not been made prime minister to preside over the dissolution of the British Empire, it would virtually cease to exist within three decades.

The Predicted Demise of Nationalism After World War II

While visiting London in 1897, Mark Twain was astonished to read in the paper one morning that he had died. Reasonably sure that in fact he was alive, Twain hastened to assure the world: "The reports of my death are greatly exaggerated."

This anecdote and World War II relate to nationalism because in the aftermath of the second world conflict, there were reports that nationalism was dead or dying. These predictions were also greatly exaggerated.

The assumptions that a postnationalist period would occur were based on the belief that we had learned from the horrors of war that the anarchistic system of sovereign states could no longer continue. E. H. Carr suggested (1945:34) that "certain trends . . . suggest that . . . nations and international relations are in the process of undergoing . . . clearly definable change. . . . [Current nationalism] can survive only as an anomaly and an anachronism in a world which has moved on to other forms of organization." The development of nuclear weapons, in particular, led scholars such as John H. Herz (1959) to theorize that the sovereign state could no longer carry out the primary task of protecting the nation and therefore was doomed. The emphasis on free trade and growing economic interdependence also seemed to augur an end to the nationalist age. Indeed, the newly established (1945) United Nations served as a symbol of progress away from conflictive nationalism and toward cooperative universalism.

In the years after World War II, some analysts predicted that nationalism was dying. This obituary notice proved premature, at least in the short run. To the contrary, nationalism has remained a strong characteristic of the international political system, although there are some signs that nationalism and the related concept of sovereignty are weakening.

Nationalism Resurgent

These rosy projections turned out to be wrong. Nationalism not only refused to die, but it has been rejuvenated as a world force. The primary force behind the resurgence of nationalism has been the anti-imperialist independence movement in the Third World. As Figure 6.1 on page 148 indicates, the number of new nation-states gaining independence has accelerated greatly.

If anything, nationalism in the newly emergent states is stronger than in the older, more established countries. Given their recent colonial bondage, these countries are especially sensitive about their independence. The new states are often ethnically divided, and their governments stress nationalism in an attempt to foster political unity. Since modernization has broken down traditional family, village, and other group ties and values, Third World regimes often try to substitute the country for these earlier foci of identity and loyalty. This may be done by both extolling the country and by emphasizing outside enemies.

It should also be noted that there is resurgent nationalism in Europe. Countering the trend toward European unification, a number of nationalist movements are reasserting themselves. Great Britain has Irish, Welsh, and Scottish separatist sentiments. Spain has Basque and Catalan movements; Belgium has Flemish and Walloon movements; Yugoslavia is strained by conflict between Serbs and Croatians. In North America, the French Canadians of Quebec are demanding greater cultural and political self-direction. And as will be detailed later, national separatism is threatening to break up the Soviet Union.

As John Herz (1969:77), in a commendable reevaluation of his earlier prophecy, admitted, "Developments have rendered me doubtful of the correctness of my previous anticipations. . . . There are indicators pointing . . . to retrenchment . . . to a new self-sufficiency . . . toward a 'new territory' "—in short, to a new nationalism.

Whither Germany?

The abiding strength of nationalism has recently been powerfully demonstrated by German reunification. Once the threat of a Soviet intervention to prevent it disappeared, the one German people of the two Germanys hurtled toward *ein Deutschland.* Virtually no one expected it to occur as quickly as it did. The Soviet foreign minister predicted it would take many years. Diplomat and scholar George Kennan, one of the most respected U.S. analysts, skeptically observed in late 1989 that a lot of "loose talk . . . has marked the discussion of recent days about German reunification. Many people talk about this as if it were something that could naturally occur. . . ." (*Manchester Guardian Weekly,* 11/19/89:9). In January 1989 East German leader Erich Honecker estimated that the Berlin Wall might remain as a symbol of German division for another century. His prediction was off by 99 years. The Wall was breached that November, and on October 3, 1990, Germany became one state in close parallel with the one German nation.

Along with the reality of one Germany, there are some other clear facts. West Germany was the leading economic power between the Atlantic and the western Soviet border. Even at current levels, united Germany will expand its status as an economic superpower. Its two Germanys' 1988 combined exports were $354 billion compared to France's $168 billion and Great Britain's $145 billion. The German combined GNP stood at just over a trillion dollars compared to France's $762 billion and Great Britain's $755 billion. If and when the economic productivity of the former East German area reaches West German levels, the gap between Germany and France or Great Britain will be even greater. For example, with a fully revitalized East Germany adding to the German economy at the same per capita level as the West Germans, Germany's total GNP would equal about three-quarters of the combined French and British GNPs. Continuing the comparison, the German population (78 million) is 37 percent larger than the populations of either France or Great Britain. Germany also has the potential to be a military superpower. As separate countries, the two Germanys had a combined total of 667,000 troops, 840 combat aircraft, and 8,145 tanks. Developing nuclear weapons would present no insurmountable technical difficulty for the Germans. It is also a matter of record that, while not always bearing sole responsibility, the history of Germany from the 1860s through World War II was marked by repeated and exceedingly destructive warfare with its neighbors and others.

Those are the facts. The question is what, if anything, do they mean about the future? At their extremes, there are two visions of the future international role of Germany. One is of a peaceful Germany that is an integral and cooperative member of the European Community (EC) and of NATO or whatever security organization follows NATO. The other vision is a power-seeking Germany that once again will exert its economic, diplomatic, and military muscle to dominate the Economic Community, Central and Eastern Europe (*Mittle Europa*), and perhaps even a wider sphere of influence.

There are many optimistic signs that the new Germany will be very different from the old Germany of Otto von Bismark's blood and iron policy, of Kaiser Wilhelm II and World War I, and of Adolf Hitler's Third Reich. To win final Soviet acceptance of rapid unification, Chancellor Helmut Kohl pledged at Zheleznovodsk in the Soviet Union to limit future German troop strength to 370,000 and to renounce forever nuclear, chemical, and biological weapons. After some early hesitation, the Germans also agreed to reaffirm the existing German-Polish border and, thereby, the 1945 loss of German territory to Poland. Germany also has remained a part of NATO, an association that many believe would make it difficult for Germany to try to achieve military superpower status. Germans have also taken pains to dispel fears of renewed persecution of Jews and others. At the September 12, 1990, signing of the treaty ending the 45-year Allied occupation of Germany, Foreign Minister Hans-Dietrich Genscher apologized to Jews for the Holocaust and said, "In this hour we remember the victims of war . . . particularly . . . the Jewish people. We would not want their agony ever to be repeated" (*HC,* 9/13/90:A1).

The public statements of most political leaders and analysts accept the optimistic vision of Germany's future. "I am not afraid of [German] reunification," French president François Mitterand proclaimed early in the process (*WP,* 11/4/89: A18). "This is a delightful surprise," U.S. secretary of state James Baker gushed when he learned of the Kohl-Gorbachev agreement at Zheleznovodsk (*Time,* 7/30/90:24). "We have closed the book on World War II and started a new age," proclaimed Soviet foreign minister Eduard Shevardnadze as he signed away his country's occupation rights. "We cannot continue to live in the past. . . . We are now dealing with a new Germany that has drawn its lessons from history" (*HC,* 9/13/90:A1). It was magnanimous statement from a man whose older brother was killed fighting Germany in World War II. In fact, German chancellor Kohl could not help but wonder about the intelligence or motives of those who do not accept the optimistic vision of Germany. "Whoever speaks of a Fourth Reich," Kohl instructed, "has either not understood history or consciously wants to defame Germans" (*HC*, 2/2/90:A9).

There are those, however, who are neither assured by the vision of the optimists nor chastened by Kohl's admonitions. British prime minister Margaret Thatcher and her government were among the least convinced. In July 1990 a furor broke out over a series of leaked and public statements by British government officials. Speaking at the NATO summit on July 6, the prime minister evoked memories of the two world wars, and counseled the national leaders that "the wise man guards against the future as if it were the present." Then, in an unsubtle further allusion to Germany, she urged a continued strong NATO even though the Soviet threat had declined because "you never know where the next threat will come from" (*WP*, 7/6/90:A28). Just a week later, British Cabinet member Nicholas Ridley was forced to resign as the result of his published comments that moves toward European monetary integration were a "German racket," and that the French were "poodles" of the Germans (*HC*, 7/15/90:A12). Only five days elapsed before yet another disclosure came. This time it was a leaked memorandum that summarized a March meeting Thatcher had held with British experts on Germany. Excerpted in the *New York Times* (9/20/90: A27), and written by the prime minister's private secretary Charles Powell, the memorandum recalled, "We started by talking about the Germans and their characteristics . . . which you could identify from the past and expect to find in the future." These included "insensitivity to the feelings of others . . . [and] their obsession with themselves. . . . Some even less flattering attributes . . . mentioned as an abiding part of the German character: in alphabetical order, angst, aggressiveness, assertiveness, bullying, egotism. . . ."

The British are not alone, and some Europeans are favorably recalling French novelist François Mauriac's tongue-in-cheek comment that "I love Germany so much that I am glad there are two of them." A January 1990 poll found two of every three Poles opposed to German reunification (*NYT*, 2/20/90:A10). Hungary's deputy prime minister has expressed concern that "in Europe today there exists a certain balance, and with one Germany this balance will change." Austria's chancellor has added that "considering the painful events of this century, it would be wrong and unrealistic to ignore the anxieties manifested in all corners of Europe" (*NYT*, 2/5/90:A10). Or, as a

A West German youth presents a bouquet of flowers to an East German border guard at the Berlin Wall near the Brandenburg Gate, November 18, 1989.

military official of a small NATO country bordering Germany told this author in the summer of 1990, "Now that the cold war is over we aren't sure which way to point the army."

Having started out with some facts and then having turned to contrasting views about the nature of Germany, let us return to a certainty. It is, as Chancellor Kohl put it, that "Nobody knows how a reunified Germany will look" (*Time*, 12/11/89:45). Perhaps the best advice has been given by Simone Weil, a woman who has served in the French Cabinet and who has been president of the European Parliament. She is also a survivor of Auschwitz, where her parents perished. Weil is optimistic about the future of Germany and Europe, but she admits "I could be wrong in all this." The wise course, Weil counsels, is that "we must never forget. And that means that we must be very vigilant, very demanding that we never forget" (*NYT*, 9/27/90:A8).

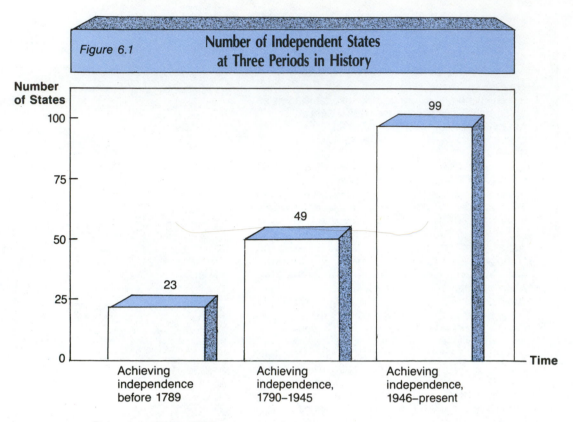

Figure 6.1

**Number of Independent States
at Three Periods in History**

Number
of States

Data source: Paxton (1990).

One of the important changes in the international system since World War II has been the rapid growth in the number of independent countries. It took all of political history through 1945 for 72 states to evolve but then only another 40 years for that figure to more than double.

As laudable as Herz's academic courage may have been, it is not at all certain that he is correct. Certainly the strength of nationalism in the newly independent countries and its persistence in many older countries cannot be denied. There are other trends, however. As we shall discuss more fully in the last part of this book, world-consciousness is slowly growing and the concept of sovereignty is steadily being chipped away. There is also a vast and increasing array of international organizations and transnational connections, all of which dilute nationalism and may subtly shift an individual's political focus. Especially in Western Europe, there are extensive ties, principally through the European Community, that are slowly building a regional identity. These trends are not yet dominant, but it may be that Herz was not so much wrong as simply premature in sounding the death knell for nationalism and sovereignty.

Indeed the dialectic between the thesis of old-styled nationalism and the antithesis of post-nationalist internationalism is one of the pivotal struggles facing the world. Will the international political system continue to rest on the concept of sovereign states as the primary political actors, or will the system evolve toward a more hierarchical structure in which states surrender some or all of their sovereignty to supranational law and order? British scholar James Mayall (1990:145), for one, believes that the evolution toward internationalism will be slow and limited at best. "There is no immediate prospect of transcending the national idea, either as a principle of legitimisation or as the basis of political

After 45 years of division there is now, again, one Germany. A key question to the future of international politics is, whither Germany? The boy and the East German soldiers you see here are symbolic of two pasts and two possible futures. One of these pasts is the cold war represented by the soldiers who were participating in the last changing of the guard in late September 1990 at an East Berlin war memorial. Now East Berlin, the East German army, and the cold war are no more, and the boy will probably not remember them. The soldiers also represent Germany's often militaristic past. The question is whether the boy will grow up in a peaceful Germany or whether he will see a Germany that once again asserts its military power in Europe and elsewhere.

organisation for the modern state," Mayall writes. "The nation-state (or the would-be nation-state) remains the basic political unit. . . . We must live in the world we have made. Our task is not god-like: we cannot hope to transform the world, if we are very lucky we might just improve it." Another British scholar is not so pessimistic. Future history, Eric J. Hobsbawm (1990:182) writes, "will inevitably have to be written as the history of a world which [could] . . . no longer be contained with the limits of 'nations' or 'nation-states' as . . . defined." "It would be absurd to claim that this day is already near," Hobsbawm admits, but "the phenomenon [of the nation-state] is past its peak."

Whichever path world political development follows, on this all can agree: nationalism remains a controversial as well as powerful force in the world. It would be well to consider the positive and negative roles that nationalism plays in world politics.

Nationalism: Builder and Destroyer

Earlier in this chapter Janus, the two-faced Roman god of gates through which roads passed, was mentioned. Janus had two faces because wayfarers had to choose which path to travel by once they had passed outward through the gate. Janus might well have been the god of nationalism because that concept, that movement, has taken the world in two divergent directions, one of harmony and one of conflict.

The Beneficent Face of Nationalism

Most scholars agree that in its philosophical and historical genesis nationalism was a positive force. It has a number of possible beneficial effects.

Nationalism promotes democracy. One analyst notes that through nationalism "the concept of popular sovereignty replaced the concept of the divinely or historically appointed ruler; the concept of citizen replaces the concept of subject" (Kamenka, 1976:14). In short, nationalism promotes the idea that political power legitimately resides with the people and that governors exercise that power only as the agents of the people.

Nationalism encourages self-determination. In modern times, the notion that nationalities ought to be able to preserve their cultures and govern themselves according to their own customs has become widely accepted. The English utilitarian philosopher John Stuart Mill (1806–73) argued that "where the sentiment of nationality exists . . . there is a prima facie case for unity of all the members of the nationality under . . . a government to themselves apart" (1861; in Snyder, 1964:4). Self-determination was also a key element of Woodrow Wilson's Fourteen Points (1918), and in recent years it has been especially strong in the Afro-Asian countries.

Nationalism discourages imperialism. A closely related impact of nationalism is that in the postcolonial world it strengthens countries to resist renewed outside occupation. Even a Third World government of a relatively new country that has little support from its population would almost surely be able to rally fierce national opposition to any foreign invader (Neuberger, 1986). Similarly, nationalism has emboldened countries to resist new or continued indirect control. It was widely thought that the Egyptians could not properly manage the Suez Canal when they nationalized it in 1956. Similarly, there are gloomy predictions about the upkeep of the Panama Canal under the control of the Panamanians. The Egyptians have managed their canal well, however, and it is probable that the Panamanians will do the same.

Nationalism allows for economic development. Many scholars see nationalism as both a facilitator and a product of modernization. Nationalism created larger political units in which commerce could expand. The prohibition of interstate tariffs and the control of interstate commerce by the national government in the 1787 American Constitution is an example of that development. With the advent of industrialization and urbanization, parochial loyalties of the masses were loosened and replaced by a loyalty to the nation-state.

Nationalism allows diversity and experimentation. It has been argued that regional or world political organization might lead to an amalgamation of cultures or, worse, the suppression of the cultural uniqueness of the weak by the strong, whereas diversity of culture and government promotes experimentation. Democracy, it could be said, was an experiment in America in 1776 that might not have occurred in a one-world system.

The Troubled Face of Nationalism

Despite its possible good, many contend that nationalism has become primarily a destructive force. Pope John XXIII, in his 1963 encyclical *Pacem in Terris*, reviewed nationalism and sovereignty and found that "the present system of organization and the way its principle of authority operates on a world basis no longer correspond to the objective requirements of the universal common good." The ills that nationalism brings are many and serious and can be subdivided into three categories: (1) how we relate to others, (2) the lack of fit between states and nations, and (3) the issue of microstates.

How We Relate to Others

Nationalism can lead to insularity. Because we identify with ourselves as the "we-group," we tend to consider the "they-group" as aliens. Our sense of responsibility—of

Nationalism has its dark side, one aspect of which is the feeling of superiority. German nationalism in the 1930s and 1940s ran out of control and led, in part, to the attempt to exterminate Jews and other peoples. The result was the Holocaust with its horrific concentration camps, such as Buchenwald shown here.

even human caring—for the "theys" is limited. This is an especially pronounced effect of the American national experience. Isolationism was a standard sanctioned by George Washington and Thomas Jefferson that lasted for a century and a half. It has retreated somewhat, but the isolationist impulse still can be felt.

   Domestically, we Americans accept the principle that we have a responsibility to our least fortunate citizens. The social welfare budget in the United States is in the hundreds of billions of dollars, and we engage in countless acts of charity, from donating blood to distributing toys for tots. Internationally, to be blunt, most of us don't care much. An illustrative 1989 poll found that of those Americans surveyed, 60 percent strongly agreed and 28 percent somewhat agreed that "America has a moral responsibility to concentrate on domestic policy before concentrating on foreign policy" and 69 percent did not consider aiding the world's less developed countries to be "important" (Myers, 1989:300). A tidal wave kills hundreds of thousands in Bangladesh, an earthquake kills a million in China, disease and hunger debilitate millions in Africa and Asia, and, well, we yawn and wonder what is at the movies. We may give a few pennies for UNICEF at Halloween, donate a few dollars at religious services for international relief work, or buy one of the "aid" records like "We Are the World," but, all in all, Asians, Africans, and others seem far away, not like us, and certainly not our responsibility.[1]

   Nationalism often leads to a feeling of superiority. It is a small step from feeling different and liking your group to feeling superior. At its extreme, this manifestation

---

   1. This is not meant to belittle the private humanitarian aid that is given. Those who give are to be admired, and their efforts do help. The problem is that too few help and too few are helped.

festered in Nazi Germany. The German nation—or race—was at the top of a ladder, which descended downward to where, at the bottom, Slavic peoples were to be kept as virtual and expendable slaves in segregated and degrading conditions, and Jews and Gypsies were "nonpeople" and "racial vermin" to be exterminated. "The highest purpose of a *folkish state,*" Hitler preached in *Mein Kampf,* "is . . . preservation of those original racial elements which bestow culture and create the beauty of a higher humanity. We, as Aryans, can conceive of the state only as a living organism of . . . [German] nationality . . ." (Sargent, 1990:199).

Nationalism is sometimes xenophobic. **Xenophobia** is suspicion, dislike, or fear of other nationalities. It is often closely associated with feelings of national superiority, although these sometimes actually stem from a sense of national insecurity, even inferiority. The belief that other nationalities are hostile is widespread and leads to world tension. Xenophobia is also responsible for the human misery and occasional international conflict that occurs when alien residents are oppressed by or expelled from one country or another. The expulsion by Vietnam of ethnic Chinese in 1978 was one cause of the border war with Vietnam.

When mutual xenophobia occurs between two peoples, good relations can be especially imperiled. This phenomenon is a growing concern for relations between the United States and Japan. There is a history of anti-Japanese sentiment in the United States. During World War II, for example, Japanese-Americans were confined to prison camps; German-Americans and Italian-Americans suffered no such injustice. In the 1980s and 1990s these, for a time latent, feelings have begun to resurface in the face of Japanese economic success. Many Americans believe Japan's prosperity has been achieved at their expense and as a result of unfair practices by Japan. Americans are alarmed, for example, by the rise of Japanese ownership of property and companies in the United States. "This year when they turn on the lights of that Christmas tree in Rockefeller Center," U.S. senator Joseph Lieberman lamented after Japanese investors bought the cultural symbol, "we Americans are going to have to come to grips with the reality that this great national celebration is actually occurring on Japanese property" (*Time,* 11/13/90:83). What those who worry about an economic Pearl Harbor seem less concerned about is investment from European countries such as the United Kingdom (whose U.S. investments are larger than Japan's) and the Netherlands, or, for that matter, the massive U.S. investments in Japan and elsewhere.

The Japanese are increasingly likely to regard American criticism of Japanese investment, in contrast to American acceptance of Canadian and European investment, as racially motivated. Indeed, some Japanese believe it reflects overall American racism. Shintaro Ishihara, a member of Japan's parliament, has written a book, *The Japan That Can Say No,* that lists SONY chairman Akio Morita as a (probably passive) coauthor. The book has not been published in English, but a pirated translation, paid for by the U.S. defense department, was published in the November 1989 edition of the *Congressional Record.* Among other things, Ishihara contends that "the only reason" Americans dropped the atomic bomb on Japan in 1945 was "their racial attitude toward Japan." Ishihara also argues that American racial attitudes toward Japan are "based on the cultural belief that the modern era is the creation of the white race," and he believes that the "roots of the [current] U.S.–Japan friction lie in the soil of racial prejudice . . . [the American] sense of superiority toward the Japanese" (*NYT,* 1/29/90:A16).

Further adding fuel to mounting mutual American-Japanese xenophobia, incidents of Japanese racial stereotyping of Americans have begun to surface. In September 1990 Japan's minister of justice Seiroku Kaijiyama watched as police rounded up foreign prostitutes in Tokyo's red-light district. These prostitutes ruin neighborhoods, Kaijiyama

One destructive aspect of nationalism is that it tends to promote dislike of other nationalities. Overtones of racism are intensifying mutual resentment over economic difficulties between the United States and Japan. Americans are more alarmed by economic difficulties with Japan than they are over similar problems with European, Caucasian countries. Another racial ramification is pictured here. A Japanese official made a racist remark about American blacks in September 1990. In response, offended U.S. blacks demonstrated outside the Japanese embassy in Washington, D.C. (shown here), and elsewhere. They demanded a boycott of Japanese products.

told reporters; "It's like in America when neighborhoods become mixed because blacks move in and whites are forced out" (*HC,* 9/28/90:A2). Two weeks later Kaijiyama apologized for his "inappropriate" remarks. The damage had been done, however. U.S. black leaders dismissed the apology as inadequate, and protest demonstrations organized by the NAACP occurred at Japan's embassy in Washington, D.C. Demonstrators wore signs proclaiming "Nix Nissan," "Kream Kawasaki," "Sayonara SONY," and other alliterative calls for an anti-Japan boycott. "No Japanese goods under the Christmas tree in 1990," one protest leader urged, and the chairman of the National Association of Black-Owned Broadcasters called on the 225 black-owned U.S. television and radio stations to pull Japanese-owned programming from the air waves. This would include the products of CBS Records, a subsidiary of SONY Corporation. "Our dignity is more important to us than any black entertainer," and "We're ready to stop listening to Michael Jackson," other demonstrators declared (*HC,* 9/29/90:C9). However just the reactions may be against specific incidents, the growing, mirror-image sense of racism is symptomatic of a trend from which neither nation will profit.

Nationalism is jingoistic. Too often nationalism leads to **jingoism**, the belief that your country can do no wrong. It combines with patriotism—or love of country—to the point that a Stephen Decatur can say, to our applause, "Our country! . . . may she always be in the right; but our country, right or wrong."

Nationalism can be messianic. If you like yourself or your we-group too much, it is easy to imagine that your fate—indeed, your duty—is to "save" others and bring them to the "way of truth"—that is, your way. This is, essentially, **messianism**. Consider, for example, the messiah complex found in Fyodor Dostoyevski's *The Possessed:* "If a great people did not believe that truth is only to be found in itself alone, if it did not believe that it alone is destined to save all the rest by its truth, it would . . . not remain a great

Israelis and Palestinians: A Tale of Two Nations

The facts are simple. There are two nations: Israeli and Palestinian. They are separated by religion and divided by their respective national ambitions. The fundamental issue is that both peoples claim approximately the same expanse of territory as their national homeland. That territory is now controlled by Israeli Jews; the Palestinian Muslims mean to get it back or at least carve out a new Palestinian state in the region (Gerner, 1990; Goldschmidt, 1983).

The origins of the dispute go back to Abraham and his two sons, Isaac, who founded the Jewish nation, and Ishmael, the symbolic father of all Arabs. This and other biblical stories are matters of considerable conjecture, but they are important because the Jews partly base their claim to Israel on Yahweh's (Jehovah's) promise (Exod. 3: 8) to Moses that he would deliver the Hebrews out of Egypt to "a land flowing with milk and honey." The catch is that God was also directing the Hebrews "unto the place of the Canaanites"—occupied territory.

After a millennium of struggle and conquest, the last vestige of Jewish control in the region was ended by the Romans' destruction of the Second Temple in A.D. 70. Judaism did not end, however. Most Jews dispersed throughout the known world and existed among groups that had converted to Judaism in other lands.

The origins of the Palestinian people is unclear, but they have existed in the region for at least seven centuries, and some even trace them back to the pre-Hebrew tribes in the area. In any case, Palestinian Arabs were the area's primary inhabitants for many centuries and comprised 90 percent of the population as late as World War I.

In Europe, however, Zionism began to gather strength in the nineteenth century. **Zionism** holds that Jews are a nation that should have an independent homeland. As such, Zionism is a nationalist, not strictly religious, cause. During World War I, Great Britain needed European Jewish financial support and to get it, the British issued the *Balfour Declaration* in 1917. This placed Britain on record in "favor of the establishment in Palestine of a national home for the Jewish people" and pledged that if the

British captured Palestine (which they soon did) from the Ottoman Empire (Turkey), the British would "facilitate the achievement of this object."

The tide of Jewish emigration to Palestine became a tidal wave in the face of the ravages of Nazi Germany. The Jewish population swelled from 56,000 in 1920 to 650,000 by 1948, approximately 40 percent of the total population of Palestine. Tension was high and fighting common between Arabs and Jews and between Jews and British. Britain washed its hands of the matter by turning it over to the United Nations. A UN partition plan in 1947 called for the division of Palestine into a Jewish state and an Arab state. Arab leaders did not accept the plan; on Israel's independence in 1948 fighting immediately broke out. Israel survived and incorporated some of the areas designated for the Arab state. At least a half million Palestinian Arabs fled their homes to refugee camps in Egyptian-controlled *Gaza* and elsewhere, 150,000 stayed behind, and another 400,000 came under the control of Jordan in an area called the *West Bank* (of the Jordan River).

Israel has fought four major and victorious wars (1948–49, 1956–57, 1967, and 1973) with its Arab neighbors. In the 1967 war Israel captured considerable territory—most importantly the West Bank. Military triumph, however, did not bring Israel peace or security. The reasons for this can best be explained in terms of *UN Resolution 242* (1967). It called for (1) Israel to withdraw from the territories occupied in the 1967 war and for (2) a recognition by the Arabs of Israel's right to "live in peace within secure and recognized boundaries free from threats and acts of force."

Israel has been reluctant to withdraw from the territories before peace. In fact, Israel claims that some of the territories must be retained to meet the "secure" borders provision of 242. Some of the lands captured in 1967 are culturally and emotionally central to Jews. Israelis call the West Bank by its biblical names of Judea and Samaria. Israel would find it especially difficult to surrender control of East Jerusalem, which lies in the West Bank, and which is a holy city for Jews, Muslims, and Christians alike.

Palestinians and most other Arabs want Israel to give up its occupied territories as a precondition to peace. They also want Israel to negotiate directly with the Palestinians, which Israel refuses to do on the grounds that they are terrorists. Many Israelis also contend that any Palestinian state would inevitably be hostile and threaten Israel's existence (Ramati, 1989). Many Arabs are also reluctant to recognize Israel's right to exist, although many have moderated their stand in recent years. The most significant issue, though, is the fate of the Palestinian people and the prospects for a Palestinian homeland.

The Palestine Liberation Organization (PLO), which came into being in 1964 and which has been headed by Yasser Arafat since that time, claims to represent all of the Palestinians. Given the growing Arab realization that Israel is a permanent reality, Arabs now focus on the political future of the Palestinians rather than on the dissolution of Israel. The logical place for a Palestinian homeland is the West Bank, and in November 1988 the Palestine National Council, the PLO's so-called Parliament in exile, declared an independent Palestinian state centered in, but perhaps extending beyond, the West Bank. The PLO's National Council also called for peace based on Resolution 242. At virtually the same time, however, the Israelis selected a government that is opposed to giving up the West Bank or negotiating in any form with the PLO. There are, then, still a number of intractable questions to be answered: (1) Will Israel negotiate with the PLO? (2) Will the PLO accept Israeli sovereignty over what was formerly the traditional Palestinian homeland? (3) Would Palestine be autonomous or independent? (4) Would it coexist peacefully with Israel?

Two things are clear. The situation is explosive and Israel's international position has begun to deteriorate. Since 1987 West Bank Palestinians have been engaged in a now simmering, now fiery revolt called the *intifada* against what they consider Israeli colonial occupation (Peretz, 1990). Israel has reacted to the uprising with occasional brutality that even one Israeli general characterized as "totally unacceptable under the standards of . . . any civilized norms" (*HC*, 2/18/90:A10). Israel has also been intransigent on negotiating with the PLO and has rejected peace plans offered by U.S. secretary of state James Baker and Egyptian president Hosni Mubarak that included such face-to-face talks. Furthermore, the flow of Jewish settlers into the West Bank that began in 1967 has continued, and Arabs and others are worried that the increased influx of Soviet Jews into Israel will be channeled into the West Bank to displace its Arab residents and to intensify Israel's attempt to annex the area.

Whatever the balance of justice in the region may be, international attitudes have begun to turn against Israel. The UN General Assembly condemned "Israel's violations of the human rights of Palestinians" by a wide vote, and a similar Security Council resolution was only averted in February 1989 by a U.S. veto in opposition to all fourteen other members of the council (*UN Chronicle*, 6/89:32). Even Israel's strongest supporters have become partially disaffected. U.S. diplomats held their first official meetings with PLO representatives in Tunisia in late 1989, and the Bush administration has regularly voiced frustration with Israel. Furthermore, American-Jewish leaders have begun to criticize Israeli policy more frequently. One study found nearly three-fourths of them favoring discussions between Israel and the PLO because, according to John Ruskay, vice chancellor of the Jewish Theological Seminary, "there is a great sadness toward Israel shared by a growing number of American Jews. The sadness is that after 40 years and a Holocaust we end up occupying [the homeland of] thousands of Palestinians against their will" (*Time*, 5/7/90:28).

Is there a solution? One hopes that the Palestinians will all come to accept both the reality of Israel and a smaller homeland. One hopes, with equal fervor, that the Israelis will come to recognize the reality of the Palestinian movement and negotiate with it.

Figure 6.2   The Expansion of the Israeli State

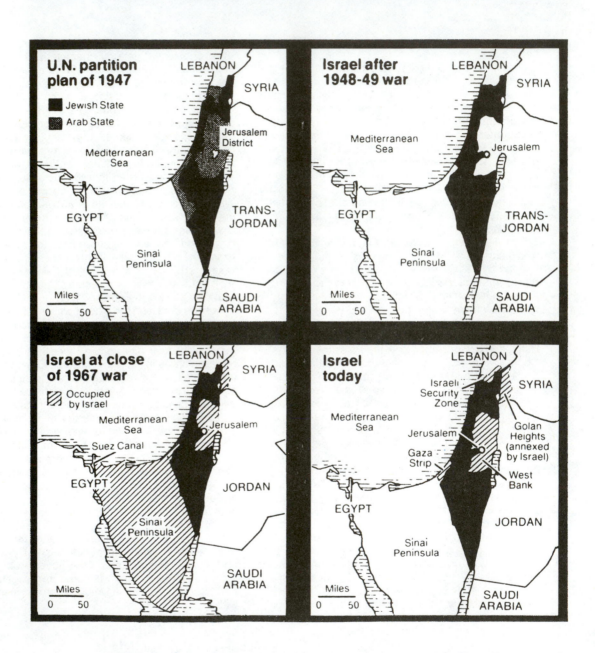

Source: From *NYT,* 2/28/88:E3. Copyright © 1988 by The New York Times Company. Reprinted by permission.

The conflict between Israeli Jews and the Palestinians and their Arab supporters presents one of the most difficult diplomatic issues facing the world. These four maps show the shifting borders of Israel and its Arab neighbors since 1947. In particular they highlight the changing status of the West Bank, the focus of struggle between Israel and the now self-proclaimed Palestinian state.

people. But there is only one truth, and therefore only a single one out of the nations can have the true God. That is the Russian people" (Snyder, 1977:213–14).

Nationalism can be aggressive. Feelings of xenophobia, superiority, jingoism, and messianism can easily lead to aggressive behavior. Hitler's Germany and the supposed destiny of its Aryan super-race to be master of the world is an especially strong example. But there are many others. Nationalism has been a major factor in the aggressiveness of the United States, the Soviet Union, and, to a lesser degree, China, and has led each of these powers to expand, colonize, and/or try to dominate its neighbors.

The Lack of Fit Between Nations and States

Nations and states often do not coincide. This means that the concept of a nation-state in which ethnic and political boundaries are the same is more ideal than real. In fact, most states are not ethnically unified, and many nations are not politically unified or independent. This lack of "fit" between nations and states is a significant source of international (and domestic) tension and conflict. There are two basic disruptive patterns: (1) one state, multiple nations, (2) one nation, multiple states. Sometimes the two troubling patterns can even intertwine, as in the case of the Israeli and Palestinian peoples (see the box on pages 154 and 155).

States With More Than One Nation   The number of **multinational states** far exceeds that of nationally unified states. One study found that only about 9 percent of all countries truly fit the nation-state concept, as Figure 6.3 on the following page shows. The rest of the countries fall short of the ideal by at least some degree, with, at the extreme, 29.5 percent having no national majority.

The Union of Soviet Socialist Republics is the most important current example of a multinational state. We are used to referring to Soviet citizens as Russians. In reality, only about half of the people in the U.S.S.R. are ethnic Russians. Additionally, there are 14 other major nationalities and dozens of smaller national/ethnic groups. The geographic distribution of the major nationalities is depicted in Figure 6.4 on page 159. Because the Russian population has been static and some of the other nationalities have had a high birth rate, current estimates are that about 50 percent of the population is Slavic Russian, with another 20 percent also Slavs (Belorussians and Ukrainians). Twenty percent of the Soviet population is Muslim (Uzbeks, Kazakhs, Azerbaijanis, Tadzhiks, Turkmen, Kirghiz, and others) and ethnically related to the people to their south in countries such as Iran and Afghanistan. Caucasus Christians (Armenians and Georgians) and Balts (Estonians, Lithuanians, and Latvians) each constitute about 3 percent of the population, the Rumanian-related Moldavians are about 1 percent, with the remainder of the population divided among small groups.

Because of its national diversity and the process of conquest by which Russians acquired dominance, the Soviet Union is an anomaly in that it is the last of the great multinational empires. Once these were common, but with the breakup of the Ottoman Empire and the Austro-Hungarian Empire at the end of World War I, the Soviet Union became the last survivor.

Given the steady tide of national self-determination, it might have been possible after World War I to conclude that the Soviet Union also would someday succumb to a flood of separatist sentiment by its national minorities. Yet the Soviet Union persisted, bound together by a totalitarian central government and by a transnational ideology. In recent years, both the authoritarianism of Moscow and the strength of Communism have ebbed, and as a result strong nationalist feelings have surfaced. The recent economic crisis has further heightened these emotions.

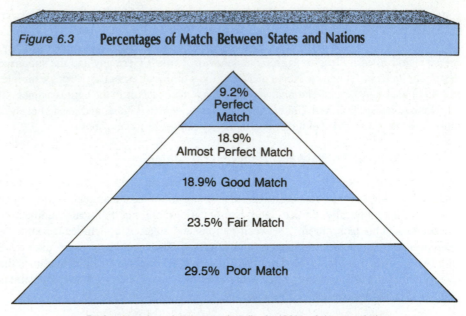

Figure 6.3   **Percentages of Match Between States and Nations**

9.2%
Perfect
Match

18.9%
Almost Perfect Match

18.9% Good Match

23.5% Fair Match

29.5% Poor Match

Perfect match = Largest nationality is 100% of the population.
Almost perfect match = Largest nationality is 90%–99% of the population.
Good match = Largest nationality is 75%–89% of the population.
Fair match = Largest nationality is 50%–74% of the population.
Poor match = Largest nationality is 0%–49% of the population.

Data source: Connor (1979).

Ideally the coincidence (match) between nationality and the total population of a state would be 100%. As this graph shows, however, this is true in only 9.2% of the states. More than 90% of states have two or more nationalities, and the largest nationality is less than a majority of the population in 29.5% of the states.

Although the bulk of international attention has focused on the Lithuanians, their struggle for independence or autonomy is mirrored by most of the other nationalities. By August 1990, 11 of the 15 Soviet republics had declared at least limited sovereignty from Moscow. So far, no republic has successfully seceded, but there is considerable turbulence, including violence in some areas that has left over 400 people dead. Even the Russian Republic under its charismatic leader Boris Yeltsin has asserted its sovereignty. The ethnic Russian movement was further activated by a remarkable letter published in *Komsolmoslkaya Pravda* by Russian novelist Aleksandr Solzhenitsyn. His novels, including the *Gulag Archipelago,* are highly critical of the Marxist regime, and his work earned Solzhenitsyn two forms of recognition. In 1970 he won the Nobel Prize for literature; in 1974 he was expelled from the Soviet Union. Solzhenitsyn's September 1990 letter was notable for both what it said and the fact that it was published in a Communist party newspaper. In the letter he predicts that in the national republics "the centrifugal forces are moving at such speed that . . . the Soviet Union will fall apart." Rather than attempt to forestall that end, Solzhenitsyn calls on his fellow Russians to lead in the dismemberment of the Soviet Union and the liberation of the national minorities. His reasoning is based less on concern with the other nationalities than on his desire to see Russia revitalized, and he argues that "by this seeming sacrifice, Russia . . . will liberate itself for precious inner development" (*NYT,* 9/19/90:A8). An ironic note to Solzhenitsyn's call for the end of the Soviet Union is that less than a month before his

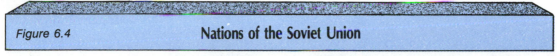

Figure 6.4   **Nations of the Soviet Union**

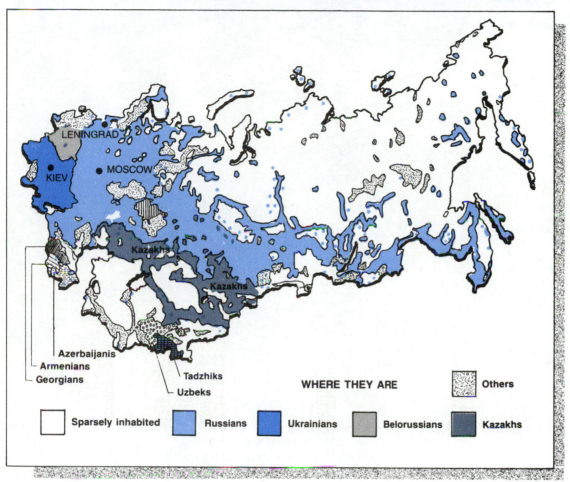

The Major National Groups of the Soviet Union

Nationality	Population (millions)	Percentage of Population	Nationality	Population (millions)	Percentage of Population
Russians	145.1	50.8	Georgians	4.0	1.4
Ukranians	44.1	15.4	Moldavians	3.4	1.2
Uzbeks	16.7	5.8	Lithuanians	3.1	1.1
Belorussians	10.0	3.5	Turkmen	2.7	1.0
Kazakhs	8.1	2.8	Kirghiz	2.5	0.9
Azerbaijanis	6.8	2.4	Latvians	1.5	0.5
Armenians	4.6	1.6	Estonians	1.0	0.4
Tadzhiks	4.2	1.5			

Note: The population figures are based on the Soviet census of 1989. The Soviet population was 286.2 million at that point; a total of 125 nationality populations are recorded.

Source: Map from *Newsweek* (3/14/88) by Ib Ohlsson. Copyright 1988 by Newsweek. Reprinted by permission. Table based on data from Hough (1990).

One curious symbol of the domestic turmoil in the Soviet Union is the renewed interest in and even adulation of the czar (tsar). In this photograph, Russian Orthodox faithful gather in September 1990 outside their newly reopened Upensky Cathedral in Moscow carrying a banner proclaiming "God is with us" and displaying a portrait of the last Russian czar, Nicholas II. He and his family were captured by the Bolsheviks in March 1917, and in July 1918 Lenin ordered them all shot to death in the Ural Mountains city of Ekaterinburg (now Sverdlovsk). According to historian Roy Medvedev, the interest in the czar is "all connected with the fact that the prestige of the Communist Party is falling" and as people move to oppose the party they are apt to be sympathetic to the victims of the party, even the tyrannical czar (*HC,* 11/4/90:A25). In fact, Sverdlovsk's Russian Orthodox Archbishop Melkhisedek predicts that the czar "will of course be canonized as a saint. It is a matter of time" (*NYT,* 11/16/90:A1).

letter, Soviet president Gorbachev issued an executive order restoring Soviet citizenship to 23 prominent exiles, one of which was Solzhenitsyn.

What will happen to the Soviet Union next is uncertain. President Gorbachev has proposed a looser federation, and he may succeed in holding the country together (Motyl, 1989). On a rational level, it is hard to imagine the Soviet Union completely collapsing into 10 to 15 independent countries. One problem would be the economy, which has become highly interdependent. For example, the Russians produce 75 percent of the natural gas; the Uzbeks produce two-thirds of the country's cotton; and the Ukrainians are major grain producers for everyone. There would also be massive population disruptions. Partly because of Moscow's desire to dilute the national minorities, a total of 60 million Russians and other nationalities live outside their own ethnic republics. Perhaps a half million people have already become refugees because of the national unrest, and further devolution would intensify the problem with possible violent consequences. Nationalism is not a rational process, however. Therefore in the last analysis the future of the Soviet Union and its constituent parts as one state or as many states will not be determined as much by rational discourse as by emotional imperative.

There are many international ramifications of the national fate of the Soviet Union apart from the fact that it might cease to exist as such. National minority unrest could bring support from nearby ethnic cousins and, in turn, confrontation with Moscow. The struggle for independence by Lithuania, Latvia, and Estonia has captured the imagination of many in the West, and Moscow's policy, especially the 1991 military crackdown, has been the subject of considerable criticism from and tension with the Western countries. It is even possible that Gorbachev's nationalities problem, along with his other travails, could lead to his peaceful or violent overthrow by old-guard forces bent on preserving the old idea of a union of soviet socialist republics, restoring Communist ascendancy, and resuming the cold war.

Multinationalism also besets the Third World. Many multinational states there are unstable because the various ethnic groups perceive that they have little in common, and one or more may wish to establish an independent political entity. Indeed, in many African and Asian countries "nationality" is largely a fiction based on former colonial boundaries. Nigeria, Africa's most populous country, is a prime example. When Nigeria became independent in 1960, most of its people politically identified themselves as being Hausas, Ibos, Yorubas, or members of other ethnic groups rather than as being a Nigerian. Tensions built up, and in 1967 the Ibo nation declared its independence and established the Republic of Biafra. The result was a tragic, three-year civil war in which 1.5 million Nigerians were killed before Ibo independence died in the ashes of Biafra. This pattern has been repeated too frequently, with the latest example occurring in Liberia. In 1990 a vicious civil war partly based on ethnic rivalries between the Krahns and the Gios raged, and before the Krahn-dominated government was finally toppled by the Gio-led rebels, 5,000 mostly noncombatant Liberians were slaughtered.

A civil war, like Nigeria's or Liberia's, is of course a domestic event and not formally a part of international affairs. But very often humanitarian concerns, power politics, or sympathy for ethnic kin in the warring country tempts other countries to intervene. In recent years, Sri Lanka, the Sudan, Ethiopia, Angola, Uganda, Mozambique, and other countries have all been torn by civil war at least partly related to national or ethnic groups' rivalries, and each of these conflicts also occasioned at least indirect outside intervention.

Nations in More Than One State   A second type of departure from the nation-state ideal involves **multistate nationalities**. This phenomenon occurs when a nation overlaps the borders of two or more states. There are three basic patterns of multistate nationalities. One pattern that can be found is a nation-state with elements of its national group in one or more surrounding states. Such a situation creates the potential for conflict since the nation-state serves as a magnet for those of the same nationality who live across the border in the neighboring state. They may wish to join the "fatherland" and the fatherland may lay claim to the area in which they live. This demand is called *irredentism,* after the phrase *Italia irredenta* ("Italy unredeemed"). An example of the conflict this pattern may cause occurred in the 1930s when Germany sought to incorporate into a greater Germany the German nationals who lived in Austria, Poland, and the Sudetenland region of Czechoslovakia.

A second pattern of the multistate nationality phenomenon occurs when a national group is a minority in two or more states and does not have a nation-state of its own. As such, the national group constitutes a *non-state nation.* The Palestinians, who are spread throughout Israel, Lebanon, Jordan, and Egypt, are one example. Another is the Kurds, who live in Iran, Iraq, Turkey, Syria, and the Soviet Union. The sporadic and continuing attempts of the Kurds to establish an independent Kurdistan have led to conflicts with the countries in which they now live. One result in the late 1980s was chemical weapons attacks by the Iraqi government on its rebellious Kurds.

The third pattern occurs when a nationality is split between two states and is a majority in both. North and South Vietnam, North and South Korea, East and West

TABLE 6.1

Characteristics of a Microstate, a Canadian Province, and a Canadian City

	Nauru	Prince Edward Island	Toronto
Population (1989)	8,100	130,000	650,000
Territory (sq. mi.)	8	2,180	37.5

Data source: Canadian World Almanac (1990).

Germany, and the two Yemens are or were examples. Such a division causes almost a natural urge to reunite, and today only Korea remains divided. But there is often conflict over which of the two political systems will dominate. This has led to armed conflict in three of the examples (Korea, Vietnam, Yemen) and considerable cold-war tension over Germany.

Overall, then, the lack of fit between nations and states has been a major source of conflict. Given the rampant nationalism that still exists, it is likely to continue as a problem. One study, for instance, found some 61 national groups with separatist potential (Gastil, 1981). Areas like Africa are such a patchwork quilt of nations and states that the Organization of African Unity has refused to give aid to secessionist movements. As President Julius Nyerere of Tanzania put it, "African boundaries are so absurd that they need to be recognized as sacrosanct" (Jensen, 1982:58). That may be a good thought for states that are, but it will surely meet with violent objection from nations that wish to be.

The Issue of Microstates

The rapidly growing number of independent countries, many of which have a marginal ability to survive on their own, has increasingly raised the issue of the reasonable limits to the principle of self-determination. At what point does a lofty principle become pragmatically unrealistic? The basic issues revolve around the wisdom of allowing the formation of what have been called **microstates**, or countries with tiny populations, territories, and/or economies. In one sense, such countries have long existed, with Monaco, Andorra, and San Marino serving as examples. But in recent years, as colonialism has become discredited, more of these microstates have become established.

Many of the current microstates do not have the economic or political ability to stand as truly sovereign states as can be seen in Table 6.1's comparison of the South Pacific island Republic of Nauru, Canada's smallest province, and one of Canada's leading cities. There are 38 states, almost one-quarter of all the world's countries, with populations less than 1 million. In fact, as Figure 6.5 depicts, if you added up all their populations, they would amount to only 10,668,000 people, slightly more than the population of Cuba, less than half the population of California, and even less than the population of Mexico City.

The perplexity about microstates is that it is simultaneously possible to support the theory of self-determination and to worry about the political liability that microstates

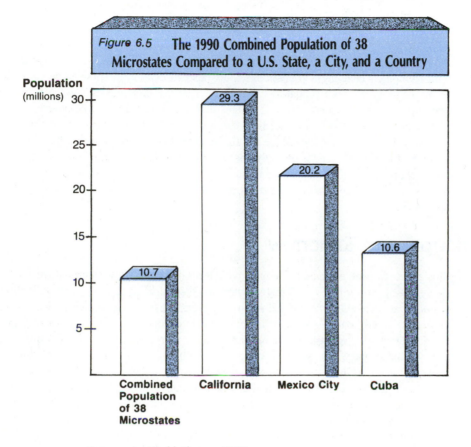

Figure 6.5   The 1990 Combined Population of 38 Microstates Compared to a U.S. State, a City, and a Country

Data source: World Almanac (1991).

cause. This quandary is made all the more difficult by the fact that it is usually not the microstates themselves but the larger powers, which are tempted to intervene, that are the real danger. Further, the problem is apt to multiply. There are another 30 or so colonial dependencies that have at least some potential for national unrest and perhaps statehood. What does one do about Britain's Pitcairn Islands, of *Mutiny on the Bounty* fame, with a population of 63 that has been restive? How should we view the aspirations of the people of the Torres Strait Islands, a tropical archipelago of 15 islands, including the charmingly-named Tuesday, Wednesday, and Thursday, that is inhabited by 5,000 Melanesians and lies off the north coast of Australia?

In a perfect world, the military and economic strength of a state would not matter. But in the imperfect world in which microstates exist, it does count. Countries that are unable to defend themselves and that have a marginal economic existence invite outside interference by and clashes between stronger powers. "Clearly," one scholar put it, "the world's microstates . . . have the ability to cause macropolitical havoc" (Harden, 1985:4). Grenada serves as a good example. A small island of 110,000 people that lies off Venezuela's north coast, Grenada became a victim of the cold war. Its leftist government had received Soviet and Cuban help, including Cuban military advisers and the laying out of an airfield on which the CIA thought high-power military aircraft could land and take off. Whatever the truth of the matter, the result was an American invasion in 1983 that toppled the leftists, ousted the Cubans, and added to the violence of the world.

Shridath Ramphal, the (British) Commonwealth secretary-general, was undoubtedly correct when he observed, "The truth . . . is that the world community has not yet thought its way through the phenomenon of very small states." One can even sympathize with Ramphal's challenging question, "Must [a small country's] survival be contingent on its capacity to repel predators?" (Harden, 1985:5). It is easier for the secretary-general to raise the question of microstates than it is to resolve the conundrum. In an ideal world, where the lambs and lions lie down together and where universal mutual responsibility reigns, independence for any self-identifying group would be admirable. In the real world, this idea is not only unattainable, it is destabilizing. It may well be that levels of domestic autonomy and guarantees of human and political rights for subcultural groups are a wiser course than the support of self-determination to the point of *reductio ad absurdum*.

Nationalism: Tomorrow and Tomorrow

This discussion of nationalism began with the observation that nationalism has not always been, nor will it necessarily always be, the world's principal form of political orientation. What will follow it and when, however, is difficult to predict. At least for the immediate future, barring a major upheaval, nationalism seems to have a firm grip on our consciousness. We still revere Nathan Hale for regretting that he had but one life to lose for his country, and we still sympathize with Philip Nolan, the tragic figure in Edward Everett Hale's *Man Without a Country*.

There are voices, however, that see nationalism as a weakening philosophy and those who advocate its end. Louis Snyder, one of the leading scholars on nationalism, has listed the arguments of those who see a coming end to nationalism: (1) Increased cross-cultural interaction is lessening the nationalistic we/they image of other peoples in the world. (2) The intermestic (merging of *inter*national and do*mestic* issues) nature of politics is creating a heightened sense of internationalism. (3) The nation-state can no longer cope with problems such as ecology, food production, and disease prevention. (4) In a supersonic, nuclear age, the nation-state can no longer protect its people. (5) Given its history of causing conflict, nationalism is condemned by the moral judgment of history. (6) Multinational corporations and interdependence are ending economic nationalism. (7) There is an indefinable, but real, psychological trend toward a new world order. International organization is expanding, and transnational philosophies (such as communism) have a strong appeal (1976:266–69).

Still, Snyder and others conclude that, for a variety of reasons, nationalism remains the world's most powerful and resilient "ism." We can bemusedly tolerate a politically powerless Albert Einstein saying, "It is beyond me to keep secret my international orientation. The state to which I belong as a citizen does not play the least role in my spiritual life; I regard allegiance to a government as a business matter, somewhat like the relationship with a life insurance company" (Snyder, 1976:ix). But it is a different story when a presidential candidate like Edmund G. Brown, Jr., tells us that we all live together on "spaceship Earth," as he did in 1976, and that we should have to sacrifice our own wealth for humanity's common good. In this case, we sighed and wrote Brown off as one of those overly mellow Californians and his campaign soon died. Again, in 1988, nationalism became a presidential campaign issue when George Bush criticized Michael Dukakis for vetoing a proposed Massachusetts law requiring teachers to lead the pledge of allegiance before class. Governor Dukakis tried to explain his action as protecting freedom of speech, but many Americans were dismayed, and the issue was one of many that helped elect President Bush.

Chapter Summary

1. Nationalism is one of the most important factors in international politics. It defines where we put our primary political loyalty, and that is in the nation-state. Today, the world is divided and defined by nationalism and nation-states.

2. This focus has grown for about five centuries.

3. After World War II, some predicted an end to nationalism, but they were wrong. Today nationalism is stronger, and the independence of the Afro-Asian nations has made it even more inclusive.

4. Nationalism has both positive and negative aspects.

5. On the plus side, nationalism has promoted democracy, self-government, economic growth, and social/political/economic diversity and experimentations.

6. On the negative side, nationalism has led to isolationism, feelings of superiority, suspicion of others, jingoism, messianism, and aggressiveness. Nationalism can also cause instability when there is a lack of fit between states and nations. Domestic instability and foreign intervention are often the result of such national instability. Nationalism has also led to a multiplicity of microstates.

7. In a world of transnational global forces and problems, many condemn nationalism as outmoded and perilous. Some even predict its decline and demise. Such predictions are, however, highly speculative, and nationalism will remain a key element and powerful force in the forseeable future.

Thrice is he armed that has his quarrel just.

Shakespeare, *Henry VI*, Part II

The devil can cite Scripture for his purpose.

Shakespeare, *The Merchant of Venice*

The ruling ideas of each age have been the ideas of its ruling class.

Karl Marx, *The Communist Manifesto*

You are either in favor of evil or you are in favor of good. You are either on the side of the oppressed or on the side of the oppressor. You cannot be neutral.

Bishop Desmond Tutu,
address to the U.S. Congress, 1984

CHAPTER 7

IDEAS, IDEOLOGY, AND MORALITY

The great French philosopher René Descartes defined the essence of being a human when he wrote, "I think, therefore I am." People can think abstractly. They can conceive of what they have not experienced, and they can group ideas together to try to explain existence and to chart courses of action.

This chapter is about the force of ideas in international relations. The essential task is to look at the great "causes" that help shape world politics. We have already covered the force of ideas in a number of contexts. The role of individual perceptions is one example. Nationalism has also been classified as an ideological force by some scholars, and, in fact, some aspects of nationalism, such as messianism, could just as well be included in this chapter as in the previous one.

The ideas and ideologies we will explore here, however, are distinguished by several characteristics. First, they are transnational. This means that large numbers of people hold a similar concept and that adherents are not confined to a single country. Second, they are internationally action-oriented. They urge a course of action on their believers. Third, they have a coherent set of symbols. Often such "gospels" have a "bible" such as the Koran or *The Communist Manifesto*. Prophets, be they Muhammad or Marx, are another symbolic anchor. Other ideas, such as democracy, are less focused, but they still have their important writings and philosophers.[1]

---

1. The entire issue of *The Jerusalem Journal of International Relations* (1987:9:1) is devoted to an excellent discussion of ideology and its role in international relations. In addition to general discussions, there are articles relating to ideology and the Soviet Union, the United States, France, Great Britain, and the African states.

We will explore these motivational forces by first discussing several broad categories: (1) religious, (2) social, (3) economic, (4) political, and (5) humanitarian and moral ideas. A second important point will be discussion of the role ideas play in world events.

Before going further, it would be wise to define and distinguish between ideas and ideologies. Ideas are more specific and less complex than ideologies. Believing or not believing that we human beings have a moral obligation to oppose the apartheid policies of South Africa's white regime is an idea. An **ideology**, by contrast, is more complex and includes:

> a set of fundamental beliefs, a belief system that explains and justifies a preferred political order for a society, either one that already exists or one that is proposed, and offers at least a sketchy notion of strategy (processes, institutional arrangement, programs) for its maintenance or attainment. Ideology thus refers to a preferred domestic political order, but by extension it may imply or even articulate the notion of a preferred international order as well. (George, 1987:1)

Democracy is an example of an ideology. It is primarily a domestic political doctrine, but it also has profound international political implications, which were discussed in chapter 5, as well as social, religious, and humanitarian consequences. Of course, the line between a simple idea and a complex ideology is fuzzy in practice. A religion, such as Islam, is not an ideology in the strictest sense, but it certainly involves conceptual complexity with impact on the secular as well as spiritual life of the world. This is particularly true when the adherents of a spiritual concept actively apply their beliefs to secular political goals, such as pan-Islamic solidarity and assertiveness.

Types of Ideas and Ideologies

When "ideology" is mentioned, it is probable that "communism" is the word association you make. But communism is only one, and a recent one at that, of the many ideas that have shaped the world.

Religion

Religion is one of the most ancient forces that have influenced world events. It has played a dual role in world politics. In one sense it has been the source of humanitarian concern and pacifism. The Roman Catholic Church, or elements therein, has been part of the antinuclear movement and has acted as a sponsor of social reform through liberation theology in Latin America, and has played other roles as discussed in chapter 3. Hinduism was an important element in Gandhi's pacifism and continues to influence India's foreign policy.

At the other extreme, religion has played a role in some of the bloodiest wars in history. The expansion of Islam following the death of Muhammad (A.D. ?570–632) and the doctrine of the jihad, or holy war, set off a series of clashes, including the Crusades (eleventh through thirteenth centuries), between the equally expansionist Islamic and Christian worlds that lasted for a thousand years. The Protestant Reformation (1517) divided Christianity, and the resulting rivalry between Protestants and Catholics was one cause of the Thirty Years' War (1618–48) and other conflicts. Religion also played a role in the imperial era. Catholic and Protestant missionaries were early European explorers and colonizers of North America, Africa, Asia, and the Pacific. Whatever its good intent and works, the missionary movement also served in many cases to promote and legitimize the political, economic, and cultural subjugation of local people by outsiders.

Religious conflict, despite its archaic sound, is not a thing of the past. Religious differences continue to be a source of conflict or to serve as an aggravating factor. When Great Britain gave up its colonial control of the Indian subcontinent after World War II, that area was divided between the Muslims and the Hindus. Countless members of each faith were killed in the ensuing conflict and in the subsequent wars between India and the newly created state of Pakistan. Recently, discontent within Kashmir, which is mostly Muslim but which lies within India adjacent to Pakistan, has led to attacks and reprisals that threaten to plunge India and Pakistan off the precipice of war once again. Divisions within religions also continue to cause conflict. The conflict among the Sunni and Shi'ite sects of Islam, discussed below, played a role in the war between Iran and Iraq. Religion sometimes serves to define and sharpen ethnic and national differences. The Jews of largely European heritage versus the Muslim Arabs, the conflict among the Christians, Muslims, and Druze in Lebanon, and the struggle between the Catholics and Protestants of Northern Ireland are three examples of current importance.

The Role of Islam

Of all the dimensions of the interaction between religion and politics that exist in today's world, none is so important as the role of Islam. Given the importance of the Middle East, where Islam was founded and where it is still centered, given the strength of recently resurgent Islamic fundamentalism and assertiveness, and given the fact that the Western secularization of politics makes the idea of any religion acting as an autonomous political force a novel thesis, we ought to halt here to examine in some detail this ancient yet modern force (Pepes, 1984).

There are in this world nearly 1 billion Muslims, about one-fifth of all humanity. They are a majority not only in the Middle East but also in countries like Pakistan, Turkey, Indonesia, Iran, and Algeria. There are other countries, such as Nigeria and the Philippines, in which Muslims constitute an important political force. Indeed, only about one of every four Muslims lives in the Middle East. Wherever their location, during most of this century they were dominated by non-Islamic powers. Direct political domination ended with the collapse of colonialism, but foreign control frequently persisted through indirect neocolonialist techniques. Indirect domination has been at least partly eclipsed by the growth of oil power, and there has been a concurrent growth of Islamic fundamentalism, pride, and militancy that have interacted with and supplemented the nationalism of Islamic countries.

Islam and the Non-Islamic World   The impact of Islam on world politics has been sharp and can roughly be divided between the interaction between Islam and the non-Islamic world on the one hand, and the ramifications of intra-Islamic rivalry and its international impact on the other.

A central Islamic concept is the *ummah*, the spiritual, cultural, and political community of Muslims. The great prophet Muhammad founded Islam and was the first leader of the *ummah*. When he died, his successor Abu-Bakr took the title of *khalifat rasul Allah* (successor of the messenger of God). This is an important title because it relates to the basic belief of Muslims that they theoretically should be united politically as well as religiously and headed by a khalif (caliph). Muslims distinguish between the lands controlled by Muslims, those inside the *ummah*, which they call "the house of Islam," and the lands controlled by non-Muslims, which are termed "the house of war." One of the fundamental tenets of Islam is the jihad, a holy war or "struggle in the way of God," and Allah's holy warriors are sometimes called *mujahedin*. Muslims believe that mujahedin who become martyrs by dying in a jihad are assured a place in paradise.

In the early days of Islam, these beliefs translated into a period of rapid religious and political expansion, partly by conversion, partly by the conquest of others, that led at its height to Muslim domination of large areas including Spain and south-central Europe. That does not mean that the concept of jihad makes Islam perpetually aggressive, however. It can just as easily be interpreted as meaning the defense of the house of Islam from outside encroachment—spiritual, political, or cultural.

This latter meaning is the main thrust of the current Islamic revival. Muslims who have escaped formal colonial rule wish also to rid themselves of indirect domination by outside powers. Fundamentalists also want to return to a true Muslim society governed by Islamic law and purged of Western cultural influences. In the words of one student of the Middle East, fundamentalists reject the "Coca-Colaization" of their way of life (Goldschmidt, 1983:320).

These drives have had a number of impacts on world politics. One is the upsurge of anti-Western (and in some cases anti-Soviet) feeling in Iran and elsewhere in the Middle East. Islam's new assertiveness is part of what might be called a "Muslim pride" movement. After centuries of outside domination during which their culture and economic circumstances declined along with their political power, the people in the region that stretches from Morocco to Afghanistan have begun to try to reclaim true independence. Part of that independence is political, and it involves rejecting direct interference by outside powers, be they the Soviet Union in Afghanistan or the United States in Lebanon. Independence also means mutual support for the strengthening of the Muslim countries. This idea is symbolized by the Organization of the Islamic Conference (depicted in Fig. 7.1). Islamic solidarity's policy impacts have ranged from coordination to protect Islamic holy places, through support of the Palestinian Liberation Organization, to the backing of some Muslim leaders for Pakistan's efforts to be the first Muslim country to build a nuclear weapon (referred to by some as the "Islamic bomb").

Second, the common tie of Islam has helped promote pan-Arab sentiment among many Middle East Muslims. This pan-Arab feeling has led to the establishment of some regional cooperation (the Arab League, for example) and even attempts to merge countries. A third impact of the Islamic revival is that the concept of the *ummah* has also led Muslim countries to support the political and economic aspirations of their co-religionists. Iraq's invasion of Kuwait appalled most Muslims, for example, but many were also upset by the intervention of non-Muslim military forces, as the box on page 172 explains.

An interesting question is whether the upsurge of Islamic fundamentalism and pride will lead to a truly united *ummah* and a rebirth of the Islamic confrontation with the house of war. The answer is uncertain, of course, and there are Muslims, especially among the most zealous Shi'ites, who advocate such a course. In all likelihood, though, a number of factors will prevent this. One is ethnic differences (Mozaffari, 1987; Shepard, 1987). Iranians, Afghans, and Pakistanis, for example, are not Arabs and do not speak Arabic. A second factor is nationalism. Individual Muslim countries, like most newly independent states, are fiercely nationalistic. Thus, it is probable that divisions within Islam, especially between Sunnis and Shi'ites, will continue to frustrate any attempts to establish a politically unified *ummah*.

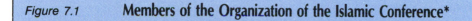

| Figure 7.1 | Members of the Organization of the Islamic Conference* |

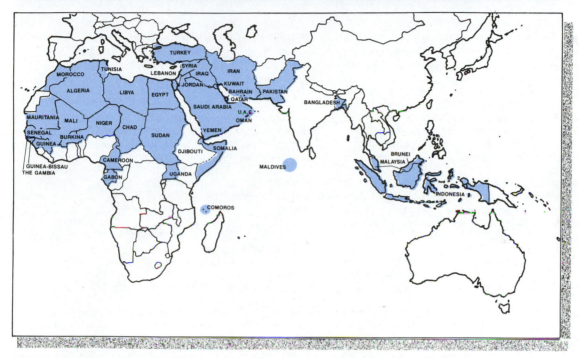

*While not depicted on the map, the Palestine Liberation Organization is a member of the Islamic Conference.
**United Arab Emirates.

As you can see from this map of the Islamic Conference, Muhammadanism is not confined to the Arab states in the Middle East.

Islamic Sectarianism and World Politics   As just noted, religion is not always a source of Islamic unity. Instead, within the house of Islam, intrareligious differences are one of the main sources of conflict. All the various sects condemn outside intervention in Islamic affairs, but they also struggle among themselves.

The most important division is between the majority Sunnis and the minority Shi'ites.[2] The fundamental issue between the two sects is the proper leadership of the *ummah*. Sunnis recognize Abu-Bakr and his successors and other caliphs as legitimate heirs to Muhammad's leadership of the *ummah*. Shi'ites reject this ascendancy. Instead they believe that the only proper *imams* (spiritual leaders) are those who are descended from Ali, who was both Muhammad's first cousin and his daughter's husband. Among other things, the Shi'ites remain bitter about the fate of Ali's son (and Muhammad's grandson) Hussein, who was tortured and beheaded when he tried to claim the caliphate in 680.

2. The word "Sunni" comes from "sunnah," or the "tradition of the Prophet," that is, the sayings and actions of Muhammad that teach Muslims the correct interpretation of their faith. The sunnah is next to the Koran as a guide for Muslims. Shi'ite (sometimes Shi'i) stems from the phrase "Shi'at Ali," or "Party of Ali," the early name of those who believed in his line of caliphs. It should also be noted that there are other sects and subjects of Islam. The Wahabi, for example, are a particularly strict, puritanical Sunni subsect centered in Saudi Arabia.

Islam, Neocolonialism, Zionism, the House of War, and the Appeal of Saddam Hussein

Many Americans and others in the West found it very difficult to understand Muslims' often ambivalent attitudes toward Saddam Hussein in the aftermath of Iraq's August 1990 invasion of Kuwait. After all, wasn't it clear that Hussein had attacked and swallowed up a small neighbor, an Arab and Muslim neighbor at that? Hadn't Iraq fought an extremely bloody eight-year war with Iran and threatened Saudi Arabia? And if Hussein had done all that, didn't he represent a threat to all the countries in the region?

Westerners could further reason that their response to Iraq's aggression was rapid and generous. Soon there were over a hundred thousand American, British, French, and other troops enduring scorpions and sandstorms in the Saudi Arabian desert and sweltering in the heat of the Persian Gulf. At home, jobs and loved ones were temporarily forsaken by the responding troops, and the cost of Operation Desert Shield soared into the billions of dollars.

Yet for all of Saddam Hussein's sins, the UN's condemnation, and the readiness of the West to respond, there seemed to be a current of Muslim sympathy for, even admiration of, Hussein. How could that be? It was true, of course, that Islamic Saudi Arabia had requested the protection of the United States and other non-Muslim countries. It was also the case that several Muslim countries such as Egypt and Syria had joined in the international effort to deter further Iraqi aggression and to restore Kuwait's independence. Still, Hussein seemed to have a wide appeal.

Hussein's emotional magnetism for many Muslims was grounded in Islam and the history of the Middle East. There are important differences within Islam, and there are also national rivalries among Muslim states. But these religious and secular rifts tend to be subordinated to Islamic unity when there is a threat to an Islamic state from non-Muslims. This reaction to the traditional Islamic view of struggle between the house of Islam and the infidels' house of war is increased by Muslim resentment of colonial and neocolonial domination by the West. From this perspective, the Iraqi call for a *jihad* against the Western interlopers in order to restore Islamic ascendancy was appealing to many Muslims. "I love any Arab leader who will unite the Arabs, even by force" a Jordanian military officer said. "We want to see one empire restoring our culture to its former glory" (*Time*, 8/27/90:26). A taxi driver in Amman agreed. Hussein "is really fighting for the people who are suffering ever since the [Muslim] Ottoman Empire disappeared," he rea-

soned. "Even if Saddam invaded Jordan, he will be at least an Arab, at least a Muslim" (*HC*, 9/23/90:E4). The strength of this image of confrontation between the house of Islam and the house of war in many Muslim minds was evident in the reaction of Iran's clergy. These Shi'ite clerics who had led the long, terrible *jihad* against Saddam Hussein's Sunni regime urged Muslims to unite to destroy the infidel invaders. The Ayatollah Ali Khamenei, who became Iran's spiritual leader after the Ayatollah Khomeini's death in June 1989, branded the Western intervention "greedy, bullying, and shameless. . . . Anyone who fights America's aggression, its greediness, and its plans to encroach on . . . the region has engaged in *jihad* in the cause of Allah, and anyone who is killed on that path is a martyr [and will go to paradise]," the Ayatollah promised (*HC*, 9/13/90:A14).

Iraq was also able to exploit the vast gulf between the opulent existence of Kuwait's emir (and other oil sheiks and monarchs) and the poor Arabs in Jordan, Yemen, and elsewhere. Resentment over the chasm in circumstances was further exacerbated by the belief of many in the region that the royal families of Kuwait and some of the other oil-producing states in the region were neocolonialist pawns of the Western countries. "Make it clear to your rulers, the emirs of oil, [who] serve the foreigner," Saddam Hussein told the Arab masses, that for "traitors there is no place . . . on Arab soil after they humiliated Arab honor and dignity." Many poor Arabs felt little sympathy with the Mercedes-driving emirs. "The oil belongs to all Arabs," agreed a Muslim newspaperman. "This wealth is our only chance to develop the Arab world. People know that Saddam wants to help the poor Arab nations" (*Time*, 8/27/90:26).

Saddam Hussein also adroitly worked to merge Arab hostility toward Israel and their feeling of oppression by the West. He charged the West with practicing a double standard: condemning his move into Kuwait while supporting Israel's occupation of the West Bank. That struck a chord in many Arabs, including a Jordanian cleric who complained that "the big trouble with the Americans is that they don't propose sanctions against Israel, but only against Iraq. They are blinded by Zionist influence" (*Time*, 9/27/90:28).

Culture is a product of religion, history, and other forces. It creates the perceptions of good and evil discussed in chapter 4. Because of culture, what seemed surely evil to Westerners seemed less certainly so to Muslims. It is not necessary to agree with an opponent's point of view, but it is always wise to understand it.

In recent years the sometimes quiescent Sunni-Shi'ite rivalry was reignited by Iran's Ayatollah Khomeini. Iran is Shi'ite, and some Shi'ites believed that Khomeini was the messianic *Mahdi* who they believe will come to lead Shi'ism first to triumph over the Sunnis within the house of Islam (thereby resurrecting the *ummah*), and then to ascendancy over the house of war. Clashes with other Muslim states have been caused by the Shi'ite effort to achieve victory over the Sunnis as encouraged by Khomeini and as continued by Iran's other ayatollahs (a Shi'ite title of scholarship in the *Shari'ah,* or Islamic law). The most serious was Iran's war with Iraq (1980–88) with millions of casualties. There were territorial and other nationalistic causes behind the war, but it was complicated by Khomeini's determination to overthrow Iraq's Sunni-dominated regime. Iran's relations with Saudi Arabia have also been troubled. The Saudi monarchy is Sunni, and it controls Mecca and Medina, which (along with Jerusalem) are the holiest cities of Islam. Iranian Shi'ites consider Sunni guardianship of the holy places to be illegitimate and wish to replace it with Shi'ite protection. This view helps explain Iran's inconsistent policy during the 1990 Middle East crisis based on the policy struggle between Iran's ayatollahs and the somewhat more moderate secular government of President Hashemi Rafsanjani.

The lesson you should draw here is not that religion and politics are an explosive mix. That is not true. In some cases, such as the American Catholic bishops' general disapproval of nuclear arms, religion is a force for peace. It is also not true that resurgent Islam is an aggressive, violent movement. To a substantial degree, it is merely reacting against what Muslims perceive to be the wrongs of the recent past and attempting to uplift the status and circumstances of Muslims everywhere.

The point is that religion, with its political and social ramifications, is an important factor in international relations. Like any set of coherent ideas, it helps define who is on which side, and it often plays a powerful role in shaping the perceptions of political leaders and the actions of the countries they command.

Social Theories

Social theories—theories about the nature of world society and about the roles and the importance of various types of people—have also had an impact on world politics. Racism, for example, combined with nationalism to help encourage and justify imperialism. The ideas of biologist Charles Darwin in *The Origin of Species* (1859) were thoroughly corrupted to allow the exploitation of the "unfit" (nonwhites) by the "fit" (whites). Racism also joined with religion to build a case in the Western mind that subjugation was in the interest of the uncivilized and pagan—that is, nonwhite, non-Christian—societies. Symbolic of this racist self-justification is Rudyard Kipling's "White Man's Burden," penned in 1899 to urge Americans to seize the Philippines.

The appeal of Saddam Hussein to many non-Iraqi Arabs is difficult for Westerners to understand. Many Arabs supported the Iraqi leader, even if they feared him, because of Muslim unity against the "infidels." Saddam Hussein was also seen by some poor Arabs as their champion against the wealthy oil royalty. He was also perceived by some as a leader who could restore the Arabs to the political and cultural world prominence that they once held. Saddam Hussein encouraged these images, as can been seen in this regal billboard. He also posed in a chariot resembling that of the great Babylonian king, Nebuchadnezzar, and compared himself to Saladin, a warrior king who united the region and battled the invading Christian crusaders 800 years ago. Ironically, Saladin was a Kurd; Saddam Hussein described the Kurds in Iraq as traitors and has attacked and killed thousands of them with chemical weapons.

Take up the White Man's burden—
    Send forth the best ye breed—
Go bind your sons to exile
    To serve your captives' need;
To wait in heavy harness
    On fluttered folk and wild—
Your new-caught sullen peoples,
    Half devil and half child.

Take up the White Man's burden—
    And reap his old reward:
The blame of those ye better
    The hate of those ye guard—
The cry of hosts ye humor
    (Ah, slowly!) toward the light:—
"Why brought ye us from bondage,
    Our beloved Egyptian night?"

This sort of bastardized **social Darwinism** also reared its head as a component of Italian fascism and the related German credo of National Socialism. The Führer proclaimed that war and conquest were "all in the natural order of things—for [they make] for the survival of the fittest." Race was a particular focus of conflict because, Hitler asserted in *Mein Kampf*, "all occurrences in world history are only expressions of the races' instinct of self-preservation." This racist social theory was an important part of the Nazi *Weltanschauung* (world view) and gave Hitler what one scholar called "a universal missionary objective" that helped determine his foreign policy (Blum, 1971:212).

Horribly laughable as that sort of doctrine may seem, we should not delude ourselves into thinking it died in the ashes of the Third Reich. It is, among other places, alive and well in the Republic of South Africa. There, 6.5 million whites completely dominate the rest of the 29 million people in the country. The white South African policy of *apartheid*, or race separation/segregation, has become an international issue (1) because human rights have become more of a world concern, (2) because of growing tension between South Africa and (especially neighboring) black African countries, and (3) because under the guise of "separate development" the South African government has tried to set up "independent" black homelands (Transkei, Kwazulu, Bophuthatswana, Ciskei, and Venda). These "countries" are totally within the Republic of South Africa, economically unviable, and politically dependent on the white regime. In fact, they are little more than large concentration camps, but they let South Africa pretend it has eliminated its racial problems because, it says, very few blacks remain in the country.

The issue of South Africa has also become a foreign policy issue in many countries as they debate what to do about the problem. The British and American governments, for instance, have favored applying only limited pressure on South Africa while following a policy called "constructive engagement," that is, continuing diplomatically to persuade Pretoria, the administrative capital, to moderate its political and socio-economic oppression of blacks. Sanctions including trade restrictions and disinvestment (ending one's financial investment in South African companies) have been in place for several years at a cost of $27 billion to South Africa. There is continuing disagreement, however, over how strict sanctions should be and over their past and future impact. The debate during 1990 focused on whether to ease sanctions in response to reforms instituted by the government of South Africa's president, F. W. de Klerk. The most symbolic of these changes was the release of black leader Nelson Mandela after more than a quarter-century imprisonment. Additionally in 1990, de Klerk suspended the long-standing state of emergency in most of the country, legalized Mandela's African National Congress (ANC) and other formerly banned political parties, repealed some laws on social segregation, and opened constitutional-revision discussions with Mandela and other black leaders. De Klerk has not, however, ended many other limits on blacks, and he has not reversed his stand that "majority rule is not suitable for a country like South Africa." This would lead, de Klerk argues, "to the domination and even the suppression of minorities," a state of affairs that he evidently believes is more onerous than the domination and even the suppression of the majority (*HC*, 4/18/90:A12).

De Klerk has argued that his reforms should be rewarded by lessened sanctions, and in the autumn of 1990 he carried his case directly to President Bush in Washington. The South African president also argues privately that unless sanctions are eased he may lose power in the 1994 general elections to the most conservative white elements. The apartheid-forever Conservative Party already controls two-thirds of the country's municipal councils, and many of its adherents are arming themselves and are dedicated to reversing de Klerk's reforms.

Apartheid is an example of a social theory that affects both domestic and international politics. The oppression of South Africa's black majority by its white minority has caused many nations to place sanctions on South Africa. It has also led to the attitude exhibited in this photograph. Riot police used shotguns on protesting blacks in Capetown in October 1990. One of the dead protesters is shown here. We can also see his proud assailant who dared the press to take a picture of him and his trophy. In December 1990 the European Community voted to ease sanctions on South Africa in response to what the EC said was "progress" there.

Mandela and other ANC leaders oppose any move to moderate the sanctions. Speaking to the UN General Assembly in June 1990, Mandela argued that the "sanctions that have been imposed by the United Nations . . . should remain in place" (Mandela, 1990a). As he explained four days later in an address to a joint session of the U.S. Congress, "We still have a struggle on our hands. . . . The purpose for which [the sanctions] were imposed has not yet been achieved" (Mandela, 1990b).

For all of Mandela's prominence and symbolic power, however, he does not represent all South African black opinion. Mangosuthu Buthelezi, who heads both the Zulu nation and the Zulu-based Inkatha political and cultural movement, opposes international sanctions. He argues that they most severely penalize blacks, who are apt to be the first to lose their jobs in times of economic distress, and are likely to thrust South Africa "into the cauldron of revolution and . . . Third World chaos" (*HC*, 6/10/87:A9). Even more troubling, the ANC–Inkatha rivalry by 1990 was undermining the blacks' anti-apartheid struggle and had escalated into bloody clashes that by the end of the year had left more than 400 dead.

Economic Theories

The role of economic nationalism has already been noted in chapter 6. Beyond that limited application, though, **economic theories** have become one of this century's most important ideological forces. **Communism** is, in its origins, essentially economic in nature. It is an important factor in the foreign policies of the Soviet Union, China, and other communist-dominated countries. **Capitalism**, though a more amorphous doctrine, also has its committed adherents and affects world politics. These ideologies will be discussed fully below, but for the moment, it is sufficient to note that the clash between communism and capitalism has been a main element of the East/West struggle referred to in chapter 1.

Communism

Although now in steep decline, communism has been one of the most powerful forces of the twentieth century and deserves our attention here. Before we look at this far-reaching ideology, though, three caveats must be noted. First, communism is a complex set of ideas. We will be concentrating only on those with international political ramifications. Second, communism is not monolithic. Whatever its "pure" roots, it has been interpreted over time, place, and circumstance to meet the perspectives and needs of its adherents. Third, communism is flexible and has been only one part of the foreign policy equation in communist countries. You cannot understand Soviet or Chinese policy by only studying communism. But, equally, even today you cannot understand the foreign policy of those countries unless you take communist perceptions into account.

You do not have to read very widely these days to encounter an analytical obituary for communism or at least a grave report on its terminal illness as an ideology. It may well be that future historians will record the late twentieth century as the time of communism's death as a domestic and international political force. It is still too early, however, to treat communism as a matter of history rather than current events. There are several reasons to proceed cautiously before assigning communism to the dustbin of history. One is that there are still a number of countries, most prominently China, which advocate only slightly modified Marxism. To the Chinese leadership, the reforms instituted in the U.S.S.R. by Mikhail Gorbachev are tantamount to "subverting socialism" (*NYT,* 2/28/89:A1).

Second, even in the Soviet Union it is premature to discount the continuing influence of communism. Mikhail Gorbachev and most of the country's other leaders have spent their entire lives being schooled in communism, advocating it, and as members of the Communist party. They are no more capable of erasing this lifelong perspective than George Bush would be of suddenly becoming a Marxist. Furthermore, Gorbachev insists that his goal is reforming, not abandoning, communism. He maintains that his aim is to succeed in "the difficult challenge of reviving the authority of Marxist thought, the Marxist approach to reality" (*NYT,* 11/27/89:A12). Gorbachev even seems amused by those who are "probing my ideological position." "Well, I am a communist," Gorbachev smilingly told a recent interviewer. "I'm sure that answer doesn't make you too enthusiastic, but it shouldn't make you panic either. It's quite normal" (*Time,* 6/4/90:27).

A third reason for not prematurely joining the funeral cortege of communism is that the future remains, as always, uncertain. It is possible, for example, that Mikhail Gorbachev and his reforms may not survive politically. He and they may be toppled by old-guard elements of the Communist party and the state bureaucracy. As time passes this appears less likely, but it remains possible.

Communist ideology, associated with Karl Marx, tells its believers that history proceeds by means of a historical dialectic, or clash of opposing ideas (thesis versus antithesis), with a resulting new order, or synthesis. Communists also believe that the economic (material) order determines political and social relationships. Thus, history, the current situation, and the future are determined by the economic struggle, termed dialectical materialism.

The first Soviet Communist party chief, V. I. Lenin, applied dialectical materialism to international politics. Lenin argued in *Imperialism: The Highest Stage of Capitalism* (1916) that capitalist, bourgeois leaders had duped their proletariat workers into supporting the exploitation of other proletariat peoples through imperialism. Thus, the material dialectic was transformed, in part, from a domestic class struggle to an international struggle between bourgeois and proletariat countries and peoples.

Communism came crashing down in Eastern Europe during 1990. Symbolic of the downfall of the ideology and the collapse of the previously Soviet-backed communist governments in the region is the dismantling of a red star by Hungarians in Budapest.

During the 75 years that have elapsed since Lenin's declaration of international class struggle, successive Soviet leaders have gradually moved away from advocating confrontation, to proclaiming peaceful competition, to urging today what might be termed competitive cooperation. "Economic, political and ideological competition between capitalist and socialist countries is inevitable," Mikhail Gorbachev wrote in his book *Perestroika* (1987:148). "However, it can and must be kept within a framework of peaceful competition which necessarily envisages cooperation." In a September 1989 speech to the Council of Europe (of the European Community) in Strasbourg, France, Gorbachev (1989:705) called on all European countries to join with the Soviet Union in building a "Common European Home" based on the "interdependence and joint destinies of the European states." He continued to argue that "differences among the states are not removable," but he also suggested that they could even prove "favorable— provided, of course, that the competition between the different types of society is directed toward creating better material and spiritual living conditions for all people."

In the past, communism has influenced the states that espouse it in several ways. Because of the presumed conflict with the capitalist world, communist states have had something of a sense of insecurity. The communist countries have also often been ready to support revolutionary movements in the Third World, especially when they served to bedevil the major capitalist powers. As a messianic doctrine, communism has further urged its followers to spread the revolution when they could. As noted, however, the weakening of communism as a doctrine and the divergence of its application by the remaining communist countries make current generalizations difficult and predictions perilous. As Gorbachev himself said in a mid-1990 interview, the Soviet Union has undertaken a "shift in direction comparable in magnitude to the October Revolution" and it is "very demanding . . . to analyze where we are and anticipate where we are going" (*Time,* 6/4/90:30).

Capitalism

Perhaps more than any other "ism" that we cover, capitalism is an amorphous set of ideas. Many of the current texts on ideologies do not treat capitalism as a separate subject. But the idea of private enterprise as the main characteristic of a country's economic structure has played a role in world politics. The United States, in particular, has often equated economic capitalism with political freedom and has often confused economic socialism with the political suppression usually found in communist states.

177

This political opposition to noncapitalist states was most pronounced in the 1950s and has since declined. It made something of a comeback, however, under President Reagan. He blamed the problems of many Third World countries on their socialist systems. In particular, the Reagan administration was reluctant to give aid to most Third World countries; it argued that greater reliance on private enterprise, competition, and the profit motive, rather than foreign aid, was the route to economic development for the less developed countries. The Bush administration is less ideologically strident than its predecessor, but it continues to intermingle capitalism, freedom, and the possibility of good relations in its thinking. During a major foreign policy address, Secretary of State James A. Baker III (1989:1) optimistically explained that "there are two reasons why we think that the prospect for a lasting improvement in U.S.–Soviet relations is better than ever before." One factor, Baker said, was that "we in the West have demonstrated . . . [that] democracy and free market economics work, and work well together." By contrast, "the alternative vision advocated by the Soviet Union has failed to produce either prosperity or a free society. Simply put—freedom works! Communism doesn't!" Even better, the secretary said, the Soviet's "perestroika promises radical reform" in foreign policy because (here Baker approvingly quoted Gorbachev) "there exists an indissoluble link between the new foreign policy and perestroika within the country."

The concepts of capitalism have also contributed to imperialism and then neoimperialism, or the state of *dependencia* (see chapters 1 and 14), between much of the Third World and the industrialized countries. Individuals and corporations consider it legitimate to set up businesses in other countries and, some would say, exploit the host country's resources and workers in order to gain profits. As we will discuss fully in chapters 13 and 14, these multinational (or transnational) corporations (MNCs/TNCs) have often conducted operations that sought to maximize profits with little thought of the development of the host country. MNCs have frequently been supported by their home governments. During the early part of this century, for example, the United States urged an "Open Door" for China, that is, equal access for all countries, in order to protect U.S. trade opportunities there. The United States additionally practiced "Dollar Diplomacy" and sent its gunboats and marines to protect private investments in Latin America. United States insistence that its corporations be free to trade with all belligerents helped bring the country into World War I. After World War II, the United States pushed free trade so that its industry could expand and profit by filling the needs of the devastated world. And in recent years, the United States has often opposed moves by Third World countries to control the foreign economic enterprises within their borders, as exemplified by the U.S. cooperation with ITT and other U.S.–based MNCs to overthrow Chile's president Salvador Allende in 1973.

Political Theories

Although it has its own chapter in this book, nationalism, in its theoretical sense, has been treated by many scholars as a political ideology. Insofar as it is one, nationalism has had a tremendous impact during this century as the world rapidly changed from a system of a few states to a system of many. Another political ideology with an important historical role was *monarchism*. As a belief system, dynastic monarchism (which held that political loyalty should extend to the monarch, who ruled by right) struggled against liberal nationalism (which tended to favor democracy with power resting with the nation). For most of the 1800s the outcome hung in the balance. At times monarchism won out, as in the case of the restoration of the Bourbon monarchy in France in 1815, and the crushing of Hungarian nationalism by the czar's troops in 1848. By the end of World War I, however, with the overthrow of the German kaiser, the Austro-Hungarian emperor, and the Russian czar, the idea of dynastic monarchism was permanently eclipsed.

Next to nationalism, *democracy* is the political ideology with the greatest impact in the twentieth century. Although belief in and advocacy of democracy have not been confined to the United States, this country has been its particular champion. From the time that Woodrow Wilson called on Americans to follow him to war in order to "make the world safe for democracy," the United States has strongly, if not consistently, judged others by the standards of its democratic-liberal ideals. Even when the American government has supported authoritarian regimes, it has often faced a drumfire of domestic criticism. In recent years such events as the slackening of U.S. support for and the fall of the regimes of the Shah in Iran, President Anastazio Somoza in Nicaragua, Ferdinand Marcos in the Philippines, and Jean-Claude Duvalier in Haiti have been linked to the democratic impulse. Political freedom has not yet quite joined basic human rights as a universally acclaimed (if not practiced) standard, but democracy is a benchmark of legitimacy to many people.

At first thought, it is easy to assume that supporting democracy is a good practice. Yet there are a number of troubling issues involved. One is that it is not always clear what is democratic and what is not. Americans tend to equate democracy with procedure. If citizens are periodically allowed to choose among competing candidates, then there is democracy. Many other cultures in the world, by contrast, view democracy as a product; they equate it with equality. Americans also put a great stress on individual civil liberties, such as free speech. Other cultures stress the collective's welfare. During one of his first visits to the United States in the late 1980s, Mikhail Gorbachev was asked by a reporter about allowing democracy in the Soviet Union. An angry Gorbachev lectured the reporter about inequality in America, about the huge gap between the way people live in Hollywood, California, and in the Watts section of Los Angeles just a few miles away. In the U.S.S.R., Gorbachev said, there was only one party but there was also social and economic equality. That, he argued, was true democracy. From a related perspective, leaders of Third World countries have often argued that their struggle to create economic development and to feed, clothe, and otherwise attend to the needs of their people does not allow the "luxury" of Western-style democracy, which many observers believe is contentious and inefficient. Scholar Jacques Barzun (1989:23) makes much the same point when he suggests that "freedom calls for a government that governs least; equality for a government that governs most," and asks, "What is it exactly that we want others to copy?"

A second issue involved with democracy is whether democracy is always possible. In most of the West, where democracy exists most firmly, it has evolved slowly and often fitfully. Democracy is also the most secure in countries where the people are well educated and can maintain a reasonable standard of living. These circumstances do not exist in many countries, however. This may mean that attempts to promote full-fledged democracy in these countries is tantamount to trying to impose an alien political system on a socioeconomic system that is not ready for it. To quote Barzun (1989:20) again, democracy "cannot be promoted from outside by strangers; and it may still be impossible when attempted from inside. . . . Just as life on earth depended on a particular coming together of unrelated factors, so a cluster of disparate elements and conditions is needed for a democracy to be born viable."

A third issue about democracy is how to promote it in others—assuming that is a good idea in the first place. The debate in the United States is whether to promote democracy by example only or whether to be a more active democratic missionary—using persuasion, trade and aid, and sometimes military force to spread the doctrine. Interestingly, both options have biblical, messianic origins for Americans. The example option is often referred to as the "city on the hill" model. This refers to a lay sermon delivered by John Winthrop, first governor of Massachusetts, in 1630. In the manner of the day, Winthrop called on his fellow colonists to follow high standards of conduct "for wee must Considr that wee shall be as a Citty upon a Hill, the eies of all the people are uppon us" (Paterson, 1989:28). Winthrop's imagery was drawn from the Sermon on the Mount in the New Testament gospel of Saint Matthew: "Ye are the light of the world. A city that is set on a hill cannot be hid. . . . Let your light shine before [people] so that they may see your good works." This image of leadership by example has influenced the foreign policy beliefs of many Americans up to the present, but one of the most eloquent expositions was by John Quincy Adams, who wrote in 1823:

> Wherever the standard of freedom and Independence has been or shall be unfurled, there will her [America's] heart, her benediction and her prayers be. But she goes not abroad in search of monsters to destroy. . . . She well knows that by once enlisting under other banners than her own, were they even the banners of foreign independence, she would involve herself beyond the power of extrication. . . . The fundamental maxims of her policy would change from liberty to force. (Clifford, 1989:15)

A competing democratic impulse is to spread the gospel. Wilson's attempt at making the world safe for democracy extended beyond setting a good example; it included going off to war in Europe. This motive has continued through the balance of the century, and it figured prominently in the explanations of Ronald Reagan's arming the Contra rebels in Nicaragua and George Bush's ordering the invasion of Panama. Some critics cynically dismiss such rhetoric as a cover for less noble power politics or imperialism. They also point to repeated instances of U.S. support of right-wing dictatorships in the past. These charges are true to a point, but they miss Americans' messianic, liberal-democratic impulse to democratize the heathens, especially when it meshes with other U.S. objectives. The United States dubbed its invasion of Panama "Operation Just Cause," because, as one senior U.S. official happily explained, "It's always nice when you can intervene on behalf of . . . [democracy], but that's not always possible" (*Time* 1/1/90:23).

Moral/Ethical/Humanitarian Ideas

Morality as a force in international politics is both part of and also very much different from the ideas we have been examining. In one sense specific concepts of moral behavior may stem from religious beliefs, from any one of the secular "isms" discussed in this chapter, or from a wide variety of other philosophical bases. But here we will also be looking at morality in a different, broader sense. There are several issues we will need to examine: (1) whether or not ethical concepts affect world politics, (2) some of the difficulties in determining what is moral and what is not, and (3) the age-old debate over whether or not moral principles can—or even should—be applied to international politics.

Israel's standing in world public opinion has been damaged by what many consider the morally questionable use of lethal force to suppress Palestinian protesters in the West Bank. In October 1990 Muslims threw rocks at Israeli civilians marching near Temple Mount, a site holy to Christians, Jews, and Muslims. Nearby Israeli forces opened fire on the rockthrowers, wounding many and killing 18 to 20, according to varying reports. The bloody handprints of the victims may be seen here on the wall behind a mourning Palestinian woman.

Ethics—Who Cares?

Ethical concepts do play a role in world politics. It is madness, given the wars, starvation, and violations of human rights that occur, to imagine that morality is a predominant force. Yet it is there.

Stanley Hoffmann (1981) has defined three great ethical issues facing the world: the use of violence, violations of human rights, and the maldistribution of economic resources. It is important not to exaggerate the progress, but strides have been made. Violence is gradually moving from being considered legitimate—even glorious—to unfortunate (even when "necessary") or even reprehensible. Some weapons, such as poison gas, have been outlawed. There have been occasional reports of use of poison gas in Laos, Cambodia, Afghanistan, and Yemen in recent years, and gas warfare was used in the Iran-Iraq war by both sides and by Iraq against Kurdish rebels, but generally the fear of offending world opinion keeps employment of gas limited. The Nuremberg and Tokyo war trials following World War II established the principle that individuals could be tried and executed for war crimes.

Advances have also been made in the area of human rights (Shelley, 1989). By the latter part of the 1800s, the international slave trade had been largely halted by international action. There have been actions and agreements condemning genocide, setting down principles of human rights, and condemning violations in South Africa and elsewhere. This has not halted offenses, but governments are warier of violations. Forty years ago Soviet dissidents were shot. Twenty years ago they were sent to Siberia. Now they are sometimes expelled to the West. Moral pressure also helped end the racist rule in Zimbabwe (Rhodesia) and is pressuring South Africa to ease the social aspects of apartheid. Israel's sometimes brutal tactics against Palestinian protesters in the West Bank and Gaza have set off waves of international condemnation. Progress is slow, but it exists.

Still, a huge gap continues to exist between the ideal of freedom and the reality of widespread oppression. As Figure 7.2 on the next page shows, countries that allow a high degree of political and personal freedom remain the exception rather than the rule in the world. A study (Gatsil, 1990) that rated countries on scales of 1 (good) to 7 (horrendous) for both political rights and civil liberties found that of the 167 countries rated, 61 (37 percent) could be described as "free," while 44 (26 percent) were "partly free," and 62 (37 percent) were "not free" at all. This distribution is represented in Figure 7.3, which also shows the changes since 1985. The proverbial good news is that in the five years that elapsed between the two studies, the percentage of free countries

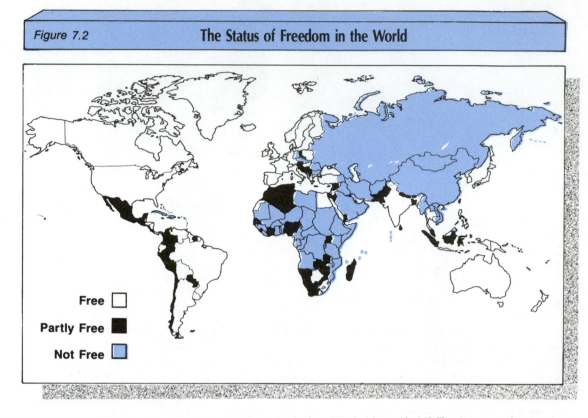

Figure 7.2   The Status of Freedom in the World

Free ☐
Partly Free ■
Not Free ▨

The Most Free Countries (rated a 1 on both political rights and civil liberties): Australia, Austria, Barbados, Belgium, Canada, Costa Rica, Denmark, Iceland, Ireland, Italy, Japan, Luxembourg, Netherlands, New Zealand, Norway, Sweden, Switzerland, Trinidad & Tobago, Tuvalu, United Kingdom, United States

The Least Free Countries (rated a 7 on both political rights and civil liberties): Albania, Angola, Benin, Bulgaria, Cambodia, Equatorial Guinea, Iraq, Mongolia, North Korea, Romania, Somalia

Sources: Map adapted from *Freedom in the World 1987–1988,* by Freedom House. Reprinted by permission. Data for table drawn from Gastil (1990:42–46).

improved significantly. The bad news is that the percentage of not-free countries also improved, albeit less dramatically. The percentage of partly-free was more than halved, indicating that there is a growing polarity between free and not-free countries.

The problem of resource redistribution has been the area of the least progress. As chapter 6 discussed, nationalism has helped retard the willingness of developed nations to significantly aid less developed nations. And, as chapter 14 will detail, the needs are great. Still, there have been advances. Organizations such as the United Nations Conference on Trade and Development have been working to press the developed "North" countries to take on more responsibility for the less developed countries (LDCs) of the "South." In a step with promise for the future, 8 industrialized and 14 developing countries met at Cancún, Mexico, in October 1981 on "global negotiations" to assist the poorer nations. Although the meeting met with wide criticism, especially because of the United States' desire to stress private economic investment, it did help promote the principle that the "North" has a responsibility for, as well as an interest in, aiding the LDCs.

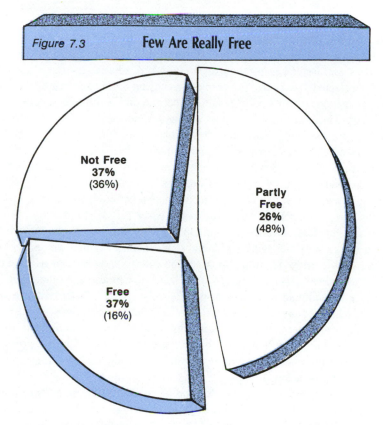

Figure 7.3   **Few Are Really Free**

Not Free
37%
(36%)

Partly
Free
26%
(48%)

Free
37%
(16%)

Data source: McColm et al. (1990).

A combined rating of 5 or less on the political freedom and civil liberties scales resulted in a "free" rating. A rating of 6 through 10 equaled "partly free," and 11 through 14 was rated "not free." Figures in parentheses are from Gastil (1985) for comparison.

Moral Uncertainties

Despite the slow improvement of moral behavior, many questions remain concerning the basic nature of morality.

Is there any universal morality? Some scholars argue that it is difficult or impossible to develop universal moral standards, for the world is too diverse and there are too many different cultures to allow agreement. Former presidential adviser Arthur Schlesinger, Jr., contends that "[we] may eventually promote a world moral consensus. But for the present, national, ideological, ethical, and religious divisions remain as bitterly intractable as ever" (1973:72).

Although most advocates of the development of moral standards would not be foolish enough to claim that such norms are in place, many are hopeful that they can be developed. Indeed, for over 2,000 years philosophers, scholars, and theologians have been attracted by the notion that rational humans could come to a common conception of moral behavior. One basis is the concept of **natural rights**, which contends that people carry into a society the same rights—such as the right to life—that they had in a "state of nature" before communities were organized.

Is justice a matter of process or results? A difference of perspective that separates Western democratic thought from the views of a good deal of the rest of the world is how justice is determined. Western democratic thought emphasizes process, that is, whether or not policies are arrived at through democratic procedures. By this standard, if a country has an elected legislature, freedom of speech and other basic political rights, and a political opposition, then its policies are democratic and legitimate. There are many, especially in the Third World, who dismiss this view as superficial. They believe that the policy-making process is dominated by elites and argue that the outcome of a policy, not the process by which it was made, determines whether it is just or not. There was, for instance, widespread Western criticism of China in 1987 and 1988 for its suppression of demonstrations and other civil rights and liberties in Tibet. The Chinese rejected that charge strongly, and argued that they had made Tibet a better, more equal society since they had reasserted control over the area in the early 1950s. Huan Xing, director of China's Center for International Studies, opined, "Regarding American attacks on China under the guise of safeguarding human rights, I must say that we define the term 'human rights' differently, according to our value concepts. Neither of us should force his views on the other" (*NYT*, 2/16/88:A3). In fact, the Chinese and others point to the gross social and economic inequities in the capitalist West; to the existence of huge economically, educationally, and socially deprived underclasses in most of the capitalist countries; and they argue that countries in which there are both slums and mansions cannot be countries in which human rights are respected. For the Chinese government, the 1989 military suppression of the protesters in Tiananmen Square and elsewhere was a justified crushing of a few to preserve the social revolution for the many.

Is there one standard of morality that applies to both individuals and states? It is common practice for states to act legitimately in ways that would be reprehensible for individuals. If you are in your country's air force and shoot down five enemy pilots, you are an "ace"; if you, as an individual, shoot five people, you are a mass murderer. Of course, we recognize differences between justifiable and inexcusable actions, but where do you draw the line? Some have argued that the state cannot be held to individual moral standards. Niccolò Machiavelli wrote in *The Prince* (1517) that "a prudent ruler ought not to keep faith when by doing so it would be against his interest. . . . A prince . . . cannot observe all those things which are considered good in men, being often obliged, in order to maintain the state, to act against faith and charity, against humanity, and against religion."

The controversy between the convergence and divergence of individual and state morality is more than a theoretical dispute. In 1793, when France was at war with England, the United States debated whether or not to assist France because earlier the French had aided the revolutionary American colonies.[3] The problem for the United States was that siding with France would mean war with England and place America in peril. Secretary of the Treasury Alexander Hamilton argued for proclaiming neutrality:

> The rule of morality . . . is not precisely the same between nations as between
> individuals. The duty of making its own welfare as the guide of its actions is

---

3. Hamilton and Jefferson's arguments and positions were complex, and space does not allow a full exposition here. Jefferson did not favor war with Great Britain on France's behalf. Indeed he argued that the earlier Franco-American alliance was defensive, and since France was the aggressor in 1793 the United States was not legally obligated to support France. Jefferson did, however, oppose neutrality. The proclamation of neutrality had the effect of favoring British seapower by prohibiting privateers that preyed on British shipping from operating from U.S. ports, and by not allowing U.S. citizens to enlist in the French cause.

much stronger [for countries]; in proportion to the greater magnitude and importance of national compared to individual happiness. . . . Millions . . . are concerned with the present matters of government; while the consequences of the private actions of an individual ordinarily terminate with himself. (Graebner, 1964:61)

Secretary of State Thomas Jefferson held that the United States was morally obligated to help France, at least to the extent of not proclaiming neutrality, allowing privateers to operate from U.S. ports against British shipping, and permitting American citizens to enlist in the French cause.

The moral duties which exist between individual and individual in a state of nature accompany them into a state of society and the aggregate of the duties . . . constitutes the duties of that society toward any other; so that between society and society the same moral duties exist as between the individuals composing them. (Graebner, 1964:55)

Jefferson lost the argument, for President Washington proclaimed neutrality.

Do ends justify means? Another philosophical debate with real-world impact is the ends/means controversy. Is an act that is, by itself, evil justifiable when done for a good cause? The great eighteenth-century philosopher Immanuel Kant argued in his *Groundwork on the Metaphysics of Morals* (1785) that from a position of moral absolutism ends never justify means and urged us to "do what is right though the world should perish."

Clearly, most of us do not adhere to such an absolute position. Most of us explicitly or implicitly accept capital punishment or the atomic bombings of Hiroshima and Nagasaki as somehow justified as retaliation or even an unfortunate necessity to a better end. The problem, again, is where to draw the line. How about assassination? Think about the smiling Adolf Hitler in the photograph below. What if you had a time machine? Given what you know of World War II and of the genocide of 6 million Jews, would you be justified traveling back to 1932 and assassinating Hitler? How about the Reagan

Would you shoot this man? If it were the 1930s and you could foresee the horrors of World War II and the Holocaust, and you were standing just out of this picture with a gun in your hand, would you assassinate Adolf Hitler? Would the end justify the means? This and other issues are raised if one attempts to apply moral standards to the formation and conduct of foreign policy.

administration's alleged attempt to kill Libya's leader Muammar Qaddafi by dropping bombs on his house in the 1986 U.S. air raid, or the disclosure by U.S. Air Force chief of staff General Michael Dugan that there were U.S. plans to target Saddam Hussein, his family, and his mistress?[4] Or what about the successful attempt (probably by Mossad, the Israeli intelligence agency) to assassinate Khalif al-Wazir, the PLO military chief? Are all, some, or any of these actions morally acceptable?

What about terrorism? Consider, if you will, the following two arguments, the first by PLO head Yasser Arafat speaking before the UN General Assembly in 1974, the second from "Freedom Struggle by the Provisional IRA" published by the Irish Republican Army.

> *Arafat:* I am a rebel and freedom is my cause. . . . The difference between the revolutionary and the terrorist lies in the reason for which each fights. For whoever stands by a just cause and fights for freedom and liberation of his land from the invaders . . . cannot possibly be classed a terrorist. I appeal to you to aid our people's return to its homeland from an involuntary exile imposed upon it by force of arms, by tyranny, by oppression. (Laqueur, 1978:510)

> *IRA:* [Our] strategy [is] to carry out selective bombings . . . as a legitimate part of war, the targets chosen being military and police barracks, outposts, customs offices, administrative and government buildings, electricity transformers and pylons, certain cinemas, hotels, clubs, dance halls, and pubs [frequented by British personnel]. . . . The effect of the IRA bombing campaign . . . [has] struck at the very root of enemy morale . . . [and has] hit Britain where she feels it most—in her pocket. (Laqueur, 1978:132)

These arguments, then, maintain that killing people who are innocent bystanders is justified by what, the terrorists claim, are their just goals. Are these justifications merely self-serving or are they legitimate?

When is war justified and how can it be justly fought? Western tradition has predominantly believed in *jus ad bellum* (just cause of war) in cases where the war is (1) a last resort, (2) declared by legitimate authority, (3) waged in self-defense or to establish/restore justice, and (4) fought with the intention of bringing about peace. The same line of thought maintains that *jus in bello* (just conduct of war) includes the standards of proportionality and discrimination. Proportionality means that the amount of force used must be proportionate to the threat (Lackey, 1989). Great Britain, for instance, would not have been justified in using nuclear weapons against Argentina in the Falkland Islands War. Discrimination means that force must not make noncombatants intentional targets.

One difficulty with these standards, even if you try to abide by them, is that they are vague. What, for example, is self-defense? As we saw in the earlier discussion of perceptions, President Reagan believed that Nicaragua's leftist government posed a threat to Texas and, by extension, to the entire United States. Rightly or wrongly, he clearly saw the U.S. campaign against Nicaragua as self-protection. Establishing justice is another troubling

---

4. Dugan was fired for this and other disclosures in September 1990. U.S. defense secretary Dick Cheney said specific targeting of individuals was barred by presidential directive, and such an attack "might" violate the directive. Neither Cheney nor Bush ever denied, however, that such a contingency plan existed.

ambiguity. There are few who would not condemn South African apartheid as unjust. Would black African nations then be justified if they mounted a multinational invasion of South Africa to topple the white regime?

The availability of nuclear weapons makes these complex issues even more difficult (Nye, 1986). The standard of proportionality is the first hurdle. Certainly a U.S. nuclear attack on Vietnam or a Soviet nuclear attack on Afghanistan would have violated proportionality. But what if nuclear weapons were needed to save Washington from Moscow—or Moscow from Washington? Many would find that proportionate, as indicated by one survey that found that of those with an opinion, 69 percent of Americans would risk destruction of the United States rather than be dominated by the Soviets (*Public Opinion*, Summer, 1986:25). The second standard, discrimination, is almost totally irrelevant in a nuclear war. Certainly more civilians than soldiers would be killed by weapons too powerful to allow differentiation between kinds of people.

The availability of nuclear weapons in particular brings up the moral issue of whether or not it is wrong to threaten to do what it would be immoral to do. Deterrence not only rests on the foundation that you have the capacity to annihilate an opponent who attacks you, but it also is based on your willingness to do so. In an all-out nuclear attack, that means your second strike retaliation would not really be self-defense. In fact, you would be dead before your weapons reached the attacker, and, therefore, the retaliation would be an act of vengeance.

Even though relatively few people are actually killed by terrorists (compared to deaths caused by war, drunk drivers, disease, and other scourges), terrorism has a strong impact because its grisly images rivet our attention. On Pan Am flight 103 from London to the United States on December 21, 1988, a bomb detonated in the aircraft over Lockerbie, Scotland. The Boeing 747, named the Clipper Maid of the Seas, blew apart at 31,000 feet; 258 passengers and crew plunged to their deaths. Another 22 persons on the ground were killed by the falling wreckage. Among the passengers were 35 Syracuse University undergraduates who had been studying abroad and who were returning home for the holidays. The point is made in this book in many places and in many ways that international politics may affect you whether you want it to or not.

The Debate Over Whether or Not to Apply Moral Standards to Foreign Policy

In addition to the more philosophical issues about the nature of morality, there are some very practical matters to consider. In essence, these center on the questions of whether or not, when, and to what degree to apply moral standards to the conduct of foreign policy.

The Argument Against Moral Standards

The uncertainties discussed above and other issues have led some to argue that it is futile, even dangerous, to attempt to govern policy by moral standards. One such argument is that states should act in their citizens' interests. Leaders should act in the national interest, not according to their own concept of morality. A second contention is that because not all states act morally, those who do are at a disadvantage: "Nice guys finish last." It can also be said that requiring that others act morally is **cultural imperialism**, since we always apply our own moral standards. If, for example, we demand that a country hold free elections before we give it foreign aid, then we are imposing our standards. Democracy is not highly valued in some cultures. A fourth argument against applying morality holds that there is no universal morality. As we will see in chapter 17, this particular argument complicates the possibility of achieving globally accepted standards of international law. Yet another objection to applying morality is that insisting on one form of moral behavior violates other states' sovereignty. Americans have been quick to condemn the Soviet Union's treatment of Jews, South Africa's oppression of its blacks, or Israel's handling of West Bank Arabs. How would Americans react, though, to a demand by the UN that blacks and Hispanics be treated equally in America, an investigation by the Organization of African Unity (OAU) of why Jesse Jackson was denied the 1988 Democratic presidential nomination, or a call by the Organization of American States (OAS) for an end to U.S. colonial domination of Puerto Rico? It is safe to bet that Americans would be outraged, and would tell the UN, the OAU, and the OAS in very undiplomatic language to mind their own business. Perhaps, then, we should follow the advice of diplomat and scholar George Kennan and promote "morality primarily in our own behavior, not in our judgment of others" (1986:217).

It may even be that we cannot agree within our own country about what is moral. Discussing the United States, scholar Ralph Carter (1989:301) argues that while "moral considerations are essential in the making of democratic foreign policy," trying to agree explicitly on whether or not to apply them and which ones to apply will produce "strain . . . on a political system already fragmented by the forces of hyperpluralism."

Some also contend that a country's policy should be based on its own national interest rather than on another country's civil and political rights conduct. Some Americans wondered in 1990 what their country's troops were doing in the Saudi Arabian desert defending an extremely retrograde regime. Saudi Arabia escaped a bottom-of-the-barrel 14 rating in the Gastil freedom survey by only one point (see p. 182). King Fahd ibn Abdul Aziz and the rest of the Saudi royal family run virtually everything, live in astronomical opulence, and permit no voting, independent legislature, or other democratic practices or institutions. In part because polygamy is widely practiced, there are perhaps 5,000 princes descended from the original king, Ibn Saud (1880–1953) and his 40 sons, and a (not very loud) quip in the country is that it has more princes than taxi drivers. Furthermore, there is heavy political and cultural censorship, and all religious practice except Islam is forbidden. Women are not allowed to work in most jobs; they are forbidden to drive or travel unescorted; and they are required to wear a head-to-toe garment which leaves only their eyes visible. The *mutawa,* the Saudi religious police, prowl the streets ready to cane those who violate minor strictures, and there was at least one incident when a *mutawa* tried to punish a U.S. servicewoman because her uniform exposed her face and bared her arms. For criminals, penalties are even heavier. Public squares are occasionally the scene of minor felons being flogged, thieves having one of their hands cut off, adulterers being stoned to death, and rapists and murderers suffering decapitation.

Of course, the tendency to be less concerned with the human rights practices of one's allies than with those of one's opponents is nothing new. An aide supposedly once complained to Franklin Roosevelt about dealing with dictator Rafael Trujillo of the Dominican Republic. "The man's an SOB!" the aide objected. "Ah, yes," FDR replied, "but he's our SOB."

A seventh and last objection to applying morality is that it may be counterproductive. The United States pressured the regime of the Shah to give more freedom to dissidents in Iran. That in part led to the revolution that brought the Ayatollah Khomeini to power and resulted in the seizure of the American embassy and the political and religious persecution of an untold number of Iranians. Similarly, U.S. involvement helped end nearly three decades of dictatorship by the Duvalier family in Haiti in 1986 and brought hopes of democracy. What followed, though, was a sham government backed by the military and the shooting, machete massacre of large numbers of voters as they waited to cast ballots during the country's first attempt at an election, and four years later the country is still almost routinely in turmoil.

The Argument for Moral Standards

Despite the obvious problems with applying morality, there are also excellent reasons for acting according to moral standards. One is that the dignity of the human race depends upon it. The strongest argument for demanding moral responsibility by states, both internationally and domestically, is to uphold the basic tenets of civilized behavior. Internationally, we have witnessed aggressive war, the use of chemical warfare, genocide, and a host of other atrocities. Domestically, racism, religious and political persecution, and the brutal denial of civil rights and the economic rudiments of human existence are regularly reported, as Figure 7.3 on page 183 shows.

These numbers are dry and do not convey the gruesome reality of life in some police states. To bring the figures to life, consider an Amnesty International (1981) report on Chile:

> [Thirty-three prisoners] were kept hanging upside down by their feet for hours at a time; they were stripped naked and then taken outdoors where icy jets of water from a high-pressure hose were turned on them (it was winter in Chile); they were punched and kicked, and given electric shocks in the most sensitive parts of their bodies. . . . [Some were] treated with particular cruelty . . . forced to swallow human excrement and urine.

Proponents of morality would argue, first, that people have an obligation to oppose the continuance of these conditions. Neither national interest nor sovereignty legitimizes crimes against humanity. Second, they would argue that it is possible to work toward and arrive at a universal morality that could be widely recognized and be incorporated as part of international law governing human rights and national conduct (Donnelley, 1989; Rentelin, 1990). The slow growth of internationally acclaimed (if not always practiced) norms of behavior has been mentioned. Proponents argue that standards like the Universal Declaration of Human Rights and the International Covenant on Civil and Political Rights, which declares, "No one shall be subjected to torture or to cruel, inhuman, or degrading treatment or punishment," are beginning to form at least basic agreement on moral conduct. One indication of the willingness of countries to agree to universal human rights practices is shown in Figure 7.4. This figure details the number of countries that have adhered to six major international human rights treaties. As you

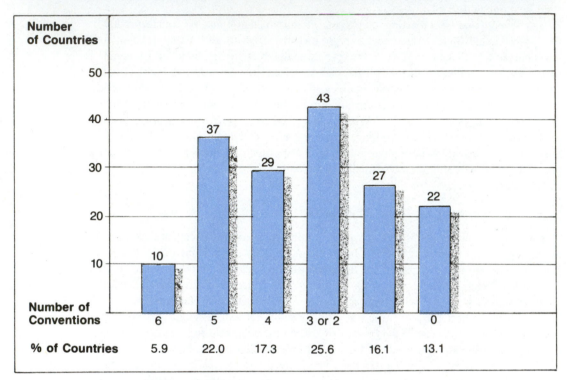

Figure 7.4 **Number of States Agreeing to Main Human Rights Conventions**

Data source: Tomasevski (1989:Table 14)

The six treaties are: (1) the International Covenant on Economic, Social and Cultural Rights, (2) the International Covenant on Civil and Political Rights, (3) the International Convention on the Elimination of All Forms of Racial Discrimination, (4) the International Convention on the Suppression and Punishment of the Crime of Apartheid, (5) the Convention on the Elimination of All Forms of Discrimination Against Women, and (6) the Convention against Torture and Other Cruel, Inhuman, or Degrading Treatment or Punishment. The data are accurate to December, 1987. This author eliminated the ratifications of Belorussia and the Ukraine, both technical members of the United Nations, from the count of countries that ratified all six treaties and from the total count of countries.

can see, only 76 of 168 countries listed, or 45.2 percent, have agreed to the majority (four or more) of the six treaties. Twenty-two countries, including the United States, had not agreed to any of the treaties at the time of the study on which the figure is based.

A third argument is that greater justice is necessary for world survival. This argument, mentioned in chapter 1 and again in chapter 19, basically deals with resource distribution. It contends that it is immoral to maintain a large part of the world both impoverished and without self-development possibilities. The inevitable result will be a world crisis that will destroy order. "The reasons for making such a right [not to be impoverished] universal are now pragmatic and moral," Richard Barnet (1979:48) tells us. "Unless such clear norms are created and supported by an overwhelming international consensus, the politics of scarcity . . . will keep the world in a permanent state of grotesque and dangerous conflict."

Pragmatically, one can also argue that pursuing moral policy is good power politics. The reasoning here is that being moral can win you friends and dismay your enemies. Critics of U.S. policy, for example, say that the gap between America's moral preaching and cynical practice has damaged its reputation. They argue that a more righteous stand in deed in addition to word would gain widespread world support and draw a sharp distinction between the United States and its international opponents. One scholar and diplomat recently argued, for example, that "including a strong human rights component in U.S. foreign policy would express political vision, contribute to individual development and dignity, build coalitions in a multipolar world, and further world order" (Shestack, 1989:28).

The Standard of Practical Morality: A Compromise Position

The problem with the preceding debate on applying moral standards to your evaluation of your country's or another country's international conduct is that unless you are an absolute moralist or are profoundly amoral, the pros and cons illustrate the issues better than they answer the fundamental question of whether or not to try to act morally. They also do not address the conundrum you face when, as Israeli professor Yehoshafat Harkabi (1989:79) lamented with regard to a possible Palestinian state in the West Bank, "The choice before Israel is not between good and bad, but between bad and worse."

There is also the difficult matter of degree of immorality. What do you do, for instance, about Kurt Waldheim? Waldheim has had a distinguished career as a public servant. Among other posts, he served as secretary-general of the United Nations from 1972 through 1982 and was elected president of Austria in 1986. Waldheim also served as a junior officer in the *Wehrmacht*, the German army, during World War II. He has been accused of sending Jews, partisans, and others to concentration camps from his posts in Yugoslavia and Greece. A commission of international historians appointed by the Austrian chancellor found that Waldheim was "often present at . . . important meetings [where deportation issues were discussed], assisted in them and was therefore one of the staff members who was especially well informed" (*NYT*, 2/10/88:A10). The commission additionally concluded, however, that Lieutenant Waldheim "had only extremely modest possibilities for resisting the injustice. . . . For a young staff member, who had no power of command on the army group level, the practical possibilities of opposing action were very slight and in all probability could scarcely have led to a tangible result." The issue, of course, is what, if anything, should be done about Austrian president/*Wehrmacht* lieutenant Waldheim. Many in Austria and elsewhere favor his resignation (for, if nothing else, distorting his military record), and the United States has placed him on a list of those barred from entering the country. Perhaps he should suffer the fate of John Demjanjuk, a retired Ohio autoworker, who was accused of being the sadistic guard "Ivan the Terrible" at the Treblinka death camp. He was deported to Israel, tried and convicted of war crimes, and sentenced to death by hanging. Or perhaps, as Waldheim said in his own defense, "Every person who served in the war knew about events . . . but [while] from today's perspective it is easy to criticize, to deduce that knowledge constitutes some kind of crime simply is not correct" (*NYT*, 2/9/88:A1).[5]

---

5. Some contend that there is evidence that Waldheim was directly involved in sending people to concentration camps. Among others, the U.S. Justice Department may hold such evidence (on which it based its decision to bar Waldheim from entering the United States), but the department refused to release the information to the commission of historians.

The debate over the career of Austria's Kurt Waldheim (second from left) illustrates the difficulty of many issues of morality. Waldheim has had an illustrious career including service for 10 years (1972–82) as secretary-general of the United Nations and, currently, as the president of Austria. Waldheim, however, also served in the German army during World War II; he has been accused of being involved in the deportation of Jews and other prisoners to concentration camps. Although Waldheim almost certainly did participate in the deportations, it is also true that he was a junior officer who had little control over policy. Furthermore, had he refused to carry out the deportations, he might himself have been imprisoned or even executed. Is Waldheim a war criminal who should be prosecuted and punished as others have been?

Another problem with the debate over applying moral standards is that it often does not fully deal with the argument that morality is but one of the standards of conduct by which states and their leaders should be governed. Realists, for example, maintain that national interest (see next chapter) sometimes precludes the application of otherwise laudable moral principles. Hans Morgenthau (1984:347) represents this point of view with his contention that:

> the principle of the defense of human rights cannot be consistently applied in foreign policy because it can and it must come in conflict with other interests that may be more important . . . in a particular instance. . . . [This is necessary] if you are not a Don Quixote who foolishly but consistently follows a disastrous path of action. . . . [Y]ou cannot be consistent in the defense of human rights, since it is not your prime business as a state among other states to defend human rights, and . . . you cannot pursue human rights without taking into consideration other aspects of your relations with other nations, which may be more important than those connected with human rights.

Morgenthau may be right, but even if you agree with his contention that morality cannot always, or even primarily, govern policy, you still cannot answer the question: "When can it?"

One way out of the dilemma may be to begin with the observation that you do not have to choose one standard or the other—morality or amorality. There is a middle ground. Kenneth Thompson (1984:387), who writes a great deal on these issues, suggests adopting the standard of "*practical morality*," which he defines as "the reconciliation of what is morally desirable" with what is "politically possible." That may sound like mumbling rather than deciding, and Thompson admits that practical morality "offers few absolutes." It does, however, offer "many practical possibilities." Prudence would be the cardinal precept of Thompson's approach, which would allow leaders to consider ethics as a component of their decisions without making it the only factor. Two questions, then, "What is ethical?" and "Is it prudently possible to be moral?" would influence decisions.

The Impact of Ideas and Ideology

Identifying categories of ideas is easier by far than analyzing their precise, or even general, impact. No nations and few decisionmakers are *pure ideologues* who make choices based solely on theoretical correctness. Even if a decisionmaker is an ideologue, it is likely that reality will rudely intrude to disrupt his or her theoretical world. A classic example involves Russia's surrender to Germany in 1918. The newly-in-power Bolsheviks, even in the face of the total dissolution of the Russian army, refused at first to act defeated. The Bolsheviks expected social unrest to spread to Germany, and when they arrived at the negotiations, they handed out leaflets to the German guards calling on them to join the workers' revolution. The Soviets proclaimed the war a capitalist conflict, declared that they would no longer participate, and called on Germany to withdraw. When the Germans pressed for capitulation, the Russian foreign commissar, Leon Trotsky, said they would neither surrender nor fight. "We interrupt the war and do not sign the peace; we demobilize the army" was Trotsky's formula—no war, no peace. "Unerhört!" ("Unheard of") was the German reaction. The German armies began to move forward again, and the Bolsheviks learned their first diplomatic lesson. Within days they agreed to Germany's terms (Segal, 1979:196–212).[6]

At the other extreme from being an ideologue, it is also rare to find people who operate without any belief system. Some leaders like to imagine themselves pure power pragmatists, but it is self-delusion. They are not only influenced by their idiosyncratic beliefs (see chapter 4), but they are also part of and affected by their nation's belief system. As Richard Sterling has noted, ideology, whether it be "translated as doctrine, creed, belief system, [or] social myth," is "an essential component of social organization and, as such, cannot be eliminated from human existence" (1974:157–58).

Between the two unlikely poles—pure ideologue and pure pragmatist—ideology plays several important roles.

First, belief systems act as *prisms*. A prism is a lens that distorts reality, and deeply held beliefs have a similar effect. They help us, for example, define enemies. Leftist regimes in Cuba in the 1960s, Vietnam in the 1970s, and Nicaragua in the 1980s all met with American hostility. "Good" and "communist" seemed to be a contradiction in terms for many Americans. Similarly, Islam is a belief system that disposes many Muslims to view non-Muslims, especially Westerners, with suspicion, as evident in the 1990 Middle East crisis. A bit surprisingly, ideological similarity does not necessarily

---

6. It should be noted that there is disagreement on Trotsky's motives. Some scholars claim he was cleverly stalling for time. Additionally, other Bolsheviks, especially Lenin, were more realistic. Still others, such as Karl Radek and Nikolai Bukharin, were even more radical than Trotsky.

mean friendship. One study found that between 1815 and 1939 ideological similarity did not predict the stability of alliances (Sullivan, 1964). Indeed, the Chinese-Soviet (Sino-Soviet) split shows that intraideological competition can be just as much a cause of conflict as interideological competition. A more recent study, however, found that democratic countries are likely to ally with one another, although the long-term stability of these alliances is not established (Siverson & Emmons, 1990).

Belief systems also *restrict options*. A country's belief system makes it difficult or even impossible for it to select certain policy options, even if they make pragmatic sense. Israel and Iraq have been implacable enemies, and an Israeli bombing attack on Iraq's Osirak nuclear reactor in 1981 stalled Iraq's nuclear weapons development program. In 1990 Iraq attacked Kuwait and threatened Saudi Arabia. Egypt and Syria sent thousands of troops to join European, American, and Saudi soldiers in defense of the country. In a perfectly nonideological world, Israel with its impressive military might would have eagerly joined and been welcomed by the coalition against the common enemy, Iraq. That was ideologically impossible, though. Despite the threat from Iraq, no Muslim country was ready to take up arms with the Jewish state against another Muslim state. Indeed, when Palestinian *intifada* riots broke out in Jerusalem in October 1990 and were met by the Israelis with deadly force (killing 19 rock-throwing protesters and wounding another 140), the warring Muslim states—including Iraq and Kuwait[7]—put aside their differences and in UN Security Council proceedings joined in condemning Israel's action.

Belief systems also often *rationalize and legitimize policy*. Especially in an era when gunboat diplomacy and the naked, self-interested use of power have become déclassé, ideology has become a legitimizing standard by which policymakers can justify their actions to themselves, to their countrymen, and to the world. When President Bush spoke on television to Americans on August 8, 1990, he told them in the first few seconds that he had ordered the 82nd Airborne Division to Saudi Arabia, asked for citizens to support him and added, "And let me tell you why." In the balance of his address he spoke of restoring Kuwaiti sovereignty, deterring further Iraqi aggression, protecting American lives, and generally "beginning a new era" of international relations, an "era . . . full of promise, an age of freedom, a time of peace for all peoples." He spoke of "sanctions now enshrined in international law" and pledged that "America will stand by her friends." After all, he concluded, "Standing up for our principles is an American tradition." What was nearly lost amid the lofty rhetoric was the major threat to the economic prosperity of the United States and its industrialized allies that would be created by Iraqi control of the Middle East's oil resources. Certainly the president mentioned the economic issues, but the predominant role of principle in his explanation did not accurately reflect the hard, realpolitik considerations that were the primary motivation behind U.S. policy.

Belief systems also serve to *differentiate*. The world's diverse religious, social, political, economic, and moral belief systems help perpetuate our feeling of distinctiveness. Here the divergent ideas act much like nationalistic concepts. They make us see ourselves not only as different but also often as superior to, hostile to, and threatened by those of differing and, especially, opposing philosophies.

It can also be said that those who have strong belief systems use them to interpret people, countries, and events. This occurs whether or not the belief system is relevant. Until recently, for example, the superpowers approached the Third World issues and needs from the perspective of the East-West power and ideological struggle rather than

---

7. Through its still legally recognized, though exiled, government and UN mission.

in terms of economic and social development. Addressing this factor, Pope John Paul II's 1988 encyclical *Sollicitudo Rei Socialis* (The Social Concerns of the Church) condemned the East-West ideological rivalry for creating a "direct obstacle" to Third World development and denounced both sides' beliefs because each "harbors in its own way a tendency toward imperialism" and employs "structures of sin" in seeking riches and power at the expense of the world's poor.

In sum, then, ideas and ideologies are part of the complex of international and domestic forces that affect world politics. Decisionmakers and nations are neither devoid of belief systems nor completely captivated by them. The role of ideas varies greatly. Ideas are most potent, for example, in revolutionary times when new ideas challenge established ideas. Scholars have also found that belief systems are more important in establishing general policy than they are in making decisions on particular issues. Finally, ideologies may be more important than such domestic factors as economics, but they are usually less important than power and national security factors.

Chapter Summary

1. The single most important factor that separates humans from animals is that we can think abstractly.
2. This ability to carry ideas in our heads profoundly affects world politics. In this chapter, we have seen that many types of ideas based on religion; social, political, and economic theories; and on concepts of morality help structure our perceptions and actions.
3. Morality is a particular type of idea that we should consider. Slowly, concepts of morality are playing an expanding role in foreign policy-making.
4. Yet there are many questions about the basic nature of morality.
5. There are also important arguments for and against

trying to apply moral standards to foreign policy formation.
6. Important as they are, though, ideas do not exist in a vacuum. Time, events, and individual predispositions all interact with ideas.
7. Ideas, then, are not often absolute guides to action. Rather, they are flexible parts of a number of factors that create mind-sets and determine action.
8. Most important, ideas influence perception. They dispose policymakers to view other actors, events, and possible policies from a predetermined perspective. Thus ideas limit options and point in the "proper" policy direction.

I do perceive here a divided duty.

Shakespeare, Othello

Our true nationality is mankind.

H. G. Wells, The Outline of History

NATIONAL INTERESTS AND ORIENTATIONS

National interest is one of those terms that bedevil political scientists. There are three things about the idea that aggravate scholars. First, many analysts claim that objective national interest is impossible to discern. This line of thought asserts that national interest is entirely subjective, that it is a function of each individual's or group's perceptions. Second, some scholars argue that a country's national interest is too complex to define or use analytically. That is, even if an objective national interest does exist, it is beyond rational comprehension. Third, there is a school of thought that contends that concern with national interest is destructive. This group of scholars argues that in a divided, quasi-anarchistic world, advocacy of national interest is tantamount to national selfishness and is the source of dangerous conflict among nations.

This combination of objections to national interest has led many scholars to ignore or quickly pass over national interest in introductory texts and other works. Indeed, one critic accused the academic community of "copping out" on the study of national interest (Neuchterlein, 1979:74). His argument is that whether we academics approve of it or not, or whether we fully understand it or not, national interest is important because foreign policy is made based on ideas about what is in the national interest. Therefore it exists as a driving force behind the actions of countries, and as students of world politics we have to study it.

There are two benefits of studying national interest. One is to understand *what is*. This means that by analyzing how our own country and other countries perceive their national interest we can better understand past and present policy—and perhaps even gain some insight into what future policy might be. The object here is to look for patterns in the way a country defines its national interest, and then to use that understanding to analyze and forecast policy.

The second benefit of studying national interest is that it will help us form more intelligent opinions about *what ought to be*. The object here is to achieve a more organized way of thinking about the national interest. This will enable us to form

The United States has long defined the Central America–Caribbean region as an area of particular national interest and has frequently used military force there. The latest incident was the U.S. invasion of Panama during the third week of December 1989. The U.S. soldiers in this photograph are taking up a position in the populous San Miguelito section of Panama City. Between 200 and 300 Panamanian civilians died in the fighting in addition to U.S. and Panamanian military casualties. Washington labeled the invasion "Operation Just Cause," but it was condemned by the UN and the OAS; the private, U.S.–based human rights organization, Americas Watch, charged that the United States had violated the Geneva Convention by using excess force that resulted in unnecessary civilian deaths.

opinions about national interest that are independent of those supplied by national leaders. Consider, for one, the 1989 U.S. invasion of Panama. As it is, we are too often at the mercy of leaders like George Bush, who said "Operation Just Cause," as the invasion was codenamed, was in the national interest, or leaders like Senator Edward Kennedy, who argued with equal conviction that Bush's justifications for the action were "threadbare and legalistic" and that the invasion caused "long-term damage to [U.S.] foreign policy" (*Congressional Record,* 1/23/90:513). We may agree with Bush or Kennedy, but unless we are able to think about the national interest in a systematic way our reasons for doing so lack persuasive substance.

With these thoughts in mind, this chapter on national interests is aimed at accomplishing three goals. The first is to address the issues of subjectivity, complexity, and destructiveness that some scholars use to justify casting the study of national interest into the shadows of academia. This writer's view is that national interest is only partly subjective; that it *is* complex, but that we are able to at least see the outlines of it; and that national interest is not necessarily destructive.

Having examined these issues, we will then turn our attention to look at how national interest is thought of and applied in world politics. To do this, we will also look at how three of the world's leading powers, the United States, the Soviet Union, and China, define their national interests.

Third, because it is important that you be active in world politics, we will discuss how to think systematically about national interest. To encourage you to form a broad view of national interest this chapter will outline for you the dimensions of national interest and will propose principles for evaluating national interest claims.

National Interest: An Idea That Many Reject

As the introductory remarks indicated, many scholars reject the concept of national interest on the grounds that it does not really exist, that it is impossibly complex, or that it is potentially destructive. Each of these objections is detailed in the following section.[1] Each will also be partly disputed in later sections of the chapter.

National Interest Does Not Really Exist

A first objection to national interest is that it is *subjective*, that it exists entirely in the eye of the beholder. Analysts can accurately point out that national interest has been used to describe every sort of good and evil. As used by decisionmakers, it is a projection of the perceptions of a particular regime or even a single political leader in a given international or domestic environment. We have seen, for example, that President Kennedy engaged in the Cuban missile crisis in part to save his own political skin. Thus, the national interest can be interpreted, all or in part, in terms of a regime's interest or an individual's interest.

A related argument is that national interest claims are often used as *retroactive justification* for policies already adopted. Ideally, a decisionmaker should fashion policies to meet the national interest. In practice, leaders often react to events with less than perfect rationality. Top American leaders defined South Korea as outside the perimeter of American interests in 1950. Yet when North Korea invaded South Korea later that year, President Truman's feisty personality led him to resist militarily. It was only later, with hindsight, that justifications on the basis of national interest were made to Americans and the world. It may well be that defending South Korea was in the national interest of the United States and that it was the initial evaluation, rather than the decision to react, that was wrong. The point here, though, is that the definition of national interest shifted with events.

Numerous scholars have argued that national interest cannot exist because of *societal heterogeneity*, that is, because every "society" is a collection of diverse subgroups, each of which has its own set of interests. It can also be said that the "intermestic" mingling of international and domestic issues has increased both the number of subgroups concerned with foreign affairs and the level of the stakes involved, thus making the search for a single national interest even more difficult. Beyond this, if we accept that a national interest does exist, the question of transcendency remains. At issue is whether or not the national interest takes priority over the interests or rights of subgroups or individuals. Jews are oppressed in the Soviet "national interest." The World War II confinement of Japanese Americans in concentration camps was also justified by that lofty term. The question is, then, what is the balance between majoritarianism and minority rights?

National Interest Is Too Complex to Use for Policy Evaluation

The thrust of this contention is that national interest includes a multitude of variables that make it so complex that it is useless as a standard of evaluation or as an analytical concept. This view is evident in political philosopher Raymond Aron's judgment that

1. The following section owes much to the analysis of Sondermann (1977).

Determining what is or is not in the national interest is a complex process. The 1990 Middle East crisis sparked a sharp debate in the United States over whether or not intervention, especially liberating Kuwait, was in the national interest. The Administration decided it was and moved a full-scale invasion force into the region. Part of that deployment is evident here as the nuclear aircraft carrier, the USS *Dwight D. Eisenhower*, traverses the Suez Canal on its way from the Mediterranean Sea to the Persian Gulf in early August 1990. Understanding national interest will help you make informed, independent judgments about what your country's interests are.

"the plurality of concrete objectives forbids a rational definition of national interest" (1966:1991). Not everyone agrees with Aron, but even those who do not must concede that it is difficult to define national interest in terms that are clear and widely acceptable or that can be applied to describe, predict, and prescribe the actions of countries.

Consider, as an illustration, the U.S. "national interest" in the Middle East/Persian Gulf region. Twice in recent years, U.S. presidents have sent forces there, first in the form of naval contingents during the Iran-Iraq war, then on a much larger scale after Iraq's invasion of Kuwait and threat to Saudi Arabia. In February 1991 those forces moved against Iraq in Operation Desert Storm. We can identify any number of arguments for and against being there. Arguments for intervention included: (1) maintaining the oil flow to the industrial countries; (2) keeping the price of oil down; (3) avoiding domination of the region by any single power (be that Iran or Iraq); (4) protecting conservative Arab regimes from outside threats; (5) bolstering U.S. prestige and credibility by showing it can act decisively; and (6) deterring or responding to aggression in the interest of international law and world peace. Arguments that intervention in the region was against the U.S. national interest included: (1) keeping forces there was expensive, costing billions of dollars in the case of the 1990–91 intervention, at a time when the U.S. financial position is threatened by huge budget deficits; (2) American lives could be and were lost; (3) some neutral Arabs saw the use of U.S. force in the region as a form of neoimperialism; (4) terrorists might retaliate by committing acts in the Untied States and elsewhere; and (5) a protracted war could have led to an even greater interruption in oil supplies than occurred. It would be possible to add more national interest considerations on either side of the argument, but the purpose here is to demonstrate that national interest is not a simple matter, but rather almost always multifaceted. Whether or not that makes it beyond analytical comprehension is another matter, one we will take up in the section on how to decide for yourself what the national interest ought to be.

National Interest Is a Destructive Standard

A last issue is whether or not operating according to one's self-defined national interest is inherently destructive of international stability and equity. As one student of the subject points out, national interest is "frequently criticized in the contemporary study of international relations as an ambiguous term that lends itself to the support of unethical state policies by justifying single-minded national selfishness" (Clinton, 1986:495). This indictment is closely related to the attack on nationalism discussed in chapter 6. According to this view, the concept as used has become a synonym for national egoism and must be abandoned to avoid world-shattering conflict. In the estimation of one such critic, "The bird's-eye view of the political will of mankind in relation to global problems and their solutions does not present an encouraging picture. People are intent on their immediate material benefits, [and] leaders play the game of power and wealth while the clouds of doom gather overhead" (Herz, 1981:182).

National Interest: Three Countries' Definitions of What It Is

One way to begin to find our way out of all this confusion is to admit that national interest cannot be approached from a single perspective. Instead, it must be viewed subjectively and objectively (see p. 212), each of which is important to our understanding of international politics.

The first way to study national interest is to analyze various countries to ask whether there are any consistent ways that they define what their **subjective national interest** is. In other words, *what is* a country's perceived national interest? It is true that political leaders almost always justify what they do in terms of national interest, but no matter how subjective these claims are, they do represent their perceptions of reality. Unless we characterize a given country's foreign policy as random, we must concede that there are certain principles, norms, or concepts that give some structure and consistency to the actions of that country. It follows, then, that by examining the claims and actions taken in the name of national interest, we can begin to understand a country's past actions, current policy, and, perhaps, future policy.

A country's definition of its national interest is based on its values and perceptions. *Values* involve what we define as good or bad, for ourselves and others, and we use values to evaluate past, present, and future events and goals. If, for example, you value human rights, then you are apt to judge yourself and (especially) others according to that standard (Kerry, 1990). *Perceptions* are also important determinants of policy, as we saw in the discussion of individual-level analysis. Whether or not you are accurate, how you imagine yourself and others to be will influence goals and policies. Whatever his real character, the rapid demonization of Iraq's Saddam Hussein into a modern Hitler initially persuaded 75 percent of Americans to favor deploying troops to the region.

As we saw in chapter 4, individual values and perceptions heavily influence leadership decisions. These factors extend beyond the individual, however, and can affect the broader political society. It is this second level of values and perceptions, those that are *widely held* in a society, that is important here. This is because they are more likely to determine policy at any given time, and, being relatively stable, they are more apt to have a long-lasting influence.

Before proceeding, several comments should be made. One is that generalized values and perceptions are not static. To the contrary, they are always changing, albeit usually slowly. The views of old, fairly stable political systems, like the United States, are particularly likely to evolve rather than be changed by revolution. The views of new political systems, like China's, whose Communist revolution occurred only four decades ago, are prone to dramatic shifts as changes occur in their ideologies.

A second cautionary comment is that values and perceptions sometimes clash.

Americans were appalled by the invasion of Kuwait by Iraq, by its threat to Saudi Arabia, and by its general behavior. An August 1990 *Time/CNN* poll of Americans found that 75 percent initially favored sending troops to the area, even given the fact that 80 percent viewed the move as either very or somewhat likely to lead to war. Yet based on other values about remaining at peace and avoiding regional wars, such as Vietnam, 53 percent of Americans opposed action if it endangered U.S. citizens in the region; a majority rejected a war designed to keep oil prices down; and, indeed, a slight majority (52 percent) opposed war to achieve any of the initially announced U.S. objectives. In short, values clashed, and Americans were of two minds at once.

It should also be noted that the values and perceptions that combine to determine national-interest conceptions have many sources. To simplify matters, these can be divided between (1) the national experience and (2) the national belief system. The *national experience* is the culmination of the events that have shaped a country and its citizens. The fact that the United States has never been seriously invaded while the Soviet Union has suffered many devastating invasions makes the orientations of the two countries very different. The second component, the *national belief system,* involves the ideas and ideologies that a people hold. Whether it is capitalism in the United States, Shi'ism in Iran, communism in China, or Zionism in Israel, these intellectual orientations are important determinants of how a country and its polity define their national interest.

To illustrate the application of these theoretical points, the following pages will examine the ways that the United States, the Soviet Union, and the People's Republic of China define their national interests. The discussion will divide orientations among those that involve (1) protecting and enhancing a country's national core, that is, its main territory and its population; (2) a country's views about creating and maintaining a favorable world order; and (3) its disposition toward projecting its values, that is, judging others by and converting them to those values. Each of these three concepts will be explained further.

National Interest, American Style

A great deal of American policy is influenced by the ideas and experiences of the past. These, of course, are not static. Instead, they are evolutionary and are modified by intervening experiences and current needs (Vorys, 1990). The convergence of these influences leads to some consistencies in the United States' particular definition of its national interest.

National Core. Americans' sense of secure insularity from core destruction, except for nuclear attack (from which there is no defense), leads them to a lingering attachment to what might be called *nostalgic isolationism.* As we saw in chapter 5, about one-quarter of Americans are isolationist, and others hanker for the "simpler" days when the country was not so heavily committed internationally. This has led, to give one policy example, to persistent calls by some to get out of NATO, and a general lack of understanding or sense by most Americans of why the United States should be involved in the defense of Western Europe. This sense of security from invasion also strongly influences the domestic debate over the defense budget, and in the post–cold war era, the lingering isolationist impulse may become stronger as the sense of threat from the Soviet Union and communism fades.

Another core orientation for Americans is *expansionism.* American history through the early 1900s is a story of territorial conquest. First the continent was conquered, then the outward impulse led to the taking of Hawaii and other mid-Pacific islands, Puerto Rico, Cuba (for a time), and the Philippines. Other areas and countries came under U.S. control, in fact, if not in name. It was this expansionist impetus that first led to a major U.S. navy, and it culminated in the post–World War II projection of American power around the world. The expansion of American power in this period was by indirect influence, rather than by direct colonization or annexation. It is symbolized by the far-flung network of U.S. military bases overseas and the worldwide deployment of the U.S. forces.

Favorable World Order. Like most countries, the United States has general ideas about the type of world order that would be most favorable to it, and because it is a major power, it has some ability to shape the international environment to its liking. This influence on world affairs combined with its own nostalgic isolationism has led to a period of *reluctant globalism* since 1945 that has seen U.S. power thrust outward in every direction. The flood tide from the United States has now begun to ebb. The United States was never really able to create the world it wanted, but it was not for lack of effort.

One important world order component of American national interest is the *protection of trade.* From its beginning, the United States has been a trading nation, and this factor worked against early isolationism and led the country to expand its international activity. Unlike isolationism, however, trade continues to be a significant and growing part of American national interest. The United States' economy and its national security are heavily dependent on trade. Protection of American trading partners in Western Europe and Japan is a mainstay of current American policy. Energy dependence also makes the Middle East–Persian Gulf area a vital concern. For all the rhetoric about deterring aggression, the U.S. move against Iraq in 1990 was primarily about oil. "Even a dolt understands," one Bush adviser expostulated, that "we need the oil. Its nice to talk about standing up for freedom, but Kuwait and Saudi Arabia are not exactly democracies, and if their principal export were oranges, a mid-level . . . official would have issued a statement [rebuking Iraq] and we would have closed Washington down for August [vacation]" (*Time*, 8/20/90:21).

Another basic tenet of the U.S. view of a favorable world order is *maintaining a* **sphere of influence** in the Caribbean, Central America, and (to a lesser degree) South America (Bogdan & Preda, 1988). Rejection of Old World influence and belief in the special status of the New World led, in part, to the formulation of the *Monroe Doctrine*, which proclaimed that the New World should not be dominated by the Old and that the United States has a special role in ensuring that no such domination be allowed to develop or persist. Later presidents distorted this noninterventionist ideal to mean the United States could intervene when countries in the Western Hemisphere violated U.S. interests or values. Since Franklin Roosevelt announced the Good Neighbor Policy, the United States has in theory stopped trying to be the hemisphere's police officer, but in practice American troops or U.S.-supported rebels have moved against the governments of Cuba, the Dominican Republic, Grenada, Nicaragua, Panama, and others in recent history.

A third basic part of America's preferred world order has been the *containment of communism.* Soviet-style communism has been antireligious and totalitarian and thus antithetical to American democratic-liberal ideals. Communism is also dedicated to the overthrow of capitalism, or the free-enterprise system and private property, which is the basis of the American economic system. Added to all this, many Americans have perceived communism to be wedded to the Soviet Union, and thus a physical as well as a spiritual and economic threat. As such, containment was a major part of America's post–World War II policy.

The reverses in Vietnam, the Sino-Soviet split, and other obvious rivalries within the communist world modified some of the automatic anticommunist aspects of U.S. policy. The domestic battering that communism has suffered in the Soviet Union and elsewhere and the perceived moderation of Soviet foreign policy behavior have pushed containment to the background of U.S. foreign policy decisions. Indeed, it is tempting to consign containment to history, but that may be premature. The Soviet Union and China are still communist-led countries, and a future in which a revived Soviet Union or a strengthened China again confronts the United States could resuscitate containment as a centerpiece of American national interest.

It should be noted that *maintaining the status quo* is a fourth world order orientation common to Americans. Because the United States so strongly dominated the world politically and economically at the end of World War II, almost any change in the status quo was equivalent to a diminution of U.S. power and control. "We are not," Senator William Fulbright told Congress in 1965, "as we like to claim in Fourth of July speeches, the most revolutionary nation on earth; we are, on the contrary, much closer to being the most unrevolutionary nation on earth" (Rourke, 1983:152). This has led the United States not only to oppose communism, but also to be suspicious of Third World independence movements, their frequent desire to experiment with socialism, and their attempts to redefine the norms of the international system. The U.S. government's reluctance to condemn South Africa's racist regime because of fears of a revolutionary, perhaps leftist, successor black government serves as a good example.

Projection of Values. Despite their domestic political pragmatism and self-image of tolerance for diversity, Americans possess a distinct *messianic impulse* that urges them to judge others by American values and to urge or force others to follow the "American way." As early as 1765, John Adams proclaimed that America was at the forefront of a "grand . . . design in Providence for the elimination of the ignorant and the emancipation of the slavish part of mankind all over the earth" (Snyder, 1977:207). Whether the standard is capitalism, democracy, or the American concept of justice and human rights, Americans often favor those who most closely conform to their standards. This has led to substantial **cultural imperialism**.

As a result, *making the world like America* is an impulse that underlies a good deal of American policy. Americans believe in themselves and their system, and their heritage convinces them that they can and should bring the blessings of the American political and civil libertarian system to the world. Despite warnings from John Kennedy (1962) and others that "we must reject . . . the theory that the American mission is to remake the world in the American image," there is a tendency to try to pressure others to live up to American ideals.

National Interest, Soviet Style

Just like the United States, the Soviet Union has a history of ideas and experiences that combines with its current needs to influence its concepts of national interest.

National Core. Of all its core orientations, *defense of the motherland* is a key element of Soviet thinking. All countries, of course, emphasize defense of the home territory, but the Soviets share a sense of impending danger unknown to Americans and many others. Conflict is a mainstream of Russian history. War has been the exception in American history. Peace has been the exception in Russian history, and the Russians have suffered staggering losses. In this century alone, they have gone through a major revolution and suffered greatly during two world wars. During World War II, for example, 75 Soviets died for every American who was killed. Thus, in part because of their expansionism but in larger part because they have been repeatedly bludgeoned from nearly every direction, the Soviets have reason to regard danger and struggle as the norm of international relations.

The Soviet Union's adoption of communism enhanced this feeling of struggle and of being surrounded by hostile capitalist forces. The rise of China as a power and as an ideological rival, particularly against a history of earlier conflict with Asiatic peoples, further added to Soviet fears and defensiveness.

The Soviet stress on massive military might has been one result of this defensive psychology. The Soviets' refusal until 1987 to allow on-site nuclear inspections and their 1983 downing of a South Korean jet airliner are probably further examples of their suspicious fear of outsiders. As we noted in chapter 4's discussion of Mikhail Gorbachev, there is now a new generation of leaders that has neither personally experienced the early days of the Communist Revolution nor the devastation of World War II. This has eased the defensiveness of the Soviet Union, but suspicion is the product of a millennium of history, not just ideology and a single war, and it will remain a strong force in the Soviet psyche.

Somewhat paradoxically, Russian/Soviet history is also a record of *expansionism*. From its beginning 500 years ago as the 15,000-square-mile Duchy of Moscovy, half the size of Maine, the Soviet Union has grown to be the world's largest country (Fig. 8.1). Thus, the Russians have a long history of expanding their borders and areas of control. Indeed, recent history has witnessed an increase in the size of the Russian/Soviet state.

The messianic element of communism also helps drive Soviet expansionism. What has changed is that communism and the growth of Soviet power have urged and allowed that country to project its influence far from its borders.

Russia, and then the Soviet Union, has long considered Eastern Europe a sphere of particular interest. Soviet tanks have rolled on several occasions since World War II to preserve Moscow's control. In this photo, Soviet armor is again on the move, but it is being hauled back to the U.S.S.R. on railroad cars. The tank shown here is part of the first contingent withdrawn from Czechoslovakia in March 1990. The Soviet officer is directing operations, but he could have been waving good-bye to Czechs.

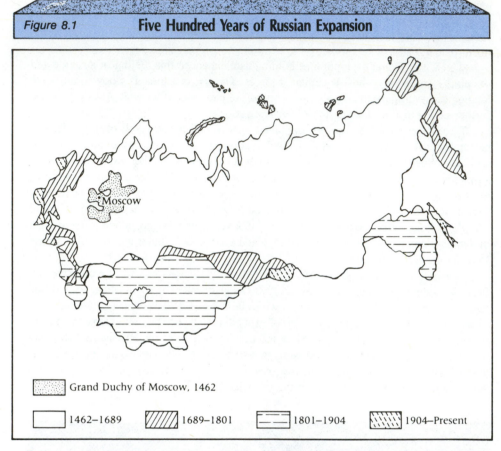

Figure 8.1   **Five Hundred Years of Russian Expansion**

·Moscow

Grand Duchy of Moscow, 1462

1462–1689   1689–1801   1801–1904   1904–Present

Territorial expansion has been one characteristic of the Russian/Soviet concept of national interest as it relates to the national core. The current Soviet Union, which is the world's largest state geographically, began 500 years ago as the relatively small Grand Duchy of Moscow, as this map shows.

The desire to be a true superpower in influence as well as in might also stems from the Soviet Union's reaction to its own *sense of inferiority*. Because they were so often besieged, and because they lagged behind Europe culturally and economically, Russians tend to be insecure and suspicious of outsiders; their strong pride makes them react very negatively to any sense of being regarded by others as second class or to any real, or perceived, insult. They intend to put their country in a position where no one can ever look down on them again.

Favorable World Order. The Soviet image of a favorable world order is a mixture of the status quo orientation of an established superpower and the tendency to foment change that is characteristic of an ideologically revolutionary country—and a country that is trying to achieve true equality with the United States.

As is common with great powers, the Soviet Union has tried to dominate some contiguous geographical areas as a *sphere of influence*. During a significant part of its history, whether as Russia under the czars or the Soviet Union under the commissars, the country has particularly been concerned with Eastern Europe. In the aftermath of World War II, the Soviets dominated this area as a defensive buffer against Western Europe, which seemed to threaten them once more in the form of NATO. Outer Mongolia, Afghanistan, and the Soviet Siberian areas taken from China in the 1800s are, in the same sense, buffers against danger from Asia. The current difficulties that Moscow is suffering have caused it to retreat from its forward positions in most of these buffers. But the history of Russia/the Soviet Union is one of an ebb and flow of influence depending on the country's circumstances. One can hope for a permanent "good neighbor" Soviet Union, but a future, rejuvenated Soviet Union may once again seek to dominate its near neighbors. If that is the case, Eastern Europe could become the arena for a volatile contest for influence between the Soviet Union and another great power, Germany.

The Soviet Union's world order orientation also favored *selective instability*. Beyond Eastern Europe, the U.S.S.R.'s aim has been to change what it calls the world "correlation of forces" in its favor. Because the United States was so dominant after World War II, changes in the status quo almost by definition worked in the Soviets' favor, either by directly strengthening them or, indirectly, by weakening the Americans. Thus they have supported revolutionary movements around the world. In recent years the Soviet Union has become more confident of its superpower status. Because of this, and because of other factors, the Soviets' support of international instability has weakened.

A third, and relatively new, aspect of the Soviet concept of a favorable world order is *strategic economic considerations*. In recent years Soviet client states and the cost of high arms levels have become more financially burdensome as the Soviet economy has lagged and as the Soviet Union itself has had to import food, technology, and even natural resources, in which they were heretofore self-sufficient. These factors have caused increased concern in Moscow about the economic aspects of international relations. Gorbachev's recent drive to achieve better relations with the United States is linked to his desire to increase economic ties with the West. Gorbachev told Great Britain's prime minister Margaret Thatcher in March 1987 that "we need a lasting peace to concentrate on the development of our society and to proceed to improve the life of the Soviet people" (Rourke, 1990:41). Given the state of the Soviet economy, that development needs the Soviet Union's erstwhile enemies to increase private investment, to grant trade concessions, to relax technology export restrictions, and perhaps even to extend foreign aid. These needs have been a prime factor in Gorbachev's peace offensive and in some of his specific policies. It was not a matter of coincidence that Gorbachev's final agreement in July 1990 with Chancellor Helmut Kohl to accede quietly to German reunification came when Germany extended billions of deutsche marks in trade credits and other economic benefits to Moscow and suggested other Western countries do the same. Some of Gorbachev's domestic policies, such as Moscow's restraint in the face of independence moves from the Baltic and other republics and the relaxation of emigration restrictions on Soviet Jews, have also been moves to avoid antagonizing the West and endangering more favorable economic relations. Furthermore, the retreat of the Soviet Union from East Europe, its role in urging peaceful elections in Nicaragua, and other policies stem from the fact that it is financially no longer willing or able to support client states and other foreign adventures.

Projection of Values. The ideological fervor of a political system is apt to wane as time passes after the revolution and as the original revolutionary leaders die or retire. This has been true for the Soviet Union, and, especially under Gorbachev, ideology has become a declining variable in Soviet policy. It would be wrong, however, to view Gorbachev or other Soviet leaders as ideology-free. He spent a life rising through the Communist party's ranks and continues to profess belief in the tenets of Marxism-Leninism. Gorbachev has been flexible as necessity has wrung many concessions from him, but it is too soon to pronounce ideology dead in the U.S.S.R. or to proclaim that the influence of communism on its foreign policy has dissipated.

With this in mind, we can say that Russians, like Americans, have a strong *messianic tradition*. They saw themselves as the political successor to the great Western empires centered in Rome and Constantinople after those capitals fell to the barbarians and Muslims respectively. In fact the Russian royal title, czar (tsar), is a derivative of Caesar. Rome and Constantinople were also the centers of Christendom (Catholicism and Orthodoxy respectively), and the Russian messianic tradition considered Russian Orthodoxy to be the true faith. Russian messianism showed itself in the years before World War I in the form of "Slavophilism" when the Russians attempted to lead all their ethnic (Slavic) kin. This, in part, led to World War I when Russia sided with (Slavic) Serbia against Austria-Hungary.

In recent years, the messianic tradition has dovetailed with the messianism inherent in communism to urge the Soviets to export their secular faith around the globe. This has lessened as revolutionary fervor has subsided, but it is still there. Among other orientations, it gives the Soviets an image of *continued world struggle of ideas and the eventual victory of communism*. This disposes the Soviets to support leftist movements where practicable. It also makes them view the capitalist countries as dangerous opponents. Gorbachev has downplayed this, but he openly continues to portray capitalism and communism as competitive. Détente for the Soviets has been more of a means of avoiding destructive war with the West than a path to friendship. Messianism also contributed to the strains between the Soviet Union and China. As a messianic culture and as the first communist country, the Soviet Union had difficulty accepting any communist movement that did not follow Moscow's ideological line. China's self-direction was viewed as heretical by Soviet ideologues.

National Interest, Chinese Style

Like the United States and the Soviet Union, China's national-interest concepts are based on historical experience and a national belief system. Unlike the other two, though, China's historical tradition is much older and some of its belief system is much newer, dating back only 40 years to the victory of its communist revolution in 1949.

National Core. Whatever their political orientation, the Chinese have a tremendous consciousness of and pride in their nearly 3,000-year-old culture and history. This pride is not total, however, because like most of the Third World (and different from the Americans or Soviets) the Chinese suffered under a relatively recent colonial experience. They consider the period of outside domination that extended from the mid-1800s through the early part of this century to be a period of humiliation.

Therefore, *anti-imperial independence* has become an important drive behind Chinese foreign policy. From this perspective, a great deal of China's history in this century can be interpreted as part of the struggle of the Chinese people to regain their pride and to rid their country of the last vestiges of outside influence.

One very important aspect of this has been China's effort to regain "lost territories." Significant areas were lost during China's period of weakness, and the country is now reasserting its claim. Tibet, which had become independent, was reincorporated in the 1950s. Britain's Hong Kong and Portugal's Macao will soon (1997 and 1999, respectively) revert by treaty to China. There are still, however, two major territorial claims that remain unfulfilled. One is Taiwan. This island was traditionally part of China, but was seized by Japan late in the 1800s. After World War II it was

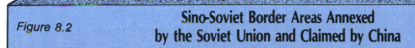

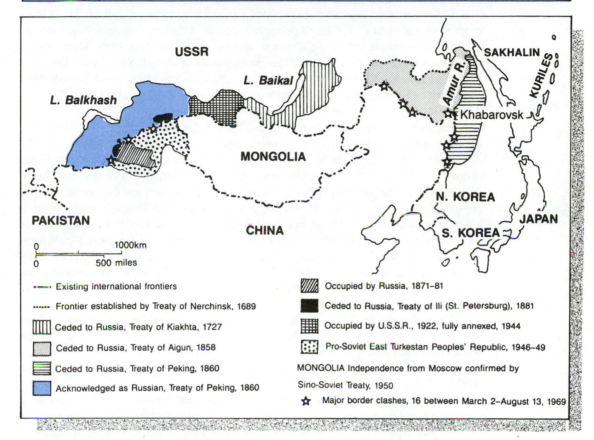

Figure 8.2 Sino-Soviet Border Areas Annexed by the Soviet Union and Claimed by China

Source: From *The Soviet Superpower,* by Peter J. Mooney, 1982, p. 172, London: Heinemann Educational Books, Ltd. Copyright 1982 by Heinemann Educational Books, Ltd. Reprinted by permission.

The recovery of territory that once was part of China is an important aspect of the Chinese concept of national interest as it relates to the national core. This map delineates the vast areas that once were China's but that have been incorporated into the Soviet Union. These remain a source of conflict between the two countries.

returned to China, but again became separated when the remnants of the Nationalist government fled there after Mao's communist victory. For years, the United States recognized Taiwan (Nationalist China, the Republic of China) as the legitimate government of all China, and the island remains an independent country. Although President Carter shifted full diplomatic recognition to Beijing in 1979, the United States continues to supply Taiwan with military equipment and is a major trading partner. By inference, Washington has also warned that it will not tolerate any attempt by the mainland to conquer the island. Thus, the status of Taiwan continues to be a major impediment to better relations between Washington and Beijing.

Perhaps even more portentous is the territorial dispute between China and the Soviet Union. During its period of imperial humiliation, China was forced to cede approximately 1.5 million square kilometers along its northern and western frontiers to Russia (see Fig. 8.2). China continues to claim these areas, and in 1969 there was large-scale fighting along the border that was partially related to these claims. Talks have dragged on inconclusively. China does not have the military might to challenge Soviet "occupation" successfully, but as China develops in the future the territorial dispute may escalate from diplomatic disagreement to a more serious level of confrontation.

China's colonial experience has created a strong urge to be *self-reliant*. There is an element of isolationism in China's policy orientation. This was evident during a period of domestic turmoil called the Cultural Revolution in the late 1960s when China withdrew virtually all its diplomatic representation from abroad. Self-reliance has also made China reluctant to seek economic ties with Western countries. This has moderated somewhat in recent years, but the Chinese are still very cautious about becoming too dependent on Western trade and technology.

Another of China's central-core orientations is *defensiveness*. Here, the Chinese fall between the near paranoia of the Soviets and the less concerned attitude of the Americans. China has been attacked and overrun many times in the past, and that history is reinforced by communist ideology's view of struggle with the capitalists/ imperialists. In the past two decades, China's image of its primary danger has shifted from the United States to concern with the Soviet Union, which Beijing considers both a potentially dangerous power and, because of Gorbachev's "subversion of socialism," as one Chinese Communist party memorandum put it, a threat to the party's continued control in China (*NYT*, 2/28/89:A1). China is intent on building itself up both as an industrial and a military force. The Chinese are particularly intent on increasing the power of their nuclear force. So far, they have refused to participate in nuclear-arms-limitation negotiations.

Favorable World Order. As both a developing and a communist country, China desires to see significant shifts in the status quo. *Sinocentrism* is one factor in China's worldview. The Chinese word for their country, "Chung-kuo," means "middle country" and symbolizes their image of themselves as the center of the political and cultural world.

This view has several foreign policy ramifications. One is that China has been seeking an *enhanced world role*. During the last two decades, China's diplomatic activity has expanded considerably. Its most important concerns have been regional, with a particular emphasis on ending Vietnam's domination of Cambodia (Kampuchea) and the Soviet occupation of Afghanistan. As China's power grows, however, its focus will increasingly extend beyond its region to include a greater array of global concerns.

China's world-order orientations may be leading toward a reassertion of China's traditional regional *sphere of influence*. Imperial China dominated smaller countries around it, especially to its south. This ended during the period of its own colonial humiliation, but the reemergence of China as a power has rejuvenated its interest in the region. There is disagreement over China's interest in and ability to reestablish some or all of its traditional sphere of influence (for example, see Burton et al., 1985), but China's opposition to Soviet influence in Southeast Asia, its border war with Vietnam in the late 1970s, and its support of anti-Vietnamese rebels in Cambodia, can all be taken as indicative of a potential reassertion of the middle kingdom's historic geopolitical domination of the region (see Fig. 8.3).

Another part of China's worldview is increased *international economic interchange*. This is a fairly recent orientation, and it conflicts somewhat with the self-reliance discussed above. In essence, China is intent on modernizing itself economically and has come to realize that it needs Western technology and investment to do so. As a result, China has moderated some of its disputes with the capitalist-industrial countries and has sought greater trade and foreign capital. China has even begun to cooperate with

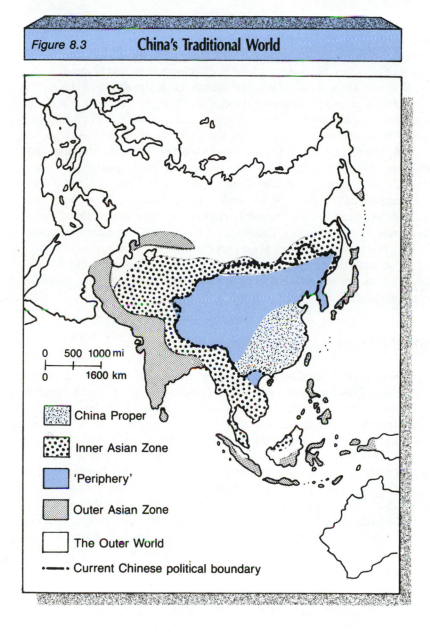

Figure 8.3 **China's Traditional World**

China Proper

Inner Asian Zone

'Periphery'

Outer Asian Zone

The Outer World

Current Chinese political boundary

0   500 1000 mi
0   1600 km

Source: From "On the Chinese Perception of World Order," by N. Ginsburg, in *China's Policies in Asia and America's Alternatives,* vol. 2, edited by Tang Tsou, 1968, Chicago: University of Chicago Press. Copyright 1968 by The University of Chicago. All rights reserved. Reprinted by permission.

Both of the two superpowers, the United States and the Soviet Union, dominate a sphere of influence that each feels especially affects its interests. Some analysts believe that China will become a superpower and that it will try to establish its own sphere of influence. This map shows the areas of China's special authority during its imperial height several centuries ago. If modern China reestablishes a sphere of influence, these areas are likely to be the focus of China's assertion of special interest. In recent years China has involved itself in confrontations with Vietnam and in the complex diplomacy of settling the multifaction civil war in Cambodia. The rise of China as a regional power could also set off a competition with two other increasingly powerful regional countries, India and Japan. The result could be a regional tripolar interaction.

the World Bank and other international economic institutions that not long ago it condemned as tools of capitalist imperialism.

Projection of Values. As with the Soviet Union, the role of communist ideology in China's foreign policy has waned. China is still closer to its revolution than the Soviet Union, however, and while the ideological content has declined it still plays an important role. Refering to events in Eastern Europe, China's premier Li Peng has pledged, for instance, that "regardless of whatever stormy waves appear on the international scene, socialist China will stand rock firm in the East" (*LAT,* 3/21/90:A5). A historical orientation, however, based on Confucianism's tenet of leading by example rather than forceful conversion, has made China less intent on actively spreading its ideology to others. This position also stems from China's resistance to Soviet ideological domination and its insistence that countries be free to define communism in their own terms. These priorities do not mean that the Chinese do not continue to support both anti-imperialism and eventual communist victory. Their support can be seen, for example, in their voting in the UN, where they are almost always on the other side of the issue from the United States. In general, though, the Chinese do not have the messianic inclinations of the Americans or the Soviets, and thus they are less intent on imposing their values on others than the two superpowers.

National Interest: Limits to Understanding

The American, Soviet, and Chinese national interest orientations outlined above are far from absolutes. They are general guides to the behaviors of the respective countries, but they have exceptions. Individual leaders or unusual circumstances may cause a country to depart from the norm. In addition, they sometimes conflict with one another. In the United States, for example, policy toward Cambodia has wavered over supporting rebels opposed to the Vietnam-dominated Cambodia communists. Vietnam is both communist and an old adversary, but the dominant rebel faction is the Khmer Rouge, which while in power (1975–79) caused 1 million Cambodian deaths (12 percent of the population). After years of U.S. support for the rebels, the Bush administration switched sides in mid-1990. Perceptions of national interest are also dynamic and mutable. Examining any country's conceptions of national interest, then, can provide some guidelines for understanding and even predicting policy, but it can never be certain or a substitute for careful analysis.

National Interest: How to Decide for Yourself What It Ought to Be

The final, and most important, task of this chapter is to suggest how each of us, as citizens of our country and the world, can best evaluate current policies and future options in the context of the national interest. It is important to have standards to use in evaluating the national interest claims of our own country and others. If we have none, it leaves us in the position of having to accept at face value the policies of decisionmakers or, if we reject them, of doing so without applying any systematic criteria of our own. Falling into this trap leaves us rightfully subject to the charge that our concept of how the national interest "ought to be" defined is no more valid than anybody else's.

Thus, if we want to be informed, rather than just opinionated, it is important to be able to evaluate any given policy within the broad context of our country's national interest. In this section we will explore some ideas that can help us accomplish this task.

National Interest—as in Nation

Before going further it is necessary to understand what is meant by *national*. The existence of the nation-state has caused the two parts of that hyphenate to be confused or considered synonymous. As discussed earlier, states and nations are very distinct, the state being a physical, political entity and the **nation** being a people who have common characteristics and experiences and a perceived sense of kinship.

When we speak of national interest, we mean the goals of the state and its regime based on its representation of the nation. What we are not discussing is the interests of the state or its regime, as such. In other words, the function of the state is to act as an agent of the nation, or, as another author put it, the state's "principal, if not its only care, is the welfare of its citizens. . . . The test of its utility is the faithfulness with which it reflects" the nation's interest (Perry, 1968:6).

This focus on the nation (the people), not on the physical state or the political regime, is a critical point in understanding what national interest ought to be. "Public interest" is a term that has been suggested to clarify whose interest is properly considered (Kratochwil, 1982:4). Whatever the term, the point is that the interests of the state and the nation are not synonymous. They are normally closely related, but they are not identical.

It is, for instance, possible for the demise of the state as such to be in the national interest. Imagine a situation in which the Soviets achieved a position where they could attack your country with nuclear weapons and escape retaliation. The president faces two stark choices: surrender or be annihilated. Can a war that kills almost everyone be in the national interest? Most Americans say that they would risk death by fighting a communist attack, but faced with an absolute certainty of total annihilation it would seem to be in the national interest to submit so that they might rise again, as did the phoenix.

If we focus on the concept of nation, it is possible to identify various dimensions of national interest. Inasmuch as a nation is (1) a people (2) with feelings of kinship (3) based on common cultural characteristics, then the national interest is whatever enhances those three factors. Policies that foster physical safety, economic well-being, and the freedom of a people to order their own sociopolitical processes can be properly identified as in the national interest. In subsequent sections we will see how these can be included in a working definition.

National Interest—Majoritarian

To form our concept of national interest, we also have to deal with the contention that there is no *single* set of interests in any society. Several points can be made in response. First, the diffusion of interests within a nation does not mean that an interest cannot be national. It is axiomatic that in most cases different subgroups will have varying interests. Not all these can be met all the time. That is true for any policy, domestic or foreign.

Instead, national interest can properly be defined as goals that will benefit all, if possible, but, when that is impossible, goals that will (1) either maximize positive results or minimize negative results for the majority; and also (2) either minimize negative results for the minority or minimize the size of the minority that suffers negative results.

Basically, this comes down to **majoritarianism** as the primary guideline for goal selection, with minority protection an important, but secondary, standard. Any other guideline would be inconsistent with the proper state/nation relationship. Obviously, this does not establish a precise standard between majority and minority interests or clearly delineate which policy benefits the majority. This is properly left to the political process. It does, however, objectively eliminate policies that serve the interest of politically powerful individuals or small groups at the expense of the majority. Majoritarianism also does not imply following every mass whim. As the next section shows, there are long- and short-term interests, and the former should prevail.

Principles of Evaluation

Once we have some concept of "whose" interest we are considering, our next step is to formulate some principles that we can use to judge the policies that we and others proclaim to be in the national interest. The following three principles can be applied to evaluating any such claim (Kratochwil, 1982).

1. Place the *burden of proof* on the claimant. "You said it, prove it" is a prudent stand to take in the face of claims to the national interest.
2. Apply the principle of *consequence*. Consider *all* the various dimensions of national interest. It is not enough to say a policy will enhance trade. The impact on security and other factors must also be considered.
3. Finally, consider the principle of *generalization*. This standard posits that what is right or wrong for one actor must also be right or wrong for any actor in similar circumstances. It is, for example, incompatible, by this principle, for the U.S. to intervene in Nicaragua (U.S. sphere of influence) while condemning Soviet interference in Poland (U.S.S.R. sphere of influence).

This third somewhat existential standard of conduct also helps unravel some of the issues of consequences for domestic majorities and minorities. We cannot ask farmers not to sell wheat to the U.S.S.R. unless other segments of the economic community are also ready to suffer financially. Domestically and internationally, then, you have to be ready to accept the same standards that you judge others by.

Dimensions of National Interest

With these preliminary principles in mind, the next step is to consider the possible dimensions of national interest. Some contend that there are so many complex and often conflicting national interests that ordering them is beyond human capability. National interest is, indeed, a complex phenomenon, but it is not beyond comprehension. Frederick Hartmann (1962:5) has argued that there is an "irreducible core" of interests based on the function of the state. And Hans Morgenthau has similarly identified a "hard core" of interests that are relatively permanent. What is needed, then, is to devise a hierarchy of interests that will at least begin to allow us to order our priorities. That is the task of this section, which explores the work of scholars toward that goal, and we will proceed by examining the issue dimension, the time dimension, and the importance dimension of national interest.[2]

2. All students of national interest owe a great deal to Hans Morgenthau. His work on analyzing this phenomenon is reviewed by Robinson (1969). According to Robinson, Morgenthau's many discussions of national interest delineated the concept according to priority (primary, secondary), time frame (permanent, variable), specificity (general, specific), and compatibility with the interests of other countries (identical, complementary, conflicting).

The Issue Dimension

There can be little doubt that national interest is multifaceted. As the earlier discussion of the U.S. stakes in the Middle East and the Persian Gulf disclosed, almost all policies may include a number of "gains" and "losses" for a country. One way to analyze these is to categorize areas of policy impact. The work of Donald Neuchterlein (1979) and this author (1971) can be combined to yield four basic **issue areas** of national interest: physical safety, material well-being, political environment, and national cohesion. Arguably, these four issue areas are objective in that each is a direct requirement for the welfare of the nation and, therefore, a legitimate goal of the state.

Physical Safety. This issue is largely self-explanatory. The essence of a nation is its people, and the physical survival of the people is an irreducible element of national interest. It should be noted that this does *not* necessarily include territory preservation or regime maintenance. The safety of the nation is more important than the state or its government, as such.

It is important to keep in mind, though, that physical safety is but one dimension of the national interest and that overemphasizing it can be destructive. There are those who argue that the emphasis on defense has turned the United States, the Soviet Union, and others into "national security states." It is argued that they are politically dominated by their military-industrial complexes, which, in turn, need tension and conflict to persist.

Material well-being. The state also has an obligation to ensure that its citizens enjoy adequate food, housing, clothing, medical care, and other human needs. It is unlikely, for example, that the West could long tolerate a complete cutoff of Mideast oil. Subsistence is the primary standard; wealth is desirable but not necessary.

Political environment. This dimension is akin to a nation's liberty to choose its own sociopolitical structure or favorable world order. When, in 1984, Mikhail Gorbachev was criticized by a British member of Parliament for the oppressive Soviet system, the communist leader shot back, "You govern your society, and you leave us to govern ours." There is an element of free choice here, but it is not necessarily synonymous with sovereignty. It is possible to argue, for example, that global security through a world government that allowed only limited autonomy would better ensure a favorable political environment than the current Darwinian process of survival of the fittest.

This point is extremely important to understand in the concept of national interest being argued here, and it will be reiterated in the upcoming discussion of the time dimension of national interest. Asserting your power to intervene in another country's domestic process, perhaps to overthrow its government or protect the existing government against a popular revolution that you do not favor, may, at one level, create a "plus" in political environment. It will also, however, perpetuate a world in which might too often equals success. If you live by the sword, you may someday die by it. Therefore, you need to be very specific about the political environment you favor, and judge policies by whether or not they help create that kind of international environment.

National cohesion. This is probably the most controversial issue dimension. It is akin to Neuchterlein's (1979:74) "promotion of values," which he equates with ideology or protection and a set of values that citizens share and believe to be good.

If we consider again the nature of a nation, we can see that perceived mutual identity is a crucial element. Without that sense of mutuality, potential nations do not form and existing nations dissolve. It follows, then, that any goal or action that contravenes a nation's values and thereby fosters disintegrative forces has a deleterious effect on the nation. The Vietnam War was one of the most traumatic attacks on the American self-image in the nation's history. Whatever other interests were involved, it is

National cohesion is one issue of national interest for, arguably, any policy that seriously breaks down national cohesion is, at least in part, working against the national interest. The U.S. intervention in Vietnam was one such policy, and it led to great strife within the United States. This was tragically epitomized by the confrontation between war-protesting students and Ohio national guardsmen on the campus of Kent State University on May 4, 1970. Many on both sides were frightened, but the guardsmen had guns and opened fire. The student shown here and several of his classmates were wounded. Four other students were even less fortunate; they were killed by the fusillade.

reasonable to argue that U.S. disengagement was necessary to avoid a further tearing of the national fabric.

As used here, the national-cohesion dimension includes the ideas, ideology, and morality as discussed in the preceding chapter. It allows for the introduction of moral, humanitarian values even if they are self-sacrificing (Wolfers, 1969). These types of values have been described as "transcending" the national interest, but insofar as these values promote national cohesion or, as will be discussed presently, are in the long-term national interest, they are not necessarily self-sacrificing at all.

By looking to national values, we avoid the swamp of controversy surrounding universal values. By combining the principle of generalization with nationally generated ideals, we thus have a valid set of values.

The Time Dimension

It is also important to distinguish between time frames. Usually *short-term* interests should be subordinate to *long-term* interests. Think about how you feel about foreign aid, for instance. If you are like a majority of Americans, your attitude toward foreign aid will range from skeptical to hostile. The U.S. federal budget is running a huge deficit and the country is facing other economic difficulties, and most surveys find that only a bit more than a third of respondents believe that "helping to improve the standard of living of less developed nations" should be an important U.S. foreign policy goal (Wiarda, 1990:71). Leaving aside humanitarian concerns, that majority position may even make short-term sense given deficits, domestic needs, taxes, and other factors. What about the long term, though? Canadian member of Parliament Bruce Halliday (1989:372) told the U.S. Congress that:

Uprisings and conflicts half-way around the world threaten everyone's security. . . . Some of the most volatile places in the world are home to poor and desperate people with nothing to lose by throwing their support behind anyone who promises them food, land, health care and education. . . . The effects of resource use, environmental damage and population growth are not confined within national borders but pose a threat to the integrity of the whole planet. . . . [The] final linkage between security and development concerns is the international economy. . . . As we increasingly rely on the Third World as a trading partner, it also becomes important to keep their economies growing. The . . . downturn in Third World economies . . . during the global recession in the early 1980s cost 135,000 jobs in Canada alone. . . . The consequences of inaction may not [always] appear in our lifetime, but we have a responsibility to future generations to implement sustainable human progress. . . . It is clearly in our national self-interests to do everything we can to help these countries improve their situation.

As you can see, what may seem penny-wise today may in fact be pound-foolish for your and your children's future.

The grain being unloaded in Ethiopia in this photograph is part of the U.S. foreign aid program. That effort, in terms of real dollars, has steadily declined in recent years because many Americans, as well as people in other wealthy countries, view foreign aid as an expensive giveaway program. In the short term, given budget deficits, they may be right. In the long term, however, the national interest of the developed countries like the U.S. might be better served by their making sacrifices now. Thus they stand to benefit economically later and avoid incurring now the bitterness of the impoverished Third World.

TABLE 8.1

Matrix for Categorizing National Interest Issues

	Long-Term Primary	Long-Term Secondary	Short-Term Primary	Short-Term Secondary
Physical safety				
Material well-being				
Political environment				
National cohesion				

By considering the many implications of any policy according to the various criteria of this matrix, you can reach a more systematic evaluation of the national interest.

The Importance Dimension

If we are to skillfully evaluate national interest, it is necessary to assess the relative importance of various claims to the national interest. That is, we must establish *priorities*. Of course, priorities range along a scale, but for our purposes here we can use Morgenthau's *primary* (absolutely necessary) and *secondary* standards.

The recent changes in the Soviet Union and Eastern Europe provide an illustration of how this priority dimension might be used. Imagine that Gorbachev is toppled by an old-guard faction in Moscow. The new leaders are determined to reclaim some of their Eastern Europe sphere of influence, and they refuse to continue to withdraw their troops from Poland, Czechoslovakia, and Hungary. The Czechoslovakians revolt and call for NATO paratroopers to help defend the democratic government in Prague. Sending military forces might help "make the world safe for democracy," but it would also run the risk of starting World War III. Both alternatives affect U.S., Canadian, and other countries' interests, but which is more important? The answer is a matter of values, of course, but in earlier and similar instances, such as Hungary in 1956 and Czechoslovakia in 1968, Western leaders considered peace primary and democracy secondary and fired only rhetorical barrages when Soviet tanks clanked into Budapest and Prague.

Possibilities and Limits

One thing you can do with the analytical criteria put forth under the issue, time, and importance dimensions is to construct a matrix, as illustrated in Table 8.1. The matrix is a beginning tool for understanding and evaluating the use and abuse of national interest. First, by plugging in what decisionmakers say, we can gather evidence on why they acted or how they might act.

Second, we can also use the matrix as a tool for planning and evaluation. Is foreign aid in the national interest? What are the long- and short-term consequences? Are the impacts primary or secondary? Use of the matrix helps ensure that we follow the principle of consequences. We need to consider *all* the consequences *all* the time. Dropping bombs on Baghdad in August 1990 would have felt good to a lot of Americans, but would it have been worth it? *All* things considered, probably not.

There are also distinct limits to the matrix. Assigning policy questions to one or another category (short-term, long-term; primary, secondary) will often be debatable. Making trade-offs between interests will also be controversial. What if two primary, long-term interests are mutually exclusive? No matrix can account for all possibilities or substitute for informed, rational judgment. In real life, though, such dilemmas exist and choices must be made, and a matrix helps us see the myriad factors. Finally, calculating consequences cannot be accomplished by this or any matrix, but we can begin. There is no mechanical substitute for insight. This is what the study of world politics is all about.

Chapter Summary

1. National interest is one of the most difficult concepts for international relations analysts to define and evaluate. In the first place, it is used in two different ways: subjectively, as a rationale for political action, and objectively, to evaluate goals and policies.

2. Even from an objective viewpoint, there are many troubling questions that complicate attempts to come to a meaningful conceptualization of national interest. Many dismiss any such attempt on the grounds that, as a concept, national interest is hopelessly vague, confuses ends and means, is necessarily subjective, and ignores the diversity of elements in society.

3. Despite these very real difficulties, it is important to understand national interest from two perspectives.

4. One perspective is to examine the policies and pronouncements of countries to look for consistencies in the ways they define their interests. This will enable us to better understand the ways an ally or antagonist is acting and what path the future may hold.

5. The second perspective relates to our evaluation of the policies of our own country. If we can form a systematic conception of national interest, even a rudimentary one, then we are in a much better position to support or oppose policy in an informed manner. To that end, we need to understand that national interest implies goals that are in the interest of the nation, not necessarily the state or the regime.

6. We also need to apply certain principles of proof, consequence, and generalization to our evaluation. Finally, we need to define various dimensions of national interest according to issue area, time frame, and level of importance.

7. These steps will not allow us to predict flawlessly what policy will be, nor will they yield a foolproof formula for evaluating policy. What the steps will do is organize our thinking so that we can reach conclusions on a systematic and informed basis.

PART III

THE INSTRUMENTS OF

We now come to the "action" of our world political drama. The stage was set, the actors were cast, and the critical approaches were established in Part I. Then, in Part II, the plot—the actors' motivations—was outlined. Thus it is time in Part III to bring down the house lights, raise the curtain, and begin the play.

Chapters 9 through 14 will look at the way the principal actors—the states—play out their parts. You should be forewarned that some of the action is not pretty. It certainly would often get an "R" rating,

220

INTERNATIONAL POLITICS

perhaps even an occasional "X," and it is definitely not suited for young children. This is because the instruments we will explore—force and coercion, diplomacy, penetration and manipulation, and economic maneuvering—are normally applied in the narrow, self-serving way that national interest is normally construed. Clash, therefore, is more common than cooperation. We will reach the happier subject of international cooperation in Part IV, but first there is considerable turbulence to contemplate.

Before specifically discussing the ways (instru-ments, tools, means) with which the actors pursue their goals (ends), we must discuss the concept of power. For good or ill, it forms a backdrop to all the means that constitute this part of the text. Power is not everything in world politics. Some states and other international actors even play a part and survive without much of it. Their actions are limited, though, and their welfare, even survival, often rests on the sufferance of other, more powerful, actors.

221

Then, everything includes itself in power,
Power into will, will into appetite;
And appetite, a universal wolf
So doubly seconded with will and power,
Must make perforce a universal prey,
And at last eat up himself.

Shakespeare, *Troilus and Cressida*

Power is the supreme law.

Adolph Hitler, *Mein Kampf*

We have, I fear, confused power with greatness.

U.S. Representative Stuart Udall, speech

CHAPTER 9

POWER

Power is a crucial factor in world politics. Indeed, some analysts argue that it is *the* single most important element in determining the course of international interactions. Most political scientists agree that this view is an overstatement, but it does serve to emphasize the importance of power. National goals and interests often conflict, and when they do, whose interests will prevail becomes a central question. The resolution of that issue is heavily influenced by power.

Power: Defining and Understanding a Controversial Concept

Like a number of other terms we have covered, *power* is both important and elusive. "Power in international politics is like the weather," prominent political scientist Joseph Nye (1990:12) tells us. "Everyone talks about it, but few understand it." Within the space of a page, Nye goes on to confide that "power, like love, is easier to experience than to define or measure," and to warn that we cannot always assume that others do things in response to our power, "Otherwise, we may be as mistaken about our power as was the fox who thought he was hurting Brer Rabbit when he threw him into the briar patch." Yes, power is perplexing. If its intricacies can throw the dean for International Affairs at Harvard University into such a literary bramble bush within a mere three paragraphs, then it is understandable that you, as an undergraduate student taking an introductory international relations course, will have to think carefully. It is not appropriate here to delve too far into the academic debate about the nature and use of power. It is, however, important to come to a clear understanding of how this text uses the word so that we can proceed from a common point.

Ends and Means: Confusion About the Nature of Power

Treating power as a means. The preceding chapter examined the confusion of ends and means—or goals and methods—and considered power as an example. In the discussion here, the term *power* should be understood as a means, a tool. Not that countries do not seek to enhance power as an end in itself—they certainly do. Here, though, we are concerned with power as a resource, or tool, that enables countries to pursue their national interests successfully. Some authors have distinguished between power and influence by saying that the former is a key factor in conflictive situations and the latter operates in cooperative relations. The relation between the two terms is complex, but in this text power is conceived of as the larger, more inclusive of the two terms. Power, whether it be obvious military armament or more subtle diplomatic skill, gives one country the ability to bend a second country to its will. Whether that is done by coercion or by persuasion, the success or failure of the first country is based on its power (Boulding, 1989).

The impulse to treat, and danger of treating, power as an end. Power is best thought of as a tool, not a goal in and of itself. This viewpoint is important because of the drawbacks of becoming obsessed with acquiring power. In the next few paragraphs, we will compare power with money. This idea, that power is a sort of international currency that gets you what you want, can help us understand why treating power as a goal is dangerous.

If you think about it, money is a tool. We use it to achieve goals like going to college, buying a car, or getting a pizza on Saturday night. By itself, money is pretty useless. It is inedible, you would not want to make clothes out of it, and it will not even burn very well if you need to keep warm. Thus money is a means to an end.

Some people become obsessed with having money for its own sake, though. For them, acquiring money is an end in itself. Such individuals are the subject of many tragic dramas, ranging from Molière's *The Miser* to Dickens's classic, *A Christmas Carol*, and its sad story of Ebenezer Scrooge. In both of these tales, the miser gave up love, friendships, and life's other pleasures to get and keep money. Each was paranoid, haunted that he would lose his money. In the end, each miser found that his money became a burden rather than a source of betterment.

There are many theories about the lure of amassing power in the international system. Realists, for instance, might contend that the quasi-anarchistic nature of the international system makes it prudent for a country to amass power to protect itself in a dangerous world. One psychological theory argues that at least some people have a need to control their environment and seek power to do so. Yet another idea, discussed in chapter 4, is that power-seeking is a particularly male psychosexual impulse.

Whatever the exact source of the urge to amass power, there are clear dangers associated with overemphasizing the acquisition and preservation of power, especially military power. Three such perils deserve special mention. One is the "spiral of insecurity." This was briefly discussed in the section on perceptions in chapter 4, but to reiterate, it means that our attempts to amass power to achieve security or gain other ends is inevitably seen by others as a danger to them. They then seek to acquire offsetting power, which we see as threatening, causing us to acquire even more power . . . then them . . . then us, *ad infinitum*, in an escalating spiral. As we will see in the chapter on disarmament (chapter 17), the arms race is a complex phenomenon, but the interaction of one country's power and other countries' insecurity is an important factor in world politics.

A second problem with acquiring power for its own sake is that it is often extremely

Military capability is a powerful instrument of international relations. It is expensive, though, and some people argue that acquiring too much military power is wasteful. In this picture U.S. first lady Barbara Bush, accompanied by her husband, christens the aircraft carrier, USS *George Washington.* The ship cost $3.5 billion. That is enough to send 17,500 students to the most expensive U.S. private university. By another standard, $3.5 billion is approximately equal to the combined annual GNPs of the small, poor countries of Chad, Laos, Malawi, and Togo.

expensive. We have reached the stage in technological development where the cost of a single new aircraft carrier begins to boggle the imagination. The latest U.S. aircraft carrier, the USS *George Washington,* cost $3.5 billion, and that is the "factory-equipped model" without much of what is needed to arm and protect the ship, including much of its peripheral equipment, its 85 aircraft, and its carrier battle group of 2 cruisers, 4 destroyers, and 2 submarines. All these escalate the cost to about $15 billion to acquire and $500 million a year to operate the ship and its flotilla. Surely, a nuclear-powered, nuclear-armed supercarrier is an impressive and powerful machine. The *George Washington* weighs 100,000 tons; has a three-football-fields-long, 4.5-acre flight deck; and can theoretically steam one million miles between refuelings. The ship projects U.S. power around the world rapidly, and, given its nuclear weapons, it has the power to flatten most small countries in a matter of minutes. Maybe it is needed and worth the money, but one has to wonder. Even considering just the ship's base $3.5-billion price tag, and mindful of the need to make choices in an era of aircraft carrier–size budget deficits, the money might be better used for other things. If we chose, as one alternative, to build modest senior citizen housing at $85,000 each, we could construct 41,176 units for the same total cost. Or the United States could give the money for just one such carrier to the World Health Organization. In that unlikely event, the WHO estimates that it could immunize every unprotected child in the Third World for a year against a variety of maladies, save the lives of 7.5 million children annually, and still have a billion dollars left over (*HC,* 4/30/90:D8).

On a grander scale, we should also consider the recent argument of historian Paul Kennedy in *The Rise and Fall of the Great Powers* (1988). Kennedy examines the growth and decline of the world's great powers between 1500 and the present. He finds that wealth is usually needed to acquire military power, and military power is usually required to achieve and protect wealth. Kennedy continues, however, that military power is often illusory, even destructive, because countries pour too many resources into it. This saps resources that should be devoted to economic growth, eventually leading a powerful country to an inexorable decline and fall. Kennedy predicts that countries that overextend themselves, including the United States and the Soviet Union, face perilous times in the future unless they address the painful need to reduce their global interests and obligations to a level that matches their financial resources.

"Declinism" is the label that has been attached to Kennedy's thesis by some of his critics, of which there are many (Cohen & Wilson, 1988; Rasler & Thompson, 1988). Some of the objections to Kennedy's thesis have been overtaken by the end of the cold war. Others, however, remain. There are criticisms of Kennedy's application of the lessons of history, especially the nineteenth-century decline of Great Britain, to the United States in what critics contend is a different set of circumstances. Other critics suggest that the propensity of "declinists" to measure current U.S. power in terms of its percentage of world gross national product or trade against the U.S. position in the late 1940s is misleading. The critics reason that the U.S. position at that time, generating 50 percent of the world GNP, for example, was an anomaly related to the destruction of World War II. No scholar would deny that the United States has declined relatively as Japan, Germany, and others have become stronger, but that is different from the implications of the reasoning of Kennedy and others. Harvard's Joseph Nye (1990:42–47), for one, argues that Yale's Paul Kennedy is "mistaken." Nye makes many counterpoints, including the suggestion that Kennedy and others overemphasize "hard power" and overlook "soft power" (noncoercive power, influence). In sum, Nye concludes that far from being about to join Kennedy's ranks of the fallen great powers, "the United States is likely to remain the leading power in world politics."

Third, the accumulation of power creates the temptation to use that power. Merely having global power sometimes means that a country may try to project itself into an area that is of peripheral interest. Earlier we saw how the United States went to war in Vietnam, a place that President Johnson derided as a "raggedy-ass fourth-rate country." It can be argued that one reason Americans went to war there was that they had the power to do so. Had U.S. military power been more modest, the United States might have emphasized diplomacy, or maybe even ignored the communist/nationalist reunification of North and South Vietnam. One can never be sure, but it is certain that it is hard to shoot someone if you do not own a gun.

Does this mean disarm? Not necessarily. The prudence of acquiring some power reserves in our quasi-anarchistic world was noted earlier in this section. It does mean, though, that in excess of reasonable needs, power can be a burden and a dangerous temptation.

The Gap Between Potential and Actual Power

To be effective, power normally must have the capacity to be used. It does not have to be actually employed to count, but there must be either the real or the perceived possibility of its use. **Potential power** is less of a factor in world politics than **actual power**. China has oil reserves off its coast, and Brazil has extensive mineral deposits deep within its Amazon region. Their ability to extract these resources, however, is limited, and consequently the resources are only potential power factors. Prior to both world wars, the United States had vast military potential, but its readiness was at a low ebb. Peter Beckman (1984:89) has calculated, for instance, that in 1910 the U.S. basic power level (potential) was more than twice Germany's. American "projectable" power (actual, usable), however, was only about one-third of Germany's. That disparity between potential and actual powers profoundly affected German calculations of submarine warfare against U.S. merchant shipping. When asked for his evaluation of the American military in 1917, a German admiral replied, "Zero, zero, zero." Potential power was not enough to deter the U-boat campaign; only after American power was activated did it contribute to Germany's defeat.

Distinguishing Between Real and Perceived Power

We have seen on several occasions that international politics is influenced both by what is true and by what others believe to be true. **Real power**, or the power that you objectively possess and can use, is, of course, a major factor. Yet, insofar as power has to do with making others conform to your wishes, it may be sufficient for them only to believe that you have both the *capacity* and the *will* to act. When a robber confronts a bank teller with his hand in his jacket pocket, the teller's decision to hand over the money or not will depend on whether the threat is believed.

This **perceived power** also occurs on a global level. Richard Nixon and Henry Kissinger long argued that unilateral U.S. withdrawal from Vietnam would damage American power. In his memoirs Kissinger (1979:292) writes: "Rightly or wrongly—I am still convinced rightly—we thought that capitulation . . . would usher in a period of disintegrating American credibility that would only accelerate the world's instability." Measuring the loss of power is difficult, but it is hard to escape the conclusion that the defeat in Vietnam and the subsequent uncertainty of U.S. foreign policy did diminish world perceptions of American power in terms of resolve and purpose. That decline almost certainly emboldened the country's adversaries and alarmed its friends.

The gap between objective and subjective power and its impact on influence were documented by one researcher who compared capability and influence during the period from 1925–30.[1] He found that the seven great powers at the time ranked by capability and, by contrast, in influence were:

Capability	*Influence*
1. United States	1. France
2. Germany	2. Great Britain
3. Great Britain	3. Italy
4. France	4. Germany
5. Russia	5. Russia
6. Italy	6. Japan
7. Japan	7. United States

As can be seen for the 1925–30 period, the United States, which ranked first in objective measurement of capability, scored last in its ability to extend influence.

Power as Money

In trying to characterize power, Karl W. Deutsch (1978:46) has written that "just as money is the currency of economic life, so power can be thought of as the currency of

---

1. Simonds (1939), discussed in K. J. Holsti (1977). I express my appreciation to Robert B. Charlick at Cleveland State University for pointing out Holsti's original source.

politics." It is useful to equate power and money because both are assets that can be used to acquire things you want. Economically, money buys things. Politically, power causes things to happen.

Even Deutsch, however, is careful to caution that "the similarities between power and money should not be overstressed" (p. 47). As another analyst points out, "Political power resources tend to be much less liquid than economic resources" (Baldwin, 1979:164). That liquidity factor means that it is harder to convert power than money. Among other differences, power, unlike money, has no standard measurement that allows all parties to agree on the amount involved.

Measuring Power

The difficulty of agreeing on the "value" of power brings us to the last issue of this section—how do we measure power? Candidly, the answer is that political scientists have not been very successful at doing that, although there have been some encouraging recent efforts to do so (Merritt & Zinnes, 1989; Kugler & Arbetman, 1989).

Two problems, as will be discussed in the next section, are that power is multifaceted and also varies from situation to situation. This means that "estimates of capabilities covering all [countries] . . . in all imaginable contingencies would run to millions of combinations and permutations" (Baldwin, 1979:167). Second, measuring things like the number of guns, oil production, or population is easy. Measuring other aspects of power, such as leadership or morale, is much more difficult. When you add in the perceptual factor of how others evaluate your capacity, you have an unimaginably complex equation.

These difficulties have not deterred some political scientists from trying to measure power. One of the most ambitious and comprehensive approaches was formulated by Ray S. Cline (1977:34; 1980). According to Cline's formula, perceived power (P_p) equals critical mass (C), comprising population and territory, plus economic capability (E), plus military capability (M), times strategic purpose (S), or coherent planning, plus will to pursue national strategy (W). In symbolic representation, then,

$$P_p = (C + E + M) \times (S + W).$$

Using this formula as a basis, Cline compiled numerous indicators of power components and arrived at a final estimation of national power for 1978. Table 9.1 shows Cline's ratings for the top 10 countries among the 77 countries evaluated.

It must be stressed that Cline's formula is at best a guideline and is subject to all the qualifiers discussed in the next section. How to count even the tangible factors (C + E + M) is highly controversial. Quantifying the intangible factors (S + W) is beyond our current capability and may well be impossible. Thus, in the final analysis, trying to use Cline's formula as a measuring device includes many, many subjective assessments. Still, there is value in Cline's formula because it emphasizes the fact that sheer numbers of things (C + E + M) must be modified by such intangible factors as strategy and will (S + W) in order to truly evaluate power. The United States, according to Cline, has the highest C + E + M rating, yet Cline's substantially higher evaluation of the U.S.S.R.'s S + W total leaves the Soviet Union with a stronger final P_p rating. Cline highly rated Soviet strategy because he believed that, "whatever current tactics might be at any moment, Soviet strategy toward the outside world is coherent and clear" (1980:153). By contrast, Cline contends that U.S. strategy is characterized by "drifting and passivity" and is "reactive," designed in response to situations created by other nations (pp. 157, 162).

TABLE 9.1

World Power Rating, 1978

Rank	Country	Per-ceived Power* (P_p)	=	Tangible Power Weights (C + E + M)	×	Strategy (S)	+	Will (W)	Total (S + W)
1	Soviet Union	458		382		0.7		0.5	1.2
2	United States	304		434		0.3		0.4	0.7
3	Brazil	137		98		0.6		0.8	1.4
4	W. Germany	116		77		0.7		0.8	1.4
5	Japan	108		77		0.6		0.8	1.4
6	Australia	88		73		0.5		0.7	1.2
7	China	83		139		0.4		0.2	0.6
8	France	74		82		0.4		0.5	0.9
9	Great Britain	68		68		0.5		0.5	1.0
10	Canada	61		87		0.3		0.4	0.7

*P_p is rounded.

Source: From *World Power Trends and U.S. Foreign Policy for the 1980s,* by Ray S. Cline, 1980, pp. 173–74, Boulder, Colorado: Westview Press. Copyright 1980 by Ray S. Cline. Reprinted by permission.

Power is multifaceted and also varies from situation to situation. When you add in the perceptual factor of how others evaluate your capacity, you have a complex equation. For an explanation of how Ray S. Cline came to grips with this problem and a commentary, see the facing page. Clearly these ratings have changed, especially for the Soviet Union. Power, as discussed later, is dynamic.

Another insight into the difficulty of measuring power has recently been published (Taber, 1989). This study compared several other studies that measured and ranked power by equating the various formulas to a theoretical standard of 1,000 for the United States. Some of the results are shown in Table 9.2 on the following page. Note especially the different rankings and the differences in the relative scores. Two of the approaches, for example, rank the United States first, two place the U.S.S.R. first. Two rate U.S. power as about twice that of the U.S.S.R.; one rates Soviet power more than 30 percent higher than U.S. power. The fifth study ranks China first by a great distance.

Each of the studies arrives at its power score by a different formula. For example, the study that ranks China first highly values population. To help further examine the data Taber has collected and correlated, this author has added two calculations to Table 9.2. The first, shown in the column "average points," totals the points assigned by Taber and divides by five. The second column finds the average rank each study assigns various countries.

There are several things that you might note in Table 9.2. One is that Third World countries receive the most inconsistent treatment, a point Taber stresses. China makes all the lists, but ranks between first and eighth. India ranks as high as fourth on two lists, and Brazil ranks third on another list, but the two countries fail to make the top 10 on two other lists. A second point evident in Table 9.2 is that, apart from China, India, and Brazil, the industrialized countries receive rather consistent treatment, and the averages reached in the two furthest right columns make at least intuitive sense. Indeed, only 12 countries make the top 10 on any of the five lists, another indication of consistency in power rating.

TABLE 9.2

Comparative Power Ratings, 1980

1 GNP		2 Cline		3 Singer		4 German		5 Fucks		6 Average Points		7 Average Rank	
US	1,000	SU	1,309	SU	1,127	CH	2,858	US	1,000	US	1,000	SU	1.6
SU	496	US	1,000	US	1,000	SU	1,253	SU	577	SU	952	US	1.8
JP	406	BZ	452	CH	782	US	1,000	CH	212	CH	848	CH	4.4
WG	319	WG	380	IN	366	IN	694	JP	195	JP	306	JP	4.4
FR	253	JP	355	JP	356	JP	220	WG	101	WG	233	WG	5.4
UK	200	AU	288	WG	238	UK	217	UK	76	FR	191	UK	7.0
IT	152	CH	275	FR	187	FR	207	CN	76	UK	177	FR	7.2
CH	115	FR	243	UK	166	WG	128	IN	73	IN	227	IN	7.6
BZ	95	UK	224	IT	127	UK	120	FR	65	BZ	133	BZ	8.8
CN	95	CN	200	CN	93	BZ	120	IT	50	CN	93	CN	9.6
										IT	66	IT	9.6
										AU	58	AU	10.0

AU - Australia, BZ - Brazil, CH - China, CN - Canada, FR - France, IN - India, IT - Italy, JP - Japan, SU - Soviet Union, UK - United Kingdom, US - United States, WG - West Germany

Data source: Taber (1989) for columns 1–5.

The first five columns are based on Gross National Product and the work of Ray Cline, J. David Singer, F. Clifford German, and Wilhelm Fucks. For full bibliographic information and methodological data, see Taber (1989). He converts and standardizes the power rating arrived at by these studies by using 1980 data and making them relative to a 1000 score for the United States. The sixth column is calculated by averaging the adjusted points assigned by Taber. The seventh column is calculated by averaging the rank (1–10) each country holds in the first five columns. Countries falling below the top ten were assigned a rank of 11 for calculation.

Power: A Definition

For all the various problems in defining and measuring power, it is still important to arrive at a common understanding of the term. As we use it here, power is equated with national capabilities. Power is a multifaceted, ever-changing political resource and is the sum of the various elements that allow one country to have its interests prevail over the interests of another country. In short, national power is *the sum of the attributes that enable a state to achieve its goals even when they clash with the goals and wills of other international actors.*

Characteristics of Power

Power is anything but a simple phenomenon. Indeed, it is very much a political chameleon, constantly changing even while it remains the same. The complexity of power can be seen by examining four of its characteristics.

Power Is Relative

In his discussion of power, Hans Morgenthau (1973:154) has observed that "it is one of the most elemental and frequent errors in international politics to neglect . . . [the]

relative character of power and to deal instead with the power of a nation as though it were an absolute." When assessing capabilities, then, **relative power**, or the comparative power of the national actors, must be considered. We cannot say that China is powerful unless we specify *in comparison to whom*. If, as stated above, power is the ability to prevail, then China is not as powerful when compared with the Soviet Union as it is when compared to Vietnam.

A related issue is whether power is a *zero-sum game*. The question is whether a gain in the power of one country inevitably means a loss of power for other actors (zero-sum) or whether an increase in power for one does not necessarily mean a loss of power for the others (non–zero-sum). Without delving too far into this controversy, we can say that the relative nature of power implies that, at least potentially and in times of conflict, power changes approach zero-sum. However, it should also be noted that the situational nature of power, which will be discussed next, means that power changes can at times be non–zero-sum. If we agree that, even if provoked, China is unlikely to use nuclear weapons against Vietnam, then increases in China's atomic arsenal do not affect the Chinese/Vietnamese power relationship.

Power Is Situational

A country's power varies according to the situation, or context, in which it is being applied. A country's **situational power** is often less than the total inventory of its capabilities. During the Iranian hostage crisis, the preponderance of American military power was virtually useless given the goal of freeing the hostages alive. Similarly, the U.S. defeat in Vietnam did not occur because the communists were more powerful in an absolute sense. Rather, it happened, in part, because the U.S. was restrained. Air Force general Curtis Lemay once suggested bombing North Vietnam "back into the Stone Age," and the United States had the resources to do it. It did not, however, have the "will" to annihilate the Vietnamese, and, therefore, its power was dissipated. Will might be equated with "price." Power is modified by our willingness to "pay the price," economically, politically, physically, or spiritually, to achieve an end. There is no implication here that lack of will implies weakness in a macho sense. Indeed, prudence is often laudable. But inevitably, right or wrong, lack of will decreases power.

The horror of nuclear war and, indeed, the rising world opinion against using force in any context are having the general effect of decreasing the weight of military might as a power factor. The ability of the two superpowers to destroy each other has, to a degree, rendered the huge nuclear stockpiles impotent. As Henry Kissinger once exclaimed, "What, in the name of God, is strategic superiority? What is the significance of it politically, militarily, operationally at these levels of numbers? What do you do with it?" (Draper, 1977:192).

On the conventional level, some analysts have also observed that although armed force is far from ended, there are many, and an increasing number of, situations where it is a null power factor. The United States and Canada have had and will probably have serious disputes, but it is hard to imagine the countries clashing militarily. Once Mikhail Gorbachev renounced the Brezhnev Doctrine, asserting the U.S.S.R.'s right to intervene militarily in other socialist states threatened by revisionism, and once people came to believe him, Soviet military might declined precipitously as an element in Soviet influence in Eastern Europe. The region's countries broke out of the Soviet orbit while Moscow watched in peace and the rest of the world watched in amazement.

The applicability of virtually all aspects of a country's power is situational. The 1990–1991 Middle East crisis exposed some limits to U.S. military power. Insufficient transportation capabilities meant that it took months for the United States to build a force confident of challenging the million-soldier Iraqi army. Symbolic of that difficulty, this October 1990 picture shows Colonel Harold Burch riding to a change of command ceremony of the U.S. First Cavalry Division in Saudi Arabia. At that point the army was still short some of the equipment it needed to operate effectively. It was also unable to procure a horse, which tradition called on the colonel to ride during the ceremony. Undaunted, Colonel Burch broke with history and mounted a camel.

Power Is Dynamic

The complexity and relative nature of power make it a dynamic phenomenon. Even simple measurements show that power is constantly in flux. Economies prosper or lag, arms are modernized or become outmoded, resources are discovered or are depleted. Saudi Arabia and Iraq provide one example of the dynamics of relative power. Based on the Taber (1989) study and using the averaging methods in column 6 of Table 9.2, in 1980 Saudi Arabia had 46 average points, while Iraq finished less powerfully with 19 average points. Only a decade later, Western and regional powers were obliged to come to Saudi Arabia's aid because of the threat that Iraq, having acquired a battle-tested and well-armed million-soldier army, could quickly erase Saudi sovereignty.

Not only can the specific power of a country change, but there is a significant body of opinion that believes the very nature of power is changing. There are scholars who contend that some power factors, such as military force, population size, raw materials, and geography, are declining in their importance as part of the power equation, while other factors, such as technological excellence, education, and economic growth, are becoming more important. Robert Wesson (1990:ix) writes, for example, that "the traditional contentions of nations, called 'powers,' are rapidly giving way to a new kind of international relations more appropriate to an age of high technology and sophisticated civilization." Wesson and others of this view focus on the world's growing economic interdependence and cultural interchange, which they believe will decrease the role of coercion and enhance cooperation. There are even scholars, such as John Mueller (1989), who argue that war is nearing obsolescence because countries have learned that war usually is not worth the goal even if you win.

Even if Mueller is right in the long term, that day has not arrived yet, as the Middle East crisis shows. Iraqi arms swept away Kuwait's defenses in one day, and if it had not been for the immediate U.S. military reaction (the international effort came days and weeks later), Saddam Hussein's forces might well have continued southward, overrunning the Saudis, the Omanis, and others. In the end, it was allied armed forces, not diplomacy, that were called on to expel Iraq from Kuwait. Like many scholars, Joseph Nye (1990:183) believes that coercive "hard power" ("command power," the ability to make another country do or not do something) is declining in importance, and "soft power" ("co-optive power," the ability to persuade) is increasing. But he also concludes that "military force will remain an important factor," as will self-serving economic strength, including the ability to command trade markets and access to natural resources.

Power Is Multidimensional

Power is multifaceted. People often think of international power only in terms of military capability. As we have seen, though, military might cannot always be used, is costly for all involved, and is only one of a number of power factors. We must, when analyzing power, avoid what Morgenthau (1973:158) calls "the fallacy of the single factor," or "attributing to a single factor an overriding importance, to the detriment of all the others."

Just as we did with national interest, it is important to consider *all* the aspects of power *and* to place them in their proper relative and situational contexts. Only then can we begin to answer the question of who is powerful and who is not. To help with that process, our next step is to identify the various elements of national power.

Elements of Power

Attempts to categorize political phenomena are almost always frustrating. The world is a complex place, and applying categories to concepts is often more of a teaching tool than a meaningful task in any real sense. This difficulty is especially acute for power. Scholars have grouped power factors according to a variety of categories and subcategories, with the most common distinction being between tangible and intangible facets of power.

This distinction is an important one. The elements of **tangible power** are those that can be readily measured. Population, industrial output, and number of soldiers are examples. Elements of **intangible power** are those that cannot be measured easily. Leadership is an example. There are problems with the distinction between tangible and intangible, though. Consider education, for example. An educated populace is an asset, but is it tangible or intangible? Being educated is a state of existence and not tangible. Yet we can count the number of people educated and measure the amount of their education. This makes education somewhat tangible, but then there is the quality of education. Vastly greater numbers of American students go to college, but many critics of U.S. education claim that Japanese (and many other countries') students are better educated. Another problem of treating tangible and intangible elements of power separately, which this textbook did in the last edition, is that the practice uncomfortably divides subjects. Under tangible military factors one can discuss numbers of tanks. Then there is the subject of the tanks' technological sophistication (tangible, intangible?), and finally some pages later a discussion of the intangible morale of the troops who operate the tanks. The problem is that on the battlefield all these factors work together. Therefore, the following discussion of the elements of power will group them into four major categories: (1) The National Core, including a country's physical characteristics, its people, its government, and its reputation; (2) The National Infrastructure, including a country's technological sophistication, its transportation system, and its information and communications capabilities; (3) The National Economy, including a country's financial position, its natural resources, its industrial output, and its agricultural output; and (4) The National Military, including a country's military equipment and it troops. Remember, though, that these categories are an attempt to make some sense of the phenomenon of power; in action they are highly interrelated, and it is their impact, not their category, that is most important.

The National Core

We discussed the nation-state in chapter 6, and this hyphenated concept forms the basis of this grouping of national power elements. The essence of a nation-state can be roughly divided into four elements: its physical characteristics, its people, its political system, and its reputation.

Physical Characteristics

Shakespeare's King Henry VI proclaimed:

> Let us be backed with God and with the seas
> Which He hath given for fence impregnable, . . .
> In them and in ourselves our safety lies.

Henry's homage to God and the English Channel—the latter of which, at least, has helped save England from European conquest for nine centuries—is an apt reminder of the importance of a country's physical characteristics.

Geopolitics   Within the more general discipline of political geography, the study of geopolitics is concerned with the interrelationship of geography, power, and international politics. First formulated as a theory in the late 1800s, geopolitics later fell into disrepute because of its use by the Nazis to justify German expansion in order to gain *Lebensraum* (living space). They and many of the early advocates of geopolitics maintained that the state had an "organic" dimension and that it had to expand or die. This theory has been discredited, as has the idea that geography necessarily determines power and policy.

Other geopolitical theories, however, have influenced history and continue to do so. Alfred Thayer Mahan, an American naval officer, argued in *The Influence of Seapower on History* (1890) that world power was determined by control of the seas and the acquisition of colonies for that purpose. Mahan's theory supported both British and American imperial expansion. Kaiser Wilhelm II was also influenced by Mahan, leading to Germany's naval expansion and search for colonies in the years before World War I.

Taking the opposite view, British geographer Sir Halford Mackinder in *Democratic Ideals and Reality* (1919:150) classified Europe, Asia, and Africa as the "world island" with the Eurasian "heartland" at its center. Control of the heartland was vital because

Who rules East Europe commands the Heartland
Who rules the Heartland commands the World Island
Who rules the World Island commands the world.

Nicholas J. Spykman (1944) took a geopolitical position between Mahan's and Mackinder's. Spykman, an American, emphasized the "rimlands" of Europe, the Middle East, Africa, South America, and Asia as the keys to U.S. security. These lands form a sort of fence that can be used to wall the Eurasian powers out of the New World or, conversely, if controlled by a hostile power, to encircle the United States. More contemporarily, Saul Cohen (1973) has divided the world into "geostrategic regions," with the two dominant areas, the maritime and the Eurasian continental, confronting each other in the Middle Eastern and Southeast Asian "shelterbelts."

Despite the bad reputation that the Nazis gave geopolitical theory, it has continued to have an important impact on politics. The rimland theory, for example, played a central role in the thinking of George Kennan, the father of the policy of containment that dominated U.S. foreign policy for four decades after World War II. With the decline of the Soviet threat and the end of U.S. containment, geopolitical theory is again part of the search for a new U.S. political and military strategy. Militarily, for example, the massive, ground-based weapons needed to contest the heartland and protect the rimland of Europe are very different from the lighter, more mobile weapons systems most appropriate to controlling the rimlands of Asia and the Middle East, or for securing the sea lanes. During the cold war the United States emphasized a "continentalist" approach anchored in NATO. There are those who argue that the United States should shift the configuration of its forces toward a "maritime" approach. In support of their argument these critics point to the fact that in the recent Middle East crisis it took 10 weeks or more for the U.S. military to become fully ready to operate there, despite the fact that its movement into the region was unopposed.

National Geography Whether or not one subscribes to broad geopolitical theories, it is hard to escape the impact of geography on individual countries. Geographic factors comprise (1) location, (2) topography, (3) size, and (4) climate.

The *location* of a country, particularly in relation to other countries, is significant. The fact that China and the Soviet Union share a border has power implications for both. The huge Chinese army can do little at present to threaten the United States. By contrast, the People's Liberation Army can walk into Siberia. Some have argued that an American military intervention in Nicaragua would have been another Vietnam, but the proximity of Central America, in contrast with Vietnam's distant location and its border connection with China, implies that the outcome might have been very different in Nicaragua.

Location can be an advantage or a disadvantage. Spain was able to avoid involvement in either world war in part because of its relative isolation from the rest of Europe. Poland, sandwiched between Germany and Russia, has a distinctly unfortunate location. The Israelis would almost certainly be better off if their promised land were somewhere—almost anywhere—else.

A country's *topography*—its mountains, rivers, and plains—is also important. The Alps have helped protect Switzerland from its larger European neighbors and spared the Swiss the ravages of both world wars. Topography can also work against a country. The broad European plain that extends from Germany's Rhine River to the Ural Mountains, which separate Europe from Asia in the Soviet Union, has been an easy invasion avenue along which the armies of Napoleon, Kaiser Wilhelm, and Hitler have marched. In the current era, topography has been of major importance in the Middle East, where such points as the Suez Canal, the Golan Heights, the Jordan River, and the Straits of Tiran have played crucial roles, and in Afghanistan, where the rugged terrain worked to the guerrillas' advantage.

A country's *size* and *shape* can be an advantage, a disadvantage, or both. The immense expanse of the Soviet Union, for example, has saved it in each of the major invasions of the modern era. Although overwhelmed at first, the Russian armies have been able to retreat into the interior and buy time with geography while they regrouped their forces. That saving distance, however, has also proved a liability. During the Russo-Japanese War (1904–1905) the Russian armies had to traverse thousands of Siberian miles to engage the Japanese along the Pacific coast. By contrast, Israel's size gives it no room to retreat, and, in particular, its east-west narrowness leaves it in constant danger of being cut in two.

A country's *climate* also plays a power role. The tropical climate of Vietnam, with its heavy monsoon rains and its dense vegetation, made it difficult for the Americans to use effectively much of the superior weaponry they possessed. At the other extreme, the bone-chilling Russian winter has allied itself with size to form a formidable defensive barrier. Many of Napoleon's soldiers literally froze to death during the French army's retreat from Moscow, and 133 years later the German Wehrmacht was decimated by cold and ice during the sieges of Leningrad and Stalingrad. In fact the Russian winter has proved so formidable that Czar Nicholas I commented, "Russia has two generals we can trust, General January and General February." Most recently, the United States and other forces have found that the sweltering heat and blowing sands of the Arabian desert provide a hostile environment that enervates troops and clogs machines.

People

A second national core power factor is a country's human characteristics. Tangible demographic subcategories include population in sheer numbers, age distribution, and

Geography is still an important power consideration. The Middle East is distant from where most U.S. forces were stationed; the climate and physical characteristics of the region created difficulties. The heat and blowing sands of the desert damaged some of the U.S. high-technology weaponry; some armored vehicles had trouble maneuvering in the deep sands and high dunes. The human ability to fight only during the (relatively) cool winter months pressured the U.S. administration to take action rather than wait. One thing that the Saudi desert did provide was an abundance of material for U.S. Sargent Karyl Gibson to use filling sandbags around her unit's position.

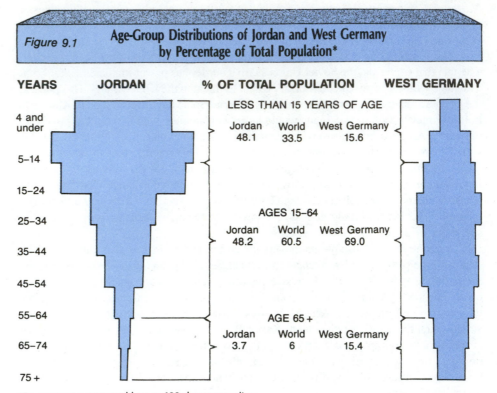

Figure 9.1 Age-Group Distributions of Jordan and West Germany by Percentage of Total Population*

YEARS	JORDAN	% OF TOTAL POPULATION	WEST GERMANY

LESS THAN 15 YEARS OF AGE

Jordan	World	West Germany
48.1	33.5	15.6

AGES 15–64

Jordan	World	West Germany
48.2	60.5	69.0

AGE 65 +

Jordan	World	West Germany
3.7	6	15.4

YEARS: 4 and under, 5–14, 15–24, 25–34, 35–44, 45–54, 55–64, 65–74, 75 +

*Percentages may not add up to 100 due to rounding.

Data source: UN (1990a).

The age-group distribution of a country's population can be a source of strength or weakness. This figure shows two variations of less-than-optimal distribution. Of them, Jordan has the greatest percentage of people younger than the statistical working years (15–64), and West Germany (and now Germany) has the greatest percentage of people other than the working-age group.

such measurable quantitative factors as health and education. There are also intangible population factors such as morale.

Population   Because a large population supplies military personnel and industrial workers, sheer numbers of people are a positive power factor. It is unlikely, for instance, that Kiribati (pop. 60,000) or Liechtenstein (pop. 30,000) will ever achieve great-power status.

Pure numbers, however, are not directly translatable into power. It is important that the population be in balance with resources. If it is not, then people can become a negative factor. India (pop. 833 million) has the world's second-largest population, yet because of the country's poverty (1989 GNP per capita: $295), it must spend much of its energy and resources merely feeding its people.

Age Distribution   It is an advantage for a country to have a large number and percentage of its population in the productive years (roughly 15–65). Some countries with booming populations have a heavy percentage of children who must be supported. In other countries with limited life expectancy, many people die before they complete their productive years. Finally, some countries are "aging," with a geriatric population segment that consumes more resources than it produces. Worldwide, 33.5 percent of the

TABLE 9.3

Selected Educational and Health Factors of Canada and Mozambique

	Life Expectancy (years)	Infant Mortality (% per year)	Physicians per 10,000 Population	Per Capita Daily Protein Gram Supply	Adult Literacy* (%)	Percent of Adults Who Have a Secondary School Degree or Higher
Canada	77	0.7	19.6	96.4	99	82
Mozambique	47	4.7	0.4	28.4	14	7

*A high percent (83%) of Mozambique's children now receive at least some elementary education and the country's literacy will rise.
Data sources: U.S. AID (1990); UN FAO (1989); World Bank (1989); *Canadian World Almanac* (1990).

The quality of life in developed and less developed countries is very different, as these health and education statistics for Canada and Mozambique show.

earth's population is less than 15 years old, and 6 percent is 65 or over. This leaves 60.5 percent of the world population in the normal productive years. Figure 9.1 on page 236 takes the extreme cases of Jordan and West Germany and analyzes their age distributions. It is obvious that West Germany is aging, while Jordan is a very young society. Neither extreme is a balanced population.

Other Factors There are a variety of ways to measure the strengths of a population. It goes without saying that an educated, healthy population is important to national power. Table 9.3 above illustrates selected educational and health factors by contrasting Canada and Mozambique. It should be noted that such statistics are helpful but not conclusive. Educationally, for example, they do not tell us how good the schools and teachers are.

Another population factor is how well the society trains and utilizes its population. Sexism limits the utilization of women to their highest capacities in virtually all countries, and in some it is rampant. In India, for example, 45 percent of all males in the appropriate age group are enrolled in secondary school; only 24 percent of the equivalent females are in school. Racial, ethnic, and other bases of discrimination add to this failure to maximize a population's potential. Blacks in South Africa, Catholics in Northern Ireland, Arabs in Israel, Shi'ites in Saudi Arabia, Jews in the Soviet Union, and a host of other groups are substantially lost as a resource to their home countries.

Morale A final factor that affects the population element of national power is the morale of a country's citizens. At the positive extreme, World War II demonstrated the power of strong civilian morale. Early in the war, Great Britain and the Soviet Union reeled under tremendous poundings by the Nazi forces. Yet the Allies hung on. Winston Churchill told the British nation during the darkest days of 1940, "Death and sorrow will be the companions of our journey; hardship our garment; constancy and valor our only shield. We must be united, we must be undaunted, we must be inflexible" (Report to the House of Commons, 10/8/40).

They were; they held; they prevailed.

At the negative extreme, the collapse of national morale can bring about civil unrest and even the fall of governments. In 1917 the Russian people were hungry and

"WE CAN'T EAT PEACE."

Public morale is an intangible but important aspect of a country's power. Sometimes this factor results in a country collapsing from within; the Soviet Union is on the edge of such a fate. When Soviet president Mikhail Gorbachev won the Nobel Peace Prize in October 1990 the world cheered, but many hungry Soviet citizens jeered.

oppressed. They revolted, they overthrew the czar, and they took the country out of the war. During World War II, Hitler's armies devastated the Soviet Union, but the people rallied and held on despite a ferocious assault. Now, the morale of Soviet citizens has again plummeted, and the greatest threat to the current Soviet government, even the continuation of the Soviet Union as such, is the mood of the Soviet people. Separatist sentiments in many of the Soviet Union's national groups, as discussed in chapter 6, are being spurred in part by the shortages of food and other necessities; by a widespread feeling among many people that the Communist system and government have not only failed, but betrayed them; and by anxieties about the future.

In May 1988 a survey in Moscow found 73 percent of respondents favoring perestroika, and only 18 percent of Muscovites expected that Gorbachev's program would decrease their standard of living. Polls in late 1989 and early 1990 showed a dramatic reversal. Ninety percent of Soviets believed the country's economic situation was bad or critical, and 57 percent had no confidence in the future (*NYT,* 5/27/90:A10). When miners went on strike in Siberia, one of their strongest demands was soap, and there have been riots in Soviet cities because of the lack of tobacco. The world was impressed when Gorbachev won the 1990 Nobel Peace Prize, but the immediate radio reports of reactions in Moscow were less enthusiastic. Typically, one member of the national legislature was glad that Gorbachev had won the peace prize, but added, "Let's be honest, he would never win the Nobel Prize for Economics."

What could happen? "If we don't see improvement in the stores, we will soon see riots in the streets," a Soviet lawyer predicted. "Anything could spark it" (*Time,* 12/4/89:62). What is especially galling for Soviet would-be consumers is that they have a huge store of $165 billion in rubles (at current exchange rates) that have been hoarded for the lack of anything to buy. Showing the resiliency of the Soviet people, the situation has spawned a sort of gallows humor. One story, considered riotously funny in Moscow, is about the man who finally saves enough money to buy a car (the average Soviet has to work 7,935 hours to earn the equivalent cost of a small car; the average American has to work 686 hours). The Soviet goes to the car commissar and orders the car. The commissar says the car will be delivered on Tuesday, August 1, 2006. The buyer asks the commissar whether it will be delivered in the morning or the afternoon. "What the hell do you care so many years from now?" the commissar explodes. "Well," the man replies, "the plumber is coming in the afternoon."

Government

The quality of a country's government is a third power element associated with the national core. The issue is not what form of government, such as a democracy or authoritarian system, a country has. Instead the issue is *administrative competence*. This is important because a state must have a well-organized and effective administrative structure to utilize its power potential fully. The current Soviet crisis stems in part from the country's massive and inefficient bureaucratic structure. "The management of the state is failing fast. Ministries are completely paralyzed," Leningrad Communist party chief Boris Gidaspov complained at a 1990 party conference. Hardly anyone there disagreed, and many were pessimistic, including Vladimir Brovikov, the Soviet ambassador to Poland. "We have," the discouraged diplomat admitted, "brought the motherland to an awful state, turning it from an empire admired throughout the world to a state with an inglorious present and an indefinite future" (*Time,* 2/19/90:33–35). Mikhail Gorbachev is trying to restructure the system (perestroika), and he has made significant changes. But whether he will succeed is in doubt.

Leadership skill is another element that adds to the government's strength. Here, the Soviet system is strengthened by the personal leadership skills of Mikhail Gorbachev. Domestically, his popularity has slipped badly, and he is criticized by both those who think he is moving too fast and those who think he is moving too slow. The changes he has instituted, however, are far-reaching. Furthermore, his ability to survive politically despite the country's travails is related to the fact that even his opponents recognize that without his individual presence the system might well dissolve into chaos. Internationally, Gorbachev has also provided strong leadership. This can be said whether you see him as a world statesman of vision who is trying to better the international system or a pragmatic nationalist leader who is cutting the Soviet Union defense burden and other costly international involvements to save his country economically. For, whatever his motives, he has radically changed the direction of the Soviet Union's foreign policy, and, at least for now, those changes can only be greeted with enthusiasm. Furthermore, his efforts have paid off as arms spending has declined and as loans, credits, investments, and other financial benefits have begun to flow to the Soviet Union from the West. Individual kudos for Gorbachev have also mounted. In addition to winning the Nobel Peace Prize in October 1990, *Time* (1/1/90:43–45) named Gorbachev Man of the Decade. The magazine began its award essay with an allusion to Shakespeare's *The Tempest,* casting "Gorbachev [as] playing [the enlightened] Prospero in a realm ruled by [the degenerated] Caliban for the past 72 years." The magazine then equated Gorbachev with Franklin Roosevelt; declared that "Gorbachev is the Copernicus, Darwin and Freud of communism all wrapped in one"; and proclaimed him "a sort of Zen genius of survival." Perhaps, but even if one is not swept up in such editorial adulation, it is hard to disagree with U.S. secretary of state James Baker's observation that "no cliché does Gorbachev justice. To say that he is a piece of work is an understatement."

Reputation

Another power consideration is a country's reputation. Whatever real power a country may possess, its ability to exert that power and influence on others will depend partly on how those others perceive its capacity and will. Even if inaccurate, those perceptions will at least initially become the operational reality.

National leaders commonly believe that weakness will tempt their opponents, while a reputation for strength will deter them. Although there is evidence that a strong reputation does not always dissuade an enemy or reassure a friend, it is clear that decisions are made based on the images of others. This idea, sometimes called the Munich syndrome (see chapter 4), has strongly affected Western diplomacy, as presidents and prime ministers have drawn the line rather than compromise with "aggressors."

Non-Western leaders also recognize the operational importance of reputation. Soviet premier Nikita Khrushchev once observed, "It is quite well known that if one tries to appease a bandit by giving one's purse, then one's coat, and so forth, he is not going to be more charitable because of this. He is not going to stop exercising his banditry. On the contrary, he will become ever more insolent" (Jervis, 1976:61).

Given the significance of reputation, an important aspect of diplomacy is projecting an advantageous image of power. If you are truly strong, you will usually want to convey that to opponents accurately so that they will give way without a struggle. If you are weak, then you may want to mislead others into believing that you are stronger than you actually are. We will examine these strategies in chapter 12, on diplomacy.

The National Infrastructure

The infrastructure of a state might roughly be equated with the skeleton of a human body. For a building, the infrastructure would be the foundation and the framing or girders. To examine the infrastructure of the state as an element of national power, the following sections will discuss technological sophistication, transportation systems, and information and communications capabilities. Each of these factors strongly affects any country's capacity in the other elements of power.

Technological Sophistication

Technology undergirds a great deal of national power. Air conditioning modifies the impact of weather, computers revolutionize education, robotics speed industry, synthetic fertilizers expand agriculture, new drilling techniques allow for undersea oil exploration, microwaves speed information, and lasers bring the military to the edge of the Buck Rogers era. Thus, technology is an overarching factor and will be discussed as part of all the tangible elements.

There are predictions that the coming hundred years will be the "Pacific Century." That estimate is based in substantial part on the technological advances centered in that region (the Pacific rim), especially including Japan, Taiwan, South Korea, Hong Kong, and Singapore. One way to gauge the technology is by international trade, because this reacts to both quality and price. This standard is shown in Figure 9.2, which shows the shifts in the percentages of world exports of several high-technology items. Note especially the increase in the percentage of this trade commanded by the Pacific rim countries.

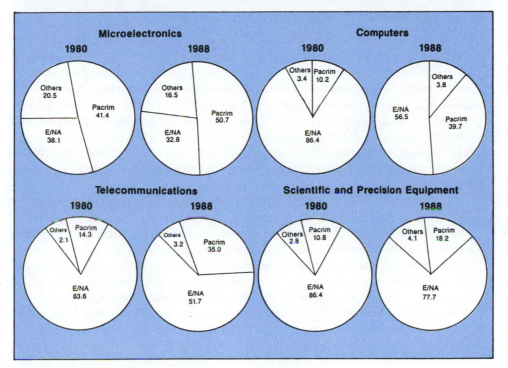

Figure 9.2   **Share of World Exports of Selected High-Technology Products in Percent**

E/NA = Europe and North America (United States and Canada).
Pacrim = Pacific rim (Japan, South Korea, Taiwan, Hong Kong, and Singapore).
Excludes internal trade including intra-EC and intra-CMEA trade.

Source: CIA (1989:18). Statistics and categories in the original condensed for this figure.

The countries of the Pacific rim control an increasingly large share of high-technology exports in international trade. This is one measure of these countries' increasing technological sophistication and power.

Transportation Systems

The ability to move people, raw materials, finished products, and sometimes the military throughout its territory is another part of a country's power equation. Part of the food crisis in the U.S.S.R. is a result of the country's decrepit transportation system, which contributes to the fact that up to 40 percent of all agricultural products spoil before they reach consumers. In late 1989, for example, the official Tass news agency reported that 29 million tons of grain, 1 million tons of meat, and 25 percent of vegetables are lost annually between farm and table. Tass also reported that 1,700 trains were stalled because of lack of fuel or repair parts. The same sort of discouraging figures also apply to the country's trucks. Even if the equipment were operating well, the Soviets would still have a relatively limited transportation system. As one standard, for every 1,000 square miles of its territory, the Soviet Union has 100 miles of paved roads and 10.4 miles of railroad track. The United States has 1,049 miles of paved roads and 45 miles of railroad track for the same amount of territory. Inadequate transportation systems are also a problem for Third World countries. Nigeria, for one, has 213 miles of paved roadway and only 6.1 miles of railroad track for each 1,000 square miles.

Information and Communications Capabilities

A country's information and communications capabilities are becoming increasingly important. The advent of satellites and computers has accelerated the revolution begun with radio and television. Photocopying machines and now fax machines have dramatically changed communications. Enhanced communications technology increases the ability of a society to communicate within itself and remain cohesive. It also increases efficiency and effectiveness in industry, finance, and the military. The trilateral countries (Western Europe, United States and Canada, and Japan) have a wide advantage in this area. Eastern Europe and the Soviet Union are a distinct second. Some Third World countries such as India, which launched a communications satellite in 1983, have some capability, but most have not entered the microchip age.

China is a good example of a country whose communications infrastructure is insufficient to meet the needs of development. Canada is a good example of a country with sophisticated and widespread capabilities. As is true for most less developed countries (LDCs), China has neither the capacity to produce a great deal of modern communications equipment nor the funds to buy it overseas. In China's case, its limited communications technology is also based on the government's political desire to restrict communications equipment in order to maintain control. Comparing Canada and China, there are 63 televisions, 11 radios, and 4 newspaper copies in Canada for every one in China. Among the basic communications technologies, the availability of telephones is an even more telling figure because telephone lines also form the basis for fax and other types of more sophisticated data transmission. Here Canada has 751 telephones for every 1,000 Canadians. By contrast, there are only 5 telephones in China for every 1,000 Chinese. Indeed, the extent of Third World limitations in communications technology is apparent by contrasting the people and phones in Canada with the combined people and phones of China, India, Bangladesh, Indonesia, Pakistan, and Nigeria. These six LDCs have 100 times the population of Canada (and nearly half the world's population). Yet these six countries have a total among them of only about half as many telephones as Canada. In the realm of more sophisticated information and communications technology, if you could get an accurate count on photocopying and fax machines and computer data transmission capabilities, you would find the gap even greater.

The National Economy

A country's economic strength has always been an important element in its power equation. Beginning with the industrial revolution, and accelerated by the technological revolution, however, the relative weight of economics has grown steadily. Indeed, as noted earlier, there are some analysts who view economic factors as the key element of national power. Whether or not that is the case, the increased role of trade in national strength, the mounting energy dependency of the developed countries, and the cost of military technology, among other things, all enhance the importance of economic capacity. To examine the national economy as an element of national power, the following sections will discuss a country's financial position, its natural resources, its industrial output, and its agricultural output.

TABLE 9.4

Comparative Financial Position of Selected Developed and Less Developed Countries

Country	1 GNP Growth	2 International Reserves	3 Balance of Payments	4 Surplus or Deficit (%)
Canada	3.0	19,525.4	− 14,091	− 12.78
India	5.4	7,089.4	− 5,192	− 35.39
Italy	1.4	41,540.1	− 10,362	− 27.36
Japan	4.1	77,378.2	+ 57	− 12.23
Nigeria	− 1.5	1,765.5	− 143	− 35.83
U.S.	3.0	149,460.8	− 110,060	− 13.91

Column 1: Average annual growth in percent of gross national product in constant dollars, 1980–1987.

Column 2: International Reserves (including gold) expressed in millions of U.S. dollars. International Reserves, minus gold, calculated based on IMF source calculation in SDRs (Special Drawing Rights) of the IMF to $ U.S. based on an August 1990 rate of 1 SDR = $1.37719/$1 = 0.76094 SDR with a market basket mix of 42% U.S. dollars, 19% West German marks, 12% French francs, 15% Japanese yen, and 12% British pounds. Gold expressed in troy ounces converted to $ (U.S.) at an August 1, 1990, price of $387.75/troy ounce.

Column 3: Surplus (+) or deficit (−) of balance of payments expressed in millions of U.S. dollars.

Column 4: Surplus (+) or deficit (−) of central government including all receipts and expenditures expressed as a percentage of the positive or negative difference between receipts and expenditures.

Data sources: IMF (1989); UN (1990b); *Statistical Abstract* (1990).

There is an old saying that you need money to make money. To a degree this is true for countries as well as people. As the data in this table indicates, the developed countries (Canada, Italy, Japan, and the United States) have substantial financial reserves. By contrast, the less developed countries (India and Nigeria) have scant financial reserves and their central government budgets have the highest percentage deficits.

Financial Position

The center of any country's economic health is its basic financial position. This factor includes many related financial measures such as the basic health of its economy measured in growth of the gross national product. International reserves, both monetary and gold assets, which can be used for international financial transactions, such as trade, are another measure. The balance of payments, the sum of all the flow of money in and out of a country, is a third consideration. A fourth measure that will be discussed here is the budget surplus or deficit of the central government. There are many other measures, such as a country's total public and private foreign debt, that could be mentioned, but these four and the issues associated with them are adequate to begin to understand how to evaluate a country's financial position.

One aspect of financial condition relates to the different conditions of the developed and less developed countries. Table 9.4 details the position of several such countries and explains the various categories of measurement. Notice the relatively poor reserve position (column 2) of India and Nigeria, a condition that gives them little ability to purchase technology, services, and other needs for development. You can also see Nigeria's negative GNP growth (column 1), mostly due to the decline in the price of its oil exports. In the balance of payments category (column 3), the U.S. negative balance is huge, making the United States the world's greatest debtor country; and in the last column the large percentage budget deficits of India and Nigeria show the struggle that LDC governments face in meeting expenses.

While these statistics are complex and may seem a bit abstract, the impact of a country's financial position on its foreign policy is very tangible. The Soviet Union provides a good example. Its foreign reserves, even with its 77 million troy ounces of gold included, are minimal. Soviet GNP has slowly decreased its growth, and some sources believe it actually declined 1 percent in 1989 and is continuing to decline in 1990. Soviet foreign debt has climbed steeply in recent years, rising from slightly over $20 billion in 1984 to almost $50 billion in 1989. Inflation is up from 1 percent to over 9 percent in the same period, and the Soviet budget deficit has increased over these six years from 2 percent of the gross national product to about 10 percent of GNP (compared to 3 percent for the United States in 1989). In short, the Soviet central government is just about broke, and that fact has been a major factor in persuading Moscow to reduce its defense spending, get out of Eastern Europe, cut support to allies around the world, and in general assume a much less adventuresome posture in the world.

Natural Resources

The possession or lack of natural resources has become an increasingly important power factor as industrialization and technology have advanced.

Among the myriad raw materials needed to become a modern industrial power, petroleum, iron, and coal are three of the most important. But there is also a host of other natural resources that are important. Some of these, such as bauxite (for aluminum), copper, and lead, are well known. Others, including manganese, tungsten, and cobalt, are more exotic. They are all necessary, however, for a strong economy.

In the power equation, natural resources have an impact in four related ways: (1) The greater a country's *self-sufficiency* in vital natural resources, the greater its power. In other words, the relation between output and consumption is important. (2) Conversely, the greater a country's *dependency* on foreign sources for vital natural resources, the less its power. (3) The greater a country's *surplus* (over domestic needs) of vital resources needed by other countries, the greater its power. The United States, for instance, is the world's largest petroleum producer, but U.S. consumption is so high that the country is also the world's largest oil importer. (4) The greater a country's *reserves* in terms of ability to meet future (especially emergency) needs, the greater its power.

Each of these four related points plays a key role in determining international relationships. As Figure 9.3 shows, the Soviet Union, for example, is self-sufficient in most of the range of important resources. Japan, by contrast, has been able to construct a strong economic base because of its efficient industrial capacity, but it is vulnerable. The Japanese import virtually all their primary energy supplies (oil, natural gas, and others) and have become increasingly dependent on foreign sources for natural resource needs because of depletion of their own resources. Hence, if its resource supplies were cut off—say, by hostile naval action—Japan would be in perilous straits, especially since it has scant reserves. The European Community is also very vulnerable. The United States stands between the two extremes in its level of dependency on resource imports and is at least moderately vulnerable because of its foreign dependency for many minerals.

A vital resource surplus is a third power factor that the world imbalance of oil production and consumption, as is evident in Figure 9.4, has dramatically underlined. Oil resources of the Middle East have allowed that region's countries to amass huge financial reserves. In 1988, for example, oil-exporting countries earned $86 billion from

THE KISS OF DEATH?

Many people argue that dependence on foreign sources for a vital natural resource (or any other critical product) is dangerous for a country's military security and economic prosperity. The August 1990 Middle East crisis dramatically increased oil prices and alarmed Americans about dependence on foreign oil. This cobra was part of an advertisement placed in *Newsweek* by a private trade organization, the U.S. Council for Energy Awareness. The answer to the problem, the advertisement said, was to build more nuclear power plants. Others advocate a U.S. energy policy to promote conservation and develop less-dangerous energy supplies. But no such policy exists. Representative of that, former Saudi Oil Minister Ahmed Zaki Yamani was asked in an interview about the U.S. energy policy. His reply was an incredulous, "Oh, is there a U.S. energy policy? I understand that your policy is no policy. And this in itself is supposed to be a policy, according to some people in the Administration" (*Time*, 12/3/90:22).

Figure 9.3 **Selected Commodities: Net Imports as a Share of Consumption, 1987[1]**

	United States	Japan	European Community	Soviet Union
Primary Energy	15%	80%	40%	0%
Petroleum[2]	35%	100%	70%	0%
Bauxite	93%	100%	100%	35%
Copper	32%	92%	100%	0%
Cobalt	92%	100%	98%	15%
Iron Ore	37%	98%	82%	0%
Manganese	100%	100%	100%	0%
Chromium	100%	100%	100%	0%
Platinum Group Metals	98%	98%	98%	0%

[1]Most data rounded to nearest 5 percent.   [2]Data are for 1986 and include products.
Data source: CIA (1989:17).

The less reliant a country is on others for resources, the more powerful it is. This figure shows the foreign dependence for minerals. As you can see, in this area the Soviet Union is in the most advantageous position; Japan is in the weakest position.

their product. Oil has also increased diplomatic power. By turning off the oil tap, or threatening to, the Arabs have been able to gain a stronger voice in world affairs. More subtly, control of this vital resource has also given a psychological uplift to the Arab world both in their own eyes and in the perceptions of others. They used to get very little respect—now they demand and receive much more. The world's dependency on oil from the region has also raised the chance for conflict if there is a threat to the oil flow, as the 1990–91 Middle East conflict shows.

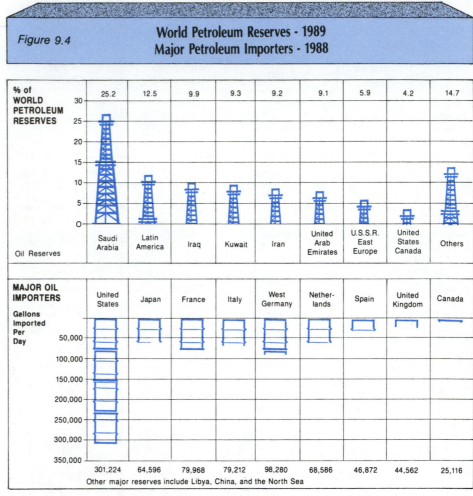

Figure 9.4

World Petroleum Reserves - 1989
Major Petroleum Importers - 1988

% of WORLD PETROLEUM RESERVES	25.2	12.5	9.9	9.3	9.2	9.1	5.9	4.2	14.7
Oil Reserves	Saudi Arabia	Latin America	Iraq	Kuwait	Iran	United Arab Emirates	U.S.S.R. East Europe	United States Canada	Others

MAJOR OIL IMPORTERS Gallons Imported Per Day	United States	Japan	France	Italy	West Germany	Nether-lands	Spain	United Kingdom	Canada
	301,224	64,596	79,968	79,212	98,280	68,586	46,872	44,562	25,116

Other major reserves include Libya, China, and the North Sea

Data sources: CIA (1989:97); *HC* 8/4/90:A5.

There is a wide gap in the world between where petroleum is located and produced and where it is consumed. The concentration of reserves in the Middle East and the massive import needs of the industrialized countries create a volatile political mixture, one which exploded on January 17, 1991, in the Kuwait war theater.

Industrial Output

Even if a country is bountifully supplied with natural resources, its power is limited unless it can convert those assets into industrial goods. Both China and India have extensive reserves of iron and coal, and China is finding new oil possibilities, but because of their limited industrial capacity, these countries have not been able effectively to transform potential into power.

Japan, by contrast, efficiently converts imported resources into manufactured products and has become an industrial power despite its lack of natural assets. Despite, for example, the disparity in iron ore mining between Japan and the United States (the United States producing approximately 150 times as much), the Japanese in 1989 exceeded U.S. steel production by about 22 percent or 19.5 million metric tons. Table 9.5 on page 247 illustrates a variety of economic production statistics, including per capita gross national product, that serve as measures of industrial capacity.

TABLE 9.5

Industrial Indicators

Country	Per Capita GNP ($ U.S.)	Aluminum (1,000s metric tons)	Cement (1,000s metric tons)	Pig Iron (1,000s metric tons)	Crude Steel (1,000s metric tons)	Motor Vehicles (1,000s)	Electricity Production (million kwh)
Brazil	1,500	396	26,508	24,384	26,112	1,248	214,116
Canada	14,503	1,536	11,820	10,140	15,456	1,524	512,592
China	258	420	204,114	59,136	59,814	255	593,520
Egypt	686	179	8,484	500	2,000	0	40,600
India	295	420	44,568	12,300	14,112	180	36,854
Italy	6,447	264	39,708	11,784	25,176	2,100	213,000
Japan	19,410	1,680	80,316	81,360	107,904	12,384	753,732
Mexico	1,431	120	23,760	5,280	7,392	636	101,880
Nigeria	927	0	3,084	0	0	0	9,900
Poland	6,815	4,700	17,112	9,492	15,096	336	145,488
Soviet Union	8,662	2,400	140,304	112,334	160,104	2,160	1,722,000
United States	18,570	5,592	71,388	50,676	88,392	10,872	2,778,648
West Germany	10,680	1,284	28,500	33,048	41,076	4,752	440,592

Data source: World Almanac (1990); UN (1990b). Figures are for 1989 or latest data available.

The level of industrial production is a major factor that distinguishes the North's relatively wealthy countries from the South's relatively poor countries. This table gives data for seven developed and six less developed countries.

Agriculture

It is common to equate steel production or numbers of soldiers with power; it is less common to think of food in those terms. Yet a country's agricultural capacity is an important factor. As with natural resources, the contribution of agriculture to power depends on whether or not a country can adequately supply its domestic needs and on whether it has a surplus of a commodity others need. A third factor is the percentage of its total economic energy that a country must devote to feeding itself.

Self-sufficiency varies widely in the world. The United States is basically able to supply its own needs. With less than 6 percent of the world's population, it produces (1988) 11 percent of the world's wheat, 17 percent of its meat, and 51 percent of its protein-rich soybeans. Other countries are less fortunate. Some are able to import to meet their needs; others face widespread hunger. Many parts of Africa are in particularly desperate shape. Compared with the Americans and Canadians, Africans consume less than two-thirds the calories, only about half the grams of protein, and rank far below in the intake of a variety of vitamins and minerals. In the Third World overall, 16 percent of the people have a calorie intake that falls below 80 percent of the World Health Organization standard, a deficiency serious enough to cause stunted growth and serious health risks. That figure rises to 25 percent in Sub-Saharan Africa.

Among LDCs, the overall daily per capita calorie availability remained static (at an unsatisfactory 2,094 calories) between 1965 and 1986, and 19 of 35 Sub-Saharan African countries actually declined in their daily per capita calorie availability. Another 4 countries made no progress, and only 2 countries (the Ivory Coast and Mauritius) in the

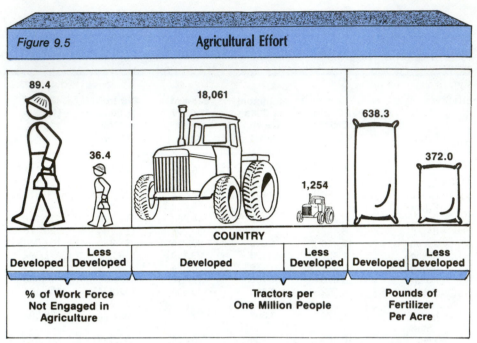

Figure 9.5 **Agricultural Effort**

Data sources: FAO (1989, Table 95); World Bank (1989, Table 4).

For many Third World countries, simply feeding their population consumes a great deal of their economic energy and resources. As this figure shows, LDCs, compared to developed countries, have less than half the percentage of their population working in nonagricultural endeavors, have 14 times fewer tractors per capita, and use about half the fertilizer per acre.

region were able to achieve a daily per capita calorie availability of 2,500. This contrasts with the world daily figure of 2,708 calories (a 13 percent increase, 1965–86), and 3,390 calories (a 9 percent increase, 1965–86) in the industrialized countries. Protein availability is a particular problem in many LDCs. Even in relatively sedentary, developed countries, people need about 50 grams of protein a day for good health. Pregnant women need an extra 30 grams a day, and lactating women need an extra 20 grams a day. The needs are somewhat higher in societies that engage in more manual labor. The developed countries have more than enough protein availability. The daily grams per capita in the developed countries is 101, but it is a just barely adequate 60 in the LDCs, and only 57 in Sub-Saharan Africa. Given the relatively high consumption by a wealthy few in most of these countries, that means that a substantial portion of the population is protein deficient. In some countries, such as Mozambique (28.4 grams daily) and Zaire (34.3 grams daily), the problem is critical. Perhaps most tragically, the most severely affected victims of protein deficiency are children who need protein for physical development and brain development.

By contrast, a surplus of food can be a plus, primarily by helping in the balance of trade, and is, for example, an important U.S. export. As a diplomatic "weapon," however, food has not proven highly successful. An attempt by the United States, for example, to withhold wheat and other grains from the Soviet Union in retaliation for the invasion of Afghanistan was ineffective. The Soviets were able to "tighten their belts," to buy grains from other countries, and even to get U.S. grain transshipped through third countries. That is, U.S. grain went to, say, French importers, who, in turn, sold it to the Soviets.

Another significant agricultural factor is the percentage of economic effort that a country must expend to feed itself. Countries that have larger percentages of their work force available for manufacturing and other non-agricultural pursuits, that use a large per capita number of tractors and other mechanical farming machines, and that use significant amounts of fertilizer to boost per acre production are more agriculturally efficient. Figure 9.5 uses these three standards to contrast the agricultural efficiency of the developed and the less developed countries.

The Military

The final category of tangible power that we will consider is the military. Throughout the world, countries have scrambled to increase their military might. In contrast to the few countries like Costa Rica, which has no army as such and which relies on the strategy that it would be too embarrassing for an aggressor to invade it, there are dozens of countries with a ravenous appetite for weaponry. We will look at the use and effectiveness of force in the next chapter, but we first need to consider the level of national armament and the fact that the military is the world's largest single economic consumer.

Levels of Spending

In the century between 1865 and 1965 the share of the world's annual economic production devoted to military expenditures rose 262 percent, according to one source (Hoffman, 1978). Defense spending continued to soar, rising 27 percent (in constant dollars) during the 1970s and reaching $958 billion in 1988. Just two countries, the United States and the Soviet Union together, accounted for almost 60 percent of the world total. The developed countries spent the vast majority of defense money, but the LDCs also spent $116.1 billion.[2]

A good way to consider defense spending is to relate it to overall economic productivity. In 1988 the developed countries spent 3.7 percent of their collective GNP on defense, and the LDCs spent 3.9 percent of their much smaller collective GNP on defense. The defense burden varied widely, though. As Table 9.6 shows, 17 percent of the 144 countries examined for 1988 spent 10 percent or more of their GNP on defense. By contrast, 9 percent of the countries spent less than 1 percent of their GNP on defense. One telling figure is that among the poorest countries ($0–999 per capita GNP), a third spend 5 percent or more of their scant GNPs on defense instead of being willing or able to fund development and pressing social spending.

As the decade of the 1990s begins, there are indications that defense spending is leveling off, even declining. This is especially true in constant dollars. Between 1980 and 1988, constant dollar spending on defense declined in 12 of the 60 countries with the highest defense expenditures, and the percentage of GNP spent on defense declined in 22 of these 60 countries. Furthermore, while the nearly $1 trillion spent on defense for 1987

2. This data is drawn from Turner (1990) and ACDA (1988) with several adjustments to modify Soviet defense expenditures and to shift GDP (gross domestic product) to GNP. There are significant controversies over measuring the Soviet defense budget and the relative values of GDP and GNP as an economic measure. The conversions were made so that this data would have continuity with data used earlier. The estimate of Soviet defense spending here uses a relatively conservative 12 percent of GNP. This equals $276 billion. The International Institute for Strategic Studies, on which Turner relies in part, estimates 1988 Soviet expenditures at $119.2 billion; the CIA estimate is $303 billion.

TABLE 9.6

Relative Burden of Military Expenditures Against Per Capita GNP

Military Expenditures as a Percentage of GNP (1988)	Number of Countries			
	GNP $0–999	GNP $1,000–2,999	GNP $3,000 +	GNP $10,000 +
10% +	10	5	8	1
5–9.99%	12	4	7	4
2–4.99%	30	13	5	13
1–1.99%	8	6	2	3
– 1%	5	4	2	2

Data source: U.S. ACDA (1989).

Some countries spend much of their wealth on defense; some spend relatively little. There is also little relationship between a country's level of wealth and the proportion it spends on its military. Ten countries with per capita GNPs of $999 or less spend 10 percent or more of their GNP on their armed forces.

could be considered bad news, the good news is that when controlled for inflation over the preceding year, 1987 was the first year since 1971 when world defense spending did not grow. Even more recently, the U.S. defense budget five-year (1992–97) plan issued by the Bush administration is $200 billion lower than the Reagan administration had projected for the same period, and it is likely that Congress will appropriate less funding than Bush requests. Also, the Soviet defense budget is being cut. It fell between 4 and 5 percent from 1989 to 1990, with, for example, a drop in tank production from 3,400 to 1,700 units. The reductions in personnel and weapons levels agreed to by Germany from the former totals of East and West Germany will also lower defense spending. Additionally, a conventional arms accord reached by the 34 countries of the Conference on Security and Cooperation in Europe in late 1990 will slash weaponry in Europe and will require the destruction of tens of thousands of tanks, artillery pieces, helicopters, and other weapons systems. This treaty is detailed further in chapter 17. How much these reductions will be offset by increased expenditures in the Middle East and elsewhere is not clear, but it seems that world totals will be at least relatively static and may even decline.

Quality Versus Quantity

Very often when you see a comparison of two countries' or alliances' military might you see a map with an overlay of small figures (such as blue for the U.S. and red for the U.S.S.R.) representing troops, tanks, planes, and other weapons. Such graphics emphasize quantity, and it always seems like the other side's figures far outnumber your own.

Quantity is an important military consideration, but the relative value of those little figures must be modified by the quality of the weapons and troops. The West, especially the United States, has tended to favor acquiring fewer, high-technology weapons. The Soviets, because of their technology lag and preferences, have favored masses of weapons. There is a general agreement that most important Western military weapons systems are technologically superior to Soviet weapons systems, but it is difficult to calculate with any precision what the balance is. A U.S. F-16, for one, is a better fighter than a Soviet MiG-29, but how many MiG-29s it would take to overcome, say, 10 F-16s is unclear.

Furthermore, high technology has its drawbacks. Besides expense, it often malfunctions more frequently than simpler weapons, and high-technology weapons are difficult to fix under battle conditions. During the late-1980s Persian Gulf crisis, a U.S. warship, the USS *Stark,* was accidentally attacked and nearly sunk by an Iraqi jet firing a French-made Exocet missile. One reason that the Stark was unable to defend itself was that the radar that guided its anti-aircraft weapons had been turned off to avoid overheating and failure in the heat of the Persian Gulf.

It should also be remembered that the effectiveness of soldiers and military hardware is very situational; it depends on circumstances. In Vietnam, the United States possessed vastly superior weapons and its troops were excellent. Yet it lost the war, in part because U.S. military power was limited by political decisions (such as not risking war with China by invading North Vietnam and not using nuclear weapons) based on the U.S. desire to keep the war limited. The Soviets faced a somewhat similar situation in Afghanistan. They soon found, for example, that their tanks were not effective in the rugged mountains there. After nearly a decade of struggle, Moscow withdrew its troops and ended what has been called the "Soviet Vietnam."

There are also a variety of considerations about the quality of military personnel that are even less tangible than technology levels. Especially in the modern, technological era of warfare, the ability to use and maintain complex weapons systems is vital and requires educated and well-trained troops. The declining pool of military-age people in the Soviet Union, the United States, and many other developed countries is raising concerns about their ability to recruit able volunteers without resorting to a draft. Readiness also affects power. The general slowness of the United States to activate and upgrade its armed forces prior to its entry into both world wars not only tempted the enemy to strike at U.S. shipping and naval forces, but it also meant that its allies had to bear the brunt of the war while the Americans prepared.

A country's military systems also need to be appropriate to the challenges it will face. The United States found that its emphasis on the types of weapons required to fight a NATO–Warsaw Pact war in Europe created difficulties in moving to counter Iraq in the Middle East. There were too few modern transport ships and aircraft, and many of the weapons systems had such limited mobility and required such extensive logistics support that it was not until many weeks after the August 2 beginning of the crisis that the full U.S. ground contingent was operational in the Saudi desert. The main U.S. tank, for example, weighs over 60 tons, and it is very difficult to move by air. As a result, the bulk of U.S. armor was moved by the few available ships and did not reach Saudi Arabia until mid-October.

Leadership and Morale

Military leadership, in the form of both inspiration and tactical skills, plays a significant role. It is difficult, for instance, to understand the long resistance of the Southern Confederacy to the overwhelming numerical superiority of the Union unless the brilliant generalship of Robert E. Lee is considered. By contrast, French generals in the middle part of this century made a series of classic errors. In the 1930s they relied on the fortified, but static, Maginot Line and were routed in 1940 by the Germans' more creative coordination of a highly mobile and mechanized army with air support. In 1954, again relying on a static defense, the French garrison at Dien Bien Phu in Indochina was surrounded and decimated by Vietnamese forces under the command of the able General Giap.

In the face of determined rebels operating in inhospitable mountainous terrain, all of Moscow's armor and all its men could not secure Afghanistan as a Soviet satellite again. This headstone of a Soviet soldier killed in Afghanistan symbolizes what became known as "the Soviet Vietnam." "He showed heroism and courage," the inscription tells us; he died at 19, it also says. The Soviet Union found out in Afghanistan, as the United States had in Vietnam, that massive firepower does not always mean victory.

Military morale is a key factor in a country's military power. In the aftermath of the massive U.S. deployment to Saudi Arabia in 1990, the press regularly carried stories detailing the low morale of the soldiers. This photograph shows U.S. Marine Corps commandant General Alfred Gray addressing that problem. According to a press account, the "crusty" general was "fed up with the complaining in the ranks." So he "bluntly dressed down" the troops living in "tents half-buried in the sand" near the desert's front lines. "There will be no morale problems," Gray ordered, "because I say [so]. . . . There also will be no boredom. Suck in that gut." It hardly needs saying, but Gray's performance violated the basic tenets of psychology and military leadership training and, based on subsequent press reports, did not work.

Another intangible military factor is morale. An army that will not fight cannot win. The Soviet-trained and well-equipped Afghan army was almost totally ineffective against the initially poorly armed, but highly motivated, rebel forces. Large numbers of regular army troops deserted, and Soviet soldiers had to do most of the fighting. The Afghan soldiers on both sides were no different except that the army was fighting for an unpopular government backed by an alien army, while the rebels were highly dedicated to a popular cause. Interestingly, once the Soviets withdrew from Afghanistan, the resistance of the government troops stiffened, and despite near-universal predictions of an early rebel victory, Afghan government troops achieved a stalemate.

Now there are significant concerns about the morale of Soviet troops. Cuts in the defense budget, generally poor living conditions, rivalries among national groups, and changing attitudes toward the government have created major worries for Moscow. The Soviet military paper *Krasnaya Zveda* (Red Star) reported that the Spring 1990 conscription in the Soviet Union was met with mass draft-dodging in parts of the country. An amazing 92.5 percent of all Armenian draftees failed to report. Some other republics and their ethnic group's resistance percentages were: Georgia (72.5), Estonia (59.8), Latvia (45.8), and Lithuania (66.4). And of the draftees that did report, 18 percent said they did not wish to serve. Perhaps the greatest personnel concern for Soviet military commanders is the ethnic rivalries that apparently are straining military cohesion. Almost 10 percent of draftees speak little or no Russian. Furthermore, there are reports that as many as 2,700 Soviet soldiers were killed in 1989 as a result of fighting among ethnic groups and because of abuse, especially by Russian troops, directed at Uzbeks, Armenians, and other non-Russian soldiers (*WP,* 8/19/90:C4). This has all created what one U.S. analyst called a "crisis for the Soviet military [that] is unprecedented" since 1945. And another U.S. expert told Congress that the deteriorating quality of the Soviet army suggests that a "Soviet commander would not want to take [it] into battle" (*LAT,* 4/26/90:A13). The resistance to the draft is also one of the factors that led to the Soviet military crackdown on the Baltic republics beginning in mid-January 1991.

Chapter Summary

1. Power is a key concept in a conflictual world. It is, in essence, the ability to get one's way even when opposed by others who have different interests and goals. Beyond that sort of simple characterization, the study of power becomes quite complex.

2. To fully understand power, one must consider all its aspects. Actual power, which can be used now, is important, but potential power also plays a role. Real power, that which one actually possesses, is another key element, but so is perceived power, or how others evaluate your capacity and will.

3. Measuring power is especially difficult. In this chapter we looked at several analysts' attempts to do so, but their efforts are more notable for the attempt than for any real success in accurately measuring power.

4. The power-measurement formula is also valuable because it highlights the fact that power is both tangible and intangible. Tangible elements of power, such as tanks or petroleum production, are relatively easy to visualize and measure. Intangible elements of power, such as morale and reputation, are much more difficult to operationalize.

5. It is also necessary to remember that power is dynamic and ever-changing.

6. Power is also relative, which means that its effectiveness depends partly on the power possessed by other (particularly opposing) international actors. Finally, power is situational.

7. Not all types of power can be used in all situations, and, therefore, only applicable power can be validly considered.

8. For all its complexity, a thorough understanding of power is crucial to a sophisticated analysis of international relations. It is prudent policy to have goals that are in realistic balance with one's power. Overly ambitious goals invite disaster. If goals and power are not in sync, then either the goals should be modified or an effort should be made to enhance one's power. In either case, a realistic assessment of both national interest and power is a necessity to the successful pursuit of international relations.

9. The major elements of a country's power can be roughly categorized as those that constitute (1) its national core, (2) its national infrastructure, (3) its national economy, and (4) its military.

Cry "Havoc!" and let slip the dogs of war.

Shakespeare, *Julius Caesar*

Not believing in force is like not believing in gravity.

Leon Trotsky, *What Next?*

There will be no veterans of World War III.

Walter Mondale, campaign speech, 1984

FORCE

It is February 1945. Marine Sergeant John Stryker, played by John Wayne, dashes across the beach after 90 minutes of celluloid heroics in *The Sands of Iwo Jima*. A machine gun barks, the sand spurts up at his feet. The leatherneck falls, a few telltale dark spots on his fatigues. There is just enough time for one last speech, a tribute through stoically clenched teeth to God, glory, and the girl back home. Fade to an image of the Stars and Stripes waving bravely over Mount Suribachi and the stirring strains of the "Marines' Hymn." Goosebumps, applause, lights up, go home safe and sound!

This 1949 classic is a typical image of war. There is an air of nobility, plumed knights, dashing air aces, and, of course, Sergeant Stryker.

There is another image of war. In our unromantic age we saw it in *Platoon*; but even the horrific imagery of this movie could not fully bring home the impact of war. Perhaps nobody can when the buttered-popcorn machine is close at hand. The real war is out there. It is marines with crushed skulls, mangled testicles, and charred bodies. It is naked and frightened Vietnamese children, Lebanese parents wailing over their fallen sons, and widowed Iranian mothers whose babies will never know their fathers. War is ear-shattering, mind-warping, terrifying, and dirty, and it has a stench all its own. "I am tired and sick of war," General William Tecumseh Sherman told a class of graduating military cadets in 1879. "Its glory is all moonshine. It is only those who have neither fired a shot nor heard the shrieks and groans of the wounded who cry aloud for more blood, more vengeance, more desolation. *War is hell*" [emphasis added].

War: The Human Record

Politically, war is a paradox. It has been condemned by almost all leaders during every period of history. The monetary and human costs of war are becoming ever higher. We may have come to the eve of Armageddon. There is truth in the observation of President

War is hell! This was true of the American Civil War, which prompted General William Tecumseh Sherman's blunt characterization of conflict. This 1972 Pulitzer Prize-winning photo of a 9-year-old girl, Kim Phuc, and other terrorized South Vietnamese children fleeing a misdirected napalm attack is graphic evidence that, more than a century later, war is still hell.

John Kennedy in a September 1961 address to the United Nations that "mankind must put an end to war, or war will put an end to mankind."

Whatever the accuracy of Kennedy's caution, the paradoxical reality is that wars are fought almost as regularly as they are condemned. There are varying estimates of the number of wars that have occurred depending on how different scholars have defined war. These studies on the incidence of war have found that, depending on methodology, between 224 and 559 international, internal (civil), and colonialist (separatist) wars occurred between 1816 and 1980 (DeMars, 1990). Our concern here is not to unravel these methodological differences. Instead, the key point to grasp is that by any standard many wars have occurred in humankind's recent history. Indeed, another study estimated that during the entire 5,500-year history of "civilization" there has been war somewhere in the world 94 percent of the time and total peace during only 292 years. During the 14,500 armed struggles that have occurred, 3.5 billion people have died as a direct or indirect result of warfare (Beer, 1981).

In addition to the overall incidence and impact of war, it is important to consider its frequency and severity. *Frequency* is mixed news. On the up side, according to one study, the percentage of countries involved in an international war in any given year has declined from 9.8 percent (1816–1945) to 6.9 percent (1946–80). On the down side, the percentage of countries experiencing a civil war increased from 3.2 percent (1816–1945) to 3.7 percent (1946–80). Even this mixed news becomes all bad when you consider that it is the increasing number of countries, not the decreasing number of wars, that has decreased the percentage of countries involved in international war in recent decades. In absolute numbers (still comparing 1816–1945 and 1946–80), the average number of countries involved in a war in any given year increased from 3.5 countries to 7.5 countries for international war and from 1.4 countries to 4.3 countries for civil war (DeMars, 1990).

Severity is the truly bad news. Since 1700, over 100 million people have been killed in war. Of the dead, an astounding 84 percent have died in this century (Eckhardt, 1988). Not only have we become much more efficient at killing soldiers, we also now kill larger numbers of civilians as part of the war effort. During World War I, 8.4 million soldiers and 1.4 million civilians died. World War II killed 16.9 million troops and 34.3 million civilians, for a staggering 8 million deaths per year (Beer, 1981). The worst news of all is for the future. A general nuclear exchange between the superpowers would certainly escalate the casualty count from millions per year to millions per minute. President Kennedy's cataclysmic characterization will have come true.

There are some analysts who contend that war is a fading form of international interaction. John Mueller (1989) argues that war among the more modernized nations has become unthinkable, and other analysts agree with the general trend of this thinking (Ray, 1989). Many other commentators, however, reject such conclusions as overly optimistic (Kaysen, 1990; Huntington, 1989). They might cite the recent events in Kuwait as evidence that armed strength and conflict are still important international political factors.

The Causes of War: Three Levels of Analysis

Why war? This question has challenged investigators over the centuries. Philosophers, world leaders, and social scientists have come to many conclusions. A survey of their divergent findings brings the inescapable conclusion that there is no single reason that people fight. Indeed there are often multiple causal factors present in crises that lead to war (James, 1988). There are many causes of war, which, for our purposes here, can be classified according to the three levels of analysis discussed in chapter 1: individual-level analysis, state-level analysis, and system-level analysis. As we look at the different types of war later in this chapter, we will also consider causal factors specifically related to each class of conflict.

A related question is, why study war? As you will see in the following pages of this chapter and in subsequent chapters, there are several reasons. One reason to study war is to know how to be best prepared to fight if necessary and to prevail. A second reason to study the use of military power is so that you can intelligently address the perpetual defense budget debate over "how much is enough." You cannot reasonably argue that the country is spending too much or, alternately, too little, if you do not understand weapons, strategies, threats, and other national security considerations.

A third reason to study wars focuses on what causes them. If you begin to understand what causes war, then you have a better chance to prevent it. If one or just a few root causes underlie war, then perhaps you can eliminate those root causes. Or, even if you cannot, then if you can recognize the symptoms of approaching conflict, maybe you can move to head it off through diplomacy or other dispute resolution procedures, such as UN peacekeeping or an International Court of Justice decision. A fourth reason for studying war is that if you study how wars are fought, you can begin to see better ways to control them, to limit the damage and death they cause, and to find paths to an early conclusion of the fighting. In short, if you want to know how to fix something, you first have to know why it is broken. Simply ignoring or condemning it does not help at all.

Individual-Level Analysis and War

It may be that the roots of war lie in the nature of human beings, either based on the characteristics of individuals or on the inherent nature of the human species. It is clear that human behavior is predominantly learned, but there are also behavioral links to the primal origins of humans. Territoriality, which we examined in chapter 4, is one such possible instinct. Another possibility, some social psychologists argue, is that human aggression, individually or collectively, can stem from stress, anxiety, or frustration. The reaction of the German society to its defeat and humiliation after World War I is an example. A sociopsychological need for power is yet another possibility. At least some leaders have a power drive that may cause aggressive behavior. While discounting some of the more strident characterizations of Saddam Hussein as a madman, most personality analyses of Iraq's leader characterized him as driven to seek power and to dominate. At the human level of analysis, misperception is a cause of conflict. The inability of leaders and nations to perceive events objectively is caused, in part, by factors that may be inherently human. Our proclivity for seeing our opponents as more hostile than ourselves is but one example.

State-Level Analysis and War

War may also result from causes related to the internal political dynamics of countries. As we discussed in chapter 5, there is a great academic debate over what is called the externalization of internal conflict, or the degree to which external aggression is linked to domestic unrest (James, 1988; Levy, 1988). Social scientists know that sometimes governments will engage in war to rally the populace and divert attention from domestic problems.

Some analysts also believe that some types of systems (democratic, authoritarian) are more aggressive than others. Additionally, some observers charge that some political cultures are more warlike than others. The reunification of Germany has rekindled this debate. Most published comments on the nature of German political culture have been optimistic. Lord Shawcross, the chief British prosecutor at the Nuremburg war crimes trials of the Nazis, expressed support of reunification. He believes that the German people have "accepted the fact that the Nazi leadership" was "an evil regime" and that the Germans "are a very different people to what [they were] . . . during the war" (*NYT,* 9/27/90:A8). Similarly, a summary of opinion at a conference held by Prime Minister Margaret Thatcher in London indicated that the conferees "had no serious misgivings" about the current German leaders. Still, there are nagging doubts, and the report wondered, "What about 10, 15, or 20 years from now? Could some of the unhappy characteristics of the past re-emerge with just as destructive consequences?" (*NYT,* 7/20/90:A27).

Economic factors can also cause conflict, as the 1990–91 Middle East crisis shows. The radical economic perspective argues that capitalism causes imperialism. Others contend that the military-industrial complex or other domestic factors cause aggressive behavior. Additionally, national growth is related to both internal conflict and economics. Various growth factors, such as population expansion and economic modernization, may lead to pressures and dislocations that cause aggressive behavior. Finally, nationalism in the form of ethnocentrism, xenophobia, and the strains caused by the lack of fit between states and nations is a common cause of conflict at the state level of analysis.

System-Level Analysis and War

From a third analytical perspective, wars may be caused by a number of factors that are related to the general nature of the world's political system (Levy, 1988b; Alt, Calvert, & Humes, 1988). There is, for example, a "contagion theory" of conflict. It argues that persistent crisis or recurrent warfare breeds more hostility because of heightened tension, the tendency to become inured to violence, and similar phenomena. In addition, the uneven distribution of world resources and the needs of strong countries can cause conflict such as colonial conquest (Eckhardt, 1990).

The distribution of power in the world is yet another possible system-level cause of conflict. Numerous studies have found that power vacuums can cause conflict as opposing powers move to fill the void. There is a lively debate over whether the end of the cold war, the changes in Eastern Europe, and the strengthening of Germany will result in instability and a power struggle in Central and Eastern Europe (Mearsheimer, 1990b; J. Snyder, 1990). Some scholars have also argued that relative equality, between countries or between alliances, may cause conflict because each side calculates it can win a war (Vasquez, 1987). As chapter 3 explained, there is also some speculation that the number of poles in political systems determines their degree of stability.

A related phenomenon, also detailed in chapter 3, is that periods of power transitions in the world system are prone to conflict (Houweling & Siccama, 1988). Dominant states may be tempted to strike a rising rival. Declining states may act to try to preserve or regain their glory. New powers may attack to exert their new strength (Anderson & McKeown, 1987). Changes in power will often lead to miscalculations of the actual power of the states involved. In an era of rapid technological innovation, the power transition factor is especially important. It led the Soviet Union in 1969 to contemplate a nuclear attack on China to destroy that rising power's nuclear weapons development program.

Moreover, at least to some degree, the *world arms spiral* is a result of the nature of the international system. Countries acquire arms in part because other countries do, creating a tension-filled cycle of escalating arms → tensions → arms → tensions until a flash point is reached. Finally, some systems analysts argue that wars occur because the international system is quasi-anarchical. Therefore there is little to prevent conflict. Unlike domestic societies, the international society has no effective system of law creation, enforcement, or adjudication.

Force as a Political Instrument

Because war is the most cataclysmic of all political events, it is the focus of ever-increasing research. For all this effort, though, political scientists have only begun to be able to identify the causes, conditions, and consequences of conflict. It may be that social scientists in the future will be able to write of war in the past tense, but for the present we must recognize conflict as a fact of international politics. Having discussed the human record, we should also consider levels of violence, the effectiveness of force, the changing nature of warfare, and the classification of wars. Among other things you might gain from the following discussion, remember that the possession of arms and the threat of violence have important *psychological* and *diplomatic impacts* in addition to their strictly military role.

As a last point before embarking on the discussion of how force is used in the international system, we should again, as in chapter 7, consider when to threaten and

The 1990–91 Middle East crisis included the use by both U.S. president George Bush and Iraqi president Saddam Hussein of all the possible levels of force from intimidation to attack.

fight. This is, of course, a very personal decision. Pacifists and some others consider war to be wrong under all circumstances (Holmes, 1989). Most people are not true pacifists, however, and are willing to use force in some circumstances. In such cases, it is well to keep the standards of *jus ad bellum* (just cause of war) and *jus in bello* (just conduct of war) in mind. The following discussion, then, is not an advocacy of war as a legitimate tool of politics. Rather it is an examination of how force is used and some suggestions about how, if fight we must, we can conduct that unhappy exercise with moderation and success.

Levels of Violence From Intimidation to Attack

A country's military power may be used in several escalating ways: (1) as a diplomatic backdrop that creates perceived power through military potential; (2) by explicitly threatening its use against an opponent; (3) through limited demonstrations of violence; and (4) by direct use of military forces to defeat an opponent.

Military power does not have to be used or even overtly threatened to be effective. Its very existence establishes a *diplomatic backdrop* that may persuade potential opponents not to risk confrontation. This is especially true when there is gross inequality—when it is clear that one side will lose—or when both antagonists have a great deal of relatively equal power and, thus, face not only a 50/50 chance of losing but almost certain significant damage, win or lose. The calculation of these odds, it should be noted, is highly subject to decisionmakers' misperception, especially during periods of power fluctuation, about their country's or an opponent's relative power, about their own military credibility, or about the opponent's willingness to take military action.

All types of weapons can be part of a diplomatic backdrop, but nuclear weapons play a particularly important psychological role. Atomic weapons, of course, have been physically used by one country against another only twice, and both of those attacks were more than 40 years ago. This does not mean that they do not play a role in world politics today. Deterrence will be discussed in detail in a later section of this chapter, but we can say here that one role of nuclear weapons has been to persuade the two superpowers to avoid direct confrontations with one another. Even when conflict threatened between the superpowers, or between a nuclear power and a nonnuclear country, the existence of nuclear weapons has sometimes played a role. There is, for example, no evidence that the United States explicitly threatened the Soviets with nuclear force during the Cuban missile crisis, but there can be little doubt that superior U.S. nuclear capabilities influenced the Soviets' decision to give way.

The next level of military application is *overtly threatening* an opponent. This may be done verbally, or it may involve shifts in the readiness or deployment of a country's armed forces. During the 1973 Arab-Israeli War, for example, the Soviets readied airborne brigades and threatened to intervene if Israel attempted to annihilate the encircled Egyptian army. The prospect caused sufficient alarm in Tel Aviv and Washington to restrain the Israeli forces.

As with the diplomatic backdrop, nuclear weapons can play an important role in overt or explicit threats. A key concept is the idea of **extended deterrence**. This means threatening to use your forces, particularly your nuclear forces, to deter an opponent from an attack with conventional weapons on a third party or part of your territory (including colonies) that is distant from your territorial core. Recent studies found, for example, that threatening to use nuclear force in some circumstances does enhance the chances of a favorable political outcome for the threatening power, although it does not ensure success (Geller, 1990; Huth, 1990; DeMars, 1988), but there are some studies that question the validity of extended deterrence at all (Lebow & Stein, 1990). DeMars's analysis showed that since 1945, defenders possessing nuclear weapons succeeded in 12 of 15 (80 percent) attempted uses of extended deterrence. Nonnuclear defenders succeeded in only 2 of 9 (22 percent) attempts. The study concluded, therefore, that "while nuclear weapons do not guarantee success, they appear to be almost standard equipment for a nation to play the extended deterrence game on a large scale in the nuclear era."

Limited demonstration of your capability and commitment is a third military option. This involves actual combat use of the military but in a way that is aimed at intimidating rather than defeating an opponent. In the mid-1980s, for example, France sent fighter aircraft and troops to Chad and warned invading Libyan forces not to move south of a demarcation line. When Libya crossed that line, French forces struck back in a demonstration of superior military power that dissuaded the Libyans from further incursions.

Direct action is the most violent option and involves using full-scale force to attempt to defeat an opponent. Within this context, the level of violence can range from highly constrained conventional conflict to unrestricted nuclear war.

Additionally, the choices provided by the four levels of violence form a *multiple menu*. That is, they are often exercised concurrently. While fighting in South Vietnam (direct use), for example, the Nixon administration mined North Vietnam's Haiphong Harbor (demonstration) and issued warnings (threat) that the communists either had to negotiate more seriously or face the full force of American arms (backdrop).

Effectiveness of Force

Another aspect of the threat and use of force is a question of whether or not it works in a utilitarian way (Lalman, 1988). It does, and one of the reasons that weapons and war persist in the international system is that they are sometimes successful. The use of force may accomplish its intended goal, and the threat of violence may successfully deter an enemy from attacking you or an ally. There is a great deal of controversy over the conditions for successful deterrence (Orme, 1987), but it is clear that it works at least some of the time. Beyond these passive uses of force, we can also ask ourselves if force is a utilitarian instrument when actually employed as a demonstration or in full force. Answering this question necessitates looking at measurements and conditions for success.

Measurement

There are two ways of measuring the effectiveness of war. One is by trying to apply *cost/benefit analysis*. Was the result worth it in terms of the loss of life, human anguish, and economic destruction? Although such trade-offs are made in reality, it is impossible to arrive at any objective standards that can equate the worth of a human life or political freedom with dollars spent or territory lost (Beer, 1981). A pacifist would argue that no political objective is worth a human life. A militarist would argue that war actually improves the human condition, or, as Benito Mussolini declared, "War alone brings up to its highest tension all human energy and puts the stamp of nobility upon the people who have the courage to face it."

The second way to judge the effectiveness of force is in terms of *goal attainment*. The issue is whether the accumulation and use of military power achieve the desired results. Wars are often caused by specific issues and fought with specific goals (Diehl, 1990). Furthermore, the choice for war is not irrational insofar as leaders usually calculate, accurately or not, their probability of success. This calculation is called the "expected utility" of war. The validity of this calculation is supported by the fact that military force sometimes does work, especially when a major power is the initiator of the war. One study found that "analyses of data on the initiation and outcome of international wars involving Great Powers from 1495 to 1985 reveal that initiators have won 58.1 percent of the time" (Wang & Ray, 1990:i). What is more, the initiators' success rate is going up. During the first three centuries (1495–1799) analyzed, the initiators won only very slightly more (51.5 percent) of the wars than they lost. During the last two centuries (1800–1985), the initiators won 69.2 percent of the wars. The U.S. actions against Grenada (1983) and Panama (1989) are examples of successful uses of military force. It is equally clear, however, that initiating military force sometimes backfires, and that rational calculations are sometimes wrong (Maoz, 1989). Egypt's attack across the Suez Canal (1973), the Soviet movement into Afghanistan (1979), and Argentina's seizure of the Falkland Islands (1982) are three examples in which the country that chose action was routed.

Conditions for Success

The next question, then, is: When does force succeed and when does it fail to accomplish its goals? Several studies have begun to outline some of the conditions for successful application of conventional force. Two studies (George, Hall, & Simons, 1971; Blechman & Kaplan, 1979) have analyzed instances of threatened or actual use of the military. The 1971 study identified eight requisites of politically successful military action. The study examined three crises and found that in two (Laos, 1961; Cuba, 1962) in which the United States was successful, all eight of the requisites were present. By contrast, only two of the elements for success were evident in Vietnam, which was a failure.

Blechman and Kaplan's study, asking somewhat different questions from the earlier analysis, found that the military option was most successful when viewed as a short-term measure designed to supplement diplomacy and give leaders time to seek more permanent solutions. The two authors also came up with a list of 10 elements that make successful use of the military more likely.

In an interesting parallel to the work of these scholars, U.S. secretary of defense Caspar W. Weinberger in a 1985 speech outlined six conditions that he felt should be met before committing U.S. troops to combat (Hudson & Kruzel, 1985:3). The secretary's analysis was not based on scholarly study, but it did reflect the view of practical experience. What is most important is that it is possible to synthesize these three analyses and arrive at some rudimentary rules for the successful use of military force.[1] These are:

1. Action should be taken in areas where there is a clearly defined, preferably long-standing and previously demonstrated commitment.
2. Your felt and announced commitment should be strong.
3. Military force is most successful when used to counter other military force, rather than to try to control political events.
4. If you are going to use military force, it is better to do so early and decisively (with sufficient force) than to threaten and then escalate slowly.
5. Establish clear goals.
6. Work to secure widespread domestic support of the action and goals.

These correlations between military action, political circumstances, and success are only preliminary, and they do not guarantee success. They do, however, give some indication of factors that contribute to successful use of the military instrument.

One telling exercise is to apply these six standards to the 1990–91 Middle East crisis. For the United States' defense of Saudi Arabia, all six criteria were met, and, therefore, the United States stood a good chance of being successful. With regard to the U.S. goal of getting Iraq out of Kuwait, the picture was somewhat less clear. Criteria 1, 2, 3, and 5 were mostly met, but 4 was not, insofar as early use is concerned. And the long crisis saw much ambivalence in the public's willingness to support initiating action to liberate Kuwait, thereby affecting criterion 6 in a negative way. For Iraq, the invasion

1. George's elements were (1) strong U.S. determination, (2) a less determined opponent, (3) clear U.S. goals, (4) a sense of urgency to accomplish these goals, (5) adequate domestic political support, (6) usable military options, (7) fear of U.S. escalation by the opponent, and (8) clarity concerning terms of the peaceful settlement. Blechman and Kaplan's elements were (1) the opponent finds the threat credible, (2) the opponent is not yet fully committed to a course of action, (3) the goal is maintaining the authority of a particular regime abroad, (4) force is used to offset force by an opponent, (5) the goal is to have an opponent continue current behavior, that is, to deter a change in behavior, (6) the action is consistent with prior policy, (7) there has been previous U.S. action in the area, (8) U.S. involvement begins early in the crisis, (9) military action is taken rather than threatened, and (10) strategic forces become involved, thus signaling seriousness of purpose. Weinberger's six criteria included (1) vital U.S. interests must be at stake, (2) there must be a clear intention of winning, (3) political and military objectives must be clearly defined, (4) sufficient military force must be employed to gain the objective, (5) there must be reasonable congressional and public support, and (6) combat should be a last resort.

Even traditional (conventional) weapons have increasingly longer ranges and greater destructive power. These U.S. Marine F-18 Hornets can take off from aircraft carriers and can also refuel in flight from KC-130 tankers, one of which is seen in the background. The Hornets shown here are aloft over the Persian Gulf in November 1990. A few weeks later, a Navy F-18 was the first U.S. plane lost during Operation Desert Storm.

of Kuwait fulfilled criteria 1, 2, 4, and 6. Whether or not Iraq fulfilled criterion 5 is in some doubt. Iraq has long claimed Kuwait's territory, but Iraq's pre-invasion goal was to redress certain grievances with Kuwait. The countries that later confronted Iraq might have accepted this initial, limited goal. Iraq's goal was changed after the attack, however, to absorbing Kuwait. Criterion 3 was not met, since Kuwait was not a military threat. From this perspective, one could have predicted that the defense of Saudi Arabia would succeed. The criterias' support for the U.S. liberation of Kuwait or Iraq's defense of its conquest were mixed, however. These may have caused miscalculations by both sides about the other's resolution, but in the end the preponderence of force made the difference.

The Changing Nature of War

The nature of war has changed greatly over the centuries. Two factors, technology and nationalism, have radically altered the scope and strategy of war.

It goes without saying that the *technological ability to kill* has escalated rapidly. Successive "advances" in the ability to deliver weapons at a distance (hand-held, then thrown, then bow and arrow, then rifle, then cannon, then plane, then missile) and in killing power (individuals, then gunpowder, then TNT, then nuclear weapons) have resulted in climbing casualties, both absolutely and as a percentage of soldiers and civilians of the countries at war.

Nationalism has also changed the nature of war. Before the nineteenth century, wars were generally fought between noble houses with limited armies. The French Revolution changed that. War began to be fought between nations, with increases in intensity and in numbers involved. France's Grand Army was the first to rely on a mass draft and the first to number more than a million men.

As a result of technology and nationalism, the *scope* of war has expanded. Entire nations have become increasingly involved in wars. Before 1800, no more than 3 of 1,000 (.3 percent) people of a country participated in a war. By World War I, the European powers called 1 of 7 (14 percent) of their populations to arms. Technology increased the need to mobilize the population for industrial production and also increased the capacity for, and rationality of, striking at civilians. Nationalism made war a movement of the masses, increasing their stake and also giving justification for attacking the enemy nation. Thus, the lines between military and civilian targets have blurred.

Finally, the *strategy* of war has changed. Two concepts, the power to defeat and the power to hurt, are key here (Schelling, 1966). The **power to defeat** is the ability to seize territory or overcome enemy military forces and is the classic goal of war. The **power to hurt**, or coercive violence, is the ability to inflict pain outside the immediate military sphere. It is hurting some so that the resistance of others will crumble. The power to hurt has become increasingly important to all aspects of warfare.

Traditionally wars were fought with little reference to hurting. Even when hurting was used, it depended on the ability to attack civilians by first defeating the enemy's military forces. During the American Revolution, for example, the British could have utilized their power to hurt—to kill civilians in the major cities they controlled—and they might have won the war. Instead they concentrated on defeating the American army (at first they could not catch it, then it grew stronger) and lost.

In the modern era, the power to defeat has declined in importance relative to the power to hurt. Guerrilla and nuclear warfare both rely extensively on terror tactics to accomplish their ends. Even conventional warfare relies partly on terror tactics to break down the opponent's morale. Iraq's use of hostages as human shields to try to deter an attack also utilized the power to hurt as part of conventional warfare.

Classifying Wars

The changing nature of war, the increased power of the weapons available, and the shifts in tactics have all made classifying wars more difficult. One way to classify wars is by intensity, with limited and total at the two extremes. Another classification scheme would divide wars into tactical (battlefield) wars and strategic (targeted cities and economic centers) wars. Yet another is to classify wars by weapons usage, with nuclear and nonnuclear two obvious categories. Here we will use four classifications: traditional wars, limited nuclear-biological-chemical (NBC) wars, strategic wars, and interventionist wars. As is frequently the case in any explanation, the exact boundaries between various types of wars or other political phenomena are imprecise and are, to a degree, mere pedagogical devices to group and explain things. Therefore, you should be concerned mostly with the issues involved in planning for and fighting wars. Of the four categories of war, the first three will be defined and analyzed in this chapter. The fourth, interventionist wars, will be discussed in the next chapter. This type of warfare includes guerrilla operations, terrorism, the supplying of arms and logistical support to other countries or groups that you support, and the stationing of military advisers or even a limited number of military specialists with specific combat roles in another country. The reason for the placement of interventionist war in the next chapter, rather than this chapter, is to emphasize how frequently countries now intervene militarily in other countries without resorting to the traditional use of significant numbers of their own military personnel.

Traditional War

The term traditional war has two implications. One is that the war is being fought with traditional weapons. This excludes NBC weapons. The second implication is that the war is primarily designed to defeat an opponent's military forces by overcoming them on the battlefield. Therefore, attacks on civilian population centers, economic facilities, and other targets not immediate to the battlefield are absent or limited. It is true that wars have not always been fought by this tradition, with World War II (a strategic war) being a prime example. Historically, however, most wars have more or less refrained from attacking purely civilian targets, and even bitter conflicts such as the repeated wars between Israel and the surrounding Arab countries have mostly adhered to a traditional war pattern.

Goals and Conduct

The classic statement on the proper goal of war was made by the nineteenth-century German strategist Karl von Clausewitz. He argued that "war is not merely a political act, but also a political instrument, a continuation of political relations, a carrying out of the same by other means" (*On War*, 1833).

Clausewitz's point is well made, and it implies several principles that should be kept in mind by civilian and military decisionmakers. First, it stresses the principle that wars, if they are to be fought, should be governed by political, not military, considerations. Often commanders chafe under restrictions, as General Douglas MacArthur did in Korea over his lack of authority to attack China. When generals become insubordinate, as MacArthur did, they ought to be removed from command, as he was.

Second, Clausewitz's statement emphasizes that war should be fought with clear political goals in mind. When these goals are subordinated to military factors or when the flush of victory escalates these goals, disaster looms. Harry Truman's accomplishment of firing MacArthur is offset by the president's earlier error in crossing into North Korea. After the North's invasion of the South, Truman's stated aim was to drive the communists out and restore the border. The spectacular victory at Inchon and subsequent disintegration of North Korean forces, however, emboldened the president to move north of the border. That brought in China, with a resulting cost of two years and tens of thousands of casualties in a war that had already been "won" according to initial U.S. goals.

Third, Clausewitz's statement includes the idea that war is not a substitute for diplomacy. During combat, channels of communication to the opponent should be kept open in an attempt to limit the conflict and to reestablish peace.

These principles derived from Clausewitz suggest that sometimes losing or compromising is preferable to continuing to fight or even winning. Green Bay Packer coach Vince Lombardi once said that "victory isn't the most important thing; it's the *only thing*." It is doubtful if this is a very good standard on the football field, and it is certainly wrong on the field of battle. Starting from the idea that war is an instrument, not a goal, you can reason that winning may cost too much. Americans could have continued and escalated the war in Vietnam, but they found the cost (in lives and economics) too great. An escalation of that war, such as the invasion of North Vietnam, might have brought China into the war, and increased the cost monumentally. There were also psychological costs. Many Americans were sickened by the human cost to both sides; if the war had been continued or escalated, there would have surely been an increase of deep divisions within the United States. Ultimately, the United States could have achieved a military victory by "nuking" North Vietnam and killing everyone there. Americans finally realized, though, that victory wasn't the only thing. It wasn't even the most important thing, and the United States settled for defeat only thinly disguised as a compromise rather than continuing to fight. Many believe it was a wise, if unfortunate, choice.

Keeping Limited War Limited

The idea of limits is inherent in traditional war. At times, as in World War II, near-total war occurs, but even then weapons such as poison gas were not used in combat. Most writers have observed that conventional wars have a number of explicit or implicit rules of the game by which they are usually fought. These include limits on objectives, weaponry, targets, geography, mobilization, and direct superpower confrontation. Not all of these limits are always observed, and in some especially brutal wars like the Iran-Iraq conflict many were violated. The use of chemical warfare by both sides, including a few attacks on civilians, was particularly disturbing. But even in this war there was considerable restraint.

Goals are limited, usually falling short of eliminating the opponent as a sovereign state. Even where unconditional victory is the aim, obliteration of the enemy population is not a goal. *Weapons* are also restricted. The use of nuclear, biological, and chemical weapons has generally been avoided despite their ready availability. This is based on the principle that the level of force used should be no greater than the minimum necessary to accomplish war aims. It must be added here, though, that the power of **conventional weapons** should not be underestimated. The spreading availability to countries of weapons systems (especially missiles) capable of accurately delivering extremely powerful explosives over a long range strains the outer boundary of traditional warfare. Intelligence reports, for example, indicate that Iraq is one country to develop fuel-air explosives (FAEs). Essentially, this bomb or warhead is a double-detonation device by which a first explosion disperses a fuel such as propane or ethylene oxide in the air over a wide area, then a second explosion ignites the fuel-air mixture creating a huge fireball and shock wave similar to a nuclear explosion. In the laconic estimation of one U.S. defense official, an FAE is "not your garden-variety weapon" (*HC*: 10/5/90).

Traditional wars also usually have *target* restrictions. Despite their close proximity, the Arabs and Israelis have never tried to bomb each other's capitals. Iraq's launch of Scud missiles against Tel Aviv and other Israel cities was, by contrast, a serious escalation.

There is often an attempt to limit *geographical scope*. American forces refrained from invading China during the Korean War. On a more global scale, the Soviets passed up the temptation to blockade Berlin in 1962 in response to the U.S. blockade of Cuba. Geographical limits thus help define and confine conventional war. Further, by limiting the extent to which they *mobilize* their troops and economic power, countries assure their opponents that rapid escalation is not in the offing. Since 1945 another mark of limited war has been *avoiding big-power armed clashes*. Often the superpowers used lesser powers, such as Israel and Syria, to test their arms against one another, but the superpowers have been wary of direct confrontations.

A particular method of avoiding confrontation has been noninterference or giving way in each other's **sphere of influence**. Generally, the United States and the Soviet Union during the cold war avoided direct intervention in each other's spheres of influence (United States: Latin America/Caribbean; Soviet Union: Eastern Europe). The United States encouraged, but did nothing to help, dissidents in Hungary (1956), Czechoslovakia (1968), and Poland (1980s). Similarly, U.S. anticommunist moves in the Dominican Republic (1965), Chile (1973), and Grenada (1983) occasioned only protests from the Soviets. The single direct confrontation between the powers (Cuba, 1962) resulted in a Soviet retreat in the American sphere.

As an evolving big power, China has not yet defined its sphere or had it tacitly accepted by other countries. Southeast Asia, however, may well become in the future what it was in the past—an area of primary Chinese influence. Events such as the post-Vietnam withdrawal of American influence, Sino-Soviet rivalry in Indochina, the Sino-Vietnamese clashes, and China's involvement in Cambodia's civil war are all part of that evolutionary process.

Escalation and De-escalation

The fact that limited wars are fought by rules of the game does not mean that sometimes those boundaries are not violated. **Escalation** occurs when the rules are changed and the level of combat increases. Conversely, *de-escalation* is a decrease in the level of fighting.

The dynamics of changing the level of combat are truly complex, but we can basically say that they can be either irrational and destructive or positive and productive.

If we begin from the principle of fighting limited wars according to political rules, for political goals, and with an economy of force, then it follows that escalation or de-escalation should be a deliberate, controlled strategy designed to signal a political message to the enemy. Accordingly, it is also important to send signals through diplomatic channels or public pronouncements so that the opponent will not misperceive the escalation as an angry spasm of violence or the de-escalation as a weakening of resolve.

Escalation at its worst occurs when the pressures of military conflict career beyond political control or when the opponent misperceives the message. In such cases, an action/reaction spiral is more likely to occur, leading to total, even nuclear, war.

The object of escalation or de-escalation should be to achieve peace by changing the rules to signal intent. Changes in the level of combat require careful conflict management and communication to emphasize its political rather than military meaning. It is a dangerous strategy, but when it is used skillfully, it can persuade an opponent that it is better to switch than fight.

Limited Nuclear-Biological-Chemical (NBC) War

The potential for limited, on-the-battlefield use of NBC weapons has created a controversial zone between traditional and strategic (and between conventional and nuclear) warfare. For our purposes here we will be considering the use of NBC weapons as part of a battlefield strategy. Even in this limited context, however, NBC weapons pose a special set of considerations because of the horror with which these weapons are regarded and because their use on even a limited basis will significantly increase the chances of escalation. There are many analysts who argue that a crucial "firebreak" (barrier) exists between traditional and NBC war, and once that NBC threshold is crossed, there is danger of careening into total holocaust. To these critics, a term such as "limited nuclear warfare" is an oxymoron. Other people argue that a "weapon is a weapon," that they all kill and how they do it is not important. While that view has some philosophical justification, there are political considerations that make even small NBC weapons qualitatively different rather than merely quantitatively more efficient killers. Many "small" tactical warheads, for example, are of the size dropped on Hiroshima (12.5 kt) and larger, and the United States alone possesses about 11,000 such devices.[2] In addition, once the nuclear threshold is crossed, even with relatively low-yield weapons, three very important factors will change. First, just because the threshold will have been crossed, it will probably be easier psychologically to escalate from tactical battlefield to intercontinental strategic weapons than it was to cross the line to begin with. Second, the mind-warping tensions that will occur once the nuclear threshold is crossed will increase significantly the chances for errors in judgment, even hysteria. Third, even limited nuclear strikes will probably have such a disruptive effect on communications that leaders will find it very difficult to gain accurate information or to issue orders. In short, once the first mushroom cloud rises, no matter how small, the fate of the world will be very much in doubt. The physically and psychologically destructive impact of some biological and chemical weapons might have similar effects and carry an equal danger of uncontrolled escalation.

2. Discussion of weapon yield (explosive power) will be given in kilotons. A kiloton is equal to 1,000 kilos. A kilo equals 2.2 pounds. Therefore, a kiloton equals 2,200 lb. or 1.1 tons. Pounds can be roughly converted to kilos by multiplying pounds by 0.45.

Whether or not this line of thinking is correct, the reality is that both the superpowers and some of the lesser nuclear powers arm and plan for the possibility of NBC conflict. Therefore it is important to understand the issues surrounding these weapons and the doctrines associated with their use.

Limited NBC Weapons

Some of these weapons have existed for centuries. What has caused mounting concern in this century is their increasing lethality and the increasing ranges at which they can be delivered.

Tactical Nuclear Weapons

Weapons in this category are defined loosely by their explosive power and by their delivery vehicles and the ranges of those vehicles. Some of the weapons, especially bombs, can be used in both tactical and strategic warfare scenarios, and some delivery vehicles are both nuclear- and conventional-capable, leading to some disagreement among various estimates of national inventories. U.S. battlefield nuclear weapons have explosive yields as low as less than 0.1 ($^1/_{10}$) kt for the W-48 artillery shell fired by a 155mm howitzer over a range of a few miles. Tactical weapons also potentially include the new B-83 nuclear gravity bomb with a variable yield up to 1,200 kt, almost 100 times that of the Hiroshima bomb. In addition to being delivered by artillery and aircraft, tactical nuclear weapons can be delivered by short-range and intermediate-range (high-speed) missiles and by cruise missiles launched from the air, ground, or sea.[3]

The United States has about 11,000 tactical nuclear devices, as noted, and the Soviet Union has about twice that number. Additionally, Great Britain, France, China, and Israel combine for about 1,200 nuclear explosive devices, many of which could be delivered in a tactical situation. Until recently the focus of planning for a tactical nuclear war was along the front between NATO and Warsaw Pact forces, and there are still more tactical nuclear weapons there than anywhere else. Because these weapons are highly transportable, though, they could be used almost anywhere. The aircraft carriers deployed by the United States in or near the Persian Gulf against Iraq, for example, all carry a significant number of nuclear and chemical weapons.

Biological Weapons

The production, possession, and use of biological (germ-based) weapons was outlawed by the 1972 Biological Weapons Convention, which has been signed by 112 countries. Nevertheless, there are indications that the United States and the Soviet Union retain the ability to build biological weapons, and there have been reports that Iraq has been trying to develop them. The use of biological warfare in a tactical or strategic environment would be

3. There is a difference between short-range (0–500 km) and intermediate-range (500–5,500 km) delivery systems that is important to the discussion on the Intermediate-Range Nuclear Forces (INF) Treaty discussed in chapter 17. Intermediate-range is sometimes termed "theater-range," meaning a general region. Some of the warheads and delivery vehicles discussed in this chapter are being destroyed or dismantled under the INF Treaty, but the number represents only a very small fraction of the U.S. and Soviet stockpiles. When discussed, weapons delivery systems' ranges will be given in kilometers (km). A mile is equal to approximately 1.6 km. Kilometers can be converted approximately to miles by multiplying kilometers by 0.6.

tricky because of the difficulty of controlling the toxins and protecting your own troops and people from what is called the "boomerang effect." At least potentially, though, a biological attack could be horrendous. During World War II, the British experimented with anthrax (a bovine-based disease causing malignant pustules in humans) on a small island off their coast, and a half-century later the island is still uninhabitable.

Chemical Weapons

The use of chemicals in warfare dates at least back to 600 B.C. when the Athenians poisoned their enemy's water supply with a diarrhea-inducing substance. Today's chemical weapons (CW) are much more sophisticated, and can be divided into three classes. The first includes incapacitating chemicals including tear gas and CS gas. While they have military applications, and were used by U.S. forces in Vietnam, these gases are nonlethal and are even used by domestic police forces. Indeed, some people argue that they are "humane" because they allow you (sometimes) to capture, rather than kill, an enemy. Blister agents such as mustard gas, phosgene, and lewisite are a second category. Mustard gas was used extensively during World War I. When inhaled, mustard gas destroys the inner lining of the lungs and the ability to take in oxygen. Agents that attack the bloodstream (hydrogen cyanide) or the nervous system (tabun, sarin, VX) and kill rapidly are the third category of chemical weapons agents. All of these agents can be delivered by missile, bomb, artillery shell, and other means.

There are huge stocks of U.S. and Soviet chemical weapons, and there are at least a dozen other nations that possess what has been called the "poor man's atomic bomb." So far, international treaties, fear of retaliation, and world opinion have limited chemical use. There is also the danger of a boomerang effect, although some CW agents such as sarin are nonpersistent, that is, they evaporate rapidly. These inhibitions have not, however, stopped the use of chemical weapons. Both Iran and Iraq used them during their war, and Iraq used them to attack rebellious Kurds in Iraq's northern provinces. Concerns about chemical warfare most recently resulted from Iraq's threats and ability to launch CW attacks with its extensive array of blister, blood, and nerve gases both on the military forces arrayed against it and on Israel.

Issues About the Use of Limited NBC Weapons

A significant issue relating to NBC weapons is whether it is moral, under any circumstances, to use them. Since the earliest days of recorded history there have been strictures about limits on the way war should be fought (*jus in bello*). These are founded on such concepts as necessity, proportionality (of the response to the provocation), and discrimination (between military and civilian targets). In the book of Deuteronomy, for example, the Hebrews had been "utterly destroying the men, women, and children, of every city" (3:6) they defeated. Jehovah put a stop to that. Moses' followers were told that after taking a city to "proclaim peace unto it" and to refrain from killing "the women, and the little ones, and the cattle" (20:10). Jehovah even decreed that "thou shalt not destroy the [fruit and nut] trees" (20:19). Given the destructiveness of modern NBC weapons, many people argue that they are unnecessary, never proportional, and incapable of discriminating between soldiers and women, little ones, cattle, fruit and nut trees, and other impermissible targets.

Be that as it may, some types of NBC weapons have been used, there are considerable stockpiles of them, and there are contingency plans to use them again. Therefore, we need to consider the issues of timing and targeting.

Chemical warfare is not just a horrific possibility, it is also a reality. The most outrageous use in many years was the chemical weapons attacks by Iraq on Kurds in the northwest part of that country. The Kurds, who live in several countries in the region, have long sought to establish an independent Kurdistan. There are unconfirmed reports of chemical attacks on as many as 65 Kurdish villages. This included an attack on Halabja which, it is said, killed 5,000, including the woman and baby shown here.

Timing: When to Use NBC Weapons

The debate over timing is twofold. One controversy is over the question of *first use*. If you are faced with an overwhelming traditional attack, should you use NBC weapons to try to defeat it? This was an important question during the cold war, when many analysts doubted the ability of NATO to defeat a Warsaw Pact attack without using nuclear weapons. The U.S. military is now confident that it can withstand a nonnuclear attack in Europe without resorting to nuclear weapons, but the concern over first use has increased in the Middle East in particular. One factor is capability. Israel possesses nuclear weapons; and Egypt, Iran, Iraq, Israel, Libya, and Syria all have major CW capabilities. These countries also have increasing abilities to deliver their weapons over long range. Israel, for one, has the Jericho II missile with a range of 1,450 km. Iraq has the 900 km al-Abbas missile and has tested the 1,950-km-range Tammuz 1 missile. Whether Israel would use its NBC weapons faced with an undefeatable Arab attack, or whether Iraq would take a similar step if faced with defeat by U.S.–led forces is unclear.

The advantage of first use is, of course, that it may defeat your opponents by destroying them or by convincing them to withdraw because the cost of defeating you will be too great. There are also disadvantages. One is the risk of retaliation or even escalation. If Iraq had launched a CW attack on Israel's cities, would the Israelis have responded with nuclear weapons against Baghdad? A second concern is the long-term diplomatic damage that might well result from first use (or perhaps any use) of NBC weapons, especially on a large scale. U.S. military sources claimed that tactical nuclear weapons would not be used under any circumstances against Iraq because there was no need and because, in the words of one senior army planner, "you lose the moral high ground if you use one of those stupid things" (*LAT,* 10/2/90:A6).

A second time-related issue assumes first use and asks *when is the optimal time* to use NBC weapons. One option is to use them early in a war to defeat the attack and to show resolve. The danger here is early retaliation or escalation. The other option is to wait until your back is against the wall, the last-gasp approach. If you wait until then, though, the attacking forces will be inside your territory, and the NBC weapons you use to assail the attacker may well kill many of your own people. Military commanders also worry that delay could mean defeat, especially in a situation involving NATO in the European theater. In order for NATO military commanders to launch nuclear weapons they must obtain permission at approximately seven military and political levels; this might take, at the quickest, 24 hours. This means, in the estimate of one U.S. general, that "the delays that are attendant upon asking for and receiving nuclear weapons release always create a situation in which, if you wait until they [the enemy] get into your territory to ask for the use of nuclear weapons, it is always too late" (*NYT,* 5/1/89:A10).

Targeting: What to Attack

Targeting decisions are related to whether you are the first to use NBC weapons and, if so, when you use them. Given these circumstances, what do you attack: invading front-line military forces, second-echelon military command and support facilities, or rear-area military, political, and civilian targets? The immediate military gain from attacking oncoming forces is offset by the extensive NBC defense preparations of some countries and by the dangers of detonating NBC weapons within the territory you are supposed to be protecting. Yet the temptation to launch NBC weapons at an enemy's rear areas that are less protected and also away from your own civilians carries with it the extreme risk of escalation.

Strategic War and Nuclear Weapons: Preliminary Considerations

The Bible's Book of Revelations speaks of an apocalyptic end to the world: a "hail of fire mixed with blood fell upon the earth; and . . . the earth was burnt up. . . . The sea became blood . . . and from the shaft rose smoke like the smoke of a great furnace and the sun and the air were darkened." Revelations continues, "Woe, woe, woe to those who dwell on earth," for many will die a fiery death, and the survivors "will seek death and will not find it; they will long to die, and death will fly from them."

Whatever your religious beliefs, such a prophecy is unnerving. We now have the capability to sound "the blast of the trumpets" that will kill the living and make the living wish to die.

Strategic War

As the earlier section on The Changing Nature of War indicated, the targets of warfare have increased. This is because of the increased range and destructive power of weapons. Expanded targeting is also a result of the increased importance of a country's population and economy as supports for the country's military forces. These factors have created the ability to wage and, some argue, the legitimacy of conducting strategic warfare against population and economic centers far away from the battlefield. Strategic warfare can be conducted with a variety of weapons including, but not limited to, nuclear weapons. Indeed, use of conventional weapons to firebomb Dresden and Tokyo during the concluding days of World War II produced more deaths in each city than the atomic attacks caused in either Hiroshima or Nagasaki.

For all of this, though, the number and power of modern nuclear weapons mean that the ultimate strategic war would be fought with nuclear weapons. Therefore, the following discussion of strategic war will concentrate on nuclear weapons considerations, although many of the same issues are also relevant to nonnuclear weapons.

The Continuing Role of Nuclear Weapons

The role of nuclear weapons has been discussed at various points in this chapter, but it would be well to reiterate quickly the uses here. One is that nuclear weapons form part of the "backdrop" of power and influence. There can be little doubt that the massive nuclear capability of the United States and the Soviet Union is part of what makes them superpowers and gives them extraordinary impact on international events. In this sense, nuclear weapons are highly symbolic, and "the United States and the U.S.S.R. now wage a post-war against each other through displays of deterrent force" not only to avoid nuclear war with one another, but also to maintain their positions as superpowers (Lake, 1989:360). Second, nuclear weapons are part of direct deterrence. Whether or not nuclear weapons will always deter superpower confrontation and nuclear attack is uncertain, but they have been a restraining factor so far (Blight, 1990). Third, nuclear weapons have been an important part of successful extended deterrence. Whether overtly or implicitly, they are a utilitarian tool with which to threaten opponents. Finally, nuclear weapons can be used. That has happened only twice, in 1945, when the atomic attacks on Hiroshima and Nagasaki were effective—even if ghastly and of questionable morality. There are those who contend that it may be necessary to fight and win a nuclear war in the future. Far from being solely looming horrors that threaten one day to end civilization, it must be recognized that nuclear weapons exist and play a role in world politics today.

A reasonable question is whether this assessment of the role of nuclear weapons remains valid in the current, post–cold war atmosphere of cooperation between the United States and the Soviet Union. Is nuclear war possible? The answer is yes. It may be that continuing U.S.–U.S.S.R. cooperation and successive and successful conventional and nuclear forces reduction agreements among all countries will someday eliminate the necessity of having sections on limited or strategic nuclear war in an international relations text. That day is neither at hand, nor will it come in the foreseeable future. First, we cannot be sure of the future of superpower relations. There have been periods of détente before (although never as extensive as now), but they have not lasted. Among other factors, the future of the Gorbachev government in the Soviet Union is uncertain, and the attitude of any successor regime is unknowable. Second, the superpowers' nuclear arsenals are huge, and even when the START talks (see chapter 17) are concluded the nuclear stockpiles will remain potentially globe-shattering. As Figure 10.1 shows, the United States has 12,102 strategic nuclear explosive devices and the Soviet Union has 11,320. These weapons possess 10,052 megatons of explosive power: the equivalent of 20,104,000,000,000 (20.104 trillion) pounds of TNT.

Third, both sides are developing new weapons and improving existing designs. The United States, for example, continues to produce eight types of warheads at its Plantex plant near Amarillo, Texas; has just revised its nuclear war–fighting plan (Strategic Integrated Operational Plan, SIOP); and is experimenting with several nuclear warhead designs to implement SIOP if necessary. One proposed warhead would generate a huge microwave burst to destroy enemy communications and other electronic and computer capabilities; another warhead would focus its nuclear burst to enhance its power rather than having it dissipated in concentric circles like a pebble dropped in the water; and a third design would burrow into the ground before detonating in order to attack underground command centers. The 1991 U.S. budget also continues funding for the B-2 strategic bomber, the strategic defense initiative (SDI), mobile strategic missile development, an antisubmarine nuclear depth charge, and a variety of other strategic warfare projects.

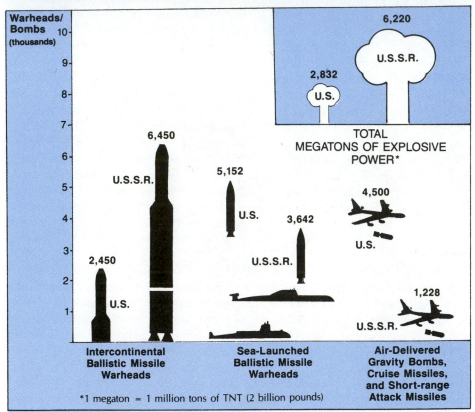

Figure 10.1

Number of U.S.–U.S.S.R. Warheads by Delivery System and Total Explosive Power (in megatons)

*1 megaton = 1 million tons of TNT (2 billion pounds)

The 1990 strategic arsenals of the United States and the Soviet Union carry destructive power beyond true grasp. The missiles of one U.S. nuclear submarine have more explosive power than all the munitions exploded in all the wars of history.

Fourth, nuclear weapons developments are not simply confined to the two superpowers. China, Great Britain, France, and other countries possess nuclear weapons; several countries have nuclear weapons development programs; and another 30 countries have or are near the technology needed to build nuclear weapons. Thus, as chapter 17 discusses, nuclear weapons proliferation is a global concern. Also, more and more countries are acquiring the capability to deliver weapons, including nuclear devices, over extended ranges. Israel's Jericho II and Iraq's Tammuz 1 missiles have already been mentioned. To this list could be added Argentina's Condor II, Brazil's SS-1000, and, most powerful of all, India's Agni (Sanskrit for "fire") missile with its 2,500-km range and its capability of carrying a one-ton warhead.

In sum, nuclear weapons remain with us; new nuclear weapons and new nuclear weapons–capable countries are on the horizon; significant nuclear arms reductions (much less complete disarmament) are hopes rather than realities; and nuclear war remains a possibility. Therefore, we need to consider the possibilities of and issues associated with strategic nuclear war.

How a Nuclear War Might Start

For all its horror, nuclear war is within the realm of possibility. Strategic analysts envision many possible scenarios including (1) an accident, (2) an unbalanced leader, (3) an unprovoked attack, (4) a last-gasp defense, (5) an inadvertent error in judgment, and (6) an escalation.

Before looking at each of these scenarios, two preliminary points should be made here. One is that all of these scenarios are not equally likely. As we shall see, inadvertent war and escalation are much more likely than an accident or some of the other scenarios. Second, the six are not necessarily mutually exclusive. They may combine into *multipath scenarios*. For example, a crisis in Europe with the possibility of escalation could lead to a partial release of nuclear weapons safety controls, thereby increasing the chances of accidental war (Allison, Carnesale, & Nye, 1985).

An *accident* is one way a nuclear war might start. It is possible that a technical malfunction or a human technical error could start a nuclear war. There have been several instances when U.S. computers warned of an incoming missile barrage (U.S. Congress, 1980). Corrections were made, of course, but as response times shorten, the ability to verify computer warnings will decline. There have also been instances of "escaped" (but thankfully unarmed) American and Soviet nuclear weapons or delivery vehicles that have landed in such diverse spots as Canada, Spain, Finland, and in the United States in Arkansas and New Mexico. Overall, the chance of an accidental nuclear detonation is slim, but an accident at a time of high international tension could cause a spasm reaction that could take the world across the nuclear firebreak.

A related concern involves the possibility of an accidental explosion of the multiple detonators on nuclear devices. These detonators must be exploded simultaneously to cause a nuclear explosion by the weapon's plutonium core, but a single detonator explosion could shatter the weapon, releasing deadly radioactivity. Information came to light in 1990 that in the previous two years the United States had restructured its W-79 nuclear artillery shell because computer studies had concluded that a W-79 detonator might be set off by a single bullet striking the shell. There was such concern for the shell's stability that, in the words of one military official, "for a while, we were also worried that these things might go off if they fell off the back of a truck" (*HC*, 5/23/90:A1).

An *unbalanced leader* is another possible cause of nuclear war. What if Adolf Hitler had had the bomb? Or the Ayatollah Khomeini? Control of nuclear weapons by a fanatical or even crazy leader is possible, and the proliferation of such weapons increases the chances of havoc. When Germany invaded the Soviet Union in 1941, Josef Stalin suffered a mental breakdown. There is substantial evidence that Richard Nixon suffered the same incapacity at the time of his resignation, and there are hotly contested rumors that the secretary of defense instructed the military's nuclear-launch commanders to ignore any sudden presidential order to act. There is also the possibility that a berserk military officer might try to use nuclear weapons, although there are numerous safety devices such as the "dual key" system and electronic "permissive action links" designed to limit such a possibility. The odds of this scenario occurring are still slim, although in a time of crisis with tensions high and safety systems partially or fully relaxed, the probability would rise sharply.

An *unprovoked attack*, or "bolt out of the blue," could also happen. This might occur if one nuclear country felt that it could successfully disable all or most of its opponent's strategic forces or if a country believed an attack combined with defensive measures would result in a victory with "acceptable losses." Such a possibility is remote in the current nuclear environment because each of the superpowers has sufficient capability to launch a devastating retaliatory attack. An unprovoked nuclear attack could also come as a result of a nuclear country attacking a nonnuclear country. The Soviets approached the United States in 1969 to probe the U.S. response if Moscow ordered a preemptive nuclear strike on China's nuclear arms development facility at Lop Nor. The United States expressed alarm, and the Soviet strike never came to pass. Such an unprovoked attack is unlikely in the future, but it is a possibility.

Nuclear war could come as a *last gasp*, an attempt to fend off final conventional defeat. One scenario with real possibilities is to imagine a beleaguered Israel, its vaunted army finally overwhelmed by numerically superior Arab invaders, launching a last-gasp strike against Egyptian, Jordanian, and Syrian armies pounding the last Israeli defensive positions around Jerusalem.

Of the various scenarios, an *inadvertent nuclear war* caused by misperceptions is one of the two most likely. False intelligence that a nuclear attack is imminent, for example, might cause a leader to strike first. There is a nuclear strategy called "damage denial" that looks to reduce your damage by, among other things, destroying an opponent's offensive capability before it is launched.

Imagine that you are the U.S. president and you have become absolutely convinced that the Soviets are about to launch a major nuclear strike. What do you do? You can wait and pray, you can surrender, you can contact the Soviets on the hot line. (But do you believe it when they deny your accusation? Should you tip them off by calling and eliminate your chance of a preemptive, damage denial strike?) Or, you can strike first to destroy as many enemy missiles as possible, thereby hoping to limit the damage to your country. Your decision is perhaps the ultimate example of operational reality. It is hard to imagine anyone launching an attack, but the psychological pressures under such circumstances on the president would be immense. Both the United States and the Soviets possess missiles (MXs and SS-18s, respectively) that are first-strike weapons, intended for just such damage denial missions. As the power and accuracy of missiles increase, and as the launch-to-touchdown times decrease, the pressure to use your weapons before they are destroyed becomes ever greater.

Escalation is the final, and most likely, single path to nuclear war. This path to nuclear war could occur in a number of ways. One is tactical → regional → strategic escalation. Once even low-yield tactical weapons are used against oncoming, front-echelon troops, the breakdown in communications and the psychological pressure on decisionmakers could easily lead to wider strikes. Americans are a people who tend more than most others to believe that they can control events. Therefore, they are more apt than others to initiate tactical nuclear warfare in the belief that they can contain it at that level. Soviet military analysts, by contrast, are much more skeptical about the possibility of limiting nuclear war once it has begun. Therefore, NATO tactical use of weapons would push the Soviets to the brink of massive retaliation, and a NATO attack on rear-echelon supply areas, reserve forces, and/or command centers in or near the Soviet homeland would almost certainly occasion a huge Soviet response.

We should return to the *multipath* possibilities mentioned above. Many consider this the most likely route to nuclear war. Consider the escalation/inadvertent scenario in the box on the next page. Treat the scenario very seriously. It is not outlandish. Some analysts believe Europe will become unstable. If so, the European war events are real possibilities. Land-based missiles are very vulnerable to attack and destruction. You are in charge, but remember that your communications with the outside world will be spotty at best and that you and your advisers may be near nervous collapse.

You Are the President

Here is the situation, Mr./Madam President. It is day three (D + 3) of war in Europe. Several years after reunification, rightist political forces won control of the German government. Berlin demanded the return of Polish territory taken from it in 1945 and once again pressed its demand for the Sudetenland region of Czechoslovakia. The Poles and Czechoslovaks asked the U.S.S.R. for protection. It is not clear what spark caused the conflagration, but fighting broke out along the Polish and Czechoslovak frontiers, and the Soviets launched a massive attack with conventional weapons against Germany (D day). The attack engaged U.S. and other NATO forces still in Germany and still obligated to defend Germany. NATO forces began to collapse under the weight of Soviet armor, and the Supreme Allied Commander in Europe (SACEUR) asked on D + 1 to be permitted to use tactical nuclear weapons. At first you refused because you hoped conventional forces could stabilize the front, but new reverses created a desperate situation on the battlefield. Confronted, as you were, by the imminent loss of the entire American army and all or most of Western Europe, you transferred tactical/theater nuclear control on D + 2 to SACEUR. Rather than having large numbers of friendly civilians killed by extensively attacking Soviet combat units already in Germany, SACEUR launched bombers from the few remaining European air bases and missiles from a U.S. ballistic-missile submarine assigned to NATO to attack second-echelon Soviet logistic and command centers in Eastern Europe, some near the Soviet border. As a precaution, Mr./Madam President, you collaterally ordered a full strategic nuclear alert to warn the Soviets not to escalate the fighting.

The good news is that SACEUR's nuclear strikes and the resulting panic and devastation in Eastern Europe have so disrupted the Soviet-led attack that NATO forces have been able to at least temporarily hold their ground. There are even sketchy reports of Soviet disorganization and withdrawal. The bad news is that your strategic alert appeared to the Kremlin's leaders (who, remember, have nuclear detonations destroying facilities just outside the Soviet border) as the first step to a strategic strike. The Soviet leader wavered for some hours, but finally gave in on D + 3 to the pleadings and demands of his entire military staff that the only response to the impending American nuclear strike was to launch a preemptive strike as damage denial. The Soviet leader authorized a strike using SS-18s and SS-24s against U.S. intercontinental ballistic missile (ICBM) silos in the Midwest and some Strategic Air Command (SAC) bomber bases near the polar route to the Soviet Union.

You have been evacuated to the national airborne emergency command post. Following the doctrine of "launch on impact" designed to prevent inadvertent war, you chose to "ride out" the attack. Although communications have been massively disrupted, reports seem to indicate that approximately 2,300 Soviet ICBM warheads have destroyed virtually all of your ground-based missiles in their silos and a substantial part of your manned bomber fleet. Most of these missile and air bases were relatively remote from population centers, but at least 15 million Americans are dead from blast damage, and another 10 million will die soon from wounds or radiation. Reports also indicate hysteria among the American population and a widespread collapse of civil order.

The chairman of the Joint Chiefs of Staff and your secretary of defense are pleading with you to authorize use of U.S. submarine-launched ballistic missiles (SLBMs) to destroy Soviet nuclear targets that are capable of launching their remaining 9,000 strategic warheads and bombs in a second strike that will utterly decimate the United States. Your secretary of state has mentally collapsed and has been crying in the cabin. Your national security adviser is screaming at the generals that if you launch SLBMs against the obviously alerted Soviets, they will be able to get their weapons off before your weapons destroy them. The second Soviet wave will attack U.S. population centers. The same 9,000 weapons you hope to destroy will kill most of the remaining 225 million Americans. Your spouse is weeping that if you launch a strike, your children and grandchildren in San Francisco and Chicago will all be killed.

It's your move, Mr./Madam President.

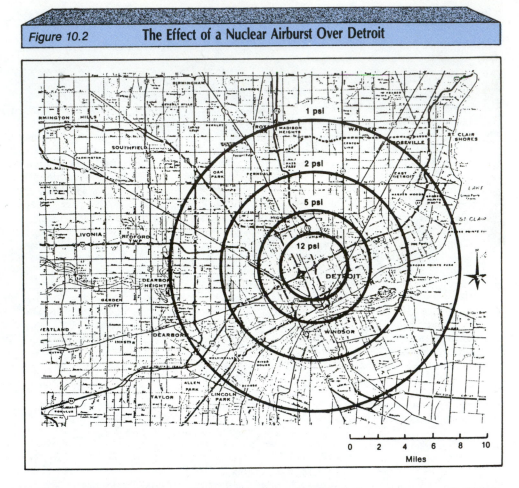

Figure 10.2   The Effect of a Nuclear Airburst Over Detroit

This map of Detroit, Michigan, with concentric circles shows the psi (pounds per square inch) that a 1-megaton nuclear airburst at 6,000 ft. would generate. It gives you some idea of what the range of damage would be. Within the 12 psi circle (a radius of about 1.7 miles) everyone would be incinerated and everything would be destroyed. Even at a distance of 6 miles, near the 2 psi circle, the explosion on a clear day would inflict anyone who is not behind a building or in some other way shielded from the direct thermal burst with second degree burns; casualties would be about 50 percent.

The Impact of Nuclear War

If nuclear war is possible, then we should know what the impact of nuclear weapons would be. The trouble is that we do not know—precisely. Certainly, it would be terrible for those in immediate blast areas. But what would be the global impact of massive strategic war? Some scholars have made dire predictions ranging from biological devastation through a modern ice age (nuclear winter) caused by dust clouds screening the sun's rays (Turco et al., 1990; Robock, 1989). Other analysts, while not sanguine about the impact of nuclear war on our biosphere, are a good deal more cautious about making dire predictions. Stephen Schneider of the National Center for Atmospheric Research argues the result of an extensive nuclear war would be "nuclear fall, not

It is difficult to imagine fully what a nuclear attack would be like. On August 6, 1945, one atomic bomb destroyed the Japanese city of Hiroshima and killed 130,000 people, more than half the city's population. That stark devastation can be seen here set against the delicacy of the parasol the woman carries. The power of the Hiroshima bomb was miniscule by today's standards. Today, the Soviet SS-18 missile carries up to 10 warheads, each of which has at least 36 times the explosive yield of "Little Boy," the atomic bomb that demolished Hiroshima, or "Fat Man," which destroyed the city of Nagasaki three days later.

nuclear winter." And MIT's George Rathjens has charged that "all the hype about a lot of freezing following a nuclear exchange is hyperbole" (*NYT,* 1/23/90:C8).

There is less disagreement about the immediate effect of a nuclear attack. Let us assume a 1-megaton warhead, one-twentieth the size of the Soviet's largest (see Fig. 10.2). Its detonation a mile above your city creates a huge fireball with temperatures in the range of 20 million degrees Fahrenheit. Within 2¹/₂ miles everything and everyone is set on fire. All is quickly snuffed out, however, by an atomizing blast. Death and destruction are total. In a second 2-mile ring, flesh is charred, blast winds reach 160 mph, and collapsing buildings and flying glass and metal crush and shred nearly everyone. Yet another 2 miles out, most homes are on fire, half the population is dead, the remainder probably lethally exposed to radiation. Still another 4 miles out, a third of the population is wounded, normal services are destroyed, and civil chaos threatens as panic sets in and people fight for medicine, food, and water. Those who survive will face uncertain futures of psychological trauma and devastated life-styles. Only by stretching the imagination can they be called the lucky ones (U.S. Office of Technology Assessment, 1979).

There is another view of nuclear war that foresees neither the end of the world nor a society-shattering catastrophe. It makes two points. First, it argues that a nuclear attack may not be total and that a country must be ready to make "appropriate" nuclear responses to limited strategic strikes. Second, it claims that the development of defensive measures, such as antiballistic missile weapons and enhanced civil defense, would reduce deaths significantly. As one Reagan defense department official, Thomas K. Jones, optimistically put it, "If there are enough shovels to go around, everyone's going to make it" (Scheer, 1982:18).

It should be stressed that the debate over the impact of nuclear war is not meaningless speculation. Instead, it has an important impact on nuclear strategy, as we shall see presently.

Strategic Nuclear Weapons and War: Planning a Nuclear Strategy

Now that we have briefly examined some of the preliminary considerations involved with strategic nuclear weapons and war, we can proceed to discuss planning a nuclear strategy. There are crucial issues of what a country's nuclear arsenal and doctrines should be that seldom really enter the political debate. The questions involve such issues as (1) the extent of the nuclear force, (2) targeting, (3) control, (4) types of weapons systems (delivery systems and warheads), and (5) whether or not to try to defend against nuclear attack. To a large degree, these issues are decided within a relatively small world of military and technical specialists, the *Wizards of Armageddon* as one author (Kaplan, 1983) has aptly named them. Even when these issues are publicly debated in the United States and elsewhere, it is often done in terms of general antinuclear feeling, arms control, budget considerations, or (in the case of SDI) technical feasibility. These matters are certainly important, but they do not address many other vital considerations. Usually, too, they are debated in isolation without trying to place them in the general context of nuclear strategy.

The aim of the following section is to examine the five policy issues listed in the previous paragraph and to put them into a general framework so that you can see their relationship to one another. To do this, we will examine each issue according to the views of those who favor second-strike deterrence as the best route to safety and the contrasting views of those who contend that it is safer to be ready, if necessary, to fight a nuclear war. These two sides can be characterized by the bizarrely colorful acronyms of **MAD** (Mutual Assured Destruction) proponents versus **NUT** (Nuclear Utilization Theory) advocates (Keeny & Panofsky, 1981). Of course, as with most of the issues examined in this book, the debate reflects a wide range of opinions that most properly fall along a scale, and the stark dichotomy of MADs vs. NUTs is an explanatory device (Rathjens & Reed, 1986). There are many intermediate positions, and there are also some who reject both positions and argue for rapid nuclear disarmament. Still, it should help simplify the issues for those who are beginning their study of these matters.

MAD vs. NUT: The Basic Positions

Those who favor the mutual assured destruction strategy (whom we will call MADs) believe that as long as nuclear weapons exist, safety is best achieved through each nuclear power possessing (1) a sufficient number of weapons that are (2) capable of surviving a nuclear attack by an opponent and (3) delivering a second-strike retaliatory attack that will destroy that opponent. If each nuclear power has this capability, a mutual standoff or mutual checkmate type of deterrence is achieved, and no power (so the theory goes) will start a nuclear war because doing so will lead to its destruction (even if it destroys its enemy). Thus, MAD is fundamentally a doctrine that rests on deterrence by punishment.

MADs additionally tend to oppose any weapon or doctrine that could lessen mutually assured destruction. This means they reject offensive (first-strike, counterforce) weapons capable of destroying an opponent's retaliatory system. MADs are also apt to dismiss attempts to create defensive systems like SDI or civil defense. MADs believe that the ideas of a limited nuclear war and nuclear war management are not only impossible but dangerous. It is impossible, they say, because the force of nuclear weapons is so great that they will both destroy technological control channels and so psychologically devastate leaders that even an initially limited nuclear exchange will inevitably escalate into world-ending war. The peril that MADs see in all of these notions (first strike, defense, limited war, and war management) is that they make the *unthinkable thinkable*. The MADs' point is that the further you get away from (what they see as) the fundamental truths that nuclear war will lead to total destruction and that the only way to avoid this is through assured destruction, the greater danger you are in. Therefore, thinking the unthinkable, that is, planning to manage a nuclear war, trying to construct defenses, and planning doctrines that contemplate first-use, all delude you into thinking that you can survive and win a nuclear war. According to the MADs, these thoughts make nuclear war seem less horrific, thus increasing the likelihood that you will start or provoke one.

Those who favor nuclear utilization theory see things very differently. In the first place, NUTs contend that deterrence theory is a mad gamble. Strategist Colin S. Gray (1982:87), for example, argues that any circumstances that would cause a war between the superpowers "are likely to be so desperate that there is no good reason to believe that deterrence would function." Critics of deterrence theory also point out that more accurate, quicker weapons enhance the possibility of a disabling first strike. NUTs point out that deterrence theory relies on rationality and clear-sightedness when, in reality, decisions are often emotional and are based on misperception.[4]

Because nuclear utilization theorists believe deterrence will not always necessarily work, they argue that plans must be made to fight, survive, and win a nuclear war. The NUTs favor defensive measures such as SDI and civil defense. They also favor developing contingency plans for fighting a protracted war involving a series of nuclear exchanges. They believe in building a first-strike capability and using highly accurate and powerful warheads that could, if necessary, disable the other side's ICBMs before they could strike. Thus, they do not rule out first-strike preemptive war.

It is possible to summarize NUT thinking in five ways. One is that like MADs, NUTs stress the survivability of weapons. They do not totally rely on it, however, as MADs do. Second, NUT strategy is partly based on *damage denial*, in contrast to the punishment strategy of MADs. This means NUTs want to be able to destroy enemy weapons before the weapons detonate; and the NUTs want to provide civilian and military protection if there is an attack. Third, NUTs are not nuclear maniacs, as their opponents sometimes charge. They certainly do not want to start a nuclear war. NUTs believe, though, that nuclear war might come, and that if it does, their strategy gives the best chance for containing, surviving, and prevailing in the conflagration. Therefore, a fourth part of NUT thinking is that you must have the plans and technical capabilities to fight such wars. In the United States, for example, this would include the evacuation of the president to the National Emergency Airborne Command Post, a modified Boeing 747 sometimes called the "doomsday" plane, from which the president would conduct a nuclear war according to the military's Strategic Integrated Operating Plan (SIOP). Fifth, NUTs believe their strategy enhances deterrence by adding damage denial to punishment. They argue that technological factors have made it possible for an enemy to launch a strike like the one envisioned in the box on page 277. Such an attack can be avoided, however, by either damage denial or by convincing the opponent that you are capable of a counterattack that will punish severely but not be so damaging as to prompt wholesale third-strike attacks on your population.

4. "The Rational Deterrence Debate: A Symposium," the January 1989 edition of *World Politics* (42/2), is a good source on recent analysis.

Deterrence

Persuading an enemy that attacking you will cost him more than any potential gain is worth is called **deterrence**. As such, deterrence is not new and can be applied to conventional as well as nuclear threats. Nuclear deterrence has taken on particular significance, though, because of the ability of a major nuclear power to deter by assuring the destruction of an opponent if it should strike.

Both MADs and NUTs favor deterrence. Their dispute is over *how* to deter (Huth & Russett, 1990). Basically, there are two ways, both of which have been mentioned. One is *deterrence through punishment*. This is a punitive strategy that relies on your ability to inflict unacceptable damage on any opponent that attacks you. MADs favor this deterrence strategy, the core of which is the ability to launch a major retaliatory second strike even after a massive first strike by an enemy. As proof that the strategy works, MADs point to assured destruction, that is, the certainty that your opponent will be destroyed too. MADs can also cite as evidence the fact that the superpowers, despite over four decades of bitter cold war, have remained at peace with each other.

The second approach is *deterrence through damage denial* (or *limitation*). This strategy is closer to the concept of defense. It means that you deter enemies by preventing them from inflicting enough damage on you to make you surrender, cease to exist, or comply with their wishes. NUTs favor this strategy and want to combine it with deterrence by punishment.

Whatever your exact position, though, deterrence is based on two factors: capability and credibility.

Capability. Effective deterrence requires that you have the capacity to respond after an attack on your forces. This need has been the primary cause of what seems to be the "overkill" capacity of the superpowers. Figures on how many times over each nuclear arsenal can kill everyone are largely irrelevant. The issue is how many weapons will survive. As each power acquires more weapons, the other, it can be argued, must get more to ensure its capability to launch a retaliatory second strike. This, in turn, creates pressure on the first country to get yet more weapons, and the result is the arms spiral. This search for invulnerability based on numbers and types of weapons will be discussed more fully in the section on strategic posture options.

Credibility. It is also necessary for other states to believe that you will actually use your weapons. Perception is a key factor, and some NUTs argue that the nuclear-freeze movement and other such causes run the risk of deluding the Soviets into thinking the West might not have the will to respond before its capability is destroyed. This misperception could be more dangerous than the arms race.

One of the reasons that NUTs favor limited nuclear war planning is because they believe that without it, it is not believable that a U.S. president would respond to a number of possible nuclear-attack scenarios, including the one in the box on page 277. They contend, therefore, that credibility is enhanced if enemies know you are ready and willing to fight a blow for blow nuclear war.

Extent of Nuclear Forces

Along a scale of nuclear strength and assuming that countries have nuclear weapons, there are three key points: superiority, sufficiency, and minimum deterrence. The *superiority* option argues that you can be secure only when you can overwhelm your opponent. The problem with this line of thought is that superiority and absolute security for one side means inferiority and absolute insecurity for the other. In reality, neither superpower has or is seriously trying to gain nuclear superiority. Although few advocate superiority openly anymore, it is almost inherent in the NUT position, and thus one of its weaknesses. Logically, fighting a nuclear war must contain some idea of "winning," and if that is so you must have superior weapons (and strategy) to prevail. If all powers are intent on being superior, stability is very difficult to achieve.

The doctrine of *sufficiency*, or enough forces to survive and strike back, is the announced doctrine of both superpowers and the basis of the MAD strategy. It also implies the willingness of each side to let the other achieve "essential equivalence" or "strategic parity." The difficulty is that, in the complex world of nuclear arms, equivalence is hard to measure and the chances of misperception are high.

The final nuclear force size option is *minimum deterrence*. Some MADs would advocate this. This is the strategy of some of the "lesser" nuclear powers (France in particular). It relies on a small nuclear force for deterrence on the theory that even if you could not utterly destroy your opponent, the damage you could inflict would be so horrendous that no enemy would risk it. This strategy has the benefit of restraining the arms spiral, limiting the budget drain of defense spending, and perhaps limiting nuclear war, should it occur, by convincing your opponent that it is not necessary to obliterate you. On the negative side, if a crisis does occur, your capability is limited, the temptation for a preemptive strike is high for the aggressor, and your credibility is doubtful. Would, for instance, France really use its weapons against the Soviet Union, knowing that utter destruction would end French civilization forever?

Targeting: Countervalue vs. Counterforce

Another area of disagreement between MADs and NUTs is targeting—what to shoot at. MAD and NUT proponents are also divided over the types of targets to attack. MADs tend to favor a "countervalue" strategy, while NUTs lean toward a "counterforce" approach.

Countervalue Targeting was the underlying assumption of MAD strategy through the early 1960s. It was based on the idea of targeting an aggressor's civilians and infrastructure in retaliation for an attack on your forces or cities. U.S. defense secretary Harold Brown specified in 1978 that the punishment deterrence strategy would include the destruction of the 200 largest Soviet cities, an attack that would kill 34 percent of the Soviet population and demolish 62 percent of Soviet industry (Snow, 1987:193).

Both the Soviet Union and the United States forswear targeting civilians. "As a conscious matter of policy," one U.S. defense official explained in 1982, "we have not planned for the deliberate destruction of the [Soviet] population" (Ball, 1985:32). Both sides do, however, target a large number of industrial, communications, transportation, and other infrastructure targets, and given the proximity of most of these to civilian populations, the distinction between civilian and infrastructure targeting is more a matter of theoretical nicety than differing impact (Shue, 1989).

Counterforce Targeting emphasizes deterrence through damage denial. This essentially NUT strategy targets an opponent's strategic nuclear forces and command, control, communications, and intelligence (C^3I) capabilities. Counterforce targeting could be used in two scenarios. One is a first strike in which the object would be to destroy both an opponent's strategic weapons and the C^3I functions the opponent needs to launch a counterattack. Second, and a bit less dire, counterforce targeting could be used in a less than total, multiple-exchange nuclear war. Advocates of this latter approach, including some MAD advocates, argue that you have at least a chance of controlling nuclear war if you only retaliate against military targets.

There are numerous drawbacks to counterforce strategy. One is that in some cases it requires a first strike. Even deploying the nuclear weapons systems required for a first strike is likely to be seen by an opponent as proof you are contemplating such a strike. This results in higher tension and instability and a higher chance of inadvertent war by presenting your opponent with a "use 'em or lose 'em" quandary when war threatens. Second, if you destroy your opponent's political and military command structure you destroy his ability to retaliate, but you might also destroy your opponent's ability to negotiate or even surrender, and his uncontrolled subordinate nuclear commanders might well retaliate without restraint.

Whatever the validity of the arguments for and against the countervalue and counterforce options, U.S. policy has moved steadily toward counterforce targeting. This strategy began to find its way into U.S. strategic doctrine as early as 1961 when President Dwight D. Eisenhower signed the first Strategic Integrated Operational Plan (SIOP) into effect. It accelerated in 1980 when President Jimmy Carter signed Presidential Directive 59, the first full-scale war-fighting plan. Under President Ronald Reagan and now under President George Bush there has been a mounting emphasis on counterforce targeting, building the weapons to carry it out, and implementing the rest of the NUT approach to strategic nuclear planning. Much of this is discussed in other sections of this chapter, but in the area of targeting the latest SIOP gives ample evidence of this trend. Called SIOP-7 by most outside analysts, and SIOP-6F by the Administration in order to downplay its changes, the new war-fighting plan, which entered into effect on October 1, 1989, puts the first emphasis on the early destruction of Soviet leadership targets and relocatable targets such as the mobile SS-24 and SS-25 ICBMs. At least 120 warheads are aimed at Moscow alone. One critic argues that given the decline of the cold war SIOP-7 "isn't strategy, it's pathology" (*Time,* 7/16/90:19). Other critics contend that "the new SIOP will increase the risk that the Soviets will go first in a crisis" (*HC:* 7/23/90:A3). Somewhat paradoxically, they also criticize SIOP-7 on the grounds that it is "designed primarily for such challenging, perhaps impossible tasks as locating and destroying a significant proportion of Soviet relocatable targets and leadership targets" (Ball & Toth, 1990:92).

Soviet doctrine is harder to assess confidently, but it appears to emphasize NUT strategies, including counterforce targeting. Interestingly, the Soviets appear to have begun to move slowly toward the MAD approach, while the United States has moved in the other direction, resulting in something of a convergence in the strategic approaches of the two superpowers. In 1977, then–general secretary Leonid Brezhnev declared the U.S.S.R. was not seeking first-strike superiority, and his successors, especially Gorbachev, have continued to voice that line. At least in terms of rhetoric, the changes in Soviet strategy have been profound. They have shifted away from an emphasis on massive offensives and have begun to use terms such as "security interdependence" to describe international relations, "reasonable sufficiency" to characterize the level of force needed, and "defensive defense" to portray the types of weapons needed. This third idea implies having weapons (such as antiaircraft missiles) that are primarily defensive in nature and have much less offensive capability (Papp, 1990). Furthermore, there is evidence from the significant unilateral reductions in conventional forces announced by the Soviet Union and by its willingness to give up a massive amount of equipment in the 1990 conventional forces agreement that Moscow is taking a more defensive posture. On the strategic nuclear level, however, the retention and upgrading of such first-strike weapons as the SS-18, Mod 5 ICBM indicate that counterforce targeting and a war-fighting approach are still part of Soviet doctrine. The real test for both sides will be what weapons they are willing to give up as part of the START agreement, which is discussed in chapter 17.

Control of Nuclear Weapons

Another set of nuclear-doctrine issues comes under the classification of control. One issue involves questions of who can authorize the use of nuclear weapons and how tightly that control is kept. The second issue centers on when to launch a nuclear strike.

The Authority to Use Nuclear Weapons

In the United States and the Soviet Union, the presidents hold the authority to authorize the use of strategic nuclear weapons. They are each followed day and night by an individual holding the nuclear release codes in a satchel, dubbed "the football" in the United States. Each side has elaborate and highly secret plans for transfer of the national command authority (NCA) in case the leader is killed or unable to communicate. Both the United States and Soviet Union have elaborate safety systems on most (but not all) weapons delivery systems to prevent them from being fired without order by the NCA.

Few would dispute this basic structure, but there is a good deal of controversy over how tightly control should be held. In case of surprise attack, when the NCA is destroyed or out of communication, what should be the authority of subordinate military levels to fire their nuclear weapons? What, for example, should be the authority of the commanding officer of a ballistic missile submarine if (1) that officer is convinced there has been a nuclear attack on his country, and (2) he has been unable to communicate with higher military authority for an extended period of time?

Tight control, one with multiple authorizations needed before launch, has the advantage of minimizing the possibility of a nuclear war being started by an accident or by a fanatic. *Loose control* lessens the chance that country's retaliatory forces could be rendered inert by a breakdown in the chain of command.

The MADs and NUTs are not so neatly divided on this issue as they are on some of the others. Both would want to avoid a situation where an opponent could launch a *decapitation attack* designed to disable your C³I functions, either by physical destruction or by a nuclear explosion–generated *electromagnetic pulse* (EMP) that could disable your communications and computer systems long enough to leave the country unable to launch a countervalue retaliation (the MAD concern) or conduct counterforce operations (the NUT concern).

Where MADs and NUTs would diverge is over how much control provides the greatest safety. Overall, MADs worry that each degree of lessened control would increase the chance of an accidental or unauthorized release. NUTs share that concern, but they believe that it is a necessary risk to ensure that ongoing (but limited) nuclear operations could be conducted during a prolonged nuclear war.

Launch Doctrines

A second crucial control issue is *when to launch* a nuclear counterattack. Basically, there are three options. One is to ride out an attack, that is, wait until enemy warheads have detonated. This option is called "launch on impact" (LOI). The second possibility is to

The photo shows one of the grim ironies of world politics. In the foreground we can see Mikhail Gorbachev and Ronald Reagan in Moscow's Red Square during the 1988 summit there. The two are doing what comes naturally to veteran politicians: kissing babies and smiling. Not smiling is the U.S. military officer on the right in the rear. He is carrying, chained to his wrist, the briefcase dubbed the "football." It contains the codes that the U.S. president would use to authorize a nuclear strike on the Soviet Union or anyone else. Nearby, perhaps one of the two figures on the left in the rear, is a Soviet official carrying Gorbachev's "football." It is fascinating to wonder whether Reagan would have actually called down on his own head the dozens of U.S. nuclear warheads targeted on Moscow if an international crisis had, at that instant, called on him to release the apocalypse.

launch your weapons during the approximately 30 minutes it would take an enemy warhead to reach you after it was launched. This is called launch under attack (LUA). Third, there is a preemptive launch, termed launch on warning (LOW), authorized when you become convinced that an enemy intends to launch a strike against you.

MADs generally favor LOI on the grounds that it prevents inadvertent war. They contend that even if a country's ICBMs were wiped out in an attack, its other nuclear forces, especially SLBMs (sea-launched ballistic missiles), would be sufficient to assure the attacker's destruction. NUTs believe such a doctrine only serves to tempt opponents. This is especially true given the steadily decreasing time that a nuclear attack would take from launch to detonation. Submarines could launch nuclear warheads against C^3I and other targets using a low-trajectory arc that would take little more than 10 minutes to target. This increases the "use 'em or lose 'em" pressure to launch retaliatory weapons. For these reasons, NUTs support LUA and even, in some scenarios, LOW (launch on warning) preemption.

Currently, U.S. declared doctrine is LOI. However, the chairman of the Joint Chiefs of Staff has said that "the Soviets have no assurance that we will ride out an attack" (*NYT*, 5/6/83:A1). If we consider such statements, as well as the construction of the B-2 bomber and the MX missile, there appears to be good evidence that LUA is the more likely "real" U.S. doctrine—with preemption at least a possibility. It is more difficult to deduce Soviet doctrine, but there are several factors that make it doubtful that they would be willing to ride out an attack. One is that 57 percent of all Soviet strategic nuclear devices (warheads/bombs) are on ICBMs. This means the Soviets are more vulnerable to a disarming first strike than is the United States, with only 20 percent of its explosive devices on ICBMs.

Types of Weapons Systems

Perhaps the most crucial decisions in nuclear strategy involve the types of **strategic nuclear weapons** systems to be deployed. Weapons systems vary considerably in capability, cost, and strategic impact, and there are often sharp disputes between MADs and NUTs over the value (or liability) of a given weapons system. The normal controversy over the level and mix of nuclear weapons systems has become even more heated in the last few years because of declining defense budgets, because of improved Soviet-American relations, and because arms reductions create the necessity of deciding to keep some systems, to give up others, and to reduce still other systems in order to balance other countries' nuclear forces.

Ideally, decisions about what weapons systems to develop and deploy should be based on what seems to be required. That is, civilian and military strategists should identify a need and then develop a doctrine and a weapons system to go with it. In reality, what often happens is that technology drives both doctrine and acquisition. Weapons systems such as MIRVs, cruise missiles, and SDI (all of which we will discuss) all began their development because the technology to build them was available or envisioned rather than because of any demand by leaders for a weapon to fill a gap in deterrence or defense. In the case of SDI, for example, President Reagan did not initiate the idea. Rather, he was persuaded by his science and military advisers that a nuclear defense system could be built. Such is the work of the Wizards of Armageddon. It is important, therefore, for us nonwizards to understand the implications of current and proposed weapons systems so that we can have a say also. To explore weapons systems, we will consider the advantages and disadvantages of (1) land-based intercontinental ballistic missiles (ICBMs), (2) sea-launched ballistic missiles (SLBMs), (3) penetrating bombers, and (4) various types of warheads.

Land-Based Intercontinental Ballistic Missiles

ICBMs are the most numerous delivery vehicles in both the superpowers' arsenals. Land-based missiles have several advantages. One is accuracy. The MX has an advertised **circular error probability** (CEP, accuracy) of 265 feet after a 6,500-mile flight, and a late-model SS-18 has a CEP of 1,000 feet.[5] This degree of accuracy, plus the ability of each of these missiles to carry 10 warheads (each 20 to 50 times more powerful than the Hiroshima bomb) means that they are effective as first-strike weapons that could destroy an enemy's underground ICBM silos and C^3I facilities. Because of this ability, missiles like the MX are favored by NUTs, while MADs consider them dangerously destabilizing and prefer to rely on less accurate, less powerful ICBMs like the U.S. Minuteman IIIs.

Another advantage of ICBMs is cost. They are relatively inexpensive (in the astronomical scale of defense expenditures) per unit of firepower, easy to maintain, and require few support personnel.

5. There is some dispute over the reliability of accuracy figures. Missiles are tested along an east-west axis in the respective countries' Pacific Ocean test ranges. In combat, the missiles would be fired over the North Pole, thereby encountering very different magnetic influences that, some argue, could significantly effect CEP. From the MAD point of view, this uncertainty casts enough doubt to negate the argument that first-strike weapons could be effective in a counterforce strategy. Thus deterrence is preserved. Additionally, the MX CEP cited is the U.S. Air Force claim. MX testing problems cast some serious doubt on the missile's reliability.

Land-based intercontiental ballistic missiles (ICBMs) are vulnerable to attack by powerful first-strike weapons, such as the U.S. MX and the Soviet SS-18 missiles. This vulnerability arguably decreases deterrence and increases strategic instability. One solution is to build mobile ICBMs. The Soviet Union has done so, constructing SS-24 and SS-25 missiles which are mounted on railroad cars or huge tractor trailers. So far, political considerations have been one of the factors that have delayed the building of U.S. mobile missiles. One fear of some strategic planners is that the sight of mobile missiles might alarm the American public so much that there would be tremendous pressure to make too many disarmament concessions to the Soviets. Although this cartoon is, as cartoons usually are, hyperbolic, just think about how you would feel if you were stuck in traffic with a mobile ICBM in front of you.

The primary disadvantage of ICBMs is increasing vulnerability. If CEP estimates are correct, ICBM forces are vulnerable to destruction, even given the ability of U.S. silos to withstand a blast effect of 2,000 pounds per square inch. As indicated, the Soviet Union is particularly vulnerable to such a disarming attack because it relies extensively on ICBMs.

One solution to ICBM vulnerability is to build mobile ICBMs. MAD proponents favor mobile ICBMs because by decreasing vulnerability they increase deterrence. The Soviet Union has single-warhead SS-25 and multiple-warhead SS-24 mobile ICBMs.

The United States has debated the mobile missile option since the late 1970s but has moved forward slowly. The Bush administration finally announced in late 1989 that it was going to place 50 MX missiles on 25 trains located in six states (Louisiana, Texas, Washington, North Dakota, Arkansas, and Michigan). During crises, these rail-mobile MXs will then be deployed throughout the country's 120,000 miles of commercial railroad track to complicate Soviet targeting. The Bush administration is also seeking funds to continue development of the single-warhead, potentially road-mobile Midgetman missile.

There are two problems. One is cost. The conversion of 50 MXs from silo-based to rail-based missiles will cost at least $5.6 billion, and the development cost of the Midgetman is estimated to be $30 billion. Political concerns are the second inhibiting factor. Members of Congress are reluctant to have mobile missiles roaming their states or districts, and NUTs fear that such a sight (especially the road-mobile Midgetman) would create an acute antinuclear reaction in the American public and strengthen the hand of defense critics in Congress and elsewhere.

Sea-Launched Ballistic Missiles

Both superpowers have extensive SLBM forces. Britain, France, and China also have SLBM forces. The primary advantage of SLBM forces is their near invulnerability. U.S. ballistic missile submarines (SSBNs) are almost totally invulnerable despite advances in Soviet antisubmarine warfare (ASW). Because of their poorer technical quality and the more advanced U.S. ASW capability, Soviet SSBNs have been relatively more vulnerable. Still, it is unlikely that U.S. forces could carry out an effective counterforce strike against Soviet SSBNs. Meanwhile, Soviet technology is steadily advancing and narrowing the gap between the two forces.

Because of their relative invulnerability, SSBNs and their SLBMs are favored by MAD proponents as an effective deterrent system. NUTs also support SLBMs because the same invulnerability allows for their controlled use. The U.S. program to equip its SSBNs with the powerful D-5 missile, called a seagoing MX, is also favored by NUTs. The Soviets are farther behind in their development, but their SS-N-23 has counterforce potential.

Currently, the main disadvantage of SSBNs and their SLBMs is cost. A fully equipped U.S. SSBN approaches $3 billion, and it is expensive to operate. Another difficulty is communications. Since they will be far away and deep underwater, SSBNs could well lose contact with their command centers after an effective C^3I attack on their home country.

Penetrating Manned Bombers

Aircraft are still employed as weapons delivery systems by all the nuclear countries. What we will be discussing here are penetrating bombers, those that are flown to or near targets to deliver their weapons by gravity bomb or by short-range (150 km) attack missiles (SRAMs). These bombers are distinct from U.S. and Soviet aircraft that are being converted or being especially built to fire air-launched cruise missiles (ALCMs). These planes are not really bombers at all; they are cruise missile platforms (CMPs).

The United States has maintained a large fleet of B-52 bombers, but these are being converted into CMPs. The Soviets have only a very limited bomber capability, especially for reaching the United States, although they began deploying a few strategic-range Blackjack bombers in 1988. The United States deployed the B-1B bomber in the mid-1980s, but it has been dubbed the "flying Edsel" by critics and its effectiveness is dubious. This project has been followed with the B-2 Stealth bomber, which is the focus of great debate (Brown, 1990; Rice, 1990).

Manned bombers have some advantages. One is flexibility. They are both nuclear and nonnuclear capable. Unlike missiles, they can also be started toward their targets then recalled if desired. Bombers can be moved from base to base, kept on runway alert, and even kept in the air on rotation. These capabilities provide them with some level of protection. For these reasons, MADs tended to favor manned bombers. Development of the B-2 changed that.

The B-2 supposedly overcomes the leading disadvantage of manned bombers: vulnerability to air defense measures. The U.S. Air Force claims that a variety of technologies make the B-2, which is a black flying wing that looks remarkably like the batplane, electronically invisible to air defense radars. For those who favor MAD, this invisibility is the problem. For NUTS it is an advantage. If the B-2 is invisible as advertised, then it becomes a potential first-strike nuclear delivery system. An enemy might theoretically not know a nuclear war had started until nuclear explosions started destroying its weapons and C³I capabilities. By reducing the warning time to potentially zero, MADs say the B-2 dramatically heightens instability.

A second drawback of the B-2, as discussed in chapter 1, is cost. At current production levels (and allocating already spent development costs), the cost of each B-2 will approach $1 billion. Because of the economies of scale, which allow (for example) research and development costs to be allocated among all units acquired, the original unit cost estimate of $515 million each for 132 B-2s has soared as Congress has reduced the total number of B-2s to be acquired.

The fate of the B-2 has been further cast in doubt by the change in U.S.–Soviet relations. Even when the cold war existed, critics questioned the need for a high-cost manned bomber in an era of cheaper missiles. With that era fading, the B-2 utility is even more questionable. The Air Force has switched the emphasis of its rationale for the B-2 and argued that crises like the 1990 confrontation with Iraq prove the need for a penetrating bomber. Congress has been largely unimpressed, though, and the FY 1991 budget authorizes the acquisition of only two B-2s.

Cruise Missiles

These are slow (600 mph), low-flying (500 feet), but powerful (up to 150 kt) missiles, with a range of up to 1,500 miles. One advantage is that they are highly mobile and can be launched from the ground, from surface ships or submarines, or from aircraft. They have conventional as well as nuclear capability, and Tomahawk cruise missiles, armed with conventional warheads and launched from ships, were some of the first weapons to strike Iraq in January 1991. Thus, they are highly versatile. Second, cruise missiles are inexpensive by military standards. These factors make them attractive to NUTs. There are, however, disadvantages. Cruise missiles can be shot down. More importantly, they create significant arms control problems. Because they are small (20 feet long, 21 inches in diameter) and can be easily concealed, it will be difficult to devise a plan that assures each side that the other is not hiding some.

Types of Warheads

The most significant development in warhead technology has been multiple independent reentry vehicles (MIRVs). This technology allows a single missile to carry several warheads that can strike separate targets independently. MIRVs have the advantage of greatly adding to Soviet and U.S. firepower at relatively low cost. A single SS-18 carries ten 750 kt warheads, and an MX carries an equal number of 300 kt warheads. That means one SS-18 carries explosive power equal to about 600 Hiroshima bombs.

What makes MAD proponents leery of MIRV technology is that when combined with missile accuracy it substantially increases counterforce capability and thus (MADs say) decreases nuclear stability. MIRVs complicate arms control because it is difficult to verify how many warheads a MIRVed ICBM or SLBM is carrying.

Defending Against Nuclear Attack

The concept and possibility of nuclear defense plays an important role in today's nuclear arms planning and diplomacy. There are two types of nuclear defense. One is *active*, consisting of measures to destroy attacking weapons. The other is using *passive* measures, such as civil defense, to survive an attack, but the nature of nuclear war makes such measures largely ineffective.

Mounting many warheads, called multiple independent reentry vehicles (MIRVs), on a single missile vastly increased the firepower of the U.S. and Soviet strategic missiles, as well as considerably complicating arms control. In this picture you can see several of the MIRVs being mounted on a U.S. MX missile. Amazingly each warhead is only about 6 feet tall, much smaller than the Hiroshima bomb, yet 20 times as powerful as the 15 kt atomic bomb dropped on Japan in August 1945.

The current debate over the idea of building a ballistic missile defense (BMD) system began in March 1983, when President Reagan announced that the United States would try to develop and deploy such a system. The project became known as the Strategic Defense Initiative (SDI) to its proponents and as **Star Wars** to its opponents. There is also substantial evidence that the U.S.S.R. is working on such a project (Broad, 1987); President Gorbachev confirmed as much in his December 1987 televised interview on NBC with Tom Brokaw.

Reagan initially talked in terms of a comprehensive defense system using lasers, particle-beam weapons, and other extraordinary technologies to destroy attacking missiles at all phases between launch and detonation. Few if any technologically knowledgeable people ever believed this was possible in the foreseeable future, or perhaps ever, and in the intervening years the daunting technological problems coupled with budget restraints have steadily decreased the aims of SDI development. As it stands in mid-1990, SDI developers are concentrating on a concept called "Brilliant Pebbles," an approach, in the words of one SDI scientist, "many orders of magnitude short" of Reagan's original vision (*NYT,* 2/13/90:C1). Brilliant Pebbles envisions thousands of radar-controlled, nonnuclear rockets circling the Earth in low orbit waiting to intercept attacking warheads. Thus far, defense officials have not issued an estimate of what percentage of warheads might be interdicted, but what is known about Brilliant Pebbles indicates that it would only be intended to intercept a portion of a massive Soviet attack. As such, it would be at best a limited defense system.

There are two levels at which to debate this issue. One is the possibility and advisability of any BMD system. The second is the value of the Brilliant Pebbles system itself.

The Arguments For and Against SDI   Proponents of SDI are of the NUT persuasion and make a number of arguments in support of developing and deploying the system.

One is that in the event of a Soviet strike, even a limited BMD system would save tens of millions of lives. A second contention is that SDI will vastly reduce the vulnerability of land-based missile and C³I facilities, thereby reducing the temptation to launch a preemptory strike against them. Further, NUTs say, the same factor will mean that future U.S. presidents will be under less pressure to "use 'em or lose 'em" and that will lessen the chances of inadvertent nuclear war.

SDI advocates also claim the system is morally superior to punishment by deterrence because it is a defense rather than a threat to wreak nuclear revenge. A fifth pro-SDI argument is that it will make arms control easier to achieve by lessening concern about cheating and the related need for strict verification. Sixth, SDI's supporters claim that it will provide a good shield against small attacks, such as an accidental launch, an unauthorized launch by a deranged subordinate, or an attack by a small country (a growing possibility given the proliferation of nuclear weapons). Seventh, proponents point to Soviet BMD activities and say that the United States would be at a disadvantage if the U.S.S.R. had a defensive system and the United States did not.

As for the contention that SDI is technologically impossible, its proponents express confidence that science can overcome the technological obstacles to building a system that can detect, evaluate, and successfully counter a nuclear missile attack. SDI advocates reject the claim that the system will be too expensive (about $20 billion has been spent so far; Brilliant Pebbles would cost at least $35 billion more) and reply that its potential for saving lives, increasing deterrence, and other benefits are well worth the cost.

Critics of SDI, who are generally of the MAD point of view, say that developing and deploying the system will cost too much; it is technologically impossible; and it is dangerously destabilizing as well. First, opponents say that in a time of budget deficits, the $55 billion price tag to get to just a first-phase deployment is simply too expensive, especially for a system that provides only a partial defense at best. Detractors also deride SDI as technologically impossible. One skeptical member of Congress declared, "It's time we stopped listening to snake oil salesmen in white lab coats" (*NYT,* 2/13/90:C8). His comment is echoed by the doubts of many eminent scientists, as well as by organizations such as the U.S. Office of Technology Assessment (OTA) that doubt that science can develop a system that under the pressures of a nuclear attack can perform the equivalent of "hitting a bullet [traveling at perhaps 30,000 mph] with a bullet" (*NYT*, 4/25/88:A1). Yet another point made by SDI critics is that the Soviets could counter the proposed SDI capabilities by techniques such as launching decoy warheads to overwhelm Brilliant Pebbles. Opponents also argue that the Soviets could simply build a tremendous number of new offensive missiles to overcome the defense.

Finally, and most importantly, SDI opponents claim that trying to develop and deploy such a system would be dangerously destabilizing. First, they say, it would militarize space. Second, critics contend that the SDI will push the Soviets to develop a massive number of new nuclear delivery devices capable of overwhelming any defensive system. Some analysts even worry that the Soviets, rather than face a situation in which American missiles could attack them but their missiles could not counterattack, might decide to launch a preemptive first strike to avoid being put at such a decided disadvantage. It is also within the realm of possibility that an SDI would lull its possessor into a false sense of security, make the "unthinkable" a bit more "thinkable," and convince some future leader that a planned nuclear attack on an opponent was a rational choice. Finally, critics charge that pursuing the SDI program will further entangle the already horrendously complex nuclear disarmament problem.

What to Believe There is no right answer. Whether or not an effective SDI system would be worth the huge cost is a matter of subjective value. Whether the proposed weapons are technically feasible or Buck Rogers nonsense also depends on whom you listen to. Much of the proposal sounds beyond comprehension, but so, not long ago, did traveling in space. Many great inventions have been laughed at before their time.

Finally, the safety or danger of such a proposal depends on a series of assumptions. Critics, most of whom are of the MAD school, argue that deterrence has worked and are willing to gamble that it will continue to work. They are unwilling to destabilize deterrence by provoking more Soviet offensive weapons and making the unthinkable thinkable. Proponents of the SDI program (generally NUT theorists) have their doubts about the (continued) effectiveness of deterrence. They say a defensive system will both enhance deterrence and provide an alternative to certain destruction if deterrence does fail. Where you stand on these issues depends on what frightens you most. As such, SDI has been and remains highly controversial, and its future is uncertain. President Bush supports SDI, but not with the ardor of his predecessor. Furthermore, the technical difficulties and cost of SDI have resulted in the downgrading of its aims from a comprehensive defense system to defense of some strategic sites, or to counter a small number of warheads launched by accident or by a small nuclear power. Research will continue, but at reduced budget levels, although this will still be about $2.5 billion for FY 1991.

Chapter Summary

1. War is organized killing of other human beings. Virtually everyone is against that. Yet war continues to be a part of the human condition, and its incidence has not significantly abated.

2. Scholars, philosophers, and diplomats have tried to understand why wars occur in hopes of preventing them. To date, although much valuable research has been done, about the best we can do is to point out that war is a complex phenomenon that seems to have many causes. Some of these may stem from the nature of our species, some from the existence of nation-states, and some from the nature and dynamics of the world political system.

3. It is insufficient, though, merely to condemn war or to try to understand its origins. We must also understand how war is waged and its impact on international politics.

4. As we have seen, force can be used, threatened, or merely exist as an unspoken possibility. However it is operationalized, its successful use requires planning and skill. (It is important to remember that if force is to be used, it must be employed as a means, or tool, rather than, as sometimes happens, as an end in itself.)

5. The nature of war is changing. Technology has enhanced killing power; nationalism has made war a patriotic cause; entire populaces, instead of just armies, have become engaged; and the power to hurt has equaled or supplanted the power to defeat as a goal of conflict.

6. Force, it must be remembered, does not have to be used to have an impact. The possession of military power creates a backdrop to diplomacy, and the overt threat of force increases the psychological pressure even more.

7. When it is used, force can range from very limited demonstration to full-scale nuclear attack.

8. To look at the conduct of war, we examined traditional warfare and limited nuclear-biological-chemical (NBC) war, and strategic nuclear war. Guerrilla and terrorist violence will be discussed in the next chapter. For each of the types of conflict examined in this chapter, we examined a variety of factors such as weapons and strategy. We also saw that the ability to conduct war is continuing to change as new technology develops new weapons.

9. The study of force involves several major questions. When and why does war occur? When it does happen, how effective is it, what conditions govern success or failure, and what options exist in structuring the use of force? The final question, discussed in chapter 17, is how can we prevent war? This may be the most important question, but it is not the only question.

Rumor is a pipe
Blown by surmises, jealousies, conjectures,
And of so easy and so plain a stop
That the blunt monster of uncounted heads,
The still-discordant wavering multitude,
Can play on it.

Shakespeare, *Henry IV,* Part II

All propaganda has to be popular and has to adopt its spiritual level
to the perception of the least intelligent of those towards whom it
intends to direct itself.

Adolf Hitler, *Mein Kampf*

CHAPTER 11

PENETRATION
AND
INTERVENTION

Sates, as noted in chapter 5, are huge organizations that include many internal sources of policy pressure. Much of foreign policy and, by extension, international politics, is a reflection of those pressures. A country's policy-making substructures are increasingly subject to manipulation (penetration and intervention) by other countries. Thus, penetration and intervention are important determinants of the course of international relations.

Penetration and Intervention: Ends and Means

We can define penetration and intervention as processes by which one country affects the internal politics of another country. *Penetration* means gaining access to another actor's internal structure, and *intervention* means manipulating the penetrated actor's political process. Often, intervention is thought of in terms of "armed," but as we shall see presently it is also possible to intervene with nonviolent means.

The traditional image of international politics involves "direct interaction" between governments. By contrast, penetration and intervention are a process of "indirect interaction" based on the ability of one international actor to affect the substructure (the domestic political actors) of a country. By doing so, say by manipulating public opinion, the penetrating actor indirectly influences the penetrated country's government and policy. Penetration and intervention usually are carried out by governments, as depicted in Figure 11.1 (see next page). Sometimes, though, transnational actors, such as international terrorist groups, can also penetrate and manipulate a state's policy.

There are many forms of penetration, some of which involve intervention and some of which do not. These can be roughly divided into three categories. The first is *passive*

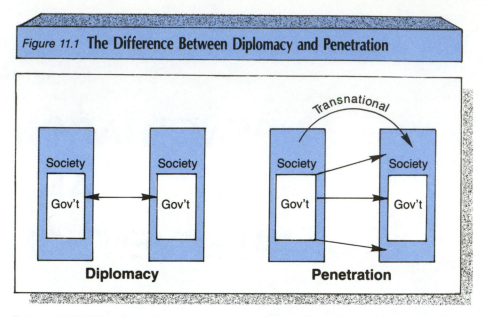

Figure 11.1 The Difference Between Diplomacy and Penetration

Diplomacy is traditionally carried out between governments. Penetration occurs when a government or other domestic actors in one country bypass the (executive branch of) government of another country and interact with the various other political actors in that society.

penetration, or information gathering. A more active form of penetration is *manipulative intervention* through propaganda and other techniques. Third, there are various forms of *coercive intervention*, some of which include armed intervention. As we shall see, each of these is an increasingly important instrument of international politics.

Before looking in detail at these activities, it is appropriate to survey the general nature of penetration and intervention, including their increasing importance, the organizations that carry them out, and their limits and dangers.

Penetration and Intervention: Increasing Importance and Ability

The history of penetration and intervention is a long one. Indeed, internal activity is as old as diplomacy and war. In ancient Greece, names such as Odysseus and Alexander the Great are closely identified with spying and propaganda. The Bible is also full of references to these activities. Joshua was an expert propagandist who sapped the morale of his enemies by spreading the news of his miraculous victories and the story that God had promised victory to the children of Israel. Moses, who sent 12 spies into the land of Canaan (Num. 13:3), may have been the first spymaster, and Delilah used her charms to gain intelligence (Judg. 16:9) and to neutralize Samson. For this she received 1,100 pieces of silver from the Philistines, a magnificent sum, especially when compared with Judas Iscariot's mere 30 silver pieces.

The use of intelligence about an enemy, attempts to affect morale and opinion, and efforts to foment trouble in an opponent's camp have long been important tools of international politics. As Joshua learned, if you can crumble the enemy's resistance by blowing your horns, the victory can be just as sure as if you gain it by force—and less costly.

While internal activity has been important throughout history, it has become even more vital and prevalent in the twentieth century. Only 60 years ago, U.S. secretary of state Henry L. Stimson disbanded his department's intelligence operation with the offended comment, "Gentlemen do not read each other's mail." Today, such an attitude is nearly inconceivable. Spying, propaganda, and subversion are common methods of international activity. The two superpowers are the leading practitioners, and they both have intelligence operations that spend billions of dollars yearly. In his first six years in office alone, President Reagan approved at least 50 secret operations designed to intervene in the internal affairs of countries such as Afghanistan, Angola, Cambodia, Nicaragua, Libya, Ethiopia, and Chad. What is perhaps most startling about the 50 covert operations is that they represent a sharp drop from the 900 large- and medium-size operations and thousands of small programs that occurred in the 1960s and 1970s.

Three general factors account for the increasing importance of penetration and intervention. They are (1) the need to know, (2) the ability to gather information, and (3) the ability to intervene. There are also some very specific factors that have led to the increased use of particular forms of internal activity; we will discuss these as we take up each type of activity.

The Need to Know

Intelligence about the assets and intentions of others has always been valuable. Recent world changes, including advances in technology and the growth of interdependence, have made such information absolutely crucial.

Advanced *technology* has made information more important in two ways. First, the speed and destructiveness of modern weapons mean that the time to make defensive decisions may be extremely limited. Second, keeping up technologically with others has become essential. The technology gap between the Soviets and the Western allies is a matter of real concern for the Kremlin. A great deal of Soviet bloc espionage against the West is aimed at gaining computer technology and other electronic/industrial information.

World *economic interdependence* has also enhanced the importance of good intelligence. Governments use human and technical means to monitor allies and neutrals as well as enemies. Mexico, Nigeria, and Venezuela all have friendly relations with the United States, but since they are all also major sources of U.S. petroleum imports, it is prudent for Washington to monitor political developments in those countries. All three of these countries have faced significant internal tensions in recent years, and an upheaval in any one could seriously affect the U.S. energy picture.

Economic interdependence has also led to increased industrial espionage. A significant focus of Soviet intelligence efforts is gaining industrial technological secrets to allow the U.S.S.R. to cut the technology gap with the West. Allies also conduct industrial (and traditional) intelligence activities against one another. In May 1990, for instance, the French newsmagazine *L'Express* reported that U.S. counterintelligence agents had uncovered an effort by the French intelligence service, *Direction Général de la Sécurité Extérieure,* to infiltrate European branches of IBM, Texas Instruments, and other U.S. computer companies in order to channel secrets to the struggling French computer manufacturer Compagnie des Machines Bull, which is largely owned by the French government. For each microfilm of a missile design that secret agents gather, thousands of pieces of data on Soviet wheat fields, Iranian oil production, and the Brazilian coffee crop are amassed and analyzed by intelligence agencies.

The Ability to Gather Information

Technology has vastly improved information-gathering techniques. Sensitive listening devices, high-resolution optics, infrared sensing equipment, computers that sort and assemble information, and a variety of other means have revolutionized the intelligence-gathering field. Electronic transmission of information, computerization, rapid transportation, and modern media capabilities have also opened advanced societies to penetration. Currently, in the United States, 70 percent of all domestic telecommunications and 60 percent of all traffic abroad is transmitted via satellites or microwave towers and is easily interceptible. Stories have even circulated in recent years that both the United States and the Soviet Union are experimenting with clairvoyance, extrasensory perception, and other psychic techniques to gather information. Additionally, advances in transportation and communication have greatly increased contacts. Even authoritarian countries, such as China, are visited by increasing numbers of foreigners who bring back information about the country. Cultural contacts also provide propaganda opportunities.

Related to this expansion in the level of contact is the increase in the size of diplomatic missions. Intelligence agents, with **diplomatic cover** titles, are an integral part of the missions of many countries. These agents are not only stationed in capital cities, they are also often placed in consular and other missions throughout the country. The Soviet Union and East European countries have 2,100 diplomats in the United States (including those accredited to the UN), and between 600 and 850 of these were, and may still be, intelligence agents. These are supplemented by spies planted among tourists and immigrants and by agents recruited from among American citizens. This network is, in turn, countered by 2,000 U.S. counterintelligence agents.

Spying has also gained increased tacit acceptance. It is an open secret that the "diplomats" attached to the embassies of most major countries include a contingent of intelligence agents. One reason countries tolerate this is so that other countries will reciprocate and allow limited intelligence activity by their agents. Second, both the Americans and Soviets realize that accidental or inadvertent war can be prevented in part by letting the other side keep track of their activities. Neither side tries to interfere with many technical monitoring programs (for example, satellites); diplomatic spies are tolerated as long as they are not too blatant; the NATO and the Warsaw Pact armies have invited each other to observe military maneuvers in Central Europe, and on-site inspection is a part of the 1987 Intermediate-range Nuclear Forces Treaty.

The Ability to Intervene

The third factor in the increasing importance of internal activity is the ability to manipulate. This aspect has been enhanced by advances in technology and a growing knowledge of psychology.

Technologically, the advent of electronic media—first radio, then television—meant an inevitable lessening of the barrier that a national border can pose to the flow of information and propaganda. As we shall see, the major powers—and some lesser ones—spend billions of dollars broadcasting their views to the world.

Furthermore, governments are more willing than before to accept penetration and even limited intervention tacitly and, in some cases, explicitly. This acquiescence is partly a matter of an inability to prevent it. Radios, for instance, are common even in authoritarian countries, and that combined with the difficulty of effectively jamming radio signals from other countries has led to a marked decrease in this activity.

There have also been advances in the understanding of social psychology. Especially since World War II, behavioral scientists have become involved in the design of propaganda. Persuasion will probably always be partly an art, but it is also very much a science.

Public Opinion

The importance of internal activity has also been enhanced by the rising role of public opinion in foreign policy. Morale has always been a target of propaganda, but the increased role of public opinion in foreign policy-making (see chapter 5) has broadened opportunities to affect another country's policy. This is particularly true in more democratic countries. The war between Sandinista troops and Contra rebels, for instance, was waged with words in Washington as well as with bullets on the battlefields of Nicaragua. Each side sent its leaders to the United States to make its case, both invited sympathetic U.S. public figures to visit, both held regular news briefings, and both hired public relations firms to give gloss to their message to the American people and Congress.

The Limits and Dangers of Penetration and Intervention

Despite advances in both the importance of penetration and intervention and the ability to carry on these activities, intelligence operations are limited in their impact and can be dangerous for the country conducting them.

Limits

Target resistance is one limit. It stems from the ability of targets to frustrate intelligence efforts. All countries employ sophisticated coding of signals and other procedures to guard their secrets. Countries can also use double agents or other **disinformation** techniques to mislead an opponent. Additionally, all major governments have counter-intelligence units designed to thwart penetration.

Unpredictability is another limiting factor. Often the best that intelligence analysts can hope to achieve is to predict probability. An intelligence estimate is often made from the unenviable position of trying to predict a decision before it is made. International events are highly complex, especially where human decisions are involved, and projecting the future is always hazardous.

Lack of resources further restrains intelligence activities. Even in the age of the computer, it is impossible to gather and analyze all relevant information. Intelligence agencies are also subject to budgetary and other domestic political pressures. The substantial reduction of the CIA's covert operations in the 1970s left the agency short of agents skilled in covert operations and other functions. Lack of specialized educational training has also left the American intelligence community short of analysts in such areas as Eastern Europe.

There are also self-imposed limits. Intelligence activity may be limited by a variety of ethical or political considerations. Later, for example, we will consider the morality of assassination. In the political realm, the United States was reluctant to cooperate with the (supposedly radical, "communist-leaning") African National Congress in South Africa, even though intelligence indicates it is the strongest black movement there and will likely play a pivotal role if/when white rule crumbles.

A number of factors limit how well intelligence consumers utilize intelligence. Unexpected information or analysis that goes against "prevailing truths" may be perceptually rejected. There were estimates in the 1960s that the United States could not prevail militarily in Vietnam, but given American might and arrogance, any thought that heavily armed U.S. forces could not defeat their lightly armed opponents was perceived as too outlandish to believe. More recently, U.S. satellites detected a massive buildup of Iraqi armor and troops on Kuwait's border on July 28, 1990, five days before the subsequent invasion. Based on this intelligence information, the CIA increased its estimate of an attack from possible to highly likely. Yet the White House and State Department seemingly ignored the warning, and three days later on July 31 the assistant secretary of state for the Middle East publicly told a congressional committee that the United States was not obligated to defend any Persian Gulf state. In short, despite the best evidence, decisionmakers often see and hear what they want to.

A last, and related, factor is organizational restraints. Prevailing truths also inhibit analysts from forwarding dissonant conclusions. Unusual analysis is often not applauded for its fresh approach. Rather, it is rejected as odd and misconceived, and the analyst's credibility is cast into doubt. Even if the analyst is brave enough to press an unusual idea, it will probably be suppressed at an intermediate level. Secretary of State Dean Acheson once unwisely opined: "You think Presidents should be warned. You're wrong. Presidents should be given confidence" (Betts, 1978:77). Finally, intelligence sometimes just falls through the bureaucratic cracks. A warning from Washington to military commanders in Hawaii that Pearl Harbor might be bombed simply moved too slowly in 1941 to be of any use: it arrived after the Japanese attack. A last-minute alert was sent by Western Union rather than by military cable.

Dangers

Although penetration and intervention can bring success, these methods have potential drawbacks to the user. One conundrum for open societies is the inherent conflict between secret operations and democracy. Intelligence activities sometimes require secrecy to succeed and to avoid danger to a country's agents and their contacts and operatives in other countries. Yet these exigencies conflict with the fundamental premise of democratic government, that the people and their legislative representatives need to know what is happening in order to have some say in whether it should happen at all.

A related danger is that intelligence operations can run amok, escaping the control of even those who are supposedly in charge. The Tower Commission, for instance, charged in March 1987 that the Irangate operation conducted by Lieutenant Colonel Oliver North "functioned largely outside the orbit of the U.S. government [and] was not subject to critical reviews of any kind." The result was a rogue operation that, among other things, shipped antitank weapons to a very hostile Iran and violated a number of U.S. laws by misusing funds and shipping combat equipment and supplies to Nicaraguan rebels.

Intelligence operations can also backfire and have unintended and negative impacts. It is alleged, for instance, that in 1985 the CIA arranged through Saudi Arabia to assassinate the leader of a militant Muslim faction in Lebanon. When the bomb in a car in a suburb of Beirut went off, the leader was unharmed but 80 bystanders were killed (Woodward, 1987).

Additionally, clandestine operations can severely embarrass a country. An imbroglio occurred in 1985 when French agents blew up and sank the ship *Rainbow Warrior* and killed one crew member in a New Zealand port. The vessel was owned by Greenpeace, the international environmental organization, and had been slated to sail to protest French nuclear tests in the Pacific. France earned a considerable international black eye when its agents were caught, tried, and convicted in New Zealand.

Even when the intelligence operation is simply gathering information there is the potential for disastrous results. During the Cuban missile crisis, the KGB discovered that one of its ranking officers, Colonel Oleg Penkovsky, was a CIA double agent. As the KGB stormed into his Moscow apartment, Penkovsky sent to the CIA his last coded signal: nuclear attack imminent! The message may have been an error or it may have been the final act of a desperate man, a Samson trying to bring the temple down with him. In either case and in the midst of a nuclear confrontation between the two superpowers, Penkovsky's warning could have had apocalyptic consequences. Such alerts have also been received in Moscow. KGB defector Oleg Gordievsky discloses in his 1990 book *KGB: The Inside Story* that in 1983 the KGB warned the Kremlin that a NATO exercise code named Able Archer 83 was actually the guise for an attack on the Soviet Union. In the end, a crisis was averted, but this sort of warning could lead to an inadvertent war as discussed in the preceding chapter.

Finally, some types of penetration and intervention are subject to moral objection. This issue was raised in chapter 7, but it is worth pondering again. Tactics such as carrying out assassinations or supplying terrorists who do the work for you raise serious ethical questions. There is also serious concern about the morality of supplying other countries with arms that potentially add to the violence in the world.

One disadvantage of conducting foreign intelligence operations is that they can sometimes embarrass you. France found this out when its agents were arrested and convicted in New Zealand for blowing up and sinking the *Rainbow Warrior* while it was in Auckland harbor. The ship was owned by Greenpeace, an environmental group, and was in New Zealand prior to sailing to France's Pacific Ocean nuclear testing area to protest a scheduled test.

Organizing for Penetration and Intervention

All major countries have one or more important agencies involved in intelligence or counterintelligence. The largest and most important of these, though, are the intelligence bureaucracies of the United States and the Soviet Union; they deserve a brief look.

Among *American intelligence organizations,* the Central Intelligence Agency (CIA) is the most well known. Formed in 1947, it employs about 15,000 people and has a budget of at least $3 billion, although the exact figure is secret and may be considerably greater. CIA activities range from routine monitoring of foreign publications through high-level analysis and policy recommendations. The director of the CIA is a regular adviser of the president. The CIA is also involved in a range of field operations through personnel stationed at American embassies and through special operatives. The various types of activities will be detailed in the pages that follow.

The National Security Agency (NSA) is less well known than the CIA, but it is said to be a larger organization. It specializes in electronic intelligence and uses advanced technology to monitor the activities of the Soviet Union and others. There are also a variety of other intelligence agencies, including the Defense Intelligence Agency (in the Department of Defense); the Department of State Bureau of Intelligence and Research, the United States Information Agency (propaganda); and army, navy, and air force operations. The Federal Bureau of Investigation is responsible for counterintelligence operations. All these activities cost at least $30 billion a year.

Little is known for sure about the size and operations of the *Soviet intelligence organizations,* but estimates run as high as 90,000 civilian intelligence personnel and a budget several times that of the CIA. There are two main organizations. The Committee for State Security, known as the KGB (Komitet Gosudarstvennoi Bezopasnosti), has responsibilities for both internal security and external intelligence gathering and operations. The activities of the KGB run the gamut from suppression of internal dissent, through intelligence gathering, to active measures such as subversion. Its agents are attached to all diplomatic missions. In the era of glasnost in the Soviet Union, the KGB has been widely criticized for its internal activities, but there is no evidence that its size, especially for foreign intelligence, has been reduced. The other main Soviet intelligence agency is the military's Chief Intelligence Directorate of the General Staff, known as the GRU. The GRU specializes mainly in military intelligence, and it also maintains specialized troops.

In total, these organizations are probably considerably larger than their American counterparts, but it should be remembered that they carry out many domestic and paramilitary functions that are beyond the scope of the CIA and others.

Passive Penetration: Information Gathering

All major countries gather information about friends and foes alike using a variety of techniques. These can be roughly divided between **overt** (open) and **covert** (secret) methods.

Overt Information-Gathering Techniques

Despite popular stereotypes about cloak-and-dagger intelligence, the greatest volume of information, if not the most sensitive, is gathered through overt methods. The three primary methods of overt intelligence gathering are (1) observation, (2) monitoring of public information, and (3) the use of **national technical means** (NTM), such as satellites. These methods attempt to gain traditional military and political information, but they also focus on gaining industrial and technology intelligence.

A great deal of information can be gained through simple observation. The openness of the American system gives other countries an excellent chance to gather information. Soviet scientists and technicians regularly visit the United States and attend conferences on such topics as lasers, optics, high-energy physics, computer software, engineering, and particle accelerators. Other technical experts are associated with leading American scientific university programs through scholar exchange programs. Soviet operatives also regularly attend or watch American political events, just as U.S. observers never miss a May Day Parade in Red Square. Soviet embassy officials regularly visit Capitol Hill offices, socialize with members of Congress and staff members, and attend committee meetings. The bits of information gained by such methods are seldom significant individually; they are more like pieces of a jigsaw puzzle. "They're looking for bits and pieces," one Senate source explained. "Every hearing on foreign relations, agriculture, or international economics the Soviets are going to cover. They're trying to see which way the decisions are going, what the thinking is" (*HC,* 3/28/81:A20).

Monitoring public information is another major intelligence source. Most CIA professionals are involved in monitoring the print and broadcast media of other countries. They read journals, books, and whatever else they can obtain. *Red Star*, the leading Soviet military journal, is read with as much interest in Washington as in Moscow.

Here again, countries with closed political systems have an advantage over those with more open systems. The amount of technical, defense, and political information available in the United States, Canada, Western Europe, Japan, and other open political systems through the press, professional journals and conferences, and public documents is immense. As many as 10 Soviet embassy officials have signed up for reports and hearing transcripts issued by the U.S. Senate Armed Services Committee, and during the height of the MX-basing controversy, the FBI trailed two Soviet officials to Ely, Nevada (a potential MX site), where they were gathering data from the local library about the area.

National technical means (NTM) are also important sources of information (Krepon, 1989). Technological advances have created sophisticated equipment that can accomplish almost unbelievable feats, and to a substantial degree, NTM operates in the open and with tacit acceptance. The United States and others use satellites that transmit photographic, computer-graphic, heat-sensitive, and other types of information back to Earth. These spy satellites crisscross the globe from 80 to 200 miles aloft or, even farther out (22,000 miles), travel at the same speed as Earth and seem to hang motionless over the equator. The images they transmit are highly accurate, and some can even pick up the faint signals that leak from microwave phone communications. There are also a wide variety of high-flying spy planes and undersea and ground monitoring stations. One U.S. radar, the giant Great Dane, is reportedly able to spot a baseball at a range of 2,300 miles. Satellite intelligence, for example, was a major factor that allowed the allies to locate and destroy most Iraq warplanes and missiles in January 1991 before they could be used. The limits of even the most sophisticated NTM were demonstrated, though, by the fact that several Scud missiles were launched against targets in Israel and elsewhere.

Covert Information-Gathering Techniques

The area of covert intelligence is the stuff of John Le Carré spy novels. Spy activities include either traditional HUMINT (human intelligence) or more technological methods, such as SIGINT (signal intelligence), which includes ELINT (electronic intelligence) and COMINT (communication intelligence).

Human intelligence includes both members of a country's intelligence service and agents recruited from among the citizens of the country it is penetrating. As noted, intelligence personnel are often assigned to embassies under diplomatic cover. Soviet efforts, for example, were dealt a severe blow in the mid-1980s when a senior KGB officer fed

The United States, the Soviet Union, and other countries spend considerable effort to recruit spies. The United States in recent years has been rocked by a number of major espionage scandals. One of these involved Edward Lee Howard, pictured here in front of the Kremlin in Moscow, who worked for the U.S. CIA and spied for the Soviet KGB. Howard was uncovered, but he was able to flee to Moscow before being captured.

information to France's counterintelligence agency about Soviet agents attached to embassies in France and other Western nations. As a result, 47 agents were expelled from France and another 101 were ejected from other countries. A grim footnote is that the KGB informer was uncovered and executed before he could defect to the West.

People become spies against their own countries for a number of reasons. In some cases, political reasons are involved. Arkady Shevchenko, a high-ranking Soviet diplomat serving as under secretary-general of the United Nations, worked for two years as an American spy and then defected to the United States in 1978, claiming he could no longer tolerate the Soviet political system (Shevchenko, 1985). Another recent incident involved a now-imprisoned American couple, the Pollards, who turned over secrets to Israel because of their belief in that country's importance.

Probably the most common method of recruiting spies is with money. A serious case unraveled in 1986 with the exposure of the Walker ring, a group of U.S. Navy personnel who spied for pay. Ring members provided code books that allowed the Soviets to decipher over 1 million messages and information that compromised the communications circuits used by the National Command Authority in time of nuclear crisis. In return, the spies received up to $332,000 each. They and others, including CIA operative Edward Lee Howard, were uncovered when KGB officer Vitaly Yurchenko defected to the United States. For their trouble, the spies received sentences of up to 365 years in prison and fines of up to $410,000. A strange sidelight to the tale is that after exposing the Walkers and others, Yurchenko "undefected" by returning to the Soviet Union, claiming he had been kidnapped and drugged by the CIA.

The reunification of Germany and the opening of the files of East Germany's Stasi intelligence organization has resulted in some sensational disclosures. One is that West Germany's top counterintelligence agent against East German spies was himself a double agent receiving $2,500 a month from the Stasi. The woman who was in charge of preparing the weekly top-secret intelligence report for Chancellor Helmut Kohl was also a Stasi agent, and sometimes East German leader Erich Honecker got to read the reports before Kohl did.

The United States has also had some spectacular successes by trading cash for secrets. Throughout the 1980s, Marin and Ille Ceausescu, brothers of since-executed Romanian dictator Nicolae Ceausescu, sold Soviet and Warsaw Pact military secrets to the CIA in exchange for $40 million. Among other things, components of the most advanced Soviet air defense radars obtained from the Ceausescus significantly aided in the development of U.S. Stealth (radar-invisible) aircraft technology.

Signal intelligence has become increasingly important as technology has improved. The ability of the Allies to crack the German code and monitor communications, for instance, significantly shortened World War II. The dividing line between overt and covert technical means is at times vague and not overly important, but essentially, covert means are those in which there is an attempt to mask their use from the target.

Electronic eavesdropping on conversations is one method. Soviet workers put so many listening devices in the new U.S. embassy being built in Moscow that in late 1988 President Reagan ordered the entire building torn down and rebuilt. Modern technology has replaced old-fashioned microphones with amazing devices. One, if placed in an electric typewriter, can pick up each key's distinctive signal, broadcast them, and reconstruct what is being typed. Another is a laser-based device that can intercept conversations by interpreting the voice-generated vibrations of a window pane.

The use of computers for generating, storing, and transmitting all sorts of data has also vastly increased monitoring possibilities. Computers can be an asset by sorting, analyzing, and storing vast quantities of information that previously would have been beyond human processing capacity. They can also be a liability. Computers give off microwave signals that can be intercepted and translated. They can also be directly accessed without authorization. The U.S. government operates over 26,000 mainframe computers, two-thirds of which are used by the Department of Defense. One indication of their vulnerability came to light in 1988 with the disclosure that a West German computer science student had gained access to 30 computers used by the U.S. military or its contractors at locations including the Air Force Systems Command in California and the Naval Coastal Systems Command in Florida. None of the information was classified, but experts were worried about the "very real dangers" of computer penetration (*NYT*, 4/25/88:A1). Not only is it possible for data to be stolen, but it is also possible to plant a "virus" in a program, perhaps one that controls a weapons system, causing it to malfunction at a critical moment.

Manipulative Intervention: Noncoercive Techniques

There are a range of techniques by which one country can attempt to manipulate the political situation in another country. Two such methods that deserve some attention here are (1) political support of one faction or another in a foreign country and (2) propaganda.

Political Support

One way to intervene in another country's affairs is to give political support to one of that country's competing political elements. When you are supporting the government, foreign aid, trade concessions, and other such benefits are common. These are more fully discussed in chapter 13. The Bush administration has attempted to shore up Gorbachev in the Soviet Union through these techniques, and Washington has also refused to press such issues as the independence of the Soviet Baltic republics in order to ease pressure on Gorbachev.

Less commonly, governments may overtly support a challenging faction in another country. Financial support is one way to give such assistance. The United States gave $7 million to the UNO coalition that elected Violeta Chamorro as president of Nicaragua, thereby ending the rule of Daniel Ortega and the Sandinistas. Similarly, the Bush administration in March 1990 asked Congress to appropriate funds to support the African National Congress (ANC) in South Africa. Increased U.S. support of the ANC was also demonstrated by the cordial welcome, including an invitation to address a joint session of Congress, extended to ANC leader Nelson Mandela during his visit to the United States. It should also be mentioned that such support does not always come from government sources. U.S. labor unions gave funds to the Polish Solidarity movement in support of its ultimately successful quest to topple the communist government in Poland.

Propaganda

Propaganda is an attempt to influence another country through emotional techniques rather than logical discussion or presentation of empirical evidence. It is a process of appealing to emotions rather than minds by creating fear, doubt, sympathy, anger, or a variety of other feelings. Although the use of propaganda is as old as history, increases in communication, democratization, and the understanding of psychology have made propaganda increasingly important. In essence, if you cannot persuade another country's leaders through force or diplomacy, you can try to affect policy by persuading its people through propaganda.

Before proceeding with our discussion of the techniques and impact of propaganda, we should quickly distinguish between propaganda and public diplomacy, which will be discussed in the next chapter. In practice, the two flow into one another, but for our purposes here, we will construe propaganda to be information and messages put out by government agencies for the explicit purpose of influencing opinion in other countries. Public diplomacy is the direct public actions and statements made by political leaders and diplomats. These often have persuasive intent, and propaganda agencies regularly use them in their messages, but they are distinct in that public diplomacy is "original" and propaganda is the institutional interpretation of what has been said and done.

The extent of propaganda efforts. By any standard, propaganda is big business. In the mid-1980s, the United States, the Soviet Union, and 19 other countries each operated radio networks that broadcast 300 or more hours a week to foreign audiences. U.S.- and Soviet-originated broadcasts each totaled over 2,000 hours a week in several dozen languages. Many countries also have extensive efforts through other media. The United States Information Agency (USIA), for example, staffs over 200 foreign posts in 126 countries, and the agency sponsors magazines, exhibits, films, speaking tours, and cultural exchanges. U.S. propaganda is also broadcast through WORLDNET, a satellite network that beams television into 50 countries.

The end of the cold war, the growth of freedom in many countries, and the increasing availability of many sources of information around the world have increased criticism of government propaganda efforts. One charge is that propaganda agencies, such as the U.S. Voice of America (VOA) radio network, too often ignore truth in the interest of diplomacy. According to one report, a February 1990 VOA editorial that condemned Iraq's use of secret police drew strong protests by Saddam Hussein to the U.S. State Department. As a result, the department apologized to Iraq, and the secretary of state instructed the USIA to get written approval for all future editorials (*NYT,* 9/10/90:A23). Another concern is that overt propaganda is no longer effective and may be counterproductive. This worry has led one former USIA assistant director to call for an end to government editorial control of VOA in order to allow it "to establish itself as a credible, authoritative, and consistently reliable source of information" (Davies, 1990:14).

The techniques of propaganda. There are a variety of *techniques* for projecting effective propaganda. One of these is telling the truth (White, 1971:26–35). Sometimes the truth can be very damaging to the other side. The Soviets have regularly used reports and pictures of racial disturbances in the United States as propaganda in Africa. Similarly, when the Soviets shot down a South Korean airliner in 1983, the United States reaped a propaganda windfall. On the positive side, images such as American astronauts standing on the moon require little doctoring to create a favorable impression.

Lying is another technique. Outright lies are not a common practice, perhaps because they are difficult to support and because they run the risk of being exposed. When that occurs, the former target can become the aggressor and try to embarrass you and attack your credibility. Still, lies, which are sometimes called "disinformation," play a role. In April 1986, U.S. warplanes raided Libya in retaliation for alleged Libyan involvement in terrorist acts against U.S. personnel in West Germany. Later that summer, President Reagan approved a disinformation campaign that fed false information to the U.S. and foreign press that further raids and perhaps even an invasion were imminent. The object was to frighten Libyans and perhaps even cause them to overthrow their leader. Not only was the effort unsuccessful and (as far as feeding false information to the U.S. press was concerned) illegal, but when it was exposed it caused considerable embarrassment to the U.S. government. This led Bernard Kalb, assistant secretary of state for public affairs, to resign in protest.

Half-truths are a more common technique than lying. One common ploy is to take a kernel of truth and project it as a general statement. The existence of some Soviet support of European peace activists has been used by the United States to try to discredit the entire movement as a communist front. Presenting controversial information as fact is another approach. There has been a degree of scientific doubt about alleged Soviet-backed chemical warfare in Southeast Asia, Afghanistan, and elsewhere, but that has not stopped the U.S. propaganda machine. A third half-truth technique is deliberate omission. In this case, the information presented is true but is incomplete.

Coercive Intervention

The last of our three categories of internal activity is coercive intervention. This type of penetration and intervention is by far the most controversial. There are a variety of ways to intervene coercively. The use of economic sanctions against a country and bribes to co-opt foreign leaders or others are two ways. Both of these are discussed elsewhere (chapter 13 and above, respectively). Blackmail is also sometimes possible. If, for example, you can discover that a target has committed a sexual indiscretion, or you are able to trap your victim into one, you may be able to gain cooperation through blackmail. There is also growing concern that military and other computers could be penetrated and, through viruses or other means, disabled at a time of crisis. The most powerful coercion, though, involves the threat or use of violence, and in this section we will concentrate on these means by investigating (1) direct military intervention in another country's internal affairs, (2) the supply of arms in support of domestic and international political violence, and (3) terrorism.

Direct Military Intervention

The most overt form of coercive intervention is dispatching one's own military personnel to another country. The exact junctures where military aid becomes military intervention and where military intervention (in the sense we are using it here) becomes full-scale war are debatable. What is implied here, though, is the direct but limited use of military personnel on one side or the other of another country's internal conflict. There was a time, for example, in South Vietnam in the late 1950s and in the very early 1960s when U.S. military personnel advised the army of South Vietnam (ARVN) in its struggle with the indigenous Viet Cong rebels. Then, during the presidency of John Kennedy, these advisers were augmented and became involved increasingly in the fighting, either along with the ARVN or operating independently in small counter-guerrilla forces such as the Green Berets. By the mid-1960s, U.S. forces had grown to 500,000, and their combat with the North Vietnamese Army (NVA) moved the U.S. involvement out of the interventionist category discussed here and into traditional warfare.

The past few decades have witnessed numerous instances of limited intervention. The attraction of doing so is that it may be successful. The December 1989 intervention of the United States in Panama to topple the military dictatorship of Manuel Noriega is an example. Iraq's persistent refusal to quit Kuwait finally evoked a U.S.–led attack in January 1991. There also have been recent instances of U.S. shows of force, but not fighting. Such demonstrations have occurred in the Philippines to support President Corazon Aquino during some of the several military attempts to overthrow her.

There is, however, also the danger that direct intervention will fail or that it will escalate into full-scale war that, in turn, may itself fail (Shafer, 1990). The U.S. experience in Vietnam is an example of an intervention that both escalated and failed, as is the long, and ultimately unsuccessful, Soviet involvement in Afghanistan throughout most of the 1980s. Another U.S. example is the 1983 intervention in Lebanon. That effort collapsed in the aftermath of the suicide truck-bomb attack on the marine barracks that killed 241 servicemen. In retrospect, President Reagan has evaluated "sending the marines to Beirut [as] the source of my greatest regret and greatest sorrow" (*HC,* 11/5/90:A3).

The issue of the legitimacy of intervention is also controversial. Panama provides a good case in point. General Noriega was abhorrent by almost any political or ethical standard. The U.S. intervention ended his rule, and Panama is well rid of him. Does this legitimize the U.S. intervention? Certainly President Bush thought so, and others have agreed. One former state department official has written on Panama, for instance, that Washington acted properly in not turning "a blind eye to the fate of democracy [in Latin America] at a time when it [democracy] is sweeping the globe" (Kagan, 1990:63). Yet intervening in the internal affairs of any sovereign state is troubling, especially when you have been friendly in the past with the government you are now overthrowing or you continue to be on good terms with regimes in other countries that are similarly distasteful. It may well be, as Senator Edward Kennedy observed, that "the United States [or anyone else] does not have the right under international law . . . to roam the hemisphere to bring dictators to justice or . . . to impose democracy by the barrel of a gun on Panama or any other nation" (*CR,* 1/23/90:S12).

Furthermore, a victory through intervention may only be short-term. One drawback is that it may only draw out the conflict and may even undermine the credibility of the old government supported or the new government installed. When a display of U.S. air power in the Philippines aided in the defeat of rebels led by Lieutenant Colonel Gregorio "Gringo" Honasan in December 1989, he condemned the U.S. action as morally wrong because it would mean more bloodshed. The intervention also arguably decreased President Aquino's long-term ability to survive. As a columnist in a pro-Aquino Manila newspaper wrote in the aftermath, "When a government cannot overcome a rebellion without 'outside' help, I hope that this does not make it a colony, a satrapy, or a banana republic all over again" (*Time,* 12/11/89:51). Short-term victory may also cause long-term diplomatic loss. In addition to concerns about continuing to conduct international relations through the use of armed force, there is the damage done to the international image of the intervening power. The United States won a military victory in Panama and ousted Noriega, but Washington did so at the cost of condemnation by both the Organization of American States and the United Nations. Even though many Americans thought the operation was on behalf of a just cause, many in Latin America and elsewhere viewed it as simply another instance of big power muscle-flexing, one more example of Yankee imperialism.

The Arms Trade as Intervention

The international supply of arms is big business, involving tens of billions of dollars. The arms trade is a multifaceted issue and might be considered part of the use of military force (chapter 10) or an economic factor under exports and imports or even, in some

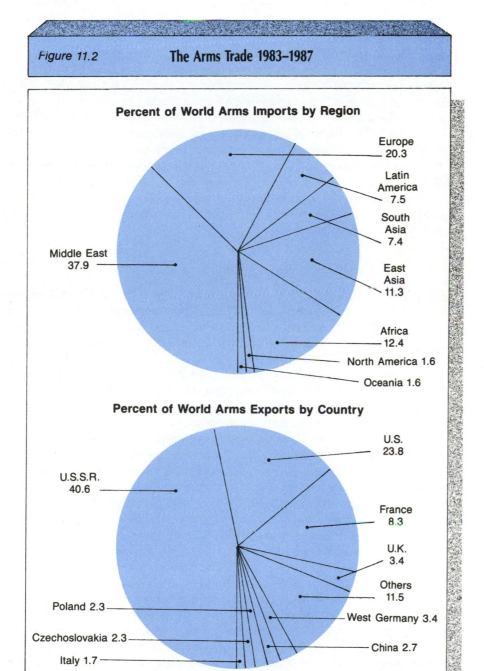

Figure 11.2   **The Arms Trade 1983–1987**

Percent of World Arms Imports by Region

Europe 20.3
Latin America 7.5
South Asia 7.4
East Asia 11.3
Middle East 37.9
Africa 12.4
North America 1.6
Oceania 1.6

Percent of World Arms Exports by Country

U.S. 23.8
U.S.S.R. 40.6
France 8.3
U.K. 3.4
Others 11.5
Poland 2.3
West Germany 3.4
Czechoslovakia 2.3
China 2.7
Italy 1.7

Data source: U.S. ACDA (1988).

The total 1983–87 arms trade with the Third World amounted to $237 billion in current dollars. The United States and the Soviet Union were the primary exporters, while Middle East countries were the primary importers.

cases, foreign aid (chapter 13).[1] The international flow of arms can also be considered a form of penetration and intervention because, whether intended or not, it has an impact on events within countries and between countries (other than the supplier). This is particularly true where the exports are to countries in the Third World.

Of the total $237.7 billion world arms imports between 1983 and 1987, $188.1 billion (79.1 percent) came into Third World countries. During these five years, Iraq was by far the largest arms importer ($29.9 billion), followed by Saudi Arabia ($18.3 billion), India ($11.0 billion), Syria ($10.4 billion), and Iran ($8.9 billion). Regional percentages of arms imports are shown in Figure 11.2 on page 309.

The arms that flowed in the world largely came from the developed countries, as also is evident in Figure 11.2. The Soviet Union gave or sold 40.6 percent ($96.4 billion) of the arms, and the United States exported 23.8 percent ($54.6 billion) of the arms. The only LDC with arms exports over 1 percent of the world total was China, with 2.7 percent ($6.5 billion) of the transfers.

The Arms Trade in Support of International Warfare

One way that the arms trade intervenes is through support of international warfare between other countries. Until recently the U.S. supply of Israel and the Soviet supply of Syria, for example, were partly a method of fighting through "surrogates." In a sense the arms trade also intervened in the affairs of Israel and Syria by strengthening them and arguably making them more bellicose.

Often the flow of arms into an international war situation is predicated in substantial part on the desire for profit rather than on political considerations. As Figure 11.3 shows, a large number of countries sold weapons to both Iraq and Iran in their long, bitter conflict. Total deliveries to the two warring countries during 1980–87 amounted to $55.1 billion, with the Soviet Union the biggest single supplier, delivering $20.2 billion worth of arms (mostly to Iraq). France, China, North Korea, West Germany, and perhaps others were also multibillion-dollar suppliers, although the extensive use of intermediary arms brokers by the Iranians masks some totals.

There can be little doubt that Third World countries have legitimate defense needs, but it is also true that the massive flow of arms to LDCs has increased the level and perhaps frequency of violence. In the decade 1978–87, weapons deliveries to LDCs included among other systems 20,660 tanks, 5,563 jet combat aircraft, and 44,859 surface-to-surface missiles (Neuman, 1989). The 1990–91 Middle East crisis increased this flow. A $20-billion arms deal was concluded in September 1990 to send 385 U.S. main battle tanks, 24 F-15 fighters and a host of other heavy weapons to Saudi Arabia. Egypt was promised hundreds of U.S. tanks, Israel was promised F-15s and Patriot air-defense missiles (to offset, in part, the Saudis' new F-15s), and the list goes on with London, Paris, Moscow, and other capitals joining Washington in the search for new arms sales. One estimate is that if all pending deals are consummated, U.S. sales alone to the region could reach $30 billion for 1991 (*CSM,* 10/17/90:18).

The end of the cold war and the resulting decline in defense spending in many countries has heightened pressure to increase foreign arms sales. The Soviets earn needed foreign exchange currency through foreign weapons sales, and in the United States some arms companies such as McDonnell-Douglas and General Dynamics have foreign sales amounting to 10 percent or more of total sales in some years. France, Great

---

1. For an excellent symposium on the arms trade, see the summer issue of the *Journal of International Affairs* (1987:40:1).

Britain, and some other countries are even more dependent on weapons sales. In the early 1980s up to 42.5 percent of all French arms production was sold abroad, and the figure for the British was about 30 percent. Third World countries such as China and Brazil have also become enthusiastic merchants in the international arms bazaar. In the mid-1980s, for instance, arms sales accounted for 6.3 percent of all China's exports, which include weapons such as the M-1B surface-to-surface missile, produced solely for export (Krause, 1989).

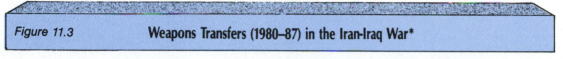

Figure 11.3   **Weapons Transfers (1980–87) in the Iran-Iraq War***

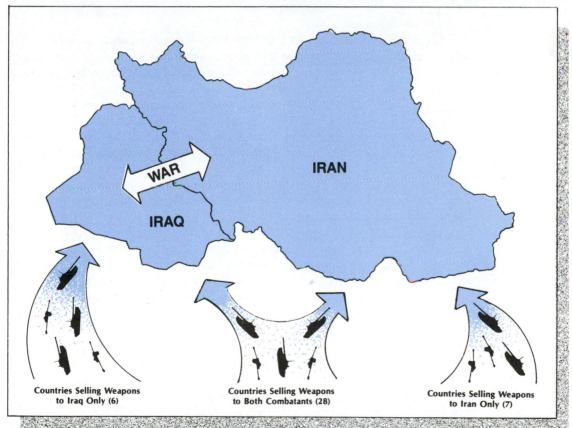

Countries Selling Weapons to Iraq Only (6)   Countries Selling Weapons to Both Combatants (28)   Countries Selling Weapons to Iran Only (7)

*Weapons transfers include weapons, ammunition, and explosives. Still other countries sold military support equipment or supplied advisers during the war.

Data sources: SIPRI (1987); U.S. ACDA (1988).

Without an eager willingness by many countries to sell weapons to the combatants, the Iran-Iraq War would have almost certainly been shorter and less severe. Most countries sold weapons to both sides. One irony is that many of the weapons sold to Iraq in the 1980s were in August 1990 deployed against the troops of the countries that exported the weapons to Iraq. This includes F-6 and F-7 fighters bought from Egypt, Milan antitank missiles from France, 155mm howitzers from Saudi Arabia, and Saboteur armored vehicles from Great Britain. Indeed, some of the tanks that clanked into Kuwait from Iraq were Chieftan-5s—produced by Great Britain, sold to Kuwait, and resold to Iraq by the Kuwaitis.

The Arms Trade in Support of Civil and Guerrilla Warfare

The incidence of civil war and intervention. Far from being minor, civil wars are lethal and, by most estimates, account for more battle deaths than wars between states (especially if the two world wars are factored out). There is also evidence that internal violence is on the rise. Between the end of World War II and 1980 some 44 civil wars broke out, for an average of 1.3 per year, the highest for any period since the end of the Napoleonic era in 1815. Furthermore, civil wars as a percentage of all world conflict have increased by about 20 percent over the 1816–1945 period and now account for about two-thirds of all mass conflict. A third discouraging statistic is that the length of civil wars has increased. During the 1816–1945 period, the average civil war lasted a bit less than a year; between 1945 and 1980 the average civil war went on for a little over three years (DeMars, 1990). Data does not exist on the historical level of arms transfers, but the massive sale of arms is an increasing phenomenon, and it can therefore be at least suggested that there is a relationship between arms transfers and the frequency and length of internal conflict.

Given the high frequency of civil war and the fact that outside countries often support one or both sides, it follows that internal war is a concern of the international community. In fact the two superpowers, who are the primary interveners, involved themselves in about 50 percent (31 of 59) of the civil wars fought between 1945 and 1987. U.S. interventions were mostly (81 percent) on the side of the government, while the Soviet Union's were split evenly between government and opposition. The impetus behind intervening is evident in the fact that of those civil wars that have ended, the interveners were successful in approximately 75 percent of the cases (Sensi, 1988).

The role of guerrilla warfare. One of the hallmarks of civil war is that the opposition often fights using guerrilla tactics. Often these are confused with terrorism, and it is important to distinguish between the two. Not all guerrillas are terrorists, nor are all terrorists guerrillas.

Guerrillas are part of an organized force that uses hit-and-run tactics to attack a superior military force. In a strict sense, any army can contain guerrilla elements (like the Green Berets in Vietnam), but in common usage, guerrilla usually refers to a rebel force that is using irregular tactics to try to bring down its country's government.

Terrorists, by contrast, are individuals or groups who use tactics such as assassination, kidnapping, and bombing to achieve a political goal. The goal may be as broad as the overthrow of a government. Or the goal may be much more specific, as in terror tactics in the Middle East and elsewhere aimed at gaining the release of captured terrorists held in Israel, West Germany, and other countries. More will be said about terrorism presently.

The confusion between guerrillas and terrorists comes because guerrillas sometimes use terror tactics as part of their campaigns. This is because both groups are faced with much the same problem—namely, defeating an opponent that is much stronger. To do this, it is often necessary to attack opponents where they are weakest, rather than meeting their strengths head-on as in conventional warfare. Tactics include elements of both terror and propaganda, but the goal is the same: to break down an opponent's military and civilian morale and support.

Guerrillas and terrorists attack supply, communications, and transportation facilities. They also attack lightly defended outposts or patrols or individual members of the military/police. Guerrillas and terrorists also sometimes use random violence against civilians, either to get others to comply or to create a state of fear that will erode the public's faith in the ability of the government to protect them and, in turn, lead to a breakdown in governmental authority and control. In this sense, as noted in chapter 10,

The increase of guerrilla warfare results from many factors, including the desire of one country to intervene in another country's affairs and the comparative ease of obtaining weapons. The leftist rebel member of the National Revolutionary Movement (FMLN by its Spanish initials) shown here is holding her position against government troops in San Salvador, the capital of El Salvador. The FMLN has received support from the Soviet Union, Cuba, and Nicaragua, but note that the weapon shown here is a U.S. M-16 made in Hartford, Connecticut.

guerrilla and especially terror tactics depend heavily on the ability to hurt rather than the ability to defeat.

Propaganda is another key element of guerrilla activity. To achieve their goals, guerrillas (at least successful ones) use propaganda methods to win popular support and undermine loyalty to the government. Mao Zedong once observed that in order to prosper, guerrillas need to "swim" among the people like fish in the sea. Mao's point is that popular support will greatly strengthen guerrillas by providing intelligence, food and other supplies, and hiding places. Popular opposition will almost certainly doom a guerrilla movement.

Increasingly, guerrilla movements also use propaganda methods to win international support, which can be vital in gaining money and political support from outside governments. They distribute literature, make speakers available, hold press conferences for foreign journalists, and even invite reporters to join them and observe their (most commendable) activities. Dan Rather of CBS, for example, was spirited inside Afghanistan, where he darkened his face, donned the distinctive Afghan garb, and traveled with the guerrillas to bring back their story. It was a million-dollar press coup for the Afghan guerrillas.

The increase in guerrilla warfare. Most analysts agree that guerrilla warfare is becoming increasingly common. One cause is the growth of mass armies and military technology. In the days when armies were small and weapons were primarily swords or rifles, the difference in weaponry between government and rebel forces was limited. Today, governments use tanks, aircraft, and other sorts of sophisticated weapons with greater firepower and longer ranges usually unavailable to insurgents, who, therefore, increasingly must adopt guerrilla tactics. A second factor is that the advances in army strength and technology have a dangerous flaw: they require more repair parts and other logistics support. Therefore, modern weapons make the military much more dependent on its supply lines, which are primary targets for guerrilla strikes.

A third cause of the increased use of guerrilla tactics is that outside countries supports guerrilla activity because it avoids the label of aggression. Instead of directly trying to overthrow the Sandinistas in Nicaragua, for example, the United States supported the Contra rebels. Even though the support was overt, it avoided the avalanche of criticism that an invasion would have brought. A fourth, and closely related, factor in increased insurgency is the willingness of outside forces to supply rebels. In particular, this has been a trademark of the communist support of revolution, but under the Reagan Doctrine, the United States supported rebels attempting to overthrow leftist governments in Latin America, Africa, and Asia. Outside support is also spurred by the desire of the more established powers to fight "proxy" wars and avoid direct involvement, especially if there is a risk of confrontation with another major power. Soviet and Chinese support of the Vietcong was an effective effort that temporarily weakened their prime international opponent, the United States. Similarly, Western aid was dispatched to the rebels in Afghanistan as a way of tormenting the Soviets.

The dangers of arms sales. Supplying weapons to guerrillas may avoid direct military intervention, but it has its drawbacks. One, of course, is the expense. A second is the chance that the weapons you supply today will be used against you tomorrow. The CIA's arms-supply program to the Afghan rebels illustrates the difficulties of controlling the use of weapons. At least 20 to 30 percent of the $2 billion in arms meant for the Afghan rebels through 1988 never arrived at their destination. For example, 29 of 40 Swiss Oerlikon anti-aircraft guns went astray out of a $50-million CIA purchase. Furthermore, of those weapons that did reach Afghanistan, a significant number were sold. These include Stinger surface-to-air missiles, one of the United States' most sophisticated missiles. Ironically, some of the funds gained by the rebels were used to buy Soviet-made AK-47 automatic rifles. These were the principal infantry weapons of both sides in the struggle and were for sale at about $1,400 each in the Peshwar arms bazaar in Pakistan.

Where did all the missing U.S.–supplied weaponry go? The Soviet Union is one place. When the Soviets began to withdraw from Afghanistan in May 1988, one of their officials boasted that his country had acquired several Stingers for analysis. Other Stingers wound up in Iran, sold to the Shi'ite government there by Shi'ite factions among the Afghan rebels. At least one of these missiles was used in October 1987 to attack a U.S. Navy helicopter patrolling in the Persian Gulf.

Still other weapons wound up in the arsenals of criminals. Drug merchants in Pakistan are particularly well armed; one displayed one of the missing Oerlikon anti-aircraft guns on the roof of his place of business. Observed a U.S. drug-enforcement official in Pakistan, "Every doper [here] has got [heavy weapons]. I mean, dope peddlers anywhere in the world are going to have guns, but these guys are armed to the teeth. . . . Where do you think the weapons come from? Allah?" (*HC*, 2/22/88:A1).

Terrorism as a Form of Intervention

It is a mistake to view most terrorism as meaningless and random violence carried out by crazy fanatics. To the contrary, terrorism is usually the result of calculated acts carried out for political reasons. Most people condemn terrorism as immoral, but this does not mean that terrorists are psychopaths; most are not. Therefore, it is important to examine terrorism in its political context. To do that we will explore the incidence, sources, causes, techniques, and impact of terrorism and the methods of responding to it.

The incidence of terrorism. A variety of measures can be used to gauge the level of terrorism. One is the frequency of terrorist acts. Generally, terrorism has increased in frequency during the last quarter-century. The number of attacks rose from 165 in 1968, to 496 in 1981, to 782 in 1985, to 856 in 1988. It should be noted that these figures are a minimum number insofar as they are based on U.S. statistics and do not include acts such as the U.S. attempt to kill Libya's leader Muammar Qaddafi in an F-111 bombing raid on his home in 1986, which some would label as a terrorist act. If there is any good news in all of this it is that terrorist attacks declined by 38 percent to 528 incidents during 1989. Whether this is a trend or an anomaly is not yet clear.

Deaths due to terrorism are another measure. Perhaps 6,500 people have died from terrorist attacks and another 11,500 have been wounded during the past quarter-century. This includes the 270 holiday travelers killed in one of the most tragic and spectacular terrorist attacks in recent years: the December 21, 1988, bombing of Pan Am flight 103 over Lockerbie, Scotland. While individually and collectively these deaths are a tragedy, the statistics need to be kept in perspective. They represent a small fraction of the people who died in Africa last year from starvation or the 1 million Iraqis and Iranians who died or were wounded during their countries' long war. Indeed, the total of terrorist-caused deaths since 1968 is only about half of those caused in the United States by drunk drivers in 1989 alone. The point here is not to diminish those who have died in terrorist attacks, but to understand the psychological, ability-to-hurt techniques and impact of terrorism that we will discuss presently.

Geographically, most terrorist attacks (40–45 percent in any given recent year) occur in the Middle East. Slightly less than 30 percent occur in Europe, and about 15 percent happen in Latin America. There are very few terrorist attacks in Canada or the United States, although Americans are apt to be targets in other parts of the world. Figures for 1989 show that 31 percent of all terrorist attacks were against American targets, and 64 percent of all attacks on American targets occurred in Latin America. Only 16 Americans were killed in 1989 and 19 were injured, but this was an unusually low figure, having declined from 192 killed and 40 wounded in 1988 (U.S. Department of State, 1990). Political figures and business leaders are the most frequent targets, with each category being the object of about a quarter of all terrorist attacks.

The sources of terrorism. Transnational groups such as the Japanese Red Army, Italy's Red Brigade, or various Muslim factions use terrorism to gain recognition for their causes. Even more worrisome is **state terrorism**: terrorism carried out directly by, or specifically encouraged and funded by, an established government. Countries such as Libya, Syria, and Iran have been widely accused of supporting terrorism. In 1988, for instance, hijackers forced the landing of an airliner in Iran where passengers said the terrorists took on a variety of heavy weapons with the open assistance of Iranian authorities before flying on to Algeria where they murdered a passenger.

Despite repeated denials by Washington and Moscow there is repeated evidence that both superpowers have engaged in state terrorism and continue to do so. In the 1960s, for instance, the CIA encouraged the Cosa Nostra, especially through Chicago mob boss Sam Giancana, to assassinate Fidel Castro; and the U.S.–sponsored Phoenix program in Vietnam led to the assassination of a large number of Vietcong officials in order to collect the price that the CIA had put on their heads. In the 1980s there were reports that the CIA was involved in a car-bomb attack on a Muslim leader in Lebanon, and a CIA-sponsored manual advocated the "neutralization" of Sandinista leaders in Nicaragua. Most recently, the U.S. Air Force chief of staff was fired in 1990 in part for disclosing that the United States was contemplating an air attack to kill Iraq's Saddam Hussein and his family. The Soviets similarly have engaged in such activities. In

Although it has never been proved, it may well be that even the pope has been the target of state-sponsored terrorist assassination. Pope John Paul II is shown here minutes after he was shot in St. Peter's square in May 1981 by Mehmet Ali Agca, a Turkish terrorist. There were charges that Ali Agca had connections to the Bulgarian secret service and, through them, to the Soviet KGB. The assassination attempt may have been a Soviet response to the impact of the first Polish pope on Polish nationalism and the Poles' resistance to their communist government.

Those who report on terrorism face a dilemma. Media exposure works to the advantage of terrorists insofar as they rely on the media to spread news about, and fear of, their attacks. Yet, in a free society with a free press, we are entitled to know what is happening. The line for press responsibility is very fine. Some people argue that NBC anchorman Tom Brokaw stepped over that line when he conducted a live interview with Abul Abbas. Just 6 months earlier, Abbas had allegedly masterminded the attack on the cruise ship *Achille Lauro* that resulted in the murder of an elderly invalid American tourist.

December 1979 a KGB assault force wearing Afghan army uniforms stormed the residence of Afghanistan's communist prime minister Hafizullah Amin, whom Moscow considered a weak leader, and murdered him. The KGB officer who led the attack ordered all witnesses shot, and with ironic justice the Soviet colonel (wearing an Afghan uniform) was killed by his own troops in the wild gunfire that followed. Persistent stories have also linked the KGB to the 1981 shooting of Pope John Paul with the help of Bulgarian agents and Turkish fanatics.

The causes of terrorism. The causes of terrorism are complex and controversial, and we can only begin to address them here (Sederberg, 1989). At one level we can say that terrorism occurs because many of those who use it consider it a necessary and legitimate tool to rid themselves of what they consider oppression. The notorious Palestinian terrorist Abu Nidal argued, for example, that his tactics are necessary because the weaponry available to Israel means that "neither the Palestinians nor the PLO will ever be in a position to achieve a military victory over the Zionists." This fact also justifies to Abu Nidal the use of terror tactics because "fair struggle means the right of a people to fight against the usurpation of their land by all available means" (*Der Spiegel*, No. 42, 1985).

From a different perspective, terrorism occurs because it sometimes accomplishes its ends. One aim of terrorism is to gain attention for its cause. It regularly accomplishes that because, in part, the media conveys the terrorists' images and messages. To a degree, there is a relation between terrorist acts and their impact that is related to the old question, "If a tree falls in the forest, and there is nobody there to hear it, does it make a sound?" Similarly, the aim of terror is often not to terrorize those who are attacked but rather to intimidate others. In this sense, there can be little doubt that media reporting supports terrorist activity; but we can also surely support a free press that reports all important events. This uncertain balance between the importance of a free press and not aiding terrorism creates significant dilemmas. Consider the example of anchorman Tom

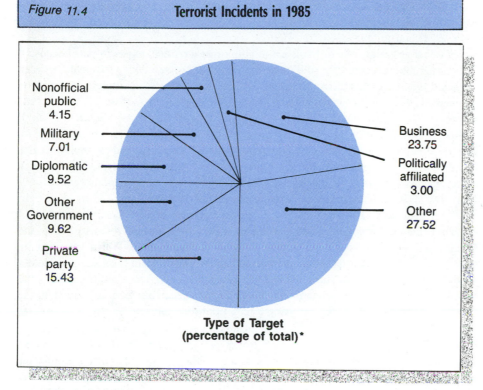

Figure 11.4   **Terrorist Incidents in 1985**

Nonofficial
public
4.15

Military
7.01

Diplomatic
9.52

Other
Government
9.62

Private
party
15.43

Business
23.75

Politically
affiliated
3.00

Other
27.52

**Type of Target
(percentage of total)***

*These percentages are based on numbers that are higher than the total number of incidents because of multiple recordings of victims and/or installations attacked.

Data source: U.S. Department of State (1985a).

Terrorism is aimed at destabilizing political systems and winning recognition of and concessions to terrorist groups and their causes. Terrorism, however, is a relatively minor problem when compared to many other things that threaten humans.

Brokaw's NBC evening news interview of Abdul Abbas, who allegedly masterminded the attack on the Italian cruise ship *Achille Lauro*. That interview added to our information, which is good; it also promoted Abdul Abbas, which many found objectionable. If you were Brokaw, would you have conducted the interview?

The techniques of terrorism. As noted above, terrorists use indirect violence to try to accomplish their ends. That is, the real targets are not those whom they attack. Ninety-five percent of all terrorist actions involve bombings, assassinations, armed attacks, kidnappings, hostage taking, or hijackings, with bombing (50 percent) and hostage taking (33 percent) by far the most common forms of attack. For the most part, though, those murdered or kidnapped are only important, from the terrorists' point of view, insofar as their fates create terror in others, thereby, the terrorists hope, destabilizing the government that is their true target or winning specific concessions. It is this randomness of violence, the impression that no one is safe, that is the essential weapon of terrorists. In fact, as shown in Figure 11.4, only about 7 percent of terrorist attacks were aimed at military figures, and another 12 percent at diplomatic and politically affiliated targets.

The impact of terrorism. It is difficult to measure the impact of terrorism because its effect is primarily indirect. According to one leading authority, however, in the long run most terrorism has made "no political difference one way or another—in some ways, it [has] caused the exact opposite of what the terrorists hoped and intended to achieve" (Laqueur, 1987:246).

Be that as it may, it is difficult not to admit that terrorism exists in part because it does sometimes succeed. One study that analyzed 549 hostage-taking incidents between 1968 and 1984 found that terrorists achieved "logistical success" (completed the mission as planned) 475 times (87 percent) and scored a "negotiated success" (also received some or all of their demands) 147 times (27 percent) (Sadler & Scott, 1987:37). Although most countries have declared they will not negotiate with terrorists, many do. In early 1988, for instance, it was widely reported that France had paid ransom to Iranian or Lebanese Shi'ite extremists for the return of French hostages. Irangate also included an unsuccessful attempt by the Reagan administration to trade weapons (which were sent) to Iran for U.S. hostages (who were not released).

Terrorism can also sometimes succeed on a larger scale. The assassination of Austria-Hungary's archduke Franz Ferdinand in 1914 by a Serbian terrorist group, the Black Hand, led (by a path the terrorists certainly did not foresee, World War I) to the destruction of the Austro-Hungarian Empire and the founding, in a sense, of a greater Serbia (part of present-day Yugoslavia). More recently, the 1983 terrorist bombing of the U.S. Marines barracks in Lebanon that killed 241 servicemen was a key factor in the subsequent withdrawal of U.S. military forces from that country.

Responding to terrorism. The issue of how to respond to terrorism is complex. State terrorism and terrorism carried out by private groups present different issues. So do immediate responses and long-term solutions. Often, especially in the immediate aftermath of a bloody terrorist attack, people are apt to respond viscerally and want to exact biblical, "an eye for an eye" justice. Indeed, a military response may work. Some raids have freed hostages, others have killed or captured terrorists who will terrorize no more, and after the U.S. bombing raid on Libya, terrorism sponsored by the Qaddafi government declined. Related to this hard-line approach is the stand of the United States and many other governments that proclaims that no deals will be made with terrorists. The argument is that you should not reward terrorism, and that doing so will only encourage more terrorism.

Sometimes these positions may be appropriate and successful, but insofar as terrorism is complex, simple solutions are often apt to be inappropriate and unsuccessful. One problem is that the military actions may miss targeted terrorists, result in the deaths of hostages, and kill innocent bystanders. There is also the moral question of whether certain actions make you part of the problem, rather than the solution. The U.S. raid on Libya, even though it was an apparent success in terms of stemming terrorism, has its dark side. On the morning of April 15, 1986, five huge F-111s, each carrying four 2,000-lb bombs, attacked Qaddafi's residence. The Libyan leader was not there, but others were not so lucky. Qaddafi's 15-month-old adopted daughter was killed by the American bombs, as were another 100 people who lived in nearby residential neighborhoods.

There is also doubt about whether the "no concessions" policy actually reduces terrorism. One analyst argued that the U.S. position was "dangerously rigid" and that "U.S. policy toward hostage incidents has actually had little effect on the outcome" (*BG,* 11/5/89:A23). He went on to argue that some countries, such as France, regularly bargain with terrorists, while the Americans and British are particularly resistant to such maneuvers, yet there is no demonstrable shift of terrorist activity away from the hardliners and toward those willing to make concessions.

A last point about responding to terrorism is related to long-term solutions. One approach to ending terrorism is to create an international climate that is intolerant of terrorism. This requires more than rhetorical and military attacks on terrorists who assail you. It also requires that countries that condemn terrorism refrain from it themselves and also condemn the terrorist activities of allies as well as enemies. As suggested in earlier sections of this chapter and in chapter 7, Western countries have not always practiced what they preached about the evils of terrorism. This occasional double standard helps perpetuate the climate of violence and violations of international law that engender terrorism.

Second, while terrorism is immoral by most people's standards, it is not irrational. Therefore, another long-term approach to terrorism is to eliminate the poverty, the political oppression, and the lack of peaceful avenues of change that lead to terrorism. Many terrorists argue they have little other choice; they may not.

In sum, then, as one analyst aptly put it, "Terrorism is diverse in source and form; responses to it must reflect this diversity. Those attempting to deal with terrorism must act with restraint so that the cure does not cripple or kill the patient. They must also act with intelligence; both in the sense of military/police intelligence and the wisdom to recognize what they confront" (Sederberg, 1989:158).

Chapter Summary

1. Not all of international relations is carried on between governments through accepted channels. Some interactions are carried on clandestinely and/or are aimed at changing the internal workings of another state.

2. Spying, propaganda, and fomenting trouble among your opponents have long existed as tools of international relations.

3. In recent years, however, penetration and intervention have become more important aspects of international relations than they once were. There is an increased need to monitor what other countries are doing. There have also been advances in the ability to gather information and the ability to manipulate the internal situation of others.

4. Internal activity can be roughly divided into information gathering, noncoercive manipulation, and coercive intervention.

5. Contrary to popular images, most information gathering is carried on through overt means, which range in sophistication from public media monitoring to the use of satellites and other national technical means.

6. Covert information gathering, though a minor activity, is also important. Again, techniques range from traditional human agents who engage in James Bondian spying to the use of highly sophisticated and secret national technical means.

7. Propaganda, or broadcasting information—some true, most altered—at a target audience, has great potential because of new understanding of psychological factors, advanced techniques, and the greater impact of the people on policy in many countries.

8. Coercive intervention is the most troubling aspect of the activities discussed in this chapter. It involves secret attempts to disrupt an opponent internally. Limited military intervention, the support of guerrilla warfare, and even terrorism are among its techniques.

9. Few support such activities in the abstract, but when discussed relatively, as a choice among perhaps greater evils, such practices become more difficult to condemn (or support) absolutely.

The better part of valor is discretion.

Shakespeare, *Henry IV*, Part I

And sheathed their swords for lack of argument.

Shakespeare, *Henry V*

Blessed are the peacemakers on earth.

Shakespeare, *Henry VI*, Part II

To jaw-jaw is better than to war-war.

Winston Churchill, June 26, 1954

CHAPTER 12

DIPLOMACY

We often think of diplomacy in stereotypic terms. There is an image of somber negotiations over green-felt–covered tables in ornate rooms. Modern diplomacy certainly includes such interactions, but it also extends much further. Indeed, diplomacy includes the entire range of communications between two or more governments.

Diplomacy as Communication

As a *communications process*, diplomacy has three elements. The first element is *negotiation*. When two parties are talking with each other, either directly or through an intermediary, they are negotiating. The second element of diplomacy is *signaling*— saying or doing something with the intent of sending a message to another government. When leaders make bellicose or conciliatory speeches, when military forces are alerted or relaxed, when trade privileges are granted or sanctions invoked, or when diplomatic recognition is extended or relations are broken, these events are, or at least should be, signals. Indeed, the use of military power is a form of signaling. As Clausewitz, the great German military strategist, said, war is not the end of diplomacy but a continuation. Military action can be designed as a signaling process to attain goals rather than to defeat enemies, and nonviolent signals and negotiation should continue during conflict.

Public diplomacy is the third element. Here diplomacy moves away from its traditional mode of communication, which is between governments, and enters the more modern practice of trying to persuade a wider audience, including public opinion in another country and world opinion in general. This comes close to propaganda, but it is distinct in that public diplomacy involves what is actually said and done by political figures, while propaganda includes the follow-up messages put out by information agencies interpreting events and statements by leaders.

The Evolution of Diplomacy

Diplomacy is as old as recorded history and almost certainly even predates it. Modern diplomacy has its origins in the practices of the Greek city-states, and this section will examine their contribution as well as the diplomatic practices of Rome, Byzantium, the Italian city-states, France, and nineteenth-century Europe. This historical review will bring us to about World War I, which marks the transition from the "old" diplomacy to the "new" diplomacy. Current diplomatic trends will then be discussed in the following section.

From Ancient Greece to Eighteenth-Century France

The histories of Greece and Rome hold the origins of diplomatic practice. In the writings of ancient Greece we first encounter many of the terms, such as reconciliation, truce, alliance, and commercial treaty, used in modern diplomacy. Diplomatic missions are also described in the Homeric epics. Ambassadors were dispatched on an ad hoc (case-by-case) basis. Negotiations were conducted orally, but treaties were written. The Greeks also recognized neutrality, used arbitration, and had officials charged with furthering commercial relations. Rules concerning the declaration and conduct of war, maritime practice, the status of aliens, and other principles that remain important today were also evident in Greek practice.

Rome, which practiced conquest more than diplomacy, was important for organizational improvements on Greek practice. Ambassadorial appointments, instructions, and status became more formalized. Diplomatic immunity became more widely recognized, at least in theory. The Romans, with their penchant for laws, also stressed the sanctity of contracts, thus elevating the status of treaties.

The Byzantine Empire, which flourished after Rome's collapse, was noted for the beginnings of "professional" diplomacy. Diplomats were specifically trained as negotiators, and the first department of foreign affairs was established. In an age of chaos, and surrounded by powerful barbarian foes, the Byzantines also emphasized the darker sides of diplomacy, such as deceit and spying. They also created elaborate protocol procedures for military reviews and homage to the emperor designed to enhance beyond reality the image of Byzantine strength.

The diplomacy of the Italian city-states beginning in the fifteenth century is best known for its improvements on the Byzantine practices of cunning and artifice. The names Niccolò Machiavelli of Florence and Cosimo de' Medici, duke of Florence, are synonymous with scheming conduct. Machiavelli counseled in *The Prince* (1532) that it was best to be as powerful as a lion and as sly as a fox and summed up his estimation of human nature with the observation that one "must start with assuming that all men are bad and ever ready to display their vicious nature whenever they may find occasion for it."

The Italian city-states also made more positive contributions to the evolution of diplomacy. They first established permanent diplomatic missions. Treaty making and protocol were improved. Summit meetings were also introduced as a diplomatic practice.

The French system is the direct predecessor of modern diplomacy. This system is strongly identified with the contributions of Cardinal Richelieu in the seventeenth century. He was the first to see diplomacy as an ongoing process rather than an expedience. He also began the practice of building public opinion support. Honoring treaties became an ethical as well as a pragmatic responsibility. Richelieu also insisted on precision in drafting agreements and consolidated all foreign affairs functions under one ministry.

Under Louis XIV, the minister of foreign affairs became a member of the king's cabinet, and permanent embassies were established in all the major capitals, with lesser-ranked missions in minor capitals. It was also during this era that the first diplomatic manual *On the Manner of Negotiating with Sovereigns* (1716) was written by François de Callierres.

Diplomacy in Nineteenth-Century Europe

The post-Napoleonic international conferences at Vienna (1815) and Aix-la-Chapelle (1818) were important in codifying the status and functions of diplomatic agents. The nineteenth century was also both the height and the beginning of the end of the "old" style of diplomacy. Kings and emperors still held sway, for example, but the American and French revolutions signaled the onset of the decline and fall of that system. Diplomacy of that day was characterized by Eurocentrism, great-power status, executive control, elite conduct, secrecy, and bilateral negotiations (Nicholson, 1979:43).

The 1800s were Eurocentric, with Europe at the center of the political globe. America was isolated behind its oceans, and the rest of the world was either impotent or colonized. The six great powers (Great Britain, France, Italy, Austria-Hungary, Prussia-Germany, and Russia) were considered to have both special status and special responsibilities.[1] Lesser states were bullied and sometimes divided up among the big six. Intervention and imperialism were common. The powers also had a special ability to maintain order, both by "policing" minor powers and colonial dependencies and by consulting and maintaining a balance of power among themselves. It was a system that worked reasonably well for a century before it collapsed catastrophically with World War I.

Foreign policy-making was still under executive control, that is, it was dominated by the king. In the previous century Louis XIV had quite literally believed, "I am the state." (*L'état c'est moi*.) And although Richelieu had concerned himself with public opinion, and while legislatures were gaining power in Britain and America, democracy in the nineteenth century was still the exception rather than the rule. Foreign policy was conducted by elites. The diplomatic corps was recruited exclusively from the nobility and gentry. It was an era when that class had shared values and members who were often related. Great Britain's King Edward VII, Germany's Kaiser Wilhelm II, and Russia's Czar Nicholas II were relatives. Nationalism was developing, but to a substantial degree the elite diplomats were "men of Europe" who had as much loyalty, or more, to the "system" of elite and great-power dominance as they did to their national entities. In part, this elitism provided a common frame of reference and a mutual confidence that benefited negotiations.

Diplomacy was further marked by secrecy. Diplomats of the nineteenth century adhered to the belief that public negotiations caused undue posturing and a reluctance to compromise. Negotiations were almost always confidential and treaties were often secret. Although there were a few noted multilateral conferences, such as the Congress

---

1. Italy became a great power toward the end of the century. Spain was in a twilight zone, no longer a great power but to a degree living on past glory. Turkey was a power but declining and outside the confines of Europe. The United States had yet to assert itself.

of Vienna, **bilateral diplomacy** (direct negotiations between two countries) was the normal form of negotiation. Practitioners felt not only that conference diplomacy was slow and cumbersome but also that it confused the power relationships on which international relations hinged.

Modern Diplomacy

Although diplomatic practice has evolved slowly over the centuries, the years around World War I—symbolized by Woodrow Wilson's Fourteen Points—are generally recognized as a benchmark in the transition to modern diplomacy as part of the modern political era. The Great War was the beginning of the end of European world dominance. It also marked the fall of the German, Austrian, Ottoman, and Russian emperors. Nationalistic self-determination was on the rise in Europe and other parts of the world. New powers—the United States, Japan, and China—were beginning to assert themselves, and they joined or replaced the declining European powers. The "old diplomacy" did not vanish, but it was substantially changed in the decades following the "war to end all wars." As will become clear, the "new diplomacy" is characterized by an expansion of geographic scope, multilateral diplomacy, parliamentarianism, democratization, open diplomacy, leader-to-leader diplomacy, and public diplomacy. Each of these new practices has been greeted as a "reform," but as we will see, the changes have not necessarily been for the better.

Expansion of Geographic Scope

The diplomacy of the twentieth century has been marked by expansion of its geographic scope. The two Hague Conferences (1899, 1907) on peace, particularly the second, with its 44 participants, included countries outside the European sphere. President Wilson's call for national self-determination foreshadowed a world of over 170 countries. Today, the United Nations, with its nearly universal membership, symbolizes the truly global scope of diplomacy.

Multilateral Diplomacy

Although conferences involving a number of nations occurred at times during the nineteenth century, that practice has expanded greatly in the modern era. The rise of **multilateral diplomacy** is symbolized by Woodrow Wilson's call for a League of Nations. There are now a number of permanent world and regional international organizations. Ad hoc conferences and treaties are also more apt to be multilateral. Before 1900, for example, the United States attended an average of one multilateral conference per year. In recent years, American diplomats have averaged more than one such conference per day (Plischke, 1979).

Multilateral diplomacy has increased for several reasons. Technological progress is one. Advances in travel and communications technology allow faster and more frequent contacts among countries. Second, multilateral diplomacy has increased because more countries and leaders recognize that many of the issues, such as arms levels, the environment, and economic growth, facing the world cannot be solved through the domestic policies of any one country or through traditional bilateral diplomacy alone. Instead, global cooperation and solutions are required. Third, diplomacy through multilateral organizations has been attractive to smaller countries as a method of influencing world politics beyond their individual power. One study of Canadian multilateralism, for example, observed that it is through "coalitions with other middle powers [that Canada] . . . can exercise an influence on policy-making and seek to catalyze change" (Doxey, 1989:29).

A fourth reason behind multilateral diplomacy is the existence of numerous multilateral organizations, such as the United Nations, and increased international criticism of unilateral decision-making, especially involving the use of force. These have increased pressure to obtain at least symbolic multilateral cooperation. The United States clearly valued the participation in Operations Desert Shield and Desert Storm of Egypt, Syria, and other Muslim states in order to defuse the image of a non-Muslim, developed country attacking a Muslim, Third World country. The United Nations also became important in the U.S. strategy, and Washington worked hard to get the UN Security Council first to condemn Iraq's invasion of Kuwait and post-invasion actions, and then to obtain UN authorization for the January 1991 offensive move to oust Iraq from Kuwait. It is also clear that Egypt, a U.S. military ally in the war, and the Soviet Union, which has a key Security Council role, both desired to give diplomacy and economic sanctions a full chance to work, and their wishes restrained for awhile the inclinations in Washington to move quickly to the attack.

Parliamentary Diplomacy

A vehicle of diplomacy, **parliamentary diplomacy**, which includes debate and voting in international organizations, now sometimes supplants negotiation, compromise, and accord. Furthermore, with the decline of the legitimacy of great-power special status and responsibility, voting is often done on the basis of sovereign equality. China and Chad, for example, each cast one vote in the UN General Assembly. The old system has not completely died out, however, and the UN Security Council, dominated by the five permanent members and their veto power, is the primary example (see chapter 15).

The role of parliamentary diplomacy was strongly evident during the crisis that followed Iraq's invasion of Kuwait. Because of the veto power in the Security Council, the United States and Great Britain, both of which favored strong action, had to move cautiously to gain consent to resolutions by the other 3 permanent members and the 10 nonpermanent members of the council. In the aftermath of an incident during which Israeli security forces killed a score of rock-throwing Palestinian protesters in the West Bank, the United States also had to refrain from vetoing the council's condemnation of Israel and call for a UN investigation. Blocking these proposals might have weakened Washington's ability to get the Security Council to go along with condemnations of Iraq and the authorization to attack after January 15, 1991.

Democratization

The elite and executive-dominant character of diplomacy has changed in a number of ways. One is that diplomats are now drawn from a wider segment of each country's society. This has the advantage of making diplomats more representative of their nations and more sympathetic to the individuals therein. It also means, though, that diplomats have lost their common frame of reference once provided by their similar cosmopolitan, elite backgrounds. Diplomats are now more likely to have their attitudes rooted in their national cultures and are more apt to suffer from the antagonisms and misperceptions that nationalistic stereotyping causes.

A second democratic change is the rise of the roles of legislatures and public opinion in foreign policy-making. Executive leadership still dominates this process, but it is no longer the exclusive domain of princes, presidents, and prime ministers. The rise in representative and popular power is certainly in accord with democratic theory, but it has its drawbacks. Democracy is too often impatient, crusading, and xenophobic, and executives have lost a degree of flexibility. For example, concern in Washington that Americans would not support a prolonged confrontation with Iraq increased the pressure on the Administration to order an attack.

This question of the proper balance between executive leadership and input from other political actors, such as legislatures and the public, is the source of debate in many countries. Some members of the Supreme Soviet have criticized the new constitutional language that gives the Soviet president the authority to go to war. There is a similar concern in the United States; during the 1990–91 Middle East crisis members of Congress and other U.S. commentators expressed increasing concern that the Bush administration would launch a war against Iraq without congressional authorization. In an interesting commentary on comparative democracy, Soviet foreign minister Eduard Shevardnadze assured his country's legislature that "any use of Soviet troops outside the country demands a decision of the Soviet Parliament" (*NYT,* 10/16/90:A18). By contrast, U.S. secretary of state James Baker told Congress that while he hoped to include it in a decision, "I cannot give you a blank-check commitment that we will, in every case, do nothing until we have consulted with . . . Congress" (*NYT,* 10/26/90:A1). Apart from jealousy of its asserted constitutional authority, the White House was reluctant to seek a supporting congressional resolution for fear, according to one source, that "if you brought [a resolution] . . . to a vote . . . , you would have a significant number of votes [in Congress] against it, and that would be a crack—a significant one—in the policy we're now engaged in. That would not be a good signal at this time" (*CSM,* 9/24/90:1). In the final week before the war broke out, Congress did take up the issue, and by a wide vote in the House and close vote (52–47) in the Senate did give Bush the authority (which he asserted he already had) to act. The issue of who in Washington has the war power remained unresolved.

Open Diplomacy

Of Wilson's Fourteen Points, his call for "open covenants, openly arrived at" is the best remembered. One advantage of **open diplomacy** is that it fits nicely with the idea of democracy. It also has the potential of avoiding perceptual errors that can occur if an opponent misjudges your commitments. Offsetting these advantages are several drawbacks. The majority of scholarly and practitioner commentary favors both open discussion of foreign policy goals and publications of treaties. It is the "openly arrived at," or negotiation phase, that is troublesome. Here, most analysts agree that confidentiality is important. Early disclosure of your bargaining strategy will compromise your ability to win concessions. Public negotiations are also more likely to lead diplomats to posture for public consumption. Concessions may be difficult to make amid popular criticism. In sum, it is difficult to negotiate (or to play chess) with someone kibitzing over your shoulder. Secret diplomacy is also a way to pursue a policy that is under heavy fire from domestic critics. Just weeks after the massacre of Chinese students in Tiananmen Square by the government, and amid strong calls in the United States for sanctions against China, the Bush administration sent a secret mission to China. National security adviser Brent Scowcroft and Deputy Secretary of State Lawrence Eagleburger traveled to Beijing to reassure Deng Xiaoping and other top Chinese leaders that U.S.

There is less secret diplomacy than there once was, but it still exists. Ironically, the secret is not always being kept from the opponent: sometimes a government conducts secret diplomacy to avoid criticism by its own citizens. Many Americans were outraged after Chinese troops killed many pro-democracy protesters in Beijing's Tiananmen Square in June 1989. The Bush administration condemned the action and imposed sanctions that included pledges to cut off high-level contacts. Within two months, however, the president sent Deputy Secretary of State Lawrence Eagleburger and National Security Advisor Brent Scowcroft to Beijing to reassure the Chinese government that Washington did not wish relations between the United States and China to deteriorate. The Eagleburger-Scowcroft mission was kept a secret from the American people. Here we can see Scowcroft meeting with Chinese leader Deng Xiaoping during a second (and this time public) visit to Beijing in December 1989.

reactions would be mild. The point that is important here is to note whom this secret mission was a secret from. It was the Administration's domestic critics that were the foe from which the delicate mission had to be hidden.

It should be added that even secret treaties and understandings are not totally without merit. There are times when a desirable agreement cannot be made in public. The agreement ending the 1962 Cuban missile crisis included an oral pledge by the United States to remove missiles from Turkey, a NATO ally. President Kennedy would have found it difficult to give that assurance in public. U.S. involvement in the Vietnam War ended with North Vietnam seeming to agree not to conquer the South forcibly in return for a pledge of 3.5 billion capitalist dollars in U.S. foreign aid. Neither country could have made that agreement in public.

Leader-to-Leader Diplomacy

Modern transportation and communications have spawned an upsurge of high-level diplomacy. National leaders regularly hold bilateral or multilateral summit conferences, and foreign ministers and other ranking diplomats jet between countries, conducting shuttle diplomacy. One hundred thirty years of American history passed before a president (Woodrow Wilson) traveled overseas while in office. Richard Nixon departed on his first state visit to Europe only 33 days after his inauguration. The once-rare instances of meetings between heads of state has become so common that in some cases it has become a routine. The leaders of the Group of Seven (G-7) largest industrialized countries meet annually, for example.

President Bush surpassed the enthusiasm of all his predecessors for leader-to-leader diplomacy by having 135 meetings with other leaders during his first year in office. He left for a Far East tour within weeks of assuming office, has since traveled extensively, and has held scores of meetings with foreign leaders in Washington. The November 1990 meeting between Bush and President Gorbachev in Paris was the 23rd U.S.–U.S.S.R. summit since Franklin Roosevelt first met with Josef Stalin in Teheran, Iran, in

CIRCLING, CIRCLING

IRAQ

Summit meetings between U.S. and Soviet leaders are becoming almost commonplace. There are advantages and disadvantages to the summit process. One possible advantage is that a good working relationship may be established between leaders. This seems true for Presidents Gorbachev and Bush, and it may have helped bring about the unprecedented level of cooperation between Moscow and Washington during the confrontation with Iraq. Only a year or two earlier, when the Soviets supported Iraq as an ally, the 1991 U.S.–led action against Iraq would have been more dangerous, perhaps impossible.

November 1943. Thus, Soviet-American summit meetings have occurred on an average of 1 about every 2.5 years. Counting the meeting in New York while Bush was president-elect, the Bush-Gorbachev meeting in Paris was their fifth face-to-face negotiation, an average of 1 about every 4 months.

In addition to his urge to meet with his counterparts from other countries, President Bush has used the telephone to contact foreign leaders so frequently that this practice has been dubbed "Rolodex diplomacy." During his first year in office, Bush spoke on the telephone with other national leaders about 190 times, including 3 calls to Gorbachev. Other leaders, foreign ministers, and high-ranking diplomatic personnel are also hooked on the telephone, personal meetings, and other rapid communications methods. German chancellor Helmut Kohl likes the telephone and the fax machine, and U.S. secretary of state James Baker uses a 41-line telephone in his inner office to make and receive calls to and from around the world on a regular basis.

The advent of globe-trotting, leader-to-leader diplomacy, or **summitry**, and the increased frequency of Rolodex, telecommunications diplomacy, is a mixed blessing. There are several *advantages*. The first is that leaders can sometimes make dramatic breakthroughs. The 1978 Camp David accords, which began the process of normalizing Egyptian-Israeli relations after decades of hostility and three wars, were produced after U.S. president Jimmy Carter, Egyptian president Anwar Sadat, and Israeli prime minister Menachem Begin isolated themselves at the presidential retreat in Maryland.

Second, advocates of rapid diplomacy believe that it can help dispel false information and stereotypes. President Bush argues that the telephone helps avoid specific misunderstandings. "I want to be sure [that U.S.–U.S.S.R. disagreements are] real and they're based on fact, not misunderstanding," the president explains. "If [Gorbachev] knows the heartbeat a little bit from talking [with me], there's less apt to be misunderstanding" (*Time,* 4/9/90:39). More general cross-cultural stereotypes are also an issue. Ronald Reagan (1990:60) recalls in his memoirs that at his first summit (Geneva, Switzerland, November 1985) with Gorbachev, the Soviet leader believed "a lot of the propaganda he'd heard about America: that munitions makers ruled our country, black people were treated like slaves, half our population slept in the streets." For his part, Reagan's "evil empire" rhetoric and images were equally a caricature of the Soviet leader and his country. Yet the two leaders had the good sense to recognize, as Reagan (p. 62) has written, "that the myths and misconceptions on both sides of the Iron Curtain had contributed to misunderstanding and our potentially fatal mistrust of each other." Less than three years and several summits later (June 1988), the once-consummate cold warrior was in Moscow, confessing, "I never expected to be here" (Rourke, 1990:286). From his peregrinations President Reagan learned "on the streets of Moscow, looking into thousands of faces" and by "talking with ordinary Soviet citizens" that "they were generally indistinguishable from people I had seen all my life on countless streets in America—ordinary people who longed, I am sure, for the same things that Americans did: peace, love, security, a better life for themselves and their children" (Reagan, 1990:73). Progress had been made.

A third advantage of personal contact among leaders is that mutual confidences or even friendships may develop. The public images of the priggish Richard Nixon and the dour Leonid Brezhnev were far from accurate. Behind the closed doors of summit meetings the two found that their shared taste for scatological humor and Brezhnev's love of flashy gold watches, fast cars, and souped-up motorboats provided a basis for the strange comaraderie that developed between the two. Similarly, Reagan (1990:72) recalls that "there was a chemistry between us that produced something very close to a friendship. . . . I liked Gorbachev." By some accounts, that chemistry has worked between Bush and Gorbachev. At their September 1990 summit in Helsinki, Finland, they shared a podium for a statement. Bush stepped to the microphone. It didn't work, and the president whacked it. Still nothing. "Hit it again," Gorbachev suggested, karate-chopping the air. Then Gorbachev tried to say something, and his microphone didn't work either. "Should I hit it again?" Mikhail asked George as, the press reported, they "grinned at each other in an uncommonly warm and fuzzy way" (*NYT,* 9/10/90:A10).

Clear vision and good feelings are laudable, but there are also several potential *disadvantages* to leader-to-leader diplomacy. Former secretary of state Dean Rusk warns that "summit diplomacy is to be approached with the wariness with which a prudent physician prescribes a habit-forming drug—a technique to be employed rarely and under the most unusual circumstances, with rigorous safeguards against its becoming a debilitating or dangerous habit" (Stefan, 1987:31). One concern is that summits may lead to ill-conceived agreements. According to Kissinger (1979:142), "Some of the debacles of our diplomatic history have been perpetrated by Presidents who fancied themselves negotiators." An irony of modern diplomacy is that the interdependent and technical nature of global issues are making them increasingly complex at the very time when leader-to-leader diplomacy is becoming more frequent. There is, one Bush administration official worried, a tendency to oversimplify problems and "we assume five or six people can do anything, and it makes it a lot easier." "But," the official warned, "if we push the experts aside, we suffer in the end" (*WP,* 4/13/90:A7).

A second problem with leader-to-leader diplomacy is that it may lead to misunder-standings. At the U.S.–Soviet summit in Reykjavik, Iceland, in October 1986, Reagan and Gorbachev departed from what had been planned, and began spontaneously to discuss huge cuts in nuclear and conventional weapons. Reagan recalls (1990:69), "I felt something momentous was occurring . . . we were going to achieve something remarkable." As it turned out, he misunderstood Gorbachev's position, and when Reagan's false hopes were dashed by Gorbachev's unwillingness to allow SDI development, Reagan felt betrayed. "I couldn't believe it and blew my top." It was, the president remembers, one of the "most disappointing—and ultimately angriest—days of my presidency." The telephone may present even greater difficulties. Henry Kissinger, for example, argues that "the telephone is generally made for misunderstanding. It is difficult to make a good record. You can't see the other side's expressions or body language" (*WP,* 4/13/90:A7).

Third, while mistakes made by lower-ranking officials can be disavowed by their superiors, a leader's commitments, even if not well thought out, cannot be easily retracted. "When Presidents become negotiators no escape routes are left," Kissinger (1979:12) warns. "Concessions are irrevocable without dishonor." Fourth, and closely related, leaders may make agreements based on their sense of personal goodwill with another leader rather than on the substance of an issue. American politics and culture often lead U.S. presidents to seek very personal relations with other leaders, despite the more formal relationships those leaders' cultures often dictate. The first time Reagan talked with Japan's prime minister he addressed him by the shortened version of his first name, only to discover that such familiarity is considered effrontery in Japan. When Gorbachev first came to the United States in June 1990, Bush initially thought it would be neat for Mikhail to come up to the Bush summer home in Kennebunkport to do a little fishing, pitch a few horseshoes, and maybe even try tennis. The Soviet ambassador quickly quashed the idea. There is in Russian an old proverb, *Sluzhba sluzhboi, druzhba druzhboi,*—"Business is business, friendship is friendship." Still, it is understandable, although not always appropriate, that American presidents are apt to perceive relationships through American culture and imagine they are becoming buddies with their counterparts. Typically, Reagan recalls telling Gorbachev a joke in which an American and a Soviet are discussing their respective political systems. The American says he can go to the White House and criticize Reagan. The Soviet says he can go to the Kremlin and do the same thing; he can say (here's the punch line), "I don't like the way President Reagan is running his country." "Gorbachev howled," Reagan recalls (1990:72), reveling in their goodwill. Another U.S. official who was often present at these meetings remembers it differently. "When Ronald Reagan told his patented funny stories, Gorbachev would roll his eyes, and you could see him thinking 'Oh, no, not another story!' " (*Time,* 7/11/90:17).

Fifth, specific misunderstanding and general chemistry can work to damage working relations between leaders instead of improving them. Kissinger (1979:142), who should know, has observed that most world leaders are characterized by a "healthy dose of ego," and when two such egos collide, "negotiations can rapidly deteriorate from intractability to confrontation." An insensitive remark can also injure feelings. Amid a 1982 Israeli attack on Lebanon, President Reagan called Israel's prime minister Begin to protest. Reagan used the word "holocaust" to characterize the effect of the attack. Begin is a survivor of the World War II Holocaust, and he wrote the next day that the "anger" of Reagan's comments "hurt me personally and deeply, especially through the use of the word 'holocaust,' of which I know some facts that may be unknown to my fellow man" (Reagan, 1990:68). Relations between the two were never the same again. Sixth, and last, the failure of summitry can lead to increased tensions. High-level negotiations create hope; when they collapse, the resulting disappointment and mutual recriminations can leave matters worse than before. If a summit conference is the ultimate negotiation, then its failure makes it seem that no solution is possible. In such a case conflict may be the response (Schaetzel & Malmgren, 1980).

Public Diplomacy

Modern international relations are also increasingly conducted through **public diplomacy**. The communications revolution has placed leaders and other diplomats in public view more than ever before, and their actions have an impact on world opinion that is often distinct from their specific negotiating positions. Additionally, a leader's image has become more important because of the democratization of the foreign policy process discussed above. Thus public diplomacy can be defined as a process of creating an overall international image that enhances a country's ability to achieve diplomatic success.

Scholar Raymond Cohen, for instance, envisions a "theater of power" that is a "metaphor for the répertoire of visual and symbolic tools used by statesmen and diplomats." Cohen continues that leaders "must be sensitive to the impression they make on observers. . . . They surely [are] subject to the same sort of 'dramatic,' if not aesthetic, criticism of other kinds of public performances" (1987:i–ii).

Governments also recognize this change. One official U.S. publication argues that:

> International events are increasingly played out, and their outcome shaped, in the arena of world public opinion. Public diplomacy is part of the worldwide transformation in the conduct of international affairs. . . . [G]overnment-to-government communications [have] become less important as world leaders compete directly for the support of citizens in other countries. . . . Put simply, instant global communications are breaking down rigidities and isolation, and public opinion is increasingly influential in shaping foreign policy. (U.S. Advisory Commission on Public Diplomacy, 1986:10)

The Soviets are also demonstrating a heightened awareness of the potential for public diplomacy, and in Mikhail Gorbachev they have a skilled performer. In the estimate of one British diplomat,

> Public relations have been both an instrument and an integral part of Mr. Gorbachev's foreign policy. He has set out to reburnish the Soviet Union's image. He has innovated; he has been subtle; and he has made it harder to distinguish between propaganda and substance. . . . [Gorbachev] has amply justified . . . George Bush's assessment of him as "an impressive ideas salesman." (Lyne, 1987:218)

Among his other international performances, the Soviet general secretary's flair has been repeatedly evident during his visits to the United States. Prior to arriving for the first time, in December 1987, Gorbachev appeared on U.S. network television in an interview, and while in Washington he played to the mass audience, even alarming his security force by getting out of his car to "press the flesh" with the crowds there. This and similar performances left the Soviet leader with a public opinion standing nearly equal to the hometown star, Ronald Reagan.

Public diplomacy was also very evident during the Middle East crisis that began in August 1990. The clearest example was the taped messages by George Bush and by Saddam Hussein that were aired on the television networks of each other's country. Other examples were only slightly less obvious. The Bush administration issued increasingly stark threats against Iraq and mounted an invasion force on the theory that even if President Hussein would not back down, the pressure might cause his overthrow. The Iraqi president countered, by contrast, with attempts to seem reasonable. Several

Public diplomacy is the attempt by one country to present an image that will influence public opinion in other countries. During the Middle East crisis, both sides used television as part of their public diplomacy campaigns. After detaining foreigners in Iraq and Kuwait as "guests," the Iraqis tried to show their guests were being well treated. Here we see Saddam Hussein, trying hard to look benevolent, with a young British "guest" in an image broadcast on Iraqi television. The boy does not look as if he is convinced that Saddam is his friend.

foreign dignitaries, including President Kurt Waldheim of Austria and former West German chancellor Willy Brandt, traveled to Baghdad to seek the release of hostages; in each case some were released. In a counterpoint, Iraq's ambassador in Washington regularly spoke to the U.S. press, asking why huge numbers of American soldiers should die in the Arabian desert when Iraq had done nothing to the United States.

Given the increased democratization of foreign policy-making, public diplomacy can be a valuable tool. It must be carried out skillfully, however. Saddam Hussein's message to the American people was over an hour long, statically delivered while seated at his desk, and read in a flat voice, emulated by his interpreter. The broadcast was consigned to the wee hours of the morning by the networks, and few Americans saw it. Saddam Hussein also misjudged public reaction when he had himself telecast hosting some of the hostage children. The image telecast was the Iraqi president patting the head of a small British boy. Saddam Hussein undoubtedly saw himself as benevolent; the boy was clearly intimidated, however, and to most of the rest of the world the Iraqi looked chillingly sinister.

Diplomacy: A Game of Angels and Devils

Ambassador William Macomber (1975) has described diplomacy as "the angels' game." This is in sharp contrast to Sir Henry Wooten's infamous characterization of a diplomat as an "honest man sent to lie for his country." In fact, neither characterization is true. Diplomacy is not the domain of the heavens or the darker regions. Nor is it as mysterious as many bystanders and practitioners make it out to be. It is a combination of human interaction and state policy-making. It is a necessary art that requires a breadth of vision and a precise mind. In the following sections we will explore diplomacy by looking at the functions of diplomacy, national diplomatic styles, the rules for effective diplomacy, diplomatic options, and conflict resolution.

Functions of Diplomacy

Diplomacy is carried on by a variety of officials with titles such as president, prime minister, ambassador, or special envoy, and it is worthwhile to explore the roles that these officials and other diplomats play.

One role is to *observe and report*. A primary diplomatic role has always been to gather information and impressions and to analyze and report these back to the home office. This mostly includes routine activity, such as reading newspapers and reporting observations, but it also may involve espionage. As the last chapter indicated, many embassies contain a considerable covert element. Whatever the method, it is important for policymakers to know both the facts and the mood of foreign capitals, and the embassy is a primary source.

In some ways, the importance of the ambassador as an observer and reporter has declined. High-level policymakers are more likely to visit countries themselves, and they also bring back and share valuable insights and information. Countries are also far less isolated from one another, and there are many new information-gathering techniques. The result is that diplomatic reports compete with many other sources of information. As one Bush White House official put it, "There is a diminished value in classical diplomatic reporting. If you had a choice between reading the [diplomatic] cables in your box and tuning in to CNN three times a day, you'd tune in to CNN" (*WP,* 4/13/90:A7). This fact is offset, however, by the expansion of diplomatic focus. Diplomatic reporting now includes economics and culture as well as politics as such, and thus there are many more facets of a foreign state to ascertain and analyze.

Negotiating is a second important function of diplomacy. Negotiation is a combination of art and technical skill that attempts to find a common ground among two or more divergent positions. For all the public attention given meetings between national leaders, foreign ministers, and other high-level officials, the vast bulk of negotiating is done by ambassadors and other such personnel. Most issues are not weighty enough to merit the attention of those at the top, but in sum these matters make up a substantial part of international relations. And even those negotiations that do finally reach the summit, such as arms talks, usually have most of the groundwork laid and agreements achieved through myriad meetings between diplomatic specialists.

Substantive representation is a third task of diplomacy. This includes the "explanation and defense of national policy" (Barston, 1988:2). As noted many times, misperception is dangerous in world politics, and the role that diplomats play in explaining their countries' actions and statements to friends and foes alike is vital to accurate communications.

The misimpressions that may have been conveyed to Baghdad about U.S. resolve just prior to Iraq's invasion of Kuwait illustrate how important it is for diplomats to convey their countries' positions accurately. On July 25, just eight days before the attack, U.S. ambassador to Baghdad April Glaspie told President Saddam Hussein that President Bush "personally wants to expand and deepen the relationship with Iraq," and she assured Iraq's president that Americans "don't have much to say about Arab-Arab differences like your border differences with Kuwait. All we hope is that you solve those matters quickly." On July 31, three days before the invasion and two days after a CIA warning that an Iraqi attack was highly likely, assistant secretary for the Middle East John Kelly told a congressional committee that the United States was not bound by a defense treaty with any Persian Gulf state. This is technically true. Still, the implications of Kelly's remark ran against a long-standing U.S. commitment to stability in the area. It also may be that, as the chairman of the House Foreign Affairs subcommittee on the

One role for diplomats is to represent their countries symbolically. President Reagan appointed Ambassador Edward J. Perkins, pictured here in South Africa, as an antiapartheid symbol as well as in recognition of Perkins's long diplomatic service. Ambassador Perkins made a point of frequently meeting with South African blacks as another symbol of the United States' disapproval of apartheid.

Middle East charged Kelly, "You left the impression that it was the policy of the U.S. not to come to the aid of Kuwait" (all quotes from *Time,* 10/1/90:54). There are some who have argued that these, as it turned out, inaccurate signals may have helped convince Iraq it could get away with invading Kuwait.

Diplomats also *symbolically represent* their countries. Diplomats, to a degree, personify their countries. Ambassadors who speak the language and respect the customs of the country to which they are accredited, who are intelligent, dignified, tactful, charming, and discreet, and have integrity and patience are apt to make a good impression. Diplomats, be they presidents or ambassadors, can be as winning as fine wine, and "champagne is the lubricant of diplomacy" (Bailey, 1968:35–43). The reverse characteristics can quickly alienate people. To describe President Carter's attack of diarrhea while he was on a state visit to Mexico as "Montezuma's revenge" was roughly equivalent to telling a Polish joke in Warsaw. Mexicans were not amused.

Certainly, with today's modern communications and transportation, there are many images of any one country that are projected. But day in and day out, the ambassador represents *the* official image of his or her country and society.

Diplomats can sometimes *intervene* to tell a country what to do. Soviet representatives to some Eastern European countries until recently combined the roles of diplomat and proconsul. They attempted to persuade, but they could also issue directives. American diplomats can also play that role in some weaker and/or dependent states. When South Vietnam resisted the U.S.–negotiated settlement, President Nixon cabled President Thieu that "all military and economic aid will be cut off . . . if an agreement is not reached" and that "I have . . . irrevocably decided to proceed . . . to sign [the agreement]. . . . I will do so, if necessary, alone . . . [and] explain that your government obstructs peace." As the United States' chief diplomat, Nixon was being distinctly undiplomatic. "Brutality is nothing," he told Kissinger. "You have never seen it if this son-of-a-bitch doesn't go along, believe me" (Kissinger, 1979:1420, 1469). Thieu went along.

Finally, diplomacy is also sometimes conducted for its *propaganda value*. Even where there is little hope for settlement, it may benefit a country's image to appear reasonable or to make opponents seem stubborn. As Nikita Khrushchev told a diplomat, "Never forget the appeal that the idea of disarmament has to the outside world. All you have to say is 'I'm in favor of it,' and it pays big dividends" (Shevchenko, 1985:246).

National Diplomatic Style

Before going further with this discussion of the common elements of diplomacy, it is important to note that there are also distinct differences in the ways that various countries negotiate. These culturally based variations are important to understand in order to avoid misinterpreting what another country's diplomats are doing or are trying to convey.

A full discussion of differences in national style is beyond the scope of this book, but a few illustrations may be useful. American negotiators, for instance, are often legalistic and pragmatic. They tend to haggle over details and treat negotiations as a spirited contest in which winning is best but compromise is better than not reaching an agreement. The Japanese, by contrast, tend to avoid formal negotiations because for them, "the art of understanding, empathizing, satisfying the concerns of others—all while pursuing one's own interest" is so culturally valued that it even has a name, *haragei*, "the art of the belly." Haggling is left to merchants, who are low in the traditional social order (Thayer & Weiss, 1987:55).

Chinese negotiators similarly avoid haggling, but they are more direct about their position than their Japanese counterparts. Henry Kissinger (1979:1056) recalls that the Chinese "never stooped to petty maneuvers; they did not haggle; they reached their bottom line quickly, explained it reasonably, and defended it tenaciously." Like the Japanese, though, the Chinese are very solicitous, and, according to Kissinger, they "use friendship as a halter in advance of negotiations; by admitting [you] to at least the appearance of personal intimacy, a subtle restraint is placed on the claims [you] can put forward."

Soviet diplomats also have distinctive traits. Unlike the legalistic Americans, the Soviets are apt to make generalized proposals and want to come to an agreement in principle while discounting the fine print. One U.S. diplomat has characterized this as trying to get the other side to buy a "pig in a poke" (Graybeal, 1986:40). Once the haggling begins, though, the Soviets are very stubborn, an often frustrating experience for the Americans who want to compromise and move quickly to strike a deal. Furthermore, for all Gorbachev's polish, Soviet diplomats are often intentionally obnoxious in an attempt to intimidate their opponent. Helmut Sonnefeldt, a former American ambassador to Moscow, characterized the Soviets as "mostly unpleasant. . . . [They] antagonize you right away when they start out; they try to put you on the defensive right away" (U.S. House Committee on Foreign Affairs, 1979:505).

The Rules of Effective Diplomacy

Diplomacy is an art. There is therefore no single formula for conducting successful negotiations and signaling. There are, however, a number of standards that can enhance the chances of effective diplomacy (Morgenthau, 1973; Bailey, 1968).

Be realistic. It is important to have goals that match your ability to achieve them. As Kissinger (1970:47) has pointed out, "The test of a statesman . . . is his ability to recognize the real relationship of forces." President Roosevelt has been criticized for "acquiescing" at Yalta (1945) to Soviet domination of Poland, but the fact is that the Red Army had already occupied the country, and only war would have dislodged the Soviets. Roosevelt wisely accommodated himself to the inevitable and concentrated on winnable points. "Dreaming the impossible dream" makes for a charming Don Quixote, but it is not effective diplomacy.

Avoid being dogmatic. A good negotiator shuns the temptation to think his or her position is morally superior. Crusading is better for rhetoric than for diplomacy. Almost any negotiation will involve some concessions, so it is important to maintain a degree of flexibility and not to slam the door on proposals before they are fully explored. It may be that Kuwait's refusal to be flexible helped bring on the invasion by Iraq. According to Jordan's King Hussein, the Kuwaitis refused to bargain with Iraq over the two countries' differences. The king recalled that the Kuwaitis said they would not "give up an inch of territory," a resolve strengthened by their confidence that "if they [the Iraqis] attack us, we would call the Americans." King Hussein reports that even King Fahd of Saudi Arabia said in the hours after the invasion that because the Kuwaitis were "this adamant" they had "brought this about" (*NYT,* 10/16/90:A18).

Understand the other side. Information about the facts, personality, and point of view of the other country is invaluable. It helps the diplomat know what his or her bargaining opponents may concede, what they will not, and what they have to back up their position. "Know thine enemy," as the old saying goes. As a corollary, it is also wise to make sure that thine enemy knows thee. Errors are a major cause of conflict and they result from misperceptions based on cultural differences and the lack of or wrong information.

Search for common interests. Unless you want war or are willing to surrender to any demand to avoid conflict, it is necessary to search for common ground. This can include shared interests (such as avoiding war); compromises (on the theory that half a loaf is better than none); or barters, in which each side trades concessions on different issues.

Compromise on nonvital issues. Most diplomats counsel that it is important to distinguish your central from your peripheral values. Intransigence over a minor point, when a concession can bring a counterconcession on an issue important to you, is folly. There is some research indicating that concessions, even unilateral ones, are likely to engender positive responses.

Be patient. It is also important to bide your time. Being overly anxious can lead to concessions that are unwise and may convey weakness to an opponent. As a corollary, it is poor practice to set deadlines, for yourself or others, unless you are in a very strong position or you do not really want an agreement.

Leave avenues of retreat open. It is axiomatic that even a rat will fight if you trap it in a corner. The same is often true for countries. Call it honor, face, or prestige, it is important to leave yourself and your opponent an "out." "Either/or" ultimatums, especially public challenges, often lead to war. Austria's timed ultimatum to Serbia in 1914 led to World War I, and the UN's timed ultimatum to Iraq similarly led to war. By contrast, President Kennedy's care to allow the Soviets to withdraw their missiles gracefully from Cuba in 1962 may well have averted World War III.

Options in Negotiation and Signaling

There are several good rules to follow in diplomacy, but the practice is still more art than science. Effective diplomacy must tailor its approach to the situation and the opponent. In doing so, diplomats have to choose the channel, level, visibility, type of inducement, degree of precision, method of communication, and extent of linkage that they will use.

Direct or Indirect Negotiations

One issue diplomats face is whether to negotiate directly with each other or indirectly, through an intermediary. *Direct negotiations* have the advantage of avoiding the misinterpretations that an intermediary third party might cause. As in the old game of "Gossip," messages can get garbled. Direct negotiations are also quicker. An additional plus is that they can act as a symbol. When, in 1969, the United States was finally ready to talk directly with China, Henry Kissinger (1979:179) instructed the U.S. ambassador to Poland (where periodic secret U.S./PRC meetings had been taking place) "to walk up to the Ambassador of the People's Republic at the next social function they both attended." It was a precedent-breaking move meant to signal not only China but also the Soviets of impending U.S./PRC collaboration. Also indicative of the heavy symbolism of the U.S. gesture was the Chinese ambassador's reaction. Ambassador Stoessel's chance to speak to the Chinese chargé d'affaires finally came at a fashion show sponsored by the Yugoslav embassy. A model appeared wearing a see-through wedding dress, and the always decorous Chinese diplomat got up to leave. He was further unnerved to see Stoessel heading in his direction. "He looked scared and made for the stairs," the ambassador recalls. "He was running down the stairs and I was right behind him." Out the door they raced. "It was dark. It was snowing. It was cold. . . . I [finally] got him," Stoessel triumphantly concluded. Public Sino-American contact had begun (*NYT*, 9/24/82:A14).

Indirect negotiations may also be advisable. Direct contact symbolizes a level of legitimacy that a country may not wish to convey. Israel, for instance, has refused to recognize or openly and directly negotiate with the Palestine Liberation Organization, because that would symbolize acceptance. It is reliably reported, however, that necessity has led to contact with the PLO, at times through intermediaries, to exchange prisoners and to explore other matters.

Indirect diplomacy can also avoid the embarrassment of a public rebuff by the other side. During the opening moves between the United States and China, oral messages were sent through the "good offices" (friendly intermediaries) of Pakistan and Romania, and written messages were exchanged on photocopy paper with no letterheads or signatures.

High-Level or Low-Level Diplomacy

The higher the level of contact, the more seriously a message will be taken. It implies a greater commitment, and there will be a greater reaction. Therefore, a diplomat must decide whether to communicate on a high or a low level.

A *high level of diplomacy* has its advantages. When a president, premier, or Communist party leader speaks or writes, it is seriously noted in other capitals. Thus, when you wish your communication to be both immediately received and given great weight, it is best to have it issued from the highest level. When President Bush wanted to let Iraq know that harming the hostages would cause a dangerous U.S. reaction, he said publicly that "I've had it" with Iraqi cruelty to the hostages (*HC*, 11/1/90:A1).

The significance of statements by national leaders can also have a deleterious effect, and that is a lesson presidents and prime ministers sometimes have to learn. President Reagan's first-term rhetoric was full of caustic references to the Soviet Union as the evil empire that would lie and cheat to accomplish its ends. Once, preparing for a regular Saturday radio talk, Reagan tested the microphone with something akin to "testing, testing, bombing the Soviet Union, testing one, two, three." Unfortunately for East-West relations, the microphone was live at the time, and Reagan's test message was broadcast. Reagan (1990:62) argues in his memoirs that this rhetoric was justified because he "set out to say some frank things about the Russians, to let them know there were some new fellows in Washington who had a realistic view of what they were up to and weren't going to let them keep it up." According to KGB defector Oleg Gordievsky, the message received in Moscow was very different. He argues that Moscow's "tendency to paranoia" combined with Reagan's rhetoric produced "a potentially lethal mixture." It convinced KGB head and later Soviet Communist party general secretary Yuri Andropov that the United States was preparing to launch a nuclear war and was in the grips of an "outrageous military psychosis" (Christopher & Gordievsky, 1990:81).

There are other times when *low-level communications* are wiser. One attempt to negotiate with Iran during the hostage crisis involved sending two former U.S. officials to Teheran. Their mission collapsed, however, "due to the announcement that they were presidential emissaries" (Vance, 1983:276). The Ayatollah Khomeini decreed that no Iranian official would meet with any American official. "It was a bad mistake," former secretary of state Cyrus Vance recalls. "Had their mission been kept unofficial and out of the spotlight, Khomeini might have received them."

Low-level communications also avoid overreaction and maintain flexibility. Dire threats can be issued as "trial balloons" by generals and then, if later thought unwise, disavowed by higher political officers. Lower level communications are also read as "trends in thinking" or "one viewpoint" rather than "official policy" and can be backed away from with no loss of face.

Public or Private Diplomacy

Another diplomatic choice is whether to communicate in public or in private. *Public communications* have high symbolic value, just like direct communications. They increase credibility. During the U.S./PRC diplomatic dance, a major advance was achieved when the American ambassador to Warsaw was invited to the Chinese embassy there. He offered "to arrive discreetly at the rear door" but was told by the Chinese that "the main entrance was eminently suitable," presumably, Kissinger (1979:188) concludes, "to avoid any chance that Soviet intelligence might miss the occasion."

Public communications also have the advantage of speed. During the Cuban missile crisis, urgent messages between Premier Khrushchev and President Kennedy were communicated at times via Radio Moscow and the Voice of America.

Private communications can also be useful. They may allow messages that, for diplomatic or domestic reasons, would be difficult to state publicly. In particular, they allow for the exploration of new and unpopular paths while avoiding outbreaks of domestic or international opposition. It is also far easier to retreat from a position taken in private than from one taken in public. Hence, when bluffing or uncertain, it is better to communicate confidentially.

Using Coercion or Rewards to Gain Agreement

Yet another diplomatic choice is whether to use carrots or sticks. To induce an opponent to react as you wish, is it better to offer rewards or to threaten punishment?

Coercive diplomacy, as we have seen, can be effective when you have the power, will, and credibility to back it up. Such action can be directly communicated, as was done by blockading Cuba in 1962. Coercion was also a key U.S. strategy in the months that followed Iraq's invasion of Kuwait. President Bush regularly made statements such as "Sand is running through the glass. I don't think the status quo can go on forever" (*HC,* 11/2/90:A11). When such metaphors failed to move Iraq, Bush dispatched another

100,000+ U.S. troops "to ensure that the coalition has an adequate offensive capability" and reasoned, "I think it sends a very strong signal, another strong signal, to Saddam Hussein that we are very, very serious" (*HC,* 11/9/90). The Iraqi leader was still not convinced.

At other times, *offers of rewards* may be a more powerful inducement. The alternative, coercion, may lead to war with high costs and uncertain results. It may also be possible to "buy" what you cannot "win." One song in *Mary Poppins* includes the wisdom that "a spoonful of sugar helps the medicine go down," and an increase in aid, a trade concession, a state visit, or some other tangible or symbolic reward may induce agreement. This is particularly true when dealing with allies or with stronger, hostile countries.

Often, the best diplomacy includes a mixture of carrots and sticks. In its 1989–90 diplomatic maneuvering with Moscow to achieve an accord that would ease the conflict in Nicaragua and El Salvador, Washington used both coercion and rewards. The idea, according to a strategy memorandum by Assistant Secretary of State for Inter-American Affairs Bernard Aronson, was to make Moscow see "tangible signs that they will pay a high price in bilateral relations if they obstruct [a settlement], but also tangible benefits from cooperation" (*Time,* 6/4/90:39). Confrontation might bring a breakdown in U.S.-Soviet arms talks and perhaps even a U.S. military move in the region; cooperation would result in U.S. support for trade and other economic incentives for the Soviet Union and acceptance of the Sandinistas in Nicaragua if they won a democratic election. An agreement was reached.

In contrast, U.S. diplomacy during the 1990–91 Middle East crisis emphasized coercion with little said (at least publicly) about positive incentives for a change in Iraqi policy. Complete Iraqi withdrawal from Kuwait and even reparations were the sole U.S. position. As President Bush told the nation during his mid-September 1990 address to a joint session of Congress, "Iraq will not be permitted to annex Kuwait. That's not a threat, not a boast. That's just the way it's going to be." Some commentators criticized what they saw as a one-sided approach. In an article entitled "For Saddam, Where's the Carrot?" Professor Roger Fisher (*CSM,* 10/15/90:18) argued that coercion was "barely half" of what was needed to resolve the crisis. The author of the book on bargaining, *Getting to Yes,* argued that the United States should be "building a golden bridge for Saddam's retreat." Fisher contends that U.S. diplomacy erred by increasing the level of threat without providing simultaneous, positive signs of what would happen if Iraq withdrew.

Being Precise or Being Intentionally Vague

Most diplomatic experts maintain that it is important to be precise when communicating. There are times, however, when purposeful vagueness may be in order.

Precision is a hallmark of diplomacy. Being precise when communicating and, especially, when negotiating agreements helps avoid later misunderstandings. Diplomats are often accused of wrangling over minute and seemingly inconsequential details, but those nuances may turn out to be very important. The seeming triumph of the 1978 Camp David accords on the Middle East was later tarnished by Israel's refusal to refrain from building new settlements in disputed Egyptian/Israeli territory. Because there was room for interpretation, each side felt it had been betrayed by the other (Vance, 1983:229).

In some instances *vagueness* may be a better strategy. Such a tactic may paper over an irreconcilable difference. It is especially appropriate when it allows a country in a weak position to retreat with honor and/or when an agreement between countries is more important than the details. The American/North Vietnamese peace accord called for the withdrawal of all "foreign" troops from the South. American troops were obviously foreign, but were North Vietnamese troops also foreign? That ambiguity allowed each side to do what it wanted. The United States left; North Vietnam stayed.

Communicating by Word or Deed

Diplomacy utilizes both words and actions to communicate. Each method has its advantages. *Oral and written communications* are appropriate for negotiations and are often a good signaling strategy. They can establish position at a minimum cost and are more apt to maintain flexibility than active signaling.

Signaling by action also has its uses. It is often more dramatic than verbal signaling. During the 1961 Berlin crisis, President Kennedy could have affirmed the U.S. commitment to that city by making a statement in Washington. Instead, he took the more demonstrative step of going to West Berlin. There, dramatically standing before the free citizens of the city, the president proclaimed himself a symbolic fellow citizen. "*Ich bin ein Berliner*," his words rang out in a message to West Berliners to take heart and to the Soviets to beware of any attempt to absorb the city. Both sides understood the import of the president's declaration, and the crisis eased. They all got a good chuckle too, because the president's speech writers had made a minor grammatical error. "*Ich bin Berliner*" (I am a Berliner) is what they had wanted to say. By adding the "*ein*," however, they had inadvertently changed the meaning of Berliner from a citizen to a favorite local confection, a jelly doughnut known locally as a berliner. Thus what the leader of the free world actually declared was "I am a jelly doughnut" (*NYT,* 4/30/88:31).

There is an old saw that actions speak louder than words, and it is applicable here. Verbal threats of military action are one thing; alerting forces, changing deployments, or actually committing to combat are even more persuasive. It must be remembered, however, that as hard as it is to take back words, it is even harder to undo deeds, and they are also more likely to cause a strong counterreaction and intransigence by an opponent.

Here again, the 1990–91 Middle East crisis provides a ready illustration. Jordan's King Hussein believes that Iraq merely wanted to force the settlement of several outstanding issues with Kuwait, matters on which Kuwait had refused to negotiate, and that Iraq would have withdrawn from Kuwait within a week. There is some disagreement about exactly what the king said, but he reports telling President Bush and Egypt's President Hosni Mubarak that Iraq's Saddam Hussein had assured him (the king) by telephone of an early withdrawal. The king also warned Bush and Mubarak that Iraq's leader "would not respond positively to threat or intimidation" (*NYT,* 10/26/90). Within a day, however, Egypt, the United States, and others had condemned Iraq, and soon thereafter Egyptian, U.S., and other troops began pouring into Saudi Arabia. That buildup, especially the shift from defensive to offensive capability in November and its accompanying rhetoric comparing Saddam Hussein to Adolf Hitler, made war increasingly more likely and a diplomatic settlement less probable. The argument here is not that a quick and firm response in this or any other crisis is necessarily wrong. Rather the point is that such moves carry burdens as well as potential payoffs, that each diplomatic signal should be considered carefully in light of specific circumstances and specific goals, and that reactions based on the lessons of history, including the Munich syndrome, should be handled judiciously.

Separate or Linked Negotiations

A final question diplomats must decide is whether to link negotiations on one issue to the overall state of two countries' relations (Morgan, 1990).

Proponents of **linkage diplomacy** contend that it is foolish to try to deal with another country outside the general framework of relations. Henry Kissinger (1979:129) explains that he and Nixon believed that "events in different parts of the world . . . were related to each other; . . . we proceeded from the premise that to separate them into distinct compartments would encourage the Soviet leaders to believe that they could use cooperation in one area as a safety valve while striving for unilateral advantages elsewhere. This was unacceptable."

Opponents of linkage argue that if an agreement, such as an arms treaty, is in your national interest, you should sign it regardless of what the other side is up to elsewhere. If a treaty is not in your interest, you should not sign it no matter how well behaved your opponent is. Cyrus Vance (1983:102) told President Carter that "we should accept the fact of competition with the Soviets, and we should not link Soviet behavior in the Third World to issues . . . [as] fundamental . . . as SALT." Indeed, linkage opponents are apt to argue that even in a time of ill will and worse behavior, an agreement on one issue may create a positive climate that will allow settlement of other issues.

Crisis Management

A special area of diplomatic practice is crisis management. In many ways, the process is related to general negotiating and signaling, and the "rules" and "options" discussed above apply to crisis diplomacy as well as less perilous interactions. Skilled crisis management also involves sound decision-making (chapter 5), including a careful evaluation of one's national interest (chapter 8) and power (chapter 9).

A **crisis** is a situation in which (1) two or more countries have important national interests involved, (2) there is the possibility of war, and (3) there is a limited time to reach a solution. The high national values, threat of war, and time constraints compress and intensify the diplomatic process and create a special set of considerations.

Assuming that a realistic evaluation of interests and power has occurred and that decisionmakers are willing to engage in the perilous process of crisis diplomacy rather than immediately fighting or giving way, then there are three simultaneous strategies that can be employed. Two of these involve the power formula—namely, increasing your capabilities and increasing your credibility. The third approach is decreasing your opponent's stakes/values in the confrontation.

Increasing Capability

Military power is the asset that can be most readily increased in a crisis, given its limited time frame. *Assets* can be increased to some degree by speeding up production, calling up reserve forces, or taking equipment out of mothballs. Even if it is impossible to produce equipment or train troops fast enough to be used immediately, initiation of these moves may persuade an opponent that in a protracted conflict your power resources will prove superior.

Readiness is a second capability factor. Undertaking procedures to move your forces from peacetime status to a war footing increases your ability to respond quickly and effectively.

Given the relative nature of power, capability increases have the effect of raising the "net cost" the opponent will have to pay if war occurs. This strategy works best if you have greater potential than the other side. Even if you are weaker, though, it shows that victory will not come cheaply, and it may convince the opponent that victory is not worth the price.

The Middle East crisis that began in August 1990 provides a good case study of crisis management attempts by both sides. One step taken by Iraq was to increase its capability by calling up its reserves, including this female member of the Iraqi People's Army.

Increasing Credibility

The second vital power element is credibility. Your opponent must be convinced not only that you can but that you *will* act. Your resolve can be demonstrated in several ways:

Proclaim willingness. Statements by leaders that war is better than retreat help create an air of resolve.

Invoke larger principles. Saying that the issue is linked to world peace, the communist (or capitalist) conspiracy, the domino theory, or other such transcendent values increases your apparent concern. Applying doctrines, such as Monroe's, or principles of behavior, such as the Munich syndrome's "You cannot appease aggression," also increases your apparent resolve.

Proclaim righteousness. Claiming that what you are doing is legitimate increases the perception that you will act. Invoking international law is one legitimizing technique. Obtaining a supportive vote in the United Nations or some other international organization is another. A third is getting "invited" into a country by its government, as the United States was to Lebanon and Saudi Arabia and the Soviet Union was to Afghanistan.

Invoke alliance obligations. Saying you must act because a solemn alliance leaves no choice increases credibility. The American pledge to defend Western Europe, with nuclear weapons if necessary, is more credible because of the NATO treaty than it would be if it were just administration policy.

Invoke national honor. Resolve is enhanced by statements that you will be morally disgraced and/or will lose prestige if you shirk the challenge.

Claim you are losing control. Statements that domestic pressure is too great to resist or that subordinates may take things into their own hands will increase the pressure.

Pretend irrationality. Hitler was particularly good at appearing crazily committed to war unless he got an immediate concession.

Engage in military demonstrations. Sending ships to a trouble area, having "practice" military maneuvers, or actually engaging in limited combat also increases perception of resolve.

Decreasing Your Opponent's Stakes

While you are increasing your power and credibility, and thus the perceived likelihood of conflict and the net cost to your opponent, it is also sound strategy to try to lower the other side's stakes, to make the issue seem less vital to your opponent. Whereas increasing power adds to the *costs* an opponent will have to pay, decreasing *stakes/values* is meant to make the conflict less important and not worth the cost. Tactics include the following:

Stress the limited nature of your goals. Statements that you do not want to threaten the existence or the basic position of your opponent are helpful. Saying that the issue is confined to a single country/area or that you will act only for a limited time is another approach. Saying that this is your "last demand" may also prove effective. Every time Hitler pressed for something, it was his "last" demand, and many believed him, until Poland.

Invoke community values. Call on your opponent to join you (by giving way) in preserving peace. If the two parties are in the same international/regional organization (such as the European Community), highlight your common ties and interests. This is intended to make concessions appear to be a noble gesture instead of a retreat.

Provide avenues of retreat. As discussed earlier, it is important to leave an opponent room to retreat with dignity.

Minimize the extent of duress. Inasmuch as an opponent will find it hard to back down under threat, it is important to create the appearance of mediation, negotiation, and even mutual (if only symbolic) concessions.

Assert your basic goodwill. Treating the conflict as an unfortunate but singular event in otherwise nonhostile relations will help isolate the issue and diminish its value.

These points cover most of the main tactics of the three elements of crisis diplomacy, although others and numerous nuances could be added. It must be stressed that the rules, options, and tactics described do not substitute for wisdom. They rely on accurate information and objective analysis of both your own and your opponent's power and goals. Success also depends on the native ability of decisionmakers and diplomats. Understanding how the game is played does not always make for successful diplomacy. As in any art, the fundamentals are important and must be mastered, but beyond that, individual skill is the essence of success.

Management of the Middle East Crisis

One way to look at the theory of crisis management is to apply it to a real crisis. The case we will use here is the Middle East crisis that began in early August 1990 and led to war in January 1991. The goal here is to ask which actions have or have not been taken to increase the capability of the countries (the "allies") participating in Operation Desert Shield, to increase the credibility of the allies, and to decrease the stakes of the opponent, Iraq. That may give us clues as to why the crisis was not resolved diplomatically and, instead, careened into war.

As far as *increasing capability*, the allies moved strongly. Almost a half-million U.S. troops were sent to the region. They joined with Saudi Arabia's forces (with

THE CHARLOTTE OBSERVER KEVIN SIERS

Iraq über Alles

significant contingents from Egypt, Great Britain, Syria, France, Pakistan, and Bangladesh) and with smaller forces from several other countries. There was almost no doubt that the allies could win a war with Iraq, and the early-November dismissing of Iraq's military chief of staff by Saddam Hussein indicated that the Iraqi president was worried about the resolve of his high command in the face of the imposing, U.S.–led forces poised to strike Iraq.

The allies, especially the U.S. administration, also worked hard at *increasing credibility*. Bush and other allied leaders repeatedly proclaimed their willingness to fight to oust Iraq from Kuwait. Larger principles such as freedom from aggression were regularly cited to support the allied resolve. The characterization of Saddam Hussein as a latter-day Hitler and the explicit references to the lesson of history provided by Munich in 1938 were particularly evident. There also were repeated references to Iraq's threat to a new, post–cold war era of international cooperation and peace, to the sanctity of sovereignty and freedom from aggression, and to the prospect that if the Iraqi challenge was not met the world would be thrown back into the Dark Ages. Secretary of State Baker, for instance, managed to get almost all these credibility-building references into one short speech to U.S. soldiers in Saudi Arabia. "All nations have the right to be free, free from aggression," he told them. Baker continued, "Today we . . . have an opportunity to establish . . . a whole new international order." Not content with that, the secretary went on to make a reference to Munich by suggesting that we need to avoid "that terrible mistake in the '30s when we were unable or refused to stand up to unprovoked aggression" (*HC*, 11/5/90:A5). Despite the fact that each of the allies had a self-interested stake in opposing Iraq, there was a strong effort to legitimize the action.

The allies were invited by Saudi Arabia; the emir of Kuwait invited anyone who would help liberate his country; and there were numerous UN votes condemning Iraq and supporting the allied forces. As the crisis went on, there were quiet assertions by the White House that withdrawal without victory would erode, even end, effective U.S. influence in the region; and there were numerous military demonstrations, including a practice landing by U.S. marines on the Arabian peninsula. Even though he was dismissed for them, the statements of U.S. Air Force general Michael Dugan about massive air attacks and killing Saddam Hussein and his family even lent an air of irrationality or possible loss of control to the mix.

There were, however, numerous factors that decreased the credibility of a U.S. attack in the eyes of Saddam Hussein. One was the willingness of the Saudis and others to compromise. "We see no harm in any Arab country giving its Arab sister land, a site or a position on the seas," observed Saudi defense minister Prince Sultan ibn Abdul Aziz in reference to a possible shift of strategic Bubiyan Island and the Rumalia oil field from Kuwaiti to Iraqi possession. In response, the U.S. administration increased the determination of its rhetoric in order to "dampen the talk of a peaceful settlement that wafted around Sultan," as a White House official explained (*Time*, 11/5/90:39). Additionally, the Soviets, the Chinese, and the French (each with a veto on the UN Security Council) were clearly reluctant to vote for a UN authorization of an offensive move to free Kuwait. Finally, and perhaps most importantly, the initial U.S. public and congressional support for Operation Desert Shield began to wane as the crisis went on. Many Americans were especially ambivalent about attacking into Iraq and Kuwait. Before he ordered his troops to invade Kuwait, Saddam Hussein told the U.S. ambassador that he believed that "the nature of American society makes it impossible for the U.S. to bear tens of thousands of casualties in one battle" (*Time*, 10/1/90:54). That belief is part of what sustained his intransigence in the face of growing U.S. threats. Perhaps, in this case, he was correct. Public opinion polls showed most Americans were very uncomfortable with an allied offensive move, and protest gatherings, editorials, and other antiwar evidence began to mount. Applying a lesson of history different than Munich, one Massachusetts protester greeted a visiting President Bush with a sign that read "Kuwait is Arabic for Vietnam," and protesters updated a classic Vietnam-era protest slogan and chanted, "Hell no, we won't go, we won't die for Texaco." That analogy also began to be used by members of Congress. "The last thing we need is to have . . . a bloody war, and have American boys . . . brought back in body bags and yet not have the American people behind them," influential senator Sam Nunn told "Face the Nation" (6/11/90). "We've gone that route one time," Nunn said referring to Vietnam. "We don't want to do it again." For good or ill, all the international and U.S. domestic reluctance to commit to war detracted from the credibility of the undeniable allied capability in the Gulf region.

The third possible thrust of Middle East crisis diplomacy was *decreasing the opponent's stakes*. In this area, the diplomacy seemed to be the least skilled. There were attempts to invoke community values, such as Arab fraternity and international peace, but beyond that few of the other tactics noted above received much attention. The Bush administration repeatedly said there would be no compromise. Before meeting with the Iraqi ambassador a mere six days before the January 15 deadline specified in the UN resolution for Iraq's withdrawal from Kuwait, Secretary Baker said he was not going to the meeting to negotiate, but rather to deliver the message that Iraq had to withdraw unconditionally or face dire consequences. The Iraqis replied that death was preferable to dishonor, and the crisis intensified. Worse, there was considerable talk, including a statement by Vice President Dan Quayle (quickly discounted by the White House),

The object of crisis diplomacy is to avert war and to accomplish at least some of your goals. By this definition the crisis diplomacy of the Middle East conflict of 1990–91 failed. This British Challenger tank is part of the equipment of the famed 7th Armored Brigade, the Desert Rats. As the highway sign shows, the Desert Rats were on their way to the Kuwaiti border to be in position for Operation Desert Storm.

about removing Saddam Hussein from power, significantly reducing Iraq's armed forces, and ensuring that Iraq would never again have chemical warfare capability or be allowed to attempt to build nuclear weapons. As one radio commentator put it, such statements put the Iraqis in a position of being damned if they fought and damned if they gave way—so why not fight? As noted above in the discussion of using coercion and rewards in diplomacy, there were few if any carrots offered to Iraq. Duress was maximized, and the painting of Saddam Hussein as Hitler and President Bush's equation of the Iraqi army with the Nazi SS divisions that terrorized Poland (crimes which later resulted in the Nuremberg trials and executions) did not follow the advice to assert your basic goodwill. Whatever else he may have been during the crisis, Saddam Hussein was determined. So was George Bush. Both sides brandished sticks, neither proffered carrots. At 3 A.M. Iraq time, on January 17, 1991, diplomacy ended and the war began.

Each international confrontation differs, and therefore crisis diplomacy cannot be carried out by a simple checklist of do's and don'ts. It is also not possible at the time this is being written to know what was being said privately to Iraq. Nevertheless, the public diplomacy must be given mixed grades. It was strongest in increasing allied capability. The effort to increase credibility began strongly, but was eroded both internationally and domestically. There was little attempt to decrease Iraq's stakes. In sum, the odds for a peaceful solution were slim.

Early in the morning of January 17, 1991, Iraq time, the diplomats fell silent and let slip the dogs of war.

Chapter Summary

1. Diplomacy is a communication process that has three main elements. One is negotiating through direct or indirect discussions between two or more countries.

2. The second element of diplomacy is signaling—that is, saying or doing something in order to transmit a message to the other side.

3. The third element is public diplomacy conducted to achieve a favorable image in world opinion.

4. Diplomacy is an ancient art, and some of the historical functions of diplomacy are still important. Diplomacy, however, has also changed dramatically during this century, with such practices as summits, multilateral meetings, and parliamentary maneuvering as common now as they once were rare. These changes reflect the changes in the international system and in domestic political processes and have their benefits, but they are not all positive steps. At the very least, diplomacy has become more complex with the proliferation of actors and options. It has also become more vital given the possible consequences if it fails.

5. Diplomats, who now include presidents and prime ministers as well as foreign ministers and ambassadors, have many functions, such as reporting, negotiating, symbolically representing, and (sometimes) intervening.

6. Good diplomacy is an art, but it is not totally freestyle, and there are general rules that increase the chances for diplomatic success.

7. There are also a wide variety of approaches or options in diplomacy. Whether contacts should be direct or indirect, what level of contact they should involve, whether communication should be public or private, what rewards or coercion should be offered, how precise or vague messages should be, whether to communicate by message or deed, and whether issues should be linked or dealt with separately are all questions that require careful consideration.

8. Crises are a special type of international event characterized by high stakes, short decision times, and the possibility of conflict. Accordingly, their resolution includes special considerations, and there are a number of ways to communicate your resolve and to defuse your opponent's stakes and resolve. As with any aspect of diplomacy, these methods do not guarantee success; there is no substitute for skilled practitioners.

So far as my coin would stretch; and where it would not,
I have used my credit.

Shakespeare, *Henry IV*, Part I

For herein Fortune shows herself more kind
Than is her custom: it is still her use
To let the wretched man outlive his wealth,
To view with hollow eye and wrinkled brow
An age of poverty.

Shakespeare, *The Merchant of Venice*

Monetary disorders fuel economic wars between friends.

Ronald Reagan, State of the Union, 1986

CHAPTER

ECONOMICS: THE NORTH

In your college or university, the study of politics and economics is probably divided into two separate departments. The distinction, however, between the two subjects is not so precise in the real world. Indeed, to a significant extent economics is politics and vice versa. This book has already touched on the politics-economics interrelationship at several places, and you should go back and briefly review those points. Chapter 1 outlined how international economics is related to the supply of natural resources, employment, product availability and price, and other considerations that affect you and your country's economic welfare. Chapter 2 briefly introduced the topics of increasing world interdependence and North-South economic disparity, and these subjects will be further detailed in this and the next chapter. Chapter 9 discussed the many economic aspects of national power including agriculture, natural resources, industrial capacity, and financial soundness.

This chapter and the following one will continue our examination of how economics and politics intertwine. This chapter will discuss the general nature of political economics. It will focus on the current situation of the North,[1] or the developed

1. The Soviet Union and its former East European allies are treated as industrialized countries of the North here and in most analyses. The recent collapse of the economies of these countries puts their per capita GNPs below those of some countries traditionally classified as being in the Third World South. Still, these countries have a more developed economic infrastructure than many Third World countries, and economic recovery is easier than economic development. Complicating GNP estimates are new uncertainties about the Soviet GNP. A study was conducted by the World Bank and the International Monetary Fund, as commissioned by the Group of Seven at its Houston summit in July 1990. The study, released in December 1990, estimated the 1989 Soviet per capita GNP at only $1,780. This is far below previous estimates, such as the CIA's 1988 estimate of nearly $9,000 per capita. In fact, the new estimate puts the Soviet Union below such Third World countries as Mexico, which had a 1989 per capita GNP of $2,165. As has been the normal case, factors such as measuring the true value of the Soviet currency, the ruble, make estimates difficult and controversial. Thus the traditional economic classifications, like all of world politics, are dynamic.

countries. The next chapter will concentrate on the South, or the less developed countries (LDCs). Still later, chapter 18 will further discuss trade, monetary relations, and Third World development and the attempts to promote economic cooperation within and between the two poles of the North-South Axis. Amid all these specifics, try to keep in mind that economics is a vital and inseparable part of the world's complex political structure and its operation.

Politics and Economics: Myriad Complex Relationships

There is no single, simple relationship between politics and economics; the two subjects are closely connected, as the box (pp. 352–353) on Politics, Economics, and the Middle East Crisis discusses. Politics and economics are not synonymous, however. Sometimes political issues affect economic relations (Pollins, 1990). At other times economic considerations influence political relations. Furthermore, economic power serves as both a goal and a tool of national interest and foreign policy. But the flow of international economics is sometimes at least partly separated from national policy and is conducted by various transnational actors ranging from the International Monetary Fund (IMF) to the world's huge multinational corporations.

One tangled question is *the degree to which economic interchange is governed by state political policy*. There is one level at which international trade, international investment, and other economic interchange is politically color blind. In free market economies, decisions are partly separate from political direction. Instead they are governed by considerations such as supply and demand and profit motive. As we saw in chapter 11, most countries that supplied weapons to the combatants in the Iran-Iraq war sold arms to both sides. Certainly this trade was influenced by multiple political factors, such as a country's tariff rates, but the basic urge to trade is and was economic, not political.

It is also true, however, that states manipulate economics to gain their political ends. This is sometimes called "economic statecraft" or "mercantilism" (Baldwin, 1985; Blake & Walters, 1987). Political economist Stephen Krasner (1987:327) has identified five possible mercantilist goals. These include:

1. Sovereign autonomy. States seek to maintain control over their commercial policy as a fundamental aspect of their sovereign status and as a necessary condition for using economics for other purposes.
2. Power maximization. Commercial policy is used to foster the power of the states by enhancing those power elements discussed in chapter 9.
3. Specific political objectives. States may use economics to try to achieve particular goals. The U.S. government in 1988, for example, used economic methods such as freezing Panamanian assets in U.S. banks in an attempt to topple that country's strongman, General Manuel Noriega.
4. Economic objectives. Countries may act to protect domestic economic interests. Even in an era of relatively free trade, for example, farmers in many countries have persuaded their governments to maintain trade barriers against foreign agricultural imports.
5. Milieu objectives. Krasner argues that "commercial policy can . . . be used to promote long-term . . . objectives by attempting to create a particular global

Tensions have grown among the industrialized countries in recent years over trade and associated political issues. This is illustrated in this picture of several members of the U.S. Congress smashing a Toshiba "boom-box" in 1987 to protest the U.S.–Japanese trade imbalance and the fact that Toshiba sold sensitive, defense-related technology to the Soviet Union.

environment" (p. 330). Many who advocate free trade, for instance, are less interested in inexpensive products than the idea that increased economic interdependence and interchange will promote world cooperation and peace.

Another knotty question about the relationship between politics and economics is *the degree to which international economics promotes cooperation or conflict*. In this and the following chapter and in other places in this book where international economics is discussed, you will see that it has both impacts. Idealists would point out that increased economic contact has many benefits. Some are economic, including cheaper products through specialization and the transfer of technology from more advanced economies to less developed countries. Other advantages are political. Some analysts argue that economic cooperation will expand to political cooperation. The lure of trade can also cause countries to lessen their political hostilities. Soviet and Chinese needs for Western technology and Western desires to sell their products, for example, have combined to urge capitalist and communist leaders to improve political relations with each other.

International economic issues also divide countries. The current U.S. trade deficit is causing political strains with a number of the country's allies. The greatest U.S. imbalance is with Japan, and many Americans blame the Japanese for unfair trade practices. The Japanese believe that the problem is mostly caused by poor U.S. economic management, such as the huge federal budget deficit. Whatever the causes, Japan's economy will suffer from increased U.S. protectionism. Almost inevitably, the result will be a cooling of the cordiality that has marked U.S.–Japanese political relations for the past four decades.

Political divisions are fostered by attempts to use economics as a tool of state foreign policy. An irony of increased economic interdependence is that it adds to the possibility of economic coercion. Countries regularly try to use economic sanctions, such as trade embargoes, as a means of achieving foreign policy goals. Whether or not the attempt is successful, and regardless of the loftiness or unacceptability of the goal, economics thus becomes a political weapon and promotes international hostility and conflict.

Politics, Economics, and the Middle East Crisis

The Middle East crisis that began in August 1990 is a recent reminder of the strong interaction between economics and politics. Some of the complaints that led Iraq to attack Kuwait were economic. Iraq claimed that Kuwait was siphoning too much oil from the Rumelia oil field, which is mostly in Iraq, but which just extends into Kuwait. Iraq was also angry because Kuwait was exceeding the oil production quotas set by the Organization of Petroleum Exporting Countries (OPEC). This oversupply was driving down prices. This particularly angered Iraq because it believed that it had shouldered huge costs in the 1980s protecting the oil kingdoms to the south from the Iranians. From the Iraqi point of view, the low oil prices caused by oversupply were damaging Iraq's ability to recover from the war and pay off the debts it had accrued during the war. Iraq also considered the oil kingdom's production of oil in excess of the OPEC quota as a sign of ingratitude, even hostility. Kuwait refused to respond diplomatically to Iraq's demand for economic concessions, and Iraq attacked.

In addition to political concerns about its aggression, Iraq's invasion struck at the world's most sensitive economic sore spot. By seizing Kuwait, Iraq doubled to nearly 20 percent the amount of world petroleum reserves that it controlled. If Iraq had also taken the rest of the Arabian peninsula including Saudi Arabia and the oil emirates along the west coast of the Persian Gulf, Baghdad would have held approximately 55 percent of world oil reserves and

almost 28 percent of the mid-1990 world oil production of 46.4 million barrels daily. Furthermore, given the fact that most of the oil produced in the United States, the Soviet Union, and the North Sea is consumed by the countries that produce it, Iraq would have controlled over half of the daily international flow of about 21 million barrels of oil. Any such increase in its control of the global oil supply would have vastly increased Iraq's economic and political power.

The economic impact of Iraq's seizure of Kuwait was immediate in the West. The price of oil contracts (futures) more than doubled from approximately $18 to $40 a barrel, and some analysts predicted that a protracted war in the region might drive oil prices to $100 a barrel. For consumers, the price of gasoline and home heating oil jumped in the United States 40 to 50 percent. General inflation also jumped because of the energy costs of production and distribution of almost all products. Stock markets in New York, Tokyo, and elsewhere were traumatized. In Japan, which depends on oil for 58 percent of its energy needs, the Nikkei stock index lost 2.5 percent of its value in the first week of the crisis alone, and by mid-October the Japanese stock market had declined a total of 24.5 percent from its August 1 value. A rough economic standard is that every $10 rise in the price of a barrel of oil will reduce the U.S. GNP growth by 1 percent and add nearly 1 percent to the unemployment rate. As the 1990 holiday season approached, the already sagging

In sum, then, the relationship between economics and politics is multifaceted. Each influences the other. Economics both contributes to enhanced international political cooperation and is a source of international tension. Each of these aspects will be examined further at various points in this and the next chapter, but before proceeding to those discussions, a brief survey of the historical growth of the international political economy is in order.

The Historical Growth of the International Political Economy

In world politics, economics is a means of influence as well as a power asset. As such, it is also a potential target for one's foes. While it is true that in the modern era economic factors have become ever more important, their role extends far back into history. The Book of Exodus records what may have been the first attack on a country's economic (and social) infrastructure in order to overthrow imperial domination. In his attempt to persuade the pharaoh to release the Israelites from their Egyptian captivity, Moses (with

U.S. economy was sliding into a recession. The impact of soaring energy prices was even more damaging to poor, energy-dependent Third World countries.

The political response to Iraq's aggression was also immediate. The United Nations repeatedly and almost unanimously condemned Iraq and voted sanctions against it. Numerous countries rushed support to the Middle East to protect the Arabian peninsula and perhaps drive Iraq from Kuwait. The cost of the economic sanctions and the military effort were immense. The U.S. military buildup cost the United States $2.5 billion in August and September alone, and estimates for fiscal year 1991 (October 1990–September 1991, the U.S. government's budget year) were $15 billion while the forces stayed on the defense, and up to $1 billion a day for the offensive operations after January 17, 1991. In the first month of deployment, U.S. costs ran the gamut from such obvious military costs as fuel and chemical warfare gear ($279 per soldier), through food (12.1 million pounds of meat, $21.4 million), to 305,334 bottles of sunscreen lotion ($413,000) and 604,000 tubes of lip balm ($99,237). The call-up of U.S. reservists disrupted both their personal economic lives and the operations of their employers. Other countries also contributed expensive military forces, and 54 countries pledged $20 billion to support military operations and other activities in the Middle East region.

The economic sanctions imposed on Iraq were a double-edged sword that proved costly to both sides. Many Third World countries had citizens working in Iraq, and the repatriation of the workers and their lost wages added to the negative impact on these countries. India, for one, lost at least $2.5 billion to the increased oil prices, the expense of repatriating its nationals, and the wages lost to its fleeing workers. Turkey took a $3 billion battering from increased oil costs, lost revenue from steel and other exports to Iraq, and lost income from the oil pipeline from Iraq through Turkey to the Mediterranean. Iraq's foreign loans are also going unpaid, costing the shaky East European economies $4 billion. To help these damaged countries, the newly formed, 24-country Gulf Crisis Financial Coordination Group pledged in November 1990 to provide $13 billion in relief to the countries most damaged by the sanctions. Even the wealthier countries are suffering from the sanctions. American grain farmers lost sales ($350 million in 1989); Italian banks could not collect $2.2 billion that Baghdad owed them; and in Paris five A-310 commercial jetliners worth $70 million sat undelivered to and unpaid for by Iraq.

The list could go on and on. That is not necessary, though, to make the point that economics and politics are powerfully intertwined. The political impact of Iraq's economic threat brought the world to the point of war; the economic costs of the political reaction were huge and global.

God's help) turned the Nile "to blood. . . . And all the fishes died; and the Nile became foul so that the Egyptians could not drink water." When that failed, Moses dispatched successive plagues of frogs, gnats, and flies to bedevil the Egyptians. Pharaoh still refused to release the Israelites. Next a plague was visited on their livestock, and all the Egyptians were infected with boils. Despite these travails, a very stubborn pharaoh refused to give in. Discretion would have been the better part of valor. At Moses' command, "thunder and hail and fire . . . rained upon the land of Egypt" and struck down every man, beast, plant, and tree of the fields. Adding to the Egyptians' misery, Moses then dispatched a swarm of locusts that "covered the face of the land" and "ate all the plants in the land and all the fruits on the trees . . . not a green thing remained." Economic sanctions do not always work right away, and they did not work this time. Even the locusts plus three solid days of darkness failed to convince the pharaoh to let the Israelites go. Finally God was forced to slay the first-born of every Egyptian family, and a shattered pharaoh begged Moses to lead his people out of Egypt quickly lest all Egyptians perish.

With more historic certainty, economics is also known to have affected other areas of ancient international relations. Trading records extend back to almost 3000 B.C., and there is other evidence of trade back into the Neolithic age. The earliest human records reveal warfare for plunder, resources, and other economic gain. Trade wars were also known early in history. The Phoenicians allied themselves with King David of Israel to crush their economic rivals, the Philistines. The Greek city-states also engaged in economic strife, and the Punic Wars between Rome and Carthage were also partly rooted in economics.

The Increasing Role of Economics

Whatever its ancient role, economics has become a more important aspect of international relations, as shown by expanding trade and the resulting increase in interdependence and domestic impact. International financial ties have also grown rapidly.

Expanding Trade

Trade is booming in the twentieth century, and the international flow of goods and money is a vital concern to all world states. In 1913 the entire flow of goods in world commerce totaled only $20 billion. In 1990 world trade stood at nearly $3.2 trillion. Even considering inflation, this represents a tremendous jump in world commerce. Figure 13.1 depicts the rise in the dollar volume of trade. Trade growth has been especially rapid during the post–World War II era of significant tariff reductions. During the 1913 to 1948 period of world wars, depression, and trade protectionism, trade increased at an average annual rate of only 0.8 percent. The postwar period has seen average annual increases at a rate of approximately 9.1 percent.

The rapid growth of trade has been caused by a number of factors including productive technology, resource requirements, materialism, transportation, and free-trade philosophy.

Productive Technology   The industrial revolution, which began in eighteenth-century Europe, is one factor behind increased trade. As productive efficiency increased, the supply of goods increased. From 1705 to 1780, prior to industrialization, world industrial production increased at an annual rate of only 1.5 percent, and trade increased at only about 1 percent a year. In the years that followed industrialization, however, productivity rapidly increased, and the volume of trade followed suit.

In the simplest terms, the age of machine production of goods, such as textiles, meant that more manufactured products were available and that they were available at lower prices. These manufactured goods, then, formed the "supply" side of trade development (Major, 1980). Table 13.1 on page 356 shows this relationship.

This pattern of increases in both industrial output and trade has generally continued to the present. Figure 13.2 (p. 357) shows this growth in recent years. You should particularly note that trade has expanded faster than output. This means that an increasing percentage of what is produced is traded internationally.

Resource Requirements   Industrialization and other technological advances also affected the "demand" side of international trade. During the nineteenth century and through World War II, importation of raw materials by the industrialized European countries was a primary force in trade as manufacturing needs both increased demand for raw materials and outstripped domestic resource availability. During the late 1800s,

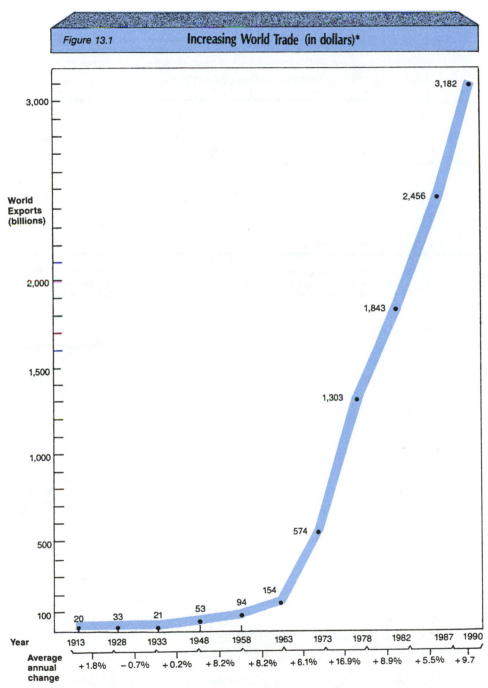

Figure 13.1 **Increasing World Trade (in dollars)***

World Exports (billions)

Year	Average annual change
1913	
	+1.8%
1928	
	−0.7%
1933	
	+0.2%
1948	
	+8.2%
1958	
	+8.2%
1963	
	+6.1%
1973	
	+16.9%
1978	
	+8.9%
1982	
	+5.5%
1987	
	+9.7
1990	

*Figures are rounded.

Data sources: The 1913–58 figures are from Root (1973:24). The 1963–82 figures are from GATT (1983:126). The 1987 figure is from UN (1988:102). The 1990 figure is from UN (1990c) and is projected from figures in the first two quarters.

Figure 13.1 shows the rapid expansion of trade measured in exports, especially during the last quarter-century when it grew approximately 1,000 percent to reach $3,182 billion in 1990. Foreign commerce and international economics in general have become more important aspects of international relations and of the domestic economic health of individual countries.

TABLE 13.1

World Industrial Production and Trade Before and After the Beginning of the Industrial Revolution

Period	Trade (percentage of average annual growth)	Industrial Production (percentage of average annual growth)
1705–1779	1.0%	1.5%
1780–1819	1.4	2.6
1820–1839	2.8	2.9
1840–1860	4.8	3.5

Data source: Rostow (1978:67).

After the industrial revolution began in the mid-1700s, both industrial production and trade expanded rapidly. Production created a supply of manufactured goods to be traded. Expanded production also created a demand for raw materials, which were obtained through trade.

for example, raw material accounted for 97 percent of all French and 89 percent of all German imports.

In the post-1945 world economy, primary resources have declined somewhat as a percentage of both total world trade and of the imports of the industrialized countries. With respect to general trade, primary resources decreased from 49 percent of all imports in 1960 to 23 percent in 1989. This is due to increased trade in manufactured goods, however, rather than a decline in the demand for primary resources, which over the long term has remained strong, if often unstable.

Materialism   The rise in the world's standard of living, especially in the industrialized countries, has also contributed to "demand" pressure on international trade. More workers were brought into the wage-producing sector, and their "real" (after inflation) wages went up. The real wages of English craftspersons held relatively steady between 1300 and 1800, for instance, but then more than doubled by the 1950s (Rostow, 1978). In short, more people had more money to buy things.

Here again, the trend has continued into the current era. The workers of the wealthier countries have especially enjoyed increased real wages. The average wage in the industrialized countries, for example, showed a 3.7 percent annual real increase between 1969 and 1990. This strengthens demand because individuals have more wealth with which to purchase domestic and imported goods.

Transportation   Technology has also increased our ability to transport goods. The development of railroads and improvements in maritime shipping were particular spurs to trade. They both increased the volume of possible trade and decreased per unit transportation costs. Imagine if automobiles still had to be brought from Japan by sailing ships and distributed by wagon train! The famous clipper ship *Flying Cloud* (1851) weighed only 1,782 tons, and the "immense" *Great Eastern* (1858) weighed 22,000 tons and could carry 15,000 tons of cargo. By contrast, the modern tanker *Seawise Giant* is 1,500 feet long (five football fields, almost one-third of a mile) and carries over one-half million tons of oil.

Free-Trade Philosophy   The 1930s and early 1940s were a period of global trauma, marked first by great economic depression, then by World War II. One cause for these successive miseries, it was said, was the high tariffs that had restricted trade and divided nations. To avoid a recurrence, the victorious United States took the lead in reducing barriers to international trade. The General Agreement on Tariffs and Trade (GATT)

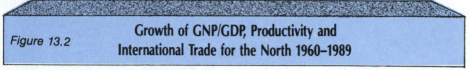

Growth of GNP/GDP, Productivity and International Trade for the North 1960–1989

Figure 13.2

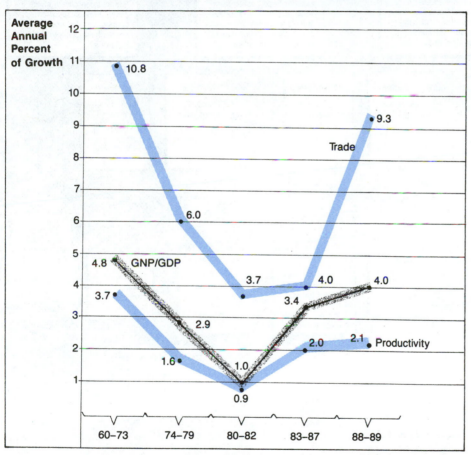

Note: Data is for the Organization for Economic Cooperation and Development (OECD) countries including Australia, Austria, Belgium, Denmark, Finland, France, Germany (West), Great Britain, Greece, Iceland, Ireland, Israel, Japan, Luxembourg, Netherlands, New Zealand, Norway, Portugal, Spain, Sweden, Switzerland, Turkey, and the United States. The figures for 1987–89 are OECD estimates. Final figures will probably be very slightly higher. Growth is an average for all OECD countries as reported in GNP (Gross National Product) or GDP (Gross Domestic Product).

Data sources: OECD (1989); U.S. Economic Report of the President, 1990.

Trade has become increasingly important in maintaining the health of most countries' manufacturing (industrial) sectors. This figure shows that exports for the OECD countries have grown faster than GNP/GDP or productivity. This means that more and more of what industrial countries produce are exported. A sharp reduction, therefore, in world trade would damage the economies of the industrialized countries.

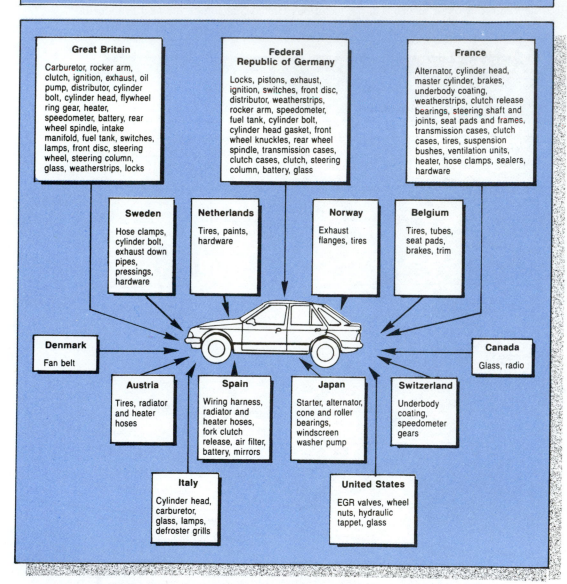

Figure 13.3   **The International Origins of Components of a European-built Ford Escort**

Great Britain

Carburetor, rocker arm, clutch, ignition, exhaust, oil pump, distributor, cylinder bolt, cylinder head, flywheel ring gear, heater, speedometer, battery, rear wheel spindle, intake manifold, fuel tank, switches, lamps, front disc, steering wheel, steering column, glass, weatherstrips, locks

Federal Republic of Germany

Locks, pistons, exhaust, ignition, switches, front disc, distributor, weatherstrips, rocker arm, speedometer, fuel tank, cylinder bolt, cylinder head gasket, front wheel knuckles, rear wheel spindle, transmission cases, clutch cases, clutch, steering column, battery, glass

France

Alternator, cylinder head, master cylinder, brakes, underbody coating, weatherstrips, clutch release bearings, steering shaft and joints, seat pads and frames, transmission cases, clutch cases, tires, suspension bushes, ventilation units, heater, hose clamps, sealers, hardware

Sweden

Hose clamps, cylinder bolt, exhaust down pipes, pressings, hardware

Netherlands

Tires, paints, hardware

Norway

Exhaust flanges, tires

Belgium

Tires, tubes, seat pads, brakes, trim

Denmark

Fan belt

Canada

Glass, radio

Austria

Tires, radiator and heater hoses

Spain

Wiring harness, radiator and heater hoses, fork clutch release, air filter, battery, mirrors

Japan

Starter, alternator, cone and roller bearings, windscreen washer pump

Switzerland

Underbody coating, speedometer gears

Italy

Cylinder head, carburetor, glass, lamps, defroster grills

United States

EGR valves, wheel nuts, hydraulic tappet, glass

Note: Final assembly takes place in Halewood (United Kingdom) and Saarlouis (Federal Republic of Germany).

Source: From *The World Development Report, 1987,* p. 39. Copyright 1987 by The International Bank for Reconstruction and Development/The World Bank. Reprinted by permission of Oxford University Press, Inc.

Fewer and fewer complex manufactured products are totally composed of parts from a single country.

came into being in 1947 when countries accounting for 80 percent of world commerce agreed to work to reduce barriers to international trade. As a result of this and a series of related efforts, world tariff barriers dropped dramatically. American import duties, for example, dropped from an average of 60 percent in 1934, to 25 percent in 1945, to just 4.3 percent in 1987. Other industrialized countries' tariffs were similarly low, with Japan's at 2.9 percent and those of the 12-member European Economic Community at 4.7 percent (Blake & Walters, 1987).

Increased Economic Interdependence

One result of increased trade is that world economics has become increasingly intertwined. Domestic economics, including employment, inflation, and overall growth, is heavily dependent on foreign markets, imports of resources, currency exchange rates, and a variety of international economic factors. Exports account for approximately 6 percent of the Canadian, 7 percent of the American, and 11 percent of the Japanese GNP. Imports make up 12 percent of American and Canadian, and 9 percent of Japanese consumption. The rise in trade is both a cause and a result of this increased international economic **interdependence**. Increased trade stimulated economies and caused new demands for, and dependencies on, foreign products and resources. This, in turn, resulted in even greater trade, because stimulated production and consumption needed even more trade to supply them. Thus, there is a circular relationship among interdependence, trade, and economic growth. The discussions of economics in chapters 1 and 9 detailed some specific statistics relating to interdependence. Even without such statistics, one can easily understand that a world is highly interdependent when Russians eat American wheat, Japanese export cars to Americans but import oil from the Arabs to fuel their own cars, and the French watch televisions built in Asia and ship wine everywhere. Another way to visualize the complex interdependence is to consider the component origins of a European-built Ford Escort as shown in Figure 13.3. The idea of **autarky**, of any country's being truly economically independent, has long since ceased to be a realistic concept.

Increased Domestic Impact: A Two-Way Street

One aspect of increased world economic relations is the escalating interrelationship between domestic and international economics. Every country's economic health, to a greater or lesser degree, is affected by the world economy. Between 1972 and 1990, for example, world exports grew at an average annual rate of 6.5 percent. The global gross domestic product (GDP) grew at an average annual rate of 3.3 percent. Therefore exports grew to be a larger part of these countries' economic output and prosperity.

To reiterate an earlier point, it is extremely important to understand the impact of world trade and monetary relations on domestic economies. Millions of jobs and entire industries can be created or destroyed by foreign sales or competition. Inflation can be accelerated or eased by currency exchange rates. Oil and other vital resources can flow in vast quantity or can be subject to rationing and long lines. You and the world economy are more intimately linked than you probably imagine.

It should also be stressed that the interrelationship between international economics and domestic economics works in both directions. Domestic economics and politics affect the international scene just as world factors affect the national situation. American inflation, as we shall see, helped cause a financial crisis in world banking during the early 1980s. The U.S. deficit is also a major concern of world economic leaders.

Economics: Technical Terms and Sources

The terms gross national product **(GNP)** and gross domestic product **(GDP)** are similar but not interchangeable. GNP measures the sum of all goods and services produced by a country's nationals, whether they are in the country or abroad. Thus GNP includes data such as the profits of a country's MNCs. GDP only includes income within a country, and excludes foreign earnings.

All monetary values in this and the next chapter are in U.S. dollars ($) unless otherwise noted. There are two ways to express monetary values. One is in **current dollars,** which means the value of the dollar in the year reported. Because of inflation, using current dollars means that, for example, the percentage increase in *value* of exports will rise faster than the percentage increase in the *volume* of exports over any period. The second way to express monetary value is in **real dollars,** or uninflated dollars. This means that the currency is reported in terms of what it would have been worth in a stated year. In this book, monetary value is in current U.S. dollars except where noted. Therefore, you could say either a car in 1991 cost $9,852 or (assuming a 4 percent inflation rate) it cost $6,400 in real 1980 dollars.

The number 100 is used as a baseline in many of the figures used in this and other chapters. It is used to show relative change. This number is an abstraction and has no value as such. It simply allows comparisons of later growth or decline. It is used instead of zero to avoid pluses and minuses before subsequent data. For example, if you earned $5,000 in 1980 and a friend earned $7,000, and you wished to compare later earning growth, you would make 1980 earnings for both of you equal to 100. Then, if in 1990, you earned $8,000, but your friend earned only $4,000 (using increments of 10 equal to $1,000), your earnings would be expressed as 130 and your friend's earnings would be 70.

You may find that the data, such as trade expressed in dollars, used in this book for any given year or period varies somewhat from what is cited by another source. Most of the data is based on extensive compilations and complex calculations completed by the sources cited or by the author. But the reporting organizations such as the United States, the United Nations, the International Monetary Fund, the World Bank, and the General Agreement on Tariffs and Trade all use slightly different assumptions and inputs in calculating their final figures. Most of the major sources used herein include careful discussion of exactly how they arrive at their conclusions. You may refer to these if you wish a detailed explanation of their methodologies. The key, then, is usually not to focus too much on specific numbers, especially if they come from different sources. Rather it is best to concentrate on patterns, such as the rate of growth or decline of trade over a period of years.

Unless specifically noted, this chapter relies on the following sources of financial, trade, and other economic data: Euromonitor (1990), *International Marketing Data and Statistics, 1990,* London: Euromonitor Publications; International Monetary Fund (1989), *Governmental Financial Statistics Yearbook 1989,* Washington, D.C.; International Monetary Fund (1990), *Direction of Trade Statistics,* June 1990; International Monetary Fund (1990), *World Economic Outlook* 28 (May 1990); International Monetary Fund (1990), *International Financial Statistics* 43/11 (November 1990); Organization for Economic Cooperation and Development (1989), *OECD Economic Outlook* 46 (December 1989), OECD: André-Pascal, France; United Nations (1990), *Monthly Bulletin of Statistics* 44/8 (August 1990) and 44/10 (October 1990); United Nations (1990), *World Economic Survey, 1990;* United Nations Conference on Trade and Development (1990), *Handbook of International Trade and Development Statistics, 1989;* U.S. Central Intelligence Agency, *Handbook of Economic Statistics, 1989;* U.S. Council of Economic Advisers (1990), *Economic Report of the President* (February 1990); U.S. Department of Commerce (1990), *Statistical Abstract of the United States, 1990;* U.S. Department of Commerce (1990), *Survey of Current Business* 70/9 (September 1990); World Bank (1990), *1988–1989 World Debt Tables,* Washington, D.C.: World Bank; World Bank (1990), *World Tables,* 1989–1990 Edition, Baltimore: Johns Hopkins University Press; World Bank (1990), *World Development Report, 1989,* New York: Oxford University Press.

TABLE 13.2

Percentage of World Exports by Major Economic Categories of Countries

Category of Country	Percentage of Exports			
	1950	**1963**	**1975**	**1990**
Western Developed	6.8%	65.0%	63.8%	73.2%
Soviet Bloc Developed	6.8	12.1	9.8	7.6
Oil Exporters	6.3	6.9	12.9	4.0
Other LDCs	24.8	14.6	12.1	15.2

Data sources: The figures for 1963 and 1975 are from GATT (1983:125); figures for 1950 and 1990 are from UN (1990c). Percentage for 1990 is based on first two quarters.

The pattern of world trade is very uneven. The export market, from which countries profit, is heavily dominated by the Western developed countries.

Domestic politics and international politics are strongly linked. The global economic downturn of the last decade has caused intense domestic pressure to raise tariffs and take other actions to protect domestic jobs and industries. Presidents and prime ministers may fancy themselves world leaders, but they are elected by domestic voters.

Uneven Patterns of Trade

In addition to the historical growth levels of world trade, interdependency, and the domestic impact of trade, it is important to consider the patterns of international commerce. Three facts stand out. First, trade is overwhelmingly dominated by the North, the developed countries. The percentage of world trade shared by less developed countries is both small and relatively static. In fact, if the oil-producing nations are considered along with the other less developed countries, the LDCs have lost ground slightly. Table 13.2, above, shows the percentages of exports in world trade in 1950, 1963, 1975, and 1990 held by various categories of states.

A second, and related, pattern of world trade is that little commerce occurs among less developed nations. North/North trade accounts for 64.4 percent of all world commerce, North/South trade 29.4 percent, and South/South trade a scant 6.2 percent.

A third important trade pattern involves types of exports. Developed countries predominantly export manufactured and processed products. LDCs mostly export primary products (food, minerals, etc.). This is discussed in greater detail in the next chapter, but we can note here that this pattern leaves the LDCs in a disadvantaged position because the prices of primary products expand more slowly than those of manufactured goods and because world demand for primary products is highly volatile.

Increased Financial Ties

Our discussion of expanded international economic activity has focused so far on trade, but there also has been a parallel expansion of international financial ties. These will be dealt with primarily in later sections on multinational corporations and monetary relations, but a preview is in order here. One aspect of increased financial ties is the growth of investment in other countries. When Americans invest in British or Nigerian companies, or when Canadians invest in U.S. corporations, then a complex skein of financial interdependency is begun. Such international investment has long existed, but it has accelerated greatly since World War II. In 1950, U.S. direct investment abroad was $11.8 billion. By 1970 that figure had risen to $78.1 billion, and in 1988 reached $326.8 billion. Investors in other industrialized countries and some in LDCs have added to the international flow of investment capital. In 1970, total world foreign **direct investment** was approximately $164 billion. Just 15 years later, that figure had reached $580 billion and by 1988 it was well over a trillion dollars, including $328.9 billion direct investments in the United States. International portfolio investment, which does not involve the control of companies, is measured in the trillions, with foreign investors holding more than $1.7 trillion in U.S. assets alone.

Another indicator of increased international financial ties is the level of international lending by private banks. In total, private banks in June 1990 had approximately $4.78 trillion in outstanding international loans. Contrary to popular myth, most of this money is not owed by LDCs. In fact, they account for only about 12 percent of the total owed to private banks, while the bulk of lending is among the industrialized countries. Of the international banks, the largest lenders are the Japanese, with a 1990 outstanding total of $666 billion, and the Americans, with loans totaling $527 billion.

It should be noted that the increased flow of trade and capital means that monetary exchange rates have become an increasingly significant factor in both international and domestic economic health. As will be detailed later, the 1980s' rapid rise in the value of the American dollar against the currencies of Japan, West Germany, and some other countries, followed by a 50 percent decline of the dollar against those currencies, had major trade and financial ramifications. It has, among other things, increased inflation in the United States and affected the balance of trade between Japan and the United States.

In sum, then, the international flow of money has reached immense proportions and has added to the interdependency of countries and their citizens.

Strains in the Economic Relations of the North

Although the North has been generally prosperous, all is not well. The industrialized countries' economic growth rate has slowed considerably, from the high levels it sustained earlier. In the 1960s average annual GNP growth for the North was over 5 percent; in the 1970s it was about 3 percent. The early 1980s were difficult times, with growth actually declining 0.3 percent in 1982. In the past few years, growth again picked up to an average 3.8 (1987–89), but OECD projections are for an average 2.8 percent growth for 1990–91. And this was before the growth-dampening Middle East crisis of 1990–91. In short, the North's economic boom era is over. There are many reasons for the deceleration of the North's economy, such as the rising cost of energy and monetary exchange rate volatility. The economies of Western Europe and Japan have also slowed after rebuilding in the aftermath of World War II, and there is the beginning of industrial competition from a few newly industrializing countries in the South. The governments of the North have generally followed policies designed to combat inflation rather than to promote growth, and consumer confidence has sagged in many countries. None of this should be interpreted as meaning that the North is in danger of plunging into an extended depression. This is always a possibility, but current indicators do not presage any immediate danger. Indeed, in the last years of the 1980s, growth patterns turned up

STAYSKAL
81 CHICAGO
TRIBUNE

BUY ★ AMERICAN

MADE IN TAIWAN

The flood of foreign-made products entering the United States and the country's trade deficit have sparked a "Buy American" campaign. It has had, at best, a limited impact.

slightly; balance-of-payments deficits (defined on p. 390) have eased somewhat for most countries, and trade has expanded a bit more quickly. There has not, however, been a return to the robust patterns of earlier decades.

Whatever the causes of the economic slowdown of the 1980s, the result has been a partial retreat from the liberal economic philosophy that predominated for 35 years after World War II. It is both alarmist and premature to talk in terms of resurgent economic isolationism, but there is a distinct disenchantment with free trade, the free flow of investment capital, and other aspects of the liberal economic era.

Even the United States, which was the strongest early advocate of dismantling international economic barriers, has taken a turn toward protectionism. During the Reagan administration, the percentage of imports into the United States that were subject to some form of trade restriction rose from 25 percent to 40 percent. In 1988, the Administration additionally rescinded some of the special trade privileges allowed under GATT's General System of Preferences for several of the newly industrializing countries such as Taiwan and South Korea.

Other issues also trouble the North. A mounting tide of international investment causes many people to worry about whether or not their country's economy is in danger of falling under the control of foreign investors. The easing of tensions between the United States and the Soviet Union and China has sparked renewed controversy over restrictions on Western technological trade with communist countries. The unsettling fluctuations of the international currency market and exchange rates have brought calls from nearly everyone for greater regulations, and there are even proposals to revert to the fixed-rate gold standard.

Despite annual economic summits among the leaders of the **Group of Seven (G-7)**, they have not been able to achieve effective economic coordination. The United States, which once provided that direction, has lost its ability amid domestic economic difficulties, a plummeting dollar, and huge trade and balance-of-payments deficits. According to economist Lester Thurow, the result of the leadership vacuum and heightened self-interest is that the industrial countries recognize that to enhance growth each country "would have to do what's good for the world economy, but they don't want to do it. . . . Coordination is easy to say, easy to praise, but very difficult to do" (*NYT*, 12/27/87:C1).

, Another recent change in the economic structure of the North is the growth of regional trading groups. The most well known is the European Common Market, which now has 12 member countries and may soon expand. The trading bloc and its umbrella organization, the European Community (EC), are also moving toward greater monetary and even political integration (Vernon, 1990). Officials of the EC maintain that "the health of the world economy depends more than ever on our markets remaining open" and argue that "construction of the single market has not led to any change in the ground rules for [trade] policy" (Krenzler, 1989:16). Still, the concern is that Europe will turn toward trade protectionism. "My fear," a U.S. Chamber of Commerce official told Congress, "is that, as European governments seek to balance political interests among [themselves], the legitimate interests of outsiders will be the first to be traded-off. 'Fortress Europe' may not be a realistic outcome, but selected protectionism . . . will be defended as necessary" (Olmer, 1989:133). Furthermore, Europe is not alone. The Canada–United States Free Trade Agreement of 1989 established a trading bloc between those two countries; Mexico is negotiating to join the pact; and President Bush has called for a Western Hemisphere trade association. In Asia, Japan, the members of the Association of Southeast Asian Nations, and other countries have also moved closer together, and a trade bloc could form there. This is especially likely if Europe and any Western Hemisphere trade groups become more protectionist.

The 1990 annual summit of the G-7 leaders in Houston, Texas, provided an example of both the difficulty of achieving economic coordination and the growing regionalization of economic concerns. President Bush acknowledged the loss of U.S. leadership. It is "a rapidly changing world," Bush said, and "we're not urging everybody to march in lockstep." "It is impossible," the *New York Times* dryly commented, "to imagine Lyndon B. Johnson or Ronald Reagan making such statements" (*NYT,* 7/12/90:A1). The differing regional views of the G-7 countries were especially evident in Houston. "There are three regional groups at this summit: one based on the dollar, one based on the yen, one on the deutsche mark," British prime minister Margaret Thatcher observed (*Time,* 7/23/90:26). The United States was more cautious than either the Germans on extending ties with the Soviets or the Japanese on increasing economic relations with China, but Washington did not prevail. As one American observer put it, "both [Germany and Japan] came to Houston, told the United States what they planned to do, and told us to take it or leave it" (*NYT,* 7/12/90:A1).

As President Bush found at Houston, the 1990s may be a time of greater disharmony and distress for the industrialized economies. During the decades of booming prosperity following World War II, the rapidly expanding international economy minimized any pressures for economic rivalry among the developed countries. The dominant position of the United States among the Western industrial countries and the need to remain united in the face of a perceived Soviet threat also served to limit economic discord. These factors have now changed considerably, and there is increasing friction among the G-7 and other developed countries. Domestic economic difficulties will probably heighten tensions, at least in the short term. There are a few analysts who are optimistic about the immediate global economic future (Morris, 1989), but most range from cautious to gloomy. As the 1990s begin the U.S. economy is in recession. The unification of Germany will strain that country's economy. Estimates of $200 billion and up for the reconstruction of what was East Germany are common, and the projected

The leaders of the Group of Seven (G-7), the major industrialized countries, meet annually to try to coordinate economic relations. Their 1990 meeting was in Houston, Texas. They were joined by Jacques Delors, president of the Commission of the European Community. Pictured at Rice University, Delors is at the left, and to his left are Premier Giulio Andreotti (Italy), Chancellor Helmut Kohl (Germany), President François Mitterrand (France), President George Bush (United States), Prime Minister Margaret Thatcher (United Kingdom), Prime Minister Brian Mulroney (Canada), and Prime Minister Toshiki Kaifu (Japan).

German budget deficit could quadruple to $80 billion by 1992. Japan has a growing sense that its economic bubble could also burst. Many analysts believe that stocks, real estate, and other Japanese investments are overvalued. Real estate in Japan, which is the size of Montana, is estimated to have a current market value of $15 trillion, four times the total value of U.S. real estate. The stock market, which traded at a much higher price-earnings ratio than U.S. stocks, suffered a huge (40 percent) decline in 1990, and in the estimate of a Japanese economist, "The stock market bubble has already burst, the land-price bubble . . . will happen next" (*Time*, 10/15/90).

These domestic economic difficulties will increase pressure to protect local economic enterprises and workers and to try to earn profits from trade. The strains are not severe enough to warrant any term such as "economic opponents"; but without a common political enemy, faced with rising intra-Western economic competition, and in a time of relatively slow growth, economic relations distinctly have become less cordial.

Several of the North's economic concerns deserve additional explanation. Therefore, the issues that involve trade, international investment, and monetary regulation will be discussed in detail in this chapter. There are still other issues, such as the formation of cartels (international trading blocs), the Third World role of multinational corporations, loans to the Third World, foreign aid, and North-South trade, that involve the North, but that are particularly related to the development of the countries of the South. As such, these issues will be discussed in the next chapter.

Trade Issues Among the Industrialized Countries

International trade is the most obvious form of economic interaction among countries, and trade relations have become increasingly difficult in the past decade. One important source of trade tension is the unequal records of the industrial countries in their export-import balance. Chronic trade surpluses for some and deficits for others create tensions. The 1980s was a decade of trade prosperity for West Germany and Japan. During 1987–90, for example, West Germany accrued a trade surplus of $337.2 billion and Japan amassed a positive trade balance of $858.4 billion. Canada also had a surplus of $19.4 billion. The United States, by contrast, had a trade deficit of $513.7 billion; Great

Britain's deficit during these years was $323.5 billion. The rest of the OECD countries also had an average trade deficit, amounting in 1989, for example, to $88 billion.

The Growth of Protectionist Sentiment and Trade Barriers

The various factors discussed above have dramatically increased the clamor within the countries of the North to restrict trade in order to ease trade deficits and to protect domestic economic enterprises and jobs. One U.S. labor leader has charged that:

> Foreign trade is the guerrilla warfare of economics—and right now the United States is being ambushed. . . . Free trade is a joke and a myth. And a government trade policy predicated on old ideas of free trade is worse than a joke—it is a prescription for disaster. The answer is fair trade, do unto others as they do to us—barrier for barrier—closed door for closed door. (Blake & Walters, 1987:28)

The current trade difficulties are evident in the latest round of trade talks being held under the auspices of the General Agreement on Tariffs and Trade (Deardorff & Stern, 1990). GATT has almost 100 members who account for 85 percent of all world trade, and since its establishment after World War II GATT has been the West's major trade coordination and regulation organization. The latest of its periodic series of trade negotiations is called the Uruguay Round because the initial meeting was held in Punta del Este, Uruguay, in September 1986. The issues and negotiations are complicated, but the bottom line is that they did not reach agreement by the scheduled conclusion date at the end of 1990. Instead they adjourned in December without success and amid mutual recriminations and thinly veiled threats of protectionist retaliation. There is concern that failure to agree on the multitude of issues about government subsidies of economic interests, trade barriers, intellectual property rights, and other sticking points could seriously undermine the entire post–World War II emphasis on encouraging free international economic interchange. As President Bush warned, the Uruguay Round is "the last train leaving the station, and countries around the world must jump aboard" (*Time,* 10/8/90:65).

Tariffs and Nontariff Barriers to Trade

If the economic war does break out, its weapons will be trade barriers. **Tariffs** are the most familiar trade barrier. At present, tariff barriers are generally low, but they are set high selectively. In 1983, in an effort to protect Harley-Davidson, the last American motorcycle company, the Reagan administration hiked by 1,000 percent the import duty on heavyweight motorcycles from Japan. Still, although it is possible that a sudden escalation of tariff rates in general could occur, the complex series of international agreements governing their level makes such an event unlikely.

A lesser-known but important way of restricting trade is by **nontariff barriers** (NTBs). These are sometimes reasonable regulations based on health, safety, or other considerations, but more often they are simply protectionist. Reminiscent of a Paul Simon song, one team of economic analysts said, "There must be 50 ways to restrict foreign trade without using a tariff." Import or export *quotas* are one NTB. These limit the number of units that can be shipped. Some of these quotas are imposed by importing countries, but many others are voluntarily agreed to by exporting countries rather than face formal restrictions. Japan, for example, has agreed to export only 2.3 million cars to the United States annually, and some 40 percent of all Japanese exports to the European Common Market are covered by "voluntary" quotas. Lest anyone mistake how euphemistic the word voluntary is, when Switzerland and West Germany refused to place voluntary quotas on machine tools, the United States set mandatory quotas that rolled back their exports to earlier, lower levels.

Technical restrictions such as health and safety regulations are another barrier and can bar goods or increase their cost considerably. One example is the dispute that broke out in 1989 between the United States and the European Community. New EC regulations banned the importation of beef grown with synthetic hormones. That cost U.S. beef exporters $140 million, and triggered U.S. tariff retaliation against various European food exports. Officials of the European Community argued the beef ban was a health regulation. United States exporters claimed it was protectionism, especially since some EC members still allowed the sale of domestic beef containing hormones. A January 1991 EC ban on U.S. pork imports, on the grounds U.S. slaughterhouses are not sanitary enough for European standards, heightened the tension.

Subsidization allows a domestic producer to undersell foreign competition at home. One reason that agriculture is one of the least competitive of all trade sectors is that many governments heavily subsidize their agriculture industries. Efforts of the G-7 countries within the EC and as part of the Uruguay Round to reduce agricultural subsidies have met with fierce domestic resistance. Agricultural subsidies in the developed countries for 1989 were approximately $250 billion, and remain a major impediment in trade negotiations.

Dumping is yet another variant of NTB. The tactic is prohibited by GATT rules, but there are frequent charges that it happens. Dumping occurs when a company sells its goods abroad at a price lower than what it sells them for at home. In 1987, for example, the Reagan administration accused Japan of dumping computer chips on the U.S. market. Japan did not admit guilt, but after U.S. trade officials imposed restrictions, such as limiting the importation of Japanese computer chips, on several types of Japanese products, Japan agreed to stop the practice and open its own market to U.S. semiconductors. By that time, however, Japan had come to dominate the U.S. market, while American manufacturers had only 10 percent of the Japanese market; the imbalance has yet to change.

There are other forms of NTBs, but it is unnecessary to list each type to make the point that there are many ways to restrict trade in addition to tariffs. Despite the popular and press focus on Japanese NTBs, the fact is that all of the industrialized countries impose these restraints. Furthermore, while Japanese NTBs are gradually being lessened, those of the United States and others are growing in number and restrictiveness. A key issue, then, is whether the industrialized countries will continue to move toward free trade or whether they will return to the protectionist policies of an earlier era.

Other Economic Factors That Cause Trade Imbalances

The flow of trade is also governed by many factors in addition to governmental policy such as tariffs and NTBs. As we saw in chapter 1, for instance, the fact that the Japanese save much more of their disposable income than do Americans means that there is less demand for imports in Japan than there is in the United States. Demand in the United States is also partly a function of the excellent reputation that many Japanese products, such as automobiles, have. American automobiles do not enjoy the same image of quality in either the United States or foreign markets. Monetary exchange rates also strongly affect prices and therefore trade.

There are also a host of factors related to the exporting country that affect trade. Many analysts maintain, for example, that the emphasis in the United States on short-term profits limits the country's willingness to invest in long-term, initially money-losing product and market development that, in the end, would maintain a competitive edge. According to Akio Morita (1989:19), chairman of Sony Corporation, "the most fundamental change American business will have to undergo is lengthening its time span required to produce a profit." Critics of U.S. industry additionally argue that one cause of high U.S. product prices has been the top-heavy character of American businesses. In response many firms recently have been slashing their white-collar staff to cut costs and increase competitiveness. Some also charge that the United States is disadvantaged by having aging industrial plants and outmoded productive technologies. Robots, for example, are much more extensively used in many countries than they are in the United States. From 1972 to 1990 U.S. productivity (the amount of GNP increase per employed person) increased an annual average of only 3.0 percent compared to 4.5 percent for Japan, 3.6 percent for West Germany, and 3.4 percent for Canada. A fourth of many criticisms is that many U.S. producers have been too complacent about domestic markets and too slow and inept in developing foreign markets. The large, gas-gulping U.S. cars were unattractive to foreigners faced with narrow streets and high gasoline costs. When Apple first introduced its computers to the Japanese market, they did not have Japanese characters and the instruction booklets were only in English. Finally, as a gauge of attitudes, it might be noted that most Japanese executives engaged in foreign trade speak English; few U.S. executives fluently speak Japanese, or any other language for that matter. Before blaming trade deficits on others, a country should examine its own economic practices to see if they contribute to the imbalance.

These and the numerous other factors that govern trade mean that even if no trade barriers existed there would not be perfectly balanced import and export figures. In fact, contrary to popular belief in the United States and elsewhere, a complete absence of trade barriers might actually increase the trade deficits of some countries. As one international economics text points out, "If Japan removed all tariff and non-tariff barriers . . . , and at the same time eliminated all voluntary restraints limiting its exports to the United States, it would appear that Japan's bilateral trade surplus with the United States would increase rather than diminish" (Blake & Walters, 1987:22).

Trade barriers, then, are just part of what determines the flow of trade. Still they are an important part, and the outcome of the debate between the advocates of free trade and of protectionism will influence the course of international economics and politics.

Free Trade: Pro and Con

During the economic prosperity of the 1950s and 1960s, **free trade** advocates far outnumbered protectionists. The lean times of more recent years have changed that, and **protectionism** has been resurrected. This is because trade policy is strongly influenced by political forces. Economic theory makes many valuable contributions, but in the end it is the political leaders who decide. Thus, international economic policy and the various positions on trade are based on a combination of systems-level economic realities such as energy needs and state-level domestic pressures from interest groups, legislatures, consumers, and others.

Free Trade: Pro

Advocates of free trade argue from a series of economic and political propositions. These include the benefits of specialization, the cost of protectionism, the promotion of

TABLE 13.3

The Law of Specialization at Work

	Wheat		Wine	
	Canada	*France*	*Canada*	*France*
Production cost	$50	$90	$70	$30
Transportation	+ 10	+ 0	+ 0	+ 10
Total cost and direction of trade	$60 →	$90	$70 ←	$40

Ideally, specialization, as illustrated above, would result in lower prices. Political and economic factors combine, however, to leave a gap between reality and the ideal.

competition, the ability of trade to promote world cooperation, and the conflict-inhibiting effect of commerce.

Benefits of Specialization   The most basic economic idea supporting free trade is the image of each country efficiently doing what it can do best. Free-trade theory has existed for a long time, dating back, for example, to Edward Misselden's *Free Trade or the Means to Make Trade Florish,* originally published in England in 1632. Free-trade theory is also associated with the ideas of Adam Smith (*Wealth of Nations,* 1776), who argued economies are most efficient when the government does not intervene. Consider the following hypothetical example: Canada produces wheat at $50 a ton and wine at $70 a barrel. France produces wheat at $90 a ton and wine at $30 a barrel. Even given transportation costs of $10 per ton and $10 a barrel, France can save money by purchasing Canadian wheat, and Canada can save money if it buys French wine. Table 13.3 shows this relationship.

This example is, of course, simplistic. Many more sophisticated modifications of the theory have been formulated, and economists adjust their thinking to real-world exigencies. Still, the vision of world prosperity inspired by the specialization that is virtually inherent in a truly free-trade world remains a powerful concept and the stated goal of the world's economic leaders. As the final declaration of the G-7 at the Houston annual summit meeting in July 1990 proclaimed, an "open world trading system is vital to economic prosperity. A strengthened [GATT] is essential to provide a stable framework for the expansion of trade. . . . We reject protectionism in all its forms."

The Cost of Protectionism   The reverse side of specialization is the cost of protectionism to the country erecting barriers. Tariffs and NTBs result in higher prices. This occurs because the tariff cost is passed on to consumers or because consumers are forced to buy more expensive domestically produced goods. In September 1990, for example, the U.S. Congress passed legislation imposing quotas and other restrictions on the importation of textile and apparel products. President Bush vetoed the bill, arguing in part that excluding lower-priced imports would increase the average American family's clothing costs by $75 a year. The United States still, however, protects its 12,600 sugar producers by limiting imports and guaranteeing U.S. producers a sugar price twice the world market price. This costs U.S. consumers about $3 billion more a year than they would pay for imported sugar.

Promotion of Competition   A third economic free-trade argument focuses on competition. Without foreign competition, domestic manufacturers have a captive market. Especially if one corporation dominates its field or if there is monopolistic collusion among supposed competitors, a variety of ill effects, from price fixing to lack of innovation, may occur. American automakers seemingly refused to offer U.S. consumers well-built, inexpensive, fuel-efficient small cars until pressure from foreign competition forced them to reform their product and their production techniques.

Competition has also spurred American manufacturers to begin to modernize and streamline their operations to boost productivity, reduce costs, and improve competitiveness. Between 1981 and 1986, for instance, General Electric shut down 30 aged plants and opened 20 new ones. The U.S. automotive industry has also responded by producing higher-quality small cars at more efficient factories. General Motors's new auto, the Saturn, produced at an entirely new plant in Tennessee, is a good and recent example.

World Cooperation   A fourth, and this time political, argument claims that free trade promotes world cooperation. *Functionalism* (to be discussed extensively in chapter 15 on international organization) argues that cooperating in certain specific functions, such as trade, can lead to habits of cooperation that can be transferred to other, more potentially conflictive areas. If countries can trade together in peace, the interactions will bring greater contact and understanding. Cooperation will then become the rule rather than the exception, and this, it is thought, will lead to political cooperation and interaction. The move toward the political integration of Europe, which began with economic cooperation, is the most frequently cited example (see chapter 18).

Conflict Inhibition   A fifth, and again political, argument for free trade is that it restrains conflict. Trade not only promotes functional cooperation, advocates claim, it also leads to interdependence, which makes fighting more difficult. The theory here is that if countries become highly dependent on each other for vital resources and products, then the cutoff of those supplies would dissuade or even prevent them from fighting. If oil and iron are necessary to fight, and if Country A supplies Country B's oil, and B supplies A's iron, then they are too enmeshed to go to war.

In reality, of course, a very high level of specialization and integration would be required to make this idea work perfectly. Indeed, dependency can cause conflict in some cases. One study has even found that conflict is more likely during periods of economic openness (Mansfield, 1988). This may be because dependence also creates vulnerability. The United States repeatedly threatened military action to protect its oil supplies, it deployed forces to the Persian Gulf in 1987 and to the Middle East in 1990, and in 1991 it went to war there to protect its interests.

From a somewhat different perspective it should also be noted that the deterioration of trade relations can also have a harmful political effect. The causes of the massive U.S. trade deficit with Japan ($49 billion in 1989) are complex and are attributable to policies and practices in both countries. The tendency in the United States is to blame all the difficulties on Japan; Japanese resentment of this has begun to erode political relations. American books such as James Fallows's *Containing Japan* have been countered by books such as Shintaro Ishirara and Akio Morita's *The Japan That Can Say No*; politicians on both sides of the Pacific have become more openly critical of each other's country; and President Bush has even spoken of China as a balance against Japan in Asia. It is important to point out again that politics and economics are closely intertwined. What has become known as "Japan bashing" will harm overall relations, and a U.S. trade war with Japan would be an economic and political disaster for both countries.

Many analysts argue that one reason for the huge and persistent U.S. trade deficit and some other U.S. economic ailments is the rampant consumerism of Americans. The Japanese electronics, German cars, Swiss watches, and other products Americans cannot afford to pay cash for are purchased on credit cards and through installment loans. Walter Cavanagh of Santa Clara, California, shown here, symbolizes that materialism. According to the *Guiness Book of World Records,* Cavanagh has over 1,200 valid credit cards, a dubious world record. Outstanding consumer credit debt (that is, short-term credit, not including mortages) rose 122 percent from $349.4 billion in 1980 to $776.5 billion at the beginning of 1990. During this period personal income rose 94 percent, meaning that Americans are deeper in personal debt than ever before. Consumer debt amounts to $3,106 per American.

Free Trade: Con

There are also several political and economic arguments for protectionism (Root, 1973:303–23). These include protecting the domestic economy, the indirect costs of lost jobs, diversification, compensating for existing distortions, national security, and using protectionism as a policy tool.

Protecting the Domestic Economy   The need for trade barriers to protect the domestic economy is a favorite theme of domestic interest groups. Threatened industries and associated labor unions seek protection from competition. They argue that domestic business will suffer and domestic workers will be unemployed while foreign companies and workers reap the profits. Whatever the objective truth of this argument—and most economists dismiss it—the political pressure for protectionism is intense. An associated argument seeks protection for "infant industry." This is an especially common contention in LDCs trying to industrialize but is also heard worldwide. Many economists give the idea of such protection some credibility but argue that supposedly "temporary" protection too often becomes permanent.

The Indirect Costs of Lost Jobs   Lost jobs and wages cannot be measured in their own terms alone. Rather they must be estimated in terms of a ripple effect that multiplies each dollar several times. A worker without a job cannot buy from the local merchant, who in turn cannot buy from the building contractor, who in turn cannot buy from the department store, and so on rippling out through the economy. Displaced workers also collect unemployment benefits and may even wind up on public assistance programs. These costs are substantial, and although the World Bank and others claim they are less than the cost of protecting jobs, the economic costs of unemployment go far toward offsetting that figure. Finally, there is the psychological damage from being laid off and from other forms of economic dislocation that cannot be measured in dollars and cents.

Diversification   Another protectionist argument holds that economic diversification should be encouraged. Specialization, it is said, will make a country too dependent on a few resources or products. If demand for those products falls, then economic catastrophe will result. In reality no modern, complex economy will become that specialized, but the argument does have a simplistic appeal.

Compensating for Existing Distortions   Yet another protectionist argument is that in the real world many trade distortions exist that are unaccounted for by pure economic theory. Factors including persistent trade barriers, government-managed economies, and state-directed trading (where the government controls trade, especially imports) have created an imperfect economic world. If the oil-producing countries set prices, if communist governments act as state traders, if France continues to leave video recorders sitting on the dock while "awaiting inspection," then, the argument goes, nice-guy free-traders will finish last.

   The answer to some of these distortions is to correct them rather than retaliate, and there has been some hard bargaining in the past few years. In June 1990, for example, the United States and Japan reached an accord aimed at ending some of the trade-restrictive practices about which many Americans had complained. Still, many existing distortions (such as consumer attitudes) are difficult to remedy by governmental action. It is also fatuous to imagine that countries will not control trade at least to some degree for economic, strategic, or domestic political reasons. Therefore, many argue that it is prudent to continue to compensate for existing distortions, and that it is imprudent to take too far a lead in free trade and suffer negative consequences while others hold back (Culbertson, 1990).

National Security   A fifth, and very political, protectionist argument involves national defense (Moran, 1990; Olsen, 1987). The contention here is somewhat the reverse of the "conflict inhibition" pro–free-trade argument above. Protectionists stress that their country must not become so dependent on foreign sources that it will be unable to defend itself. In recent years, the U.S. government has acted to protect industries ranging from specialty steels and computer components to basic textiles partly in response to warnings that the country was losing its ability to produce weapons systems and uniforms. "The world is still divided into sovereign nation-states, reinforced by substantial differences in culture, religion, ideology, and group experience," a consultant to the U.S. Business and Industrial Council recently argued (Hawkins, 1989:545). "And the age-old struggle of nations . . . continues. Thus the political order of the world still fits the mercantilist model. If the United States . . . is to maintain its identity, security, and prosperity . . . [it must] remain the political master of its economic base."

Policy Tool   A sixth protectionist argument maintains that trade is a powerful political tool that can be used to further a country's interests. The extension or withdrawal of trade and other economic benefits also have an important, albeit hard to measure symbolic value (Nossal, 1990). Many people, for example, believe the United States and other countries should end their trade with and investments in South Africa because, they argue, you should not do business as usual with an immoral regime, whether or not the sanctions are a pragmatic success in changing the oppressive government's behavior.

   One way to use trade politically is as a carrot, and economically powerful countries regularly use trade benefits to encourage and reward desired behavior. The United

States, for example, has used greater access to its markets to encourage a desired behavior on the part of the Soviet Union, such as allowing greater emigration of its Jews to Israel and elsewhere. Indeed, the entire end of the cold war confrontation has had a close relationship with the Soviet Union's need for Western trade, technology transfers, aid, and other economic benefits and the West's willingness to supply them. At the September 1990 Bush-Gorbachev meeting in Helsinki, Finland, Gorbachev replied to a reporter's question about possible U.S. aid to the U.S.S.R. with a proud and prickly, "I wouldn't want . . . to give rise to the opinion that the Soviet Union is going to align a certain sum with a certain behavior. . . . It would be very oversimplified and very superficial to judge that the Soviet Union could be bought for dollars" (*NYT*, 9/10/90:A8). That may be literally true, but it also cannot be denied that economic carrots, such as the $20 billion in credits and subsidies that Germany extended to the Soviet Union in 1990, were a powerful incentive for Moscow to support the reunification of Germany, nuclear and conventional arms negotiations, and a variety of other steps toward ending the cold war.

Economic sanctions also can be used as a coercive policy instrument, as a stick as well as a carrot. International economic sanctions have cost South Africa approximately $27 billion over the years and have helped push the country's white leadership to ease the apartheid system (Becker, 1987; Kaempfer, Lehman, & Lowenberg, 1987). It is also probable that the sanctions that the United States imposed on Nicaragua during the years the Sandinistas held power helped create the deteriorating economic conditions that undermined President Daniel Ortega's government and led to his defeat at the polls. The most important example of sanctions in recent years is the UN–imposed restrictions on Iraq. These cost Iraq approximately $1.25 billion a month in lost oil revenues, and were aimed also at creating food and other shortages in Iraq that would either pressure President Saddam Hussein to withdraw from Kuwait or topple his government.

Sanctions, however, have many limitations and drawbacks. One is that they frequently do not work. The sanctions on Iraq did not visibly change Baghdad's behavior. Confidence in their success waned as the crisis has dragged on, and the impatience for military action by some of Iraq's opponents superseded the sanctions. Indeed, after just four months of economic pressure, U.S. secretary of state James Baker gloomily argued that "no one can tell you that economic sanctions alone will ever get [Saddam Hussein] out of Kuwait" (*HC*, 12/3/90:A8). Another difficulty with sanctions is that they may harm economic interests other than those in the intended target. The negative impact that the sanctions on Iraq were having on many other countries is detailed in the box Politics, Economics, and the Middle East crisis on pages 352 and 353. Another way that sanctions can damage those who impose them more than those on whom they are imposed occurs when other countries move in to fill the economic void. The United States' embargo of grain sales to the Soviet Union in response to its 1979 invasion of Afghanistan was an outright failure. It did not change Soviet behavior, and the primary losers were U.S. grain farmers who lost their market when the Soviets turned to Canada, Argentina, Australia, and others for supplies. From this perspective, the possibility of shooting oneself in the foot played a significant role in the mild and transitory sanctions placed on China in dismay over its bloody suppression of pro-democracy demonstrators in 1989. Direct investment (1988) of $3.5 billion in China and exports of $5 billion per year to China helped inhibit the United States from truly cracking down on China with strong sanctions. Other countries had even greater stakes. At the G-7 summit in Houston, only a year after the Tiananmen Square massacre, Japan announced that it would make $5.4 billion in easy-term loans to China. The government in Tokyo had decided, according to one diplomat, that "it had waited out a decent interval" and that it could not afford to imperil the more than $50 billion Japan had invested in China or further antagonize its large Asian neighbor (*HC,* 7/20/90:A6). It may also be argued that sanctions can even harm those whom you want to assist. Some black South Africans and others argue, for instance, that the people who suffer most acutely from sanctions on their country are the impoverished blacks who are the first to lose their jobs in an economic downturn. Similarly, the attempts to strangle Iraq economically, including the cutoff of food supplies, not only harmed Iraqi civilians who have no say in the government's policy, but also had a deleterious effect on Kuwaitis and foreign nationals trapped in Kuwait and Iraq.

We will have occasion to look at trade restriction as a policy tool again in the section on strategic trade below and in the next chapter's discussion of OPEC, but as we can see here, the utility of sanctions is uncertain. Some scholars find that they are useful, especially for an economically powerful country like the United States (Baldwin, 1985). Most studies, however, stress the difficulty of using sanctions (David Brown, 1987; Licklider, 1988). This is well summarized by a recent study that examined 103 attempted uses of sanctions by the United States (Hufbauer & Schott, 1985). These two scholars found that the success of sanctions varies according to policy goals, the economic strength of the target country, the length of sanctions, and other factors. Another important point is that the overall success of U.S. sanctions has declined over time as the strength of the United States in the total world economy has waned. From being effective 44 percent of the time before 1973, the success of sanctions has declined to being effective only 26 percent of the time since then.

The Special Case of Strategic Trade

Within the general debate over the benefits and liabilities of free trade, there is a particular area of controversy over what can be called strategic trade. The issue is how far a country should go in restricting trade and other economic interchanges with countries that are or may become hostile. During most of the period since 1945 the focus of this debate has been on Western exports to the Soviet Union and other communist countries. Led by the United States, the West founded the Coordinating Committee for Multilateral Export Controls (COCOM) to establish and monitor a list of militarily applicable items that could not be exported to communist countries. Over the years, many U.S. allies came to favor more extensive trade with the Soviet Union and other East bloc countries. By the mid-1980s, 6.5 percent of all West German exports and 6.7 percent of all Japanese exports, compared to only 2.5 percent of U.S. exports, were destined for communist countries. U.S. business interests, who argued they were losing valuable markets to less restrictive exporters, also exerted considerable pressure to expand trade. According to one industry study, U.S. export restrictions cost the country $9 billion annually and 225,000 jobs in the mid-1980s. An industry spokesperson derided Washington for "trying to protect secrets which are no longer secret," and charged that "trying to regulate clear down to prune juice [is] not only wasting taxpayers' money, but hurting our exports" (*NYT,* 2/15/88:D6). The dramatic improvement in East-West relations in the late 1980s has done much to defuse this argument about the scope of export restrictions. In mid-1990 COCOM reduced the list of restricted export categories by a third.

This liberalization still leaves 78 mostly high-technological types of products on the banned list. A joint proposal by a U.S. and a British corporation to build a fiber optic cable across the Soviet Union, for example, was not allowed because of its potential

A controversial and continuing trade issue involves the level and type of exports from the West to the East, especially the Soviet Union and to other countries that might use technology imports for weapons systems. Critics of extensive technology trade charge, for example, that dual-use technologies, such as even simple computers, can be converted from peaceful to military applications.

military application. Furthermore, there are numerous other restrictions applied by individual countries on the export of certain technologies, weapons, chemicals, and other products. These restrictions continue the debate over the balance between political wisdom and (for some) moral issues on the one hand, and profitable business on the other. Restrictions also are difficult because there are many dual-use technologies that have both military and civilian applications.

As noted in the last chapter, the arms trade is a huge global business, and a combination of the end of the weapons-generating cold war and the general slowing of the world economy has increased pressures on governments to allow, even promote, the international sales of weapons. Various Western companies have also been willing, sometimes illegally, to sell technology and supply capital to allow Libya, Iraq, and others to build chemical weapons plants, construct missiles, and acquire other capabilities that, arguably, are not in the global interest. It can be said, then, that strategic trade is a special case in the debate over free versus restricted trade, and that some limits on what one sells to others are appropriate. The always unsettled issue, however, is what should be banned and to whom.

Investment Issues Among the Industrialized Countries

Trade is but one of the areas of economic interchange among the industrialized countries. The flow of investment capital is another aspect of the international political economy. Our particular concern here is the growth and practices of the **multinational corporations** (MNCs, transnational corporations) that are at the forefront of the movement of investment capital and private loans among the countries of the North. As is true for trade, the vast bulk of investment capital moves among the industrialized countries. MNCs are also an important aspect of the economic situation of the less developed countries, as the next chapter details. Finally, as we will discuss presently, MNCs are highly controversial whether they operate in the North or in the South.

MNCs: Past and Present

A multinational corporation is a private enterprise that includes subsidiaries operating in more than one state. This means more than merely international trading. Rather, it implies ownership of manufacturing plants and/or resource extraction and processing operations in a variety of countries. Additionally, multinational corporations (MNCs) invest in businesses involved in the supply of services, real estate, retail and wholesale operations, and a host of other operations. Many therefore contend that MNCs are transnational organizations whose operations transcend national boundaries. Whether or not this is true and to what degree it is, is, as we shall see, a highly controversial issue.

Historically, some have traced the roots of modern MNCs to Europe's great trading companies, beginning with the Dutch East India Trading Company in 1689. The level of multinational enterprise expanded in the nineteenth century and into the twentieth. It was not long after Henry Ford began building Model T's that his corporation had its first subsidiary in Europe. Indeed, as early as 1902 one British author wrote a book, *The American Invaders*, warning against the takeover of the European economy by such American predators as Singer Sewing Machine, Otis Elevator, and General Electric.

Not until after World War II, however, did the development of MNCs truly accelerate. Between 1945 and 1968 direct private investment in international ventures increased 10 percent annually.

Modern MNCs have become economic goliaths. As fast as trade and other forms of international commerce have grown, MNCs have expanded even more rapidly. To get some idea of the size and continuing growth of MNCs, consider some of the following statistics:

• There are about 2,000 large (operating in six or more countries) and over 8,000 smaller MNCs.

• These 10,000 MNCs control 90,000 subsidiaries.

• In 1989 the largest 50 MNCs had combined foreign and domestic sales of $1.85 trillion and amassed profits of $77.7 billion.

• Of the top 50, 42 percent are Western European, 34 percent are U.S.–based; and 20 percent are Japanese. Only 2 (Daewoo and Samsung corporations of South Korea) of the 50 are based outside the trilateral countries (the North American and West European industrialized countries and Japan).

• Even among the top 500 MNCs only 22 are in the Third World, and most of these are oil companies.

Finally, it is instructive to measure companies against countries. There is, of course, no comparison in coercive power between any corporation and a state, but corporations do wield considerable economic muscle. Table 13.4 compares MNCs' gross corporate product (GCP sales) with the gross national product (GNP) or gross domestic product (GDP) of a number of countries. According to these standards, the top 50 MNCs had a combined GCP more than three times the combined GDP ($.61 trillion) of the countries of Sub-Saharan Africa.

MNCs and International Investment: Benefactor or Burden

The growth of international investing has created considerable controversy. You will note that many of the arguments in support of encouraging the relatively free flow of investment capital are very similar to those in support of free trade. Similarly, the counterarguments are akin to those put forward by economic nationalists in favor of greater protectionism.

The Case for the Free Flow of Investment Capital

A very general argument that coincides with the liberal economic approach is that *the flow of investment capital reflects a complex and interdependent world*. In an era when

TABLE 13.4

Corporations and Countries, 1987
(figures in billions of dollars)

Corporations	Rank	GCP* ($ billions)	Countries	GNP/ GDP** ($ billions)
General Motors United States	1	127.0		
			Austria	116.8
			Taiwan	101.3
Royal Dutch/Shell The Netherlands/ United Kingdom	4	85.5		
			Argentina	76.9
			Egypt	70.2
Toyota Japan	6	60.4		
			Iraq	56.5
			Greece	46.7
Samsung South Korea	20	35.2		
			Portugal	34.9
			Colombia	33.9
Bayer Germany	38	23.0		
			Bangladesh	17.5
			Chile	17.1
			Kenya	5.6

*GCP stands for gross corporate product.

**The GNP/GDP figures are the latest available.

Data sources: Fortune (8/1/88:24); *World Almanac Book of Facts* (1990).

Many multinational corporations (MNCs) generate GCPs greater than the GNP/GDPs of many countries. Here you can see the relationship between five of the top MNCs ranked by GCP and several countries' GNP/GDP.

national boundaries are becoming increasingly permeable and when a whole range of transnational organizations and relationships are developing, transnational businesses are a natural development.

Supporters also maintain that *MNCs are part of the growth of transnational cooperation*. These supporters believe increased economic cooperation encourages increased international political cooperation. The United States and the Soviet Union sponsor numerous cultural exchange programs on the theory that contact between peoples will increase harmony. MNCs may be part of this general approach. It is noteworthy that, leaving aside questions of gastronomic sophistication, American fast food enterprise is contributing to the evolution of a common global culture. The world's largest Kentucky Fried Chicken outlet, for instance, is on Tiananmen Square in Beijing. McDonald's has over 3,000 restaurants in 52 countries outside the United States, and its largest outlet is the 700-seat restaurant on Pushkin Square in Moscow. It was the first of 20 planned McDonald's for the U.S.S.R.; when it opened on a frigid January 1990 day in Moscow, there was a 500-yard waiting line and riot militiamen to keep order. "Who cares how long we have to wait?" one eager customer exclaimed. "We stand in line for hours, sometimes days. We are accustomed to this" (*HC*, 1/1/90:A10). What made the huge crowd especially amazing was the fact that the 5.5-ruble cost of a *dvioni chizburger,*

One of the arguments for the expansion of multinational corporations and the free flow of international investment capital is that they create transnational co-operation and cultural contacts. One example of this cultural contact is the movement of American fast-food MNCs into other countries, including the opening of the world's largest Kentucky Fried Chicken outlet in Beijing, China.

kartofel-free, and a *koktel* (double cheeseburger, french fries, and a shake) was equal to almost a half a day's pay for the average Soviet worker. The Pushkin Square McDonald's and a wide variety of other Western enterprises are now possible in Moscow under new Soviet laws that allow foreign investors to own and reap capitalist profits from business in the Soviet Union. Even Michael Jackson is part of the MNC invasion of the Soviet Union. PepsiCo operates 25 bottling plants in the Soviet Union, and has run advertisements with the message, "The new generation chooses Pepsi," superimposed in Russian over a video of the rock star singing and strutting his stuff.

Another contention is that *MNC–directed investments provide the host country with a wide variety of economic benefits.* Jobs are one example. In 1990 non-American MNCs employed 3.5 million people in the United States who earned $110 billion. A related benefit is that investment can revitalize declining industries. Hondas, Subarus, and other "Japanese" cars are now made in the United States, and in Fontana, California, a joint effort by Brazilian and Japanese MNCs reopened a steel plant that had been shut for four years. Foreign investors can also bring new management techniques, as was the case with West Germany's Tenglemann Group, which took over A&P in 1980 and saved the foundering food chain from possible bankruptcy and dissolution.

A closely related point in support of international investment is that it may *inhibit conflict by creating economic interdependence.* Arguably, the more we own of each other, the more self-damaging it is to engage in economic or other sorts of aggression. Any chance of a trade war between the United States and Japan will be inhibited by the $16.9 billion in direct investments that Americans have in Japan and the $53.4 billion in direct investments that Japanese have in the United States. Therefore, American investors would be damaged by a U.S. attack on the Japanese economy, and Japanese investors would lose billions in a U.S. depression. Similarly, it may well be that the vast amounts of money that oil-rich countries have invested in the economies of the industrialized countries make the investors reluctant to increase petroleum prices too steeply, a move that would damage the industrialized economies by plunging them into a recession or even depression, which would devastate the investment portfolios of the oil producers.

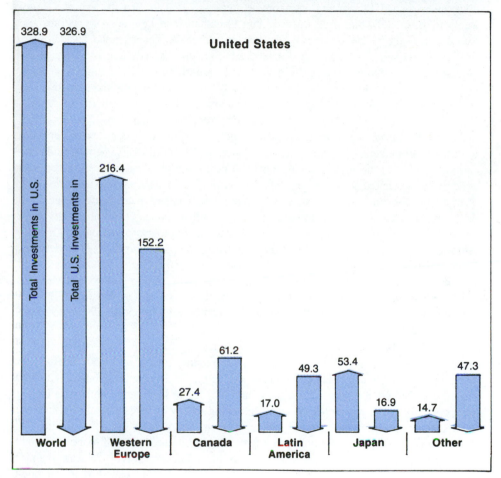

Figure 13.4 The Balance of Foreign Direct Investments, 1988
(in $ billions)

Data source: Statistical Abstract (1990:763).

The flow and balance of direct investment into and out of the United States varies significantly among countries and regions, as you can see from this figure. Overall, however, 1989's U.S. direct investment abroad ($326.9 billion) and foreign direct investment in the United States ($328.9 billion) were approximately balanced.

The Case Against the Free Flow of Investment Capital

There are also a variety of concerns about the impact of the huge sums of investment capital that characterize the international economy.

One fear is that *foreign investors will gain control of your economy* and will be able to influence your political processes and your culture. In the 1960s U.S. investment capital seemed ready to engulf other countries' economies; Jean-Jacques Servan-Scheriver's best-seller, *The American Challenge* (1968), called on Europeans to resist foreign domination. Now, Europeans and others have launched their own challenge.

Americans, after years of being net capital exporters, are now sometimes shocked by the tidal wave of foreign investment into their country. Figures for 1989 indicated that by the end of that year foreign direct investment in the United States had reached $390 billion, a 450 percent increase during the decade of the 1980s. The list of well-known U.S. companies owned by foreign investors is impressive. The British control Capitol Records, Baskin Robbins, and Burger King; Canadians run People's Drug Stores and Roy Rogers; the Germans direct Alka-Seltzer and RCA Records; the Swedes have Frigidaire and Hertz; Wilson Sporting Goods is Finnish; Ramada Inns is a Hong Kong holding; and the Japanese have 7-Eleven Stores, Fotomat, and Columbia Pictures. In fact, the U.S.–U.S.S.R. hot line, the crisis link between Washington and Moscow, was recently sold by Western Union to Tele-Columbus USA, a subsidiary of Motor-Columbus ANG, a Swiss MNC. Overall, foreign direct investment owns 12 percent of all U.S. manufacturing, including more than 50 percent of the U.S. consumer-electronics industries, 40 percent of its heavy truck production, one-third of its chemical industry, and one-fifth of the domestic banking market (Fry, 1990). This trend has caused cries of concern in the United States. Representative Joseph Gaydos (D-Pennsylvania), for one, charges that "for the first time since the Revolution, Americans are being subjected to decisions and dictates from abroad. . . . The multi-national corporation has been described as a predatory octopus, its tentacles reaching out to grasp and swallow a small American fish" (*CR*, 4/13/88:H1613). As with trade, the particular focus of anxiety has been Japanese investment. Symbolically, there was particular consternation when Japanese investors in November 1989 purchased for $846 million a 51 percent share of Rockefeller Center, with its Radio City Music Hall, Rockettes, skating rink, and Christmas tree. Critics carped that the famous center would soon be dominated by a Kabuki theater, sushi bar, and bonsai tree.

The fears occasioned by foreign investment have to be put in some perspective. In the first place, investment is spread broadly among many countries. The 50 largest direct investments in the United States are held by companies in 16 countries. Japan, with 5 of these, is only tied for third with Canada and the Netherlands and behind the United Kingdom (9) and Germany (6). Second, the strong inflow of investment capital into the United States has slowed. The 50 percent drop in the value of the dollar against the Japanese yen and the West German mark that occurred in the latter half of the 1980s had the intended impact of making American products less expensive overseas, thereby increasing U.S. exports and decreasing the U.S. trade deficit. The shift in currency values also, however, dramatically decreased the price of real estate and corporate properties in the United States. At the 1985 high of about 250 yen (¥) to the dollar, Sony's $3.4-billion purchase of Columbia Pictures would have cost ¥850 billion. In 1989, at an exchange rate of approximately ¥142 = $1, the $3.4 billion equaled only ¥482.8 billion. Exchange rates are explained in more detail in the following section. With the relative stabilization of exchange rates, and even a small increase in the value of the dollar versus the yen and other currencies, new direct investment in the United States declined 14.5 percent in 1989 (to $53 billion) from what it was in 1988 ($62 billion). Very preliminary figures indicate that during the second quarter of 1990, there was even a net $3.8-billion outflow of investment capital. Furthermore, in 1989 it was the British, not the Japanese, who accounted for the lion's share of direct investments, spending $27 billion (51 percent of the total) to acquire 158 companies (30 percent of the 521 U.S. companies purchased). Americans, it should be added, were almost equally busy with their own acquisitions. Europe was a particular target, with Americans investing $15.1 billion in 1989, of which 73 percent was in Great Britain, including Ford Motor's acquisition of Jaguar Ltd.

The purchase of U.S. companies and real estate by foreign investors has upset some Americans. The acquisition of Rockefeller Center, shown here, by Japanese investors was greeted with particular dismay. As you will discover in the text (pp. 376–382), however, there are several advantages, as well as some disadvantages, to foreign direct investment.

It is also important to place foreign direct investment within the context of the immense U.S. economic structure. If you add up the direct investment in the United States of the other six G-7 countries plus Switzerland, which are by far the largest direct investors, they control only 5.5 percent of the U.S. business sector (holdings/GDP) or an average of .92 percent each. By comparison, U.S. direct investment in those countries controls an average 4.7 percent of their GDP. Great Britain, the largest direct investor in the United States, has holdings equal to 2.1 percent of the U.S. GDP; U.S. holdings in Great Britain account for 5.7 percent of the British GDP. Overall, foreign direct investment accounts for about 7 percent of the U.S. GDP in contrast to 18 percent in Germany, 20 percent in the United Kingdom, and 27 percent in France. Japan is a major exception to this pattern at only about 1 percent.

You also can begin to see from these figures that foreign direct investment is part of an increasing pattern of global business. Indeed, it is becoming complex even to determine who owns whom. The U.S.–based Hardees hamburger chain is owned by Imasco, Ltd. of Canada, but that company, in turn, is controlled by Great Britain's B.A.T. Industries Plc. Americans worry about foreign auto competition in the United States and worldwide, yet Ford owns 25 percent of Mazda; Ford and Volkswagen have formed a joint company to produce cars in Latin America; Chrysler owns 24 percent of Mitsubishi Motors, which owns part of Hyundai; and General Motors owns 42 percent of Isuzu. As a general rule, national boundaries are no longer a major impediment to the flow of investment capital, and the MNCs are major players in resisting trade or financial protectionism (Milner, 1989). Furthermore, the communist countries, which had been the primary area barring foreign direct investment, are now eagerly seeking it. China first allowed foreign direct investment in 1979, and it amounted to $22 million that year. By 1988 the inflow of direct investment had grown to $4.5 billion (Pomfret, 1989). The Soviet Union also now allows direct investment, and there has been a similar burst of investment there.

Another concern associated with the huge global flow of investment capital relates to *political interference*. Countries often attempt to force or persuade their MNCs' foreign subsidiaries to follow the home country's political lead. The Reagan administration, for instance, tried to stop U.S. subsidiaries in Europe from participating in the

Soviet gas pipeline project in the early 1980s, a move that sparked charges of political interference in Europe. From the other direction, Pat Choate's sensationalistic *Agents of Influence* (1990) argues that U.S. sovereignty is threatened by being manipulated by foreign MNCs.

MNCs can also be the source of political controversy when they appeal to their home governments to help them resist control from host governments. In the early 1980s, for example, the Canadian government's move to bring oil companies more closely under control sparked difficulties with the United States, which attempted to protect U.S. investors' holdings in Canada.

Conversely, home countries worry that MNCs may use their subsidiaries to *escape political control*. One study contends that "the goal of corporate diplomacy is nothing less than the replacement of national loyalty with corporate loyalty" (Barnett & Muller, 1974:89). In 1987, for example, a British subsidiary of a U.S. MNC sold a substance, carbon-carbon, that is useful in manufacturing nuclear missile nose cones, to the Soviets. That sale was illegal under U.S. law, but not British law.

MNCs also raise some *national security issues* for a host country. It is probably not wise to have foreign ownership of businesses that are vital to your defense. In 1987, for instance, the Reagan administration blocked an attempt by Japan's Fujitsu electronics corporation to buy Fairchild Semiconductor, a manufacturer of computer microchips. Ironically, Fairchild was owned by a French company at the time, but it was later sold to an American firm.

Critics of MNCs and the related flow of international investment also charge that they are *harmful to the economies of host countries*. Investments are made to reap profits, and therefore at least part of that gain is repatriated to the home country rather than reinvested in the host country. As a result, a successful investment will, in the long run, create a net outflow of capital. MNCs are also sometimes charged with eliminating more jobs than they create in the host countries because they often bring in components from their subsidiaries overseas rather than buying them from host-country manufacturers. Moreover, MNCs are often belabored for creating an unhealthy socioeconomic structure in which the management class comes from the home country and the worker class is drawn from the host country. This is especially true in less developed countries, but can also be the case in industrialized countries. About half of U.S. managers resign within 18 months of a foreign acquisition. Many of the replacement managers, however, are also Americans. Cultural misunderstanding can also be a liability for a foreign investor. A poor understanding of the retail market, labor relations, or other business conditions is one reason that half of all foreign direct investment in the United States eventually ends in disinvestiture. In 1989, for example, Australian entrepreneur George Herscu was forced to put into bankruptcy his $1.2-billion holdings in U.S. retail stores (including Bonwit Teller and B. Altman). As a general proposition, though, it is in the interest of a business to adjust to the culture in which it is operating, and the cultural problems of doing business in other countries should not be exaggerated.

There are also concerns that MNCs are *harmful to the economies of their home countries*. Jobs are a major issue, and MNCs are regularly charged with exporting them. The thrust of this line of thinking is that the MNCs set up subsidiaries in countries where labor costs are cheaper rather than continuing production in their home country. There is reason for concern when one learns that in 1987 Canadian employees had an hourly average rate of $9.61 and Singapore workers received $3.69 per hour. A related contention is that by setting up manufacturing and other facilities overseas, MNCs accelerate the deterioration of their own country's economic infrastructure by not investing in plant modernization at home.

MNCs: The Value of Regulation and the Canadian Approach

As these points about the role of MNCs in the economy of the North indicate, these giant enterprises are of mixed value. The appropriate response to this balance sheet of assets and liabilities is to harness the benefits available through international investment while avoiding some of the drawbacks. This can be done through regulation.

To repeat a point, concern about foreign domination is overdrawn for countries of the North. Most of these countries have such substantial economies that they would be very difficult to dominate. Also, since foreign investments come from many sources, the economic and political manipulation that does occur is diluted because it is exercised by many corporations rather than a few. Therefore its impact is dispersed. Onetime European concern about American domination proved groundless. Current American concerns are similarly overblown. Georgetown University professor Theodore Moran maintains that with a $4.5-trillion U.S. economy, "We are not going to have our economy taken over by foreigners unless it continues to decline for 50 or 60 years" (*Time,* 9/14/87:62).

That may be true, but it is also important to use prudent regulation to avoid potential political and economic problems. Most of the developed countries, however, do not have a broad national policy to regulate foreign investment (Black, Blank, & Hanson, 1978).

Canada is an exception, though, and provides a worthwhile example of fears about, and responses to, massive foreign investment. In 1985 companies dominated by foreign investors accounted for 29 percent of Canada's industries, 57 percent of its petroleum and natural gas, 58 percent of mining and smelting, and 52 percent of its machinery production. Americans led all other foreign investors in Canada, with their 1986 direct investments standing at $66 billion (Canadian dollars), which gave America a 22 percent share of all Canadian industries.

Studies show that Canadians are concerned over the prospect of foreign control, and there have been several official studies by the Canadian government on the issue. One, the Gray Report of 1972, found that MNCs have little direct effect on Canadian public policy. Still, the country has been working to reduce and control foreign investment. Between 1973 and 1985 the percentage of foreign-owned business in Canada dropped from 34 percent to 29 percent. In 1972 Canada established the Foreign Investment Review Agency to review nearly all direct investments in the country. This agency established guidelines on acceptable investment practices; in its first eight years it rejected 10 percent of applications (Spero, 1985:144–54). Canadians still worry about possible domination; this concern was heightened by the 1989 free trade agreement with the United States. Still, many of the worst possibilities have been avoided. One Canadian economist put it this way, "We in Canada have much more foreign ownership than the U.S. will ever have, and we're one of the wealthiest countries in the world as a result" (*Time*, 9/27/87:62).

International Monetary Relations and Their Regulation

Of all the facets of international economic relations, the importance of the ebb and flow of the world's currencies is the least understood. Periodically these days we hear that after years of exceptional "strength," the American dollar is "weak" and has plunged in a virtual free-fall against the Japanese yen and the West German mark. In January 1985 the dollar was worth 258 yen. Three years later it was worth only 122 yen. Similarly, the dollar plummeted during the same period from 3.25 marks to only 1.80 marks. By mid-1990 the rates were 148 yen and 1.61 marks to the dollar. Emotionally, we might not like the dollar's decline, but is it really bad? That depends.

The dollar's decline is bad news if you are going to buy a Japanese VCR or a German automobile. They will cost more. So will traveling in those countries, because your dollar is worth less there. On a more general level, if your national currency is weakening, inflation will probably go up in your country because the foreign products you buy will be more expensive. Also, your standard of living may go down, or at least rise less rapidly, because some exports you would like to purchase will be too expensive.

If, on the other hand, you are a manufacturer trying to sell something to the Japanese or Germans, the dollar's decline is good news because your product's price will decline in those countries and you should be able to export more. The U.S. tourist industry is also pretty happy, because a lot more Japanese and Germans will be visiting sites from the Statue of Liberty to the Golden Gate Bridge. A declining currency, then, is good for businesses that export, and this may translate into more jobs as factories expand to meet new orders.

Money, you must remember, has no intrinsic value. We accept it in exchange for other goods and services only because we are confident that others will, in turn, accept it for goods or services we ourselves want. This principle is true on an international as well as a personal scale. Therefore, the stability of world **monetary relations** is vital to global economic well-being. This has always been true, but as trade and other economic relations have expanded, the importance of monetary interchange has increased proportionately.

In the rest of this chapter, we will look at the nature of exchange rates, the history of monetary regulations, current issues including balance of payments and lending practices, and attempts to reform the monetary system. The financial position of LDCs and attempts at financial cooperation are more fully discussed in chapters 14 and 18, respectively.

Exchange rates are, very simply, the values of two currencies in relation to each other—how many dollars per yen and vice versa.

The exchange rate is important because it affects several aspects of the balance of payments and the health of domestic economics. Trade, for example, is partly governed by how much foreign imports cost relative to domestic products.

The example in the box on How Exchange Rates Work (opposite) shows two things. First, it shows the mechanics of how exchange rates affect prices. Second, it demonstrates that shifts in exchange rates influence imports and exports and, therefore, trade balances. The example does not mean, however, that prices are the only factor that influence trade patterns. If price was the only factor, and the exchange rates had changed dramatically (which they did), then the trade pattern would have shifted massively between Japan and the United States (which it did not). This point will be important to remember as we discuss soon the serious monetary problems, including the huge U.S. trade deficit and balance-of-payments deficit, facing the North. Before taking up these issues, however, we should first examine the history of monetary relations during the last half-century.

Monetary Relations Since World War II

Many scholars and politicians believe that the Great Depression of the 1930s and World War II were partly caused by the near international monetary chaos that characterized the years between World War I and World War II. Wild inflation struck some countries. The depression of the 1930s caused other countries to suspend the covertibility of their

How Exchange Rates Work: Falling Dollars, Rising Yen, and Who Buys Which Cars*

To begin to understand the mysteries of how exchange rates work and the impact of their fluctuation, consider the following two scenarios: the first with the dollar ($) equal to 258 yen (¥), which was the case in early 1985; and the second with the dollar equal to ¥148, which was the case in mid-1990. For our problem, let us think about an automobile that costs ¥2,064,000 to manufacture in Japan and another that costs $12,000 to build in Detroit. Let us further suppose that an average Japanese worker makes ¥1,086 an hour; an American makes $10 an hour. Manufacturing costs and wages are not directly affected by exchange rates and, therefore, remain constant.

Automobile Imports at a ¥258 = $1 Exchange Rate

- At ¥258 to the dollar, the equivalent cost is $8,000 for the Japanese car (¥2,064,000 ÷ ¥258) and ¥3,096,000 for the U.S. car ($12,000 × ¥258).
- It will take the Japanese worker earning ¥1,806 ($7) an hour a total of 1,143 work hours (¥2,064,000 ÷ ¥1,806) to buy the Japanese car and 2,851 work hours (¥3,096,000 ÷ ¥1,806) to buy the American car. The Japanese worker will probably buy the Japanese car.
- It will take the American worker earning $10 (¥2,580) an hour a total of 800 work hours (¥2,064,000 ÷ 2,580) to buy the Japanese car and 1200 work hours ($12,000 ÷ $10) to buy the American car. The American worker will probably buy the Japanese car.
- With both the Japanese and American worker buying Japanese cars, Japanese automobile exports to the United States will rise and U.S. exports to Japan will decline.

Automobile Imports at a ¥148 = $1 Exchange Rate

- At ¥148 per dollar, the equivalent cost is $13,946 for the Japanese car (¥2,064,000 ÷ ¥148) and ¥1,776,000 for the U.S. car ($12,000 × ¥148).
- It will take the Japanese worker earning ¥1,806 ($12.20) an hour a total of 1,143 work hours (¥2,064,000 ÷ 1,806) to buy the Japanese car and 983 work hours (¥1,776,000 ÷ ¥1,806) to buy the American car. The Japanese worker will probably buy the American car.
- It will take the American worker earning $10 (¥1,480) an hour a total of 1,395 work hours (¥2,064,000 ÷ 1,480) to buy the Japanese car and 1,200 work hours ($12,000 ÷ $10) to buy the American car. The American worker will probably buy the American car.
- With both the Japanese and American worker buying American cars, automobile exports from Japan will decline and exports from the United States will rise.

*The changes in dollar-yen values are hypothetical and illustrative only. Monetary rates have an important impact on costs and trade, but there are many other political and economic factors that also are important. These are too complex to calculate here and also vary widely for different times, products, and countries. This box is meant to focus on monetary values only, and the explanation does not imply that dollar-yen values and trade will vary in exact one-to-one proportion.

currencies, and the North broke up into three rival monetary blocs: British, American, and French. Other countries, such as Germany, abandoned convertibility altogether, and adopted highly autarkic monetary and trade policies. It was a period of open economic warfare—a prelude to the military hostilities that were to follow after 1939 (B. Cohen, 1987).

The Bretton Woods System

As part of postwar planning, the Western allies met in 1944 at Bretton Woods, New Hampshire, to establish a new monetary order. The **Bretton Woods system** operated on the principle of "fixed convertibility into gold." At its root, the system depended heavily on the strength of the American dollar, which was set at a rate of $35 per ounce of gold.

As long as the American economy was strong, international confidence remained high and countries accepted and held dollars on a basis of "as good as gold."

In addition to this system of convertibility, Bretton Woods established several institutions to help promote and regulate the world economy. For our discussion here, the most important of these is the International Monetary Fund (IMF). The primary function of the IMF is short-term lending to countries with international balance-of-payments problems. If a country is spending more than it is taking in, it can draw on IMF funds to help buy back its own currency, thus maintaining exchange-rate stability.

The End of the Bretton Woods System

The Bretton Woods system lasted for 25 years, and it worked reasonably well as long as the American economy dominated the world and the dollar remained strong. Beginning in the 1960s and accelerating in the early 1970s, the foundation of the Bretton Woods system collapsed. The basic cause was the declining U.S. balance-of-payments position and the resulting oversupply of dollars being held by foreign banks and businesses. The growth of world competition, the costs of American foreign policy (especially its war in Vietnam), the astronomical rise in oil prices, domestic spending and inflation, and other factors further lowered confidence in the dollar. Countries were less willing to hold dollars and increasingly asked the United States to buy them back at the $35 = 1 ounce gold rate. U.S. gold reserves fell precipitously; a crisis was reached in 1971 as U.S. gold reserves fell to only $10 billion against $80 billion in U.S. currency being held overseas. Unable to continue under the old system, the United States took a series of steps that took the country off the gold standard. In place of fixed convertibility, a new system, one of "free-floating" currency relations, was established. Here, the value of a country's currency was basically left to supply and demand.

The Current Monetary Situation

Despite the appeal of its economic simplicity, the free-floating monetary system has not worked well. One problem is that high U.S. interest rates and the country's political stability kept the demand for the dollar, and thus its value, high despite large U.S. trade deficits. Another is that some governments, including Japan's, acted to keep their currencies weak compared to the dollar in order to stimulate exports to the U.S. market and elsewhere. Also, the huge amount of currency that is involved in international financial dealings has strained the ability of governments to regulate it. These and other factors have led to urgent calls for international cooperation and new monetary reform, but despite efforts in these directions, no plan has been found acceptable and workable. The result, according to one analysis, is that "the international monetary system since 1971 makes the Bretton Woods system look tranquil and coherent by comparison" (Blake & Walters, 1987:78).

The Globalization of Banking

Another major change in the financial and monetary state of the world is the globalization of banking. In a relatively short period of time, banks have grown from hometown to national to international enterprises. As noted earlier in this chapter, commercial banks in mid-1990 had $4.8 trillion in outstanding international loans. Chapter 3 also mentioned banks as a type of important international actor. The world's 10 largest banks have combined (1989) assets of $3.22 trillion, outstanding loans of $1.8 trillion, and net earnings of $9.8 billion. To belabor the obvious, they are huge financial

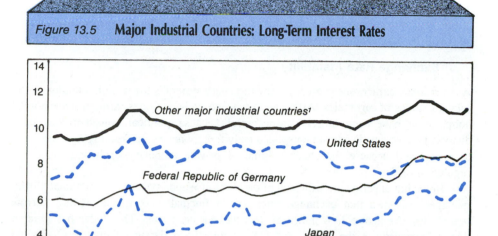

Figure 13.5   Major Industrial Countries: Long-Term Interest Rates

Source: IMF (1990).

[1]Canada, France, Italy, and the United Kingdom; composite is the average of the interest rates for individual countries weighted by the average U.S. dollar value of their respective GNPs in 1988.

enterprises, and whom they loan their money to, for what, and what interests they charge have a major impact on the global economy. One indication of this is the close relationship in the changes of long-term interest rates that is evident in Figure 13.5. As you can see, there are differences in rates among countries, but at least for the industrial countries, the rise and fall of rates are synchronous. One notable trend in the balance of international banking is the shrinking role of U.S. banks. The United States had none of the top 10 banks in 1989 measured in terms of assets (Citicorp ranked 11th). Only 3 of the top 50 and 13 of the top 100 banks are now U.S.–based. By contrast, 22 of the top 50 and 30 of the top 100 banks are Japanese. Most of the others are European, although Canada has 5 and the Third World 6 of the top 100 banks. One cause of the shift away from what once had been U.S. bank dominance was the decline of the dollar, which had the impact of doubling the relative assets of Japanese and German banks in the mid-1980s; the assets of banks were also inflated in many other countries where the holdings of the banks were, for the most part, calculated in local currency. Difficulties with international loans (especially in the Third World) and domestic economic problems have also caused a shrinking of the relative size of U.S. banks and their partial retreat from the international marketplace. Chemical Bank, for example, has cut the number of countries where it maintains loan offices from 30 to 9, and Chase Manhattan has abandoned the market in 22 of 55 countries where it formerly did business. Whether this U.S. banking retreat is permanent or will be reversed remains to be seen. There are some signs that offset the recent declining figures. Citicorp, in particular, still has the world's widest-ranging network, with 2,200 offices operating in 98 countries and serving 20 million customers.

Current Monetary Issues

There are several complex issues facing the world monetary system. Two that particularly involve North-North financial relations are the instability of exchange rates and the balance-of-payments deficits some countries are experiencing. Another important monetary issue is international lending practices, but this is more a North-South matter and will be addressed in the next chapter.

Exchange Rate Instability

As mentioned earlier, one problem in the monetary system is the wide fluctuation of the relative values of currencies. Attempts to manage exchange rates through international cooperation have been largely unsuccessful because political considerations have distorted the economic adjustments that a truly free monetary market might be expected to make, and because the sheer volume of private monetary exchange makes its regulation difficult.

In the initial period after the end of the Bretton Woods system, international money managers assumed that exchange rates would fluctuate slowly and within narrow boundaries. As Figure 13.6 indicates, this has not been true. The dollar has gyrated widely, especially in the 1980s, and U.S. exports have fluctuated inversely with the dollar's foreign exchange value. The late 1970s saw a fairly quick depreciation of the dollar by about 15 percent of its 1973 base value. Then beginning in 1980, the dollar appreciated at a rocket rate of over 56 percent of its 1980 value, leaving it 30 percent higher than its 1973 base value. Having reached this height, with the resulting massive U.S. trade deficit, public confidence and governmental action intervened to depreciate the dollar's value. In just three years it declined to about its 1973 base value, was worth less than half of what it had been against the yen, and had declined by nearly as much against the West German mark. Declines in relation to other currencies such as the British pound and the French franc were not as great but were still steep. If Figure 13.6 were extended out to 1990, you would see that, on average, the U.S. dollar strengthened a bit in mid-1989 (110.5) then declined in 1990 to 102 (1980 = 100).

In general, governments have not been able to manage international monetary exchange rates successfully. To do so, a country's central bank, for example, may choose to create demand by buying its own currency if it wishes to keep the price up. In this case the price goes up because of increased demand for a limited supply of currency. Conversely, a central bank that wishes to lower the value of its currency may create a greater supply by selling its currency. Governments might even cooperate to control any given currency by agreeing to buy or sell it if it fluctuates beyond certain boundaries. To facilitate this way of controlling currency, the International Monetary Fund even created **Special Drawing Rights (SDRs)** as reserves that central banks could draw on. SDR value is based on an average value, or "market-basket," of several currencies, and SDRs are acceptable as payment at central banks. Countries facing strong, unwanted declines in their currencies can borrow SDRs from the IMF and use them in addition to their own reserves to counter the price change.

SDRs have had a positive effect, but they have not been sufficient to check instability. Partly this is because countries sometimes work at odds with one another. Many Europeans have not been happy about the decline of the dollar because they fear that they will lose export markets to the United States. This has led some governments to take actions counter to what U.S. officials are trying to achieve.

The total value of SDRs, which stood at $65.4 billion in October 1990, even when added to other national reserves, has not risen as fast as the avalanche of money moving in international channels. In 1989, the three biggest currency trading centers (London, New York, and Tokyo) alone had an average daily volume of $431 billion. That means that in these three cities, $157.3 trillion in currencies were bought and sold in 1989 for other currencies. This represents a 119 percent increase in just three years from a daily

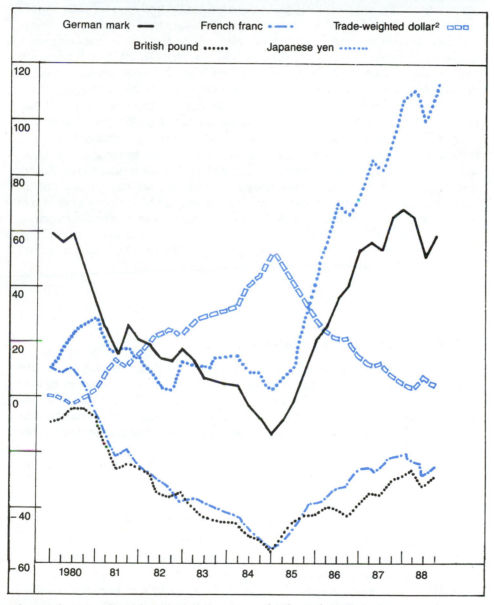

Figure 13.6   **Selected Developed Countries: Percent Change in Value of Currencies Relative to the U.S. Dollar,[1] 1980–88**

[1]Change relative to selected foreign currencies, compared with March 1973.

[2]Relative to 16 major currencies, weighted by 1979–80 trade in manufactures.

Source: CIA (1989).

In this figure, when one of the currency lines is going up, it is increasing against the value of the U.S. dollar. Therefore, the value of the U.S. dollar is decreasing. The trade-weighted dollar line is complicated, but it can be understood as the price of U.S.–manufactured goods to 16 other countries. As the dollar declines, that price goes up, and U.S. exports decline.

$197 billion in 1986. Adding in smaller currency trading markets would bring the 1989 total to about $550 billion a day in currency exchanges. What this means is that it is more and more difficult for the central banks of governments to control monetary exchange rates by buying or selling currency. Central banks use their monetary reserves (currencies, SDRs, and gold) to try to control rates, but the total reserves of the world's countries are only $667.7 billion (September 1990), hardly more than the daily flow of currency. The international flow of money also creates problems in regulating these transactions or even your own currency. In 1990, for example, a U.S. indictment was handed down against an Atlanta branch of Italy's Banca Nazionale del Lavoro for an illegal loan (under U.S. and Italian laws) to Iraq of almost $3 billion. Amazingly, it was partly underwritten by the U.S. Department of Agriculture on the theory it was promoting U.S. farm exports; in fact the loan was used, among other things, to develop Iraq's Condor 2 missile. Another unsettling aspect of currency exchange is that it is difficult to stop what has become known as money laundering by the global narcotics industry in the torrent of international currency trading. There is no accurate estimate of how large a figure narcotics money trading accounts for, but the estimate that the wholesale U.S. cocaine market alone is worth an annual $28 billion gives some idea of the volume. A final indication of the difficulty of keeping track of the world currencies is that of the $242.3 billion in U.S. currency in circulation in 1989, the government could not locate $180 billion (74.3 percent) of it. The Treasury Department thought about half of all outstanding currency was overseas, but no one was really sure.

Balance-of-Payments Problems

Many of the problems that we have already discussed including trade deficits, the ebb and flow of investment capital and investment returns, and international borrowing have combined to create problems for some countries' balance of payments. If all the economic theories worked perfectly, the flow of money between countries should remain in a state of near equilibrium. Because economics is very political, however, major imbalances occur.

The **balance of payments** is a figure that represents the entire flow of money into and out of a country—that is, credits less debits.

Credits (plus items)

1. Exports
2. Foreign travel of others to your country (military, tourists)
3. Foreign purchases of your services (for example, consulting)
4. Gifts and other transfers from abroad (foreign aid, charity)
5. Capital imports (loans to, investments in your country)
6. Profits, interest from foreign investments
7. Government receipts from foreign activity

Debits (minus items)

1. Imports
2. Your citizens' travel in other countries
3. Your purchase of foreign services
4. Gifts to those abroad
5. Capital exports
6. Profits, interest paid to foreign investors
7. Government overseas expenditures

During the 1970s, the balance of payments of the industrialized countries suffered because of high oil costs, dropping from a $9.7-billion surplus in 1971 steadily downward to a mammoth $61.8-billion deficit in 1980. Then, in the 1980s, oil prices declined, and economies recovered. The balance of payments of most of the North's countries returned to near even, with a 1990 deficit of only $1 billion for all of the North's countries combined. The failure of the North to achieve a positive balance of payments even during this favorable period can be attributed to one country: the United States.

Astronomical trade deficits and overseas spending more than offset U.S. gains from sales of services and investment returns. Also, the gaping U.S. federal budget deficit required the borrowing of large sums from private foreign investors and the paying of interest to them. By late 1989, foreigners held 21.8 percent of the $1.5 trillion in bonds and other instruments sold by the Treasury to finance the yearly deficits. These holdings resulted in tens of billions of dollars in interest payments going to the country's foreign creditors. Corporate and public spending added to the accumulation of debt. In 1987, the rate of American saving of disposable (after-tax) income fell to a 40-year low, the poorest among the major industrialized nations, and has only risen slightly since then. Among other impacts, this meant a greater reliance on foreign lenders to fund the public debt and the reinforcement of a stubborn trade deficit as Americans continued to buy imported goods at record volumes despite the falling dollar and the rising cost of imports. Corporate savings were also low. One of the ironies is that companies are not only borrowing from foreign lenders to refurbish production facilities, but that since some of the key needs, such as machine tools, are now foreign-dominated, U.S. manufacturers are using the foreign funds to import foreign goods. Thus both the purchase of modern equipment overseas and the interest on the loans are adding to the net flow of funds out of the country and to increasing the balance-of-payments deficit.

This caused the annual U.S. balance of payments to continue in the red, expanding from an average yearly deficit from 1975 to 1979 of $13.6 billion to deficits of $116.4 billion in 1985 and a peak of $153.9 billion in 1987. The deficit has eased since then, but was still $110 billion in 1989. By 1985 these annual shortfalls turned the United States into a debtor nation for the first time since 1917. Americans owed foreigners a net $111 billion (debt minus money owed). As recently as 1982, the United States was in an enviable position with a $137-billion credit (money owed minus debt). By the end of 1989 it had spiraled to a debit of $645 billion. This net debt only represents approximately 5 percent of the country's total assets, and thus is still only a warning sign, but some analysts are predicting that it could rise to over $1 trillion by the mid-1990s.

The growing U.S. balance-of-payments deficit is more than just an American problem. First of all, for all its recent travails, the U.S. economy is still the world's largest. Second, the dollar remains the basic unit of international exchange. Third, the United States continues to be the leader, albeit less dominantly so, of the economic and political noncommunist developed countries. Therefore an ailing America creates weakness in the entire system. This situation threatens to further erode economic and political cooperation and to lead the major industrialized countries toward more self-centered trade, monetary, and other economic policies.

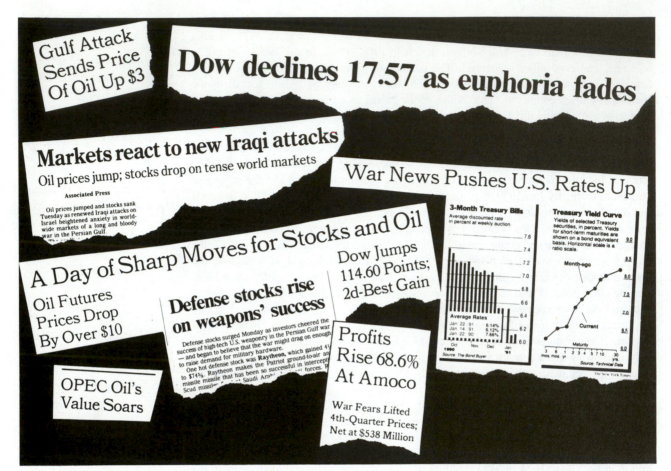

Politics and economics are closely interrelated, as this chapter began by observing. As the box on pages 352 and 353 discusses, Iraq's invasion of Kuwait, the UN sanctions, and Operation Desert Shield had both economic causes and economic effects. The headlines shown here from late January 1991, after the onset of war and the launching of Operation Desert Storm, attest to the major economic impacts of the escalation from crisis to war.

Chapter Summary

1. Economics and politics are closely intertwined aspects of international relations. Each is a part of and affects the other. This interrelationship has always been true, but it has become even more important in recent history. Economics has become more important internationally because of dramatically increased trade levels, ever-tightening economic interdependence between countries, and the growing impact of international economics on domestic economics.

2. The stronger role played by international economics means that political relations between countries have increasingly been influenced by economic relations.

Currently, for example, the most significant question in U.S.–Japanese relations is the trade imbalance (in Japan's favor) between the two allies. Conversely, politics also significantly affects economic relations. Domestic political pressures are important determinants of tariff policies and other trade regulations. Trade can also be used as a diplomatic tool. The U.S. grain embargo against the Soviet Union in response to the invasion of Afghanistan is one example.

3. Our discussion of international economics is divided into three parts. This chapter discussed economic issues that are centered primarily in the developed

countries (North). The next chapter discusses the economic situation of the less developed countries (South). Chapter 18 discusses the world's efforts to achieve greater economic cooperation, coordination, stability, and equity.

4. This chapter has focused mainly on questions of trade and on questions of monetary relations. Trade, as noted, has become an increasingly important part of world politics. The increases in trade have brought many benefits, but there are also problems.

5. The patterns of trade are one problem. Overall, the North, which produces manufactured goods, has a considerable advantage over the South, which produces mostly primary products (agricultural products and raw materials).

6. There are also problems in bilateral trade patterns. The gross imbalance in exports and imports between Japan and the United States is a previously mentioned example.

7. Another troublesome trade issue is the continued existence of a wide variety of barriers to trade. In part, these are based on tariffs, but nontariff barriers are more important.

8. There are significant arguments on both sides of the question of eliminating trade restrictions. Free-traders argue that trade results in greater efficiency and lower costs because of the law of comparative advantage. Free-trade advocates also contend that international commerce promotes world cooperation and inhibits conflict.

9. Those who reject complete free trade argue that trade barriers are needed to protect domestic industry. They further maintain that overreliance on other countries is dangerous for national security reasons and that trade can be a valuable policy tool to reward friends and punish enemies.

10. The wisdom of trade between the Western allies and the communist countries is a very special trade question. There is a good deal of dispute within the West about what level and what type of trade with the communists is appropriate. Some consider trade between East and West both good business and a method of promoting cooperation between the two camps.

11. Opponents of unrestricted trade, including the United States during the past few years, argue that trade too often supplies opponents with technology and goods that increase their strength and that it encourages dangerous dependency on an enemy for needed resources and products.

12. The question of the status and roles of international investment and multinational corporations is another issue related to foreign commerce. Today, commerce is heavily influenced by huge corporations that conduct business worldwide. In purely economic terms, some MNCs rival small countries in their output. MNCs are highly controversial.

13. Some argue that MNCs are a necessary part of today's complex international economic structure and that they provide many benefits in the form of transferring technical ability, capital, and jobs.

14. Critics of MNCs charge them with exploiting host countries, interfering with their politics, and engaging in unethical economic and social practices.

15. International monetary relations are a very important but little-understood part of international economics and politics. With the collapse of most of the post–World War II Bretton Woods economic system, monetary relations have become unsettled and troublesome during the last decade and a half. Exchange rates, which supposedly float relatively freely and adjust according to market conditions, are sometimes out of balance.

16. The mid-1980s strength of the American dollar, partly artificial, caused numerous problems, including a massive U.S. trade deficit. Then, beginning in 1985, the dollar declined sharply.

Having nothing, nothing can he lose.

Shakespeare, *Henry VI*, Part III

How apt the poor are to be proud.

Shakespeare, *Twelfth Night*

No one can . . . love his neighbor on an empty stomach.
Woodrow Wilson, speech, May 23, 1919

It's really very simple. . . . When people are hungry they die. So spare me your politics and tell me what you need and how you're going to get it to these people.

Bob Geldof, *NYT,* January 16, 1985

ECONOMICS:
THE SOUTH

The last chapter on the economics of the industrialized North dealt with strength. This chapter is about the economic weakness of the South. Surely the North has economic uncertainties, but they pale when compared with the position of and the problems facing the **less developed countries (LDCs)** of the South. To examine the reality of the economic deprivation that grips most of the globe, this chapter will detail the massive disparity between the ends of the North-South Axis and discuss some of the causes. The chapter will then take up the South's most critical need, development capital, and look at its possible sources—loans, trade, private investment, and foreign aid. As we shall see, however, none of these sources is proving adequate. Next, our attention will turn both to the Third World's increasing demand that the North share its wealth, and to the actions that LDCs are taking to try to better their economic circumstances. The North's response will also be included in this discussion. That response is marginal. While there is some progress toward improving the situation of the South, many countries are in desperate straits. Thus the chapter will end, as it begins, on a gloomy note. In a somewhat brighter picture, the beginnings of the multinational response to world poverty will be dealt with in chapter 18 on economic and social cooperation.

Existing Patterns

The world is a mixture of wealth and poverty, progress and despair, exploitation and assistance. The economic pattern of disparity that exists between North and South has existed for a long time. The issue is whether or not, pragmatically or morally, it can be allowed to continue much longer.

World Economic Divisions

Before delving into the economics of the South, it is important to understand that the world is divided economically into the developed-industrialized countries of the North

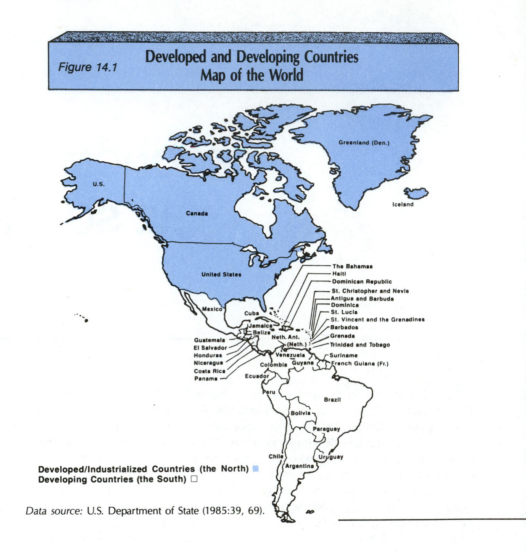

**Figure 14.1   Developed and Developing Countries
Map of the World**

Developed/Industrialized Countries (the North) ■
Developing Countries (the South) □

Data source: U.S. Department of State (1985:39, 69).

and the developing countries of the South, as shown in Figure 14.1. These two general divisions are frequently further subdivided. As with most attempts to categorize the world's political and economic divisions, the varying classifications are imprecise and subject to change. Many of the former centrally planned economies, such as Poland, are attempting painful transitions to become market economies. Even the Soviet Union has moved a significant distance in this direction. The newly industrializing countries (NICs) are still usually in the South, but there are exceptions such as Taiwan, which has a per capita GNP ($5,126) that is 50 percent greater than Portugal's ($3,380); it may be that Taiwan could be classified as a developed market economy. Furthermore, there are vast differences within the various categories. In the North, for example, Canada's per capita GNP ($15,560) is 4.6 times larger than Portugal's; and in the South, Mexico's per capita GNP ($1,701) is 7 times larger than Myanmar's (Burma) ($241).

There is, however, a very fundamental fact of world economics that these classification ambiguities should not obscure. This is that, on average, the conditions of life for the citizens in the countries of the industrialized North are dramatically different from the living standards of those people who reside in the countries of the under-

An important characteristic of the world economic system is its division into two spheres: a relatively affluent and industrialized North, and a relatively poor and nonindustrialized South. Each of these spheres can be further subcategorized by economic strength, wealth, and type of economy. The North-South Axis is a source of economic and political tension in the world.

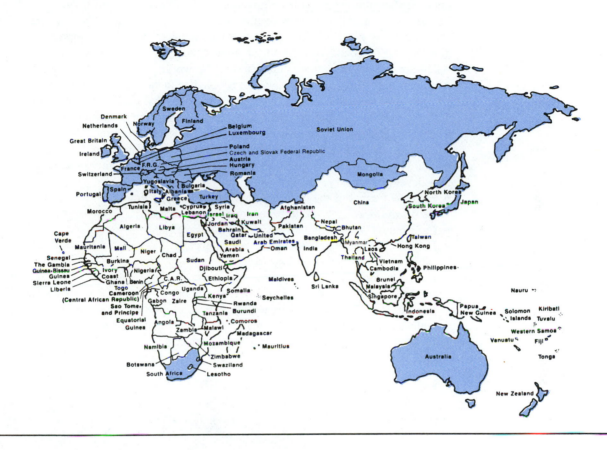

developed South. The North is a zone of relative plenty; the South is a scene of widespread deprivation.[1] The North includes the Group of Seven (G–7) largest market economies, other smaller developed market economies, and the developed centrally planned economies. The countries of the South consist of the newly industrializing countries (NICs); the underdeveloped countries; and the 42 **least developed countries**—those with a 1987 per capita GNP of $480 or less.

---

1. The data used in this chapter is the most recent available. At the time of writing, reliable GNP data from the South is usually from 1987, and although newer GNP data is available from developed countries, the same years will be used when possible to make comparisons as accurate as possible. The year of data will be specified when appropriate. The sources used herein include most of those listed in the box, "Technical Terms and Sources," in chapter 13 (p. 360). Additional sources include World Bank (1989), *Social Indicators of Development, 1989* (Baltimore: The Johns Hopkins University Press); United Nations Industrial Development Organization (1989), *Industry and Development: Global Report 1989/90* (Vienna); and *Development and the National Interest: U.S. Economic Assistance into the 21st Century* (U.S. Agency for International Development, 1989).

The South: Harvest of Poverty

Sensationalism is not the aim of this book, but it is hard to recount conditions of impoverishment in neutral, academic terms. Some of the relative North-South economic statistics have already been presented in chapter 1, but they bear elaboration here. One way to begin to grip the North-South Axis is to consider the fact that a great deal of the globe's land mass and virtually all of three continents—South America, Africa, and Asia—are part of the South. Furthermore, the world's wealth is badly apportioned. Approximately 77 percent of the world's people live in the South, yet they produce only 15 percent of the global GNP. Conversely, this means that the 23 percent of the people who are fortunate enough to reside in the North command 85 percent of the world's wealth. Additionally, the people in the South collected only 19 percent of the world's export earnings in 1990 and are cared for by only 9 percent of global expenditures on public health. On average, if you live in an LDC, you will, compared with someone who lives in a developed country:

- Have 69 percent of the caloric and 60 percent of the protein nourishment.
- Be 3 times less likely to go beyond elementary school.
- Earn only 7 percent of a North citizen's income.
- Have only 11 percent of the doctors per capita and 18 percent of the hospital beds per capita of your neighbor in the North.
- Be 8.8 times more likely to have your baby die before age 5. Nearly 16 million toddlers die each year, and a total of 240 million babies in LDCs, equivalent to the population of the United States, will die between 1990 and 2005. For those who live, malnutrition will often retard normal physical and mental growth. The mortality rate for women during delivery is 15 times higher in the South than in the North.
- Die 14 years earlier.

A stark economic reality is that a great percentage of the world population, especially in the South, lives in poverty beyond the comprehension of most of the readers of this book. Shown here are living conditions in Ciudad Bolívar, a section of Bogotá, Colombia. Ironically, this section is named after Simón Bolívar, who liberated much of South America from Spanish rule in the early 1800s, yet the people of Ciudad Bolívar remain shackled by poverty.

Indeed, for most who read this book, the state of life for many in the South is beyond comprehension. Lack of adequate nutrition, medical care, and education creates a debilitating cycle.

Nor is the future picture for many in the South optimistic. At least relative to the North, the socioeconomic plight of the South is not improving. Some indicators, such as literacy rate, physicians per capita, and life expectancy, show advances in Third World absolute conditions, but the general economic gap between North and South is widening. The per capita GDP (Gross Domestic Product) of the LDCs slowly increased a paltry $90 from $760 in 1980 to $850 in 1990, while the per capita GDP of the industrial market economy countries zoomed up $2,300 from $10,200 in 1980 to $12,500 in 1990. This means that the wealth ratio between the two groups widened from 13.4 to 1 in 1980 to 14.7 to 1 in 1990. The per capita GDP of the 42 most impoverished countries inched up to only $290, resulting in a wealth ratio—"chasm" is a better word—of 43 to 1.

The worst news is that absolute conditions are declining in some countries. Sub-Saharan Africa is a particularly depressed region. Per capita GDP in the region declined 7 of 10 years and by a total 23 percent in constant dollars between 1980 and 1990. Food production is one alarming example of the impact of the economic malaise. The rapidly rising population is overwhelming agriculture. Per capita food production declined in 88 percent of the region's countries between 1975 and 1989. The once-agriculturally self-sufficient Sub-Saharan Africa now imports approximately 40 percent of its food at an annual cost of $3 billion—a cost that the countries of this region can ill afford. The naked truth is that relatively speaking, and in some cases absolutely, the rich are getting richer, and the poor are getting poorer.

Development: Difficulties and Disagreements

An initial question that might be asked is: why did the gap between North and South develop? One factor was circumstance. The industrial revolution came first to Europe and, by extension, to North America. This occurred when earlier civilizations in Asia, the Middle East, and Africa had declined. Furthermore, once industrialization began, it initiated a process that led to the subjugation of the Third World. Industrialization brought the North both wealth and technology that, in part, could be turned into sophisticated weapons that overpowered the more rudimentarily armed people of the South. The need for primary products to fuel the North's factories and the search for markets in which to sell those products led to increased colonization. Nationalism furthered this process as expanding countries, such as Germany, sought colonies to symbolize their major power status, while declining countries, such as Spain, attempted to hold on to colonies to belie their fading glory. Another pattern was followed by the United States. It acquired few colonies, but it came to dominate Central America and the Caribbean indirectly. As a result of these factors, Asians, Africans, Latin Americans, and others were consistently and often forcibly exploited to benefit the industrialized, imperialist countries. This pattern existed for a century and in some cases much longer. Politically, most of the countries of the Third World achieved independence and theoretical equality in the decades following World War II. What has not changed, though, or approached equality is the economic relations between North and South. There are many reasons for the LDCs' inability to catch up, including the weak prices of primary products, the difficulty of obtaining development capital, and occurrences of political instability and mismanagement in the LDCs. Some also argue that the international economic system remains stacked against the LDCs. What should be done?

Development: Differing Approaches

The LDCs' goal is development. Yet the path to that end is uncertain. There are many differing development approaches advocated by analysts, and these views are related to the economic orientations discussed in chapter 1. For our purposes here, we can divide them into three groups: liberals, radicals, and mercantilists (Kolko, 1989).

The Liberal Approach

Liberals believe that development can be achieved within the existing international economic structure. This belief is related to the idealist approach to general world politics. Liberals measure success or failure in terms of aggregate economic indicators such as GNP, trade levels, employment statistics, and wage rates. Liberals believe that the major impediments to the South's development are its weaknesses in acquiring capital and its shortage of skilled labor. These difficulties can be overcome through free trade and foreign investment supplemented by loans and foreign aid. Liberal economic advocates believe that another barrier to the South's achievement of national economic aspirations is irrational domestic and international state policies such as centralized planning (domestic) and protectionism (international). In other words, liberals believe "that economic exchange within and between states should be determined principally by market mechanisms," and that "to the extent that the global economy as a whole, and individual states' policies, conform to classical liberal economic principles, *all* states' growth and economic efficiency will be maximized" (Blake & Walters, 1987:6). Therefore, the liberal approach to development looks to integrate LDCs into the current world economic system by eliminating imperfections in the current system while basically maintaining its structure and stability.

Radical Approaches

Scholars who take more radical approaches are termed Marxists (Robinson, 1987) and structuralists (Galtung, 1971; Wallerstein, 1976), and they share a **dependencia model** of the international political-economic system. Both schools maintain that GNP rates and other such indexes of growth are secondary to the patterns of production and trade. Radicals contend that while classic imperialism (direct control and exploitation of colonies) has declined, indirect control and exploitation continue, driven by capitalism's need for cheap primary resources, external markets, profitable investment opportunities, and low-wage labor. The South, for example, produces low-cost, low-profit **primary products** such as agricultural products and raw materials. These help supply the North's production of high-price, high-profit manufactured goods, some of which are profitably sold to the LDCs. It is, therefore, in the interest of capitalist exploiters to keep LDCs dependent.

What has occurred, radicals say, is **neocolonialism** (neoimperialism), which operates without colonies but is nevertheless imperialistic. This has created a hierarchical structure in which the rich states in the center of the world economic system dominate the LDCs on the periphery of the system.

The dependency of LDCs is maintained in a number of ways, such as structuring the rules and practices of international economics to benefit the North. The radicals further contend that neoimperial powers corrupt and co-opt the local elite in LDCs by allowing them personal wealth in return for their governing their countries in a way that benefits the North.

Many political figures in the South and some scholars view North-South relations from the perspective of a dependencia (or neoimperialist) model. These observers claim that the developed countries of the North continue to dominate the world political and economic system and manipulate the countries of the South exploitively.

Marxists and structuralists part ways on how to proceed with LDC development. Both believe that significant changes have to be made in the way international politics works, but structuralists are prone to stress reform of the current market system. Marxists believe that the entire capitalist-based system must be overturned, both within countries and in the world system, and replaced with domestic and international socialist systems before economic equity can be achieved.

The Mercantilist Approach

Some scholars dismiss both the liberal and radical approaches. Mercantilists believe that political considerations govern international economics. According to this theory, countries do not manipulate international economic policy for the welfare maximization, as liberal theorists believe. Nor do states adopt economic policy because of the class competition as emphasized by radicals. Instead, states are driven by the urge to accumulate and maintain power. Thus, mercantilists are related to the more general realist school of international political theory discussed in chapter 1.

From this perspective, mercantilists argue that the trade, investment, and aid policies of the industrialized countries are not especially concerned with LDC development, unless the growth of one or more of those countries is in the political interest of the developed country. Further, and this will be discussed later, mercantilist theorists maintain that the South's calls for a New International Economic Order (NIEO) that will achieve greater equity are, in essence, attempts to change the rules so that the LDCs can acquire political power for themselves (Krasner, 1985).

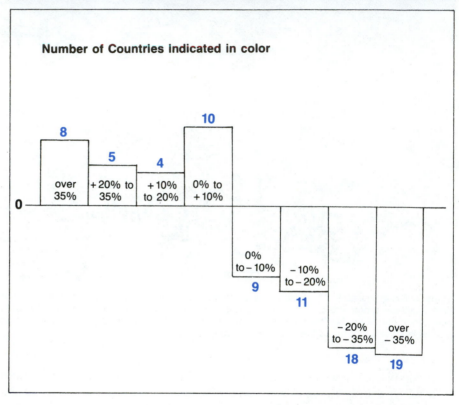

Data source: UN (1990a).

The pattern of development in the Third World is very uneven. A few countries had strong increases in per capita GNP, but 72 percent of all less developed countries (LDCs) had a loss of per capita GNP in real dollars. One-fifth had per capita GNP decline of over 35 percent. Even some of the countries with strong per capita GNP advances are still very poor. China ($471) and India ($234) are two examples.

Third World Development: A Mixed Pattern

If there is controversy over the causes and cures for the world's economic disparity, there is more agreement on the fact that the Third World presents a mixed pattern of development. First, there are wide differences within individual LDCs between small wealthy and middle classes and the many poor. Second, there are a few Third World countries that are beginning to industrialize and enjoy a measure of prosperity. Most countries of the South, however, continue to stagger under crushing economic limits. Figure 14.2 shows that in terms of real growth of GDP during the 1980s, almost three-fourths of LDCs had a loss of GDP.

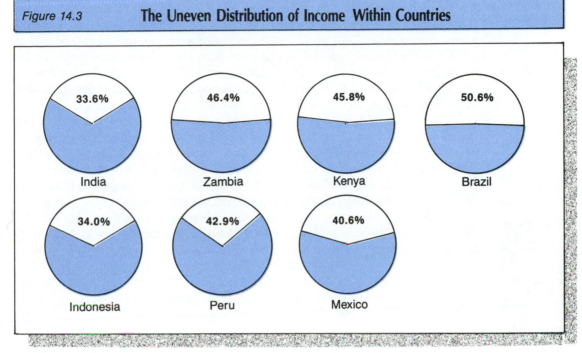

Figure 14.3   **The Uneven Distribution of Income Within Countries**

India 33.6%   Zambia 46.4%   Kenya 45.8%   Brazil 50.6%

Indonesia 34.0%   Peru 42.9%   Mexico 40.6%

Data source: World Bank (1989:221).

The area indicated in white for the Third World countries above gives the percentage of all personal income earned by the richest 10 percent of the population.

Internal Disparity

Within the Third World there are cities with sparkling skyscrapers and luxuriant suburbs populated by well-to-do local entrepreneurs who drive Mercedes-Benzes and splash in marble pools. For each such scene, there are many more of open sewers, contaminated drinking water, distended bellies, and other symptoms of rural and urban human blight. In short, the scant economic benefits that have accrued are not evenly distributed (Chan, 1989). Figure 14.3 shows the percentage of income earned by the highest income-earning 10 percent of the population in six Third World countries. For example, in Brazil the top 10 percent accounts for half of all personal income, while the poorest 20 percent of the population has a scant 2 percent of the income. By comparison, the distribution of domestic income is narrower in the North. The top 10 percent takes in 24 percent of all income in Canada, for example, and 20 to 25 percent in most other industrialized countries. The poorest 20 percent of Canada's population has just 5 percent of the country's income, equal to the United States' but slightly more disproportionate than most European countries.

A Few Newly Industrializing Countries

A second pattern of uneven economic growth in the Third World is the disparity between countries. Although it is possible to show, for example, that aggregate LDC manufacturing output, GDP, and some other factors expanded considerably in the 1970s and 1980s, these averages are misleading because much of the progress was confined to a relative few **newly industrializing countries (NICs)**. Just five of these (Taiwan, South Korea, Hong Kong, Singapore, and Brazil) accounted in 1988 for about 27 percent of all manufacturing in the Third World, and the same five were responsible for 47 percent of all manufactured goods exported by LDCs that year. Furthermore, these five countries had an average 1987 per capita GDP of approximately $2,900, 3.4 times greater than the average LDC per capita GDP, and the five accounted for 15.1 percent of the entire GDP in the Third World.

The fortunes of these five countries and the other NICs are not unmitigated success stories, however. Some of the NICs have achieved their expansion through heavy foreign borrowing, leading to what one scholar called "indebted industrialization" (Frieden, 1987). Brazil, for example, is staggering under a 1988 foreign debt of $105 billion. This is equivalent to 40 percent of its GNP, over 4 times its export earnings, and 10 times its net trade balance. It might also be said that Brazil has followed a policy of "indentured industrialization." As noted, the wealth in Brazil is extremely maldistributed with the top 10 percent of the population outearning the bottom 20 percent by a ratio of 25 to 1. A few live in splendor in Rio de Janeiro, while the mass lives in urban squalor or rural deprivation.

Thus figures for the Third World can be deceptive. There are a few relative success stories, but for most countries, and for most of the people within those countries, the economic picture is bleak.

Modernization: A Mixed Blessing

In addition to its more traditional woes, the Third World also suffers many negative side effects from the process of modernization. Medical advances have decreased infant mortality and increased longevity, but that has added to *explosive population growth*. Sub-Saharan Africa, for instance, more than doubled its population from 210 million in 1960 to 466 million in 1988. The region continues to have the world's most rapidly expanding population, increasing at 3.3 percent annually, and it is expected by the UN to triple its current population by 2025 to a total of 1.58 billion.

Economic change has also brought *rapid urbanization* with a host of incumbent difficulties. In 1970 there were 4 mega-cities with populations over 10 million in the world. One of these, Shanghai, was in a LDC. In 1990 there were 25 mega-cities, 18 of which were in the Third World. Mexico City is projected to be the world's most populous city by the turn of the century with 26 million inhabitants. By a similar measure, between 1965 and 1990 the percentage of the Third World population living in urban areas grew from 24 to 34 percent, and there is now a total of approximately 300 cities in LDCs with populations over 500,000. In the urbanization process, older tribal, village, and family loyalties are being destroyed, with few new offsetting values and other social support systems to take their place. The result is social and political instability. Struggling LDCs are also often unable to meet the employment, sanitary, housing, and other needs of the flood of people moving to or being born in the cities. At least a third of all urban dwellings in Sub-Saharan Africa have no running water, toilets, or electricity. A survey of the capital of Nigeria, Lagos, found conditions even worse there, with three-quarters of all families living in one-room dwellings, 80 percent without cooking facilities, and only 13 percent with running water (Brown & Jacobson, 1987).

Poor planning has too often led to the misdirection of attempts to improve conditions. "Spectacular" development projects such as steel mills or symbolic projects

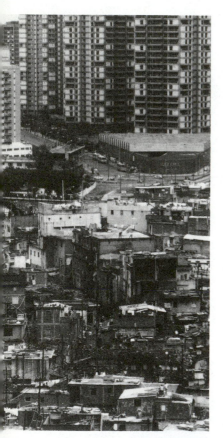

There is a great disparity of wealth within Third World countries as well as between the countries of the North and South. One country in which this disparity is particularly acute is the newly industrializing country of Brazil where more than 50 percent of the income is earned by 10 percent of the people. This leads to conditions in which many people live in shantytowns while a few people live in the luxury of highrise apartments, such as shown here in Rio de Janeiro.

such as airports have been built at the expense of slower, less obvious efforts to build an economic infrastructure and tailor it to local needs. One has to wonder, for example, about the UN–backed decision to build a $75 million conference center in Ethiopia at the same time that a worldwide relief effort was under way for the country where 300,000 people had already died of starvation.

Development has also brought *industrial and environmental dangers.* One problem is deforestation. It is a global issue but is especially critical in the Third World where increased population pressure on fuel wood, expanding farm and ranch acreage, and general urban growth are rapidly depleting the forests. Loss of these forests will increase soil erosion, negatively affect oxygenation of the air, lessen rainfall, and have numerous other deleterious effects. Approximately one-third of the globe's originally forested areas has already been lost, and 53 percent of what remains is located in the LDCs. These forests are rapidly being cut. According to the World Resources Institute (1990), another 50.4 million acres (78,750 square miles) of forest are being cut annually. That is approximately equal to the area of a small country like Uganda or Syria every year; if the current rate of cutting persists through the 1990s, nearly 7 percent of forest land, an area equal to Mexico or almost half the United States, will be cleared during the decade.

Third World industrial development is also adding to air, water, and soil pollution. This is a problem of industrialization in general, but pollution growth is especially acute in developing countries, which often cannot afford the expensive processes to cleanse emissions and dispose of waste. Industrial concentrations around cities combined with the fuel burning in the rapidly increasing number of urban dwellings have caused air pollution in Third World cities that is often much higher than in the cities of the industrialized countries. In the more prosperous NICs (newly industrializing countries), massive urban traffic jams add to the pollution. As a result, 60 percent of Calcutta's residents suffer breathing disorders; São Paulo, Brazil, exceeds the World Health Organization (WHO) standard for dangerous smog levels 226 days a year, and Jakarta, the capital of Indonesia, has airborne levels of lead that are 17 times higher than what WHO considers safe.

Capital Needs and Development

Whatever the problems and drawbacks, the LDCs are justifiably determined to increase their levels of development. To do this, the countries of the Third World need massive amounts of capital to supplement their own internal efforts to improve socioeconomic conditions. Many things can be accomplished with domestic resources and drive, but these **capital needs** require outside resources as well.

In obtaining these resources, LDCs are constrained by the limited amount of financial reserves, or **hard currency**, that they possess. Most private and many public investors and traders are selective in the currencies they will accept. American dollars are the standard currency of exchange. Others, such as British pounds, German marks, Swiss or French francs, and Japanese yen, are also widely convertible. Guatemalan quetzals, Iraqi dinars, Malaysian ringgitos, Nigerian nairas, and Seychelles rupees are another story. They and most world currencies are generally not acceptable in international economic transactions. Further, these countries have small reserves of acceptable trading currencies. More than 80 percent of all hard-currency reserves are concentrated in the industrialized countries.

A primary issue for LDCs, then, is the acquisition of hard-currency development funds. Four main sources of convertible currencies are available: loans, investment, trade, and aid. Unfortunately, as we shall see in our discussion of these sources, there are limitations and drawbacks to each. No single source is sufficient to meet the Third World's enormous and complex needs. In 1989 the developing countries had a current accounts balance-of-payments deficit of $19.1 billion, for a total deficit during the 1980s of $371.6 billion. Even when net flows of aid, loans, and investments are figured in, the LDCs had a net outflow of $31.3 billion in the 1980s. They are therefore losing ground in their quest to build up financial reserves.

Loans

One source of hard currency is loans extended by private or government sources. Borrowing within reason is a traditional approach for both individuals and countries to improve their conditions. But things got out of hand during the 1970s. A key factor was the rapid rise of oil prices. This increased the financial need of energy-importing LDCs and threatened to retard their new development programs. They borrowed money from Western banks, from other private lenders, national governments, and from international organizations to meet higher oil import costs and planned to pay back the loans and debt-service (interest) with funds earned from expanded exports. There were also a few energy-exporting LDCs—Mexico is an example—that borrowed money to finance development with the expectation of paying off the loans with future oil revenues. The oil price hikes also put huge sums of money into the hands of countries belonging to the Organization of Petroleum Exporting Countries (OPEC). A lot of these funds were deposited in Western banks, and they, in turn, had surplus funds that they needed to lend in order to receive interest (Devlin, 1989). The upshot was a frenzy of lending and borrowing that left the LDCs $849 billion in debt in 1982. This figure rose to an estimated $1.3-trillion in 1990.[2] Table 14.1 shows the growing debt of 15 particularly troubled countries that owed 38 percent of the Third World's debt at the beginning of 1989.

Banks, mostly located in the trilateral countries, are the primary private creditors. In 1990, all LDCs owed these institutions over $534 billion. Of this, approximately one-half of the debt is held by U.S. banks. Other private lenders, such as corporations, are owed $209 billion, and the LDCs owe approximately $561 billion to public lenders such as the **International Monetary Fund (IMF)**, the World Bank, international regional banks, and governments.

The Third World Debt Crisis

The bubble burst in the early 1980s. The oil price rise that fueled borrowing also impaired economic growth in the industrialized countries. As their economies slowed, they bought fewer LDC exports. Ironically, there was also a drop in oil prices, which further limited the ability of energy-exporting LDCs to repay their loans. In August 1982 Mexico announced that it could not meet payments on its foreign debt and called for $4 billion in assistance to pay its creditors, dramatically demonstrating the depth of the Third World debt crisis.

2. Like many financial statistics, loan indebtedness is complex. Some of the rise in the level of indebtedness is due to adjustments in the exchange rates rather than new borrowing. Other variables, such as whether the loan carries fixed or variable interest rates; whether it is short-, medium-, or long-term; and whether it is owed to public or private lenders, affect the financial picture.

TABLE 14.1

Escalating Debt of 15 Third World Countries, 1970–89 ($ billions)

Country	1970	1982	1989
Argentina	$ 8.47	$ 45.4	$ 45.2
Bolivia	.50	3.7	4.7
Brazil	6.84	85.3	105.0
Chile	2.58	18.0	17.1
Colombia	1.64	10.6	12.8
Equador	.26	7.5	9.4
Ivory Coast	.27	8.0	11.8
Mexico	5.97	87.6	94.4
Morocco	.75	11.3	17.1
Nigeria	.57	14.3	28.0
Peru	2.67	12.2	13.4
Philippines	1.56	29.5	23.4
Turkey	3.34	15.7	31.4
Venezuela	.97	37.2	32.0
Yugoslavia	2.06	20.0	18.2
Total	$38.05	$406.3	$463.9

Data sources: World Bank (1989); U.S. AID (1990); IMF (1990).

A number of other debt-laden countries have followed Mexico's action over the years. These actions threatened to put the debtor countries into technical bankruptcy, to strain the financial stability of private lending institutions in the North, and to damage political relations between debtor and creditor countries. On the other hand, the good-faith attempts of most countries, most of the time, to pay the debt have caused havoc with their internal social and economic development strategies. There are many social costs, including the decline in health care that is caused by shifting funds from building health facilities to paying off the international debt. As far as economic development, the principal and interest payments on the debt have lessened the ability of indebted LDCs to build the economic infrastructure needed both to prosper and to create the economic activity required to generate the funds to pay the loans. The result, it became increasingly clear in the mid-1980s, was a downward spiral in the political, economic, and social conditions in many of the indebted LDCs and worsening relations between them and the creditor countries. Just one indicator of the creditors' gloom over their ability to collect is provided by the loan discount rate. This discount rate is the percentage of the loan's face value (original amount) that the rights to collect the loan can be sold for by one creditor to another. By mid-1989 the discount rate for all LDCs' debt was 50 percent, and it was an average of 33 percent for the most heavily indebted LDCs listed in Table 14.1. Some of these countries' debts were selling at fire sale rates, such as Nigeria's (23 percent), Argentina's (18 percent), and Peru's (6 percent).

We are used to thinking of the term international crisis in association with military confrontations. They are crises, but the morass of debt that has mired both debtor and creditor countries is also a true crisis. To understand it further, we can look at its economic ramifications, its political ramifications, and the efforts to solve the crisis (Borchert & Schinke, 1990).

The economic growth plans of many less developed countries are being devastated by their heavy foreign debt. These countries must use increasing amounts of the capital they earn from trade and other sources to pay the principal and interest on their debt rather than investing the capital in the development of their economies.

Economic Ramifications

The $1.3-trillion debt has serious economic ramifications for both the South and the North. For the countries of the South, the debt means that they were scheduled to pay over $161 billion in principal and interest charges in 1990. The economies of the LDCs are not growing fast enough to do that, and they are more than $10 billion in arrears. Furthermore, the net flow of outside loans is decreasing, especially from private sources.[3] Net bank loans, for example, dropped from +$43 billion (one-third of all LDC external financing) in 1983 to +$6 billion (one-tenth of all LDC external financing) in 1989. When interest is added, the flow of private lending changed from a net of +$17 billion in 1981 to −$36 billion in 1989.

3. As in many financial statistics, *net* figures are better indicators than gross figures. Net borrowing here represents the amount of new loans minus the amount that LDCs are paying in principal and interest. If a country's income (export earnings, aid, loans, and so forth) is insufficient to meet its expenses (principal and interest payments, imports, etc.), then the country must use its reserves or go in arrears.

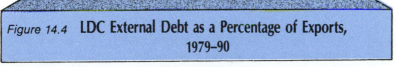

Figure 14.4   **LDC External Debt as a Percentage of Exports, 1979–90**

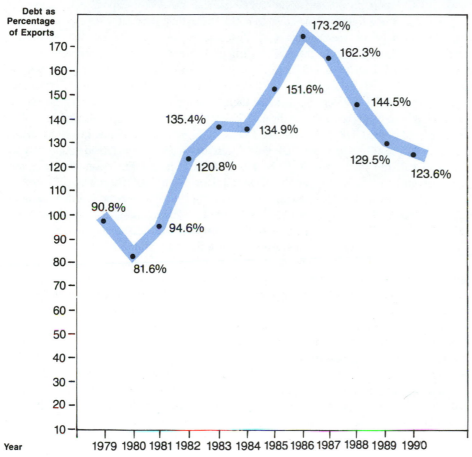

Data source: IMF (1990).

The LDCs' debt as a percentage of their exports has steadily risen, which means it is increasingly difficult for the LDCs to meet principal and interest payments. It has declined some recently, but is still burdensomely high and could rise rapidly if the global economy is troubled.

The impact on the LDCs is that their economic expansion is imperiled because to pay off loans they have to use funds that could otherwise be reinvested in their economies. The percentage of foreign exchange earnings that LDCs have had to devote to meeting their debt payments rose from 12.4 percent in 1970 to a high of 27 percent in 1986, and stood at 20.6 percent in 1990. This burden is also evident in the relationship between a country's debt and its export of goods and services that earn it hard currency to meet scheduled loan payments, as shown in Figure 14.4. In 1979 the LDCs' debt equaled 90.8 percent of their export earnings. This debt figure rose to a high of 173.2 percent of export earnings in 1986. The debt-to-exports percentage eased to 123.6 in 1990, but this is still way too high. Even these worrisome figures would, however, be welcome for many of the most burdened countries. In 1989, for example, Argentina's debt was 1,000 percent of its export earnings, Peru's was 620 percent, Nigeria's was 590 percent, and Brazil's was 553 percent. Making matters even worse, the rise in oil prices in the aftermath of Iraq's invasion of Kuwait and the constricting world economy threaten to reduce LDC export growth and again rapidly escalate the debt-to-exports percentage.

What all these figures come down to in the end is this: the LDCs are experiencing a huge hemorrhage of money that they desperately need for social and economic development. In 1980 the net transfer of all financial resources was a positive inflow of $36.1 billion for LDCs; in 1988 that figure was almost the complete inverse, with a negative outflow of $31.2 billion. Furthermore, as noted, the use of LDC financial resources to service the debt has harmed them economically and, ironically, increased their inability to meet payments. In the past 20 years, the debt has approximately doubled to 40 percent of the GDP of the indebted LDCs, and it retards economic growth. During the 1980s, for example, the real GDP growth rate of the 15 most indebted countries was less than half the GDP growth of the North American and European industrialized countries and only about two-thirds of overall Third World GDP growth.

The debt crisis has also potentially serious ramifications for the North. Just nine large U.S. banks, for example, hold $62 billion in LDC debt, and all U.S. banks in 1989 held a total of $178 billion in LDC debt. The difficulty the LDCs are having meeting their debt service payments are aggravating an already difficult period for U.S. banks. In the five years from 1984 to 1988 a total of 721 banks failed, three times as many as had failed in the preceding quarter-century. Then in 1989 and 1990, the savings and loan crisis further rocked the U.S. banking industry. Debt defaults by the LDCs could wreak financial disaster on Northern banks, endangering their depositors or requiring massive interventions by the North's governments to fend off bank bankruptcies or to repay depositors under government insurance plans. Indeed, the debts are already causing financial costs for the North's governments. One cost is the additional funds the developed countries have given to IMF (International Monetary Fund) and other international lending institutions to assist the LDCs to meet debt payments. Another cost is the loss of tax revenues to the central governments caused by banks writing off part of their LDC debt as uncollectible, thereby reducing the net profits and the taxes banks pay on those profits.

Political Ramifications

Adding to the serious economic ramifications, there are also political perils associated with the debt crisis. One is that unmet or difficult debt repayments cause strains between the lending and borrowing countries. It is all too easy for Americans to disparge supposed Latin American irresponsibility for borrowing too much, or for Latin Americans to become outraged at what they consider an example of Yankee imperialism.

Another political sore point is the conditions that lending institutions sometimes attach to restructuring loans. This especially involves the *conditionality* of IMF loans. As part of loan agreements, the IMF often requires that borrowing countries agree to economic reforms that the IMF believes will ensure that the borrower will not continue to have repayment difficulties. These conditions may include restricting imports, stabilizing or freezing wages, or eliminating budget deficits by either raising taxes or reducing expenditures. These stringent conditions hit already-poor domestic populations hard, though, and often set off explosive reactions. More than 300 people died in riots in early 1989, for example, as Venezuelans took to the streets to protest government austerity measures.

From the IMF's point of view, such demands are prudent. From the perspective of many in the Third World, they are objectionable on a number of counts. One is that the conditions are an invasion of sovereignty. A second is that the Western-dominated IMF is asking LDCs to follow policies, such as balanced budgets and reduced imports, that countries in the North, especially the United States, cannot accomplish. Third, some argue that implementation of some of the reforms are politically difficult and might threaten the continuance of new, still-tenuous democratic governments in countries such as Argentina and Brazil (Remmer, 1990). Fourth, it is not clear that IMF conditions actually improve economic performance. In fact, one recent study that examined IMF programs in Latin America concluded that "the dominant theme to emerge from this analysis of IMF programs is not that of success . . . but of failure" (Remmer, 1986:21). Finally, some critics contend that conditionality is aimed at maintaining the dependencia relationship (Cleaver, 1989). As *West Africa* (March 10, 1986:280) magazine editorialized:

> The real motives of the IMF . . . appear to some to be primarily directed at making the developing countries perform better in their client relationship with the West. The emphasis on export-led growth seems to be directed at more efficient production of primary commodities so that the poorer countries earn the foreign exchange with which to import manufactures from, and pay their debts to, developed countries.

Here we return to the importance of perceptions. Whether or not conditionality is economically or politically oppressive, and whether, even if it is neoimperialist, the IMF and others are doing it inadvertently or with intent to dominate, the reality is that many in the Third World believe it to be so. Thus, not only is the level of current lending available from private and public sources insufficient to meet the capital needs of the LDCs, but the conditions attached to the loans and the strain of repaying huge amounts add to the tension along the North-South Axis.

Attempts to Resolve the Debt Crisis

The danger of the debt crisis to both North and South has led countries in both economic spheres to search for solutions. The United States, as the world's leading economic country and the largest single holder of LDC debt, has been in the forefront of this effort. The Baker Plan of 1985 (after then–U.S. secretary of the treasury James Baker) proposed refinancing the debt with an extended period of payments and lower interest rates for the LDCs, but it proved unworkable because most banks refused to issue new loans fearing they would be throwing good money after bad. The crisis worsened.

The most recent plan was proposed in March 1989 by U.S. secretary of the treasury Nicholas Brady. In brief, the Brady Plan proposed that banks would forgive part of what was owed by LDCs, lower interest rates, and make some new loans. In return, the banks' investments would be guaranteed by the governments of creditor countries and by the International Monetary Fund (IMF) and the World Bank. These institutions and creditor country governments would also increase loans to LDCs to offset declining net bank financing and ease the overall LDC net financial outflow. LDCs would also have to continue the conditionality agreements discussed above (Brady, 1989). Several agreements have been negotiated among LDCs, their private creditors, national governments, and international institutions. The most significant was the February 1990 agreement with Mexico that cut Mexican debt by about 20 percent. Agreements were also signed with the Philippines, Costa Rica, and Venezuela.

It is too early to evaluate the Brady Plan fully. It is true that the severity of figures such as the ratio of debt to GDP or to export earnings has declined somewhat. That, however, may be more due to the relatively vigorous world economy in the late 1980s than to the debt reduction efforts as such. The less-optimistic projections for the early 1990s will provide a more difficult test for the debt relief efforts. Almost immediately after the Brady Plan was formulated, some experts were predicting it was not enough to solve the crisis (Islam, 1989). And a recent UN (1990d:93) analysis concluded that "after a year of experience, the Brady Plan does not seem to be the solution so long sought after for the debt crisis." Success, the report argued, required "a substantially larger commitment of official [government] resources. Otherwise, debt reduction is a marginal exercise serving mainly to help disaffected creditors [the banks] to exit from the debt renegotiation process." But more official resources in the form of buying up the banks' debt, the report went on, would merely transfer the risk to governments and international lenders like the IMF and not fully end the drag on the LDCs' social and economic growth. Therefore, in the end, the report advocates that "the time may finally be approaching when the international community could pledge itself to end the developing-country debt crisis instead of just managing it."

Private Investment

A second source of capital for LDCs is investment by private interests. Like loans, investments are a limited and troublesome source of development capital for LDCs. The amount of investment capital available worldwide is staggering, but only a small percentage of it is invested in developing countries. Less than 10 percent of Canadian 1988 direct investments are in LDCs, for example, and only 18.8 percent of U.S. direct investments are in these countries. And these percentages are declining. In 1986 for instance, 20.6 percent of U.S. direct investment was in LDCs. Thus, there was a nearly 9 percent drop in two years, and these figures are comparable for other industrialized countries. Moreover, what does go into the Third World is concentrated in a few oil-exporting or newly industrializing countries.

Private investment also may be an undesirable source of capital because the investments are primarily made by the huge multinational corporations (MNCs), discussed in chapter 13. Many of the pluses and minuses of MNC practice discussed in that chapter are also applicable to investment in the Third World. Indeed, they are magnified by the relative economic weakness of many LDCs. Most of these pros and cons will not be reiterated, but a few deserve further comment in the context of MNC–LDC relations.

Third World countries need and seek investment because it brings new capital, technology transfer, possible economic diversification, and other benefits. Yet there are drawbacks. One, critics charge, is that MNCs take more capital out in profits than they put in through investments. In the 1980s, for example, there was a net inflow of $68 billion in investment capital into LDCs, but there was an outflow of $101.5 billion in profit-taking. The result was a net outflow of $33.5 billion.

Detractors also complain that MNCs often fail to train host-country workers for management or skilled technical jobs, although MNCs do often pay more than local companies do for equivalent work. MNCs are also sometimes guilty of extracting primary products and natural resources from LDCs with little thought of conservation and without setting up processing facilities in the host country, thereby continuing dependencia (Cowling & Sugden, 1987). Critics charge that MNCs often take advantage

The development capital that multinational corporations invest in less developed countries is desirable, but often the MNCs are accused of practices that harm the countries in which they operate. In 1984, a chemical leak at a Union Carbide plant in Bhopal, India, killed, blinded, or otherwise injured more than 10,000 of the city's residents. The Indian government charged the company with negligence and in late 1988 issued a murder warrant for its American president. Huge civil suits have also been filed in U.S. and Indian courts. The company claims that there was sabotage by a disgruntled Indian employee.

of sometimes lax health, environmental, and other regulations in developing countries. This allows the MNCs to follow unacceptable safety techniques or to sell products that are banned in their home countries (Ives, 1985). In the realm of safety, one especially tragic incident occurred in 1984 when a chemical leak at a Union Carbide plant in Bhopal, India, killed, blinded, and injured thousands. Even an MNC with as benign an image as Swiss-based Nestlé's corporation has been criticized for trying to persuade Third World mothers to abandon breast-feeding to use Nestlé's powdered baby formula. The Nestlés program may have been commercially successful, but it was a disaster for Third World babies. Their health declined because mother's milk helps immunize a baby, because impure water was often used to mix the formula, and because impoverished mothers would skimp on the formula they could not fully afford. And in 1988, executives of Beech-Nut baby foods, a U.S. subsidiary of Nestlé's, were convicted and imprisoned for selling fake apple juice (consisting of beet juice, corn syrup, etc.) to American and overseas parents alike.

Trade

Export earnings are a third possible source of development capital. Because of the vast size of the world market, and because earnings from trade can be utilized by developing countries according to their own wishes, trade is theoretically the optimal source of hard currency for LDCs. Yet, in reality, Third World countries are severely disadvantaged by the pattern and terms of international trade.

There are several sources of LDC trade weakness. First, the LDCs command less than 20 percent of the world export market. Second, most of these countries suffer a

TABLE 14.2

The Main Export of These Countries Is One Product

Africa	The Gambia	Rwanda	Papua New	Grenada	Middle East
Algeria	*Groundnuts*	*Coffee*	Guinea	*Spices*	and
Petroleum	Ghana	Seychelles	*Copper*	Guatemala	Mediterranean
Angola	*Cocoa*	*Copra*	*concentrate*	*Coffee*	Bahrain
Petroleum	Guinea	Somalia	Western Samoa	Jamaica	*Petroleum*
Botswana	*Bauxite*	*Live animals*	*Coconut oil*	*Alumina*	Cyprus
Diamonds	Lesotho	Togo		Netherlands	*Citrus fruit*
Burkina Faso	*Diamonds*	*Phosphates*	**Europe**	Antilles (Neth.)	Iran
Cotton	Liberia	Uganda	Finland	*Petroleum*	*Petroleum*
Burundi	*Iron ore*	*Coffee*	*Wood and pa-*	*products*	Iraq
Coffee	Libya	Zaire	*per products*	St. Kitts and	*Petroleum*
Central African	*Petroleum*	*Copper*	Iceland	Nevis	Kuwait
Republic	Malawi	Zambia	*Fish and fish*	*Sugar*	*Petroleum*
Diamonds	*Tobacco*	*Copper*	*products*	St. Lucia	Oman
Comoros	Mali			*Bananas*	*Petroleum*
Cloves	*Groundnuts*	**Asia/Pacific**	**Latin America**	Suriname	Qatar
Congo	Mauritania	Brunei	**and Caribbean**	*Alumina*	*Petroleum*
Petroleum	*Iron ore*	*Petroleum*	The Bahamas	Venezuela	Saudi Arabia
Djibouti	Mauritius	Fiji	*Petroleum*	*Petroleum*	*Petroleum*
Petroleum	*Sugar*	*Sugar*	*products*		Syria
Ethiopia	Niger	Indonesia	Chile		*Petroleum*
Coffee	*Uranium*	*Petroleum*	*Copper*		United Arab
Gabon	Nigeria	Myanmar	El Salvador		Emirates
Petroleum	*Petroleum*	(Burma)	*Coffee*		*Petroleum*
		Teak			Yemen
					Petroleum

Data source: IMF (1990).

Countries that are dependent on one or a very few exports for earnings are vulnerable to loss of income due to many market changes.

chronic trade deficit. The 1990 deficit was $119 billion. Furthermore, the least developed countries suffer many of the serious deficits. Ninety-two percent of these countries had trade deficits in 1987, with imports of $116.3 billion that were 21 percent greater than their exports of $95.8 billion.

A third factor contributing to LDC trade weakness is the heavy dependence of these countries on the export of primary products, including foodstuffs, minerals, fibers, and other raw materials. The more a country depends on primary products for export earnings, the less wealthy it tends to be. Primary products in 1988 made up 44 percent of the least developed countries' exports, 40 percent of other Third World countries' exports, and only 15 percent of the exports of the industrialized market economies. Even these figures are somewhat misleading, though. The percentage of the South's exports that are manufactured has been rising. Part of the reason this has occurred, though, is because the real price of primary products has been declining. This makes the percentage of manufacturing exports as part of all exports grow considerably faster than the actual volume or value of those exports.

Even these statistics do not fully tell the story, however, because many LDCs are export-dependent on one or two primary products. Table 14.2 shows the countries that are at least 50 percent export-dependent on one product.

Dependency on primary products, especially on one such product, for export earnings leaves LDCs disadvantaged because of both market weakness and price weakness.

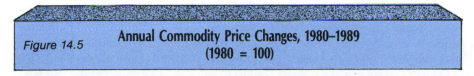

Figure 14.5

**Annual Commodity Price Changes, 1980–1989
(1980 = 100)**

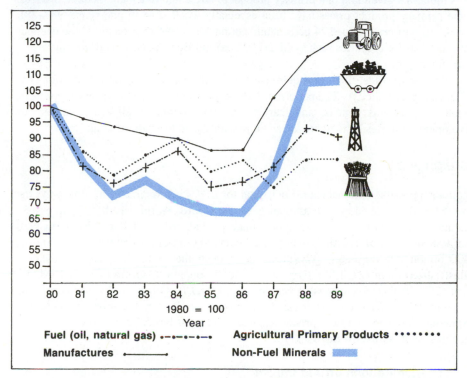

1980 = 100
Year

Fuel (oil, natural gas) .—.—.—.—.   Agricultural Primary Products ● ● ● ● ● ● ●
Manufactures ●————————●   Non-Fuel Minerals ▬▬▬

Data source: IMF (1990).

Since 1980 the real price of primary products has declined compared to manufactured products. In fact, the price of fuels and agricultural products declined absolutely. LDCs dependent on such products for export are disadvantaged in trade.

Market weakness is common for primary products. A number of factors such as damage to a crop or a downturn in world demand can quickly disrupt markets and devastate earnings. During the past decades, world trade in products such as cotton, sisal, jute, wool, and other fibers has been harmed by the development of synthetics. The sale of natural rubber has been drastically reduced by other synthetic substitutes. Sugar sales have been harmed by chemicals such as Nutrasweet and also by dietary changes. Minerals such as tin and lead have also experienced market declines. Oil is perhaps the best illustration of the havoc that changing market conditions can wreak on exporting countries. The shifts in oil markets and prices are covered extensively later in this chapter, but suffice it to note here that what was once called "black gold" turned into a "black glut" in the 1980s, and market prices plunged in the face of new sources, conservation, unchecked production, and the development of alternative energy supplies. The Middle East crisis of 1990–91 caused prices to soar initially, but the long-term effect is still unclear.

Price weakness is an additional disadvantage for primary products. Figure 14.5 (above) compares the price of primary products both to 1980 prices and to the cost of manufactured goods. It shows that the real value of agricultural and fuel primary products has declined since 1980. Even nonfuel minerals, the one primary product category worth more in 1989 than in 1980, lost ground relative to manufactured products. What this means is that it is increasingly difficult for countries that export primary products to buy the manufactured products needed to industrialize, because it takes more of a given unit of a primary product to buy a unit of a manufactured product. Some primary product prices have been especially weak. Just in one year (1987–88), world cocoa prices dropped 24 percent and cotton was down 15 percent. These declines are disastrous for countries such as Ghana (cocoa) and Burkina Faso (cotton) that rely on them for export earnings.

The use of trade, then, to acquire capital and to improve economic conditions has not been highly effective. The pattern of LDC export-dependence on primary products, balance-of-payments deficits, and market and price weakness all disadvantaged the developing countries in their trade relations with the industrialized countries.

Foreign Aid

The fourth possible external source of capital for LDCs is foreign aid. In some ways the flow of official development assistance to the Third World has been impressive, amounting since World War II to approximately a half trillion dollars.[4] Between 1980 and 1988 alone, **bilateral aid** (country to country) to developing countries came to over $400 billion. Of this, about two-thirds came from the 18 (of 24) market economy industrialized countries in the Organization for Economic Cooperation and Development (OECD) that give official development aid (ODA). Other aid donors include the communist industrialized countries, the members of the Organization of Petroleum Exporting Countries (OPEC), private agencies, and **multilateral aid** (several countries) agencies, such as the World Bank.

The Limitations on Aid Impact

Without disparaging the value or intent of this effort, further analysis of the figures shows that aid is neither a story of undisguised generosity nor one of unblemished success. Factors that tend to reduce the impact of aid include political considerations, military content of aid, recipient per capita aid, donor aid relative to wealth, and aid application (Imbeau, 1988; Lebovic, 1988).

Political considerations are one factor that limits the effectiveness of aid. The bilateral aid that makes up the bulk of all foreign aid is given more on the basis of political impact than economic need. About one-half of all U.S. economic aid is distributed through the Economic Support Fund, which provides aid to countries in which the United States has a military-political security interest. Of the Bush administration's FY 1991 foreign aid request of nearly $8 billion (a 50 percent decline over FY 1988), almost two-thirds ($5 billion) was earmarked for Egypt ($2.1 billion) and Israel ($2.9 billion). By contrast, only two countries in Sub-Saharan Africa were designated to receive aid: Djibouti ($1.7 million) and the Seychelles ($2 million), both of which have U.S. military facilities. El Salvador ($215.6 million), faced with a leftist guerrilla war, was designated for more aid than any other Latin American or Caribbean country.

---

4. This includes aid to currently developing countries from the Western industrialized countries, communist countries, OPEC countries, and multilateral institutions. It does not include aid that was given to currently developed countries, such as U.S. aid to the Western European countries under the Marshall Plan in the late 1940s and early 1950s. It includes direct grants, credits, and concessional loans.

Washington's increased political concern with Eastern Europe was best illustrated by a $227.5-million aid request for Poland, up from $3 million the year before.

Most other countries also give aid selectively. Great Britain and France have a special interest in their former colonies. Soviet aid has declined considerably in recent years, amounting in 1987 to just over $2 billion, of which more than half went to India. The Soviets also gave de facto aid through trade concessions (often swapping oil for sugar or other products at favorable rates) to Cuba, Vietnam, and Nicaragua amounting to almost $6 billion. Many of these supports have now ended. Cuba, for example, is struggling because of the higher costs of Soviet oil and other losses of aid. In fact, the Cuban government has instituted severe austerity measures, including sending office workers into the agricultural fields for three-week stints.

Some other countries, by contrast, give aid based primarily on economic need and with a more even hand. Canada's 1988 aid package was $2.34 billion. About 75 percent was distributed through the International Development Agency, rather than bilaterally. The aid was distributed to 82 countries, with the largest grant (Bangladesh, $120 million) amounting to only 5 percent of the total.

Political factors in recipient countries also disrupt the aid flow. In Ethiopia, the Sudan, and other countries undergoing civil wars, government and rebel forces have refused to allow aid to be distributed in enemy areas and, in some cases, have actually attacked aid convoys and killed aid personnel.

Military content is another factor that limits the impact of the aid figures that are sometimes reported. Egypt, with a per capita GNP of only $680, certainly needs aid, but of the total $2.1 billion in U.S. aid for 1991, 61 percent ($1.29 billion) was military aid. In the late 1980s about a third of all U.S. aid involved military transfers, and approximately 45 percent of Soviet aid was also of a military nature.

Measuring recipient per capita aid, rather than gross aid, is also useful to gain a truer picture of the impact of foreign aid. In 1987 LDCs received only $8.10 per capita. It should be added that when the few large aid recipients are eliminated, such as Israel, which received $285.90 in aid per capita (though it is not even an LDC), per capita aid is even less impressive. Some representative countries and the aid they receive are shown in Table 14.3.

TABLE 14.3

Aid and Per Capita Aid Received for Selected Countries, 1987

Country	Aid ($ millions)	Per Capita Aid ($)	As % of GNP
Ethiopia	$ 635	$14.30	11.8
Bangladesh	1,637	15.40	9.3
Myanmar (Burma)	364	9.30	5.6
Niger	348	51.20	16.1
Kenya	565	25.60	7.0
Chad	198	37.60	20.3
Indonesia	1,245	7.30	1.8
Lesotho	108	66.50	29.4
Peru	292	14.40	0.6
Guatemala	241	28.50	3.4

Data source: World Bank (1989:202).

Total aid figures often look impressive, but they can be misleading given the unbelievable poverty and daunting economic problems many countries face. For example, Bangladesh, one of the world's poorest countries, received over $1.6 billion in aid in 1985, but that averaged out to be $15.40 per person.

The Superpowers as Aid Recipients

During the cold war years the two superpowers, the United States and the Soviet Union, gave about $350 billion to allies and needy countries. Now, with the Soviet Union in a state of near–economic collapse and the United States being battered by domestic economic difficulties and by competition from Japan, Europe, and elsewhere, things have changed. In late November 1990 German chancellor Helmut Kohl and Foreign Minister Hans-Dietrich Genscher went on German national television to urge their fellow citizens to, in Kohl's words, "please help reduce the emergency in the Soviet Union." The appeal to Germans to donate money and food for Soviet relief was "an act of charity and above all a work of good neighborliness" the chancellor told German viewers (*HC*, 11/29/90:A21). And the So-

viets needed the help. "We can't live like this," Soviet president Mikhail Gorbachev said in an unusually candid televised comment. "Everything is really rotten" (*HC*, 11/29/90:A22).

Lest Americans get too cocky, they too are beginning to be aid recipients. In February 1990, the Japanese government made an administrative rule change that gives Japanese companies large tax deductions if they donate money to American hospitals, schools, or philanthropic organizations. Just in case the Americans missed noticing Japan's new generosity, a pamphlet distributed to businesses urged that "it is important in American society to take credit for good works accomplished. This is not bragging, it is a matter of getting deserved credit" (*NYT*, 2/22/90:D1).

Donor aid relative to wealth is another analytical approach that lessens the seeming significance of aid figures. This compares aid given to the donor's wealth. Particularly in the United States, there is a myth that the country is a sort of Daddy Warbucks that gives away massive amounts of foreign aid in an act of self-sacrifice that unmercifully burdens American taxpayers. Like most folktales, it is far from the truth. In 1988, the United States gave $12.2 billion in economic aid. That was more than any other country, but from another perspective it equaled only 34 percent of the $35.6 billion American consumers spent on tobacco products, 50 percent of what they spent on jewelry and watches, 63 percent of retail liquor store sales, and only half again as much as the $6.8 billion Americans spent on flowers, noncommercial seeds, and potted plants.

Ways to evaluate foreign aid are demonstrated in Table 14.4, which shows countries' relative aid-giving from two different perspectives: total dollars and aid as a percentage of GNP. Note that while the United States gives the most money (this distinction was lost in 1989 when Japan boosted its contribution to over $10 billion and U.S. aid declined), when aid is evaluated as a percentage of GNP or on a per capita basis, the American effort looks very different. The percentage of their respective GNPs given by Western industrialized countries has remained about even during the 1980s at 0.4 percent, but U.S aid has declined from almost 0.5 percent in 1965, to 0.3 percent in 1975, to 0.25 percent in 1988. This leaves the United States ranking 16th of the 18 OECD countries. If, in 1988, the United States had been as generous as Norway in GNP aid, the amount it gave would have risen from $12.2 billion to $54.7 billion.

The way aid is applied is a final factor that limits its impact. Too often aid has been used to fund highly symbolic but economically unwise projects such as airports, sports arenas, or grandiose government buildings. Inefficiency and corruption have also sometimes drained off aid from its intended applications. Aid critics also charge that some countries have used aid to allow other budget funds to be diverted to nondevelopmental uses, including the nearly $40 billion in 1987 Third World arms purchases. There is also radical criticism of aid on the grounds that it is used to maintain the local elite,

TABLE 14.4

Foreign Aid Effort of 18 Western Developed Countries Analyzed
by Amount Given and by Aid as a Percentage of GNP, 1988

Country	Total Amount Given ($ billions)	Rank	Amount Given as a Percentage of GNP	Rank
Austria	$0.3	16	0.24%	17
Australia	1.1	10	0.46	8
Belgium	0.6	13	0.39	9
Canada	2.3	7	0.50	7
Denmark	0.9	12	0.89	3
Finland	0.6	13	0.59	6
France	7.0	3	0.73	5
Great Britain	2.6	6	0.32	12
Ireland	0.06	18	0.20	18
Italy	2.7	5	0.35	11
Japan	8.5	2	0.31	14
Netherlands	2.2	8	0.98	2
New Zealand	0.1	17	0.27	15
Norway	1.0	11	1.12	1
Sweden	1.5	9	0.87	4
Switzerland	0.6	13	0.32	12
United States	12.1	1	0.25	16
West Germany	4.7	4	0.39	9

Data source: World Bank (1989:236).

Aid can be analyzed from different perspectives. In total dollars, the United States ranks 1st. But in percentage of GNP it ranks 16th. Norway is 11th in dollars, but 1st in percentage of GNP giving. Overall, Canada is closer than any other country to the median in the two analytical categories combined.

does not reach the truly poor, and therefore continues the dependencia relationship between North and South. In fact, some critics argue that aid can actually retard growth. It is possible to argue, for example, that if you give poor people food, you reduce their incentive to farm.

Evaluating Aid

It is beyond our scope here to evaluate fully the various criticisms of foreign aid and the factors that have limited its impact. Still, the aid effort needs to be put into perspective. It is neither a panacea nor a waste. Criticisms about recipient countries' defense spending, wasteful spending, and corruption have to be considered in context. Third World countries do have legitimate defense needs, and at times symbolic projects enhance national pride and legitimacy. Corruption surely exists, but the response should be to prosecute those who are corrupt rather than to indict foreign aid. As U.S. representative to the Food and Agriculture Organization (FAO) Millicent Fenwick put it, "You have to understand that we are dealing with human beings, not saints" (*Time*, 2/9/87).

Scholar Roger Riddell (1987:267) has recently published an excellent study that considers the range of arguments for and against aid and the evidence available on its impact. He finds:

Two . . . conclusions can be drawn. . . . The first . . . is that there is nothing automatic about the link between aid and development: an *a priori* positive or negative relationship between the two cannot be derived theoretically, while the evidence of aid in practice remains at present inadequate to provide a certain guide to the interrelationship. . . . [Nevertheless,] the second main general conclusion . . . is that there is a role for official aid, based on addressing the needs of the poor in the Third World, and that, while aid is by no means the necessary or even the crucial ingredient for development, it can assist in the alleviation of poverty, directly and indirectly.

Third World Responses to Economic Disadvantage

As we have seen on several occasions, the North-South Axis of international politics has become increasingly important and contentious. The poor countries of the Third World are increasingly asserting that they have a right to share in the world's economic wealth. They have acted on a number of fronts to enhance their own economic situations and to pressure the industrialized countries to redistribute part of their wealth. Some of these development efforts fall within the realm of comparative domestic politics and are beyond our scope here. There are, however, a number of aspects of development that are directly related to our study, and we will examine these in terms of Third World expectations, demands, and actions and also development of the Third World movement.

Rising Expectations in the Third World

One of the most important developments of the post-1945 world has been the independence movement among Third World countries. Dozens of former colonial dependencies in Africa and Asia demanded and won political sovereignty. Attaining political independence did not complete the revolution, however. The Afro-Asian states and countries of Latin America remained in an economically subservient and disadvantaged position in relation to the dominant industrialized states, many of which were their former colonial masters.

As early as the mid-1950s it became clear that the emerging Third World states would not docilely accept continued manipulation. A number of forces were present, emerged, or intensified in the 1960s and 1970s that incited increasing Third World demands and solidarity.

Nationalism is one factor. Third World leaders recognize that true sovereignty cannot exist without economic independence.

Relative deprivation is another factor. The rapid increase of communications technology has brought the image of the North's relative richness to the South. Whether or not their objective lot has improved, the impoverished people of the South are more aware of their relative deprivation and therefore are more discontent.

Increased moral/cooperative rhetoric is another factor that has promoted Third World assertiveness. From the time of the League of Nations and accelerating during and after World War II, there has been increased lip service to the idea of international cooperation and responsibility to promote peace, economic well-being, and human rights. This rhetoric is symbolized by chapters IX and X of the United Nations Charter, which dedicate that organization to cooperative principles and establish the Economic and Social Council. Whatever the sincerity of the North in these fine phrases, the South takes them seriously and is demanding that the industrialized states practice what they have so nobly preached.

Transnational ideology has also contributed to the Third World's assertiveness. Whether or not they have adopted Marxism, few Third World leaders have not heard the communist and socialist camps' condemnation of continuing capitalist/imperialist exploitation of the South. Given Third World economic conditions and North-South economic relations, it is a message that strikes a sympathetic note.

Economic turmoil is yet another factor motivating the South. A variety of related and destabilizing economic events, including the breakup of the Bretton Woods monetary system, the periodic worldwide economic downturns, and gyrating energy costs, occurred during the past two decades. Conditions in the South went from bad to worse, and the affected countries responded with a series of declarations of economic rights and responsibilities, detailed in the following sections.

Development of the Third World Movement

The developing identity of the Third World first took the form of *political nonalignment*. In 1955, 29 African and Asian countries convened the Bandung Conference. They discussed ways to hasten the independence of colonial territories and also rejected the idea that they had to be associated with either of the superpower blocs in the East-West conflict. Instead, many embraced the principle of nonalignment, which stressed a distinctive Third World political identity. As part of that identity, the South's states would not be passively neutral in world affairs. Indeed, they would be active, but they rejected alignment with either bloc. This political movement has continued, meeting every three or four years in various Third World capitals.

It should be pointed out that the nonalignment movement was more symbolic than unified reality. Of the 101 countries that are members, about half distinctly leaned toward one or the other of the superpowers during the cold war era. Still, the nonalignment movement has had a powerful influence on Third World political consciousness.

The Third World has also been the scene of a growing economic movement. Nonalignment provided a role model for similar economic assertiveness. A coalition of disadvantaged countries, the **Group of 77**, emerged and called for the first United Nations Conference on Trade and Development (UNCTAD), which met in Geneva (1964). This conference and the Group of 77 (now over 120 countries) evolved into an ongoing UNCTAD organization, which has also met every three or four years. UNCTAD has served as a vehicle for the LDCs to discuss their needs and to press demands on the North (Weiss, 1986).

UNCTAD and the Group of 77 have also promoted many other discussions of the Third World's economic position. The most significant of these was a 1981 meeting at Cancún, Mexico, between North and South. Fourteen states representing the Group of 77 met with eight Western industrialized states representing the Organization for Economic Cooperation and Development (OECD), a 24-member organization that serves to promote economic coordination among the Western industrialized countries. (We will explore the level of North-South economic cooperation more fully in chapter 18.) Little of substantive importance was accomplished at Cancún, although the meeting did serve as a symbolic admission by the North that it has a stake in the South and that North-South economic relations are subject to negotiation between the two spheres. Overall, the response of the North has been mixed. Aid has increased some, for example, but the percentage of LDC goods subject to trade barriers has risen from 19.1 the year of Cancún to 23.4 in 1989.

Third World Demands

The development of Third World consciousness and assertiveness has led to a series of demands on the industrialized North. These calls for reform are collectively known as the **New International Economic Order (NIEO)**. More than any other single document, the Declaration on the Establishment of a New International Economic Order outlines and symbolizes the Third World's view of, and its calls for reform of, the "old" international economic order. This declaration, adopted as a resolution by the UN General Assembly in 1974, begins by protesting the North's domination of the existing economic structure and the maldistribution of wealth. To remedy this situation, the NIEO declaration calls for a number of reforms:

1. *Trade reforms.* The NIEO envisions improved and stabilized markets for primary products. This would include removal of trade barriers and the regulation of prices and supplies.
2. *Monetary reforms.* Reforms in monetary relations include stabilization of inflation and exchange rates and increased funding from the IMF and other international monetary agencies. The NIEO also includes demands for greater LDC participation in the decision-making of the IMF and other such international agencies.
3. *Industrialization.* The 1974 resolution also calls on the North to assist the South in gaining technology and increasing industrial production.
4. *Economic sovereignty.* Additionally, the Third World asserts its right to control its own resources and to regulate the activities of multinational corporations.
5. *Economic aid.* Finally, the Third World has called on the developed countries to extend economic aid at a level at least equivalent to 0.7 percent of the GNP of each. Only five industrialized countries are currently at or above this level (see Table 14.4 on p. 419), and if that standard were met by just the OECD countries it would almost double aid (from the 1988 figure) to $95 billion. There are also calls for more nonpolitical multilateral aid to be given through the World Bank and other such institutions. These calls for reform have been supplemented and detailed in the periodic UNCTAD meetings and other Third World forums.

Third World Action

The countries of the South have not passively waited for the North to respond to their demands. They have instead taken action on a number of fronts. Not all these moves have succeeded, but they are marks of the South's growing assertiveness. Areas of action include cartel formation, nationalization and control of multinational corporations (MNCs), and protection of developing industry.

Cartels

A **cartel** is an international trading agreement among producers who hope to control the supply and price of a primary product. The first cartel was established in 1933 to regulate tea, but of the current 19 cartels, all but the tea organization were formed after 1960. In their importance to the world economy, cartels range from the Organization of Petroleum Exporting Countries (OPEC) to the Asian and Pacific Coconut Community.

The rise of OPEC and its subsequent decline illustrate many of the strengths and weaknesses of cartels. This 13-member organization (which includes both Middle Eastern states and others such as Venezuela and Nigeria) was founded in 1960 but did not immediately have a major impact. In 1970 the price of oil was still only $1.35 per barrel (bbl), or 3.2 cents per gallon. Within a few years, however, a number of factors, including increased energy needs in the North and stagnant oil production in the United States, strengthened the economic hand of OPEC. Many members nationalized (took control of) production from private foreign companies. The OPEC countries also dramatically hiked prices. The North's economy convulsed, but with OPEC members producing 68 percent of all supplies (1976) and with world supply short of demand, OPEC was in the driver's seat. By 1981 the price of OPEC oil had risen almost 2,500 percent, to $34 per bbl. Money poured into the OPEC treasuries as black gold flowed out. During the 1970s, more than a trillion dollars was accumulated, and the OPEC countries' balance-of-payments surplus peaked at an annual $109 billion in 1980.

The decline of OPEC began to be obvious in the early 1980s, although its causes were paradoxically contained in the glittering success of the seventies. The humbling of OPEC was rooted in the changing balance of production, declining demand, declining price, and intra-OPEC competition.

The changing balance of production was one source of OPEC's decline. OPEC never contained all the major oil producers. Important producing countries like the United States and the Soviet Union were not involved. Furthermore, the steep rise in oil prices spurred oil exploration and the development of previously uneconomical oil supplies such as oil shale and low-capacity wells. Offshore drilling was particularly important; major fields were developed by Great Britain and others in the North Sea and by the United States off its coasts. By 1980, non-OPEC oil production rose to over 40 percent of the world total; and in 1982 the balance shifted to non-OPEC countries, which produced 54 percent of all oil and that figure remained fairly consistent through 1989. This meant not only that some countries could meet more of their energy needs, it also meant new competition for OPEC. Great Britain, for instance, is a non-OPEC country that has moved from oil importer to oil exporter and that sells its oil below OPEC prices.

Declining demand in the 1980s was the second cause of weakness for the OPEC cartel. The spiraling oil prices of the late 1970s caused a worldwide effort to conserve energy and to develop alternative energy sources. As a result, world consumption dropped from 53.4 million bbl/day in 1979 to 45.2 million bbl/day in 1983, creating a sea of surplus oil. By 1986, consumption had begun to creep back up and during the first three months of 1990 reached 52.4 million bbl/day, nearing its historic peak.

Declining price also sapped the strength of OPEC. In demonstration of the way the fundamental economic principle of supply and demand works, the decline in demand and the increase in competition (supply) were followed by a drop in price. The 1981 price of $34 per bbl had, by mid-1986, plunged to as low as $10 per barrel. The changing price of energy is shown in Figure 14.5 on page 415. This price rose to an average of about $18 per bbl in mid-1988, although this represents only about $8 per bbl in real (1973) dollars, thus leaving the real price about what it had been 15 years earlier. Oil remained near this price until the August 1990 invasion of Kuwait by Iraq, when the price jumped briefly to $40 per barrel, settled into the low $20s by the end of the year, then jumped to about $30 as the January 15, 1991, UN deadline on Iraq's withdrawal was reached.

Intra-OPEC competition is yet another factor that weakened the cartel. OPEC could have countered declining demand and outside competition by cutting supply (production), thereby propping up prices. The cartel's members, however, have proved themselves unable to cooperate in the face of adversity. One cause is that some members, such as Nigeria and Venezuela, borrowed billions of dollars against future oil revenues to finance development. When demand slumped, export revenues fell, and those countries began to struggle to sell enough oil to pay off the principal and interest on their debts. As both prices and competition cut into OPEC sales and profits, the economic plight of some of the cartel's members grew worse, and intra-OPEC competition heated up.

In addition to economic competition, intra-OPEC political strife also debilitated the cartel. Two of its members, Iran and Iraq, were at war in the 1980s. Iran's relations with Kuwait and Saudi Arabia were also severely strained, and there was speculation that these and some other OPEC countries kept oil prices down in order to disable Iran's already war-weakened economy. Then, once Iraq emerged the victor, its relations with Kuwait were strained in part by what, Iraq said, was Kuwaiti overproduction; and an Iraqi invasion of Kuwait followed.

The lesson of OPEC for cartels is that when a cartel can act *with unity* to control the bulk of world production of a *vital resource,* then the cartel can be a success. Most cartels, however, are not so lucky, even for a short time. They are subject to demand variations, competition from nonmembers, development/expansion of substitutes, conservation/decline in demand, and intracartel competition. The result is that cartels have not proved to be a significant technique for Third World development.

Nationalization and Control of MNCs

A second area of action to accomplish the New International Economic Order (NIEO) program has involved Third World countries' taking closer control of their domestic economies. One route has been **nationalization** of foreign-owned companies. This process requires that at least a majority of any company be owned by the host country or its citizens. Between 1960 and 1976, 71 countries nationalized 1,369 enterprises at an accelerating rate.

Although nationalization is an effective method to gain control of production, it has declined because it does have its drawbacks. Nationalizations have caused some international squabbles as MNCs have looked to their home countries for support over compensation disagreements with the nationalizing country. The potential for nationalization has also inhibited foreign investment. MNCs are less willing to risk their money, thus limiting one source of capital inflow for LDCs.

As discussed in the previous chapter, recent years have seen many host countries establish rules that limit profit-taking, require local processing and capital reinvestment, and mandate training and other personnel policies. But even here, progress has been slow and uneven. The pressure to attract investment capital is so strong that some LDCs are actually easing restrictions on MNCs, and nationalizations are also now relatively rare. Thus the struggle between the desire for economic sovereignty and the need for investment capital continues unabated.

Protection of Developing Industries

A third thrust of Third World activity has been an attempt to protect developing industries from foreign competition. China is one of the most recent developing economies to fly the protectionist flag. The temptation and domestic political pressure for developing countries to use tariffs and nontariff barriers to protect infant industries are strong and may, in the earliest stages, even have some merit. Protectionist policies work against the theory of comparative advantage, however, and also invite retaliation by more economically powerful states. Most important, there is evidence that LDC protectionism does not work. As one analyst concluded, "Empirically, the record shows that those countries that have followed low tariff policies and eschewed quantitative restrictions . . . all have outstanding export performance records. On the other hand, the rate of export growth of countries following high protectionist policies . . . has been well below par" (Krauss, 1983:52–53).

The Response of the North

Some of the goals of the NIEO can be furthered by the individual and collective policies of the countries of the Third World. These actions can go only so far, though, in promoting greater economic equality. A pivotal part, then, in advancing the NIEO is the cooperation of the North. Thus far this cooperation has been limited. It is true that there have been important advances in international economic cooperation. Some of this progress has included improvements in North-South cooperation, and these will be discussed in chapter 18.

The Recalcitrant Rich   Overall, though, the governments of the North have been slow to respond. There are some analysts who contend, with a good deal of logic and evidence, that because of economic interdependence and other factors, the North has a vital stake in the South's development. Whatever the truth of this global view, it has occasioned only a limited response in the North. Traditional narrow self-interest has been strengthened by the economic turmoil of the recent past. Given the vastly superior economic and political strength of the North, its reluctance to cooperate has meant that, so far, the NIEO remains a series of conscience-disturbing demands rather than a developing program.

It is also important to note that some analysts are skeptical of the equity issue as a basis of the Third World's demands for the NIEO. Stephen Krasner (1985:3) takes the realist/mercantilist view that what LDCs want is "power and control as much as wealth." The true purpose of the NIEO, he continues, "is to change the rules of the game" to the South's benefit. This goal, Krasner believes, is generally "incompatible with long-term Northern interests." These views lead him to conclude that "given fundamental [North-South] conflicts stemming from outlandish disparities in power, there would be more security in a world with lower levels of transnational interaction. Self-reliance and collective self-reliance rather than interdependence may serve the interests of the North as well as those of the South" (p. 12). Krasner, therefore, might contend that this section should be entitled the "realistic rich" rather than the "recalcitrant rich."

The Future of the South

Even if you were to assume that the future could be foretold on the basis of the recent past, your predictions for the future would depend on whether you were an optimist or a pessimist.

On the positive side, there is progress on many fronts. A few newly industrializing countries now export a diversity of manufactured products and have robustly expanding GNPs. Many social indicators also show improvement. The population explosion is beginning to ease (although it remains alarmingly high), new agricultural techniques give hope of feeding the hungry, life expectancy has improved, and illiteracy has

Most countries of the South continue to struggle economically. Progress is possible, however, and significant strides have been made by some newly industrializing countries. The Taiwanese workers shown here on the way home from their factory jobs live in a relatively industrialized prosperous Third World country.

declined. There is also at least a genesis of recognition in the North of its interest in and responsibility for the development of the South. In short, for many, things are better than they were, and for a few, things are much better.

On the negative side, the South has long suffered under a heavy burden of socioeconomic/political problems. Economically, it continues to be disadvantaged, dependent, and exploited. Socially, many parts of the Third World are handicapped by overpopulation, illiteracy, hunger, disease, and the breakdown of traditional societal structures. Politically, LDCs are often inexperienced, internally divided, and subject to coups and countercoups as well as outside interference. Consider Nigeria, Africa's most populous state. During the last 25 years, its population has approximately doubled, but per capita food production has declined 21 percent. One obvious result is poor health. Twenty-five percent of all Nigerian babies have low birth weights. This figure is 4 times higher than in the United States and Canada. Nigeria's literacy rate is only about 30 percent, it is heavily indebted, and its annual per capita GNP is about equal to 2 weeks of the U.S. per capita GNP. Nigeria has also suffered through a civil war and military coups.

Thus, despite some of the hopeful signs, the prospects for the future are at least troubling. The world population recently hurtled through the 5-billion mark, environmental problems threaten coming generations, and there is a resurgence of protectionism and other forms of shortsighted economic self-interest. There are few signs that the North will radically reform its trade, aid, investment, monetary, or political policies. In sum, we have improved on the past, and in the future we may well improve on the present. But progress is painfully slow. It is, at best, an evolution rather than a revolution, and there are many who seriously question whether the world can progress far enough, fast enough to avoid apocalypse.

Chapter Summary

1. The economic issues facing the North and those facing the South are, in most respects, fundamentally different. The North is concerned with preserving and expanding its economic prosperity. For the South the major issue is survival, in economic terms and, all too often, in human terms. For many in the world's less developed countries, life is a struggle against starvation, disease, illiteracy, and death.

2. Measuring "progress" in LDCs is controversial. In absolute terms, there have been some advances. Relative to the North, however, the South is falling further behind. Modernization has also brought some negative consequences, including explosive population growth, destructive urbanization, and poor planning.

3. It should also be noted that *South* is a word that somewhat hides the wide disparities in the Third World. A few newly industrializing countries have expanding and modernizing economies. There is also, in most LDCs, a wealthy class of people. For most Third World countries, however, and for most of the citizens in those countries, prosperity—even comfort—is only a hope, and a dim one at that.

4. Capital is the primary need of the LDCs. They need hard currency to buy the goods and services that will allow them to develop their economies. There are four basic sources of hard currency: trade, loans, foreign aid, and foreign investment. In each of these areas, however, the LDCs face difficult problems.

5. The catch-22 of trade is that the primary products that LDCs mainly produce do not earn them enough capital to found industries to produce manufactured goods that would earn more money.

6. Loans are unsatisfactory because of high repayment costs, because they have largely dried up in recent years, and because there are conditions attached.

7. Foreign aid is minor compared with world needs and is often given on the basis of political expediency rather than economic necessity.

8. Investment capital flows least into the most needy countries and is often accompanied by unacceptable practices by multinational corporate investors.

9. In recent years, the countries of the Third World have begun to make greater demands for economic equity and have increasingly come together to press those demands on the North. These demands for fundamental economic reform are collectively referred to as the New International Economic Order.

10. The LDCs have also taken actions such as the founding of international trading agreements called cartels. OPEC is the most well known and successful of these. Most cartels, however, have not worked well because of the disadvantages that primary-product producers face in relation to the industrialized countries. The LDCs have also acted to protect developing industries and to nationalize MNCs. Each of these steps, though, has its drawbacks as well as its advantages. So far, the response of the North to the demands of the South has been extremely limited.

11. The economic and social future of the South is far from cheerful. There are some good signs, such as expanding literacy, but there are also many troubling omens. The massive starvation in Ethiopia and other countries in Africa and the epidemic economic, social, and political unrest on a global basis are very possibly Scrooge-like glimpses into "Christmas-future." In chapter 18 we will examine attempts to work together for economic betterment and equity, but these are too few and may very well come too late to avoid repeated and greater catastrophes.

PART IV

GROWING COOPERATION

This text began with a literary analogy between international relations and Shakespeare's belief that "all the world's a stage, And all the men and women . . . [are] players." The world drama, as we have followed it to this point—its actors, its plot, its action—has been a troubled tale. The actors, if not always villains, have too often been convinced of their own righteousness and have pursued their interests at the expense of others. Discord has time and again triumphed over harmony. The specters of hunger and disease continue to stalk the world, yet the rich nations content themselves with little more than expressions of pity.

Still, the world survives and has a future. It is that future, rather than a gloomy contemplation of the past, that should consume our intellects. Indeed, a major thrust of this text is to enable its readers not only to understand what has been and what is but also to contemplate what might be. As the Bard of Avon tells us in *Hamlet*, "We know what we are, but not what we can be." Another, more contemporary, analogy is between our world drama and *The French Lieutenant's Woman*. This novel, and movie, has two endings, one of love and peace, the other of conflict and tragedy. It may well be that the fate of humankind similarly hangs in the balance of the world drama.

One possible path is akin to Shakespeare's dictum that "what is past is prologue" (*The Tempest*). If this is true, then the divisions, self-interest, and conflict that

428

IN THE WORLD

have often characterized the past will continue into the future. To continue, however, does not necessarily mean that we can survive as before. The nuclear arms race, the flood of world population, modernization's threat to our ecological survival, and the seething demands of the impoverished majority of the world's population all carry potentially apocalyptic consequences.

Catastrophe is not certain. Indeed, we may continue to muddle through. But it is also possible, as Shakespeare further writes in *Hamlet*, that the world's future may

. . . a tale unfold whose lightest word
Would harrow up thy soul, freeze thy young blood,
Make thy two eyes, like stars, start from their
  spheres,
Thy knotted and combined locks to part,
And each particular hair to stand an end
Like quills upon the fretful porpentine.

On the other hand, there is the alternative of a more salutary future. It involves a world that the idealists urge upon us as discussed in chapter 2. Analysts of this school would have us avoid the experiences recounted by the ghost of Hamlet's father above by following the admonition of *King Henry VI*: "Now join your hands, and with your hands your hearts."

The final five chapters of this book are about the world's effort to find a new order. They are an exploration of the movement toward international cooperation.

There are many signs that we, as citizens of the world, are beginning to see our stake in one another and that we are beginning, however uncertainly, to move toward a process of accommodation rather than competition. The author is even more convinced that such efforts are crucial for the future. Each of the final four chapters explores one aspect of cooperative behavior. Chapter 15 addresses international organization as it is and as it might be. Next, chapter 16 discusses the concept and practice of international law. Then, in chapter 17, the painfully slow struggle to find a basis for arms control or disarmament is analyzed. Chapter 18 details the growth of economic cooperation in the world. Finally, chapter 19 examines international progress with respect to the social and environmental issues of our biosphere.

The issue that faces us all is which of the alternative endings to adopt. The time left for decision is uncertain, but pressing problems make it clear that procrastination is perilous. To end, as we began, with a thought from Shakespeare,

There is a tide in the affairs of men,
Which, taken at the flood, leads on to fortune;
Omitted, all the voyage of their life
Is bound in shallows and in miseries.

Julius Caesar

Friendly counsel cuts off many foes.

Shakespeare, *Henry VI,* Part I

[The United Nations is] group therapy for the world.

Antonio Montiero, Portuguese ambassador to the UN

INTERNATIONAL ORGANIZATION

The nation-state has, for the past several centuries, been the primary actor in world politics. Indeed, as discussed in the chapter on nationalism, it is hard to conceive of any other form of organization. Yet alternatives do exist.

International organization is one of these alternatives. Many established agencies are currently involved in promoting political, economic, and social cooperation. Many observers contend that such efforts are the hope of the future. They may be right. It is just possible that ongoing organizations will serve as prototypes or building blocks for a future, higher form of political loyalty and activity.

There are also those who dismiss the notion of international organizations as idealistic dreaming. But there was also a time when we believed that the world was the center of the universe. We now know that the sun does not turn around the earth; perhaps we can learn that the nation-state need not be the center of the political cosmos.

The Nature and Development of International Organization

The concept of international organization is not a new one, although the practice of having a continuous international organization is a relatively recent advance in the conduct of international relations. Now there are a growing number of permanent international organizations. The size and scope of these international organizations vary greatly, ranging from multipurpose, nearly universal organizations like the United Nations to single-purpose organizations with very few member countries (Feld & Jordan, 1988; Kratochwil & Ruggle, 1989).

431

Types of International Organizations

The term *international organization* tends to bring *United Nations* to mind. There are many more, however, and for our purposes they can be divided into general, regional, and specialized types of international organizations. One commonality among some of them is that their memberships consist of national governments. Therefore, they are termed international **intergovernmental organizations (IGOs)**. As pointed out in chapter 3, some of these IGOs have at least theoretical, limited supranational status. There are also a significant and growing number of international **nongovernmental organizations (NGOs** or sometimes **INGOs)**, which are transnational actors made up of private organizations and individuals instead of member states.

We have already addressed some international organization types and activities under such headings as intergovernmental organizations and nongovernmental organizations (chapter 3), parliamentary diplomacy (chapter 12), and cartels (chapter 14). In this and the next two chapters, we will further examine organizations that focus on promoting cooperation in law, disarmament, and socioeconomic endeavors. Thus, although many of the organizations discussed in this chapter have a variety of purposes, our primary focus will be their impact on the world's political order.

A universal intergovernmental organization is one that draws its membership from all areas of the world. The United Nations is the most obvious example, but there are many others, such as the World Health Organization.

TABLE 15.1

Types and Examples of International Organizations

| | Purpose | | | |
| | General | | Specialized | |
Geography	IGO	NGO	IGO	NGO
Universal	United Nations	Catholic Church	International Monetary Fund	Red Cross, Amnesty International
Regional	Organization of American States	European People's Party	Association of Southeast Asian Nations	African Football Confederation

International organizations can be classified according to whether they deal with many issues (general) or are specialized. They can also be classified according to whether their membership is universal or regional. There are many scholarly schemes for classifying such organizations as well as differences in definition and terminology. There is also disagreement over whether some organizations, such as alliances, are properly international organizations at all. One discussion of many of these points is Feld & Jordan, with Hurwitz (1983:1–40). Also see Judge (1978:28–83) and Archer (1983:36–67). For an exhaustive catalogue, see *Union of International Associations* (published annually). The 1990 edition indexed 4,939 "traditional" IGOs and NGOs and a total of 21,373 of all such organizations.

There are many nongovernmental organizations (NGOs) that are active on the international stage. One of these is AmeriCares, a private relief organization headquartered in Canaan, Connecticut. In 1990, AmeriCares was active in shipping supplies to assist refugees in Jordan and elsewhere who had fled from Iraq and Kuwait. Then the organization moved to assist the Soviets facing food and medical shortages during the 1990–91 winter. This photo, taken in December 1990, shows an AmeriCares shipment loading at Bradley International Airport near Hartford, Connecticut, destined for Minsk in the Soviet Union. The sign in Russian on the cargo reads, "To the Soviet people from the people of the United States."

Regional intergovernmental organizations are those that draw their memberships from one geographic region. Some regional organizations, such as the Organization of American States (OAS), are multipurpose, much like the UN. Others are somewhat active in a variety of areas but concentrate on one. The Association of Southeast Asian Nations (ASEAN) is an example of a primarily economic regional organization, while the Organization of African Unity (OAU) devotes most of its energy to political affairs. Additionally, there are a host of single-purpose regional organizations. Most regional military alliances would fall in this category, as would regional economic organizations such as the Economic Community of West African States.

A general intergovernmental organization is one that is active in a number of areas such as political, economic, and social development and/or cooperation. The United Nations is, again, an example, as is the (British) Commonwealth. The European Community (EC) is evolving into a general-purpose IGO. Of all the types of international organizations, those with general functions are the rarest.

Specialized intergovernmental organizations are single-purpose, or functional, organizations. A vast array of these specialized agencies exists, and they deal with almost every conceivable subject from health through postal regulations (Universal Postal Union, headquarters, Berne, Switzerland) to air travel (International Civil Aviation Organization, headquarters, Montreal, Canada).

Nongovernmental organizations is our final category. As mentioned, NGOs are different from IGOs in that they are not made up of member states. Some NGOs, such as the Roman Catholic Church, are active in several geographic and policy areas. Most NGOs, however, have limited purposes (Red Cross, Amnesty International, Socialist International) and/or are limited geographically (African Football Confederation, for example). However, this typology of organizations is not mutually exclusive, as Table 15.1 shows.

The Roots of International Organization

International organization is primarily a modern phenomenon, but its origins extend far back in history. Three main root systems have nourished the current growth.

Universal Concern for the Condition of Humanity

The roots of international organization lie, in part, in the universal concern for the condition of humanity. This has been expressed in the writings of philosophers and in the attempts to create organizations to improve human conditions.

Philosophy   The first branch of the root system is the universalistic conception of humankind. Confucius (551–479 B.C.) deplored violence, and Erasmus (1466–1536) rejected war as brutal, wicked, wasteful, and stupid. Other early philosophers agreed that all persons share a responsibility for one another's welfare. Still other philosophers, including William Penn, the Abbé de Sainte-Pierre, and Immanuel Kant, argued that the way to accomplish these ends was through general international organizations.

Organization   The first example of an organization based on these principles was the *Hague system*, named for the 1899 and 1907 peace conferences held at that city in the Netherlands. The 1907 conference was more comprehensive, with 44 European, North American, and Latin American states participating.

Organizationally, the Hague system included a rudimentary general assembly and a judicial system. The conferences also adopted a series of standards to limit the conduct of war. World War I destroyed the plans for a third Hague conference in 1915, but the move toward universal organization was under way.

The next step along the path was creation of the **League of Nations** after World War I. The League was intended mainly as a peacekeeping organization, although it did have some elements aimed at social and economic cooperation. Despite the hopes with which it was founded, the League could not survive some of its own organizational inadequacies, the unstable post–World War I peace, the Great Depression, and the rise of militant fascism. After only two decades of frustrated existence, it died in the rubble of World War II.

The *United Nations* is the latest, and most advanced, developmental stage of universal concern with the human condition. Like the League of Nations, it was established mainly to maintain peace, but it has increasingly become involved in socioeconomic issues. In addition, as we shall see, the UN and its predecessor, the League, represent the coming together of all the root systems of international organizations. They are more properly seen as the emergent saplings of extensive cooperation and integration.

Big-Power Peacekeeping

The second branch of the root system is the idea that the big powers have a special responsibility to cooperate and preserve peace. The Roman Peace, enforced by the imperial power of Rome, was viewed by Dante and others with nostalgia amid the turmoil of the Middle Ages. As early as 1625, Hugo Grotius, the "father of international law," suggested that the "Christian powers" confer to "settle the disputes of others" or even "compel parties to accept peace on fair terms" (Claude, 1971:25).[1]

1. Claude (1971) discusses the origins of international organization, and his concept of "three streams" is influential but somewhat different from that used here.

This idea took on substance with the Congress of Vienna. This conference and three others between 1815 and 1822 led to the Concert of Europe. This informal coalition of the major European powers and the following balance-of-(big-)power diplomacy managed generally to keep the peace for the century between the fall of Napoleon and the outbreak of World War I.

The persistence of the philosophy of big-power responsibility (and authority) was evident in the Council of the League of Nations. The council was granted authority (Covenant Article 4) to deal "with any matter within the sphere of activity of the League or affecting the peace of the world." Significantly, five of the nine seats on the council were permanently assigned to the principal victorious allies of World War I. The council was thus the Concert of Europe continued.

When the United Nations succeeded the League of Nations, the special status and responsibilities of the big powers that had been reflected in the League's council were transferred to the United Nations Security Council. Like its predecessor, the Security Council is the main peacekeeping organ and includes permanent membership for the big five powers (the United States, the Soviet Union, China, Great Britain, and France). Each of the major powers can cast a veto that, as a lone vote, can block Security Council action. We will further explore these issues, but for now we should notice that a conceptual descendant of the Concert of Europe is alive and well in New York.

Functional Cooperation

The third branch of our root system lies in the specialized agencies designed to deal with specific, generally nonpolitical economic and social problems (McCormick, 1989). The six-member Central Commission for the navigation of the Rhine, established in 1815, is the oldest surviving IGO, and the International Telegraphic (now Telecommunications) Union (1865) and the Universal Postal Union (1874) are the oldest surviving IGOs with global membership. As detailed below, the growth of these specialized IGOs and NGOs has been phenomenal. This aspect of international activity is also reflected in the UN through the 18 specialized agencies associated with the world body.

Growth of IGOs and NGOs

An important phenomenon of the twentieth century is the rapid growth in the number, activities, and importance of intergovernmental organizations and nongovernmental organizations (Armstrong, 1989).

Quantitative Growth

This century has seen rapid growth in the number of all types of international organizations. Table 15.2 on the next page, as well as some discussion in chapter 3, highlights this rapid expansion. As the table indicates, there are now about 10 times as many IGOs and 67 times as many NGOs as in 1900. Further, the ratio of IGOs to the number of countries has approximately doubled. Denmark, for example, is a member of 164 IGOs, the highest number of any country (Jacobson, Reisinger, & Mathers, 1989). Overall, the world's countries now have 7,573 IGO memberships, which means the average country is a member of 45 IGOs. Thus, there are not only more IGOs absolutely and relative to the number of participating countries, but the level of participation has dramatically increased.

TABLE 15.2

Expansion of International Organizations, 1900–1990

	Category				
Year	No. of IGOs	No. of NGOs	No. of Countries	IGOs per Country	NGOs per Country
1900	30	69	38	0.8	1.8
1945	123	795	65	1.9	12.2
1990	293	4,646	170	1.7	27.3

Data sources: Feld & Jordan (1988) for 1900 and 1945. Union of International Associations (1990:1723) for 1990.

The number of IGOs and NGOs and the number of countries' memberships in these organizations are expanding rapidly.

Reasons for Growth

This century's rapid growth of international organizations, both in number and in scope of activity, is the result of a number of forces.

Increased international contact has spurred the growth of international organizations. The revolutions in communications and transportation technologies have brought the states of the world into much closer contact. These interchanges need organizational structures in order to become routine and regulated. The Universal Postal Union and the International Telegraphic Union, founded in the 1800s, have been joined in more modern times by the International Air Transport Association, the Intergovernmental Maritime Association, and almost 300 others.

The world's *increased interdependence*, particularly in the economic sphere, has fostered a variety of IGOs designed to deal with this phenomenon. The International Monetary Fund (IMF) and the World Bank are just two examples. Regional trade and monetary organizations, cartels, and (to a degree) multinational corporations are other examples.

A third cause of the growth of international organizations is the expansion of **transnational** issues. More than ever before, many of the world's problems affect many states and require solutions that are beyond the resources of any single state. One such issue (and its associated international organization) is nuclear proliferation (International Atomic Energy Agency).

A fourth incentive for the expansion of international organizations is the *failure of the current state-centered system*. The agony of two world wars, for instance, convinced many that peace was not safe in the hands of nation-states. The League of Nations and then the United Nations were successive attempts to organize for the preservation of peace. The continuing problems in health, food, human rights, and other areas have also spurred the organization of IGOs and NGOs.

A fifth factor is the increased number of *transnational political movements*. Political movements increasingly extend beyond the borders of a single state. The monarchist Concert of Europe of the 1800s has given way to the Communist International, the Socialist International, and the World Anti-communist League, some of which are now themselves in decline. The (British) Commonwealth, the Arab League, and the even more loosely-knit French Community would also fall within this category.

Sixth, the *concentration of military power* in the two superpowers and the concentration of economic power in the industrialized states have led less powerful actors to join coalitions in an attempt to influence events. "Vulnerability" has, thus, motivated the nonaligned movement, the peace movement, the New International Economic Order, and their associated organizations.

Finally, the existence and successes of international organizations provide *role models* that have generated still other IGOs and NGOs. People and countries have learned that they can sometimes work together internationally, and this has encouraged them to try new ventures in international organization and cooperation.

Evolutionary Growth of Roles

An evolutionary expansion of their roles is another way that some international organizations are growing. The evolving European Community (EC), which is detailed in chapter 18, is itself the product of the 1967 merger of the European Economic Community, the European Coal and Steel Community, and the European Atomic Energy Community. Furthermore, the scope of EC activities is expanding beyond its original economic focus to a wider range of political and social concerns. It is also developing an increasingly important organizational structure, and some observers think that in the not-too-distant future the EC could evolve into a United States of Europe.

There are other international organizations that also take on new functions. In October 1990, for example, the Economic Community of West Africa (ECOWA) intervened in the three-way civil war raging in Liberia. Approximately 8,000 troops from five member countries (Gambia, Ghana, Guinea, Nigeria, and Sierra Leone) moved to end the fighting which had turned almost half of Liberia's 2.3 million people into refugees in neighboring countries. There were some criticisms of the force for lack of impartiality, but it did achieve a late-November 1990 cease-fire among the three factions during a summit meeting among the leaders of the factions and ECOWA leaders in Bamako, the capital of Mali. Additionally, Nigeria and other ECOWA countries pledged rehabilitation aid for Liberia from their already meager financial reserves.

Purposes of International Organization

The concept of international organization is complex, and its advocates are divided on proper goals and roles. These differing aims include world government, comprehensive cooperation, functional cooperation, and/or political advantage (Diehl, 1989).

World Government

The *vision* that some proponents of international organization hold is that someday there will be one **world government**. They argue for a "top down," revolutionary approach to solving world problems. According to this approach, the current national states would give up most of their sovereignty to a new, supranational organization, which would have central lawmaking, enforcing, and adjudicating authority. Within this general goal, there are several approaches that vary according to how hierarchical the organization would be. This structure could range from a *unitary* world government with subunits serving only administrative purposes, through *federalism*, in which a central authority and member units share power, to *confederalism*, in which the members are highly interdependent but retain all or most of their sovereign authority (Cleveland, 1988).

There is also dispute about the proper locus of supranational government(s). Some argue for a global system, while others propose regional supranational structures. In a recent article, originally published in *Pravda,* Georgi Shakhnazarov (1989:245–57), president of the Soviet Political Science Association, notes that "it is common knowledge that the rate of progress—economic, scientific and social—in the 20th century has been much higher" than at any time in history. These rapid changes, he contends, have created problems with population, the environment, economies, and nuclear weapons, "dictating the need for creative renewal." According to Shakhnazarov, an "indispensable" key to resolving these problems "must be the enhancement of the degree to which the world is amenable to government." After reviewing the progress and obstacles on the path he favors, the Soviet scholar optimistically concludes that "we have the right to draw the conclusion that the sphere of world governability, despite all its contradictoriness, is slowly but steadily expanding. This progress is for the good of mankind."

There is a strong *critique* of the one-world idea. While the image of a peaceful and cooperative world is highly attractive, there are many who doubt that world government can be attained. These skeptics argue that, first, there are *practical barriers* to world government. The assumption here is that nationalism has too strong a hold and that neither political leaders nor masses would be willing to surrender independence to a universal body. Are we ready to "pledge allegiance to the United States of the World"?

Critics of the world government movement also pose *theoretical objections*. They worry about the concentration of power that would be necessary even to begin enforcing international law and addressing the world's monumental economic and social problems. Critics further doubt that any such government, even given unprecedented power, could succeed in solving world problems any better than less (potentially) authoritarian alternatives. Some skeptics further argue that centralization would inevitably diminish desirable cultural diversity and political experimentation in the world. Another criticism of the world government movement is that it diverts attention from more reasonable avenues of international cooperation such as the United Nations and other existing international organizations.

Comprehensive Cooperation

Most supporters of international organizations advocate a more limited role for IGOs. This school of thought believes that IGOs can best serve as vehicles to promote cooperation among states rather than through the subordination of states to a global authority.

The United Nations and some regional organizations are designed to advance international cooperative efforts to maintain peace, better economic conditions, protect the environment, and, in general, improve the human condition. Insofar as IGOs play an "independent" role, proponents of this approach argue that it should be one mainly of mediation and conciliation rather than coercion. The object here is to teach and allow, not to force, nation-states to work together.

Functionalism

An even more limited approach to international organization is **functionalism**. Functionalists favor a "bottom up," evolutionary approach to international cooperation. They

Gradually through history our focus of primary political loyalty has shifted from smaller units such as tribes and villages to larger units, especially countries. Some people believe that this trend should continue and that a world government should be established. The image of children starting out their school day by saying "I pledge allegiance to the flag of the United States of the World" may seem strange, but a global government may evolve.

argue that by cooperating in specific, usually nonpolitical areas, we can learn to trust one another. This, in turn, will lead to broader and higher levels of cooperation. Functionalists also contend that cooperation on social and economic issues can improve conditions to the point where the causes of political conflict are eliminated.

The best-known proponent of functionalism, David Mitrany (1966:31,38), argues, for example, that "sovereignty cannot be transferred effectively through a formula, [but] only through a function." Mitrany then contends that in time "the accumulation of such partial transfers" of sovereignty will "overlay political divisions with a spreading web of international activities" that will promote world peace and integration.

Regimes   A recent extension of functional cooperation is the creation of international regimes that deal with particular issue-areas (Strange, 1989; Young, 1989). A regime is not so much a single organization as a complex of international organizations and generally accepted rules of behavior in areas such as monetary relations, trade, health, or air traffic control. Regimes represent an advance from national cooperation through one functional organization on one issue to cooperation through a complex of related organizations on a complex of issues (Snidal, 1990).

Regimes, which are also discussed in chapter 3, enhance functional cooperation in two ways (Haggard & Simmons, 1987). One is by altering the political environment in ways that promote cooperation among states. Regimes do this by creating councils, commissions, or other consultative bodies where states can meet. In such settings goals can be set, a country's actions can be explained or questioned, and cooperation incentives can be established.

A second way that regimes facilitate cooperation is by changing expectations. There is, for example, a growing regime, some people would argue several regimes, that is expanding international cooperation with regard to the world's oceans. Navigation, pollution, seabed mining, and fisheries are all areas of expanded international discussion, rule-making, and cooperation. Whaling, for example, has been virtually eliminated, and the killing of whales now violates widely held norms. Those few countries, such as Japan, that have continued commercial whaling have come under heavy criticism and some retaliatory action, including suits in U.S. courts trying to impose trade sanctions on Japan.

Neofunctionalism   A concept related to functionalism is labeled neofunctionalism. Those who advocate this idea are somewhat critical of basic functionalism. They are skeptical that nonpolitical cooperation by itself can lead to full political cooperation or that it can eliminate all the causes of war and other forms of international conflict and self-interested action. Neofunctionalists are also concerned about timetables. They are worried that the evolutionary approach favored by functionalists will not move quickly enough and will not culminate in political cooperation soon enough to head off many of the world's looming problems. Therefore, neofunctionalists advocate establishing political organizations and processes that can address political issues with an eye to greater cooperation. They argue that this speeds up the timetable by addressing the most important questions sooner. It also may enhance nonpolitical cooperation. For example, recent U.S.–Soviet political accommodations on nuclear arms and on a number of regional disputes have increased cultural and economic exchange and cooperation rather than the other way around, as a classic functionalist might assume.

Political Advantage

It should be noted that many approach international organizations and international regimes as tools to further their self-interested concept of the "correct" international order. This approach is rarely stated openly, but it is obvious in the struggles within the UN and other IGOs, where the East-West, North-South, and other struggles were or are waged with vengeance. This seemingly contradictory use of supposedly integrative international organizations to gain national advantage is part of the world's struggle between the forces of order and the forces of conflict.

Evaluating International Organizations

Thus far this chapter has been introducing the concept of international organization and laying the groundwork for addressing the most vital questions: How do IGOs work, and how successful are they? This second question, the matter of evaluation, is by far the most difficult, and it is well to stop here and consider our standards.

In the following sections (and the remaining chapters), we will spend considerable time looking at global, regional, and specialized IGOs and NGOs. We will focus especially on the United Nations, both as a generalized study of international organization and as a specific study of the world's most important IGO.

A fundamental query of this analysis will be "How well does it work?" In responding to this question, we will consider several possible *standards*. One of these is *successes and failures*. Where has the UN (or any IGO or NGO) succeeded and where has it failed? It will be important to maintain balance in this approach to evaluation. Those who optimistically support international integration are prone to emphasize progress, to see the glass half-full. Cynics—and there are many—who dismiss the UN as impotent are apt to see the glass half-empty. It is important to maintain balanced objectivity in evaluation of international organizations.

This observation brings us to the second standard, which involves *ideals versus what is possible*. The UN was founded in the anguished aftermath of World War II. As a result, the rhetoric that surrounded its creation and the language found in its Charter (constitution) are full of idealistic hope. Article One of the Charter symbolically proclaims that it is the purpose of the UN "To maintain international peace and security. . . . To develop friendly relations among nations . . . [and] to achieve international cooperation in solving international [economic, social, cultural, and humanitarian] problems."

Obviously, we have not yet come close to attaining these goals. Does this mean the UN has failed? Perhaps from the ideal perspective it has, but this is an impossible standard for now. It is more realistic to evaluate the UN in accordance with what is possible at the present time and in the near future. As we will see, the UN and other international organizations are substantially limited by the willingness of member states to cooperate or to surrender sovereignty. Thus, to a substantial degree, the UN does not always work because we will not let it. As the classic comic character Pogo observed in a different context, "We have met the enemy and he is us."

When evaluating IGOs, then, keep their limitations and the sources of these restrictions in mind. Judge them according to what it is possible for them to accomplish rather than by an idealistic standard.

It is also a good idea to keep its relative cost in mind when evaluating the United Nations or any other intergovernmental organization. As the following discussion of UN finances will detail, there has been considerable pressure in the United States and other countries to reduce contributions to the world body. These come from the feeling that it costs too much, especially given the UN's alleged limited effectiveness.

Such judgments are subjective, of course, but they can be put in perspective. The 1989 United Nations budget was approximately $1.79 billion. This certainly is a lot of money. But it is also only one-half of the $3.5 billion it costs to build just one U.S. nuclear aircraft carrier. Or, by another measure, the annual cost of funding the United Nations is less than two-tenths of one percent (.00179) of the world's approximately $1 trillion in military expenditures for 1989. This means that 1989 world military spending could finance the UN for nearly the next six centuries (559 years). By this standard, it is possible to argue that even if the United Nations serves only as a symbol of world peace and cooperation, it is well worth its relatively minor cost.

Before leaving the subject of evaluating the United Nations and other international organizations, it is worth noting the level of knowledge and the views of the UN that are held around the world. Public opinion surveys conducted by the United Nations in 19 countries during 1989 show both a high level of awareness of and approval of the global organization (*UN Chronicle* 6/90:40). Awareness was highest in developed countries such as Denmark where 99 percent of its citizens knew about the United Nations. But even in Mexico, the country with the fewest citizens able to identify the UN, the awareness level was still 70 percent. Most of those polled who had an opinion thought the UN was doing a good job. Seventy-three percent of all Danes thought so. Almost half of all Mexicans and 86 percent of Mexicans with an opinion also rated the UN positively. Only Americans, of all the nations polled, held a negative image. Only 38 percent of all Americans thought the UN was doing a good job (Alger, 1990).

Knowledge about the specifics of the United Nations was generally low, although the degree of the dearth of information varied considerably among countries. When presented with a list of the five past and current secretaries-general, only 15 percent of all respondents could correctly identify Javier Pérez de Cuéller as the current UN head. People also had trouble naming a UN agency. West Germans were the most knowledgeable on this point, with 72 percent able to name at least one UN agency. Americans (29 percent), by contrast, had knowledge levels just slightly above those found in Third World countries, and Canadians (38 percent) did not do much better. On the two scales (could identify the secretary-general and could name a UN agency), the Danes did best (50 percent); Mexicans did worst (14 percent).

Several inferences can be drawn from these findings. One is that there is a generally favorable opinion of the UN in the world. Significantly, this is especially true for those who are aware of the international organization. Second, there is a widespread lack of specific information about the UN. Third, the more people know about the UN, the more likely they are to view it favorably. These three observations lead to the fourth: strengthening the UN requires, in part, an extensive program of global public education about the UN's organization and functions.

International Organizations: Structure and Issues

One important aspect of international organizations is structure and related issues. Constitutions, rules of procedure, finance, organization charts, and other administrative details are often dismissed as inconsequential by the political novice. They are not! To the contrary, such nitty-gritty items are often extremely important in determining political outcomes. An outline of the UN's structure is depicted in Figure 15.1. In the following discussion of the structure of international organizations and the issues related to this structure, we will examine membership, representative bodies, administrative structure, and financial arrangements. As will rapidly become obvious, the discussion will focus on the UN, both as the leading IGO and as an example of the structural issues facing all attempts to organize internationally.

Membership

Theoretically, membership in most international organizations is open to any state that falls within the geographic and/or functional scope of that organization *and* that subscribes to the principles and practices of that organization. In practice, a third standard, politics, often becomes a heavy consideration in membership questions.

Most IGOs have procedures for admitting new members and one politicized issue is the standards for *admitting new members*. From 1945 to 1955 in the UN, membership was a cold-war issue, with the United States and the Soviet Union each blocking the admittance of states sympathetic to the other superpower. Then, in a compromise, 16 new members were admitted all at once. Since then UN membership has expanded quickly, as Figure 15.2 (p. 444) shows.

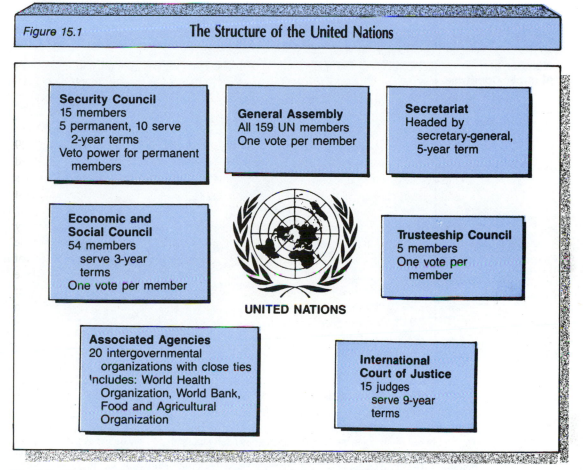

Figure 15.1 — The Structure of the United Nations

Security Council
15 members
5 permanent, 10 serve
   2-year terms
Veto power for permanent
   members

General Assembly
All 159 UN members
One vote per member

Secretariat
Headed by
   secretary-general,
   5-year term

Economic and Social Council
54 members
   serve 3-year
   terms
One vote per member

UNITED NATIONS

Trusteeship Council
5 members
One vote per
   member

Associated Agencies
20 intergovernmental
   organizations with close ties
Includes: World Health
   Organization, World Bank,
   Food and Agricultural
   Organization

International Court of Justice
15 judges
   serve 9-year
   terms

The United Nations is a complex organization. It has 6 major organs and 20 associated agencies.

Today the UN has nearly universal membership, although a few gaps and problems remain. Switzerland has never joined because of its neutrality. North and South Korea have not been admitted. So far, the United States has blocked any serious consideration of possible Palestinian membership.

Expulsion and withdrawal is another membership issue. This issue relates to members leaving international organizations. At times members have voluntarily withdrawn, usually for political reasons, from the UN. Indonesia announced withdrawal from the UN in 1965 but never followed through. Countries can also be expelled from the UN. Nationalist China was effectively, if not technically, expelled from the UN when the seat in the UN was transferred to the mainland. There also have been unsuccessful attempts to expel South Africa and Israel for alleged violations of the UN Charter. The General Assembly in 1974, however, did refuse to accept the credentials of South Africa's delegate. This action, in effect, suspended South Africa from the United Nations.

Membership, then, can be a controversial issue. It is advantageous to have all appropriate states as members. They should, however, follow the principles and rules, and this qualification sometimes opens up the issue to politics.

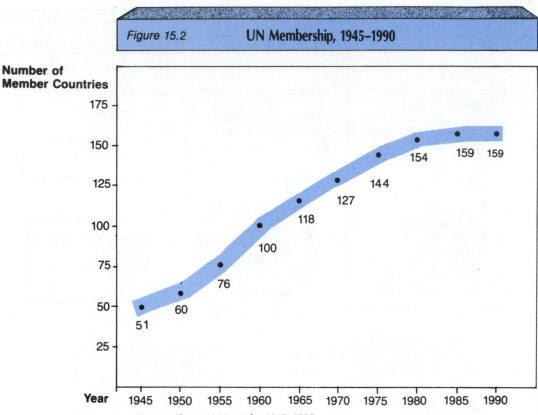

Figure 15.2 — UN Membership, 1945–1990

Data source: Riggs & Plano (1988:60) for 1945–1985.

The number of countries in the United Nations has risen rapidly, especially as newly independent countries have joined the world organization. In 1990 Namibia and Liechtenstein became members. The former East and West Germanys and the former North and South Yemens both merged into single countries with one General Assembly seat. South Africa's delegation credentials have been rejected since 1974, leaving General Assembly voting strength one less than the total membership shown after that date.

Representative Bodies

There are several important issues that relate to how the representative bodies of international organizations are structured and operate. Two such considerations are the membership basis of representative bodies and voting issues.

Membership Basis Almost all IGOs have some form of **plenary** (all members) **representative body**. The theoretical basis for plenary bodies is the collective and equal responsibility of all members for the concerns and policies of the organization.

In the United Nations, the plenary organ is called the **General Assembly**, but in other IGOs it may be termed a council, conference, commission, or even a parliament. These plenary bodies normally have the authority to involve themselves in virtually all aspects of their organizations and, thus, in theory, they are the most powerful elements of their organizations. In practice, however, the plenary organization may be secondary to the administrative structure of some other element of the organization.

A second type of representative body is based on *limited membership*. The theory here is that some members have a greater stake, responsibility, or capacity in a particular area of concern. The United Nations' peacekeeping **Security Council** has 15 members. Ten are chosen by the General Assembly for limited terms, but 5 are permanent members. These 5 (the United States, Great Britain, the Soviet Union, China, and France) were the five leading victorious powers at the end of World War II and were thought to have a special peacekeeping role to play.

Limited-membership bodies have *advantages*. First, smaller bodies function more efficiently. Second, some limited-membership bodies exist as subgroups within a larger organization. These smaller organizations include members with a specific interest in or responsibility for an area of activity.

Limited membership also has *disadvantages*. One is that it detracts from the concept of mutual responsibility. It can be argued, for instance, that in an increasingly interactive world there is little of significance that does not concern everyone. Another problem is that the existing membership may become increasingly unrealistic. The "big five" of the Security Council were something of a fiction in 1945, when, for instance, a chaotic China was seated at the insistence of the United States. After the Chinese Communist takeover in 1949, the situation became even more unrealistic when the rump Nationalist government on Taiwan occupied China's seat. This lasted until 1971 when the seat was transferred to the Beijing government.

Furthermore, the current Security Council structure does not reflect the changes in the bases of power or the strength of states that have occurred during the last four decades. The United States and the Soviet Union certainly remain *the* powers, but if France and Great Britain are powers, what about Japan and Germany, or regional powers such as India, Brazil, Saudi Arabia, and Nigeria? Should they be permanent members also?

International organizations face difficult structural issues, including how to allocate votes. The UN Security Council has 15 members. Five have permanent seats, 10 others serve two-year terms. Each permanent member can cast a veto that defeats a proposed resolution of the council. A significant action also requires a $2/3$ vote. The veto and the $2/3$ requirement were part of the challenge in securing a council decision to authorize action against Iraq. That effort was successful. The resolution passed with 12 for, 2 against (Cuba and Yemen), and 1 abstaining (China). This picture shows part of the council membership voting for Resolution 678 on November 28, 1990. At right, U.S. secretary of state James Baker III (also serving in the rotating presidency of the council) is joined by the British foreign minister Douglas Hurd and Soviet foreign minister Eduard Shevardnadze (at left) voting for the resolution. UN secretary-general Javier Pérez de Cuéllar is also shown.

Voting Issues   One of the difficult issues to face any international organization is the *formula for allocating votes* (Dixon, 1983). Three major alternatives as they exist today are majoritarianism, weighted voting, and unilateral negative voting.

The most common voting formula used in IGOs is **majoritarianism**. This system has two main components: (1) each member casts one equal vote, and (2) the issue is carried by either a simple majority (50 percent plus one vote) or, in some cases, an extraordinary majority (commonly two-thirds).

The theory of majoritarianism springs from the concept of sovereign equality and the democratic notion that the will of the majority should prevail. The UN General Assembly and most other UN bodies operate on this principle. There is, however, as discussed in chapter 5, substantial difficulty with the concept of sovereign equality. Although this idea has a level of philosophical appeal, it does not reflect reality. Should Costa Rica, with no army, cast an equal vote with the powerful United States or Soviet Union? Should Nauru, with a population of thousands, cast the same vote as China, with its billion people? It might be noted, for example, that in the General Assembly, states with less than 15 percent of the world's population account for two-thirds of the vote. By contrast, China, India, the U.S.S.R., the United States, and Indonesia, which combine for about half the world's population, have only 3 percent of the votes in the General Assembly. The one-country–one-vote formula in the General Assembly has also meant a marked change in the voting power of regions and blocs. As Figure 15.3 indicates, the voting strength of both the Western alliance bloc and the Soviet bloc has declined as many new African and Asian states have joined the United Nations.

An alternative to majoritarianism is **weighted voting** or a system that allocates unequal voting power on the basis of a formula. Two possible criteria are population and wealth. The European Parliament, for example, is based in part on population. Voting in the Council of Ministers of the European Communities is based on a mixture of size and strength, with votes ranging from ten (Germany) to two (Luxembourg). A number of international monetary organizations base voting on financial contributions. The United States, for instance, casts approximately 19 percent of the vote in the World Bank and the International Monetary Fund and 29 percent in the International Finance Corporation.

The desirability of weighted voting depends on your perspective. A good philosophical case can be made for population as a criterion, and most domestic representative institutions are based on that factor. Americans might well agree that their country should outvote Mexico four to one, but would the same Americans be as willing to be outvoted by China by a similar four-to-one margin? The financial contribution standard also makes some pragmatic sense, but as we have seen (chapter 14), many Third World states contend that "wealth-weighted" voting continues the system of imperial domination by the industrialized countries. Weighted voting is most attractive when the balance is in your favor.

A third voting scheme is *unilateral* **negative voting**, in which a member can unilaterally block action. The most common variation is a requirement for *unanimity*. The Organization for Economic Cooperation and Development (OECD) and others operate on that principle. Unanimity preserves the concept of sovereignty but can easily lead to stalemate and inaction.

A second variation is the big-power **veto**, found in the UN Security Council (Morphet, 1989). Following the theory of major-power responsibility, any of the 5 permanent members can, by its single vote, veto a policy statement or action favored by the other 14 members. Between 1946 and 1990, the veto was cast 223 times, with each of the members using its special prerogative to protect its interests. Whatever arguments might be made for or against such a system, its existence in the UN is unlikely to change because of power realities and because of the difficulty of revising the Charter, a procedure requiring a two-thirds vote of

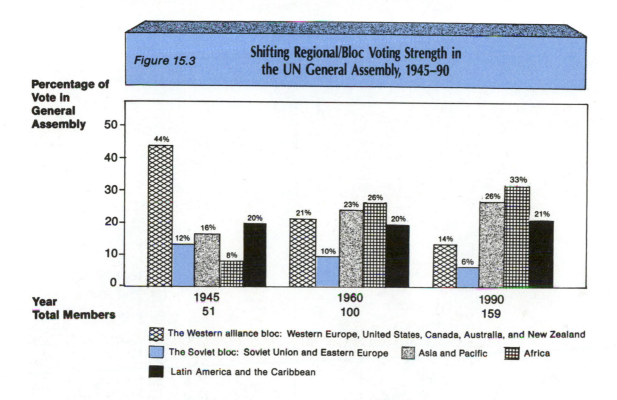

Figure 15.3 Shifting Regional/Bloc Voting Strength in the UN General Assembly, 1945–90

Post–World War II decolonization and the admission of the newly independent countries into the UN General Assembly, where each country has one vote, has shifted regional strength there. The voting strength of the Western alliance bloc has declined, while the voting strength of African and Asian countries has increased dramatically. The Eastern bloc has dissolved, but has been retained here for statistical consistency.

the General Assembly plus ratification by two-thirds of all member states, including each of the permanent members of the Security Council.

The issue of how to apportion representation in the parliamentary bodies of such international organizations as the UN will become increasingly important and contentious as they become more powerful, especially if and when they begin to have true supranational power to compel states to act in certain ways. The voting issue is not intractable, however. Numerous countries, including the United States, have had to deal with the issue as part of their development, and have successfully done so. In the case of the United States, the initial compromise was to have two houses in Congress, one based on population, the other based on equality among the states. There has also been subsequent adjustment, such as the 1964 Supreme Court decision in *Reynolds v. Sims* that required all federal House of Representative districts to have equal populations.

At least one way to think further about the ramifications of various voting schemes is to examine Figure 15.4 on the following page. It reflects the efforts of William Dixon (1989). He has gathered various voting schemes put forth over the years and has determined how many votes various traditional UN voting blocs would have under each formula. Dixon identifies 15 such formulas, of which 4 are shown in the figure. Reading from left to right, voting is based on each state having one vote, on a country's population, on a country's wealth measured by its GDP, and on a proportion of population and GDP. As you can see, bloc voting strength varies greatly. The national

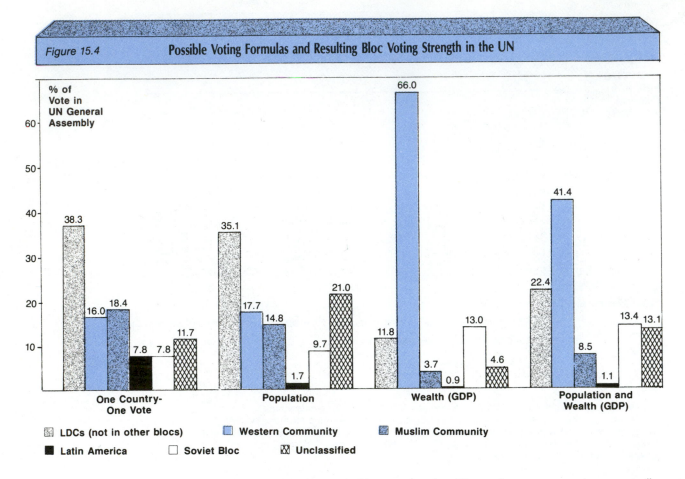

Figure 15.4   **Possible Voting Formulas and Resulting Bloc Voting Strength in the UN**

Data source: Dixon (1989:143). The bloc names are from Dixon and may vary somewhat conceptually and in country content from those used elsewhere in this text.

Voting schemes are a crucial issue for international parliamentary assemblies. This representation of bloc voting strength under four voting formulas shows how greatly voting strength would vary.

equality and population formulas each result in the Third World having a strong vote; the wealth formula empowers the Western community; the population plus wealth formula gives the North (Western community plus Soviet Bloc) 54.8 percent, the Third World 32 percent, and countries not assigned to any group 13.1 percent of the UN General Assembly vote.

Administration

In addition to representative/legislative bodies, most international organizations have an administrative structure. We cannot concern ourselves with all the details of organization and procedure here, but will focus on the issues of appointment, allegiance, and role of international bureaucracies. In the UN, the administrative structure is called the "**Secretariat**," and the "secretary-general" is the chief administrator; our discussion will use these terms in reference to all IGO bureaucracies.

Appointment   In the UN, the secretary-general is nominated by the Security Council, then elected by the General Assembly for a five-year term. The secretary-general appoints his or her principal deputies and other members of the secretariat (Weiss, 1982).

These simple facts do not, however, adequately emphasize the political considerations that govern the appointment of administrators. Because nomination of the UN secretary-general is subject to veto in the Security Council, this position has been one of intense diplomatic struggle. In the early 1960s the Soviet Union even proposed a "troika" plan that would have had three secretaries-general. Conflict was also evident when the current secretary-general, Javier Pérez de Cuéllar, was named in 1982 only after a protracted stalemate.

Politics also heavily influences the appointment of the understaff. Several of the principal deputy positions are, by tradition, reserved for and, in practice, named by one big power or another. There has also been pressure by Third World countries to distribute secretariat positions on a geographical basis. There is also big-power discontent; the United States regularly complains, for example, that its nationals are underrepresented on the staffs of the UN's specialized agencies.

Allegiance   A second administrative issue is the proper allegiance of UN officials. The issue is where their primary loyalties should lie. Are they UN officials? Or are they representatives of their home governments? Most international organizations subscribe to the principle that their administrative officers should be free from nationalistic influence and, in particular, ought not to take direction from their home governments.

In practice, however, ignoring one's home government's preferences, especially if one expects to return home someday, is difficult. At the very least, administrators may subconsciously possess orientations based on their national heritages and loyalties that affect their decisions. At worst, they may take direct orders from their home governments. The memoirs of one former UN high official, Arkady Shevchenko (1985), details his and other Soviet secretariat officers' work for the KGB. Whatever the theory, the contest in the UN and other IGOs over the appointment of administrators indicates that a pure international perspective has not fully evolved.

Role: Restraint Versus Activism   A final administrative issue is the proper role of an international secretariat. The possibilities range along a scale from relatively restrained concentration on administrative matters to activist political leadership.

The shifts in the role of the UN secretary-general give a capsule view of the possible positions along the restraint/activism scale. The UN Secretariat is, symbolically, the last major organ discussed in the Charter, and it was originally conceived as largely administrative, although the secretary-general could bring peace-threatening situations to the attention of the Security Council.

The first secretary-general, Trygve Lie of Norway (1946–53), and his successor, Dag Hammarskjöld of Sweden (1953–61), were activists who steadily expanded the role of their office. Hammarskjöld was especially assertive, broadly interpreting his powers to include taking the initiative to uphold the principles of the Charter even when the General Assembly and Security Council would not or could not act. The height of Hammarskjöld's power came during the Congo crisis in the early 1960s. The secretary-

general used UN military forces to try to avert outside intervention and to establish domestic peace during the postindependence turmoil in that African country. It is somehow symbolically fitting, if tragic, that he was killed when his plane crashed during a personal mission to the area in 1961.

Hammarskjöld's independence was not appreciated by all the big powers, however, and it caused a Soviet attempt to drive him from office and water down the position. He fended off these efforts, but since his death his successors have had to take more careful paths, although each has been active in areas of quiet diplomacy, such as mediation.

Financing

All IGOs face the problem of obtaining sufficient funds to conduct their operations. National governments must also address this issue, but they have the power to impose and legally collect taxes. By contrast, IGOs have very little authority to compel member countries to support them.

The United Nations is no exception, and it is beset by severe and controversial financial problems. The secretary-general prepares budget estimates, and the General Assembly authorizes the final budget. For reference, the fiscal year 1989 UN budget is shown in Table 15.3. It should be noted that this budget does not include such specialized agencies as the World Health Organization that are associated with the UN but not a part

TABLE 15.3

The United Nations Budget, FY 1989

Budget Category	Authorization
Overall policy-making and coordination	$ 50,213,700
Peacekeeping	109,506,600
Political affairs, trusteeship, and decolonization activities	33,419,300
Economic, social, and humanitarian activities	505,528,000
International law and justice	29,884,800
Public information	78,255,800
General administration	696,101,200
Bond payment	3,520,800
Staff assessment	263,220,100
Capital expenditures	19,096,000
Total	$1,788,746,300

Data source: U.S. Department of State (1988).

of it. Since UN revenues from operations raise only about 3 percent of the core budget, the organization is almost entirely dependent on the *assessment* it levies on member countries. This assessment is fixed by the General Assembly based on a complicated formula that reflects the ability to pay. According to the United Nations Charter, which is a valid treaty binding on all signatories, members are required to meet these assessments and may have their voting privilege in the General Assembly suspended if they are seriously in arrears. The eight leading countries and their 1989 percentage of the budget assessment are: the United States, 25 percent; the Soviet Union, 11.6 percent; Japan, 11.4 percent; (West) Germany, 8 percent; France, 6.3 percent; Great Britain, 4.9 percent; Italy, 4 percent, and Canada, 3.1 percent. There are seven other countries whose 1989 assessment was over 1 percent.[2] At the other end of the financial scale, there are a large number of countries that pay very little. Seventy-nine countries pay the minimum assessment of 0.01 percent (1/100 of 1 percent), and nine other countries pay 0.02 percent.

Several factors have come together in recent years to create a budget crunch for the United Nations and many of its specialized agencies. One is the growing cost of UN operations. Some countries have been particularly critical of what they charge is an unwarranted expansion of the UN's bureaucratic structure. Added to this, the strain on domestic budgets has engendered resistance on the part of several of the major contributors to their mounting assessments. This culminated in 1982 when the United States, the Soviet Union, and Great Britain successfully demanded that future UN budget

---

2. They were Australia (1.6), Brazil (1.5), East Germany (1.2), the Netherlands (1.7), Saudi Arabia (1.0), Spain (2.0), and Sweden (1.2). The calculation for the U.S.S.R. includes the technically separate assessments for the Ukrainian S.S.R. and the Belorussian S.S.R.

growth be restrained. The increase between the FY 1988 and FY 1989 budgets, for example, was only $19.2 million (+1.1 percent). Given inflation, this means that the UN budget declined by at least 4 or 5 percent.

A second cause of resentment stems from the differing assessments. The eight major contributors cited above collectively pay 71 percent of the UN budget, yet they cast less than 5 percent of the votes in the General Assembly. The countries that pay only 0.01 or 0.02 percent of the budget account for only one percent ($17.3 million) of the UN budget, yet they collectively command a majority in the General Assembly.

A third source of the UN's financial problems is the disenchantment with the organization sometimes felt by a number of large-contributor countries such as the United States and Great Britain. The growth in voting strength of the Third World countries in the General Assembly and many other IGOs has resulted in the United States and other Western countries usually being in the minority on most General Assembly votes. In 1989 General Assembly votes, for instance, the voting coincidence between the United States and other members was only 16.9 percent. That means that on the average vote, 16.9 percent of the other members voted the same as the United States, while 83.1 percent of the General Assembly voted in opposition or abstained. Resentment has caused the United States, especially Congress, to cut back on its appropriations to the UN and many other IGOs. For fiscal year 1990, for instance, President Bush budgeted $715 million for the UN and 46 other IGOs of which the United States is a member. Congress, however, cut the president's request by $123 million (17.2 percent), including reductions of $47 million (8.4 percent) for general IGO budgets, $30 million (27 percent) from the request for UN peacekeeping, and $46 million (100 percent) of the funds Bush had asked for to begin to make up previous shortfalls (arrearages) between the UN assessment and the congressional appropriation. Thus by the end of FY 1990, the United States' total arrearages to the United Nations and other IGOs was $621 million, including an arrearage of $157 million for UN peacekeeping operations. Indeed, U.S. arrearages in the UN are far greater than the total arrearages of all other countries combined. After the United States, South Africa owes the UN $37.3 million, and Iran is third, with an arrearage of $11.9 million. The Soviet Union was once a major debtor. Despite its own financial difficulties, however, the U.S.S.R. has steadily paid on its arrearages, and now is only behind $2.6 million.

In addition to the general unwillingness of some countries to appropriate adequate funds, a source of the UN's financial woes has been the refusal of countries to contribute to UN activities that they disapprove of. Over the years, at least 25 countries have withheld funds from the United Nations based on such political objections. Peacekeeping has been particularly controversial. The one-time Soviet bloc countries and several Arab states, for example, refused to contribute to the cost of the United Nations Emergency Force that provided a buffer between Egypt and Israel from 1956 to 1967 or to the cost of the UN force that has tried to provide a buffer between Israel and the various factions in Lebanon since 1978.

The refusal to contribute or the threat to withhold funds are also a tool large contributors use to try to influence the policy of the UN and other IGOs. There was, for example, an effort in recent years by Arab and some other states to grant the Palestine Liberation Organization (PLO) membership in the World Health Organization and other UN agencies. That brought a threat by U.S. secretary of state James Baker to "recommend to the President that the United States make no further contributions, voluntary or assessed, to any international organization which makes any change in the PLO's present status as an observer organization" (*NYT*, 5/12/89:A13). Money speaks, and the PLO remains as it was, an observer.

International Organizations: Roles and Issues

Whatever its other characteristics and controversies, the heart of any international organization is the role that it plays (Pentland, 1989). In essence, we have to ask, what is it that an international organization does; how well does this correspond to the functions we wish it to perform; and how well is it performing these roles? The following pages will begin to answer these questions by examining the scope of international organization activity with particular emphasis on international peace and security. Other roles will also be noted and then discussed more fully in later chapters.

Promoting International Peace and Security

The United Nations and many other IGOs and NGOs play a variety of roles that focus on preventing international conflict, limiting its conduct, and restoring the peace when violence occurs. Indeed, most would agree that this is the United Nations' primary goal, as symbolized by the opening words of the Charter that dedicate the organization to saving "succeeding generations from the scourge of war, which . . . has brought untold sorrow to mankind." The United Nations attempts to fulfill this goal by creating norms against violence, by providing a debate alternative to fighting, by intervening diplomatically to avert the outbreak of warfare or to help restore peace once violence occurs, and by dispatching UN military forces to repel aggression or to act as a buffer between warring countries. Note that the following individual consideration of each of these four approaches to avoiding and resolving conflict does not imply that they are used in isolation. Often just the opposite is true, and the UN will pursue several approaches at once.

Creating Norms Against Violence

One way that the United Nations helps promote international peace and security is by creating norms (beliefs about what is proper), against aggression and other forms of violence. As mentioned in the discussion of morality in chapter 7, and again in chapter 10, there is a growing rhetorical acknowledgment, as found in the UN Charter and elsewhere, that using military force except in self-defense is unacceptable. This slowly developing norm certainly has not halted violence, but it has virtually eliminated the notion of a "splendid little war," as U.S. secretary of state John Hay described the Spanish-American War. The Bush administration's repeated stress on rejecting Iraq's 1990 aggression against Kuwait, establishing a new, peaceful world order, and working through the UN may well inhibit any future U.S. inclination to launch a unilateral, "splendid little war" as it did in Grenada (1983) or Panama (1989).

The UN has been an important part of the process of creating this norm against aggression. In the Charter, the signatories pledge to accept the principle "that armed force shall not be used, save in the common interest," and further agree to "settle their international disputes by peaceful means," to "refrain in their international relations from the threat or the use of force" except in self-defense, and to "refrain from giving assistance to any state against which the United Nations is taking preventive or enforcement action."

Such pledges have at least put countries on the defensive when they violate the norm. Soviet warfare in Afghanistan, U.S. subversion against Nicaragua, Israel's invasion of

Lebanon, Iraq's invasion of Kuwait, and other such actions have been condemned in one or more UN bodies. The United Nations and other international organizations have also been important in other related arenas, such as promoting the concept of nuclear nonproliferation through the International Atomic Energy Agency, limiting chemical and biological weapons, and promoting rules for the humanitarian conduct of war when it occurs (Weisbrodt, 1987). Sometimes countries still ignore the norms, but in a world where diplomacy is increasingly affected by public communications and public opinion, such efforts and the rebukes suffered by countries that violate the norms have a subtle but important impact.

Providing a Debate Alternative

A second peace-enhancing role for the United Nations and some other IGOs is serving as a passive forum in which members publicly air their points of view and privately negotiate their differences. The UN thus acts like a safety valve, or perhaps a theater where the world drama can be played out without the dire consequences that could occur if another "shooting locale" were chosen. This process, which one scholar has called "the grand debate approach to peace," involves denouncing your opponents, defending your actions, trying to influence world opinion, and winning symbolic victories (Claude, 1971:335).

The United Nations provided an opportunity in 1988, for instance, for Iran and the United States to fire salvos of words at each other in New York rather than barrages of shells in the Persian Gulf. During the summer of that year, a U.S. guided missile cruiser shot down an Iranian commercial airliner over the Persian Gulf. The United States claimed it was an accident, that the civilian plane had been mistaken for a threatening warplane, but Iran labeled the attack aggression. To save face, if nothing else, Iran had to do something. Earlier incidents in the gulf had led to military action by both countries, but in this case Iran was able to use the United Nations to intensify international condemnation of the U.S. action. This allowed Iran to avoid further military action, and the tragic incident did not lead to escalated conflict between the United States and Iran.

Diplomatic Intervention

International organizations also regularly play a direct role in assisting and encouraging countries to settle their disputes peacefully. Ideally this occurs before hostilities, but it can take place even after fighting has started. The United Nations and other IGOs perform the following functions:

1. Inquiry: Fact-finding by neutral investigators.
2. Good Offices: Encouraging parties to negotiate; acting as a neutral setting for negotiations.
3. Mediation: Making suggestions about possible solutions; acting as an intermediary between two parties.
4. Arbitration: Using a special panel to find a solution that all parties agree in advance to accept.
5. Adjudication: Submitting disputes to an international court such as the UN's International Court of Justice.

These activities do not often capture the headlines, but they are a vital part of maintaining or restoring the peace. For example, the United Nations and other IGOs are often able to act as a bridge between warring parties when hostilities are too strong for direct talks between the combatants. The Arab League in 1979 mediated a war between North and South Yemen and worked to bring the two countries from a state of confrontation to cooperation. The ultimate proof of success was achieved in May 1990 with the two countries merged peacefully into a single Yemen. The Organization of African Unity helped end periodic fighting in 1988 between Chad and Libya over the disputed Aousou border area, and the OAU has also been working to mediate, with some success, the 15-year-old civil war in Angola between the leftist government there and the UNITA rebels. In 1988, UN officials played a useful role in the multiparty negotiations that preceded the Soviet withdrawal from Afghanistan and in arranging the cease-fire that ended eight years of war between Iran and Iraq. Most recently, UN activity in 1990 has brought raised hopes for an end to Cambodia's long agony. The Vietnamese-backed government there and the three rebel factions appear close at this writing to accepting a plan that would have them temporarily join a coalition represented by a Supreme National Council. But, in essence, the government would be turned over to the UN, which would control the key ministries of foreign affairs, interior, finance, defense, and information for about a year while the UN organized and monitored free elections. Indeed, this role of overseeing elections appears to be an increasingly common form of peaceful UN intervention. Also in 1990, the UN and the Organization of American States both monitored the February elections in Nicaragua, and the UN sent poll watchers to Haiti for the December election there.

Dispatching UN Military Forces

In addition to its diplomatic resources, the United Nations has at least a limited ability to intervene militarily in a dispute. There is also a limited history of other organizations, such as the Organization of American States, undertaking collective military action. In the UN, this process is often called peacekeeping. It is normally conducted under the auspices of the Security Council, although the General Assembly has sometimes authorized action.

Collective Security   In theory, but not in practice, the peacekeeping function of international organizations rests on the concept of **collective security**. This idea was first embodied in the Covenant of the League of Nations and is also reflected in the Charter of the United Nations. Collective security's basic tenets are these:

1. All countries forswear the use of force except in self-defense.
2. All agree that the peace is indivisible. An attack on one is an attack on all.
3. Everyone pledges to join together to halt aggression and restore the peace, and all agree to supply whatever material or personnel resources are necessary to that end.
4. A UN military force will be formed to defeat the aggressor and restore the peace.

If you think about it, this theory is something like the idea that governs domestic law enforcement. First, acts of violence are considered a transgression against the collective. If you assault someone in Ohio, the case is not the victim versus you but the society (Ohio) versus you. Second, except in self-defense, we cannot resort to violence to settle domestic disputes. Third, we rely on a collective security force, the police, and jointly support this force through taxes.

Collective security, then, is not only an appealing idea but one that works—domestically. It has not, however, been a success on the international scene. There are a number of problems of specific application, such as how to tell the aggressor from the victim in some cases. But these uncertainties also exist domestically and are resolved. The real breakdown in collective security is the unwillingness of countries to subordinate their sovereignty to collective action. Thus far, governments have generally maintained their right to view conflict in terms of their national interests and to support or oppose UN action on the basis of their nationalistic points of view. Collective security, therefore, exists only as a goal, not as a general practice.

Peacekeeping   The inability to put the theory of collective security into regular practice does not mean, however, that the UN has been ineffective in using military force to promote international security. Quite the contrary is true.

What the United Nations sometimes has been able to do more often is implement a process commonly called **peacekeeping**. Apart from using military force, peacekeeping is quite different from collective security. The latter identifies an aggressor and employs military force to defeat the attacker. Peacekeeping takes another approach and deploys an international military force under the aegis of an international organization such as the United Nations to prevent fighting, usually by acting as a buffer between combatants. The international force is neutral between the combatants and must have been invited to be present by at least one of the combatants.

The origins of the idea of peacekeeping are especially associated with the UN response to the 1956 war between Israel and Egypt, which also included British and French military action against Egypt. The Security Council was deadlocked because Great Britain and France each possessed a veto in that body. Under the leadership of Canadian diplomat Lester B. Pearson, who had been the president of the General Assembly (1952) and who later served as his country's prime minister (1957–63), the General Assembly dispatched a force of 6,000 troops from 10 countries that took up positions between the combatants in February 1957. For his innovative contribution, Pearson was awarded the Nobel Peace Prize in 1957.

UN Military Intervention in Practice   In all, since its establishment in 1945 through the beginning of 1991, the United Nations has mounted 20 missions utilizing troops or police forces from 73 countries.[3] Nine of these operations involved substantial numbers of troops: two (Korea, 1950, and the Middle East, 1990–91) can be classified as collective security, while the other seven (UNEF I, UNEF II, ONUC, UNSF, UNIFICYP, UNDOF, and UNTAG) were peacekeeping efforts. There have also been 10 UN–designated observer missions that involved more limited military forces and can be classified as peacekeeping operations. The location of the UN military operations and a brief description can be found in Figure 15.5.

3. For this discussion, the multinational force in Saudi Arabia and elsewhere in the Middle East region that confronted Iraq in 1990 and 1991 is considered a UN operation. Some might disagree with this classification since the forces there were not dispatched by the UN and were not under UN command. The forces of some countries, such as Saudi Arabia and other Gulf states were indigenous to the region; other forces, such as those of the United States, were dispatched unilaterally; Syrian and Egyptian forces were dispatched to the front partly as a result of a 12 to 3 (with 2 abstentions) vote by the Arab League. Despite this, the UN by numerous resolutions underwrote at least the more idealistic motivations behind the multinational force, and by Resolution 678 of November 29, 1990, the Security Council authorized the multinational forces after January 15, 1991, to use "all necessary means [military force]" to end Iraq's occupation of Kuwait. Therefore, by aegis if not command, the multinational force became a de facto instrument of UN collective security policy.

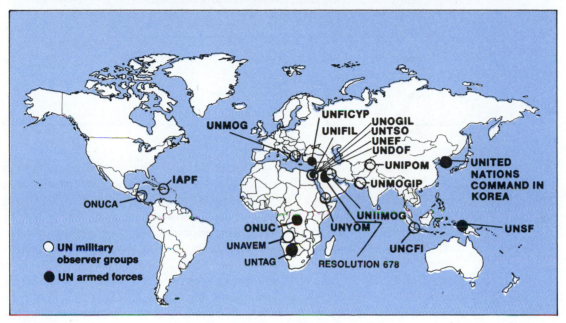

Figure 15.5 **United Nations Military Operations**

○ **UN military observer groups**

● **UN armed forces**

LATIN AMERICA

IAPF Inter-American Peace Force, 1965–66: Moderate civil strife in the Dominican Republic (dispatched by the Organization of American States; UN representative and military observer present concurrently with IAPF).

ONUCA Spanish initials for United Nations Observer Group in Central America, 1989–present: Ensure that no country in region aids rebels in another country in the region, assist in the disarming and demobilization of the Contra rebels in Nicaragua.

AFRICA

ONUC French initials for the UN Operation in the Belgian Congo (now Zaire), 1960–64: Keep peace and order, preserve unity.

UNAVEM United Nations Angola Verification Mission, 1988–present: Monitor the complete withdrawal of Cuban and South African troops from Angola by July 1991.

UNTAG United Nations Transition Assistance Group, 1989–1990: Keep various rebels and South African troops apart and supervise free elections as part of Namibia's transition from colony of South Africa to independence on March 21, 1990.

EUROPE

UNMOG UN Military Observers in Greece, 1952–54: Investigate incidents along borders with Albania, Yugoslavia, and Bulgaria.

UNFICYP UN Force in Cyprus, 1974–present: Keep law and order and peace between Greek and Turkish communities.

MIDDLE EAST

UNTSO UN Truce Supervision Organization in Palestine, 1948–present: Supervise armistice among Israel, Jordan, Lebanon, and Syria.

UNEF I and UNEF II UN Emergency Force, 1956–67, 1973–79: Prevent Israeli-Egyptian hostilities, keep peace and order in Sinai and Gaza Strip.

UNOGIL UN Observer Group in Lebanon, June–December 1958: Police Lebanon-Syria border.

UNDOF UN Disengagement Observer Force, 1974–present: Maintain cease-fire between Syria and Israel.

UNIFIL UN Interim Force in Lebanon, 1978–present: Police Lebanon-Israel border.

UNYOM UN Yemen Observation Mission, 1963–64: Report on withdrawal of Saudi Arabian and Egyptian forces.

UNIIMOG UN Iran-Iraq Military Observer Group, 1988–present: Supervise cease-fire along border between Iran and Iraq.

Resolution 678 Multinational force in Saudi Arabia and elsewhere in the Middle East–Persian Gulf region in support of UN resolutions that demanded the withdrawal of Iraq from Kuwait and authorized after January 15, 1991, the use of all necessary force to restore Kuwait's sovereignty.

ASIA/PACIFIC

UNMOGIP UN Military Observer Group in India and Pakistan, 1948–present: Supervise cease-fire in Jammu-Kashmir.

UNCFI UN Commission for Indonesia, 1949–51: Settle dispute with Netherlands.

United Nations Command in Korea, 1950–present: Established to repel armed attack by forces from North Korea and restore international peace in Korea.

UNSF UN Security Force, 1962–63: Facilitate transfer of West Irian to Indonesia.

UNIPOM UN India-Pakistan Observation Mission, 1965–66: Supervise cease-fire in Rann of Kutch.

Data source: UN (1990e).

The United Nations has played a valuable collective security and peacekeeping role. This map shows the locations around the world where UN forces have been active. In 1988, the Nobel Peace Prize was awarded to the soldiers who have served, some of whom have been wounded or lost their lives, in the interest of international peace.

TABLE 15.4

Countries Most Frequently Contributing Troops to the 20 UN
Collective Security Peacekeeping Missions (1945–90)

Canada	16	Denmark	11	Austria	9
Sweden	13	Norway	11	Australia	8
Finland	13	Netherlands	9	India	8
Ireland	12	Italy	9	New Zealand	7

Several characteristics of these actions can be noted. First, most have occurred in Third World locations such as the Middle East, Cyprus, the Congo, the India/Pakistan border, Yemen, and Indonesia. This is evident in Figure 15.5.

Second, UN forces have generally utilized military contingents from smaller or nonaligned powers. Canada has been the most frequent contributor, sending troops to assist the United Nations in 80 percent of the crises, and its and other countries' efforts are noted in Table 15.4.

Third, UN forces have generally acted as passive buffers between the conflicting parties. With the exceptions of Korea, the Congo, and the Middle East in 1991, peacekeeping forces have not conducted active military operations. Instead they usually have positioned themselves between the combatants. At times this provides an excuse to stop fighting for two combat-weary foes who are otherwise unable to find a way to disengage. Peacekeeping forces are also useful in defusing a situation before it draws in the superpowers and engages their prestige (Thakur, 1987). In other cases, UN troops provide an inhibiting presence because all but the most crazed are reluctant to attack international peacekeepers.

United Nations peacekeeping, then, is not normally the process of a stern international enforcer smiting aggressors with powerful blows. Few are willing to invest any international organization with that much power and independence. Rather, UN peacekeeping is a "coming between," a positioning of a neutral force that creates space and is intended to help defuse an explosive situation. This in no way lessens the valuable role the UN has played. In the early 1960s, UN troops kept the Congo from exploding into a cold-war battlefield, and UN forces were an important factor in allowing the disengagement of Egyptian and Israeli troops in 1973. For these, and their other contributions to world order, the UN peacekeeping forces were awarded the 1988 Nobel Peace Prize.

Effectiveness of UN Conflict-Resolution Efforts

After discussing the various approaches of international organizations to conflict resolution, the question remains: how effective are they? The answer, according to several studies, is that there is a mixed record, but the UN and other international organizations have made a distinct contribution to world security (Diehl, 1989a). One analysis found that of 282 disputes between 1945 and 1981, 123 disputes were referred to the United Nations. Of these, 28 were settled with UN assistance and another 35 were eased with UN help, for a success/partial-success rate of 51 percent (Haas, 1983). Another study using somewhat different criteria concluded that between 1945 and 1975,

The United Nations and the 1990–91 Middle East Crisis

The original focus of possible UN military action was collective security, that is, repelling aggressors. Because of many political difficulties, the single instance of the UN undertaking collective security prior to 1990 was its response to North Korea's invasion of South Korea in 1950. In the interim, the UN developed peacekeeping, separating combatants without finding fault or taking sides.

The August 2, 1990, invasion of Kuwait by Iraq confronted the UN with a grave crisis. Many nations rushed troops to Saudi Arabia to protect it from possible Iraqi attack, and the leaders of some of the responding nations pledged to also force Iraq to abandon its conquest of Kuwait. The issue was brought to the United Nations Security Council. In part because of the changing political attitudes that have accompanied the end of the cold war, the Security Council was able to take a forthright stand. In a series of 12 resolutions (August–November), the Security Council, among other things, placed a virtually total economic and travel ban on Iraq, authorized countries to use military force to uphold the embargo, and held Iraq financially liable for all damages caused by the invasion and the taking of hostages. Security Council action culminated on November 29, 1990, with the passage of Resolution 678. It demanded that Iraq comply with all 11 pre-vious resolutions, offered Iraq "as a pause of good-will" until January 15, 1991, to comply, and authorized UN members to use "all necessary means" after that date to compel Iraqi compliance. The resolution passed by a vote of 12 in favor, 2 opposed (Cuba, Yemen) and one abstention (China). Signifying not only the resolution of the UN but also the new cooperation between the United States and the Soviet Union, Moscow's foreign minister Eduard Shevardnadze traveled to New York to vote for the resolution in a Security Council meeting chaired by U.S. secretary of state James Baker (the chair rotates among Security Council members). As Baker told the council, "We must put the choice to Saddam Hussein in unmistakable terms." That is true, Shevardnadze agreed. "No member of the council wants or seeks a tragic outcome. But neither should anyone be mistaken about the collective will the international community has expressed here about its resolve and its willingness to act." (*HC,* 11/30/90:A7).

Continued UN diplomacy, however, including a last-minute trip by the secretary-general to Baghdad, was to no avail. Saddam Hussein refused to leave Kuwait, and on January 17, 1991, the UN-–sanctioned Operation Desert Storm was launched to accomplish by force what diplomacy had been unable to achieve by peace.

160 international crises occurred (Wilkenfield & Brecher, 1984), and the United Nations became involved in 59 percent (95) of these. According to this second study, the United Nations successfully resolved 28 of these crises, for a success rate of 18 percent of all crises and 29 percent of those crises in which the United Nations became active.

Synthesizing the two studies, we can see (1) that the United Nations gets involved in about half of all disputes; (2) that the UN is instrumental in resolving about a quarter of the disputes it acts on; and (3) that the United Nations contributes to easing the severity of about 15 percent of all disputes. An important addition to this is the work of regional organizations. The study done by Hass found that 80 (28 percent) of the 282 disputes were referred to regional organizations, and they had a success rate approximately equal to that of the United Nations.[4] Thus the success rates of the United Nations and the regional organizations are far from what one wishes they were, 100 percent. But they do make a significant contribution in the settlement and amelioration of international disputes.

The future of collective security and peacekeeping conducted by the UN or one of the regional international organizations is uncertain. Some observers are encouraged by the UN's resolution in the face of Iraq's aggression in 1990. International law scholar

---

4. Those regional organizations were the Organization of American States, the Organization of African Unity, the Arab League, and the Council of Europe.

Abram Chayes has argued that the UN response has set "a very significant and helpful pattern" in advancing the cause of international law and "the cause also of the Security Council [and] the United Nations." Analysts also recognized the danger to the UN credibility inherent in the crisis. As Abraham Sofaer, another international law expert, put it, "If the UN process fails this time, it will be a long time before anyone tries it again" (*HC,* 11/29/90:A10). There are even those who advocate establishment of a much-strengthened and permanent UN peacekeeping force. Most analysts agree, however, that the prospects are dim for such a step. In the end, institutional arrangements can only be marginally successful when they are too frequently faced with the unwillingness of many countries to keep the peace and the reluctance of other countries to contribute to peacekeeping operations—peacekeeping operations based on the principles of the United Nations Charter rather than on the calculations of national self-interest (Coate & Puchala, 1990; Finkelstein, 1990a; Diehl, 1989b).

Other Roles

In addition to maintaining and restoring the peace, international organizations engage in a wide variety of other activities. These are briefly noted below, and they will be discussed more fully in the following three chapters.

Law and norm promotion is one role. An important and expanding role of international organizations is defining and expanding international law and international norms of cooperation. International courts associated with IGOs help establish legal precedent. Also, the signatories to the UN Charter and other IGO and NGO constitutions incur obligations to obey the principles of those documents. International organizations additionally sponsor multinational treaties, which may establish the assumption of law.

The resolutions of international representative bodies, such as the General Assembly, also help establish international norms and even international law (Gupta, 1986). One recent study argues that the General Assembly is "a kind of global parliament . . . whose resolutions are the formal expression of world opinion on a given question. . . . There is widespread agreement that General Assembly resolutions . . . carry a moral weight and can have a significant political impact" (Marín-Bosch, 1987:705). This is short of law-creating, but establishing norms is a step toward that end. Furthermore, the General Assembly is expressing itself on a growing number of questions. As Figure 15.6 indicates, General Assembly activity increased most rapidly after 1970, a period that corresponds to the influx of Third World countries into the United Nations.[5]

Promoting arms control and disarmament is another function of international organizations. They are not only involved in individual conflicts, but they are concerned with conflict in general. Consequently, they are active on a number of fronts trying to regulate or eliminate the weapons of war, as we shall see in chapter 17.

International organizations also *promote the quality of human existence*. Perhaps the most significant contribution of international organizations to date has been in the area of individual human betterment. A wide variety of IGOs and NGOs devote their energies to problems of the environment, humanitarian causes, economic progress, and social concerns such as health, nutrition, and literacy. In 1990, for example, the UN

5. There are many problems with the General Assembly as a law-making body. One is that the voting is based on one vote per state. Therefore, as discussed earlier, a majority of the vote is controlled by a minority of the world population. Second, some resolutions, such as those condemning Zionism as racist, which are overwhelmingly passed, are of such dubious objective validity that they not only are not "law," but they may even detract from respect for the process.

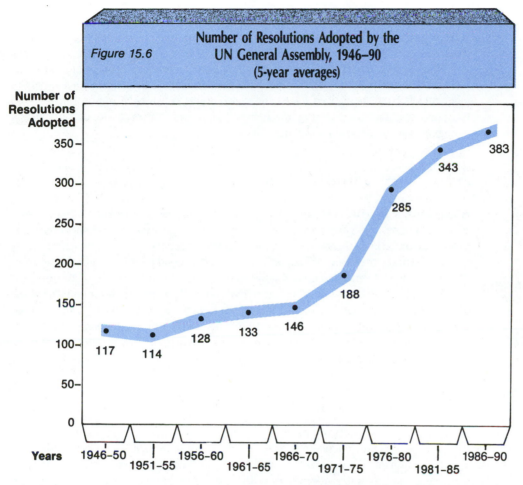

Figure 15.6

**Number of Resolutions Adopted by the
UN General Assembly, 1946–90
(5-year averages)**

Data sources: Marín-Bosch (1987:70); average for 1986–90 calculated by author from UN Security Council Records.

There has been a sharp increase in the number of resolutions adopted by the UN General Assembly. These resolutions express the strength of world opinion and have added to the establishment of international norms and law.

Children's Fund, WHO, and other agencies announced a $150-million program to develop a multi-immunization vaccine. This vaccine program will increase the number of children—estimated now to be 2 million—who will survive because of such international medical assistance. As we shall see further in chapter 18, the need is staggering, but a start has been made.

Yet another role of the UN and other IGOs is to *encourage national self-determination*. The UN Trusteeship Council once oversaw the status of a large number of colonial dependencies, but with the wave of independence in recent decades, only one trust territory, Micronesia, remains under its direct auspices. There have been, however, a number of related issues that have come before the UN. One was the case of Namibia (South-West Africa). South Africa originally governed this territory on a mandate from the League of Nations and refused to give up its hold despite UN and Organization of African Unity demands. In 1989, however, South Africa relented, and Namibia joined the world community as an independent country. The question of the Palestinian people is another issue of national status that the UN (and the Arab League) has considered, and some countries have tried to introduce the status of Puerto Rico as a subject of debate in the UN.

Promoting other international organizations and integration is one more role of the UN that deserves mention. The United Nations operates in association with a variety of other regional and specialized IGOs, and it also grants consultative status to nearly 700 NGOs. Thus, international organizations of all types cooperate to encourage and strengthen one another (Finkelstein, 1990).[6]

The Status of the UN: Three Dimensions

This Royal Canadian Mounted Policeman is part of the UN peacekeeping force that helped ensure Namibia's transition from South African colony to sovereign country. Canada is the country that most frequently contributes to UN peacekeeping missions, but the effort in Namibia was the first to involve the RCMP, including Corporal Benoit Belanger, shown here. The sign in Ombalantu, Namibia, shows the hometowns of the Canadians stationed there. The UN mission was a success; as the saying goes, "the Mounties always get their man."

Another major issue of international organization is its status in relation to its member states. Three basic positions are possible. One is to support the idea of **supranational organization**, which means that the international organization has authority over its members, which, therefore, are subordinate units. A second possibility is independence. In this case, the international body follows its own initiative in determining its action and policy. A third position is that of an interactive arena. Here the organization is the scene of cooperation and conflict among states, each striving to better its own position. Furthermore, the policy of the organization is determined by the outcome of that self-interested struggle. As we shall see, the reality of international organization is that it is a mix of all three positions.

Supranationalism

Theoretically, some international organizations possess some elements of supranationalism and can obligate members to take certain actions. In reality, supranationalism is extremely limited. Few states are willing to concede any significant part of their sovereignty to any international body. But there are limited signs that the dogged independence of nation-states is giving way to limited acceptance of international authority. In the next chapter, for instance, we will see that countries normally abide by some aspects of international law, even at times when it conflicts with domestic law.

The European Parliament also has stirrings of supranationalism. In recent years it has made several policies, including banning the importation of sealskins. Such actions may seem trivial in a world of nationalism, but they are a start and are virtually unparalleled in international political history.

Independence

A second and more developed position is that of organizational independence. Here the organization is a self-directed actor in world politics. International bodies, like any organization, develop their own norms of behavior, expectations, and policy preferences. These characteristics are especially centered in the secretariats, or administrative structures.

Although no IGO is completely, or even mostly, independent of its membership's wishes, many have developed a degree of actor status and personality. We often hear, for

6. It should be noted that, as with all political organizations, there can be rivalry and conflict among international organizations.

example, that "the UN should do something" about a situation, and at times it does.

To a degree, organizational independence is intended and established in the charters of various IGOs. The European Coal and Steel Community's High Authority was created to act independently, as was the International Court of Justice. The UN Charter directs that the secretary-general or any of his or her staff "shall not seek or receive instructions from any government or from any other authority external to the organization." And the European Parliament is a unique example of an IGO assembly whose representatives are popularly elected rather than appointed and directed by national governments.

Independence is also a product of the assertiveness of the international bureaucracies. We earlier noted the sometimes self-directed activity of the UN secretary-general and, in particular, the ideas of Dag Hammarskjöld, who argued that he had a "responsibility" to maintain peace "irrespective of the views and wishes of the various Member Governments" (Archer, 1983:148). As we also saw, however, independence can be a perilous path. It brought Hammarskjöld and his office under severe attack and led to the tacit pruning of the powers of his successors.

Independence, then, while more developed than supranationalism, is not the basic trait of international organizations. It is, instead, a growing, albeit secondary, phenomenon that is a source of struggle between the perceptions and preferences of national states and international organizations.

Interactive Arena

The most common status of IGOs is still that of an interactive arena in which member states pursue their individual national interests. The arena itself is technically neutral, but members or coalitions of members often try to use the organization as an instrument to further their goals. The Arab states, for example, have used the UN to condemn Israel for "Zionist imperialism."

To examine the "use" of the UN and other IGOs, we will briefly explore the interaction between the UN and the United States, the Soviet Union, China, and the Third World states.

The United States and the UN

United States policy in and toward the United Nations has been marked by a desire to dominate the organization and to use it as far as possible as a vehicle for furthering American policy objectives. When this has not been possible, the United States has minimized its willingness to participate in and acquiesce to the turbulence and uncertainty of worldwide multilateral diplomacy and decision-making.

For the first 20 years of the UN's existence, the United States was generally able to dominate the organization. The world body was primarily the scene of the East-West, cold-war struggle, and the Western bloc and its followers heavily outnumbered the Soviet Union and its sympathizers in all the UN's major organs. During the 1945–65 period, this pro–United States balance of power was reflected in the fact that the Soviet Union cast 103 (95 percent) of the 109 vetoes in the Security Council. The United States cast none. During the first two decades, American policy also encouraged expansion of General Assembly authority in order to circumvent the Soviet veto in the Security Council.

In the 1960s and 1970s the rapid expansion of UN membership ended U.S.

dominance of the United Nations. Many of the new Third World members were unwilling to follow U.S. leadership, and some old allies, such as the Latin American countries, showed greater independence. As a result, the U.S. position began to lose regularly in the General Assembly and other organs that use majority voting based on one vote per member. Indeed the United States became somewhat isolated, as is evident in Table 15.5. As you can see there, the average voting coincidence (percentage of votes by individual countries in agreement with the United States) between the United States and other General Assembly members in 1989 was a scanty 16.9 percent. Most of the voting blocs analyzed by the U.S. State Department had very low voting coincidences with the United States. Only the Western industrialized blocs (NATO, OECD, EC) had a higher than 50 percent voting coincidence. Of the 158 members voting in the General Assembly, only 11 (7 percent) had a +50 percent score. Israel was the highest (87.5 percent); Canada was the lowest of the supportive 11 at 60.9 percent. By contrast, 37 countries (23 percent) voted with the United States less than 10 percent of the time. Angola was the most divergent at 4.2 percent. Inasmuch as many UN votes are consensus votes or series of resolutions on single issues, the State Department also calculates the voting on those which it deems important votes. On these the United States did not do much better. The overall voting coincidence was 23.3 percent, with 20 countries (13 percent) scoring +50 percent and 32 countries (20 percent) lower than 10 percent. In fact, 6 countries (Albania, Bulgaria, the Congo, Nicaragua, Tanzania, and Uganda) scored zero.

When compared to the fact that from 1946 through 1950 the coincidence of voting in the General Assembly between the United States and other UN members was 74 percent and remained over 50 percent through the mid-1960s, the current low voting coincidence is interpreted by some Americans as evidence of increasing anti-Americanism in the world parliament. In reality, though, it is more accurately a sign of the split between the perceived interests and policy preferences of the countries of the North and those of the South. As you can see in Table 15.5, the industrialized countries (except for Eastern Europe) tend to be aligned with the United States in a minority bloc. This bloc votes in opposition to the majority bloc preferences of the South and the then-communist Eastern European countries (Holloway, 1990). This bloc pattern exists not only in the General Assembly, but it is also evident in other UN bodies and in other IGOs.

The United States' loss of control in the UN and many other IGOs has had a marked impact on U.S. policy in and attitudes toward international organizations. In the UN, the United States has shifted its emphasis to the Security Council where it and two other Western industrialized powers, Great Britain and France, can exercise a veto over Security Council resolutions. Even here, though, U.S. control has lessened, especially after the council was expanded from 11 to 15 members in 1965 to make room for more Third World countries. The result of this shift, as is evident in Figure 15.7 (p. 466), is that the United States has used more vetoes and a greater percentage of all Security Council vetoes since that time. Even these figures, however, need to be put in some perspective. The increasing U.S. use of the veto does not mean that Washington is constantly fending off hostile resolutions on a wide variety of issues. In its first 45 years of operation, the Security Council has voted on 642 resolutions, only 227 of which (35 percent) have been vetoed by one or another of the permanent members. That means 65 percent have passed. Furthermore, recent U.S. vetoes tend to be concentrated on the regular attempts of Third World countries to condemn various aspects of Israel's policy toward the Palestinians. During 1988 and 1989, for instance, 9 of 11 U.S. vetoes were on this subject.

Frustration with its minority position in the UN and other IGOs has also increased

TABLE 15.5

Voting Coincidence Between the United States and Countries by Voting Bloc in the United Nations General Assembly, 1989–1990 Session

Bloc	Voting Coincidence (%)	
	All Votes	*Important Votes*
Africa	11.3	16.7
Asia	12.0	16.6
Latin America & Caribbean	15.0	24.8
Western Industrialized (OECD)	50.3	58.5
Eastern Europe	10.1	8.3
Arab	9.8	12.4
ASEAN	12.5	19.2
EC	59.5	69.0
Islamic Conference	11.1	14.6
Non-Aligned	11.4	16.7
Nordic	42.1	43.9
NATO	57.3	68.6
Warsaw Pact	10.7	8.2
All Countries	16.9	23.3

Data source: U.S. Department of State (1990a).

Bloc designations are the State Department's.

U.S. hostility toward them (Karns & Mingst, 1990). Washington has threatened to cut off the UN and other IGOs financially if they expelled Israel or seated the PLO. As noted earlier, there has also been a marked decrease in the willingness of the United States to meet fully its assessed obligations to many IGOs. Most seriously, in 1983 the Reagan administration withdrew from the 161-member United Nations Educational, Scientific, and Cultural Organization (UNESCO), charging that it had become a hotbed of criticism of the United States and had inappropriately politicized the programs it conducted (Coate, 1990). Despite changes in UNESCO, including the 1987 resignation of its Senegalese director, Amadou-Mahtar M'Bow, Washington continues to absent itself from the organization. In its 1990 review of UNESCO, the U.S. Department of State admitted that there had been a virtual end to "vitriolic name-calling or anti-Western propaganda." However, the department worried about the willingness of UNESCO to work with the PLO, about the $50 million in dues that renewed UNESCO activity would cost the U.S. budget, and about the new UNESCO director, whom the report characterized as "well-intentioned, but a poor administrator . . . rarely in his office" (*NYT,* 4/17/90:A1).

Public opinion in the United States has also cooled on the United Nations. Most Americans continue to support U.S. membership in the United Nations, but the percentage of Americans thinking the United Nations is doing a good job has declined from 59 percent in 1954, to 44 percent in 1970, to 38 percent in 1989. A bit more positively, the percentage of Americans thinking the UN was doing a poor job dropped from about 50 percent in the early 1980s to 29 percent in 1989, with a rise from about 15

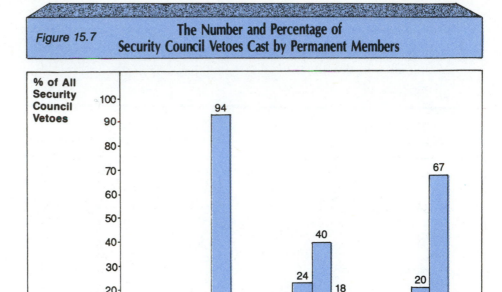

Figure 15.7 **The Number and Percentage of Security Council Vetoes Cast by Permanent Members**

Percentages may not add up to 100 due to rounding. Reflects multiple vetoes on some resolutions.

Data sources: Morphet (1989); U.S. Department of State (1990a).

Political changes within the UN and its Security Council have resulted in a decrease in Soviet vetoes and an increase in U.S. vetoes. Third World resolutions condemning Israel, calling for strong action against South Africa, and other such issues that focus on North-South tensions have frequently been vetoed by the United States.

percent to 34 percent of those with no opinion. Belief that the United Nations is ineffective is the most common reason given for negative attitudes (Alger, 1990).

On balance, it should be noted that U.S. frustrations do not reflect a situation in which American preferences and interests are regularly assaulted by an anti-American, irresponsible United Nations. The United States is far too powerful in the organization, and in the world, for that. Indeed, the evidence shows that the United States is still the most influential member of the world organization. As one study concluded, on most important issues "there has been rather close correlation between UN policies and American preferences."

Those who bewail declining U.S. influence in the United Nations and the few who even advocate withdrawal must also remember that such complaints put them in a position analogous to the proverbial spoiled kid who takes his baseball bat home once he cannot always get his way. For years the United States held sway in the United Nations and used its influence to manipulate that organization for U.S. national purposes. Now that these political fortunes are reversed, U.S. criticism seems hypocritical indeed.

The Soviet Union and the UN

The traditional Soviet view of international organization has been shaped by the mutually reinforcing factors of political reality and communist ideology. First, in terms of political reality, the Soviet Union, like its Western rival, has approached the UN primarily as a political instrument. Unlike the Americans, however, the Soviets have never had the luxury of dominating the world organization. Especially during the UN's first decades, the Soviets and their supporters were a minority in the UN, a fact that accounts for at least some of their extensive use of the veto, their refusal to pay all of their assessed obligation to the UN budget, and other forms of seeming intransigence. Second, communist ideology tends to support the feeling of being in a minority and, therefore, in a defensive position. The Soviets see the UN as an arena for struggle and one that has been dominated by the bourgeois interests of Western capitalism.

The policy orientations that traditionally resulted from their real and ideologically perceived minority status in the UN generally caused the cautious Soviets to avoid expansion of UN activity and resulted in several distinct Soviet principles of international organization participation. First, the Soviets rejected the idea of the UN as an independent actor. Secretary-General Dag Hammarskjöld's assertiveness sparked an intense Soviet reaction. Soviet writers dismissed the idea of the UN as a supranational organization as both impractical and a violation of sovereignty, and they rejected attempts "to infer that decisions taken by IGOs are of a legally binding nature" (Morozov, 1981:179).

Second, the Soviets backed the power principle in decision-making. They distinguished between the "juridical equality" of all IGO members and the "actual inequality" based on power. Given this view, the Soviets stressed the role of the Security Council, where they have a veto. Indeed, one Soviet theorist has characterized the veto as "the key principle of the Charter" (Morozov, 1981:181).

Third, the Soviets viewed the UN as primarily a political institution. They saw as secondary the organization's social and economic functions. Because the Soviets perceived the UN as dominated by the Western powers, they also saw UN socioeconomic activity as an attempt to "strengthen [capitalist] influence in the countries of the Third World" (Morozov, 1981:184).

The decline of U.S. power in the UN and the end of the cold war have not changed these traditional orientations of the Soviet Union toward international organizations completely. Among other things, the decline of U.S. strength in the UN has not meant an equal increase of Soviet strength in the UN. Moscow is no more able to dominate the Third World than is Washington. The shifts in the international systems have, however, had some impact on the Soviets' attitudes toward the UN. They have paid arrearages of over $200 million, some of it owed for 30 years. President Gorbachev has repeatedly spoken out in favor of expanding UN activity, including the "wider use" of UN peacekeeping forces "in disengaging the troops of warring sides and observing ceasefire and armistice agreements" (*NYT,* 10/19/87:7E2). The most recent indication of the change in attitude came during the 1990–91 Middle East crisis. Moscow repeatedly backed the Security Council resolutions against the Soviets' recent ally, Iraq. In fact, the Soviets even declared themselves willing to "comply with any decision, with any resolution of the Security Council." That, Foreign Minister Shevardnadze went on, "would include anything regarding the involvement of Soviet troops under the flag, under the auspices of the United Nations" (*WSJ,* 10/1/90:A3).[7]

---

7. Foreign Minister Shevardnadze was criticized in the Soviet Union for his statement, and he retreated from it soon thereafter. Still, it was an important symbol of changed Soviet attitudes about the UN.

It is too early to predict confidently whether or not the shift in the Soviet view of the UN reflects a true change in sentiments or merely a tactical change in the face of the Soviet Union's current difficulties (Haslam, 1989). Certainly, Gorbachev has a different vision of world politics than did his predecessors; he is also a skilled diplomat trying to maximize his country's position. As one analyst has pointed out, "the Soviets' enthusiasm for UN peacekeeping has coincided with their search for a dignified means of disengagement from regional conflicts," thereby saving money, while using the UN to avoid increased U.S. influence where Moscow has had to retreat (Weiss & Kessler, 1990). In fact, the analysis concludes that the Soviets see an increased UN role as one way that Moscow can continue to play a world role even during its decline as a bilateral player on the world stage. Recognition of this political reality does not mean, however, that the United States and other Western countries should reject the Soviet overtures. Instead, they present an opportunity to strengthen the norm of international cooperation through international organization (Franck, 1989).

China and the UN

China's orientation toward the United Nations is based on a mixture of ideology, nationalism, and self-identification with the Third World. These are a sometimes incompatible set of orientations that give a cautious mark to Chinese policy. Beijing's actions in the UN have also been restrained because during most of the 1970s the newly admitted country adopted a learning attitude, gaining experience without generally asserting itself.

For almost a quarter-century after its communist revolution, mainland China was excluded from the UN by U.S. opposition, as explained earlier on page 445. The U.S. Congress, for one, declared that "to seat such aggressors [as China] . . . would mean moral bankruptcy for the United Nations and destroy every last vestige of its effectiveness" (Kim, 1979: 105). For its part, a spurned China condemned the UN as a "dirty international stock exchange in the grip of a few big powers" and declared that "speaking frankly, the Chinese people are not at all interested in sitting in the United Nations" (Kim, 1979:100, 191).

Neither American opposition nor Chinese reluctance prevailed in the long run; in October 1971 reality prevailed, and China took its proper place in the UN. It was a time of dancing in the aisles by some Third World representatives and dire predictions of disruption and disaster by some in the West. The question was, how would China behave?

Overall, China's UN activity has followed a course safely between earlier Pollyanna and Cassandra expectations. Chinese behavior has been cautious. During its first five years, the Beijing delegation was reluctant to strike out boldly. In the General Assembly, it was active on only a dozen of more than 100 agenda items. China has been similarly cautious in the Security Council, casting from 1971 to 1989 only two vetoes, the least of any permanent member (United States, 61; Great Britain, 23; Soviet Union, 11; France, 12). China did not individually sponsor a single Security Council resolution from 1980 through 1986 and cast no vetoes in the 1980s (Lichenstein, 1986).

Caution is also evident in China's voting in the UN. Four possible positions are available on UN votes: for, against, abstaining (present, not voting), or not participating. In the Security Council, for example, the People's Republic of China did not participate (1971–76) in 29.1 percent of the votes, compared with 0.6 percent nonparticipation for the Soviet Union and France and 0 percent for the United States and Great Britain. The big five's respective records were similar in the General Assembly.

China's early caution, in some ways, has passed. During 1986-89, for example, China cast 87 votes in the Security Council, abstaining on none. In other ways, China's caution continues, based on its attempt to steer between its principled stands based on ideology and its realpolitik desire to support some capitalist, First World–oriented measures. This was evident, for example, in the UN resolution authorizing force against Iraq. China joined resolutions condemning Iraq and imposing economic sanctions, but abstained on Resolution 678 authorizing the use of force to expel Iraq from Kuwait.

Chinese activity in the UN also has shown a Third World orientation. One study analyzed Beijing's voting in terms of agreement with the votes cast by the Western, Communist, and Third World countries (Chai, 1979). It found that China was most supportive of the Third World and least favorable to the West, with China voting the same way as the United States only 11 percent of the time in the 1980s. Support for the Soviet Union fell about midway between the two extremes, with Moscow and Beijing in agreement just slightly over half the time.

China's Third World orientation, and its somewhat less cautious role, can also be seen in its part in selecting the UN secretary-general. China's Third World orientation led it to support Mexico's Luis Echeverria Alvarez for secretary-general over Austria's Kurt Waldheim in 1971. When it found itself alone, however, China gave way, as it did again in 1976 at the time of Waldheim's reelection. In 1981 the story was different. China was determined to block a third term for the European and supported, instead, Tanzania's Salim A. Salim. In a Security Council deadlock that lasted 5 weeks and 16 ballots, China repeatedly vetoed Waldheim, and the United States blocked Salim. The result was the compromise nomination of Peru's Javier Pérez de Cuéllar. It was an example of a new Chinese assertiveness that will probably increasingly mark its UN role.

The Third World and the UN

Given the influx of Third World countries into the UN and their rise in power in that body, it is important to consider their view of and role in the world organization and other IGOs. Third World commentators, like Marxists, are apt to portray the UN, at least historically, as a vehicle for neocolonial Western domination. Thus the UN and, in particular, the veto-dominated Security Council were and are suspect.

The growing assertiveness of the less developed countries (LDCs) and the changing balance of power in their favor in the General Assembly, in the Economic and Social Council, and elsewhere have led to a changing orientation. Now the UN and other IGOs are increasingly being used by the LDCs to band together and assert their demands for political, social, and economic equity (Holloway, 1990). In a generally power-politic world, the United Nations and other IGOs provide a ready forum for Third World complaints against the larger powers, and, insofar as there is majoritarian voting, give the collective Third World a vehicle for giving substance, in terms of passed resolutions, to its proposals and criticisms. As such, IGOs are a primary arena of the North-South struggle.

The South has pushed, for example, to restructure the UN Charter, the International Monetary Fund Articles of Agreement, and other IGO constitutions, which many LDCs view as documents drawn by and for the superpowers. The LDCs have also promoted the United Nations Conference on Trade and Development (UNCTAD) and other such IGO subunits in order to press their demands for the New International Economic Order (Murphy, 1989). It is this challenge to the established order in UNESCO that led to the United States' withdrawal. The South has also used other organizations, such as cartels, to gain collective strength. Thus the future of the UN and

The UN plays many valuable roles, including helping to create norms of behavior and pressing for their adoption. The UN has been active in trying to end apartheid in South Africa and bring equality to that country's nonwhite citizens. The UN's effort and the progress made is symbolized by this photo of Secretary General Javier Pérez de Cuéllar meeting with Nelson Mandela, vice president of the (South) African National Congress.

many other IGOs promises to be one in which the traditional patterns of dominance are challenged, and the one-time East-West political rivalry will be replaced on the stage by the economic demands of the South on the North.

International Organization and the Future

International organization has many critics. Given the continued conflict in the world and the ongoing economic and social misery, it is all too easy to dismiss international organization as inadequate, misguided, and impossibly idealistic. Even retired United Nations secretary-general Kurt Waldheim seemed pretty discouraged in an article he wrote to commemorate the United Nations' 40th anniversary. According to the secretary-general, it is "perfectly clear" in the area of peacekeeping that "the habit of international security is waning." Waldheim's assessment of UN activity in economic and social areas was equally distressed as he saw the organization approaching "zones of sensitivity that sharply pit members of different backgrounds against one another" (Waldheim, 1984:107).

The alternative is—what? Can the warring, uncaring world continue unchanged in the face of nuclear weapons, persistent poverty, an exploding population, mass starvation, resource depletion, and environmental degradation? No, it cannot! This reality leads Waldheim to cautious optimism that, in the face of these monumental transnational issues, the countries of the world will find that it is in their "enlightened self-interest" to work toward a "single great world community . . . a single global village" (Waldheim, 1984:107).

One cannot know if Waldheim is right, but it is certain that we face problems that cannot be handled in the same old ways (Renninger, 1989; Lister, 1989). Those ways have not been very successful in the past, and they carry the potential of cataclysmic disaster for the future. It is also clear that the rapid growth of international organizations during this century shows that the world has begun to try to reform its political system to meet the new challenges. It is important to concentrate on the positive impact that the UN and other IGOs have had. Peacekeeping missions, children's vaccines, agricultural innovations, and other contributions all mark the UN's 45-year history. An overall evaluation, as one *New York Times* (1/15/90:A19) story was entitled, is that there is "Amid the Jealousies, A Suspicion That the U.N. Works." What is unclear is whether old, no-longer-relevant attitudes can be changed quickly enough. It is also clear that critics of international organization are too often just that, uncreatively negative, and they disparage the organization without noting its contributions or suggesting improvements. International organization holds one hope for the future, and for those who would denigrate that effort, the answer is to make other, positive suggestions rather than implicitly advocating a maintenance of the status quo.

In the end, the United Nations and other international organizations are what we make them. It is true that they possess some independence, but it is limited. Mostly their successes and failures are a reflection of the willingness or disinclination of their member countries to cooperate and use international organizations to further joint efforts. As Dag Hammarskjöld aptly put it, "Everything will be all right—you know when? When people, just people, stop thinking of the United Nations as a weird Picasso abstraction and see it as a drawing they made themselves" (Simpson, 1988:46).

Chapter Summary

1. One of the clearest signs of the changing nature of the international system is this century's rapid rise in the number of international organizations.

2. There are many classifications of international organizations, the most basic distinction being between international governmental organizations, which are made up of member countries, and international nongovernmental organizations, which are made up of private organizations and individuals.

3. Current international organization is the product of three lines of development. One is the idea that humans constitute a single people and should live in peace and mutual support rather than in conflict and self-interested pursuit. A second is the idea that the "big powers" have a special responsibility for maintaining order. A third is the growth of specialized international organizations to deal with narrow, nonpolitical issues.

4. This century's rapid growth of all types of international organizations stems from increased international contact among states and people, increased economic interdependency, the growing importance of transnational issues and political movements, and the increasingly apparent inadequacy of the state-centered system for dealing with world problems.

5. There are significant differences among views on the best role for international organizations. Some favor moving toward a system of supranational organization, in which some form of world government would replace or substantially modify the present state-centered system. Others argue that international organizations are best suited to promoting cooperation among states rather than trying to replace the state-centered system. Still others contend that international organizations should concentrate on performing limited functional activities with the hope of building a habit of cooperation and trust that can later be built on. Finally, at least in practice, many view international organizations as vehicles that should be manipulated, if possible, toward gaining your country's individual political goals.

6. However one defines the best purpose of international organization, it is important to be careful of standards of evaluation. The most fruitful standard is judging an organization by what is possible, rather than setting inevitably frustrating ideal goals.

7. There are a number of important issues related to the structure of international organizations. One group of questions relates to membership: how and when to admit new members and when to expel members. Whether representative bodies should have plenary or limited membership is a related issue, as is the voting scheme to be used in such bodies. Current international organizations use a variety of voting schemes that include majority voting, weighted voting, and negative voting.

8. Another group of structural questions concerns the administration of international organizations: How should administrative officers be appointed, to what do they owe allegiance, and what are their proper roles and powers?

9. There are also a number of significant issues that relate to the general role of international organizations. Peacekeeping is one important role, and international organizations help maintain or restore peace through a variety of diplomatic methods. They sometimes also intervene militarily. The idea of collective security still exists in theory, but in fact the self-interest of UN members has meant that UN peacekeeping operations have been limited in scope and have relied on smaller, usually nonaligned countries for the bulk of their forces.

10. Other roles for the UN and other international organizations include promoting international law, promoting arms control, bettering the human condition, promoting self-government, and furthering international cooperation.

11. Currently, international organizations operate on three planes. The least common is the supranational level, at which IGOs have authority over nation-states. International organizations also act independently. That is, they have a will of their own, apart from the collective wishes of their members. Finally, international organizations serve as an interactive arena in which members pursue their self-interest. The brief studies of the policies of the United States, the Soviet Union, China, and the Third World provide illustrations of this interactive utilization.

The law hath not been dead, though it hath slept.

Shakespeare, *Hamlet*

Power not ruled by law is a menace which our nuclear age cannot afford.

Arthur J. Goldberg, U.S. Supreme Court justice and ambassador
to the United Nations

INTERNATIONAL LAW

Two and a half decades ago, when I was an undergraduate taking "Introduction to International Relations," the professor came into class to lecture about international law. He paused dramatically, looked around the room, flared his nostrils, shot his eyebrows skyward, and snorted a guttural "Bah!" Then, in a few short sentences, he dismissed the idea of international law as a fiction in a world of war, human-rights violations, and economic inequity.

It was, for a man who was a refugee from the ravages of World War II Europe, an understandably cynical view. It was also, however, wrong. International law exists. True, it has sometimes slept, but it is far from dead. Indeed, as we shall see in this chapter, it is not only alive, but it is growing at a healthy pace.

The Dynamic Nature of Law

Any law, either international or of the more familiar domestic variety, is a combination of expectations, rules, and practices that help govern behavior. First, we shall see that all law systems are dynamic, continually evolving systems. Second, no law system is perfect. Even in law-abiding societies, rules are broken and the guilty sometimes escape punishment. Third, law both reflects and directs a society. In other words, to a substantial degree, law mirrors the norms of a society. We legalize what we do in practice. Law, however, can also lead a society to change its behavior by enacting philosophical principles into required standards of conduct. Fourth, law depends on a mixture of voluntary compliance and coercion to maintain order.

A system of law is not something that just happens. It grows. Similarly, a political system does not just happen. It also grows, advancing from a primitive level to ever more sophisticated levels of organization. This concept of a *primitive but evolving legal system* in an evolving political system is important to understanding international law.

473

Primitive Nature of International Law

A primitive society has a number of features that we also find in international law and relations. First, there is no formal rulemaking, or legislative, process. Instead, codes of behavior are derived from custom or from explicit agreements among two or more societal members or groups. Second, there is little or no authority in any formal government to judge or punish violations of law. Primitive tribes have no police or courts. Third, a primitive society is often made up of self-defined units (such as kinship groups), is territorially based, primarily governs itself, and resorts to violent "self-help" in relations with other groups.[1]

In its current state, international law is very akin to a primitive political system. As discussed more fully below, there is at best a rudimentary legislative system. The enforcement and adjudication systems also are extremely limited. In addition, international law exists within a system of sovereign, nationalistic, territorial states that often clash in pursuit of their self-defined interests. If we accept this analogy, then we can conceive of international law as a primitive legal system. This view allows us to be encouraged by the thought that international law and its society may evolve to a higher order rather than to be discouraged by its current lack of sophistication.

Growth of International Law

Just as our "primitive but dynamic" concept would predict, international law is a growing phenomenon.

The *early growth* of modern international law coincides with the origins of nationalism as discussed in chapter 6. As sovereign, territorial states arose, there was a need to define and protect their status and to order their relations. Gradually, as this political system emerged, elements of ancient Jewish, Greek, and Roman practice combined with newer Christian concepts and also with custom and practice to form the rudiments of international law.

This early development was given voice and encouraged by a number of important theorists. The most famous of these was the Dutch thinker Hugo Grotius (1583–1645), whose study *De Jure Belli et Pacis (On the Law of War and Peace)* earned him the title "father of international law." Grotius and others discussed and debated the sources of international law as well as its application to specific circumstances such as the conduct of and justification of war, the treatment of subjugated peoples, and the relations of states.

During the late eighteenth and the nineteenth centuries, international law expanded and changed. As the international system became more complex, the scope of international law grew to cover many new areas of commercial and social interchange. Older areas of law were also refined; for example, the rules of diplomacy were substantially formalized during the immediate post-Napoleonic period. As the political focus of power shifted from rulers to the national state, the concept of the state, rather than the individual monarch, as the subject of law evolved.

The *twentieth century* has seen a significant expansion of both concern with and practice of international law. As already discussed in a number of places, ever-increasing international interaction and interdependence have rapidly increased the need for rules

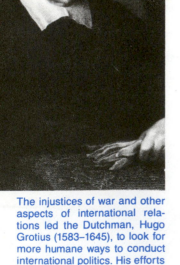

The injustices of war and other aspects of international relations led the Dutchman, Hugo Grotius (1583–1645), to look for more humane ways to conduct international politics. His efforts earned him the title of father of international law.

---

1. The comparison of primitive societies and international relations/law is based on Masters (1969). As Masters points out, the comparison between the two can be carried only so far.

to govern a host of functional areas such as trade, finance, travel, and communications. The ever-more apocalyptic consequences of war have encouraged the formation of conventions governing the conduct of war and have also promoted an increasingly accepted ethic against aggressive war.

These needs and reactions have been evident in a variety of forms. First, The Hague conferences, followed by the League of Nations, and then the United Nations were all founded on principles of international law. Second, these international organizations and others have also included the beginnings of institutions that resemble the legislative, enforcement, and judicial elements of a developed domestic legal system. A third element of growth is the increase of multilateral "lawmaking" treaties governing such subjects as genocide, atmospheric nuclear testing, proliferation, use of the oceans, and human rights. These treaty-established norms of conduct have not always been followed, but their violation has drawn increasing condemnation. This point leads to the fourth factor in current growth, which is the increased need felt by national leaders to justify actions in terms of international law and even, on occasion, to act in support of or give way to the pressure of law. All of these elements are reflected in a fifth factor, which is raised expectations. The increased rhetorical emphasis on law plus enhanced communications means that world opinion is more likely to be aware of and to condemn violations of the norms of international conduct. The Iraqi invasion of Kuwait and the response of the UN in authorizing sanctions and even the use of force against Iraq proves a good example. Amid concerns about oil, there was also a genuine global abhorrence to Iraq's aggression, the brutality with which it treated the conquered Kuwaitis, and its seizure of many thousands of foreign hostages. Furthermore, the rhetoric which was used to rebuke Iraq added even more to the verbal support of international law. Even though it did not reflect all, or even most, of U.S. motives, President Bush's characterization of Iraq's invasion as a "ruthless assault on the very essence of international order and civilized ideals" (U.S. Department of State, 1990) and his call for action against Iraq so that "a new world order" can be established which is "freer from the threat of terror, stronger in the pursuit of justice, and more secure in the quest for peace" will make it more difficult for Washington to justify a future military action against a Grenada or a Panama (*HC,* 9/12/90).

Effectiveness of International Law

One of the charges used to discredit the existence of international law is that it exists only in theory and not in practice. As evidence, critics cite the continuing presence of war, imperialism, and other forms of "lawlessness" that exist today.

The flaw in this argument is that it does not prove its point. In the first place, international law *is* effective in many areas (Chen, 1989). Besides, the fact that law does not cover *all* problem areas and that it is not *always* followed does not disprove its existence. There is, after all, a substantial crime rate in the United States, but does that mean there is no law?

International law is *most effective* in governing functional international relations. In line with our earlier discussion of functionalism (chapter 15), cooperation in and regulation of **functional relations**—that is, low-politics areas such as trade, diplomatic rules, and communications—have been rapidly increasing. This has been marked by the growth of what some scholars have termed international "regimes"—organizations and laws that regulate various functional areas.

International law is *least effective* when applied to high-politics issues such as national security relations between sovereign states. When vital interests are involved, governments still regularly bend international law to justify their actions rather than alter their actions to conform to the law.

This does not mean, however, that the law never influences political decisions. To the contrary, there is a growing sensitivity to legal standards. The virtually universal global reaction against Hussein's invasion of Kuwait and detention of hundreds of foreign hostages was partly based on Iraq's violation of international law. Any legal system is partly the product of the accepted behavior of a society (norms) based on the society's concepts of right and wrong. As such, a legal system, whether domestic or international, is more than just written statutes enacted by legislatures. It is on the basis of expectations of acceptable behavior that Iraq's violation of international norms played an important role in rallying world opinion. Certainly the reaction was based on the self-interest of oil-consuming countries and fear by Iraq's immediate neighbors, but those explanations do not account for the solidarity demonstrated in the UN and elsewhere in imposing sanctions on Iraq. Virtually all countries reacted with disdain to Saddam Hussein's declaration that Kuwait was a province of Iraq. Almost all states also honored the UN sanctions, and a number of them also committed military forces. Even under heavy pressure including threats to their diplomatic personnel, nearly half of the countries and almost all the major European countries with embassies in Kuwait refused to close their missions. The international outcry against Hussein's massive hostage-taking in violation of international law was also part of the reason that he soon began to release at least most captive women and children and in December announced all hostages were free to leave. Thus, even where international law works the least, in high-politics security issues, it works some of the time and works more often than it once did.

As a last thought on the effectiveness of international law, it, like all legal systems, will be most effective when people demand that everyone, citizens and leaders alike, abide by its principles (Falk, 1989).

The International Law System

International law, like any legal system, is based on four critical considerations: the philosophical roots of law; how laws are made; if and why the law is obeyed (adherence); and how legal disputes are decided (adjudicated).

The Philosophical Roots of Law

Before you consider the mechanics of how law works, it is important to inquire into the roots of law. Ideas about what is right and what should be established as the rules of a domestic or an international society do not spring from thin air. Rather they are derived from sources both external and internal to the society that they regulate.

External Sources   Some laws come from sources external to a society. The idea here is that some higher, metaphysical standard of conduct should govern the affairs of humankind. An important ramification of this position is that there is or ought to be one single system of law that governs all people.

Those who believe in the external sources can be subdivided into two schools. One relies on *divine principle,* or a theological basis. Many of the early Western proponents of international law relied on Christian doctrine as a foundation for law. There are also elements of long-standing Islamic, Confucianist, and Buddhist law and scholarship that can be cited as forming a basis of international conduct.

A second school of external-source thought is based on the *nature of humankind*. The **Naturalist** school believes that humans, by nature, have certain rights and obligations. Examples of rights would include life and security; obligations would include not stealing or murdering. Since states are collectives of individuals, and the world community is a collective of states and individuals, nature's individual rights and obligations also apply to the global stage and form the basis for international law.

Internal Sources   Some legal scholars reject the idea of divine or naturalist roots and, instead, focus on the *customs and practices* of society. This is the **Positivist** school. Positivists believe that law reflects society and the way people want that society to operate. Therefore, law is and ought to be the product of the codification or formalization of a society's standards and practices.

Critics condemn this approach as "amoral," and sometimes argue that it legitimizes immoral, albeit common, practice. It should be carefully noted here, though, that widespread practice, such as aggressive war, does not necessarily imply legitimacy. In the first place, statistically, peace is the norm in practice. And, second, international society condemns aggression in theory. Thus, despite frequent misbehavior, aggression is a lawless act.

How International Law Is Made

In a national society most **domestic law** is made through a constitution (constitutional law) or by a legislative body (statutory law). In practice, law is also established through judicial decisions (interpretation), which establishes guidelines (precedent) for later decisions by the courts. A lesser source of law is custom (common law), and sometimes disputes are decided based on what is fair (equity).

Modern international law differs markedly in its sources. According to the Statute of the International Court of Justice, these lawmaking sources are: international treaties, international custom, the general principles of law, and judicial decision and scholarly legal writing. Some students of international law would tentatively add a fifth source: resolutions and other pronouncements of international representative assemblies, such as the UN General Assembly. These five rely primarily on the positivist approach, but like domestic law include elements of both external and internal sources of law.

One implication of these diverse sources is that international lawmaking is *decentralized*. There is no single institutional, geographical, or intellectual source of law, and there is no central place to **codify**, or write down, the law. This fact creates difficulties as differing rules, practices, and interpretations clash, and they will be discussed further below. Decentralization does not mean, however, that international law is a meaningless hodgepodge. Consider domestic law in the United States, which contains over 80,000 municipal, state, and federal rulemaking authorities that adopt a blizzard of often contradictory standards! The American system of reconciling these differences is, of course, more established than the international law process, but in both, the alignment process is usually slow and is achieved by politics and compromise.

International Treaties   Treaties are the most important source of international law (Lukashuk, 1989). Agreements between states are binding according to the doctrine of **pacta sunt servanda** ("treaties are to be served/carried out"). All treaties are lawmaking for their signatories, but it is possible to argue that some treaties are even applicable to nonsignatories. The 1948 Convention on the Prevention and Punishment of the Crime of Genocide, for example, has been ratified by over 80 states. Some would argue, therefore, that it is "recognized" and "codified" practice and therefore is binding even on those states that have not formally agreed to it.

International Custom   The second most important source of international law is international custom. The old, and now supplanted, rule that territorial waters extend 3 miles from the shore grew from the distance a cannon could fire. If you were outside the range of land-based artillery, then you were in international waters. Maritime rules of the road and diplomatic practice are two other important areas of law that grew out of custom. It might also be noted that treaties (for example, the Vienna Convention on Diplomatic Relations, 1961) often are established to formalize long-standing custom.

General Principles of Law   According to this standard, the International Court of Justice (ICJ) applies "the general principles of law recognized by civilized nations." Although such language is vague, it does have its benefits. It allows "external" sources of law, such as "morality," to be considered. More than any other standard, it was these general principles that Iraq's aggression in 1990 violated. Even if he was being overly dramatic, U.S. secretary of state James Baker's worry that "If might is to make right, then the world will be plunged into a new dark age" catches something of the international reaction (*NYT,* 8/12/90:A10). The principle of "equity," what is fair when no legal standard exists, also has some application under general principles.

Judicial Decisions and Scholarly Writing   In many domestic systems, the legal interpretations of the courts set precedent according to the doctrine of *stare decisis* ("let the decision stand").[2] Similarly, the rulings of the ICJ, other international tribunals, and even domestic courts when they apply international law help shape the body of law that exists. Additionally, the work of legal scholars is sometimes considered by courts in their deliberations.

International Representative Assemblies   The preceding four sources of international law are generally recognized. The idea that laws can come from the UN General Assembly or any other international representative assembly is much more controversial. Clearly, to date, international law is nonlegislative. The General Assembly cannot legislate international law the way that Canada's Parliament and Israel's Knesset enact laws that govern their countries.

Members of the United Nations, however, are bound by treaty to abide by some of the decisions of the General Assembly and Security Council. Given this obligation, it is possible to argue that these bodies are quasi-legislative. Certainly, their resolutions and mandates often are not followed, but some would argue that this means that the law is being violated rather than that the law does not exist. The European Parliament, which is discussed more in chapter 18, has also begun to grow gradually as a regional legislative assembly.

Some scholars also take the position that resolutions approved by overwhelming majorities of the General Assembly's nearly universal membership constitute interna-

---

2. *Stare decisis* is specifically rejected in Article 59 of the Statute of the ICJ, but as Levi (1979:53) points out, "The fact is that all courts . . . rely upon and cite each other abundantly in their decisions."

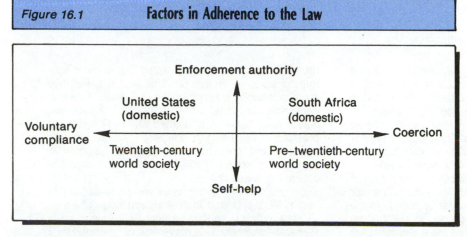

Figure 16.1   Factors in Adherence to the Law

Two crucial factors in international law are how the law is enforced and what encourages compliance. These factors differ over time and for different societies.

tional law. The reasoning here is that such votes may be construed as reflecting international custom and/or the general principles of law and, therefore, they subtly enter the stream of international law. We may, then, be seeing the beginnings of legislated international law, but, at best, it is in its genesis.

Adherence to the Law

Adherence to the law is a third essential element of any legal system. Any legal system is based on (1) what makes people comply and, when noncompliance occurs, (2) how the law is enforced.

Compliance   Obedience in any legal system, be it international or domestic, primitive or sophisticated, is based on a combination of voluntary compliance and coercion.

   Voluntary compliance occurs when the subjects obey the law because they accept its legitimacy (for example, accept the authority) and/or agree that it is necessary to the reasonable conduct of society. *Coercion* is the process of gaining compliance through threats of violence, imprisonment, economic sanction, or other punishment.

   Any society's legal system could be placed along a scale between complete reliance on voluntary compliance and complete reliance on coercion (Fig. 16.1). No society exists at either extreme, and while most rely mainly on voluntary compliance, the mixture of legitimacy and authoritarianism varies widely. Most Americans and Canadians, for example, obey the law voluntarily, whereas the black majority in South Africa are obedient to the white minority's laws and control primarily under duress.

Enforcement   In all legal systems enforcement relies on a combination of *enforcing authorities* and *self-help*, with mediation a midpoint. Here again a scale can be drawn with the two extremes (authority, self-help) at its end points, as shown in Figure 16.1. In more sophisticated legal systems, most enforcement relies on a central authority such as the police. Still, even the most sophisticated legal system continues to recognize the legitimacy of such self-help doctrines as self-defense.

The U.S., the UN, the PLO, and Compliance: What Would You Do?

In the abstract, the idea of voluntarily complying with international law and its doctrine of *pacta sunt servanda* (the treaties are to be served/honored) is eminently reasonable. So is the idea, which the United States has agreed to by treaty, that it should not attempt to use the fact that the United Nations is headquartered in New York City to interfere in the operations of the world body (Reisman, 1989).

Opposing the abstract principle of compliance is the practical reality that the United Nations has for some years accepted an observer mission from the Palestine Liberation Organization. In 1987 Congress passed legislation entitled the Antiterrorist Act ordering the mission closed and the Palestinians expelled from the United States.

The Reagan administration opposed the legislation, but once it became U.S. law, the government acted to end the PLO mission. This set up a confrontation with the United Nations. In February 1988 the General Assembly, with the United States abstaining, resolved 143 to 1 (Israel) that the U.S. move violated its 1947 headquarters treaty with the United Nations. The world assembly then unanimously asked the International Court of Justice to rule on the dispute. The court acted quickly, and in April unanimously ruled that the United States must submit the issue to arbitration. This was followed two months later by a ruling in the U.S. federal district court that concurred with the ICJ that the 1988 law was invalid because it violated the 1947 treaty. At that point, the Reagan administration, which had opposed the congressional action to begin with, declined to appeal the ruling, thereby ending the attempt to expel the PLO.

Debate over the larger issue soon arose again. In late 1988, the United States refused to grant a visa to Yasser Arafat so that he could address the UN General Assembly. This move was condemned by a vote of 151 to 2, and the General Assembly further voted to convene in Geneva, Switzerland, to hear Arafat. Legal actions in the ICJ and in U.S. courts were also possible.

Apart from the interesting details of the imbroglio, the most important question here is to ask yourself what you would do. Would you follow *pacta sunt servanda* and comply with the law even if you did not like it? Or, if you agree with Congress that the PLO is a terrorist organization, would you ignore the U.S. treaty with the United Nations and expel the PLO?

Primitive societies rely primarily on self-help and mediation to enforce laws and norms. Central authorities develop slowly and are used only in extreme circumstances (Suganami, 1989). Yet no society that has progressed beyond the most primitive has a complete absence of enforcement authority, and it is here that we can place international law.

International Law: Primitive Adherence   Because the international legal system is still primitive, enforcement and compliance reflect this stage.

Enforcement, in particular, has been slow to develop. Collective security has remained a theory, economic sanctions have been generally unsuccessful, and international law continues to rely mainly on self-help to enforce adherence, as reflected in the UN Charter's recognition of national self-defense. There have been, however, a few examples of enforcement. War criminals were punished after World War II, economic sanctions had some impact on loosening the white grip on the black majority of Zimbabwe (then Rhodesia); UN actions in Korea, in the Congo, and elsewhere did contain some elements of enforcement. And the 1990 UN Security Council sanctions on Iraq and the Council's authorizing military action against Iraq to force it out of Kuwait are strong examples of such action.

The element of voluntary *compliance* has grown more quickly than that of enforcement authority in international law, although, as the box above shows, the law is hard to follow when you do not like it. As we saw earlier, under Growth of International Law, functional international law has expanded rapidly because of the need to regulate complex international interactions in trade, finance, communications, diplomacy, and other areas. In addition, as noted, there is a growing group of concepts that restrains action in more political areas. Aggression, violation of human rights, and other unacceptable practices still occur, but they increasingly meet with widespread condemnation.

Thus, in the area of adherence, international law is a primitive but developing legal system. It is slowly moving out of the lower right quadrant of Figure 16.1 (see p. 479) and, one hopes, toward the upper left quadrant.

Adjudication of the Law

The mechanisms and processes used to judge disputes according to the law are the fourth essential element of any legal system. As primitive law systems develop into more sophisticated ones, the method of settling disputes evolves from (1) primary reliance on bargaining between disputing parties, through (2) mediation/conciliation by neutral parties, to (3) **adjudication** by neutral parties.[3]

The international law system is in the early stages of this developmental process and is just now developing the institutions and attitudes necessary for adjudication.

Institutions of Adjudication There are a number of international courts in the world today. The genesis of these tribunals extends back less than a century to the Permanent Court of International Arbitration established by the Hague Conference at the turn of the century. In 1922 the Permanent Court of International Justice (PCIJ) was created as part of the League of Nations, and in 1946 the current **International Court of Justice (ICJ)**, which is associated with the UN, evolved from the PCIJ. The ICJ sits in The Hague, Netherlands, and consists of 15 judges who are elected to nine-year terms through a complex voting system in the UN. In addition to the ICJ, there are a few regional courts of varying activity, including the Court of Justice of the European Communities, the European Court of Human Rights, the Inter-American Court of Human Rights, the Central American Court of Justice, and the Community Tribunal of the Economic Community of West African States. Additionally, domestic courts may also apply international law, as a U.S. court did in the 1988 dispute over the PLO mission detailed in the box on the opposite page.

Attitudes Toward Adjudication Although the creation of international tribunals during the twentieth century indicates progress, the concept of sovereignty remains a potent barrier to adjudication (Singh, 1989).

In theory, the authority of the ICJ extends to all international legal disputes. In reality, the court is limited by the reluctance of states to submit to its jurisdiction. States must not only agree to be subject to the ICJ, but they may also make "reservations" to that acceptance. The United States, for example, rejects ICJ jurisdiction in any "domestic matter . . . as determined by the United States." This is an extremely broad disclaimer and, in effect, means the United States can reject ICJ jurisdiction on virtually any issue.

American attitudes became even less cooperative when, in 1984, Nicaragua filed a case with the ICJ charging that U.S. support of the Contra rebels and its mining of

The ability of the UN to hear from representatives of the Palestine Liberation Organization has been challenged by the United States. The U.S. attempt to expel the PLO mission, pictured here, to the UN was condemned in 1988 by the General Assembly and rejected by both the International Court of Justice and a U.S. federal court. In late 1988, the issue arose again, this time when the United States refused to grant a visa to allow Yasser Arafat to address the General Assembly. The United States was again overwhelmingly censured by the General Assembly.

---

3. There are technical differences between arbitration and adjudication, but they are treated alike for our purposes here.

The International Court of Justice is one focus of the effort to extend the rule of law in the world. Shown here is the ICJ building in The Hague, the Netherlands.

Nicaraguan harbors violated international law. Up to that point, the United States had been one of the states that had signed what is known as the *optional clause,* thereby agreeing to be subject to the compulsory jurisdiction of the ICJ. In the Nicaraguan case, however, the United States argued that the charges were political, and therefore the court had no jurisdiction. When the ICJ rejected the U.S. objections by an overwhelming margin and decided to hear the case, the United States terminated its agreement to submit to the compulsory jurisdiction of the ICJ. The court heard the case anyway, and found for Nicaragua, giving a black eye to the United States in the court of world opinion.

On a more general level, the U.S. response was a step backward in the search for international relations governed by international law. Sovereignty overcame community (Malawer, 1988; Higgins, 1987). Domestic societies accept the principle that individuals must be subject to court jurisdiction whether or not they agree and whether or not they win their case. This wisdom does not yet extend to the international society, and only about 25 percent of the 162 countries that are a party to the ICJ Statute are adherents to the optional clause giving the ICJ compulsory jurisdiction over their international legal disputes.[4]

Third World attitudes toward adjudication are similarly influenced by the sovereignty issue and by the fact that many of these countries' legal systems rely more on mediation than on adjudication. Courts were also often instruments of white colonial oppression and are therefore viewed with suspicion.

Attitudes toward adjudication are also affected by concern that the ICJ is politicized and that its judges are influenced by their home countries' positions (Gross, 1986). Although there is a strong coincidence between judges' votes and their countries' preferences, there is no evidence that it stems from political pressure (Rourke, 1979).

Use and Effectiveness of Adjudication The result of these attitudes is that the use of the ICJ has been sporadic and declining. From its establishment through late 1989, the

4. In addition to the UN's 159 members, a special provision allows Switzerland, Liechtenstein, and San Marino to be parties to the ICJ Statute without also joining the United Nations. Fifty-seven countries have agreed to the optional clause at one time or another.

court has dealt with only 59 contentious cases and has issued another 21 advisory opinions on issues submitted by organs of the United Nations. This is a rate of 2.3 cases a year, but closer examination shows that use of the court is ebbing. In the 1950s, the rate was 3.4 cases per year, but it declined to 1.1 during the 1970s, and has only slightly recovered to 1.4 in the 1980s. That decline may be ending. In 1989, six contentious cases and one advisory opinion case were filed with the ICJ.

What this means is that the court is underutilized, rather than that it is inherently ineffective. Any court, from the U.S. Supreme Court to the ICJ, relies heavily on the willingness of those within its jurisdiction to obey its mandates and on the enforcement authority of the executive branch. As we have seen, the ICJ generally enjoys scant voluntary compliance, and insofar as the UN Secretariat is its executive branch, the court does not have powerful enforcement support.

Still, the ICJ does play a valuable role. Its rulings help define and advance international law. Furthermore, the court can contribute to countries that want to settle a dispute peacefully but that are having difficulty compromising because of domestic pressures. A recent example is the dispute between Canada and the United States over which country had territorial control over certain fishing areas, an issue which the ICJ was able to settle in its 1984 *Delimination of the Maritime Boundary in the Gulf of Maine Area* ruling.

Beyond the ICJ, there has been evidence that some of the other international courts, especially in Europe, have had some effect. The "half-full" standard must also be applied here. The international judicial system is still primitive, but each of the 149 opinions issued by the Permanent Court of International Justice and the International Court of Justice in this century is one more than the zero instances of international adjudication in the last century.

International Law and Cultural Perspective

As primitive political systems evolve and expand to incorporate diverse peoples, one problem that such legal systems encounter is the "fit" between differing culturally based concepts of law and equity. International law, in an evolving world, faces the same difficulty. Most of the law and process that currently exist are based on European and American concepts and practices, and the newly assertive states of Africa, Asia, and Latin America question and sometimes reject law based on that culture.

Differing Perspectives

The culture and international status of the Western countries, the Soviet Union, China, and the Third World each engender some differences in interpretation of international law.

The *Euro-American view* of law is based on principles designed to protect the power position of the long-dominant states of this bloc. Order is a primary point, as is sovereignty. Closely related is the theory of property, which holds that individuals (and states) have a "right" to accumulate and maintain property (wealth). This is a major philosophical underpinning of capitalism. Western law also relies heavily on the process and substance of law rather than on equity. Thus, there is an emphasis on courts and what the law is rather than on what is fair.

International law has been viewed differently from a *Soviet-Marxist perspective*. Given the Euro-American origins of international law, the Soviets viewed much of it as a

vehicle for capitalist exploitation. They particularly rejected law resulting from multinational treaties and other sources in which they did not participate. One illustrative
ramification of this stand was their belief that intervention in socialist countries to thwart
reactionary subversion or in Third World countries to overthrow capitalist elites was
legitimate. The Soviets have also supported the Third World's demands to rewrite
international economic law on the basis of equity, although the Soviets claim that since
they did not create the injustices, they should not be required to redistribute their own
resources to correct them (Dore, 1984).

In recent years, Soviet views have changed. They now give more credence to
international law, whatever its origins, and they are joining or participating more fully in
many international organizations they once condemned as imperialist pawns. The
Soviets have, in what one scholar calls "the development of a *perestroika* legal
consciousness," begun to emphasize the primacy of law, especially over the use of force
(Butler, 1989). And, to an extent, Soviet support of UN sanctions and military action on
their recent ally Iraq after its invasion of Kuwait gives substance to this change in Soviet
thinking. The Soviet foreign minister even suggested his country might supply troops to
a UN force if called upon. Another interesting development in Soviet legal thinking is a
stress on world public opinion as a source of law. As a leading Soviet legal scholar
recently wrote, states still lead in lawmaking, but "they have to take into account" the
views of nongovernmental international organizations such as "various democratic,
antiwar, and antinuclear movements" that "express values and interests common to
mankind" (Mullerson, 1989:512).

China's perspective on international law has been based on its Marxist ideology and
its history of being imperialistically exploited. The Chinese view international law as a
product of imperialism. They reject *pacta sunt servanda,* the obligation to uphold
treaties, when the treaty was imposed imperialistically. The Chinese hold that treaties
based on coercion can simply be renounced. In practice, however, they sometimes
tacitly recognize the status quo or are willing to negotiate revisions, as the recent
agreement with Great Britain on the future of Hong Kong illustrates. Also, in the years
since Mao's death in 1976, China has adhered to many lawmaking treaties, and the
country's early rejection of custom-based law has moderated (Chiu, 1987). The Chinese
disagreed with the Soviets' now-abandoned concept of legitimate interference to
maintain socialism, and they condemned the Czechoslovakian invasion as Soviet-style
imperialism. The Chinese stress equity, the idea that the law should benefit all parties.
This view places them solidly within the Third World in its demand for a New
International Economic Order.

The *Third World's view* of international law is influenced by its history of
exploitation and its "newness" as a collection of sovereign states, as well as its cultural
traditions and current status. The new nations claim that, at the point of their
independence, they entered the system of sovereign states with a *clean slate*. That is,
they are not bound by preexisting agreements or practices that work to their disadvantage. These countries support sovereignty and reject aspects of international law that
they claim are imperialistic abridgments of their sovereignty. They insist on noninterference. They support, for example, the "Calvo clause," by which Western-based
multinational corporations agree that their home governments have no right to interfere
in host countries to protect the MNCs' property. The Third World also rejects weighted
decision-making schemes, such as those in the Security Council and the International
Monetary Fund, that favor the rich and powerful. Third World countries emphasize
equity over the substance and process of law. For them, the important standard is
fairness, especially in terms of economic maldistribution.

Can There Be "One" Law?

Given the differences in perspective we have just noted, the question arises: Can the world arrive at one system of law? The answer is "Yes!" or, at least, "It is possible, if not certain."

Some scholars doubt the ability of a multicultural world to agree on a universal system of law. Others, however, argue persuasively that cross-cultural analysis can be used to discover common ground among various cultures' concepts of law, legitimacy, and rights. In the realm of human rights, for example, the debate focuses substantially on the conflicting views of *universalists* and *relativists* (Renteln, 1990). Universalists believe a basis of a global human rights law exists based on either divine authority or natural law (the nature of humankind). Relativists hold that law is based on divergent cultural custom, and, therefore, no single standard does (or, they suspect, can) exist.

Whatever the relative truth of these two schools of legal theory, it is safe to say that increasing commerce, travel, communications, and other global integrative forces are necessitating the adoption of legal standards to regulate everyday interchanges. Furthermore, increased global communications are promoting a budding consensus on at least the rudiments of legitimate political behavior. The existence and role of the International Court of Justice is but one indication of this trend. "In a world which is full of regional legal systems and parochial legal order, it is essential for the life of the international community to have one law universally applicable," reasons Judge Nagendra Singh (1989:257), past president (1985–88) of the ICJ. "To bring about this essential unity of the international legal order, the very existence of the Court is [vital], because it applies one law alone to the disputes of all States of the world, although such States may be internally governed by different legal systems."

The existence of the rudiments of universal international law does not mean, however, the global adoption of existing international law. All legal systems are dynamic, which means they change. Legal systems also rely on voluntary compliance based on a recognition of their legitimacy. To attain greater legitimacy, the international legal system needs to change some of the practices that no longer serve the system or that are anathema to non–Euro-American cultures. These divergent views are discussed in the Issues in Law section below, in the chapter 14 section on the New International Economic Order, and in chapter 19, among other places.

Issues in Law

As a developing legal system in a dynamic world political system, international law is anything but "settled." There are many unresolved issues, and in this section we will examine some of the "frontiers" of international law. For analytical purposes, the discussion will be divided between two rough categories: (1) issues between states and (2) individuals and international law.

Issues Between States

The state has been the traditional focus of international law. The state has been the *subject* of international law—the law has applied to its conduct. A great deal of international law also addresses the status of states, thus making the state the *object* of international law.

Sovereignty   Independence and equality continue to be a cornerstone of the contemporary state system, but they are no longer legal absolutes. The concept of sovereignty was extensively discussed in chapter 5, but we can add here that it is being chipped away by a growing number of law-creating treaties that limit action. Sovereignty is also ever so slowly being restricted by a growing body of general principles that govern human rights and other aspects of the relations between a state and individuals within its borders.

War   Most of the earliest writing in international law was concerned with the law of war, and this issue has continued to be a primary focus of legal development. In addition to issues of traditional "state versus state" warfare, international law is now attempting to regulate the related subjects of revolutionary and internal warfare and terrorism.

First let's consider *traditional warfare*. The question of what makes a war "just" has long been a concern of international law (Cohen, 1989). Today, aggression is outlawed by the UN Charter, and the only legitimate reasons to resort to violence are (1) in self-defense and (2) as part of a UN or regional peacekeeping effort. There are also those, called pacifists, who argue that any war is illegal and immoral (Holmes, 1989). There have also been extensive efforts to regulate the conduct of warfare. These have included such advances as prohibiting the use of certain types of weapons (such as poison gas), adopting standards for the treatment of prisoners of war, and placing restrictions against unnecessary attacks on noncombatants. The status of neutrals, their rights and obligations, is a third area of concern. All these areas contain issues of great difficulty because of the high political stakes involved and also because changes in the nature of conflict (increasingly destructive technology, mass warfare) create new problems and extend beyond traditional concepts. The next chapter will address several of these issues.

Increasing concern with *revolutionary/internal warfare and terrorism* has also brought attempts to deal with these types of violence within the context of international law. To a degree, wars of liberation have been affirmed by the General Assembly's 1974 resolution recognizing the legitimacy of the struggle of the peoples under colonial or alien domination to exercise their right of self-determination and independence by all necessary means at their disposal. This does not mean acceptance of outside intervention on behalf of wars of liberation, although non-Western legal thought is more likely to accept such acts as legitimate (Wilson, 1988).

There are also considerable efforts to agree on ways to deal with issues of terrorism, including hostages, violence against civilians, and the prosecution and extradition of terrorists. A great deal remains to be done, but progress is being made in some areas such as skyjacking, which is defined as illegitimate by almost all members of the international community.

A related subject is the validity of armed intervention by one country in another to promote or protect democracy or to redress abuses of human rights (Henkin et al., 1989). The United States invaded Panama in December 1989 in order, among other reasons, to topple the undemocratic regime of General Manuel Noriega. That armed attack successfully achieved that goal, but it also touched off a lively debate and eventual condemnation in the United Nations, the Organization of American States, and elsewhere over whether it was a violation of international law and the UN Charter provisions cited above (Farer, 1990; versus D'Amato, 1990).

Law of the Sea   The status of the world's oceans is another long-standing subject of international law. The international rules of the road for maritime shipping have long had general acceptance. The extension of a state's territorial limits to 3 miles into the ocean was another widely acknowledged standard.

One of the issues that international law addresses is which of the world's areas and resources can be exclusively exploited by individual countries or corporations and which are international and should benefit all equally. The status of the world's oceans and seabeds is such an issue. A Law of the Sea Convention has been negotiated, but some countries reject it, claiming it is unfair.

In more recent years, the resource value of the seas and harvesting and extraction technology have created uncertainty and change. Undersea oil exploration, in particular, is the source of serious dispute between a number of countries. As early as 1945, the United States claimed control of the resources on or under its continental shelf. In 1960 the Soviet Union proclaimed the extension of its territorial waters out to 12 miles, a policy that has been imitated by others, including the United States as of December 1988. Several Latin American countries claim a 200-mile territorial zone, and the United States not only established a 200-mile "conservation zone" in 1977 to control fishing but in 1983 extended that control to all economic resources within the 200-mile limit.

In an ambitious attempt to settle and regulate many of these issues, the Law of the Sea Convention (1982) seeks to define coastal zones, to establish an International Seabed Authority to regulate nonterritorial seabed mining, and to provide for the sharing of revenue from such efforts. Although the vast majority of the world's states have signed the accord, its effectiveness has been cast in doubt by the opposition of the United States and a few other states. The objection of the United States particularly focuses on what it sees as a Third World attempt to control deep-sea mining in a way detrimental to U.S. interests.

The uncertain future of the Law of the Sea Convention illustrates many of the difficulties of advancing international law and organization. First, it does not take effect until ratified by 60 countries, and by 1990 only 42 ratifications had been deposited with the United Nations. Moreover, even though ratification can eventually be expected by most or all of the 158 countries that signed the convention since the conference in 1982, the countries that refused to agree are in a position to reduce or nullify its effectiveness. The United States, along with Israel, Turkey, and Venezuela, voted no. Seventeen other countries including those of the Soviet bloc, Canada, Great Britain, West Germany, Italy, France, China, Japan, Australia, and the Scandinavian countries abstained. Many of these countries are afraid that their interests would be harmed by the convention's provisions regarding control of territorial waters or coastal resources. These countries are also concerned that the voting formula in the governing body will allow the Third World to dominate decisions to the detriment of the coastal and/or the industrialized powers that are able to exploit seabed mining and ocean fishing areas. Thus, as is often the case, the struggle over control of the seas is a case of sovereign self-interest versus international common interest.

Air and Space   Twentieth-century technology has created the need to regulate the use of air and space. The airspace above a country is recognized as part of that country by the 1944 Chicago Convention of International Civil Aviation. There have been concerns, however, with enforcement procedures, especially during accidental, innocent passage, as in the 1983 Soviet downing of a Korean airliner in Soviet airspace or the 1988 destruction of an Iranian civilian jet and its 290 passengers by the U.S. warship *Vincennes* in the Persian Gulf. There are also disputes over the dividing line between air and space, and they will escalate as satellites and space vehicles maintain positions over the territory of states. Other aspects of developing space law include agreements to ban nuclear weapons in space and to prevent countries from claiming exclusive jurisdiction over areas in space or on celestial bodies, such as the moon. As travel, military, and resource development technologies improve, space is likely to become an increasing source of conflict with need of legal regulation.

Antarctic   Regulation of the Antarctic region has been governed by agreements among 14 countries with long-standing activity in the region. These agreements include a 1959 treaty pledging to use the area only for peaceful purposes. Recent interest in resource development and attempts by some states to have the UN regulate the area have caused new and continuing negotiation.

Environment   Protection of the environment is another of the technology-related legal issues of the twentieth century. The drift of acid rain and air pollution over borders, the contamination of border lakes and international rivers, and deep-sea dumping are the subjects of disputes and have resulted in efforts to define the responsibilities and liabilities of states. These issues will be covered more extensively in the final chapter.

Individuals and International Law

In addition to states, international law is increasingly concerned with individuals. This concern has long included the treatment of individuals by states. More recently, international law has expanded to include responsibility of individuals for their acts.

THE UNIVERSAL DECLARATION OF Human Rights

Some people doubt whether all the world's diverse cultures can agree on one system of international law. It will be difficult, but in some areas there is growing agreement on at least fundamental principles. One such area is human rights. Most of the world's countries have agreed to the Universal Declaration of Human Rights.

Prisoners of War The 1949 Geneva Convention established generally accepted rules on the treatment of POWs despite some later violations. A remaining problem is how to distinguish a POW from a criminal. The Palestine Liberation Organization claims that its fighters who infiltrate Israel and are captured are POWs. Israel treats them as terrorist murderers.

Aliens In general, aliens are governed by the domestic law of the country in which they are residing or traveling. Americans, for example, do not carry their constitutional rights abroad with them. Home states therefore do not ordinarily have the right to intervene, although they sometimes do when acts against their nationals are politically motivated or do not meet rudimentary standards of justice. The treatment of hostages by Iraq provides an example. With increased travel, migratory labor, and international movement of investment capital, the treatment of aliens and their property is a developing legal area.

Human Rights International law is developing affirmatively in the area of defining human rights. The UN Charter supports basic rights in a number of provisions, as do many international instruments, such as the Universal Declaration of Human Rights (1948). The 1976 International Covenant on Civil and Political Rights and the 1976 International Covenant on Economic, Social, and Cultural Rights both expanded the recognized definitions. There are also many regional pacts, such as the 1977 Helsinki Accords, which address European human rights.

Much, however, remains to be done. The two 1976 covenants have been ratified by only about half the world's states. The United States, for example, has not, because of fears that these agreements might be used as platforms for interfering in domestic civil rights issues or as vehicles for demanding international resource redistribution under the NIEO. Additionally, there are efforts to further refine and extend agreed rights to women, children, refugees, and other classes of people. The United Nations Convention on the Elimination of All Forms of Discrimination Against Women was adopted by the General Assembly in 1979, for example, but its impact remains limited. A total of 101

International law has gradually come to hold individuals responsible for their acts. John Demjanjuk was accused of being a sadistic guard called Ivan the Terrible by his victims in a Nazi concentration camp during World War II. He disappeared, but was discovered in the United States. Demjanjuk was extradited to Israel, where he was tried and convicted in 1988 for his crimes.

countries had ratified the convention by 1990, but as Margaret J. Anstee, UN deputy secretary general put it, "We have not traveled as far or as fast as we had hoped" (*NYT,* 1/24/90:A1). Of the countries that have ratified the convention, few have taken significant legal action to implement its ideals, and other countries (such as the United States and India) have yet to ratify it. Thus, the growth of human-rights law has just begun. The acceptance of the concept of human rights has gained a good deal more rhetorical support than practical application, and enforcement continues to be largely in the hands of individual states with a mixed record of adherence. For all these shortcomings, though, human-rights obligations are now widely discussed, and world opinion is increasingly critical of violations.

Individual Responsibility   Traditionally, individuals were *objects* rather than subjects of international law. This means that international law governed their treatment but not their responsibilities. A series of precedents in this century have begun to change that concept. In the Nuremberg and Tokyo war trials after World War II, German and Japanese military and civilian leaders were tried, convicted, imprisoned, and in some cases executed for waging aggressive war, for war crimes, and for crimes against humanity. The trial (and execution) of Japanese general Tomoyuki Yamashita established the precedent that commanders were responsible for the actions of their troops. This precedent has not been expanded, although there were some calls to apply the rules to U.S. commanders for the My Lai massacre and other actions by U.S. troops in Vietnam. In recent years, the French arrested and convicted Klaus Barbie for crimes during the Nazi occupation, and there were extensive efforts to apprehend Josef Mengele, the Nazi concentration camp doctor who cruelly experimented on prisoners, before it was confirmed that he had drowned in Brazil. Israel has also captured, tried, convicted, and executed what it considers war criminals. Countries have also cooperated in deporting accused war criminals, including recent U.S. deportations of death camp guards to the Soviet Union and Israel, where they were tried, convicted, and, in the Soviet case, executed.

The capture of Manuel Noriega as part of the 1989 U.S. invasion of his country and the removal of the general to Florida, where he was arraigned on a variety of U.S. criminal charges and assigned to a federal prison, have raised a host of legal questions about the legality of seizing individuals in another country and whether Noriega is more properly a prisoner of war, as he and his attorneys have claimed. There have also been stories that in the wake of the 1990–91 Middle East crisis, U.S. Department of Justice officials have begun to draw up legal charges against Iraqi president Saddam Hussein. Whether such actions represent progress for world law or the imposition of the victor's justice on the vanquished is a highly controversial issue (Brilmayer, 1989).

International Law and the Future

As noted in the beginning of this chapter, the often anarchic and inequitable world has made it easy for some to dismiss talk of international law as idealistic prattling. This was probably never valid and certainly is not true now. An irreversible trend in world affairs is the rapid acceleration of states and people interacting in almost all areas of endeavor. As these interactions have grown, so has the need for regularized behavior and rules to prescribe that behavior. The growth of these rules in functional international interactions has been on the leading edge of the development of international law. Advances in political and military areas have been slower, but here too there has been progress. Thus, as with the United Nations, the pessimist may decry the glass as only half-full, whereas, in reality, it is encouraging that there is more and more water in the previously almost-empty glass.

All the signs point to increasing respect for international law. As a general rule, even enemies at their worst moments still respect many aspects of that law, and departures from the law draw increasing criticism from the world community. It is likely, therefore, that international law will continue to develop and to expand its areas of application. There will certainly be areas where growth is painfully slow, and there will also be law violators who sometimes get away with their unlawful acts. But, just as surely, there will be progress.

Chapter Summary

1. International law can be best understood as a primitive system of law in comparison with much more developed domestic law. There are only the most rudimentary procedures and institutions for making, adjudicating, and enforcing international law. This does not mean, however, that international law is impotent, only that it is in an earlier stage of development than domestic law.

2. As a developing phenomenon, international law is dynamic and has been growing since the earliest periods of civilization. This growth has accelerated in the twentieth century because the increasing level of international interaction and interdependence requires many new rules to govern and regularize contacts in trade, finance, travel, communication, and other areas. The possible consequences of war have also spurred the development of international law.

3. Thus far, international law is most effective when it governs functional international relations. International law works least well in areas that touch on the vital interests of the sovereign states. Even in those areas, though, international law is gradually becoming more effective.

4. The international law system has four essential elements: its philosophical roots, lawmaking, adherence, and adjudication.

5. The roots of law for any legal system may come from external sources, such as natural law, or from within the society, such as custom.

6. Regarding lawmaking, international law can be argued to spring from a number of sources, including divine principle, the nature of humankind, societal custom and practices, and lawmaking documents passed or agreed to by states. As in most primitive legal systems, international lawmaking is still heavily nonlegislative and decentralized, but it is slowly taking on those more advanced characteristics.

7. Regarding adherence, international law, again like primitive law, relies mainly on voluntary compliance and self-help. Here again, though, there are early and still uncertain examples of enforcement by third parties, a feature that characterizes more advanced systems.

8. The fourth essential element of a law system, adjudication, is also in the primitive stage in international law. But the application of international law by domestic courts and, even more important, the existence of the International Court of Justice, the Court of Justice of the European Communities, and other such international judicial bodies represent an increasing sophistication of international law in this area as well.

9. As a developing system in a still culturally diverse world, international law has encountered problems of fit with different cultures. Most current international law is based on European and American ideas and practices, and many states from the Third World and other groups object to certain aspects of international law as it exists.

10. The changes in the world system in this century have created a number of important issues related to international law. Among these are the validity and status of sovereignty; the legality of war and the conduct of war; rules for governing the surface, subsurface, and floors of the world's international seas; the regulation of air and space; and protection of the environment.

11. In general, international law has been interpreted as applying to states, but it is also increasingly concerned with individuals. Primarily it applies to the treatment of individuals by states, but it also has some application to the actions of individuals. Thus people, as well as countries, are coming to have obligations, as well as rights, under international law.

I would give all my fame for a pot of ale and safety.

Shakespeare, *Henry V*

He's mad that trusts in the tameness of a wolf.

Shakespeare, *King Lear*

As the bomb fell over Hiroshima and exploded, we saw an entire city disappear. I wrote in my log the words: "My God, what have we done?"

Capt. Robert Lewis, U.S. Army Air Corps, copilot of the *Enola Gay*

A world without nuclear weapons would be less stable and more dangerous for all of us.

Former British Prime Minister Margaret Thatcher

DISARMAMENT AND ARMS CONTROL

C hapter 10 discussed the use of force in international politics with a particular focus on the development and role of nuclear weapons. This much is certain about these weapons: the nuclear powers possess enough firepower to end civilization as we know it and, perhaps, even to destroy the Earth's ability to sustain life. What is uncertain is whether or not humans can agree to lay down their weapons, nuclear and otherwise, and live in peace. As the improbable parable in the next section symbolizes, humans have always armed themselves. The question is whether or not they can reverse the course of all of human history.

An Improbable Parable

Let us go back in time to the hypothetical origins of the arms race. It probably did not start exactly like this, but it might have.

The Opening Scene

It was a fine and sunny, yet somehow foreboding, autumn day many millennia ago. Og, a caveman, was searching for food near the cave of his not-too-distant neighbor Ug. It had not been a good season for hunting game or for berry and root gathering, and Og's stomach grumbled and his mind fretted about the coming winter and his family.

The same snows would come to Ug's cave, but Ug had been luckier. He had just killed a large antelope, grown fat from the summer's rich grazing. Ug, then, was feeling prosperous as he prepared to clean his kill in the clearing in the forest.

At that moment Og, hunting spear in hand, happened out of the forest and came upon Ug, who was grasping his gutting knife. They had met before, and though not friends, they had lived in peace. Indeed, it was a time when everyone lived in peace. It was not a matter of philosophy, really. It was just that life was hard, and a person's energy and weapons were devoted to hunting and to fending off the ever-marauding jackals. War had not been invented yet—but the arms race was about to begin.

Both Og and Ug were startled by their sudden meeting, but they exchanged the customary greetings of the day. Still, Ug was troubled by Og's lean and hungry look. Unconsciously, he grasped his knife more tightly. The tensing of Ug's ample muscles alarmed Og. Equally unconsciously, Og dropped his spear point to a defensive position. Fear was the common denominator. By this time, each wanted to escape the confrontation, but they were trapped. Their disengagement negotiation went something like this (translated):

Ug: You are pointing your spear at me.

Og: And your knife glints menacingly in the sunlight. But this is crazy, Ug. I mean you no harm; your antelope is yours.

Ug: Good, Og, and of course we are friends. I'll even give you a little meat. But first, why don't you put down your spear so we can talk better?

Og: A fine idea, Ug, and I'll be glad to put down my spear, but why don't you lay down that fearful knife first? Then we can be friends again.

Ug: Spears can fly through the air farther. . . . *You should be first*.

Og: Knives can strike more accurately. . . . *You should be first*.

And so the conversation in the clearing went on, with Og and Ug equally unsure of the other's intention, and with each sincerely proclaiming his peaceful purpose, but with both unable to agree on how their weapons could be laid aside.

The Continuing Drama

In one form or another that dialogue has continued since the days of our prehistoric ancestors. Popes and princes, peons and philosophers, presidents and presidium heads have all exalted peace and damned the weapons of war. We could survey the entire history of these utterings, but it will be sufficient here to consider the urgings of two recent world leaders.

George Bush: Securing a more peaceful world is . . . [my] most important priority. . . . We will not miss any opportunity to work for peace. . . . The threat and use of sophisticated weaponry threatens global security as never before. Chemical weapons must be banned from the face of the Earth, never to be used again. This won't be easy. . . . But civilization and human dignity demand that we try. And the spread of nuclear weapons must be stopped. . . . [We] must work every day against the proliferation of nuclear weapons. (Address to Congress, 2/9/89)

Mikhail Gorbachev: Never before has so terrible a threat loomed so large and dark over mankind. . . . [We must] advance toward the cherished goal, the complete elimination and prohibition of nuclear weapons for good, toward the complete removal of the threat of nuclear war. This is our firm conviction. (*WP*, 3/12/85)

Both the Americans and Soviets, then, are for peace and love—just like Og and Ug. If only the other side would be more trusting and put down its weapons first, then. . . .

Armaments: A Complex Debate

The debate over arms control and disarmament is one of the most complex and important in our time. More than for most subjects, it has been challenging to try to reduce this issue to proportions suitable for an introductory text without rendering the discussion superficial. To help establish a foundation for the discussion that follows, the reader can do several things. One is to review the types of arms and the issues about their use in chapter 10. This will help clarify the discussion of types of weapons and such concepts as deterrence. A second good idea is to review the glossary terms at the end of this book. The literature on arms is especially full of acronyms and the glossary will help you keep things straight.

Third, the reader should understand that there are many subtleties beyond the scope of this chapter. The following discussion of the pros and cons of arms-building must be read with the understanding that there are many intermediate points. Few favor the extremes of either unlimited armaments or absolute disarmament. Fourth, there are also many opinions concerning which types of arms are more destabilizing, which are offensive and which are defensive, and a host of other questions. We will certainly delve into some of these, but this chapter, and indeed all the chapters, should be seen as a starting place for, rather than a comprehensive end to, your studies.

Another complexity of the arms debate is that it must be subdivided into types of weapons; yet it should also be viewed by a unified perspective. This means, on the one hand, that different types of weapons have considerations that are particular to them. From this perspective, this chapter will group weapons into three categories: conventional (traditional), biological and chemical, and nuclear. Note that these three classifications vary somewhat from the classifications of warfare used in chapter 10. This is because the use and the nature of weapons make for slightly different categories; it also seems sensible to conform in this chapter to the classifications you are apt to see in other studies and in the press.

The unique characteristics of arms control issues associated with various types of weapons should not cloud the fact that, on the other hand, many disarmament issues are the same for all types of weapons. Hostility and suspicion both cause and are barriers to the control of all types of weapons: conventional, biological and chemical, and nuclear. Therefore, this chapter also treats, to a degree, arms as a singular phenomenon.

What is the Object of Arms Control and Disarmament?

If you think about arms control discussions you may have heard, you will find that people seldom start out with the fundamental question: what do we want arms control to accomplish? Basically, there are two possible foci. One is *the weapons themselves*. Some arms control and disarmament advocates operate on the conviction that eliminating or reducing armaments would be good in and of itself. They argue, as you will see below, that arms are destructive, expensive, and psychologically harmful even when not used. There are yet others who disagree with each of these contentions; but whatever the position, this line of argument focuses on the weapons, as such, rather than on their intent.

Security is the second possible focus. It is certainly reasonable to contend that the object of any arms program, whether acquisition or reduction, should be to *make people more secure*. Whether or not arms control, as such, will increase security is highly debatable. To a certain degree, this issue is discussed in the section below on whether or not arms cause war. There is also an intermediate question, however, about whether or not specific types of weapons increase or decrease security. For example, what is the relationship between nuclear arms and security?

The contention that nuclear arms decrease security is well known and was reviewed extensively in chapter 10's discussion of how a nuclear war might begin and what the impact of a nuclear war would be on the environment and the Earth's inhabitants. There is another view. Early in the atomic age, Winston Churchill observed that "it may be that we shall by a process of sublime irony have reached a stage . . . where safety will be the sturdy child of terror and survival the twin brother of annihilation" (Simpson, 1988:2). His point was that nuclear weapons may have made both nuclear war and large-scale conventional war between nuclear powers too dangerous to fight. If Churchill was right, then it follows that eliminating or perhaps even substantially reducing nuclear weapons levels could make war more possible and decrease security.

Whatever the merits of Churchill's contention, it does raise the important issue of the relationship between arms and security. If, in fact, the aim of arms control is to increase safety, then we need to ask whether any arms agreement or unilateral reduction, even one abolishing nuclear weapons, makes us more secure. If it does, well and good. If it does not, and we cannot just assume that it does, then the allure of arms control may be akin to the sirens on the rocks luring us into peril.

Caution About the Current Arms Control Climate

The issue of the wisdom of arms control is particularly current. The end of the East-West cold war has created the most propitious opportunity in decades to reduce arms levels, especially among the industrialized countries. The new climate has already resulted in several arms control agreements. Among others, the North American and European powers signed a far-ranging conventional forces reduction agreement in November 1990, and Presidents Bush and Gorbachev are slated to meet in Moscow in February 1991 to sign a new bilateral strategic nuclear weapons treaty, the Strategic Arms Reduction Talks (START) Treaty. Thus, for the first time since the beginning of the cold war, the escalating spiral of East-West hostility and arms increases has been reversed. There is now a de-escalating interaction of improving political relations and arms restraints.

There are few who do not welcome these changes, but the end of the cold war does not necessarily mean that a cascade of global arms agreements will follow or that national security systems can or should be dismantled. There are any number of clouds on the arms control horizon that give pause. One is that the relaxation of tensions between the two superpowers and in Europe cannot be confidently predicted to continue. The Soviet Union is in deep domestic trouble. In December 1990 President Bush announced that the United States would guarantee $1 billion in credits to allow the Soviet Union to buy food from U.S. suppliers. "Instability in the Soviet Union is very definitely not in the interest of the United States," U.S. secretary of state James Baker told reporters (*NYT,* 12/13/90:A1).

The Soviet domestic situation could affect arms talks in several ways. Gorbachev could be toppled from power by an old-guard element that is less amenable to relaxed tensions and reduced arms. It is also possible that the U.S.S.R. could totally or partially dissolve into separate countries. As Sovietologist Dimitri Simes put it, there is a "danger that the world will be confronted with the unprecedented specter of a nuclear superpower sliding into bloody chaos" (*WP,* 10/25/90:A23). That prospect is "very threatening and ominous," according to one U.S. State Department official (*LAT,* 11/22/90:A10). What would then happen to the Soviet nuclear arsenal and who would control it is unclear. The Gorbachev government is also concerned. Among other indications, it removed nuclear arms from some of the more restive republics. In

November 1990 Defense Minister Marshal Dmitri Yazov appeared on television to declare that the Soviet military would retain control of all nuclear weapons and defend themselves "with their weapons" if necessary (*WSJ*, 11/29/90:A9).

Even if Gorbachev survives in office and holds the country together, his domestic travails may so consume his energies and his political leverage that he may not have the psychological or political strength to concentrate on arms issues or to overcome dissent within his country. As one U.S. diplomatic official said of Gorbachev: "If you are totally preoccupied with the problems that you regard as affecting your immediate survival, how equipped are you going to be to face other issues? I mean, look what is on [Gorbachev's] plate: the economy is falling apart, the Baltics are seceding; he's being booed [in the streets of Moscow], and then someone comes into his office and says, 'What do you think we should do about the range issue on air-launched cruise missiles?' And he probably says, 'Leave me alone' " (*NYT*, 5/6/90:A20).

The escalation of arms outside the arena of the former East-West confrontation is a second cause for caution about the prospects for significant arms reductions and for caution about unilateral arms cuts by any country. Later in this chapter we will review the proliferation, increasing power, and increasing range of conventional, biological and chemical, and nuclear weapons and delivery systems throughout the world. Iraq's million soldiers, its chemical weapons, its intermediate-range missiles, its nuclear weapons program, and its virtually continual warfare throughout the 1980s and into the 1990s is the most dramatic, but not the only example. China, for instance, was peaceful during the 1980s, but it has approximately 300 nuclear explosive devices and intercontinental missiles to deliver them. China is also neither a part of current nuclear arms negotiations, nor is it a signatory of the 1968 (nuclear arms) Non-Proliferation Treaty. After several years of restraint on military spending, there are unsettling signs that China may seek to expand the conventional capabilities of its huge army as well. A mid-1990 article in a People's Liberation Army (the unified Chinese military service) journal called for a 250 percent increase in military spending during the 1990s. Chinese military journals also indicate a shift in PLA thinking toward a more aggressive posture. In the estimate of an expert at the University of Hong Kong, China is preparing to assert its traditional influence in Asia and the region's other countries "are scared" (*HC*, 12/13/90:A12).

The point here is that the international system is undergoing a time of significant transition. There are some positive signs about lessened tensions and arms reductions. But there are also worrisome developments, and there is no certainty that either peace or security is in the immediate future. The world remains a dangerous place, and therefore just as a country should only use its arms with prudence, so it should also only lay down its defenses with caution.

Does Military Spending Harm the Economy?

Another area of debate involves the economic impact of arms spending. The fundamental issue is whether arms spending contributes to or detracts from the economic health of the world and its individual countries. It is a truism that arms are very expensive and therefore represent a *budget burden*. World military expenditures amounted to approximately $1 trillion in 1990. It goes without saying that if these swords could truly be converted into plowshares, that if arms dollars could be redirected into schools, hospitals, economic development, and other peaceful purposes, then the human condition would improve. In particular, the cost of arms weighs heavily on less developed countries (LDCs). Their military spending was discussed in chapter 9, but suffice it to say that the $116 billion that LDCs spent on defense in 1989 is more than twice the foreign aid they received.

There is also some evidence that, in addition to consuming scarce budget resources, excessive arms spending can have a negative effect on a country's general economic health. For one thing, arms spending has a less-than-optimal impact on *employment*. Because military expenditures are in capital-intensive industries (those which require large sums of money but employ relatively few people to produce relatively few products), they create fewer jobs per dollar spent than more labor-intensive enterprises. It takes $13,208 in military spending to generate one job. Domestic expenditures, by comparison, require fewer dollars to create a single job. Construction spending, for example, produces one job for each $9,993 spent. Another way of looking at the relative impact is to say that each dollar spent on civilian construction creates 1.3 times as many jobs as an equal amount of defense spending.

There is additional evidence that a high level of defense expenditures can cause a *maldistribution of economic development*. Countries need to develop all segments of their economies in order to maintain economic health, and devoting too much effort and talent to any one segment is harmful. A key factor is the **research and development (R&D)** of new technologies and products, and the military has recently accounted for 25–35 percent of the world's total expenditures on R&D. That effort also uses the talents of 750,000 of the world's best scientists and engineers (Thee, 1987; Kurtz, 1988).

The maldistribution is greatest in those states with high military expenditures compared to GNP. The table below Figure 17.1 shows the 1987 R&D expenditures of five Western industrialized countries. The figure itself shows that total U.S. spending on R&D was a third higher than the combined R&D expenditures of France, Great Britain, Japan, and West Germany. However, U.S. military R&D was almost 4.5 times as much as the other four countries' combined military R&D, while its nondefense R&D was nearly equal to that of the other four countries. What this means, in part, is that Japan and the three European countries are spending their R&D funds on domestic infrastructure and commercial product development, which add to their ability to compete with the United States for world markets. The impact on the Soviet Union is even stronger. As noted in chapter 9, estimating the Soviet defense budget is extremely difficult, but a reasonable estimate is that Soviet military R&D is 3.25 percent of the country's GNP. That is quadruple the rate of even the United States, and is probably the majority of all Soviet R&D, and may help account for the dismal state of the Soviet economy.

Similarly, military needs may also use a disproportionate share of a country's manufacturing capacity; of its natural resources, such as oil; and of its products, such as electronic equipment. The result is that even if there is a demand for certain products and the money to buy them, they may be in short supply because the labor and resources to make them or the products themselves have been preempted by military consumption (Melman, 1986). Again, this is particularly true for the Soviet Union, where people have more rubles to spend than products to buy.

Defense spending also may *reduce spending on domestic programs*. No country has unlimited budget resources, and governments therefore often face the classic choice between guns or butter. One recent study of this effect on the U.S. budget found "fairly strong evidence for the existence of trade-offs," and concluded that "social programs clearly bear the significant brunt of defense spending increases" (Mok & Duval, 1988:31). There is similar evidence of the trade-off effect in the Soviet Union (Johnson & Wells, 1986; Blechman & Utgoff, 1987).

All of the above arguments about the negative impact of arms spending have their advocates, and all of the arguments have an element of truth. Still, they should only be

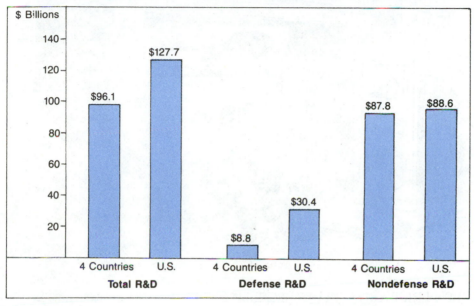

Figure 17.1   Research and Development (R&D) Spending in Five Countries

	France	Great Britain	Japan	West Germany	United States
Total R&D*	$16.4	$15.4	$41.7	$22.8	$127.7
As % of GNP	2.4	2.4	2.8	2.8	2.8
Defense R&D	$ 3.3	$ 4.0	$ 0.3	$ 1.2	$ 30.4
As % of GNP	0.6	0.6	0.03	0.2	0.8
Nondefense R&D	$13.1	$11.7	$41.4	$21.6	$ 88.6
As % of GNP	1.8	1.8	2.8	2.6	2.0

*Dollar amounts in billions.

Data source: U.S. Economic Report of the President (1990:113).

Research and development spending is important to developing both the defense and civilian sectors of a country's economy. As this figure shows, total U.S. expenditures on R&D are $31.6 billion more than four economic rivals. On just nondefense R&D, however, the United States and its competitors spend about the same amount.

accepted with caution. The relationship between defense spending and the overall economy is extremely complex, and scholars differ widely on specific impacts.

First, there is no clear evidence that lower defense expenditures necessarily lead to a reallocation of budget funds to nondefense categories. Nor is it always true that increased defense spending will lead to cuts in domestic programs. The lack of a consistent inverse relationship between changes in defense spending and domestic spending has been shown to be true in other Western industrialized countries as well as the United States (Snider & Beringer, 1990; Mintz, 1989). It is most accurate to say that defense spending may affect domestic spending, but that the impact is inconsistent, both over time and among programs. The study by Mok and Duvall (1988), for example, found that while some domestic programs, such as health and welfare, varied inversely with defense spending, other programs, such as education, were not affected. The Johnson and Wells study of the Soviet Union found parallel evidence. Housing construction and the production of durable consumer goods were affected negatively by increased defense spending, but "ideologically favored programs . . . appear to have been much less affected by marginal changes in military spending" (1986:195).

"NOW I HAVE A <u>STEALTH PAYCHECK</u>....IT DOESN'T SHOW UP IN MY BANK ACCOUNT!"

There is a vigorous debate over the impact of defense spending on domestic spending and on a country's overall economic health. Many analysts believe that defense spending is less of a stimulant to the economy than nondefense spending and saps money needed for domestic programs. Others disagree. Whatever the long-term effects, the conversion from defense to nondefense spending causes short-term hardships to many of the workers involved in defense production. In January 1991 the U.S. Defense Department ordered cancellation of the Navy's A-12 Stealth attack bomber, which would have cost $57 billion for 620 aircraft. As a result McDonnell Aircraft began to lay off 5,000 workers, mostly in St. Louis, and General Dynamics announced it would dismiss 4,000 employees in Fort Worth and Tulsa. The number of B-2 bombers the Air Force can procure has been cut, and there is a move to end production of the B-2 Stealth bomber altogether. That move may be wise nationally, but it will surely cost more workers their jobs as well.

Second, because defense and nondefense expenditures are not always related, the associated job issue is complex. It may well be that $1 billion spent on defense creates only 75,710 jobs, while a similar amount spent on construction creates 100,070 jobs. Nevertheless, each billion dollars cut from defense spending does not mean an added billion dollars for construction spending. Therefore, at least in the short term, defense spending stimulates the economy, while defense reductions cause a slowing of the economy and economic dislocation for defense workers. The U.S. Arms Control and Disarmament Agency (ACDA), for example, studied the impact of a 2 percent yearly reduction in U.S. defense spending over each of five years, for a total $56-billion reduction. Depending on whether it considered just immediate defense workers or the ripple effect (almost a triple effect if you include those whose jobs are dependent on spending by defense workers), ACDA concluded that between 135,000 and 340,000 jobs would be lost by the cuts. The agency determined, based on its preference for the lower figure as the truer standard, that "although individual firms and some localities could suffer, the impact of reductions in defense spending on jobs nationally will be minimal" (*HC,* 10/14/90:A18). Be that as it may, it will not console or feed the workers affected by the 1989 announced layoffs of such U.S. defense contractors as Lockheed (8,000),

Hughes Aircraft (7,000), General Electric Aerospace and Rockwell International (4,000 each), and Grumman and Northrop (3,000 each).

Third, many argue that there is a spillover effect from military programs to civilian economic development. While it is true, for instance, that a high percentage of all American aeronautical engineers work primarily on national defense, the technologies they develop benefit the commercial aircraft industry. Military technology is often useful only for defense, but there are some transferred benefits.

Do Arms Races Really Happen?

Another indictment of military spending is that it creates fear in other countries, causing them to buy more arms, thus setting off an arms race. This contention seems obvious, and, indeed, there is some evidence that, in some specific cases, it is true. Further, the level of the other side's arms expenditures can be used as a powerful political argument to increase military spending, even if it is not the direct cause of your expenditures (Ostrom & Marra, 1986).

As an overall phenomenon, however, the arms-race model has not been supported by social science research. Instead, technological changes, bureaucratic pressures, domestic politics, economic trends, and a variety of other factors also are related to the level of arms expenditures (Nincic, 1983). The general state of U.S.–Soviet relations also affects U.S. arms spending, as does the overall international political climate (Zuk & Woodbury, 1986).

Do Arms Cause War?

The term "arms race" has become such a common part of our lexicon that there is a widespread acceptance of the notion that acquiring arms stimulates your opponent to acquire arms, causing you to get even more arms, and so on in an upward spiral. It is further assumed by many that this reciprocal and escalating arms buildup causes increasing tension that leads to war. This is represented by Theory A in Figure 17.2.

There can be little doubt that arms both create a possibility of war and help create a climate of hostility and anxiety that is fertile ground for war. But, again, the relationship is complex. Arms may instead be amassed because of war-producing tension.

Many decisionmakers and social scientists argue that weapons are necessary for survival in a predatory world. As Hans Morgenthau (1973:398) once put it, "Men do not fight because they have arms. They have arms because they . . . fight." If wars occur because humans are violence-prone, or if even some humans and countries are aggressive, then arms are necessary. Indeed, the statement of then-British prime minister Thatcher in the quote beginning this chapter shows that she, like others, believes that arms can also be counted as a deterrent factor in preserving the peace. This logic suspects that disarmament might create instability or tempt aggressors, thus actually increasing the likelihood of war (Intriligator & Brito, 1984). If this line of reasoning is correct, then both arms and war may be the result of tension, as depicted in Theory B of Figure 17.2.

The most probable answer lies in a combination of these theories. What we can say, then, is that tension, arms, and violent conflict are interrelated. No one would deny that arms races are dangerous and that they might sometimes lead to war, but there is also no good evidence that arms directly and consistently cause wars (Morrow, 1989). Instead, arms, tension, and wars all promote one another, as represented in Theory C of Figure 17.2.

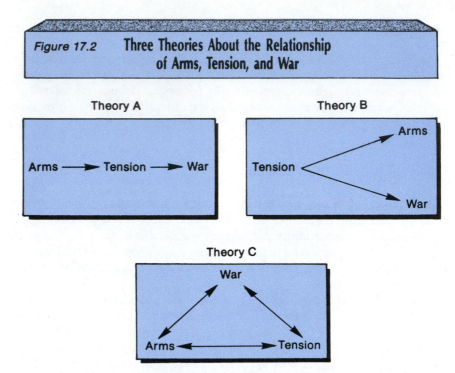

Theory A fits the idealist view of the causal relationship between arms, tension, and use. Theory B approximates the realist view. Theory C suggests that there is a complex causal interrelationship between arms, tension, and war in which each of the three factors affects the other two.

Are the Armament Stockpiles Dangerous?

When weapons are used in warfare it is tautological to point out that they are socially destructive. What is at issue here, though, is whether or not their mere existence is dangerous. Physical health issues are one aspect of this question. There can be little doubt that accidents with weapons have caused injury and death or that there is the potential for serious problems. Chapter 10 discusses the possibility of a nuclear weapons accident. The chance of a nuclear detonation is negligible; there is a higher possibility for a lethal radiation leak. According to one report, for example, 50 nuclear warheads and 9 nuclear reactors are lying on the ocean floor as a result of various naval accidents (Arkin & Handler, 1989). There is also radiation danger from the waste products of plutonium production for nuclear weapons and from testing those weapons. The Soviets have pumped waste from their Chelyabinsk nuclear warhead production facility into Karachay Lake, 900 miles east of Moscow. Now the lake is more than twice as radioactive as was the Chernobyl nuclear power plant when its reactor exploded in 1986. The Soviets have established what they euphemistically call a "sanitary alienation zone" around the lake, because standing at what one scientist called "the most polluted spot on the planet" for just one hour could be lethal (*NYT,* 8/16/90:A3). In a parallel closing, the U.S. government announced in October 1990 that its sole weapons-grade plutonium processing plant, at Hanford, Washington (which had been closed since 1988 due to environmental and health concerns and protests) would remain closed for at least another two years.

This tearful national guardsman on his way to Operation Desert Storm, and his son, who is about to be left behind, put a human face on the statistics about weapons proliferation and the conflicts that sometimes result. When you ponder the complex data in this book remember that, in the end, the numbers affect human beings and how well or poorly—and even if—they live.

Soviet citizens are also beginning to protest. Those near the main Soviet nuclear weapons test ground at Semipalatinsk, Kazakhstan, claim they have been poisoned by leaks. Their protests, followed by a national investigation, have persuaded Moscow to announce that the site will be closed by 1993 in response to what the Tass news agency described as the "extremely tense . . . socio-psychological atmosphere in Semi-palatinsk" (*WP,* 3/10/90:A1). Biological and chemical weapons also pose hazards. There are persistent reports, vehemently denied by Washington, that a good part of the U.S. chemical weapons stockpile is dangerously deteriorating. Even more alarming, there are reports that an accident at an alleged Soviet storage site for anthrax near Sverdlovsk caused an epidemic that claimed many lives (SIPRI, 1990:130).

Another indictment of the massive amount of arms, especially nuclear arms, in the world inventory is that they are psychologically damaging. A number of studies have concluded that children suffer anxiety because of their awareness of the nuclear threat. One of these studies found that most American and Soviet children thought that nuclear war would or might occur. In the event of a nuclear war, only 16.4 percent of American children and 2.7 percent of Soviet children thought they and their families would survive. Not all scholars agree with this psychological-damage argument, however. Lester Kurtz (1988:33) cites several studies that dismiss claims of children's anxiety as "sentimental balderdash."

Also, if we return to the idea discussed earlier that the object of arms control and disarmament should be to increase security, then it is arguable that getting rid of nuclear weapons might make people less secure, actually and psychologically. It may also be that the decline in East-West political tensions will decrease fear of a nuclear holocaust, even if there is not a concomitant reduction in the weapons themselves.

Approaches to Controlling Weapons

Whatever the actual merits of the arguments for and against arms, the quest for control is virtually as old as weapons themselves. This search has, through history, taken a number of varied approaches to arms control. Roughly proceeding from the most to the least comprehensive, these approaches can be subdivided into efforts to disarm, to reduce arsenals of existing weapons, to prevent the development/deployment of new weapons, and to limit arms transfers. One representation of this range can be seen in Figure 17.3. The current status of efforts along each of these approaches for conventional, biological and chemical, and nuclear weapons will be detailed later in this chapter. It should be noted that the various approaches we are about to survey are not mutually exclusive. To the contrary, they may be pursued simultaneously and may reinforce one another.

Disarmament

The most sweeping approach to arms control is to simply disarm. **General and complete disarmament (GCD)** might be accomplished either through unilateral disarmament or through multilateral negotiated disarmament.

In the case of *unilateral disarmament*, a country would dismantle its arms. Its safety, in theory, would be secured by its nonthreatening posture, which would prevent aggression, and its example would lead other countries to disarm also. Unilateral disarmament draws heavily on the idea of pacifism, or a moral and resolute refusal to fight. The unilateral approach also relies on the belief that it is arms that cause tension rather than vice versa.

503

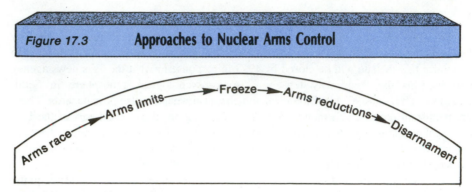

Figure 17.3   **Approaches to Nuclear Arms Control**

Data source: Based on a model provided by Abbott A. Brayton, assistant dean and professor, East Tennessee State University.

Possible reactions to the issue of arms and the future range from an escalatory arms race, through a freeze at current arms levels, to general and complete disarmament.

Negotiated disarmament between two or more countries is a somewhat more conservative approach. Advocates of this path to peace share the unilateralists' conviction about the danger of war, but they are less likely to be true pacifists, and they believe one-sided disarmament would expose the peace pioneer to unacceptable risk.

The GCD approach has few strong advocates among today's political leaders. Even those who do subscribe to the ideal tend to search for intermediate arms limitation steps. Still, the quest goes on. The UN Disarmament Committee has called for GCD, and the "ideal" is often valuable as a standard to measure the unacceptability of the "real."

An alternative approach to GCD can be termed *categorical disarmament*. This means eliminating certain classes of weapons. There has been great progress toward eliminating biological weapons altogether. The 1925 Geneva Protocol banning the use of gas or biological weapons was signed by 125 countries, including all those with any foreseeable ability to produce them. The 1975 Biological Weapons Convention banning their production or possession was signed by 112 countries including every current possible producer except Israel. Reports of the possession or even use of biological agents have occasionally surfaced, but there are no confirmed cases of use. Chemical weapons are relatively widespread, but there is a strong current effort to eliminate them also.

Arms Reductions

A second approach to arms control is to reduce the number and types of weapons in existing inventories. This alternative is one of the main thrusts of many contemporary arms control efforts. Advocates of this approach argue that the level of existing arms is so dangerous that the mere limitation of new arms is not enough. It was this view that led President Reagan to relabel U.S.–Soviet strategic negotiations as the Strategic Arms Reduction Talks (**START**) instead of Strategic Arms Limitations Talks (SALT). Washington and Moscow expect to sign a START treaty soon, and talks on reducing the conventional forces in Europe (CFE) resulted in an October 1990 agreement to reduce these forces as well.

Within the general goal of arms reductions, there are a number of different possible

TABLE 17.1

INF Treaty Reductions[1]

Missile	Number	Range[2] (km)	Warheads	Total Warheads
United States				
Pershing II	234	1,800	1	234
Tomahawk GLCM	443	2,500	1	443
Pershing IA	169	700	1	169
	846			846
Soviet Union				
SS-20	654	5,000	3	1,962
SS-23	239	500	1	239
SS-4	149	1,900	1	149
SS-22/12[3]	718	925	1	718
SS-5	6	1,200	1	6
	1,766			3,074

[1] Some of these missiles were in storage, having become antiquated. Others had not yet been deployed.

[2] Technically, the missiles are divided into two classes: those with a 1,000–5,500-km range, and those with a 500–999-km range.

[3] The SS-22 is a newer version of the SS-12. Range data is for the SS-22.

Data sources: Bulletin of the Atomic Scientists (7/90:48); SIPRI (1990:449); Turner (1990).

The number of missiles and warheads that will be taken out of service, and in many cases destroyed, as a result of the Intermediate-range Nuclear Forces treaty are important, but not as significant as the fact that for the first time the two superpowers have agreed to eliminate an entire class of weapons (intermediate-range missiles) from their nuclear inventories.

approaches. These include: absolute reductions, a build-down, and geographic reductions.

Absolute reductions, that is, reducing the number of existing weapons while building no new weapons, is one possibility. There are a few who advocate unilateral arms reductions with the idea that this would not only break the upward arms spiral but would also be a sign of good faith that could start a downward arms-reduction spiral. In 1969, for example, President Nixon announced that the United States was renouncing the possible use of biological warfare and unilaterally destroying its bacteriological weapons.

Proposals for negotiated reductions are a more common approach to arms control, with the START talks serving as a good example. Until recently, however, the goal of actually reducing the nuclear inventories had proved elusive, and arms treaties primarily limited future growth. Then in mid-1988 the United States and the Soviet Union ratified the Intermediate-range Nuclear Forces (INF) Treaty, which eliminated an entire class of nuclear delivery vehicles, those missiles with an intermediate range between 500 and 5,500 km. The specific reductions are detailed in Table 17.1.

A variation on absolute reductions proposed by the United States in the early 1980s was based on the *build-down* concept. The basic idea was that for each new nuclear weapon a country built, it would have to dismantle two or more older weapons. This idea has a great deal of surface attractiveness, but this fades with the realization that many new weapons are more than twice as powerful as old weapons and more accurate as well. Therefore, numbers might decline, but destructiveness would increase.

Geographic reductions are another variant on arms reduction and are aimed at scaling down forces in a particular area. There have been proposals, for example, to "denuclearize" Europe completely. There have also been proposals to reduce types of weapons in limited areas and the 1987 INF Treaty is an example of what is possible.

Arms Limits

By far the most common approach to arms control has been trying to limit the development and **deployment** of future weapons systems. The advantage of this is that it avoids the difficulties of scrapping existing systems. Both the Salt I and Salt II treaties took this approach. The disadvantage, of course, is that it leaves an awesomely dangerous mountain of arms in place. Most would agree, however, that while putting a cap on a stockpile is not as good as reducing it, limits are better than unfettered arms building. Figure 17.4 shows three alternatives: no caps, caps (SALT II), and reductions (START). The Soviet Union's strategic arsenal is used as an example, but the concept would be the same for any country's weapons or any type of weapons system.

Like reductions, limits are usually attempted through negotiations, but they are also possible through unilateral action. In a speech to the UN General Assembly in December 1988, President Gorbachev announced that the Soviet Union would unilaterally cut 500,000 troops from its forces by 1991 and withdraw a significant amount of military hardware from Eastern Europe and deploy it east of the Ural Mountains, which separate Europe from Asia. This was followed by announcements of unilateral force reductions by other Warsaw Treaty Organization countries that cut another 146,300 WTO troops. There were also announcements of cuts in hardware. Because some of the equipment was redeployed, the cuts were regional instead of absolute, but between the WTO frontier with NATO and the Urals the cuts amounted to approximately 15,000 tanks, 9,000 artillery pieces, and 900 aircraft. This helped pave the way for the extensive October 1990 CFE agreement.

The idea of a **nuclear freeze** is one approach to arms limitation that enjoys considerable popular support in the United States, in Western Europe, and elsewhere. At its center, the nuclear freeze movement advocates an immediate halt to the development, production, transfer, and deployment of all nuclear weapons and delivery systems. Beyond this point, the movement diverges. Some advocate a unilateral U.S. freeze, at least temporarily, as a "confidence-building measure" that will break the arms-race spiral and encourage the Soviets and others to follow suit. Others call for a "mutual and verifiable" freeze that either could be negotiated or could result from parallel policies of restraint by the nuclear powers. Critics of a nuclear freeze argue that unilateral restraint would only encourage the Soviets by showing weakness, that it would lock in a claimed Soviet advantage in strategic weapons, and that it would eliminate most of the incentive for more meaningful arms reduction talks.

There are a number of possible ways to limit new weapons, including restrictions on research and development, testing, deployment, number of weapons, and military budgets. Some of these approaches are also appropriate for arms reductions.

Research and Development   One way to avoid new weapons is to practice a sort of military birth control that would ensure that weapons systems never begin their gestation period of research and development, R&D. The advantage of this approach is that it

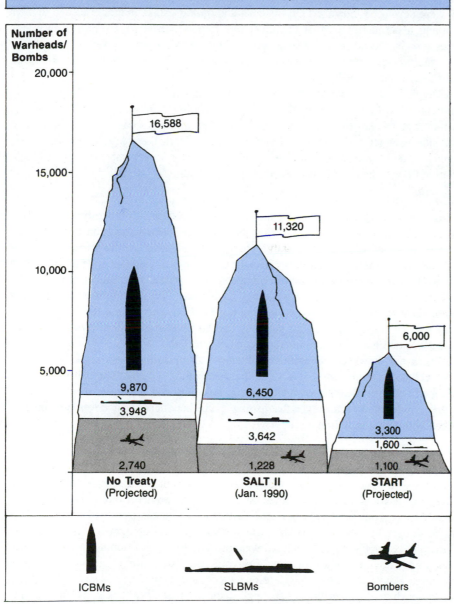

Figure 17.4 The Mountain of Nuclear Weapons in the U.S.S.R. The Scenarios for the Numbers of Soviet Strategic Nuclear Warheads and Bombs: No Treaty, SALT II, START*

*The figures for unrestrained building and for START are conjectures based on the listed data sources and the references therein. START counting rules understate the actual number of explosive devices that are likely to be deployed. SALT II was unratified, but generally observed by the contracting parties. Counting rules for START will increase the actual number of bomber devices available.

Data sources: Panofsky (1986); SIPRI (1990); Perkins (1991).

Three alternatives for nuclear weapons building are lack of treaty restraints, agreed limits, and agreed reductions. Each has a different impact on the height of the nuclear arms stockpile mountain, as can be seen in this figure.

stops a specific area of the arms race before it starts. Once R&D begins, there is a pressure on the other side to match it. Moreover, R&D initiates an arms acquisition momentum that is hard to stop because the military is reluctant to give up a weapon that is in its inventory—even experimentally. There are several U.S. systems, such as the cruise missile, that were begun as a potential "bargaining chip" with the Soviets. Once they were developed, however, the financial and military stake in them resulted in their becoming a permanent part of the inventory rather than being bargained away for concessions by the other side (Carnesale & Haass, 1987; Einhorn, 1985). In fact, the small, multiple-use cruise missiles have become one of the most contentious issues in U.S.–Soviet arms negotiations.

The difficulty in applying brakes to R&D comes from two hard-to-deny counter-arguments. The first is that R&D is not really adding arms but just seeing what is possible. The second, more potent contention is that if R&D funds are not granted, the other side may get a quantum lead and advantage. Both these arguments have been strongly made by the Reagan and Bush administrations to sell the Strategic Defense Initiative (SDI). Thus, R&D is persuasively portrayed as a "modest down-payment on the future."

Testing   A second point at which weapons can be restrained is in the testing stage. This is technically part of R&D, but it comes at the critical point when a system comes off the drawing board and is actually tried out. Restraints on testing can be effective, even if R&D has proceeded to that point, because the technological complexity of most modern weapons systems means that if they are untested their reliability is highly questionable. Countries would be prone to keep what they have rather than develop new, destabilizing weapons that are unknown. Given this, the Soviets have argued that the United States cannot test the SDI system without violating the Anti-Ballistic Missile (ABM) Treaty of 1972, a position that U.S. administrations have rejected.

There are, however, numerous problems with and objections to testing limits. These include the arguments that other evaluation methods (such as simulation) could be developed; that **verification** of nontesting is difficult; that testing is needed to keep existing arms up to date; and even that testing can be beneficial, as in developing nuclear devices with lower radiation.

Deployment   The next stage at which arms can be limited is at deployment. This approach would restrict the combat-ready positioning of weapons systems. The 1972 ABM treaty, for example, banned the further deployment of existing U.S. and Soviet antiballistic missiles. Both the United States and the Soviet Union have developed antisatellite weapons but have not deployed them. Limits can also apply to total arms bans in geographic areas, as is the case in Antarctica. Deployment limitations can additionally be applied to conventional weapons and to the positioning of conventional forces. Restrictions on the deployment of Egyptian and Israeli troops and weapons in the buffer area east of the Suez Canal are one successful example.

Although deployment limits can work, their greatest drawback is that they create the potential for dangerous violation. Nuclear missiles are increasingly mobile, and airlift and mechanization capabilities allow rapid redeployment of conventional forces. Thus, should one side choose to reintroduce its arms rapidly into an area, it would create a highly unstable and explosive atmosphere as its alarmed opponents rushed to reposition their defenses to meet the threat.

Numerical Limits   By far the most common approach to arms control limitations and reductions is to specify the number or capacity of weapons and/or troops that each side may possess. Both **SALT I** and **SALT II** relied heavily on this approach to cap future expansion rather than to reduce existing levels. Now, the START and CFE talks have taken the same approach to reducing strategic and nuclear forces.

The attraction of numerical limits lies in their seeming simplicity. The attempts, however, usually engender complex questions of what to count and how to equate different types of systems. Numerical restrictions alone also do not prevent the development and deployment of classes of weapons, and it is relatively simple to escalate numbers at a later date if tensions increase.

Budgetary Limits   Another possible approach to arms control would be to control military spending rather than weapons as such. Limiting arms by an international agreement to limit military spending has not been seriously attempted. Its advantage is that it might avoid any existing counting and verification problems by letting each country structure its armed forces subject only to monetary limitations. Spending might, for example, be limited to a per capita dollar figure or to a percentage of GNP.

There are, of course, substantial problems in determining and equating military budgets, as we saw in chapter 10. Different formulas would also tend to favor one group or another. A GNP–based formula would, for example, favor rich countries, and a per capita plan might eventually leave China stronger than the United States and the Soviet Union combined. But acceptable combinations, such as per capita or GNP base, whichever is lower, might be found.

Unilateral budget restraints, however, are having an important impact on arms limitations. The interacting factors of the high cost of weapons, improved East-West relations, and the domestic economic difficulties of the Soviet Union, the United States, and other countries are all serving to limit the development and deployment of new weapon systems and, in some cases, even to reduce existing military inventories. President Gorbachev told the Soviet legislature in 1989 that by 1991 annual defense spending would be cut 14 percent from its 1989 level. This would also be 40 percent below the annual projected spending under the most recent five-year projection (1986–1990).

Cuts in the United States' military spending are less dramatic, and were partially stalled by the Middle East crisis. Nonetheless, restraints are significant. A number of weapons programs including SDI, the B-2 bomber, and nuclear aircraft carriers and submarines have been slowed by budget cuts. As it stands, the Bush administration's projections through 1994 call for that year's defense expenditures to decline from 1989 levels by approximately 16 percent in real (uninflated, 1989) dollars, by about 5 percent of the federal budget, and by about 2 percent of the GNP. Congress cut the president's FY 1991 defense budget request by 6 percent and may well cut the requests of future administrations. Therefore the extent of reductions in U.S. defense spending are likely to be greater than the projections of administrations.

Limits on Arms Transfers

Global arms control can also be accomplished through unilateral or negotiated limits on buying, selling, or giving weapons or the technology to create weapons to other countries. The term **nonproliferation** commonly refers to the practice of nuclear-capable countries withholding nuclear weapons, material, or technology from non-nuclear-capable countries. It also means that non–nuclear-capable countries should or will not acquire nuclear weapons. In a broader sense, nonproliferation refers to the expansion of weapons capability at any level (nuclear, biological and chemical, and conventional), especially through foreign help.

Nuclear Weapons Proliferation

The first thing to be said about nuclear nonproliferation is that it continues to occur. Less than 50 years ago there were no countries with nuclear arms. Now the United States, the Soviet Union, China, France, and the United Kingdom all have acknowledged nuclear weapons inventories. Israel and India almost certainly also have nuclear weapons, although they refuse to admit it. Many experts believe that South Africa and Pakistan also probably have nuclear weapons. There are several other countries with current or recently active programs that have nuclear weapons potential. There are also many industrialized countries that could build nuclear weapons quickly. There is concern that the end of the cold war could have the ironic impact of destabilizing Europe and pressing nonnuclear countries there to develop weapons (Spector, 1990). The spread of nuclear weapons is shown in Figure 17.5.

Most observers agree that nuclear proliferation is dangerous. The more nuclear countries and nuclear weapons that there are, the greater is the chance of a nuclear weapons accident, of terrorists seizing or being given a weapon, and of an unstable leader having a nuclear weapon to use. The greatest concern is that the proliferation of nuclear weapons increases the possibility that two countries armed with them will be at war. There are, in 1991, renewed tensions between India and Pakistan, and the two have fought several wars since their independence after World War II. Any new conflict might be fought with nuclear weapons. So might a future Arab-Israeli war. Israel is alarmed by the prospect of Iraq acquiring nuclear weapons. Israeli jets bombed an Iraqi nuclear reactor in 1981 to prevent the building of such weapons and the United States and other countries bombed them again in 1991. But Iraq's program has recovered from the 1981 strike and by the time of the 1991 attacks was within a few years of creating nuclear

One way to control arms is to limit the transfers of arms from weapons producers to weapons buyers. The Non-Proliferation Treaty has had some success in restraining the spread of nuclear weapons, but little has been done to limit the massive trade in conventional arms, which amounts to over $40 billon annually. Countries in which arms are made, and companies who manufacture arms, do not usually accept responsibility for the ways in which their weapons are used. Ironically, many coalition countries involved in the Operation Desert Storm attack on Iraq had to face weapons systems that they had earlier sold to Iraq or that had been sold to Iraq by intermediaries.

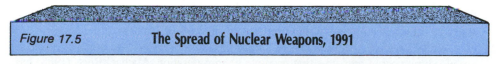

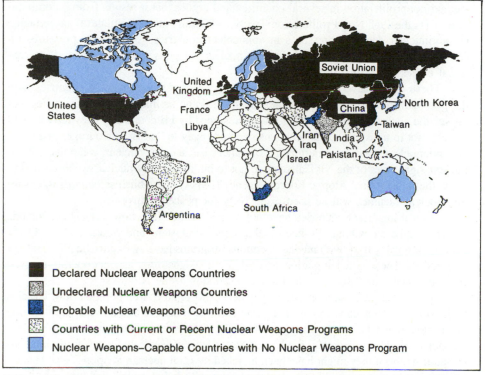

Figure 17.5 The Spread of Nuclear Weapons, 1991

■ Declared Nuclear Weapons Countries

▨ Undeclared Nuclear Weapons Countries

▨ Probable Nuclear Weapons Countries

▨ Countries with Current or Recent Nuclear Weapons Programs

▨ Nuclear Weapons–Capable Countries with No Nuclear Weapons Program

Data sources: Author's evaluation based on SIPRI (1990); various reports by the Carnegie Endowment for International Peace; Spector (1990); and press reports.

It is probable that nine countries now have nuclear weapons. Undeclared and probable nuclear countries (and their possible arsenals) are Israel (50–200), India (40–80), Pakistan (5–10), and South Africa (15–25). Arsenal counts may include weapons that could be quickly assembled from existing components and fissionable material.

weapons that could have been carried on the ballistic missiles it also had acquired. Saddam Hussein vowed, "By God, we will make fire eat up half of Israel" if it again attacks Iraq (*WP,* 4/4/90:A35). Israel has its own fire, though, and Prime Minister Yitzhak Shamir retorted that his country will know how to "defeat the evil designs of its enemies" (*Time,* 4/30/90:50). The events of Operation Desert Storm in January 1991 surely forestalled the day of possible nuclear war in the Middle East, but countries recover, new weapons programs are launched, and progress for good or ill eventually resumes.

Not all analysts agree, however, that nuclear proliferation increases the chances of war. Some maintain that safety will be increased by creating a nuclear checkmate system (Clark, 1986), although as another study pointed out, it is not the question of proliferation as such, but rather the viability of the concept of deterrence that determines whether nuclear proliferation is dangerous or not (Berkowitz, 1985). Another approach contends that deterrence has brought about peace among the superpowers and that Third World countries that might acquire nuclear weapons are no less responsible than the states that already have them (Subrahmanyam, 1986). These arguments may be true; but they are based on greater faith in the rationality of humans, whether in industrialized states or LDCs, than seems warranted by human political history.

While the forces that promote the spread of nuclear weapons are of concern, there are also a number of pressures that promote nonproliferation. Michael Reiss (1988) has studied nonproliferation in several countries and argues that it results from a combination of (1) the 1968 Non-Proliferation Treaty (NPT) and other multilateral agreements, (2) antinuclear domestic pressures in nonnuclear countries, (3) bilateral pressures on countries suspected of seeking to develop nuclear weapons, and (4) a general international consensus against proliferation.

These efforts have been successful in the sense that there are more countries with the potential to build weapons that refrain from doing so than there are countries that pursue the nuclear option. The NPT has been signed by 141 countries. They have agreed thereby not to transfer nuclear weapons or in any way to "assist, encourage, or induce any nonnuclear state to manufacture or otherwise acquire nuclear weapons." Nonnuclear signatories of the NPT also agree not to build or accept nuclear weapons and to allow the International Atomic Energy Agency (IAEA) to establish safeguards to ensure that nuclear facilities will be used exclusively for peaceful purposes.

Several important countries have not agreed to the NPT, however. These include Argentina, Brazil, China, France, India, Israel, Pakistan, and South Africa. Other countries, notably Iraq, with nuclear weapons programs have agreed to the NPT but not honored it. There is a temptation to criticize nonsignatories as uncooperative, even renegade, states, but there are legitimate objections to the NPT.

One is reasonable national security concerns. From the Arab point of view, Israel is both hostile and a nuclear threat. The Arab states also believe that powers from outside the region might be less willing to intervene if they faced Arab-controlled nuclear weapons. Would, for example, the United States have concentrated a half million troops in Saudi Arabia if they might have been attacked by Iraqi nuclear weapons? Or consider Pakistan. It borders on and has had several wars with India, which also has eight times Pakistan's population. India's nuclear weapons would make any future confrontation even more lopsided. If you were the prime minister of Pakistan, what would you do?

The NPT also sparks political sensitivities in some Third World countries. The United States, for example, has applied heavy pressure on Pakistan not to develop nuclear weapons; in October 1990 Washington cut off $582 million in foreign aid to Pakistan. The Pakistanis were hardly chastened. They accused the United States of interfering with their internal affairs, and the press called the U.S. ambassador a "viceroy" and used words like "big brother," "imperialism," "blackmail," and "exploitation" to characterize the U.S. stance. Muslim Pakistanis and others of that faith also condemn U.S. policy as part of a "Zionist conspiracy"; they resent Washington's pressure on Pakistan while remaining silent on Israel's nuclear weapons and sending billions in foreign aid to that country.

Many nonnuclear countries in the Third World are also suspicious that the NPT is mostly designed to ensure that a few countries retain a nuclear monopoly to lord over small countries. The attitudes of Brazil and Argentina provide an interesting example. In late 1990, Brazil's new president, Fernando Collor de Mello disclosed that Brazil's military had been pursuing a nuclear weapons program since the 1970s. Collor ordered the program halted and, symbolically, shoveled dirt into a 1,050-foot test shaft. Collor then met with Argentina's president Carlos Menem, and the two signed a pact forswearing building or using nuclear weapons and providing for inspection team exchanges. Still, both countries continue to refuse to sign the NPT. A Brazilian foreign ministry spokesman characterized the NPT as "an unjust instrument" (*Time,*

The Kanupp nuclear reactor near Karachi, Pakistan, helps that country produce weapons-grade uranium. Pakistan either already has or is about to acquire nuclear weapons, according to various estimates. In either case, nuclear weapons proliferation coupled with the proliferation of ballistic missile capability is an alarming reality.

10/22/90:46), and a diplomat from Argentina labeled the NPT discriminatory because "under the treaty, countries who have nuclear weapons are prohibiting others from having them" (*WSJ*, 11/29/90:A9).

Thus, the problem of nuclear proliferation continues. The NPT has had some positive impact. It must be extended in 1995, however, and some observers expect that there will be considerable controversy about its future. Third World countries, in particular, are apt to demand that renewal be linked with a deadline for complete global nuclear disarmament (Pilat & Pendley, 1990; Müller, 1990).

Chemical Weapons Proliferation

There are repeated reports of countries possessing and even using chemical weapons, and a recent independent study (SIPRI, 1990) makes reference to 17 countries that have or are alleged to have chemical weapons. The institute hastens to point out, though, that most countries deny the charges, rendering the situation "very unclear" and leaving SIPRI (1990:112) unable to "judge the accuracy of information." It is true that only the United States, the Soviet Union, and Iraq have ever admitted to having chemical weapons, yet SIPRI's caution somewhat obscures the fact that an increasing number of countries have chemical weapons, and those weapons are ever more deadly. There have also been confirmed chemical attacks, including the attack of March 1988 when Iraq unleashed mustard and cyanide gases on its own Kurdish citizens in the town of Halabja.

The gas attacks on Halabja and elsewhere, the chemical warfare used during the Iran-Iraq war, the alleged construction of a chemical weapons plant in Libya, and other concerns about the proliferation of chemical weapons sparked the January 1989 Conference on the Prohibition of Chemical Weapons, held in Paris. The conference illustrates some of the gap between the rhetorical support for and the political difficulty of controlling chemical weapons. The 149 countries represented at Paris promised not to use chemical weapons; to condemn their use; and to work toward a binding agreement prohibiting the development, production, stockpiling, or use of such weapons. Accomplishing that end will be difficult.

Some of the causes of the proliferation of chemical weapons are the same that foster nuclear proliferation. There are some Third World countries that view chemical weapons as a way to balance the nuclear weapons of other countries. Arab nations at the Paris conference objected to pressure on them to give up chemical weapons without a parallel effort to have Israel give up its nuclear weapons. The final Paris document spoke of "complete disarmament under effective international control," but that goal is not in sight. The general sense of discrimination the smaller countries feel on this issue can be sensed from the view of India's delegate. "We can't accept the principle that chemical weapons are safe in some hands but not in others. It is too much for a nation to say they are the only responsible power in the world, and others are irresponsible," he said, without directly naming the United States or the Soviet Union (*HC,* 1/12/89:A1).

There are other significant difficulties. The Soviet Union and the United States have agreed to eliminate the bulk of their chemical weapons inventories. In September 1989 the major industrialized countries, which account for 95 percent of all chemical production, also agreed to exercise caution in the export of 50 chemicals. Unfortunately, these steps are offset, at least somewhat, by illegal exports, by the development of new, superlethal toxic substances, and by the increasing availability of the knowledge and technology to create them. One of the new horrors is perfluoroisobutene. It is a choking gas that causes pulmonary edema (the lungs fill with fluid). The chemical is clear and odorless and therefore hard to detect, has a toxic effect when dispersed in the minute level of 1000 mg min/m^3, may be able to penetrate any existing protective gear, and can be formed from the same chemical (polytetrafluoroethene) used to make nonstick frying pans (Lundin, 1990).

Conventional Weapons Proliferation

The proliferation of conventional weapons can be measured in quantity and capability. The international flow of arms, especially into the Third World, is discussed in chapter 11 on pages 310–311; you might wish to review them. The fundamental point is that the magnitude of the international weapons trade is huge.

Even more alarming than the volume of the arms flow is the escalating power of the weapons being sold to and being developed indigenously by countries around the globe. Between 1985 and 1989, the U.S.S.R. and U.S. arms exports accounted for 69 percent of all world arms exports and 64 percent of the total arms exports to the Third World (SIPRI, 1990:220). The scope of conventional weapons proliferation defies easy discussion in the confines here, so we will concentrate on one aspect that has the possibility for the most devastating consequences. That is long-range missile proliferation.

The development or purchase of long-range, in some cases ballistic, missiles is increasing the ability of many countries to deliver conventional, chemical, and nuclear warheads to distant points. This increased range is alarming, even if it is only coupled with conventional warheads, because of the development of conventional explosive power, such as the fuel-air explosives discussed in chapter 10. Adding to the danger, several countries have developed or are developing space-launch vehicles (SLVs). These have a high throw-weight, the carrying capacity for a satellite—or a nuclear warhead (Hackett, 1990). In May 1989, for example, India (which already has nuclear weapons) launched the Agni (Sanskrit for fire) rocket with a one-ton payload. "Agni is not a weapons system," but an SLV, then–prime minister Rajiv Gandhi claimed. "However, the technologies proved in Agni are deeply significant for evolving national security options," he added ominously for all within Agni's range, which extends from Hong Kong to Iran on an east-west axis and from Kazakhstan to Malaysia on a north-south axis, if fired from the center of India (*HC*, 5/23/89:A12). As one indication of the degree of proliferation, Aaron Karp's (1990) analysis of weapons developments in 1989 discusses 26 countries (not including the major nuclear and industrial powers); it takes him six pages simply to list the countries and the various missiles they have bought, developed, are working on, or are planning. Fifteen of the 26 countries have or intend to get ballistic missiles with ranges over 1,000 km, and 4 (Brazil, India, Iraq, and Israel) are developing intercontinental ballistic missiles (5,500+ km).

Current efforts to restrain long-range missile proliferation center on an informal 1987 agreement among the Group of Seven (G-7) to prohibit the export of ballistic missiles and related technology. This understanding has been styled the Missile Technology Control Regime (MTCR). This is a start, but as Karp (1990:376) laconically asks, is MTCR "too little, too late?" Whether it is too late is not clear, but it surely is too little. Implementing the idea is difficult because supplier countries are under pressure from domestic economic interests to export components. Supplier countries also may wish to arm smaller allies or, at least, not to offend them. Also, even if they are not suppliers themselves, some major powers are also reluctant to offend or place sanctions on allied countries that continue to export missiles and missile technology. Such considerations have led President Bush, for example, to oppose and even veto legislation imposing automatic sanctions on missile or chemical weapons technology–exporting countries. Finally, attempts to restrain missile proliferation encounter the same resentments by Third World countries that occur over attempts to halt nuclear and chemical weapons proliferation. These countries see it as a neoimperialist plot by the big powers to ensure their continued world domination. Therefore, the Third World countries reply, with some justification, that the big powers are creating a double standard and should concentrate on eliminating their own missiles.

The History of Arms Control

The next issue to consider is the progress in the field of arms control. We have seen that arms have ill effects; that statesmen have almost uniformly condemned the arms race; and that there are a variety of approaches to controlling arms. We should therefore ask: What have we done about it?

Attempts to control arms and other military systems extend to almost the beginning of written history. In 431 B.C. Sparta and Athens negotiated over the length of the latter's defensive walls, and the Greeks also prohibited incendiary weapons. More recently, the Rush-Bagot Treaty (1817) between the United States and Canada continues to secure the world's longest undefended border. In Europe, it was not until the Hague Conferences (1899, 1907) that the first multilateral arms negotiations took place. Nothing was done at those meetings about general arms levels, but some restrictions were placed on poison gas and other weapons use.

The horror of World War I increased world interest in arms control. The Washington Naval Conference (1921–22) established a battleship tonnage ratio among the world's leading naval powers and, for a time, headed off a naval arms race. Efforts by the League of Nations led to the (unsuccessful) World Disarmament Conference (1932). There were also a number of other bilateral and multilateral arms negotiations and agreements in the 1920s and 1930s, but they all had little impact on the increasing avalanche of aggression that culminated in World War II.

The urgency of arms control was spurred by the unparalleled destruction of World War II and was further illuminated by the atomic flashes that leveled Hiroshima and Nagasaki. The horror of what had just been was thus magnified by the apocalyptic vision of what might be. As early as January 1946, the UN created the International Atomic Energy Commission to try to limit the atom to peaceful use. Later that year, the UN also called for the "general regulation and reduction of armaments and armed forces" and established a Commission for Conventional Armaments.

Progress during the 45 years that have followed these initiatives has been slow, but it has occurred, as is evident in Table 17.2. This list of treaties evokes both a sense of accomplishment and a feeling of frustration. Certainly much has been done. For nearly two decades after the first atomic explosions over Japan in 1945, nuclear weapons building and testing careened ahead unchecked. Then in 1963, the first major agreement was signed, in which most countries agreed to cease testing nuclear weapons in the atmosphere. Between 1945 and 1963, 424 nuclear devices were detonated in the atmosphere, an average of 23.6 per year. After the treaty was signed and through January 1, 1991, atmospheric tests declined to 64 (41 by France, 23 by China), an annual average of 2.4.[1] The last one of these occurred in the 1980s, and thus the alarming threat of radioactive fallout that had been increasingly contaminating the atmosphere has been largely eliminated.

In the quarter of a century since the first nuclear arms treaty in 1963, others have been signed, and each has made a contribution, as Table 17.2 relates. The 1990 CFE Treaty and the 1991 START Treaty will further enhance progress as they are implemented. Yet Table 17.2 can also be read pessimistically. Given the inherent danger of nuclear weapons, and in light of the fact that Gorbachev, Bush, and virtually every other world leader has proclaimed his or her desire to constrain, even eliminate, nuclear weapons, it can be argued that Table 17.2 is a record of scant progress in the face of a monumental problem.

Whether you are optimistic or pessimistic about the progress of arms control, the most appropriate question to ask yourself is "Why?" Why hasn't arms control moved more quickly and why hasn't it achieved more than it has? Virtually everybody says arms are dangerous. Virtually everybody says he or she wants to get rid of them. Yet the arsenals of annihilation remain. Why?

Barriers to Arms Control

There are many possible answers to the question of why greater progress has not been made. None of the factors that we are about to discuss is the main culprit. Nor is any one of them insurmountable. Indeed, you will see that important advances are being made on a number of fronts. But together, these factors form a tenacious resistance to arms control.

National Pride

The Book of Proverbs tells us that "pride goeth before destruction," and this statement is as applicable to the modern arms race as it was in biblical times. Whether we are dealing with conventional or nuclear arms, pride is a primary drive behind their acquisition.

---

1. A CIA report released in September 1990 supports long-standing suspicions that South Africa tested a weapon in the atmosphere in 1979. This would add to the total.

TABLE 17.2

Arms Control Treaties

Treaty	Provisions	Date Signed	Number of Signatories (as of January 1, 1990)
Geneva Protocol	Bans using of gas or bacteriological weapons	1925	125
Antarctic Treaty	Internationalizes and demilitarizes the continent	1959	39
Limited Test Ban	Bans nuclear tests in the atmosphere, outer space, or under water	1963	119
Outer Space Treaty	Internationalizes and demilitarizes space, the moon, and other celestial bodies	1967	93
Latin American Nuclear Free Zone	Bans nuclear weapons in the region	1967	23
Non-Proliferation Treaty	Prohibits selling, giving, or receiving nuclear weapons, nuclear materials, or nuclear technology for weapons	1968	141
Seabed Arms Control	Bans placing nuclear weapons in or under the seabed	1971	83
Biological Weapons Convention	Bans the production and possession of biological weapons	1972	112
SALT I	Limited the number and types of U.S. and U.S.S.R. strategic weapons (expired 1977)	1972	
ABM Treaty	U.S.–U.S.S.R. pact to limit antiballistic missile sites (two each) and to bar further ABM development	1972	
Threshold Test Ban	Limits U.S. and U.S.S.R. underground tests to 150 kt	1974	2
Environmental Modification	Bans environmental modification as a form of warfare	1977	55
SALT II	Limited the number and types of U.S.S.R. and U.S. strategic weapons	1979	2
South Pacific Nuclear-Free Zone	Prohibits the manufacture or acquisition of nuclear weapons in the region	1985	9
Intermediate-range Nuclear Forces	Eliminates all U.S. and Soviet missiles with ranges between 500 km and 5,500 km	1987	2

Note: In November 1990, 23 countries signed the Conventional Forces in Europe (CFE) Treaty. Presidents Gorbachev and Bush are scheduled to sign a Strategic Arms Reductions Talks (START) treaty.

Data source: SIPRI (1990).

The progress toward controlling arms has been slow and often unsteady, but each treaty in this table represents an improvement in the international political system.

For newly independent and/or less developed countries, arms represent a tangible symbol of sovereign equality. China refuses even to consider entering into arms control talks before the United States and Soviet Union reduce their nuclear inventories by 50 percent. Part of this can be attributed to security concerns, but part is also due to China's sense of itself as a potential peer of the two superpowers. Pakistan's nuclear project is partly the result of nationalistic and pan-Islamic pride. As one Pakistani official said, "The Christian, Jewish, and Hindu civilizations have [the bomb]. . . . Only the Islamic civilization [is] without it" (Dunn, 1982:45). Pride also affects countries with substantial conventional and/or nuclear arms inventories. For the United States and especially now for the Soviet Union, their immense military might is what continues to place them alone in the exclusive superpower club.

Disputes Over What to Count

Often an initial problem for arms negotiators is defining which weapons will be subject to negotiation. The Soviets, for example, have periodically tried to include British and French nuclear weapons with American weapons before negotiating equal reductions of Soviet weapons. The Americans remain adamant that negotiations include only U.S. and Soviet weapons. In recent discussions, the Soviets have backed off from their earlier position, but after the START Treaty cuts in the arsenals of the two superpowers, the Soviets will almost certainly insist on bringing British and French weapons into the equation before a second round of reductions.

China's nuclear arsenal also presents problems. Inasmuch as the Soviets deploy a significant percentage of their conventional and nuclear forces against China, Moscow is concerned with "equal security," that is, balancing its nuclear weapons against Chinese weapons in addition to those of the United States, Great Britain, and France. Washington tends to talk about "equal numbers" of U.S. and Soviet weapons. So far this issue has not been insurmountable, but it is also likely that after the START Treaty the issue of China's nuclear weapons will have to be dealt with before more reductions can be made.

There are also disputes over specific weapons. The START negotiations wrestled over the issue of whether or not the Soviet Backfire bomber was a strategic delivery system. The status of cruise missiles is also a difficult issue because their range is technically less than strategic (5,500 km), but they can be carried by ships or planes close to an opponent's border.

Concern That Arms Control Talks Are Dangerous

Earlier in this chapter we saw that the relationship between arms and war is subject to a chicken-and-egg controversy. Which came first, tension or weapons? The same issue complicates arms control.

Those who are wary of arms control efforts argue that it is both a waste of effort and potentially dangerous to address the level of arms before making progress on easing the political tensions that, these skeptics say, caused the arms in the first place. This approach is very much akin to the idea of linkage discussed in chapter 12 on diplomacy. Those who take this position make several subsidiary points. One is that focusing on arms control diverts our efforts from the root problem of political divisions. They argue that if you solve the political problems, armament levels will decline as a result.

A second contention, which was discussed earlier, is that arms provide stability in a

One of the difficult issues in U.S.–Soviet arms control negotiations is how to deal with the nuclear arsenals of other countries. This nuclear missile submarine, *Lanceur D'Engins*, nicknamed *Le Terrible*, is part of France's powerful nuclear arsenal. In negotiations, the Soviets often want to count the nuclear weapons systems of all the Western allies together before discussing reductions. The United States maintains that negotiations are bilateral and that when reductions are being calculated only U.S. and Soviet arms should be considered.

dangerous world. If this is the case, arms reductions may destabilize political relations and lead to conflict. As one study of the history of arms control put it, "Arms-limitations agreements have not contributed significantly to security and in some cases have undermined it. This has been true especially of arms limitations divorced from wider political settlements and not linked to a prior reduction in tensions" (Hawkins, 1985:32).

This line of thought leads to a third point, which is the worry of some analysts about what would occur as complete disarmament was neared. The fear is that "very low levels of arms can indirectly cause unnecessary tension if the political situation changes and one country reacts by a rearmament program which, because of the low beginning point, changes the relative strengths of the parties in a very rapid manner" (Fairbanks & Shulsky, 1987:71).

A fourth argument against attempting arms control without a political settlement is that agreements and even the negotiating process can lull you into letting down your guard. Some critics of arms control efforts maintain that democracies are especially subject to overselling arms control and losing their resolve to make the financial and personal sacrifices necessary to maintaining a strong defense.

While each of these four concerns merits thought, none are prima facie reasons to abandon arms control efforts. Many of the contentions are not supported by definitive evidence, and there are some studies that dispute the validity of one or more of them (Carnesale & Haass, 1987). It may therefore be wisest to follow a middle way between too much optimism and extreme pessimism about what arms control can accomplish and to negotiate with caution, while, at the same time, also addressing political divisions. The interlocking nature of arms, tensions, and war, illustrated in Figure 17.2 on page 502, indicates that even if we could figure out whether armed eggs or politically hostile chickens arrived first, it is probably no longer relevant and both must be dealt with simultaneously.

Complexity of Weapons Systems

A fourth barrier to arms control is the extreme complexity of the weapons systems involved. This is especially true for nuclear weapons. The main problem is how to compare apples and oranges. Technologically, a missile is not just a missile. How, for example, do you compare U.S. missiles, which are less powerful but more accurate, with the Soviets' gargantuan but less sophisticated SS-18 ICBMs? How can the fact that Soviet ballistic missile submarines are more vulnerable than their U.S. counterparts be factored into a formula to achieve parity? Given the mix of systems, how many bombers equal an ICBM, and how many ICBMs equal a SLBM?

The point is that numbers alone mean little in arguments, particularly of the nuclear variety. In addition to a vast array of different types of weapons, factors such as quality, capability, capacity, and vulnerability all greatly complicate the equation process. The result is that negotiations are extremely difficult, and agreements are subject to domestic political attack by opponents who mislead the public by pointing out numerical "inequities" without accounting for offsetting technological factors.

The Alleged Need to Test

Because new nuclear delivery systems need custom-designed warheads to match them, one way to control arms is to cease testing nuclear explosive devices. Testing continues, however, because of the argument that nuclear warheads must be periodically tested to ensure their safety and reliability; because even as the number of weapons are reduced countries strive to increase the power and sophistication of the remaining weapons; and because there has been skepticism about the ability to verify that an opponent is not testing. Despite these barriers, there has been progress on test limitations. As noted in Table 17.2 on p. 517, a 1963 treaty banned nuclear tests in the atmosphere, in outer space, or under water. Another treaty, one that limited underground nuclear testing to a maximum of 150 kt, was signed in 1974. Cold-war suspicions and concerns about inadequate verification procedures kept the United States from ratifying the 1974 treaty, although both Moscow and Washington tacitly abided by its restrictions. Both the political climate and verification techniques improved enough by 1990, however, to allow formal adherence. Presidents Bush and Gorbachev signed new inspection accords on June 1 at their summit meeting in Washington, and the U.S. Senate ratified the treaty on September 25 by a vote of 98–0.

The next goal of many arms control advocates is a comprehensive test ban (CTB) treaty. The 1989 conference of nonaligned countries in Belgrade, Yugoslavia, called for a CTB, and enough signatories of the 1963 Limited Test Ban Treaty petitioned to amend the treaty to force a conference of 70 countries which convened at the UN in January 1991. Those calling for the revision argued that, among other things, a CTB would strengthen nuclear nonproliferation by preventing countries such as Pakistan or Iraq from ever testing any weapon they might develop. This, the reasoning goes, would detract from confidence that such a weapon would actually work and, therefore, decrease the likelihood a country would take the risk of trying to use it. The Soviets have advocated a CTB, and from August 1985 through February 1987 Moscow unilaterally halted all testing and called on Washington to follow suit.

Washington, London, and Paris so far have rejected the idea of a CTB, however, and testing continues. During 1989 there were 27 nuclear weapons tests (U.S.—11, France—8, U.S.S.R.—7, U.K.—1). At the January 1991 UN conference the United States and Great Britain opposed the attempt to expand the 1963 Limited Test Ban Treaty to a CTB. Because each of the 1963 treaty's original signatories (the United States, the Soviet Union, and Great Britain) must agree to any amendment, that ended the CTB amendment attempt. The U.S. delegate, Mary Elizabeth Hoinkes, argued that nuclear tests are a "critical link" in deterrence and also necessary to correct "possible weaknesses in weapons safety, effectiveness and survivability" (*HC,* 1/11/91:A9).

Reluctance of the United States to join in a CTB has been based on the factors alluded to by Ambassador Hoinkes and other considerations. One factor is doubt about verification ability, although the recent exchange of American and Soviet scientists conducting seismographic experiments on each other's territory and the advent of on-site inspections have eliminated most of the monitoring concerns. Another factor is that the CTB would limit the U.S. ability to test new warheads, thereby possibly allowing the Soviet Union to close the technological gap in several areas of warhead design including accuracy and the yield (explosive power) to weight ratio. A CTB would also prevent the development of new warheads tailored to new missile designs, and would restrict the ability to develop new nuclear warhead concepts such as directed nuclear explosives and burrowing nuclear warheads that could attack underground weapons and command and control sites.

The key factor is the claim that even existing weapon types need to be tested. Officials have contended, among other things, that as many as one-third of all nuclear warheads in the U.S. arsenal over the years have been found to be defective because of initial design problems or deterioration. According to one official, "It could be catastrophic if you ever wanted to use [the bomb] and you pushed the button and nothing happened" (*HC*, 6/11/87:A7). In 1990, U.S. secretary of energy Admiral James Watkins told a congressional committee that "we have not identified further limitations on nuclear testing [beyond the 1974 treaty's] . . . that would be in the U.S. . . . interest." What the Department of Energy (which is responsible for developing and producing nuclear explosive devices) was willing to do, Watkins offered, was to conduct a 10-year study to evaluate whether "we can maintain the U.S. nuclear deterrent in the event of further test limitations." But, the secretary cautioned, even after the year 2000, "some level of nuclear testing will likely be required" (*WP,* 4/9/90:A10).

Two factors need to be kept in mind when evaluating such an image of nuclear weapons failure. One is that some sources outside the government, such as the Brookings Institution, have placed nuclear warhead reliability at 99 to 99.5 percent. Another point is that the image of weapons failing to go off is a hyperbole. The claims of unreliability are usually couched in more cautious language, which means, in most cases, that warheads might operate at less than optimum levels. Yield, for example, might be somewhat reduced. This is not a trivial matter, but it falls far short of the impotent arsenal portrayed by some. As one former weapons physicist put it, "The bombs work. They'll blow up a city or a dam. You don't need to test them anymore" (*HC,* 9/20/87:A12).

Suspicion

As with Og and Ug, doubts about the other side's motives are a prime barrier to arms control. The discussion of perceptions in chapter 4 pointed out that there is a propensity to perceive an opponent as more hostile and more calculating than we see ourselves. From this perspective, any proposal for arms control we make is perceived by us as a genuine effort to achieve peace. An opponent's offer, by contrast, is viewed as a grandstanding attempt to sway world opinion that must be suspiciously examined because it is undoubtedly an attempt to gain an advantage.

One way of seeing how this affects arms control is through ambivalent, somewhat contradictory public attitudes about arms control. If a poll asks a relatively general question about whether or not citizens favor arms control, the response is invariably overwhelmingly supportive. But polls also show that people are suspicious of opposing countries and are willing to risk destruction rather than submit. Throughout the cold war years, most Americans perceived the Soviet Union as hostile and dangerous. The percentage of Americans with a favorable opinion rarely rose over 30 percent, and as late as 1984 dipped to about 15 percent. People were also willing to risk war rather than submit to Soviet domination. During the early cold war years an often repeated query was whether it would be "better to be red or dead." Dead was the usual reply, and as late as the early 1980s, polls found that more than 75 percent of the people expressing an opinion in the United States, Great Britain, Germany, France, and several other countries said it would be better to fight rather than accept Soviet domination (Joffe, 1987).

The tenure of Mikhail Gorbachev in the Kremlin and the changes in Soviet policy have considerably enhanced the Soviet image since then. Even with the end of the cold war, though, surveys show that Americans are only slowly giving up their suspicions of the U.S.S.R. As late as October 1990, for example, a national poll found Americans nearly evenly split over whether the cold war was over. Just a few percent more believed it was than believed it was not. Asked whether the Soviet Union was peace-loving or aggressive, 43 percent of Americans chose peace-loving, 38 percent still saw the Soviets as aggressive, and 19 percent were unsure. Perhaps foreshadowing a new bogeyman of the future, another question found a third of those polled who had an opinion characterizing Germany as "an aggressive nation that would start a war to get something it wants" (*NYT,* 10/16/90:A12).

The link between opinion and policy begins with negative images, leads to a lack of trust, and results in a willingness to fight. The final link in the chain is that the negative image → suspicion → fear of domination makes the public often ambivalent about specific arms control agreements and prone to being swayed by the argument that the proposed agreement will reduce security.

Concern About Possible Cheating

We can list the potential for cheating as a separate barrier to arms control, although in essence it is a mélange of factors relating to suspicion, complexity, and verification. Given our suspicions, the difficulty of verifying what the other side is up to, the complexity of weapons (which makes it difficult to agree on the nature of something that both sides accept as existing), and the stakes if the other side gains an advantage, the issue of cheating is a major obstacle to arms agreements.

Do countries cheat? This question has been a major battleground in the ongoing Soviet and American nuclear negotiations. Both sides have accused the other of cheating on SALT II and other treaties, but the supposed violations are less than certain. There were some questionable moves by both sides, but they proved to be either matters of interpretation or nonthreatening ones. The point is that gross violations of Soviet/American treaties do not seem to have occurred. Arguably, neither side has cheated at all.[2] The complexity of armaments has, however, led to charges that depend on one's

2. The United States exceeded the air-launched cruise missile limit of SALT II in 1987, but this was done openly. The Reagan administration argued that Soviet cheating had abrogated the unratified, and therefore technically nonexistent, treaty.

point of view, and the difficulties of verification heighten already strong suspicions by both sides.

Those who worry about another country cheating also worry about their own country's response to violations. Possible cheating can be divided into two levels: *break-out cheating* and *creep-out cheating*. A violation significant enough by itself to endanger your security would constitute a break-out. This possibility worries skeptics about arms control. Some are also hesitant about arms control because of what they believe would be the reluctance of democracies to respond to creep-out cheating. In this scenario, no single violation would be serious enough by itself to create a crisis or warrant termination of the treaty. The impact of successive and progressive violations, however, might seriously upset the balance of forces. Western critics of arms control worry that public pressure in their democracies to maintain the arms agreements might be so strong that it would result in an unwillingness to confront alleged Soviet violations.

Verification

Because of general suspicion and the charges and countercharges of cheating, the problem of verification is one of the most significant barriers to arms control (Krepon, 1985; Scribner, Ralston, & Metz, 1985). Part of the problem is political, the other part is technical.

The *political aspect* is that without verification of treaty compliance, it is unlikely that arms control agreements can be reached. Furthermore, even in the event of an agreement without adequate verification measures, worry about the other side cheating and gaining an advantage might well lead to high anxiety and a short-lived treaty. This emphasis was symbolized by President Reagan's one, and perhaps only, Russian phrase, *Doveryai no proveryai* (trust, but verify).

The *technical difficulty* of arms control verification involves the race between the technological advances that allow more accurate verification and other technological innovations that increase the ability to evade detection.

Advances in verification are offset by other technologies that make verification more difficult. Mobile ICBMs now being deployed, for example, complicate the task of locating and counting the other side's delivery systems. Cruise missiles are only 20 to 25 feet long, and thus so small that they can be concealed in virtually any structure or even in the back of commercial-looking tractor-trailer trucks. Furthermore, cruise missiles can carry both conventional and nuclear warheads, and it is very difficult to tell the difference with satellites and other national technical means (NTM).

Given these counterbalancing detection and evasion technologies, the most important recent advance in verification is increased **on-site inspection (OSI)**. The Soviets long resisted OSI on the grounds it was a guise for an American desire to spy. In recent years, Gorbachev has changed the Soviet position. The INF Treaty contains OSI provisions; American and Soviet scientists also have conducted nuclear test–monitoring experiments in each others' countries. The United States, which long chastised the Soviet Union for its reluctance to allow OSI, has retreated from its willingness to allow Soviet inspectors access to secret U.S. installations. In another twist, both Washington and Moscow found that the NATO European countries were reluctant to allow broad OSI in the CFE Treaty. Nevertheless, the INF Treaty signaled the advent of OSI, and it is improbable that any significant future arms agreement will not include important OSI provisions.

In the last analysis, though, even the combination of more sophisticated NTM and

The Intermediate-range Nuclear Forces (INF) Treaty was an important step in nuclear arms control and reductions. For the first time, the two superpowers agreed to reduce and destroy an entire class of existing weapons. That progress is shown in this September 1988 picture of then–vice president George Bush and senior Soviet inspector Nikolai Shabalin watching the destruction of the first U.S. missiles in compliance with the treaty.

more extensive OSI does not mean that *absolute verification* can be achieved. The combination of enhanced weapons mobility and increased miniaturization of both warheads and missiles means that absolute surety is impossible (Meyer, 1985a).

Therefore, *adequate verification* is the appropriate standard by which to judge an arms control agreement. This means that your verification techniques should be sufficient to ensure that you can discover a consequential treaty violation (that is, one that will put you at a significant disadvantage) in time to either persuade the other side to desist or, alternatively, in time to rearm sufficiently to reestablish a balance of forces.

The important question, then, is not whether or not you can be absolutely sure. You cannot. The issue is which is more dangerous: (1) coming to an agreement when there is at least some chance the other side might be able to cheat or (2) failing to agree and living in a world of unrestrained and increasing nuclear weapons growth?

Domestic Factors

A variety of domestic factors also undermine arms control (Miller, 1984). Economically, arms are big business, and economic *interest groups* pressure their governments to build and to sell weapons and/or arms-potential technology such as nuclear plants (Ball & Leitenberg, 1983). American industry has been a prime supporter of military spending, and the major contractors and the myriad other smaller contractors stand to lose tens of billions of dollars as defense spending is reduced.

There is no attempt here to revive the "merchants-of-death" theory that accused arms manufacturers and exporters of encouraging World War I. It is naive, however, not to recognize the sums of money at stake in arms and disarmament decisions, the financial and political power of defense contractors, and the understandable propensity of the companies and their workers to fight to retain their contracts and jobs. If, for example, we survey the world's commercial arms-producing companies, we find that of the top 10 (in annual total sales), 9 are U.S. firms (the other is British). The 9 U.S. firms had worldwide 1988 military sales of $65.7 billion and employed approximately 440,000 workers in their military production divisions. Of the top 100 defense contractors, 48 are American, 12 are British, 10 are French, and 9 are German. Only 6 of the top 100 are located outside the trilateral countries (Japan, United States and Canada, and Western Europe), and those 6 account for only 1.7 percent of the arms sales of the top 100. The top 10, by contrast, generate 36 percent of the total arms sales of the top 100.

Although defense production is exclusively a government enterprise in the Soviet Union and China, the process of disarmament in those countries also raises opposition from what have been nicknamed the "metal eaters" in the U.S.S.R. There, Gorbachev is finding the process of *konversiya,* or conversion (from military to civilian production), is a difficult one. After reviewing the progress of partial Soviet conversion, one recent study finds that "bottlenecks and difficulties have already been encountered. Soviet economists openly speak about the . . . ill-planned process of conversion . . . [and point] to peculiarities of the arms industry that are bound to lead to frictions during the conversion process" (SIPRI, 1990:356).

Additionally, there are often *bureaucratic* elements in alliance with the defense industry. Both the United States and the Soviet Union have politically powerful military bureaucracies that resist armament reductions. Also in more democratic systems, arms control becomes entangled in the *electoral process*. The positions of executive branch policymakers and legislators are affected not only by what they think but also by the partisan implications of their positions. Members of the U.S. Congress may favor the concept of reduced arms spending, but they are apt to oppose cuts that affect the plants and workers in their electoral districts. Furthermore, because arms control is such a complex subject dealing with such a dangerous issue, advocates from all perspectives are apt to oversimplify and to appeal to popular emotions in a bid to gain support. There was grumbling in the United States even before the START Treaty was signed about its alleged poor verification procedures and its leaving the Soviets with too many SS-18 heavy ICBMs. This creates a contradiction between the general support of most Americans for arms control and their desire not to be left disadvantaged, and most elected officials are wary of making dramatic moves for fear of being charged with "giving the store away."

Arms Control: Current Progress and Future Prospects

As a final step in our analysis of arms control we can examine current arms control advances and ask, "What of the future?"

Current Progress

There has been significant arms control progress in the past few years. Some of this progress, such as the signing of the INF Treaty and the final ratification of the Partial Test Ban Treaty, has been discussed already. Two other steps that have been mentioned, but that merit further analysis, are the November 1990 Conventional Forces in Europe Treaty and the projected Strategic Arms Reduction Talks Treaty.

The Conventional Forces in Europe Treaty

Turning first to the CFE Treaty, it is primarily a product of the end of the cold war in Europe. The domestic pressures to reduce defense spending also played an important role in the conclusion of the CFE Treaty after 17 years of frustrating wrangling between the countries of NATO and the WTO. The treaty is designed to cut conventional military forces in Europe. Since this excludes forces in the United States and Canada, and also does not affect Soviet forces in Asia (east of the Ural Mountains), the formula arrived at specified cuts from the Atlantic to the Urals (the ATTU region). Like most arms

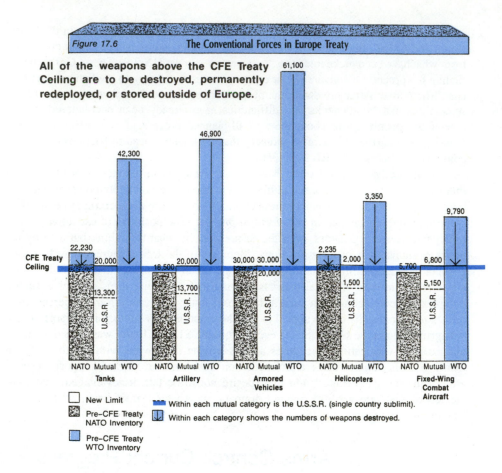

Figure 17.6   The Conventional Forces in Europe Treaty

All of the weapons above the CFE Treaty Ceiling are to be destroyed, permanently redeployed, or stored outside of Europe.

New Limit
Pre–CFE Treaty NATO Inventory
Pre–CFE Treaty WTO Inventory

Within each mutual category is the U.S.S.R. (single country sublimit).
Within each category shows the numbers of weapons destroyed.

Data source: Press reports, October–December 1990.

The 1990 CFE Treaty cuts conventional weapons in Europe between the Atlantic Ocean and the Ural Mountains in the Soviet Union. The countries in NATO and the WTO are collectively limited to the same number of weapons for each of the categories shown here. Furthermore, there is a single country sublimit shown in the white column for each weapons category. No single country in either alliance can exceed that sublimit. Given the distribution of weapons and the fact that U.S. and other countries' weapons outside of Europe are not counted in the sublimit, it will affect only the Soviet Union as far as weapons in Europe.

accords, the details of the CFE Treaty are very complex, but the broad outlines of the treaty are impressive and deserve attention.

The CFE Treaty dramatically reduces the amount of artillery, tanks, other armored vehicles, combat helicopters, and fixed-wing combat aircraft in the ATTU region. As Figure 17.6 details, the WTO countries gave up more than half of their equipment to reach the overall equal limits for the two defense alliances. NATO has to reduce some of its equipment; in other categories NATO equipment levels are already below the treaty limits. In part because of the rapid breakup of the WTO, specific sublimits were set on the Soviet Union and were diplomatically expressed in terms of the upper limit to the number of weapons per category that any one country in either alliance can have. Weapons within the ATTU region and above the limits are supposed to be destroyed, although some (but not massive) redeployments were allowed. Because of the numbers involved, Soviet destruction or redeployment of weapons was a particular concern, and there was an understanding that while the Soviets could redeploy some forces before the treaty date, most of these would be stored outside, without maintenance, and allowed to rust away. But within a month of these provisions and understandings being accepted by CFE, U.S. officials raised charges that the Soviets were removing weapons after the treaty date to avoid having to destroy them. The same officials, however, blamed at least part of the problem on various procedural difficulties, and there was no accusation of massive Soviet cheating (*HC*, 12/17/90:A1).

The number of troops was one important area of possible cuts not addressed by the treaty. In large part the decision not to include troop limits in the CFE Treaty had to do with the change of political climate in Europe. In February 1990 the United States and the Soviet Union had agreed to reduce their respective forces in Europe (and outside the U.S.S.R.) to 195,000 each. The downfall of communism in the Eastern European countries made the question moot, leaving the Soviets with a projected zero outside their borders within a year or two. Balancing that, somewhat, were a U.S. announcement in 1990 that it would reduce its NATO forces by 40,000 within a year and the agreement by the now-united Germany to limit its forces to 375,000 troops.

Before leaving our discussion of the CFE Treaty, the growing role of the **Conference on Security and Cooperation in Europe (CSCE)** should also be noted. The CSCE began in 1973 as a result of a series of meetings held in Helsinki, Finland, and the subsequent agreements (the Helsinki Accords) reached among the 35 countries, including those of NATO, the WTO, and the European neutrals, that attended the meetings. Thus far, the CSCE has been confined to a series of meetings to discuss common concerns. Now, in the changed politics of Europe, there are proposals to upgrade the CSCE to a permanent organization with a small administrative staff and a headquarters, probably in Prague, Czechoslovakia. Initial plans include a yearly meeting of foreign ministers of the CSCE member countries (reduced to 34 by the reunification of Germany) and a meeting of heads of government every second year. A Conflict-Prevention Center also will be established in Vienna. Symbolically, when the CFE Treaty was signed by the NATO and WTO members in Paris, the signing ceremony was an implied part of a CSCE meeting. Whether the CSCE will, as some predict, eventually replace both NATO and the WTO is uncertain. More certain is that, as French president François Mitterrand declared, "For the first time in history we witness a change in the depth of the European landscape which is not the outcome of a war or bloody revolution" (*HC*, 11/20/90:A1).

The Strategic Arms Reductions Talks Treaty

The provisions of the START Treaty, which is reportedly near completion, are somewhat less detailed, but the basic outlines are known. When Presidents Reagan and Gorbachev began to discuss START they set a goal of reducing the two countries' strategic nuclear arsenals by 50 percent. The START Treaty will not reach that goal; its stated limits will be about a 30 percent reduction. You will also see that because of rules for counting delivery vehicles and the warheads they can carry, the actual total of weapons permitted under the treaty is higher than the stated formal limits.

Overall, the United States and the Soviet Union will be limited to 1,600 delivery vehicles each. The two countries will also each be limited to 6,000 strategic explosive nuclear devices. Of these, only 4,900 may be carried by a mix of intercontinental ballistic missiles (ICBMs) housed in underground silos, or sea-launched ballistic missiles (SLBMs) deployed aboard submarines. The remaining 1,100 nuclear explosive devices permitted by the treaty include bombs and warheads mounted on cruise missiles and short-range nuclear missiles carried by penetrating bombers. A look at a projected division of delivery vehicles for the Soviet Union can be seen in Figure 17.4 on page 507.

The cuts in delivery vehicles and explosive devices contained in the START Treaty illustrate both the progress of arms control and the difficulties that continue to bedevil the process. There are differences between the original goals, the treaty's proclaimed cuts, and the real numbers allowed under the treaty. The goal of 50 percent cuts envisioned by Presidents Reagan and Gorbachev has not been achieved fully. Under the formal terms of the treaty, the outcome is closest for explosive devices. The Soviet arsenal will be reduced by 47 percent and the American arsenal by 50 percent. The reduction of delivery devices will be much more limited, amounting to a 35 percent cut for the Soviet Union and a 16 percent reduction for the United States.

In practice, however, the cuts will even be more limited. With respect to delivery vehicles, for example, the sea-launched cruise missiles possessed by the United States will be excluded. The Soviets' Backfire bomber will also be excluded, although it will be covered by an addendum in which the Soviets promise to refrain from giving the bomber in-flight refueling capability (thereby extending its range). With respect to warheads, there are a number of rules governing the counting of weapons that will leave the number of permissible warheads higher than the formal figures contained in the treaty. For example, each bomber carrying bombs will be counted as carrying one bomb. In actuality, a U.S. bomber can carry an average of 7.4 nuclear bombs (depending on the model) and a Soviet bomber can carry an average of 12 nuclear bombs. Bombers carrying cruise missiles will be counted as carrying 10 such delivery devices. In reality, U.S. bombers carry up to 20, so that count will be double the formal figure in the treaty. There are some estimates that the final explosive device levels permissible under the rules for counting will represent only a slight reduction of the available power of the two countries to annihilate one another.

In sum, the START Treaty represents progress. But it is not nearly as dramatic as the 50 percent cut originally envisioned, and it is even less extensive than the cuts it purports to include.

Future Prospects

What of the future? The prognosis is mixed. Among the forces working for arms control is the *chance to limit new technology*. One of the more fruitful areas of arms control has been the effort to limit the spread of weapons. Nonproliferation has had a fair amount of success and is supplemented by geographic nuclear-free zones (such as Latin America). Space is a new frontier, and treaties may be possible to expand current agreements in this area. In short, restricting the proliferation of weapons and the development/deployment of new types of weapons is a more probable area of success than reductions/limits on existing systems.

A second hopeful sign is *domestic pressure*. There is mass concern with the possibility of nuclear war (Graham, 1988). Additionally, the overall budgetary cost of military systems has caused a negative reaction in the United States and elsewhere. Especially in the West, then, but to a degree everywhere, the cost and horror of extensive nuclear and conventional weapons systems may serve as a source of restraint.

International initiatives are a third source of hope in the continuing effort to make progress. Despite periodic breakdowns, arms control talks between the United States and the Soviet Union have become a virtually ongoing process. The norm is now to negotiate. Sometimes, as with the INF Treaty, there are even successes. It is easy to be discouraged by what remains to be done, but the achievement of 13 multilateral and 10 bilateral U.S.–Soviet agreements in the last two decades is cause for hope.

There is also considerable effort on the multilateral level. The United Nations serves as a focus of effort and information and, in particular, may serve as a potential inspection agency, as the International Atomic Energy Agency now is with respect to the Non-Proliferation Treaty (Epstein & Robles, 1984).

In sum, then, there is a need for arms control and there are possible solutions. The question is whether we will do enough, soon enough.

Chapter Summary

1. From the point of pure rationality, arms control, or the lack of it, is one of the hardest aspects of international politics to understand. Virtually everyone is against arms; virtually everyone is for arms control; yet there are virtually no restraints on the explosive arms race in which we are all trapped. It is a story that dates back far into our history, but unless progress is made, we may not have a limitless future to look forward to.

2. There are many powerful arguments against continuation of the arms race. Arms are very costly, in direct dollars and in indirect impact on the economy. Arms are also very dangerous and add to the tensions that sometimes erupt in violence.

3. There are also arguments in support of arms spending, including their necessity for protection in a dangerous world and their favorable impact on some aspects of the economy.

4. There are a number of approaches to uni-, bi-, or multilateral arms control, including disarmament, arms reductions, limits on the expansion of arms inventories, and prohibitions against conventional arms transfers and nuclear proliferation.

5. There are also a number of junctures at which arms control can be applied, including the research and development, testing, and deployment stages. It is also possible to apply budgetary limits to arms spending.

6. For all the possibilities, the history of arms control has not been highly successful. There have been some important successes, though, such as the ban on atmospheric nuclear testing and the INF Treaty.

7. Despite the widespread agreement that something needs to be done, there are formidable barriers to arms control.

8. National pride is too often associated with the possession of weapons.

9. There are disagreements about how to count weapons and whose weapons to count.

10. There are also pressures to keep testing to ensure warhead safety and reliability.

11. The complexity of weapons makes trade-offs between different systems difficult to equate.

12. There are high levels of suspicion of motives, concerns about cheating, and doubts that verification methods can adequately monitor agreements.

13. There are heavy domestic pressures from the military-industrial complex and sometimes from the public against arms control.

14. For all these barriers, the possible consequences of not reaching arms control makes it imperative that efforts be continued and redoubled. There are also some limited signs that give rise to cautious optimism, including the chance to limit new technology, increased public pressure to act, and numerous international initiatives on the issue.

Happy are they that can hear their detractions, and can put them to mending.

Shakespeare, *Much Ado About Nothing*

Let us create an equitable economic climate . . . in which we will prosper because its benefits will be more widely shared and its economic growth more securely underwritten.

Michael Manley
Prime Minister of Jamaica

ECONOMIC CHALLENGES, COOPERATION, AND PROGRESS

In this, the fourth and final section of our text, we have been examining the forces of world cooperation that address global problems. The topics we have covered so far are international law, international organizations, and arms control. We have also touched in the preceding three chapters and, indeed, in many sections of the book, on the economic, social, and environmental issues that face the world. In this and the next chapter we will review briefly the related problems we face in these areas and assess the cooperative international efforts to address these issues. As we shall see, economic, social, and environmental concerns are closely interrelated, and, to a substantial degree, progress or lack of it in one area advances or retards progress in the others. Therefore, in a sense, the two chapters' division of these topics is only a pedagogical device.

The interrelationship among economic, social, and environmental issues also means that our discussion of some of the institutions that promote and practice international cooperation is necessarily fragmented. Keep in mind, though, that these organizations are not themselves fragmented and that they treat the social and economic problems as they are—as parts of an interrelated whole. Among the many institutions mentioned in this and the next chapter, keep two in particular focus. They both represent important efforts toward cooperation and integration. One, the United Nations, already discussed at some length in chapter 15, is active globally on the entire range of issues that face the world.

Another step along the path toward integration is exemplified by the European Community of Western Europe. This important regional effort has achieved a high level of integration, primarily on economic issues such as trade and monetary regulation but also on social and political issues. Among its other institutions, it has an executive authority, a judicial branch, and the world's first popularly elected international parliament. It is not yet a "United States of Europe," but there are many who hope the integration will culminate in such a union, and there are signs that their goal may someday be realized.

To Care or Not to Care

Before proceeding with our survey of international cooperation in this chapter and in chapter 19, it is important to answer the question: Why should we care about or do anything to assist the poor, malnourished, illiterate, and medically uncared-for peoples of the world?

The Case for Doing Little or Nothing

There are those who argue that attempts to aid all the less developed countries (LDCs) of the world are both *futile* and *beyond our responsibility*. The American diplomat and scholar George F. Kennan (1984:273), for instance, has written with respect to food shortages and overpopulation that "we in the United States did not create the problem . . . and it is far beyond our power to solve it."

Another, and even stronger, set of arguments against aiding the poor is based on the contention that such aid is counterproductive and even dangerous. Some see aid as *counterproductive* because they claim it increases, rather than eases, the problem. If, for example, you provide food and medicine to the already overpopulated LDCs, you only encourage more childbearing, decrease infant mortality, and increase longevity. All these effects only serve to worsen overcrowding.

The idea that aid is actually *dangerous* is even more emotionally powerful. To make this case, a **lifeboat ethic** analogy is often used. The world, it is argued, is a lifeboat that can support only so many passengers. The industrialized countries are in the boat. The billions of poor are in the sea, in peril of drowning and clamoring to get in. The dilemma is that the lifeboat is incapable of supporting everyone. If everyone gets in, the lifeboat will sink, and all will perish. The answer, then, is to sail off with a sad but resolute sigh, saving the few at the expense of the many in the interest of common sense.[1]

The Case for Selective Assistance

The lifeboat ethic is a stark choice, and its advocacy is too stressful for all but a few. Still, its rationale is appealing to some, and it has led to a "middle ground," sometimes called *social triage*. This phrase is an analogy to the medical term triage, the practice of dividing patients into three categories: (1) those whose illnesses/injuries are so minor that they will recover without medical assistance, (2) those who are seriously ill/injured but who can recover with medical aid, and (3) those who are so seriously ill/injured that they will die despite best medical efforts.

Good medical triage practice calls for concentrating on the second group, and this idea can be applied to international economic and social policy as well. The idea here is that the industrialized countries should identify those LDCs that are the strongest but still need assistance and aid them while not wasting resources trying to falsely and dangerously support and encourage the terminally poor.

---

1. For a discussion of the ideas behind the lifeboat ethic, see Garrett Hardin's "The Tragedy of the Commons" (1968) and "Living in a Lifeboat" (1974). Hardin discusses the idea that there are not enough resources to go around and that by trying to save everyone, those that are well off may only drag themselves down. That is, those in the lifeboat may sink it. This view is discussed in "Living in a Lifeboat" as well as in "The Tragedy of the Commons," which refers to overgrazing of the English villages' commons, which could be used freely by all, and subsequent damage to both the cattleherds and the commons.

" GIVE ME YOUR RICH, YOUR FAMOUS, YOUR NOBEL LAUREATES, YOUR RUSSIAN POETS AND POLISH EMISSARIES, YOUR RESPECTABLE WHITE ANTI-SOVIETS YEARNING TO BREATHE FREE......"

Who we are willing to help in the world is often limited to those whom we perceive as "good" or as similar to ourselves.

The Case for a Comprehensive Effort

A third approach to the world's economic and social problems is to cooperate in an attempt to address all the issues in all areas of the globe. Those who make this case put forth a number of arguments in favor of their position or in criticism of the lifeboat/triage mentality.

A first argument is *humanitarianism*, the idea that we have a responsibility to our fellow human beings. This, of course, is a matter of philosophy and cannot be "proved" empirically, but each reader should ask himself or herself the question: What is my obligation as a human? The pope, for example, has strongly joined those who argue that we all ought to be our brothers' keepers. John Paul II recalled, in September 1984, the Gospel of Matthew, in which Jesus said, "As you did it to one of the least of these my brethren, you did it to me." Jesus, the pontiff told a throng of 150,000, "is speaking of what today we . . . call the North-South contrast," and, like the Christian savior, the pope warned, "the poor South will judge the rich North." Whether one is Catholic or not, John Paul's is a powerful admonition.

The second argument is based on *violence avoidance*. It contends that the poor are becoming increasingly hostile toward the wealthy. The poor are also potential nuclear powers, and the prospect of embittered, atomic weapons–owning LDCs is a strong reason to act to ease the causes of despair.

It can also be argued that we are not in (or out of) a lifeboat but, rather, we are all on a spaceship, **Spaceship Earth**, and our fates are all inseparably intertwined. The growth of population is not just a problem of the poor. Instead, the resource depletion and ecological damage caused by a 5-billion and growing population count threaten the future of all people. As you will see repeatedly in this chapter and in chapter 19, the problems of economic distribution, health, human rights, and the environment, as well as population affect everyone. Also, problems in these areas cannot be solved through the efforts of individual countries acting alone. Those who advocate a comprehensive approach point out with considerable validity that many of the problems we humans face as a species are global problems that require global solutions achieved through global cooperation.

Those who favor a global effort also attack the *faulty analysis* of the lifeboat/triage advocates. Globalists point out that population can be controlled, that development is possible for all people, and that wealth can be shared with the have-nots without destroying the prosperity of the haves. It will hardly mean poverty, for instance, if Americans quadruple their aid giving by adding the amount they spend on wine, beer, and liquor. We will, in the course of this chapter, examine further several of these analytical disputes (Howe & Sewell, 1984).

Globalists also point out that we partly misidentify the problem. For example, is the problem lack of food, or is it overconsumption by some? Are there too few natural resources, or are the existing stocks being squandered by the resource-rapacious North? In short, are the problems we face caused by the poverty and population of the South or the gluttonous consumption of the North? Globalists would stress the latter.

Global Economic Issues

Let us now turn our attention to the specific subject of this chapter: the global economy. The trends and issues in the global economy have already been extensively discussed in chapters 1, 2, 13, and 14, but a brief review here is in order. *Interdependence* is one key characteristic of the global economy. The rapidly increasing flow of trade, direct and portfolio investment, and monetary interchange among countries means that our prosperity, or lack thereof, is inexorably intertwined with the products, consumption, and prosperity of others. The concept of a national economy has not completely lost its validity, but it is only a part of a much larger and even more complex global economic pattern.

There are a number of problems associated with interdependence. Many of them stem from the clash between the reality of a global economy, on the one hand, and the persisting attitudes of nationalism and the sovereign pursuit of self-interest by the nation-states, on the other. As noted in chapter 13, trade protectionism, resentment of foreign investment, and other symptoms of economic nationalism continue to play a strong role in the international political economy. But the powerful economic forces behind the growth of interdependence cannot be reversed, and there is a need and an effort to create international institutions for the management of the world economy (Segal, 1990). Still, the growth of international economic cooperation that we will review in this chapter is fitful and its future is uncertain.

The global *maldistribution of wealth* that divides the world into a relatively wealthy North and a relatively impoverished South is a second key characteristic of the world economy. The economic travails of most of the Third World countries and the human and social costs to the people who live in them were pointed out in chapter 14. The arguments based on humanitarianism and on justice to ameliorate the living conditions of many in the South and to close the gap between North and South are obvious enough. What is less apparent to most people in the industrialized and prosperous countries of the North is the degree to which it is in their interest to improve the economic conditions in the South. One advantage is security. A world sharply divided between a relatively few haves and a vast majority of have-nots is unlikely ever to achieve true peace. In a world that is plagued by proliferating weapons, poverty and the resentment it causes are dangerous.

Second, greater prosperity for the Third World would eventually benefit the North economically. After World War II the United States launched the European Recovery Program, popularly called the Marshall Plan. The ERP funneled billions of dollars to Europe in loans and grants. Part of the motivation was humanitarian; part was political. The ERP was also based, however, on the U.S. realization that it needed an economically revitalized Europe with which to trade and in which to invest. Europe recovered, and its growth helped drive the strong growth of the American economy in the post–World War II era. This example has applicability to the South. Helping the South toward economic prosperity will require an immense investment by the North. In the long run, however, there are a billion Chinese who might someday purchase Fords, more of India's 800 million people could someday afford to travel in Boeing airplanes powered by General Electric Engines, and there are 125 million Nigerians who are potential users of IBM personal computers. It is true that a developed Third World will economically compete with the North, but economic history demonstrates that increased production and sharp competition bring more, better, and cheaper products that increase the standard of living for all.

Third, as will be reviewed in chapter 19, improved conditions for the South will help ease the biosphere threats that beset us. For a variety of reasons, prosperity brings lower birthrates. That will slow population growth. Increased development assistance will also help countries take steps to protect the environment. Industrial pollution is extremely high in some Third World countries because their inhabitants do not possess the economic resources to install expensive equipment to reduce emissions and dispose of waste. Deforestation and its associated problems are also partly the result of poor countries and their people struggling to sustain themselves. Even the world drug trade is partly the result of poverty. The opium crop of Myanmar (Burma), the coca crop of Bolivia, and the marijuana crop of Mexico provide the only means of livelihood for many people in those countries. Therefore, one way to stem the tide of drugs is to give those farmers a more enticing source of income. Just saying no is not enough.

International Economic Cooperation

The principal question, and the main focus of this chapter, is, What is being done to address growing economic interdependence and the persistent maldistribution of wealth? To address that question we will first explore comprehensive international economic cooperation. Then we will turn our focus to more specialized efforts, roughly divided among those that center on trade, those that are involved with international monetary regulation, and those aimed at multilateral development.

Comprehensive Economic Cooperation

There are a number of developing and established organizations and interactions that address the broad range of international economic issues. These examples of cooperation can be divided into global and regional efforts.

Global Efforts

The United Nations serves as an umbrella organization for a host of agencies and programs that deal with economic issues through the General Assembly and the United Nations Economic and Social Council (Forsythe, 1989; Kaufmann, 1989). Many of these programs came into being in the mid-1960s in response to the decolonization of much of the Third World and the needs and demands of the new countries. The General Assembly, for example, combined a number of older programs and, by expanding them, created the UN Development Program (UNDP) in 1965 to provide both technical assistance (such as planning) and development funds to less developed countries (LDCs). The funds available for UNDP only increased slowly at a real dollar rate of 2.4 annually in the 1980s. In 1989, however, UNDP funds, albeit in current dollars, did reach $1 billion for the first time. Another important UN organization, the United Nations Conference on Trade and Development (UNCTAD) was founded in 1964 to address the economic concerns of the LDCs. These countries quickly coalesced into a voting bloc called the **Group of 77** after the number of LDCs in it at that time. Since then it has expanded to about 130 countries. The Group meets periodically in a Third World capital (such as Manila in 1987), and it has been a primary vehicle for the formation and expression of Third World demands for a New International Economic Order (NIEO), as discussed in chapter 14 (Michalak, 1989). The assertive position of the Group of 77 and the bloc's domination of voting in many of the UN's subsidiary bodies has caused discord with some of the developed nations. The U.S. decision to leave UNESCO, discussed in chapter 15, is one example. In recent years, however, there has been a "marked tempering of the confrontational drive of the G-77 majority to assert new international norms through the [international] system" according to scholar Lawrence Finkelstein (1990:11). This "new pragmatism," according to Finkelstein, has led to "the narrowing of the ideological distance" between organizations such as UNCTAD and the North's countries, and, as a result, "new patterns of cooperation may be emerging." While this is encouraging, it must be pointed out that, as will often be the case in the following discussion, the ideals of the programs far exceed the capacity of current funding levels. Still, a journey begins with a first step.

The North also has its cooperative organizations. The primary focus of cooperation among the Western industrialized countries is the 24-member Organization for Economic Cooperation and Development (OECD) established in 1961 and headquartered in Paris. The OECD is involved in a wide variety of the North's economic issues and information exchanges. Also, through its Development Assistance Committee, the OECD helps promote and coordinate foreign aid to LDCs.

Regional Efforts

While the growth of comprehensive economic organizations at the global level has been slow, the growth of economic cooperation at the regional level has been much more dramatic. Most regional efforts are still primarily trade organizations, and they will be discussed under the heading of trade cooperation below.

In contrast to other, more limited regional efforts, the **European Community (EC)** is at an entirely different level and is, by far, the most extensive example of cooperation and the most highly integrated regional effort in the world. This Western European organization of 12 member countries has not only moved strongly toward full economic integration, but there is also considerable political cooperation among the EC countries. There is even a possibility that the EC will evolve politically into a true political union. The EC has evolved through several stages since World War II. As it

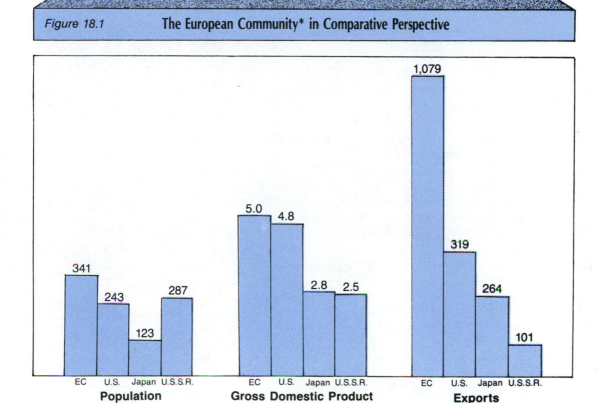

Figure 18.1   **The European Community* in Comparative Perspective**

Population (millions): EC 341, U.S. 243, Japan 123, U.S.S.R. 287

Gross Domestic Product ($ trillions): EC 5.0, U.S. 4.8, Japan 2.8, U.S.S.R. 2.5

Exports ($ billions): EC 1,079, U.S. 319, Japan 264, U.S.S.R. 101

*Data for what was then East Germany is included in the EC figures by the author.
Data source: World Almanac (1990).

The European Community economically rivals the United States and overshadows Japan and the Soviet Union.

stands, it represents the best hope for those who believe in international integration. The EC is the overarching organization that was formed by the linking in 1967 of the previously existing European Coal and Steel Community (ECSC, founded 1952), the European Atomic Energy Community (EURATOM, 1958), and the **European Economic Community (EEC**, 1958), or Common Market. Each of these three organizations continues to maintain a technical legal identity, but their individual activities are now coordinated through the policy-making and judicial institutions of the European Community.

Organizational Structure   As a developing integrated unit, the EC is a major international actor, as shown in Figure 18.1. The EC's organizational structure is extremely complex, and its full exploration is beyond our needs here. A brief look, however, is important in order to illustrate what sort of international integration is possible. Figure 18.2 gives a brief overview of this structure. The elements of the EC include a council of ministers that meets monthly. The ministers are normally the foreign ministers, but other ministers (agriculture, treasury, etc.) also represent their countries depending on the

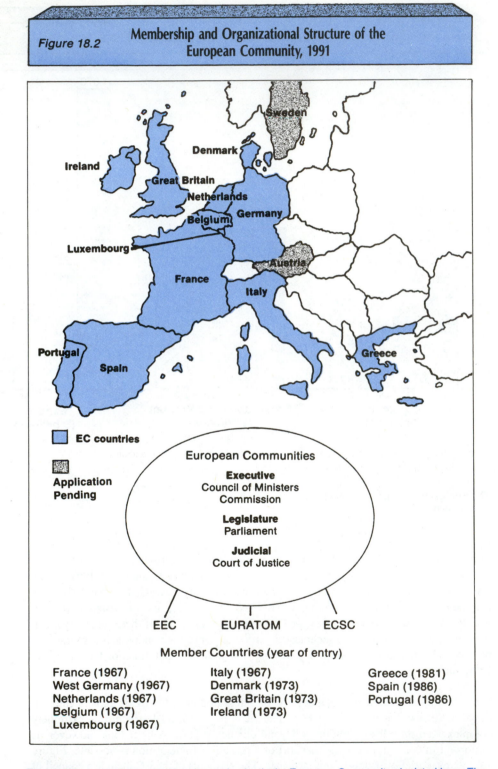

Figure 18.2   Membership and Organizational Structure of the European Community, 1991

■ EC countries

▦ Application Pending

European Communities

Executive
Council of Ministers
Commission

Legislature
Parliament

Judicial
Court of Justice

EEC   EURATOM   ECSC

Member Countries (year of entry)

France (1967)	Italy (1967)	Greece (1981)
West Germany (1967)	Denmark (1973)	Spain (1986)
Netherlands (1967)	Great Britain (1973)	Portugal (1986)
Belgium (1967)	Ireland (1973)	
Luxembourg (1967)		

The world's most advanced regional organization is the European Community, depicted here. The EC is primarily economic, but it is also involved in a variety of political, social, and environmental issues and reflects a greater level of integration than can be found in any other region.

matters to be discussed. The heads of state of the 12 EC members also meet twice each year to review the overall policy direction of the Community. The Council is the most potent of the EC's policy-making organizations. It was designed to reflect the individual views of the member states on an equal basis. As such, the Council's voting was originally on a one country, one vote basis. This has been changed, and there is now a more complicated set of rules. Most significantly, since the EC adopted the Single European Act (SEA) in 1986, Council voting on some measures is by a weighted-vote plan (termed "qualified majority voting") in which the larger EC countries have more votes on some matters. This formula ranges from 10 votes for Germany to 2 votes for Luxembourg.

The Commission of the European Community is a second powerful organizational element. Originally established to administer policy adopted by the Council, the Commission has, in the normal way of bureaucracies, become a power in its own right. Member states appoint members to the Commission, but the real heart of the organization is its president and the approximately 9,000 staff members headquartered in Brussels, Belgium. The current president is Jacques Delors, who was originally appointed in 1985 and is now in his second four-year term. Delors is French, but he is sometimes called "Mr. Europe" because of his strong advocacy of European integration. Delors and his staff, who are informally referred to as Eurocrats, have created a core structure that has a European mentality and point of view, rather than a national orientation. "We must build Europe every day," Delors says. "We must go all the way" (*Time*, 9/18/90:43).

The European Parliament is a third part of the EC's structure. It has 518 members, with representation divided among the EC countries on a modified population basis. The 4 largest countries (France, Great Britain, Germany, and Italy) each have 81 seats; the smallest country (Luxembourg) has 6 seats. Unlike most international congresses, such as the UN General Assembly, the European Parliament's members are popularly elected by voters in their respective countries. Furthermore, instead of organizing themselves within the Parliament by country, the representatives have tended to group themselves by political persuasion. One examination of the 1989 configuration listed 9 groups, including communists, the "Euro-Right," and environmentalist "Rainbow/Green" coalitions (Rose, 1990). The European Parliament meets annually in Strausbourg, France. It is largely an advisory body so far, but it is struggling to carve out a more authoritative role.

The Court of Justice is the fourth organizational element of the EC. The Court hears disputes that arise under the treaties that formed and have subsequently amended the structures and processes of the EC and its constituent units. These treaties constitute a de facto constitution for the EC. The Court is also gaining authority. In 1988, for instance, it ruled that certain value-added tax (VAT, a type of sales tax) exemptions in the United Kingdom violated EC treaties and would have to be eliminated. On hearing this some members of the British Parliament grumbled that it was the first time since Charles I's reign (1625–49) that the House of Commons had been compelled to raise taxes.

Internal Policy Direction   Discussion of the internal policy direction of the EC can be divided into economic and political considerations. Economically, the EC is pledged to become a fully integrated economic unit by the end of 1992. This planned integration has been given the sobriquet **Europe 1992**. What this means is that there are supposed to be no internal barriers to the movement of trade, capital, workers, or services. Recent decisions by the Council also are moving the EC toward integrating their members' central banks and perhaps toward adopting a single European currency. If all of this is successfully completed, there will be a free flow of economic resources, similar to the

More than any single individual, Jacques Delors represents the effort to create an integrated Europe. Delors is the president of the Commission of the European Community. He is called "Mr. Europe" by his admirers and the "head Eurocrat" by those who believe his vision of a politically, as well as economically, integrated Europe is too ambitious.

free flow among the U.S. states or the Canadian provinces. Then the members will have become a United States of Europe, at least economically.

There is also pressure for European political integration. Commission president Jacques Delors is the focus of that effort. In 1988 he said, in an unguarded moment, that within a decade he hoped that all microeconomic legislation (labor laws, social benefits policy, etc.) would be decided by EC structures. This vision would relegate national parliaments to a subordinate status, somewhat akin to the relationship of state legislatures to the U.S. Congress. Sovereignty for the 12 member states would be in eclipse.

The success of economic integration and, especially, political integration is not assured. Economically, there are many difficulties that remain to be resolved among the EC countries. Agricultural policy is one example. As elsewhere, farmers are a powerful political bloc within many of the countries who belong to the EC, and the farmers demand protection from what they consider unfair competition. This has made establishing a common agricultural policy (CAP) one of the most difficult hurdles for the EC.

Political integration will even be more difficult. There is a growing sense of being European among the people of the continent, but it is much too early to imagine people surrendering their primary political identity of being British, French, German, Italian, or some other nationality and, instead, singing a European regional anthem or enlisting in a European Army. A June 1989 survey of people in the EC countries, for example, asked whether they had ever thought of themselves as European as well as their own nationality. Of those who replied, a majority said they had in all countries except Denmark, Great Britain, Ireland, and the Netherlands. Most people, however, said the idea occurred to them "sometimes." The only two countries in which more than 20 percent of respondents said they "often" thought of themselves as European were Germany (23 percent) and France (21 percent). The most un-European-thinking country was Great Britain, where 71 percent of those Britons who answered said they "never" thought of themselves as Europeans (Hastings & Hastings, 1989:538). There is also some concern that German reunification will strengthen nationalism among its people. This concern and Germany's enhanced size and power might also cause a reactive strengthening of nationalism among others in smaller neighboring countries. Germany accounts for 24 percent of the EC's population, 30 percent of its exports, 26 percent of its steel exports, and 35 percent of its vehicle production. There is grumbling that integration might be tantamount to absorption by Germany.

Still, the strength of the European integration movement should not be underestimated. Most economic barriers among the countries of the EC have vanished. Citizens of EC countries can travel on either an EC or a national passport. There is an increasing number of joint European enterprises. The European Space Agency, for one, is a joint undertaking to develop commercial rocket and satellite ventures.

Political opposition within the EC to integration is also on the defensive. Great Britain's prime minister Margaret Thatcher provided the most dramatic example. Thatcher was the most resistant of the EC government heads to the drive toward a European currency, common microeconomic policy, and other forms of integration favored by Delors and others. In November 1990 her reluctance was one cause of her ouster from office after serving longer than any other British prime minister in modern times. Several members of her cabinet had resigned over her stand on the EC, and when foreign secretary Sir Geoffrey Howe (who had served with Thatcher since 1979) also stepped down with a melting blast at Thatcher's European policy, the "iron lady" was finished. Explaining his resignation, Sir Geoffrey told the House of Commons that the positive image of a united Europe was "a good deal more convincing and encouraging for the interests of [Great Britain] than the nightmare image sometimes conjured up by the prime minister who seems to look out on a continent that is positively teeming with ill-intentioned people, scheming, in her words, 'to extinguish democracy, [and] to dissolve our national identities' " (*HC*, 11/14/90:A9). Members of the prime minister's Conservative Party, who were already restive, revolted and challenged her control. Within two weeks Margaret Thatcher moved out of No. 10 Downing Street, and John Major became the new British prime minister. At his first (December 1990) meeting with other EC leaders in Rome, Major substantially reversed Thatcher's opposition to the EC and agreed to broad outlines for advancing EC integration and surrendering some national sovereignty.

The power of Europe 1992 also is drawing other countries into its orbit. Austria has applied for membership, and in November 1990 Sweden said it would also seek to join the EC. Norway, Finland, and others, including even quasi-isolationist Switzerland, are wondering whether they can afford to remain outside the EC. No new members will be admitted to the EC before the completion of its integration in 1992, but it is likely the EC will admit at least some of the countries who wish to join soon thereafter. The EC, especially through Germany, is also reaching out to assist Eastern Europe. The EC was the prime mover, for example, in the 1990 establishment of the European Bank for Reconstruction and Development in Eastern Europe (EBRDEE). The bank will be funded by about $12 billion in contributions from member countries and will finance development projects in Eastern Europe. Perhaps most interestingly, the Soviets are beginning to work with the EC. They are a fund-contributing member of the EBRDEE, and President Gorbachev traveled to Strausbourg in 1989 and told the European Parliament that "the idea of European unity should be collectively rethought in the process of the concerted endeavor by all nations—large, medium, and small . . . to establish a common European home."

External Relations   The economic and possible political integration of Europe have profound implications for international relations. Europe will soon complete the process of establishing joint trade and other economic relations with the rest of the world. Jacques Delors, as one symbol of the EC as a unified economic actor, attended the July 1990 Group of 7 (G-7) meeting in Houston, Texas. The G-7 may thus become the G-8, or perhaps the G-4 (the United States, Canada, the European Community, and Japan). As you can see in Figure 18.1 (p. 537), the EC will be a powerful economic unit, accounting for 37 percent of the world trade (compared to 11 percent for the United States and 9 percent for Japan). If Gorbachev's view of a common European home were to come to pass, the unit would have 820 million people and generate nearly half the world's gross national product (compared to 29 percent for the United States).

What will be the attitude of the EC toward the balance between free trade and protectionism? It is certain that there will be competition between the EC and the United States, Japan, and others. The EC can also be expected to protect its interests vigorously. Whether this competition is positive or destructive remains to be seen. Most commentary on the EC is positive, but there are worries about it becoming an economic Fortress Europe that discriminates against outside imports, investments, and other financial endeavors. This is leading U.S. and Japanese firms, among others, to increase their direct investment holdings in Europe. The sales of U.S.–controlled multinational corporations producing in Europe are, for example, already eight times higher than U.S. exports to Europe, and that figure is apt to increase.

There are also political implications of EC integration. Europe increasingly acts as a unit. The EC, for instance, exchanges ambassadors with the United States. United EC action was also evident in many cases during the 1990–91 Middle East crisis. Just two days after Iraq invaded Kuwait, the EC imposed an embargo on oil purchases from Iraq.

In September 1990 all Iraqi military attachés at all the embassies in EC countries were expelled by joint decision, and in December the EC decided that its members would not receive the Iraqi foreign minister until Iraq first began talks with the United States. Also at the meeting in Rome the EC leaders decided to ease sanctions on South Africa and to extend $1.5 billion in assistance to the Soviet Union. It is too early to claim there is a common European foreign policy on most issues, but it may not be far off.

Trade Cooperation

In addition to global and regional forms of general economic cooperation, there are a number of global and regional efforts that focus on trade cooperation.

Global Trade Cooperation

The most common form of specialized economic cooperation involves agreements and organizations to regulate trade and lower trade barriers. On the global level, the **General Agreement on Tariffs and Trade (GATT)** was founded in 1947 to promote free trade. Despite its somewhat confusing name, GATT is an organization and has its headquarters in Geneva, Switzerland. Its initial membership was 23 countries, but it has now expanded to 97 full members and 36 observer (nonvoting, nonnegotiating) members. The trade of the 97 full members accounts for more than 80 percent of all world trade. Since its origination, GATT has sponsored a series of trade negotiations that have successfully reduced tariffs and nontariff barriers, such as import quotas. The latest round of negotiations was convened in Punta del Este, Uruguay, in 1986 and is generally called the Uruguay Round. It was charged with completing a new set of trade barrier reductions by the end of 1990.

The Uruguay Round proved to be the most difficult in GATT history. It does not bode well for international trade harmony that the negotiations failed to meet their deadline for completion. A December 1990 last-ditch effort in Brussels that brought together the GATT members' top trade negotiators, including U.S. special trade representative Carla Hills, ended amid recriminations and veiled threats for retaliation for real and imagined trade transgressions by others.

The issues are complex, taking up a 291-page negotiating document, but a few of the more serious divisions can be mentioned briefly. One issue is agricultural subsidies and protection. Farmers have used their political power to obtain significant subsidies and protection in many countries. The UN estimates that OECD countries spend $185 billion annually subsidizing their farmers. This is a subsidy equal to almost 40 percent of the price of agricultural production (UN, 1990d). The subsidies caused major discord between the United States, which wants subsidies ended, and Japan and the EC. The Japanese protect their rice farmers, and the EC complained that eliminating subsidies would leave 20 percent of its farmers unemployed. It should be added that U.S. farmers also benefit from government largess. The UN study estimated that every U.S. dairy farmer gets a subsidy equal to $1400 per cow. U.S. sugar growers also cash in. Quotas on sugar imports and price supports give each of the 12,600 growers an average of $260,000 more than if they had to compete freely and sell their product at the world market price.

The United States and some of the other industrialized countries also pushed hard to extend GATT protections to relatively new areas of trade negotiation such as intellectual property rights (patents, copyrights, etc.), services (insurance, telecommunications, construction, etc.), and direct investment. Third World countries tended to oppose such innovations. They are afraid that their smaller efforts would be overwhelmed by those of the developed countries, thereby increasing the dependence of the LDCs. The Third World also argued that new directions should not be taken until the restrictions on the more traditional forms of trade were further reduced. The LDCs, for example, are affected negatively by agricultural barriers. Many Third World countries also suffer from the developed countries' frequent practice of putting quotas on the import of textile products, which bring significant export earnings into many LDCs.

The trade negotiations will continue beyond the December 1990 deadline, but as the world enters the 1990s, the prospects for further trade liberalization under the GATT system are in doubt. Domestic pressures for protection will increase as a result of the lack of success in the Uruguay Round. The difficult process of negotiating economic relations between countries and trading blocs (such as the EC) while economic barriers are disappearing between countries within the blocs will further complicate the issue.

Regional Trade Cooperation

The difficulties experienced by the Uruguay Round of GATT negotiations have been partly offset by increased regional trade cooperation. There is a substantial number of regional trade organizations, and this number has been recently expanding, as you can see in Table 18.1. Another indication of the growing importance of regional trade is the level of intrabloc trade, which accounts for 28 percent of all EC trade and 37 percent of U.S. and Canadian trade. The importance of the EC and the EEC has been discussed. Next in importance (measured in trade volume) on the regional level is the new Canada-United States bloc established by the U.S.–Canada Trade Agreement (McCulloch, 1990).

The strengthening of the European Community and the beginning of regional trade blocs on the North American continent and elsewhere are raising concerns that they could become powerful and protectionist trade rivals. The 1990 failure of the latest GATT round of trade talks to reach agreement has heightened worries. Symbolic of these, the EC has banned most beef and pork imports from the United States because of alleged health concerns. American livestock producers have charged that the health regulations are both baseless and thinly disguised protectionism, and the U.S. government has threatened the EC with retaliatory trade restrictions.

TABLE 18.1

Regional Trade Organizations and Agreements

Name	Founded	Membership
Council for Mutual Economic Assistance*	1949	10
European Economic Community	1958	12
European Free Trade Association	1960	6 non-EEC
Latin American Free Trade Association	1960	11
Central American Common Market	1961	5
Association of Southeast Asian Nations	1967	6
Andean Group	1969	5
West African Economic Community	1972	8
Caribbean Community and Common Market	1973	12
Economic Community of West African States	1975	15
Gulf Cooperation Council	1981	6
Canada–U.S. Free Trade Agreement	1988	2
Arab Cooperation Council	1989	4
Arab Maghreb Union	1989	4
Asian Pacific Economic Cooperation Forum	1989	12

*The Soviet-led Council for Mutual Economic Assistance is moribund and its future uncertain.

There are a number of regional trade organizations dedicated to improving trade among the countries in their regions, and as a result their economies have benefited.

This arrangement only moves to eliminate economic barriers between the two signatories by 1999; it does not have the organization and provisions for establishing a common external policy found in the EC.

The agreement was signed by Ottawa and Washington in 1988 and soon approved by the U.S. Congress, but final approval was blocked by the upper house of Canada's Parliament. This caused Canada's prime minister, Brian Mulroney, to call for November 1988 national elections to serve as a tacit referendum on the free-trade pact. It is worth noting that the two countries were already important trading partners. In 1986 trade with Canada accounted for 21 percent of U.S. exports and 17 percent of U.S. imports. For Canada, bilateral trade was even more important, accounting for 77 percent of all exports and 68 percent of all imports. Still, both countries practiced some protectionism, and each had specific economic interest groups claiming they would be disadvantaged by the treaty and clamoring for protection.

Especially for Canadians, the treaty debate also involved the entire question of nationalism and the country's independence from its huge neighbor to the south. Sharing the continent with the United States was likened earlier by former Canadian prime minister Pierre Trudeau "to sleeping with an elephant. No matter how friendly and even-tempered the beast . . . one is affected by every twitch and grunt" (Duchacek, 1975:146). This image worries Canadians, some of whom are afraid that their country will be economically dominated by the United States. Symbolizing Canadians' concern about becoming too entwined with the United States, opposition leader John Turner charged during the August 1988 debate that Canada's prime minister, Brian Mulroney, had "put Canada up for sale" by negotiating the free-trade pact "and wants to give away our freedom to be ourselves, to do things our own way, not the American way."

In the end, Turner's objections were in vain. A new parliamentary election was held to resolve the issue, and Mulroney's party was continued in power. On December 24, 1988, the House of Commons once again approved the measure, the Canadian Senate gave way, and the world's largest (in geography and GNP) free-trade zone came into existence.

In the two years that have followed, steps have been taken to add Mexico to the free-trade zone, thereby potentially creating a North American regional pact. President Bush met in November 1990 with Mexico's president Carlos Salinas de Gortari in Monterrey, Mexico, to begin talks on a free-trade pact between the two countries. There are many problems to overcome (such as Mexico's worry about U.S. interests gaining control of Mexican oil, and the concern by U.S. labor about competition from low-paid Mexican workers). Still, officials on both sides expressed hopes that an agreement could be reached in a year. There are also signs of interest in negotiations between Mexico City and Ottawa, which would complete the triangle. Added to all of this, President Bush in June 1990 proposed a series of negotiations among the various trade organizations in the Western Hemisphere (see Table 18.1) that could result in a hemispheric free-trade zone.

Partly as a response to the regionalization process in Europe and North America, other countries have begun to form their own groups. There are now three Arab trade groups, two of which were founded in 1989. Also joining the ranks of regional trade organizations in 1989 was the Asian Pacific Economic Cooperation Forum (APEC). This diverse, 12-member organization includes Japan, South Korea, the six ASEAN countries[2], Australia, New Zealand, and the United States and Canada. Hong Kong and

2. The Association of Southeast Asian Nations includes Brunei Darussalam, Indonesia, Malaysia, the Philippines, Singapore, and Thailand.

Taiwan are expected to join. The future of APEC is unclear. Its members have very different concerns, some of which are in conflict. The United States and Canada are part of another growing (and potentially rival) regional trade bloc. Still, the 12 APEC members account for more than half the world's GNP and for about 40 percent of all world exports. Therefore, a UN (1990d:70) analysis concluded that if APEC can established a unified policy it will "become an important force on the global economic stage."

Monetary Cooperation

Another growing area of international cooperation is the regulation of currency exchanges (Officer, 1990). As trade and the level of other international financial transactions have increased, the need to facilitate and stabilize the flow of dollars, marks, yen, pounds, and other currencies has become vital. To meet this need, a number of organizations have been founded. The most important of these is the **International Monetary Fund (IMF)**.

The IMF began operations in 1947, has 154 members, and receives its funds from member contributions and also from internal sources such as interest on loans to borrowing countries. The primary role of the IMF is to stabilize currency by granting loans to countries that are experiencing balance-of-payments difficulties because of trade deficits, heavy loan payments, or other factors. The extension of credit by the IMF to financially distressed countries is an important function. In recent years the IMF has especially concentrated on loans to LDCs. At the end of fiscal year 1990, the IMF had an extended credit line of $34.6 billion. It should also be noted, however, that after repayments to the IMF by LDCs, the net 1990 credit flow was only $2.5 billion.

Although the IMF has played a valuable role, it has not been above criticism. Indeed, in recent years, the IMF has been one focus of struggle between the North and South. This discord stems from two facts. First, voting on the IMF board of directors is based on the level of each member's contribution to the fund's resources. This formula gives the United States nearly 20 percent of the vote, with Great Britain, France, Germany, and Japan each in the 4–7 percent range. Along with Saudi Arabia (3.4 percent), these countries command nearly half the votes in the IMF. This apportionment has led to Third World charges that the fund is controlled by the North and is used as a tool to dominate the LDCs.

The second criticism of the IMF is that it interferes in LDCs' domestic affairs. As discussed in chapter 14, about 60 percent of the loans granted by the IMF are subject to strict "conditionality" requirements that the borrowing country take steps to remedy the situations that caused its balance-of-payments deficit. On the surface, the policy of requiring sound economic reform sounds prudent, but in reality it has its drawbacks. First, LDCs charge that it interferes in their sovereign domestic processes. Second, the required reforms, such as drastic budget cutting, may be politically unpopular or even impossible and may lead to political instability or even to the overthrow of the embattled government. The answers, as with most things political, are not easy, and it is likely that the IMF will continue to be criticized by some in the North for bailing out fiscally irresponsible poor countries and by some in the South for being a vehicle of continued Euro-American domination of the Third World.

Although the IMF is the most important international monetary institution, there are several others that make contributions. On a global scale, there is the *Bank for International Settlements* (BIS), with 29 (mostly European) members. The BIS is

The World Bank and its subsidiaries loan money to Third World countries for development projects. The construction shown here of a clinic in Marassol Doeste, Brazil, was financed by the World Bank.

primarily a meeting ground for its members' central banks, and it is involved in exchange rates, lending practices, and other factors that affect the Eurocurrencies. Finally, there are a number of regional monetary policies and institutions such as the European Monetary System and the Arab Monetary Fund, which are part of their previously mentioned umbrella organizations.

International Development Cooperation

A third type of multilateral economic cooperation occurs in the area of granting loans and aid for the economic development of LDCs.

The World Bank and Its Affiliates   The most significant development agency today is the *International Bank for Reconstruction and Development* (IBRD) or **World Bank**. The bank began operations in 1946 and has over 150 members. It is associated with, but independent of, the United Nations.

The World Bank is involved in making international loans for development. Its resources come from members' contributions and from interest earned on loans. In 1989, the IBRD made loans totaling $16.3 billion to approximately 50 countries. In its history, the World Bank has given over 3,000 loans, totaling $170.9 billion. Interest rates on loans vary, depending on the borrower's financial ability and other factors. The bank has instituted variable interest rates, which fluctuate according to world inflation.

The *International Development Association* (IDA) is technically a separate institution but in fact is a subsidiary of the World Bank. It was created in 1960 and has a separate pool of funds drawn from member contributions. It has 134 members, and it

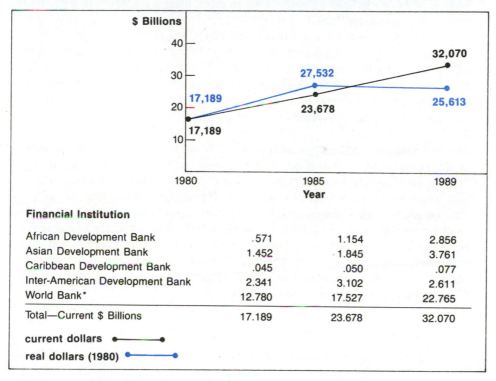

Figure 18.3   Multilateral Development Banks' Lending 1980–1989

Financial Institution	1980	1985	1989
African Development Bank	.571	1.154	2.856
Asian Development Bank	1.452	1.845	3.761
Caribbean Development Bank	.045	.050	.077
Inter-American Development Bank	2.341	3.102	2.611
World Bank*	12.780	17.527	22.765
Total—Current $ Billions	17.189	23.678	32.070

current dollars

real dollars (1980)

*Includes the International Bank for Reconstruction and Development, the International Development Association, and the International Finance Corporation.

Data source: UN (1990d:240).

Lending by international development banks has increased since 1980. The increase in real (uninflated 1980) dollars was less dramatic than the current dollar figures, and real dollar lending even decreased by 7 percent between 1985 and 1989.

focuses on making loans, usually at virtually no interest, to the poorest countries. In 1989 the IDA extended $4.9 billion in credit to nearly 50 countries. These brought the IDA's 26-year total to approximately 1,700 loans and $52.6 billion.

Like the IMF, the IBRD and IDA do a great deal of good, but they have also become a focus of struggle between the North and South. The first problem, as with the IMF, is the voting formula on the boards of executive directors. The United States has almost 20 percent of the votes in both the IBRD and the IDA. Germany, Japan, Great Britain, and France collectively account for almost another 30 percent of the IBRD and IDA vote. These proportions lead to charges of inequity by the LDCs.

The terms of the loans are a second source of contention between North and South. The World Bank is caught between many in the North who want to concentrate on "businesslike," interest-bearing loans, and the South's demands that more loans be unconditionally granted to the poorest countries at low or no interest (Bandow, 1989).

A third difficulty for the World Bank has been the desire of contributors to gain political mileage from their foreign aid. This has led some to argue that bilateral loans and aid can be better directed at friendly countries and that bilateralism more closely identifies the donor country as a benefactor. There have also been grumblings about loans to communist countries, dictatorships, and other regimes disliked by one or another of the World Bank's main backers. In short, there are attempts to politicize the supposedly nonpolitical bank.

The *International Finance Corporation* (IFC) was established in 1957, has 128 members, and is a semi-independent affiliate of the World Bank. The IFC makes loans to LDCs to promote private-sector development, whereas the IBRD and IDA make loans for public projects. In 1989 the IFC approved $1.6 billion in loans. The IFC, more than any of the other multilateral banks, has been favorably received in the United States because of its capitalism-promoting lending policies.

Other Development Efforts   In addition to the World Bank and its affiliates, a number of UN agencies are involved in development programs. The largest of these, the United Nations Development Program (UNDP), was discussed earlier in this chapter.

There are also a number of regional development institutions (Fig. 18.3). These vary greatly in funding and success, the Asian Development Bank being the largest and most active with nearly $3.8 billion in loans in 1989. The advantage of the regional banks is that they are governed by the region's countries, often the LDCs, and are not dominated by the Euro-American complex. The disadvantage is that they have scarce resources. In 1989, for example, the Caribbean Development Bank was able to loan only $77 million despite its region's pressing needs.

Economic Cooperation: A Summary

We began by noting that economic affairs are a vital part of the international power structure and that economic policy is largely conducted according to short-term self-interest. This once was the whole story, but things are changing. As we have just seen, there are a variety of organizations, almost all created in the last few decades, designed to promote international economic cooperation. It is easy to be impatient with their slow progress, but this is inappropriate negativism. They are a break with the self-interest of the past. They have made important contributions already, and they are a start on what is possible. Like all the cooperative efforts we are reviewing in these concluding chapters, they should be viewed as progress.

The stamp shown here presents a glimpse of the probable future of economic cooperation in Europe. When Italy issued this 500-lira stamp to commemorate the elections for the 12-member European Community's parliament in 1989, it printed the stamp's equivalent value in ECUs (European Currency Units). Europe does not yet have a single currency, and thus ECUs are still a technical measure rather than a spendable currency. Still, the European Community is working toward monetary union, and the ECU may well soon supplement, or even supplant, the British pound, German mark, French franc, and other national currencies.

Chapter Summary

1. This chapter has been about the socioeconomic issues that face the world and whether we should take the view that we are in a lifeboat or a spaceship. Increasingly, but only slowly so, we are taking the attitude that we are indeed a Spaceship Earth and that we have a responsibility to and a stake in the status of all the people of the world.

2. There are a variety of weighty issues that need to be addressed. Economic cooperation is probably the most advanced of all cooperative efforts.

3. The United Nations maintains a number of efforts aimed at general economic development, with an emphasis on the less developed countries.

4. At the regional level, there are a number of organizations aimed at economic cooperation and development. By far the most developed of these is the European Community, which is the great hope and example for those who favor regional integration.

5. There is also a great deal of trade cooperation, and great strides have been made through the General Agreement on Tariffs and Trade toward promoting free trade.

6. Among monetary institutions, the International Monetary Fund is the primary organization dedicated to stabilizing the world's monetary system.

7. There are also a number of international organizations established to provide developmental loans and grants to countries in need. The best known of these is the World Bank, which consists of several interrelated subsidiaries.

*Be fruitful, and multiply, and replenish the earth, and subdue it: and
have dominion over the fish of the sea, and over the fowl of the air,
and over every living thing that moveth upon the earth*

Jehovah, *Genesis* 1:28.

The sun with one eye vieweth all the world.

Shakespeare, *Henry VI*, Part I

*The world itself looks clear and so much more beautiful [from space].
Maybe we can make it that way . . . by giving everyone, eventually,
that perspective from out in space.*

Astronaut Roger Chaffee

SOCIAL AND
ECOLOGICAL ISSUES
AND COOPERATION

The beginning of chapter 18 presents three approaches that the people of the developed countries can take to the plight of many countries in the South. The lifeboat ethic recommends doing little or nothing; the social triage approach involves helping only some less developed countries (LDCs); the image of all people on the Spaceship Earth argues for a comprehensive international effort. The balance of chapter 18 then reviewed some of the economic difficulties earlier detailed in chapters 13 and 14 and examined the international efforts to address those issues.

This chapter deals with social and ecological issues and cooperation, but it is in many ways an extension of the discussion in chapter 18. One connection between the two chapters is that the question of attitude is an important consideration in addressing the issues raised. Should we care? Clearly, the view in this text is that we all should care. As chapter 18 said, part of the reason to care is based on humanitarianism. Some issues, such as human rights and health, that will be discussed in this chapter are particularly subject to humanitarian analysis. Concern over the state of the world society and its environment is not all, or even mainly, altruism, however. Self-interest, perhaps even self-preservation, compels our attention to the world's exploding population, the depletion of natural resources, and the degradation of the global environment. Yet even if we adopt a narrow perspective and only respond because it is good for us, new approaches are needed because single-country solutions will be insufficient to solve the problems we face collectively. The issues discussed in this chapter are transnational problems. Therefore, their solution requires transnational programs achieved through international cooperation.

The exploration of these issues and of international cooperation to address them will be divided into several parts in this chapter. We will first discuss social issues, including population, food, health, education, and human rights. Then the chapter will

If the world population, which now numbers more than 5 billion, continues to expand at its current rate, it may not be long before we all face "standing room only" conditions.

turn to resource concerns such as minerals, forests, wildlife, and water. Last, the chapter will take up environmental issues including pollution of the ground, water, air, and the upper atmosphere.[1]

Social Issues and Cooperation

One set of pressing problems for the world community involves the human condition. These issues are, in part, economic in nature and are being addressed by the international economic cooperation efforts just discussed in chapter 18. There are also, however, specific efforts to deal with such concerns as population, living conditions, and human rights.

Population

Identifying the population problem is simple: there are too many of us and we are reproducing too quickly. There are now more than 5 billion people in the world.

Think of this for a moment! Five billion—5,000,000,000.

Given current economic conditions, we are finding it difficult to feed this population and to provide for its other needs without depleting our resources and polluting our environment. Furthermore, the population continues to expand at an unacceptable rate. It took all of human history, to 1830, for the population to reach 1 billion. Now we are adding about 1 billion people every 12 to 15 years. China's 1990 census recorded 1.13 billion people in that country, meaning that there are now more Chinese than there were humans in the entire world only 160 years ago. Future projections are not optimistic. A

1. Several sources are particularly important to this chapter. They include: United Nations Environment Programme (1989), *Environmental Data Report,* Oxford, U.K.: Basil Blackwell; World Resources Institute (1990), *World Resources 1990–91,* New York: Oxford University Press; World Bank (1989), *World Development Report 1989,* New York: Oxford University Press; Food and Agriculture Organization (1989), *The State of Food and Agriculture (1989),* Rome: FAO; Food and Agriculture Organization (1989), *Production 1989,* Yearbook Vol. 43, Rome: FAO; U.S. Agency for International Development (1989), *Development and the National Interest,* Washington, D.C.: AID; World Bank (1989), *Social Indicators of Development 1989,* Baltimore, MD: The Johns Hopkins University Press.

May 1990 report released by the UN Population Fund indicated that a slowing of the population growth rate in the early 1980s had reversed itself, and the world population growth rate was again accelerating. Earlier predictions that the global population would stabilize at just over 10 billion toward the end of the next century no longer seem realistic. At current rates, the population will increase during the 1990s at an annual rate of 90 to 100 million people. This is roughly equivalent to adding the combined populations of Belgium, Chile, Cuba, Czechoslovakia, Hungary, Ireland, Kenya, and Syria to the globe each year. It is, therefore, not hyperbole when Nasif Sadik, the executive director of the UN Population Fund, observes that the success or failure of population control measures over "the next 10 years . . . may decide the future of the Earth as a habitation for humans" (*HC*, 5/15/90:A12). Compounding matters, the fastest population increases are occurring in Third World countries, especially those in Africa, which often are the least able to support their new people and whose economic development is further retarded by the burden of the increased population. Population increases are shown in Figure 19.1.

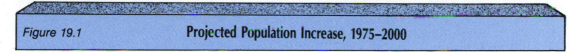

| Figure 19.1 | **Projected Population Increase, 1975–2000** |

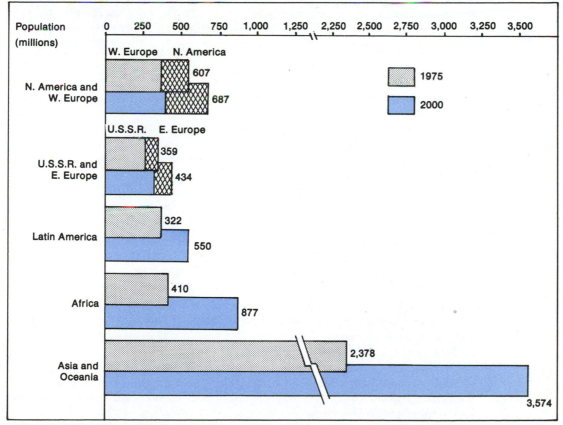

Source: U.S. Department of State (1985:48).

One of the factors that makes the world population growth particularly troublesome is that the areas of fastest growth are in the Third World regions. They are the least able to provide for the extra people.

Causes of the Population Problem There are a variety of reasons for the rapidly expanding population. One is fewer deaths. There is a lower infant mortality rate. Medical advances mean that fewer babies die. In addition, there is increased longevity. People live longer. These two factors combine to mean that even in areas where the birthrate declines, the population growth rate sometimes continues to accelerate. Africa's birth rate declined from 48.3 births per 1,000 population in 1960–65 to 44.7 in 1985–90. Yet the annual population growth increased from 2.44 percent (1960–65) to 3.00 percent (1985–90). A third reason for the alarming population growth is the huge population base of 5 billion, for which even a low birthrate means a worrisome increase.

There is a common argument that overpopulation causes poverty. The seemingly reasonable logic is that with too many people, especially in already poor countries, there are fewer resources, jobs, and other forms of wealth to go around. Logical as this may sound, it is not true. More accurately, and to the contrary, it is poverty that causes overpopulation. The least developed countries tend to have the most labor-intensive economies, which means that children are economically valuable because they help their parents farm or, somewhat later, provide cheap labor in mining and manufacturing processes. As a result, cultural attitudes in many countries have come to reflect economic utility. Having a large family is an asset in terms of social standing and is also a "major emotional counterweight to the tedium of a bleak struggle to keep alive" (Howe & Sewell, 1984:284). Thus a nonindustrial economy encourages population growth. Between 1985 and 1990, as an illustration, the population growth rate in most of the world's more highly industrialized societies was about 0.8 percent in the United States and Canada, also about 0.8 percent in the Soviet Union, and only an average 0.23 percent in the rest of Europe. The growth rate in the Third World was between 2 and 3 percent.

The International Response to the Population Problem If we reject the argument implied by the lifeboat ethic that we ought to let more poor children die in infancy and allow impoverished adults to die in their forties and fifties, then it is necessary to lower the birthrate to control population.

The move to deal with population through international cooperation is relatively recent. Its growth was symbolized by the 1984 World Population Conference in Mexico City, attended by representatives from 160 countries.

One set of solutions to the population increase involves *social approaches* to birthrate reduction. These include providing information, encouragement, and devices for birth control. Many of these efforts must come through national agencies. China, for one, annually spends approximately $1 billion on population control, and India spends more than $500 million. Given the poor economic circumstances of these countries, such expenditures represent a strong commitment. There have also been some notable successes in the Third World. In 1974 Michai Viravaidya launched a private, nonprofit organization in Thailand to promote family planning through education and the distribution of birth control devices. He also opened clinics which, for a $20 fee, perform vasectomies, and even do them for free each year on the king's birthday. As a result of Viravaidya's Population and Community Development Association, 70 percent of Thailand's couples practice family planning, the country's population growth rate has been cut in half (to 1.6 percent), and Thailand's population (54 million) is 16 percent smaller than it otherwise might have been.

Despite such efforts, the chronic economic problems found in the Third World severely limit the resources that are available locally for family planning. Thailand's success is an exception, rather than the rule in the Third World. Overall, only 43 percent of couples in LDCs practice birth control. If China, which has a strong program, is factored out, the figure falls to a mere 27 percent of couples using family planning techniques. According to United Nations Fund for Population Activities (UNFPA) estimates, world expenditures on family planning will need to grow from a current $5 billion a year to $9 billion to reach the globe's 500 million unprotected, reproductive-age couples. The World Bank estimates that such an effort could halve the world's population growth, resulting in 2 billion less people than the 10 billion projected for 2050.

The international population control effort is led by UNFPA, the nongovernmental International Planned Parenthood Federation, and other international governmental and nongovernmental organizations (IGOs and NGOs). Their efforts have had an impact, but they are limited by the lack of international funding. During the 1980s, the United States, for example, reduced its funding to international family planning efforts by more than 50 percent in real dollars. A particular objection of the Reagan administration was the funding of abortion. President Bush has not significantly changed U.S. policy, and funding ($245 million in 1989) for international family planning has remained relatively static. One cause of the U.S. position is that both Presidents Reagan and Bush are right-to-life advocates and believe that abortion is tantamount to taking a child's life. Bush vetoed the 1989 foreign aid package because it contained $15 million for UNFPA, which helps fund abortion services in China. Another White House argument is that some international agencies promote abortion in countries where it is illegal or severely restricted. Over 40 percent of all Third World women (outside of China) live in such countries. Perhaps half of the world's annual estimated 54 million abortions are performed illegally, resulting in the death of nearly 200,000 women (Jacobson, 1988). A third U.S. administration concern is that there are continuing reports that coercive techniques, including forced abortion and sterilization, have been used and continue in some countries. Reports from China in December 1990, for instance, indicate that officials in Henan Province penalize women with more than one child if they do not use an intrauterine device and men and women who do not submit to sterilization after two children. Fines for a pregnancy after two children run as high as a third of a rural peasant's annual income, leaving women little alternative to abortion. China officially condemns such policies, but its population director conceded that "China is such a big country and has so many family planning workers that I can't rule out the possibility that . . . there are cases in which coercive methods are used" (*HC*, 12/18/90:A12).

Economic approaches can also ease population growth. The evidence that poverty causes population means that the prime effort must go into easing the poverty gap both between countries and within countries. Thus, efforts must be made to develop the Third World and to equalize income distribution within countries, as discussed in chapters 14 and 17, if population is to be controlled. A related effort is to improve the status of women, because women who are more fully and equally employed have fewer children. This effort is, again, just beginning, but was symbolized by the Voluntary Fund for the United Nations Decade for Women and the 1982 Convention on the Elimination of All Forms of Discrimination against Women.

Food

The question of food is closely related to population, and as the population grows, the adequacy of the food supply becomes an increasingly critical issue.

There are two basic food problems. One is the *short-term food supply*. Regional shortages are responsible for real human suffering. Hunger—indeed, starvation—is most common in Africa, where more than 35 countries face a catastrophic shortage of food. In addition to the tens of thousands who have died, agriculture insufficiency has a host of negative economic impacts that range from sapping the vigor of the population to consuming development funds for food relief.

Second, the *long-term adequacy of the food supply* is also a significant concern. A combination of population control and agricultural development is necessary to ensure that the world's appetite does not outstrip its agriculture. Failure to meet human needs will mean a protracted world food crisis, carrying with it the potential for political instability, as well as human suffering.

Causes of the Food Problem   One cause of hunger is *underproduction*, that is, the inability of production to keep up with population in many areas of the world. Advances in mechanization, fertilization, plant and animal disease control, and other techniques are offset by declines in acreage, by agricultural supply disruption due to urbanization, by ecological damage, and by other factors. The result is that Third World per capita food production is barely expanding from its poverty base and there is the constant threat of calamity.

A second cause of hunger is *maldistribution* of food. There is, in the world, sufficient food and agricultural capacity to feed everyone adequately. Resources and consumption, however, are concentrated in a relatively few countries. In the developed world, daily food consumption averages a waist-expanding 3,390 calories a day, 62 percent more than the average in the less developed countries (LDCs). Nutritional content represents an even greater gap, with protein deficiency particularly common among the poor. Finally, and ironically, the United States and some other countries actually pay farmers to keep land out of production and warehouse surplus while starvation stalks the children of Africa and elsewhere.

A third problem results from *political strife*. In many countries with severe food shortages, farms have been destroyed, farmers displaced, and food transportation disrupted by fighting between government and rebel forces. Ethiopia, Angola, Cambodia, Somalia, and the Sudan are recent examples.

The International Response to the Food Problem   Numerous international efforts are under way. Some deal with food aid to meet immediate needs, while others are dedicated to increasing future agricultural productivity.

Food aid to areas with food shortages is a short-term necessity to alleviate malnutrition. The bulk of food aid has been bilateral, the United States' Food for Peace (or Public Law 480) program being the world's largest effort. In its more than 30-year history, P.L. 480 has distributed more than $30 billion in food and agricultural assistance, and its current annual budget is in the $1-billion range. Approximately 11 million metric tons of food aid was distributed in 1989, primarily through individual countries donating surpluses, especially wheat and other cereals. Canada is the most generous country measured on a per capita basis. It has recently averaged annual donations of 1,133,000 metric tons of cereal, or 44 kg per capita. The United States (7,357,000 metric tons, 30 kg per capita) and Australia (393,000 metric tons, 25 kg per capita) also have leading efforts. By contrast, Europe's average 1,125,000 metric tons equals only 2 kg per capita, and Japan's 413,000 kg equals only 3 kg per capita.

There are also a number of multilateral food aid efforts. The UN's World Food Program is the largest. It distributes food to needy nations and includes the International Emergency Food Reserve, which maintains a reserve food stock targeted at 500,000 tons.

The *development of agricultural techniques and capability*, especially in the LDCs, is crucial if there is any hope of future self-sufficiency. On a bilateral basis, many countries' aid programs include agricultural development aid.

There is also a multilateral effort. The oldest agency is the United Nations Food and Agriculture Organization (FAO), which was founded in 1945 as part of the UN and which has 157 members. It distributes food aid and technical assistance, and has an annual budget of approximately $800 million. The FAO has been subject to criticism for a variety of its policies, including putting too much emphasis on short-term food aid and not enough effort into long-range agricultural growth. This, in addition to the growing recognition of the food problem, has led to the establishment of several other global food efforts (Pilon, 1988; Huddleston, 1988).

A key event in these efforts was the 1974 World Food Conference held in Rome. This meeting established the World Food Council (WFC). The WFC coordinates food efforts in the UN system and is composed of 36 members nominated by and responsible to the Economic and Social Council (ECOSOC). A second organization to arise from the 1974 Rome convention is the International Fund for Agricultural Development (IFAD). This organization began operations in 1977 and has been heavily supported by OPEC, which donated 43 percent of the IFAD's initial 3-year, $1-billion capitalization. The IFAD is particularly dedicated to agricultural development projects in the poorest LDCs. These efforts are supplemented by several UN–associated organizations involved in various donor, investment, and research efforts in agriculture. Finally, there are a variety of regional and specialized organizations that address agricultural issues.

Like most of the cooperative efforts we are reviewing, the global response to hunger and the need for agricultural development has just begun and is small in relation to the problem. Yet aid for famine relief and for development does flow in the billions of dollars. Further, the various organizations serve as major clearinghouses for information on problems and possibilities. These organizations and their efforts are also a start, and there has been encouraging progress in some areas. The development of new varieties of wheat, rice, and other grains that are more prolific and heartier sparked what became known as the "Green Revolution." Cereal production slightly more than doubled in the Third World between 1965 and 1988. Other advances have further spurred agriculture in the LDCs. Fertilizer use almost tripled between 1970 and 1986, for example. As a result of these efforts, LDCs' average per capita agriculture production rose 11 percent from 1979 to 1987, and the percentage of people in LDCs who are malnourished has dropped from approximately 21 in 1970 to 16.

Progress does not mean that the problem has been solved, however. The burst of growth occasioned by the Green Revolution has not been sustained, and the growth rate of cereal production has declined in recent years from an average of 4 percent (1980–83) to 2 percent (1985–88). There is also severe pressure on croplands. In absolute terms, agricultural land is expanding, thereby creating environmental damage through deforestation, the exhaustion of marginal land, and other degradations. At the same time, however, the per capita land under cultivation or pasturage is declining and will drop by a projected 40 percent by 2025. The most immediately alarming agriculture problem area is Africa, where population growth, poor social conditions, and weak economies combine to derail development programs. The problems of Sub-Saharan Africa, in particular, are detailed in chapter 14, but suffice it to point out again here that per capita food production in the region has declined, and death by starvation, not mere malnutrition, is the fate of many Africans.

Quality of Life

Life cannot be sustained without sufficient food and water, but that is only the beginning of determining the quality of life. This section will examine issues and programs in the areas of health, education, and the collective title of general welfare. As is true in all the social concerns discussed in this chapter, there is a great disparity in regional conditions. There are also important national, regional, and global efforts to upgrade the human condition.

This baby, unlike many Third World children, is healthy. The baby's relatively happy existence is in part a result of the care being given here by a UNICEF doctor and her assistant in the Sudan. The United Nations International Children's Emergency Fund, the World Health Organization, and other public and private international efforts are improving the chances for, and quality of life for, many children around the world. The limited resources of these agencies, though, restrict the number of children the health agencies can reach.

Health

The state of medical care, sanitation, and other conditions related to health in some areas of the world is below a level imaginable by most readers of this book. The developed countries annually spend an average of $400 per capita on health care; the least developed countries spend $5 per capita. The health of the disadvantaged within developed countries and in the LDCs is an international concern because health is more than a key to personal well-being. A healthy population is vital to economic growth because healthy people are productive and because unhealthy people often consume more of a society's resources than they produce.

One way to think about health care is to consider the fate of children. As noted in chapter 14, children under age five die at a rate 8.8 times higher in LDCs than the same age children in developed countries. Of the children who die from diseases, 30,000 each day could be saved by basic medical attention. In the LDCs each year some 2.8 million children die from diphtheria, measles, poliomyelitis, tetanus, whooping cough, and other diseases for which vaccines are readily and inexpensively available in the developed world. About 4 million Third World children die annually from uncontrolled diarrhea that easily could be treated by antibiotics and oral-rehydration therapy. Pneumonia kills 4 million LDC children each year; a $4 cure is available for cases treated early.

As grim as these figures are, they were once much worse. As recently as 1974, only 5 percent of all Third World children received any vaccinations; now 70 percent receive at least some protection. Although the gap between the developed and less developed countries is still distressingly wide, average Third World health has improved dramatically in the last quarter-century. Focusing on Africa between 1965 and 1990, the mortality rate for children under five years old has declined 35 percent; the general population's death rate has dropped 32 percent; and life expectancy has grown 18 percent. Overall in the Third World between 1965 and 1984, the per capita number of physicians grew 44 percent and per capita nursing personnel rose 270 percent.

A significant part of the credit for these advances belongs to the World Health Organization (WHO) and to other IGOs and NGOs. Headquartered in Geneva, WHO was created in 1946 and is affiliated with the United Nations. It has 166 members and an approximate annual budget of $500 million. The crusade against smallpox provides a heartening example of the contributions of WHO and other agencies. Smallpox was a scourge throughout human history, and as late as 1976 there were over 131,000 cases worldwide. That year, WHO began a 10-year campaign to eradicate the disease, and by 1977 smallpox was confined to a single case in Somalia. No case of smallpox has been reported since 1979. International agencies including WHO have also been instrumental in decreasing the incidence of river blindness, a once-rampant tropical disease caused by fly-transmitted larvae that enter the bloodstream and settle in a victim's eyes. Poliomyelitis is also losing its grip thanks in part to international health agencies. In April 1990 the Pan American Health Organization predicted that it would eliminate the disease in the Western Hemisphere by year's end, and WHO believes that it can decrease the world's current incidence of polio in children from 208,000 to zero by the turn of the century. In one of the most ambitious programs to date, the United Nations announced in September 1990 that WHO, the UN International Children's Emergency Fund (UNICEF), and the UN Development Program (UNDP) will cooperate on a $150-million program to develop a vaccine that will, with one dose, protect children against 6 major diseases (diphtheria, measles, poliomyelitis, tetanus, tuberculosis, and whooping cough). Insofar as only 15 percent of the cost of inoculating a child is the cost of producing a vaccine, a single vaccine would substantially reduce the estimated $2.5 billion that it would now cost to vaccinate all the world's still-unprotected children. A single vaccine would also solve the drop-out rate in vaccination programs, which is about 15 percent for each round of shots or boosters.

Education

Education, like health, is more than just a factor in the quality of life of individuals. Education is also a key to increased national and international productivity, population control, and other positive social goals. Promotion of education remains primarily a national function, but there are a number of international efforts. For one, the United Nations Educational, Scientific, and Cultural Organization (UNESCO) sponsors several programs. The national and international efforts are slowly paying off. In the 1950s less than 30 percent of all Third World children ever attended any school; now about 70 percent receive at least some primary school instruction. Overall, those with at least rudimentary literacy have increased to just over 70 percent of Third World adults.

The increasing percentages should not disguise the crying needs that still exist. Almost 1 billion adults are still illiterate, and their personal and societal productivity is limited. There is also a gender gap in education, with males considerably more likely than females to be literate in LDCs. This higher rate of illiteracy for women has several negative effects. It limits the options for uneducated women. There is also a relationship between lack of education and high birth rates because poorly educated women are less likely to work outside the home and are less able to read or understand birth control literature. In Mexico, for example, women with less than 6 years of education have an average of 8.1 children; women with more education have an average of 3.3 children. In the Sudan those comparative birth rates are 6.5 and 3.4, and in Turkey they are 5.9 and 2.1. The statistics showing an increase of literacy in LDCs also tend to cloud the fact that for most children a few years of primary education is the extent of their training. Only about 40 percent of all children in LDCs reach secondary school, and that figure is less than 10 percent in 15 countries. Post-secondary education is attained by only 7 percent of Third World students compared with 39 percent of students in developed countries. In the technological age, the lack of advanced training is a major impediment to development. In the North there are nearly 300 scientists and engineers for each 10,000 people (3 percent). For each 10,000 inhabitants of the South, there are only 95 scientists and engineers (0.95 percent); in Africa there are only 9.6 (0.096 percent).

General Welfare

The quality of life is also determined by a variety of factors that can be grouped under *general welfare*. There are a variety of efforts to meet the needs of distressed groups. The Office of the United Nations High Commissioner for Refugees, which won a Nobel Peace Prize in 1981, spends about $500 million annually attending to the needs of populations displaced by war and political turmoil. It is assisted by some 200 private agencies. The work of these agencies was recently evident in the assistance they provided to the 700,000 refugees that fled Iraq and Kuwait in late 1990. Displacement for the refugees was tragic, but widespread disease and hunger was avoided. The International Labor Organization seeks to improve world working conditions; UNICEF is concerned with child welfare; and there are UN programs devoted to migratory workers, the disabled, the aged, women, and other disadvantaged groups.

Human Rights

Another area of international social concern is human rights. This was discussed in chapter 7 on ideology and morality and chapter 16 on international law, but it is appropriate to review some of the problems and cooperative efforts here.

Rights that most Americans, Canadians, Western Europeans, and others would consider routine are equally routinely denied to a substantial part of the world's population. Various classes of citizens are discriminated against because of race, religion, ethnicity, sex, or some other inborn characteristic. Political torture is commonplace, and free speech, assembly, and movement are regularly denied. In short, conscious violations of human rights by some are a major source of deprivation and suffering for many. Although widespread abuses continue to occur, the international atmosphere that once tolerated such practice has begun to be an increasing source of criticism and even action.

The United Nations is one focus of global human-rights activity. The basis for UN concern is the organization's charter, which touches on human rights in several places. More specific is the Universal Declaration of Human Rights, adopted by the General Assembly in 1948. This document of 30 articles proclaimed as a "common standard" an array of rights "for all peoples and all nations."

To further extend these rights, two multilateral treaties, the International Covenant on Civil and Political Rights and the International Covenant on Economic, Social and Cultural Rights, were put forth by the UN for ratification in 1966 and have been agreed to by most states. In addition, there are 19 other UN–sponsored covenants governing children's rights, genocide, racial discrimination, refugees, slavery, stateless persons, women's rights, and other human rights issues. Organizationally, these agreements and human rights in general are monitored (with debatable effectiveness) by the UN Commission on Human Rights, and there are current efforts to draft documents setting standards for the treatment of migrant workers, prisoners, and other groups.

There are also a number of regional conventions and organizations that supplement the principles and efforts put forth by the UN. The most well developed of these are in Western Europe and include two covenants and the European Court of Human Rights as well as a Commission on Human Rights.

Asia is the region of least progress and it has neither a regional covenant nor an organization. The former Soviet bloc countries are also without their own standards. They are judged, however, according to the 1975 Helsinki Accords. This was signed by 35 countries, including the Eastern European states, and expresses the intention of all signatories to respect human rights. The Helsinki Accords and subsequent meetings of the signatories provided a forum for Western leaders to criticize the Soviets, arguably encouraged the Poles and other dissidents, and helped provide the climate that led to the vast changes in Eastern Europe.

Additionally, there are a substantial number of nongovernmental organizations concerned with human rights. Some of them, such as Amnesty International and the Red Cross, were discussed in earlier chapters. These groups work independently and in cooperation with the UN and regional organizations to further human rights, and they add to the swelling of information about and criticisms of abuses.

The impact of the IGOs and NGOs active in the human-rights arena and the advancement of the rights those organizations promote have been mixed. One study of six main human-rights conventions, for example, found that as of December 1987 only 10 countries had ratified all six, only 45 percent of all countries had ratified a majority of the conventions, and 22 countries had not ratified any (Tomasevski, 1989). Political biases and domestic political concerns are two of the factors that impede the growth of human-rights observance and enforcement on the international stage.

Political bias disposes countries to be only selectively shocked by transgressions against human rights. One frequent complaint by the United States and other Western countries is that the Third World majority in the United Nations ignores many abuses by

LDC regimes while exhibiting excessive zeal decrying racism, colonial oppression, Israeli-Zionist aggression, and other alleged abuses of the West. Albeit understandably, this bias exists. A recent analysis finds that "self-determination and racial discrimination . . . have been the top human rights priorities of the Third World majority, which long suffered under pervasive violations of these rights" (Donnelly, 1989:281). The study's author points out, however, that "the West [had its own biases] when it ran the show" and, for example, "economic and social rights were not even discussed" in the Commission on Human Rights until 1965.

It can also be added that the West continues to have its political biases. The 1990–91 events in the Middle East provide ready illustrations. Iraqis and many other Arabs charged that U.S. horror at Iraq's occupation of Kuwait was not matched by U.S. horror at Israel's continuing occupation of the West Bank. The two issues certainly are not the same, but there are some parallels. The Western reaction to the torture of Kuwaitis was also magnified by politics. A December 1990 report by Amnesty International documented 38 methods, ranging from the use of electric probes to the severing of ears and tongues, used to terrorize the Kuwaitis. "Good God," President Bush gasped after reading the report, "it is so powerful you won't be able to believe it. . . . I ask you to read half of it. If you can't stomach half of it, read a quarter of it" (*Time*, 12/31/90:27). The point here is not that the report's gruesome portrayal of conditions was false; it was not. Nor is the point that we should not be aghast; we should be. Instead the point is that there have been many Amnesty International and other reports detailing mind-boggling human rights abuses in many countries, including Iraq. Yet these reports are neither regularly read in the Oval Office nor reported in the press, and they seldom spark a sharp reaction by officials or the public. Saddam Hussein's regime dropped poison gas on its own people and had been torturing victims for decades. The international community responded with only concerted tongue clucking to Baghdad's chemical attacks on the Kurds, and a mere two years before the invasion of Kuwait many Americans rooted for the Iraqis as they battled the then-enemy Iranians.

Domestic political concerns are another impediment to spreading human-rights observance and enforcement. Different societies and their regimes have divergent social values, and these complicate the adoption of treaties establishing universal human-rights standards. The problem can be seen in the reaction of the United States to two recent such multilateral treaties sponsored by the UN: the 1979 Convention on the Elimination of all Forms of Discrimination Against Women and the 1989 Convention of the Rights of the Child. President Jimmy Carter signed the women's rights treaty in 1980, but it has yet to be ratified by the Senate. President Bush joined 70 other world leaders in September 1990 at the UN's "Children's Summit," but he declined to sign the treaty delineating their rights.

James J. Kilpatrick, the widely read conservative columnist, outlined the objections to the women's rights treaty (*HC*, 8/11/90:D8). He fretted that it would compel the United States to "prohibit . . . all discrimination against women . . . [to] ensure that men and women have equal responsibility for child rearing . . . to eliminate discrimination against women in the political and public life of the country . . . [and] to enact laws providing equal pay for work of equal value." In sum, Kilpatrick found that the "document is a bummer" that would violate constitutionally enshrined national sovereignty and is a "sham" because "neither Congress nor the states could eliminate acts of wholly personal discrimination." Kilpatrick's recommendation: "Kill it!"

Domestic concerns also led President Bush to eschew joining the more than 100 countries that have signed the children's rights convention. It requires countries to guarantee the survival and development of children, to allow them to participate in

The United Nations sponsored the 1989 Convention on the Rights of the Child. These children, as their T-shirts attest, gathered with actress Audrey Hepburn at the UN for the September 1990 UN "Children's Summit." President Bush also attended, but he declined to sign the pact.

planning their upbringing, and to ensure them freedom of thought and conscience. White House officials said they were studying the ramifications of the treaty. Among other things, there was concern that the document did not define fetuses as children and, therefore, left them unprotected against abortion. Somewhat paradoxically, a clause in the convention that forbids the execution of children under the age of 18 was also under suspicion (*HC,* 9/29/90:A1).

These and other impediments should not cloud the contributions of the United Nations, Amnesty International, and other human-rights organizations and efforts. The abuses that they highlight increasingly are penetrating the international consciousness and disconcerting the global conscience. Also, the Donnelly (1989) study has found that while political biases still affect the UN's view of human rights, those biases are declining. His statistics also demonstrate that there have been shifts, with increased discussion of issues that are relatively new on the international human-rights agenda. For example, the UN General Assembly's Third Committee, which specializes in social, cultural, and humanitarian issues, spent only 1.7 percent of its time discussing women's rights from 1955 to 1965. That percentage rose to 5.9 during 1966–79 and 12.9 during 1980–85. In fact, women's rights since 1975 have been the second most extensively discussed issues (after racial discrimination) in the Third Committee.

At the end of his article, Donnelly (1989:300) asks "Where does this leave us?" His answer to that rhetorical question closely parallels the view of this author. He confesses "ambivalence" because of what the UN and others have not been able to accomplish "in large measure because of the constraints imposed by the political biases of [their] members." Nevertheless, Donnelly is encouraged by the UN's "momentous achievement" in promoting the formation of international human-rights norms, and he recognizes that considerable progress has been made through international efforts despite the flaws and shortcomings of the process of identifying, condemning, and correcting human-rights abuses.

Resource Issues and Cooperation

Throughout history, humans have taken their world for granted. They have assumed that it will always be here, that it will yield the necessities of life, and that it will absorb what is discarded. For several millennia this disregard proved justifiable. The earth was generally able to sustain its population and replenish itself.

Now, the exploding human population and technology have changed this. Not only are there 5 times as many people as there were just a little more than 150 years ago, but our technological progress has multiplied our per capita resource consumption and our per capita waste and pollutant production. The result is that the world faces the potential of no longer being able to sustain its population in an adequate manner, or being able to absorb its waste. To put this as an equation:

$$\begin{array}{ccccccc} \text{Exploding} \\ \text{population} \end{array} \times \begin{array}{c} \text{Spiraling per} \\ \text{capita resource} \\ \text{consumption} \end{array} \times \begin{array}{c} \text{Proliferating} \\ \text{waste and pol-} \\ \text{lutant production} \end{array} = \begin{array}{c} \text{Potential} \\ \text{catastrophe} \end{array}$$

Areas of Concern

Recent decades have witnessed a large number of warnings that we are using our resources too quickly. More than in any other single document, these concerns were crystallized in a study, *The Limits to Growth*, sponsored by the Club of Rome (Meadows et al., 1974). This analysis concluded that if the world system continued on its path of exponential population growth and exponential resource depletion, collapse would be the inevitable outcome.

Since that time, studies by individual analysts, governmental commissions, and private organizations such as the Club of Rome or the Worldwatch Institute have uniformly concluded that the rate of resource consumption is a matter of serious concern.[2] It should be noted that not all these studies are as dire in their predictions as *Limits to Growth*, and as we shall see, some are even optimistic. Almost all, however, express at least moderate concern about oil and minerals, forests, water, and fisheries.

Petroleum, Natural Gas, and Minerals

The supply of oil, gas, and mineral resources is one area of concern. At the forefront of these worries is the cost and supply of energy resources. The energy issue has such immense economic and environmental ramifications that it was the main motive behind the military confrontation with Iraq over its invasion of Kuwait.

The world need for energy is skyrocketing, growing 35.4 percent between 1975 and 1988, as Table 19.1 on the next page shows. There has been a growth of nuclear and hydroelectric power generation, both in terms of Btu production and as a percentage of all energy production, but as Table 19.1 also demonstrates, the world remains dependent on oil, coal, and natural gas for 88 percent of its energy. Projections of future use are tricky, as are estimates of future reserves, but at 1987 use and proven reserve levels, the world supply of petroleum will be exhausted in the year 2031 and the reserves of natural gas will be depleted by 2057. Coal is a bright spot. Current reserves will last over 1,000 years at current consumption rates. Coal, however, is a major pollutant if not controlled

2. The Club of Rome is so named because its founder, Aurello Peccei, lived in Rome. The Worldwatch Institute is based in Washington, D.C., and was founded by another noted analyst, Lester R. Brown.

TABLE 19.1

Global Energy Production

	1975		1988		1975–1988	
	10^{15} Btu[1]	Percentage of Total Energy Use	10^{15} Btu	Percentage of Total Energy Use	Percentage of Increase (1975/1988)	Shift in Percentage of Total[2]
Oil	117	47.6	133	39.9	13.7	− 7.7
Coal	66	26.8	93	27.9	40.9	+ 1.1
Natural gas	44	17.9	67	20.1	52.3	+ 2.2
Nuclear	4	1.6	19	5.7	266.7	+ 4.1
Hydroelectric	15	6.1	21	6.3	40.0	+ 0.2
Total[2]	246		333		35.4[3]	

[1]The first and third columns measure quadrillions of British thermal units (10^{15} Btu). A British thermal unit (Btu) is the amount of heat required to raise the temperature of one pound of water from 62° to 63° F. One Btu also equals 252 calories.

[2]May not equal 100 or balance due to rounding.

[3]This total represents the percentage growth of all energy produced. It is derived by subtracting column A from Column C and dividing the result by column A. (333 − 246 = 87 ÷ 246 = .3537)

Data source: U.S. Department of Energy (1989:245).

Oil supplies almost 40 percent of all commercial energy produced, and our reliance on oil is projected to increase. Supplies, however, are limited and rapidly being depleted.

by expensive technology. The development of hydroelectric power is attractive in some ways, but it is expensive to develop. In addition, the placing of dams on rivers creates environmental problems; there is also increasing concern about health hazards to those living near high-power electric transmission lines. Nuclear power is yet another alternative, but its costs and hazards are too well known to repeat here. Some people advocate developing wind, solar, geothermal, and other such sources of power. So far, though, cost, production capacity, and other factors have limited the application of these energy sources and will continue to do so unless there are major technological breakthroughs. As one example, geothermal power accounts for only about $3/10$ of 1 percent (.0003) of commercial energy production.

Dealing with the supply and demand for energy also requires understanding of use patterns. The vast majority (75 percent) of all energy is used by the developed countries, with the United States alone consuming 24 percent of all commercially generated energy. The growing demand for energy, by contrast, is a result of increased needs by the countries of the South. Between 1977 and 1987, U.S. energy consumption declined 3 percent overall and 12 percent on a per capita basis. Africa's total consumption during the same period increased 68 percent, and its per capita consumption increased 20 percent. Other Third World regions had growth rates lower than Africa's but higher than the industrialized countries.

The supply of fossil fuel resources has the highest political profile, but there are also many other minerals being rapidly depleted. Table 19.2 projects the year of depletion of several important minerals at current consumption rates for both proven reserves and undiscovered reserves as estimated by the U.S. Bureau of Mines.

TABLE 19.2

World Mineral Depletion

Mineral	Percentage of Proven Reserve Used Annually (1989)	Year of Depletion, Proven Reserves	Year of Depletion, Estimated Reserves*
Tin	4.9	2009	2010
Silver	5.1	2009	2019
Cadmium	3.7	2016	2038
Manganese	2.9	2023	2124
Iron	0.6	2145	2211
Gold	4.5	2010	2013
Copper	2.5	2028	2053
Mercury	4.5	2011	2026
Zinc	4.7	2010	2031
Lead	4.5	2011	2026

*Estimated reserves are projections of U.S. Bureau of Mines for undiscovered deposits.

Data source: U.S. Bureau of Mines (1990).

Population growth and increased industrialization are increasing the depletion rate of many of these minerals.

The figures in Tables 19.1 and 19.2 are part of the puzzle of how, all at the same time, to (1) maintain the industrialized countries' economies and standards of living, (2) promote economic development (which will consume increased energy and minerals) in the South, and (3) manage the problems of resource depletion and environmental damage involved in energy and mineral production and use. If, for instance, we were able to develop the Third World to the same economic level as the developed world, and if the LDCs' energy-use patterns were the same as the North's currently are, then global energy consumption would quadruple. Using the same energy resource patterns that exist now, petroleum reserves would be dry by the turn of the century, and natural gas and many other minerals soon would follow oil into the museum of geological history.

Land and Forests

The depletion of forests and their wood resources is a particular area of resource concern. The increase in world population and, to a lesser degree, economic development are causing havoc to the world forests. Approximately 1 billion people depend on wood as an energy source, and many forests have disappeared because of such domestic needs as cooking and heating. Forests are also being cleared to make room for farms and grazing lands. Cash-poor countries are cutting their trees and exporting the wood to earn capital to pay off their international debt and to finance economic development. The money that Brazil earns from lumber and paper products ($5.8 billion in 1988) is an important part of its economy. Forests are also being drowned by hydroelectric projects and strip-mined for minerals. Acid rain and other environmental attacks increase the toll of trees. Whatever the cause, the result is that some 50.5 million acres (78,750 sq. mi.) of forest are being lost every year. That is a loss roughly equivalent to clear-cutting the combined states of Maine, Massachusetts, and Virginia. Reforestation is at only about 10 percent of maintenance level.

Some areas have already suffered almost total devastation. Madagascar has lost 90 percent of its original vegetation; significant stretches of the Himalayan foothills, China, East Africa, Malaysia, and the coast of Brazil have been nearly denuded of their forests. More than any other type of forest, the tropical forests are the focus of current concern and effort. The tropical forest in Brazil and the surrounding countries is a particularly critical issue both because of its size and the pressure on it. This ecosystem is by far the largest of its kind in the world, covering 2.7 million square miles, about the size of the 48 contiguous U.S. states. It is also the world's most biodiverse ecosystem. A 1982 study by the U.S. National Academy of Sciences estimated that each typical 4 square miles of tropical forest contains 750 species of trees, 125 kinds of mammals, 400 types of birds, 160 different reptiles and amphibians, and perhaps 300,000 insect species. The expanding population and economic needs of the region's countries have exerted great pressure on the forest. During the 1980s, Brazil alone leveled somewhere between 65,000 and 100,000 square miles of forest.

There are numerous negative impacts of deforestation to the land and to the people and animals that depend on the forests. Where forests have been depleted, the cost of wood needed for cooking and heating goes up and may swallow up a third of a poor family's meager income in some African cities. In some rural areas, wood is so scarce that each family must have at least one member working nearly full time just gathering a supply for home use.

The devastation of the forests is also driving many forms of life into extinction. Some scientists estimate that tens of thousands of types of plants, animals, insects, and fish are becoming extinct each year. This loss of biodiversity has an obvious esthetic impact, and there are also pragmatic implications. Some 25 percent of all modern pharmaceutical products contain ingredients originally found in plants, for example. Many plants also contain natural pesticides that could provide the basis for the development of ecologically safe commercial pesticides to replace the environmental horrors (such as DDT) of the past.

Deforestation also causes soil erosion. Tropical forests, which rest on thin topsoil layers especially unsuited for agriculture, become exhausted especially quickly once they are cut and crops are planted or grazing takes place. Barren land also has little water retention ability, and the chances of drought increase as a result. With no trees to hold soil in place, runoff occurs, and silt clogs rivers and bedevils hydroelectric projects. The unchecked runoff also significantly increases the chances of down-river floods with the resulting loss of life and economic damage.

A related degradation of ground resources is termed *desertification*. More of the world's surface is becoming desertlike because of water scarcity, timber cutting, overgrazing, overplanting, and because crop and animal wastes that ordinarily recycle nutrients into the soil are now being burned as energy sources. The desertification of land is increasing at an estimated rate of 30,600 square miles a year, an area the size of Austria. During the last 50 years, approximately 400,000 square miles of once-agricultural land has become barren desert.

Wildlife

The march of humankind has driven almost all the other creatures of the Earth into retreat and, in some cases, into extinction. The impact of deforestation on this process has just been noted, and there are many other human byproducts ranging from

Each year an area of the world equivalent in size to Austria becomes a desert because of environmental abuse.

urbanization to pollution that destroy wildlife habitat. At root, as with most of the problems discussed in this chapter, population growth and mismanaged technology are the primary problems. Whatever its cause, decreased wildlife will be a loss to humans. Squibb Corporation, for example, developed Capoten, a drug used to control high blood pressure, from the Brazilian pit viper. Many of the endangered species have no immediate pragmatic value, but a world without giant pandas, hooded cranes, Plymouth red-bellied turtles, and Chinese river dolphins will be a lesser place.

Unfortunately for them, there are other species that do have economic value. The taking of feathers, pelts, ivory, and other wildlife products is endangering snow leopards, black rhinoceroses, and many species. In the mid-1980s the legal trade alone of wildlife products was 192,000 wild cat skins, 472.5 tons of ivory, and 10.5 million reptile skins. During the 1980s, legal hunters and poachers seeking ivory, which sells for up to $120/lb, slaughtered approximately a quarter-million elephants in Tanzania alone. In 1980, 1.3 million elephants graced Africa; half that number survive now. Pollution is also a threat to wildlife. Birds, for instance, are particularly affected by insecticides that enter their systems directly and through the insects and seeds they eat. Fish similarly suffer from despoiled habitats.

Human food requirements bring increasing pressure on the ocean's fish, whales and other mammals, mollusks, and crustaceans. Some species, such as the gray whale, are endangered. The average marine catch in the oceans rose 30 percent between 1977 and 1987 to 80 million metric tons. Inasmuch as the FAO estimates that the sustainable annual yield of the oceans is somewhere between 62 and 96 million tons, it is clear that any further increase in fishing, and perhaps even the current level, will mean that fish, crustaceans, and mollusks are being taken at a rate faster than they can replenish themselves.

Water

The final resource we will examine here is perhaps the most basic of all. Along with oxygen, water is an immediate need for almost all life forms. The earth's water supply is also threatened, and the cry "water, water, every where / Nor any drop to drink," of Coleridge's Ancient Mariner may foreshadow the shortages of the future. Increased use by the expanding population, industrial use, pollution, and other factors are depleting or tainting water supplies. The use of freshwater, after tripling between 1940 and 1975, has slowed its growth rate to about 2 to 3 percent a year. Much of this is due to population stabilization and conservation measures in the developed countries. Water use is still growing rapidly in the Third World, however, and a substantial number of LDCs have low or very low supplies of water per capita, a trend that may well continue into the next century, as you can see in Figure 19.2. Furthermore, a great deal of the water is being spoiled because of salinization from improper agricultural irrigation techniques, fertilizer leeching, industrial pollution, human and animal wastes, and other discharges. Only about 65 percent of Mexicans, for example, have access to safe drinking water, and Mexico's overall per capita fresh water supply is less than half of the U.S. per capita supply. Things are even worse for Kenyans. Only 28 percent have access to safe water, and the per capita supply is only 6 percent of the U.S. per capita supply.

Disagreements About the Future

After contemplating photographs of the world from space, geologist Preston Cloud wrote that "Mother Earth will never seem the same again. No more can thinking people take this little planet . . . as an infinite theater of action and provider of resources for

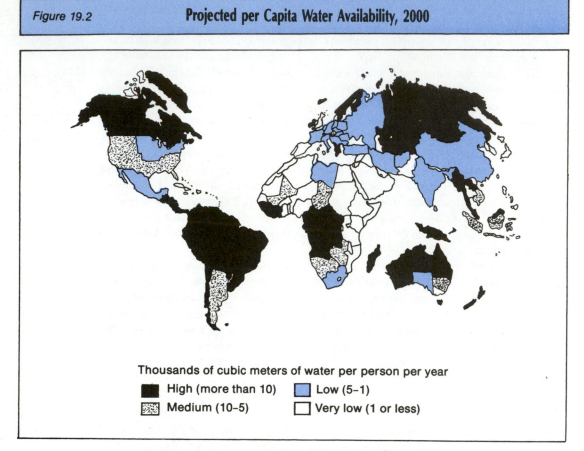

Figure 19.2   **Projected per Capita Water Availability, 2000**

Thousands of cubic meters of water per person per year

- ■ High (more than 10)
- ▒ Medium (10–5)
- ■ Low (5–1)
- □ Very low (1 or less)

Source: Council on Environmental Quality and Department of State (1980).

Water is a limited resource and in many areas of the world it is in increasingly short per capita supply as the world population increases.

man, yielding new largesse to every demand without limit" (*Time,* 1/2/89:30). That not particularly happy view of the world resource picture is the dominant theme of analysts. Many resources (for example, minerals) are not renewable, and even those that are (forests, fish) are being used faster than they can reproduce. Some analysts have reacted to these projections with true alarm. They see the potential for human suffering caused by economic deprivation. They predict an increase in international violence, dubbed ecostrife, as countries clash over scarce resources. Still other analysts predict the end of democracy as authoritarian regimes are required to control the resource-hungry masses.

There are other analysts, however, who do not share this doomsaying view. Instead, they argue that we will be able to meet our needs and continue to grow economically through conservation, population restraints, and, most importantly, technological innovation (Simon, 1983). This upbeat view has earned this group the sobriquet "technological optimists." The optimists argue that potential shortages can be met by technological advances. New technology can find and develop oil fields. Synthetics can replace natural resources. Fertilizers, hybrid seeds, and mechanization can increase acreage yields. Desalinization and weather control can meet water demands. Energy can be drawn from nuclear, solar, thermal, wind, and hydro sources. In short, as one study concluded, "The real limits to growth, rather than being scientific and technological, are political, social, and managerial. They can, with effort and good will, be overcome" (Gabor & Colombo, 1978:229).

Resources Conservation: The Global Response

While it is not clear exactly where between the views of the most optimistic and pessimistic analysts the truth lies, it is certain that mineral, forest, wildlife, and water resources must be more carefully managed and conserved. After several millennia of unchecked use, people are now beginning to act with some restraint and to cooperate in conservation causes. All the various individual and organized efforts cannot be mentioned here, but a few illustrative examples will serve to demonstrate the thrust of these activities.

Individual concern is having an important impact on preservation of forest and wildlife resources. World membership in environmental groups grew nearly 20 percent between 1988 and 1989 alone. In several European countries and in the European Parliament, Green parties have become viable, if still minority, political forces. Tropical forest and wildlife protection have become popular causes. At the global level, the International Whaling Commission regulated whaling, then banned it beginning in 1986. Several countries objected, but only Japan still hunts whales. The total annual kill of 300 violates IWC regulations, but it is confined to Minke whales, the only species not threatened. Meanwhile, blue, humpback, fin, Sei, and other species of whales driven to the edge of extinction are now free from hunters. Another marine mammal, the dolphin, is being assisted by consumer concern about the death toll of dolphins caused by fish-netting techniques. Public pressure has forced U.S. tuna canners to demand that suppliers use methods to save most of the 100,000 dolphins killed annually. StarKist, Chicken of the Sea, and Bumble Bee brands all announced in April 1990 that their tuna would be dolphin-safe, and their cans sport labels proclaiming their commitment. International pressure has also brought pledges from Japan, South Korea, and Taiwan to cease using the huge drift nets that are so destructive to marine mammals and sea turtles.

National governments are also becoming more aware and committed. Many countries have extended their coastal territorial zones and regulate fishing within them. Regionally, organizations such as the Inter-American Tuna Commission and the International Pacific Halibut Commission try to conserve fishery resources. The U.S. State Department has organized an Office of Global Change. Resource conservation and environmental cooperation are now a regular part of the discussions and the communiqués of Group of 7 (G-7) and Soviet-American summits. During President Bush's first meeting with Japan's then-prime minister Noboru Takeshita in February 1989, the president objected to the possibility of Tokyo's assisting Brazil to build a road from the Amazon forest heartland, over the Andes, and through Peru to Pacific Coast ports. The road would have carried Brazilian lumber to wood-hungry Japanese home and furniture manufacturers. Takeshita denied any interest, but he also assured Bush that Japan would not fund the road. Even the once-unconcerned Soviet Union now has a Ministry of the Environment, and in 1990 Moscow hosted a conference organized by the distinctly un-Marxist–sounding Global Forum of Spiritual and Parliamentary Leaders on Human Survival.

At the international level, the United Nations Environmental Program (UNEP) is drafting a biodiversity-conservation treaty aimed at committing countries to preserve their

Private and individual actions can improve the global condition. One recent example is the consumer pressure on tuna-canning companies to require their suppliers to use fishing techniques that will not kill dolphins. The major U.S. canners had adopted this policy, and they proudly advertise their new-found ecological awareness, as this StarKist label logo shows.

forests and wildlife and at persuading wealthy countries to provide financial incentives to assist poorer countries in the effort. Private organizations such as the World Wildlife Fund and Nature Conservancy are already implementing that concept. As part of a scheme to swap debt for trees, groups have bought from creditor banks over $20 million of Ecuador's, Costa Rica's, and Bolivia's debt bonds in return for an agreement by those countries for perpetual protection of tracts of forest. Entertainers have helped popularize the cause in efforts such as the 1989 New York City "Don't Bungle the Jungle" concert staged by Madonna, the Grateful Dead, the B-52s, and others. The increased interest in flora and fauna is also increasing the tourist trade, and many countries are beginning to realize that they can derive more economic benefit from tourists shooting pictures than from hunters shooting guns or loggers wielding chainsaws.

Internationally, the world's increasing list of endangered species is now gaining some relief from the Convention on the International Trade in Endangered Species (CITES). In 1989 elephants were added to the CITES list of endangered species by 87 countries meeting in Geneva. All ivory exports and imports are banned in signatory countries. This agreement will not end the ivory trade, but in conjunction with individual bans on importation imposed by the European Community, the United States, Japan, and other countries, CITES is a step toward prohibition.

Environment

The state of the world's biosphere is closely related to many of the economic and resource issues we have been examining. Like the concerns over those issues, international awareness and activity are relatively recent and are still in the early organizational stages.

Areas of Concern

Several resource concerns that also have an environmental impact, such as desertification, deforestation, and biodiversity diminution have already been discussed. To these the following sections will add brief looks at ground pollution, water pollution, air pollution, and atmosphere degradation (including climatic warming and ozone layer depletion).

Ground Pollution

The pollution of the land is a significant problem, but the territorial dominance of states renders this issue primarily domestic and, therefore, outside the realm of international action. Where solid waste disposal does have an international impact is through international dumping. With their disposal sites brimming and frequently dangerous, the United States and Western Europe in the late 1980s were annually shipping 1.5 million tons of hazardous wastes to Eastern Europe and Africa. Financial considerations have persuaded some governments in those regions to accept the toxic deliveries but resistance is building. "International dumping," declared Nigerian UN diplomat Saad M. Baba, "is the equivalent of declaring war on the people of a country" (*Time,* 1/2/89:47). Another international connection with ground pollution is that it is often caused by waste disposal by multinational corporations (MNCs). Indeed, the MNCs often set up operations in LDCs because they have fewer environmental regulations, which means lower operating costs for the MNCs.

Water Pollution

The discussion of this issue includes both ocean and freshwater pollution. *Ocean pollution* is a mounting problem. Some pollutants are introduced directly into oceans, seas, and other international waterways. Much more (80 percent) of the ocean pollution comes from the land. Rivers serve as a pollutant highway that, among the other degradations, damages coastal fishing grounds. Virtually all commercial fishing (99 percent) is done within 200 miles of the continents' coasts. Therefore, the fishing grounds are especially subject to pollutants carried into the marine areas from the river water that is discharged each year. Human sewage, industrial waste, pesticide and fertilizer runoff, and petroleum and other spillages all add to the problem. Many coastal and up-river cities, for example, are not served by sewage treatment facilities, and sewage is the major polluter of the Mediterranean and Caribbean seas and the ocean regions off East Africa and Southeast Asia. Industrial waste is also common. Hong Kong alone dumps 1,000 tons of plastic offshore daily. Spillage is yet another concern. The demand for petroleum has increased offshore drilling. In 1975, 8.3 million barrels a day, or 15.4 percent of world production, came from marine wells. In 1987 that figure was up to 14.7 million barrels a day, or 26.4 percent of world production. Marine oil well spillages have been relatively uncommon, but they have occurred. A 1979 blowout in the southern Gulf of Mexico, for example, dumped 176.4 million gallons of petroleum into the Gulf. Tanker accidents have been more common. The most sensational in recent years, the March 1989 grounding of the Exxon Valdez in Prince William Sound, Alaska, resulted in a discharge of 8.8 million gallons of oil. Other tanker spills have been much larger, though, with the record being the 1979 spill of 88.2 million gallons caused by a collision between two tankers off Trinidad and Tobago. The up side of the petroleum spillage statistics is that incidents have declined dramatically, down from 1,450 in 1974 to only about 100 annually in recent years. Still, of the 940 million gallons of petroleum discharged each year into the marine environment, almost half still comes from transportation spillage, with municipal and industrial waste discharge being the other major polluter at 36 percent of the total.

Freshwater pollution involving lakes and rivers is moving from being a domestic to an international issue. The direct discharge of pollutants into lakes and rivers that form international boundaries (the Great Lakes, the Rio Grande) or that flow between countries (the Rhine River) is a source of discord. Freshwater pollution also is caused by acid rain and other contaminants that drift across borders. In Canada's St. Lawrence River, for example, nitrates nearly doubled between 1970 and 1983, phosphorus rose 40 percent, and lead tripled.

Air Pollution

Insofar as the world air currents do not recognize national boundaries, air pollution has become a major international concern. There are many sources of and problems associated with air pollution, and to illustrate the problem, we will explore the acid rain issue.

Acid rain is caused by air pollutants that contaminate water resources and forests through rainfall. Sulfur dioxide (SO_2) is one component of acid rain, and each year about 25 million metric tons of SO_2 are emitted from the burning of fossil fuels and from industrial processes in Europe and North America alone. These and other pollutants have many deleterious effects, one of which has come to be termed *Waldsterben*, forest death. Canada's forests have been seriously affected, and the pollution drifting north from the United States has become an international issue between the two countries. In

Pollution shows no political or ideological preference in wreaking its damage to the world's forests. Parts of the United States, Canada, and Western Europe have suffered extensive forest death. Eastern Europe and the Soviet Union have also been hard hit. This photo of a petrochemical plant and its neighboring trees in the Bashkirian region of the Soviet Union gives mute testimony to the devastation that continues to occur.

1988 Canadian prime minister Brian Mulroney called the Reagan administration's position on acid rain "unacceptable," and angrily told Americans that the "United States would be pretty upset with me if I were dumping my garbage in your backyard. That's exactly what's happening [to Canadians], except this garbage is coming from above" (*NYT*, 4/25/88:A10).

Europe's forests are also being killed. Fifty percent or more of the forests of Great Britain, the Netherlands, Germany, and Switzerland have been damaged by acid rain. Germany, for one, is bombarded by the equivalent of 2.8 million metric tons of its own and others' sulfur dioxide annually, and 15,500 square miles of its forests (equal to Connecticut and Maryland combined), are in various stages of *Waldsterben*. As one study depicts the damage to the historic and once-beautiful Black and Bavarian forests:

> Both conifers and broad-leafed trees stand stripped of all foliage and some are covered with lichens. Dead, brittle branches litter the forest floor. . . . Among those trees still alive, many have lost 60 percent or more of their leaves and needles and will soon perish, finished off by frost, wind damage and insect attacks. . . . [E]ven the vegetation beneath the drip line of the canopy is brown and lifeless. It's almost as if the entire ecosystem has been poisoned. As the forests do, so too does the wildlife. Noticeably fewer birds and animals inhabit some *Waldsterben*-stricken forests. The same picture is repeating itself across at least seven million hectares [27,000 sq. mi.] of forest lands in 15 European countries. (World Resources Institute and International Institute for Environment and Development, 1986:206)

It is hard to overestimate the long-term effects of *Waldsterben* in Germany, the rest of Europe, Canada, part of the northern United States, and elsewhere. Millions of jobs and the entire multibillion-dollar forest industry are threatened. The tourist industry is also in danger, imperiling millions of other jobs. The decline of lumber from forests will drive the prices of housing and other consumer costs higher. Oxygenation of the air decreases, and the level of carbon dioxide increases. Rainfall patterns are affected. The death of trees and their stabilizing root systems causes increased soil erosion resulting in the silting-up of lakes and rivers. The list of negative consequences could go on, but it is not needed to make the point that *Waldsterben*, wherever it occurs, is environmentally and economically devastating.

Atmosphere Pollution

The use of the term atmosphere degradation here means the damage being done to the atmospheric envelope that surrounds the Earth. Two particular concerns will be examined. One is global warming caused by the buildup of carbon dioxide and the greenhouse effect. The second is the depletion of the ozone layer.

Global Warming The *greenhouse effect* refers to what some scientists claim is a general warming of the planet caused by carbon dioxide (CO_2) from fossil fuel burning and from other chemical gas discharges. The accumulation of CO_2 in the upper atmosphere creates a blanket effect, trapping heat and preventing the nightly cooling of the earth. Other gases, especially methane and chlorofluorocarbons, also contribute heavily to creating the thermal blanket.

There is a great deal of controversy about the existence, the causes, and the future impact of the greenhouse effect. Sorting all this out is impossible within the confines of this discussion, but a brief synopsis is in order. One thing that is certain is that both global CO_2 emissions[3] and CO_2 levels in the atmosphere have increased. This increase is associated with the industrial revolution. Global CO_2 emissions increased from 5.8 to 18.7 billion tons annually between 1950 and 1985. Some projections hold that annual emissions could reach 26.8 billion tons by 2020. This emission increase has been accompanied by an increase of residual concentrations of CO_2 in the atmosphere. Deforestation has compounded the problem in two ways. One is by destroying a huge number of trees; a large tree can absorb and convert to oxygen up to 48 lbs of CO_2 annually. By 1980, forest loss was resulting in an added 1.7 billion tons of CO_2 that would have otherwise been absorbed by the vanished trees. Second, forest clearing is often done by burning, and that process adds significantly to CO_2 emissions. As a result of burning and deforestation, the CO_2 concentration in the atmosphere has risen about 25 percent from 280 parts per million (ppm) to 350 ppm during the last century. Furthermore, the increase is accelerating. Concentrations rose an annual average of 0.7 ppm in the 1960s, 1.5 ppm in the early 1980s, and 1.71 ppm in the late 1980s, with each added 1 ppm the result of retaining an additional 2.13 billion tons of CO_2 in the atmosphere.

The past and current impact of increased CO_2 concentrations is less certain. Scientists estimate that over the last century the Earth's average temperature rose 0.5 °C (1.1 °F). That rise has been unsteady, however, and from 1940 to 1970 there was a cooling trend. Also, because the earth has natural warming and cooling trends, not all scientists are convinced that CO_2–driven warming is under way. On the other hand, the temperature has increased some, and given the rises in emissions and concentrations, it may be that a critical juncture was reached in the late 1960s or early 1970s. A 1991 report by the British Meteorological Office indicated that 1990 was the warmest (15.4 °C/59.8 °F) year in recorded history. It is also true that 1980, 1981, 1983, 1987, and 1988 were the previous five warmest years since global record keeping began in 1850.

Predictions about the future are even less certain. One widely cited estimate is that by the year 2050 the atmospheric CO_2 levels could double, and the world's average temperature could increase another 1° to 3 °C (1.8° to 5.4 °F). Rainfall, wind current, and other climatic patterns could be dramatically altered by such a change. There are predictions that in the lower and middle latitudes the chances of a drought in any given

---

3. CO_2 emissions and atmosphere levels include CO_2 equivalents of methane (20:1) and chlorofluorocarbons (18,000:1) based on the greater heat absorption properties of methane and CFC molecules.

year would rise more than sixfold. Parts of the U.S. Midwest might become a permanent dust bowl. Others would prosper, and farmers in the upper-midwestern United States, Canada, and the northern Soviet Union might have their growing seasons and bounty increased. The increase in the rate of water evaporation could produce hyperkinetic energy hurricanes and typhoons with wind speeds of 225 mph, according to another prediction. The polar ice caps would begin to melt, and sea levels would rise somewhere between 8 and 55 inches. At the extreme, a few small island countries such as the Maldives could be almost completely awash, and most of the world's great coastal cities would be partially submerged. Miami, New Orleans, Galveston, and Seattle would disappear almost completely.

It should be reiterated, though, that none of this is certain. Some scientists do not believe that increases will be huge, either because they will not occur in any case or because offsetting factors, such as increased cloudiness, will ease the effect. They also point out that significantly reducing CO_2 emissions will not be easy. It might well require substantial life-style changes in the industrialized countries. Costs will be enormous, running as high as $3.6 trillion to achieve a 20 percent reduction in U.S. emissions alone. The difficulty of balancing environmental protection with Third World development, a conundrum that thematically runs through many of this chapter's issues, is also a factor. In fact, CO_2 emissions in North America and Western Europe have declined somewhat in recent years, with the global increase coming from less developed regions of the world. Sustainable development, then, is the obvious but elusive goal.

Ozone Layer Depletion   There is little doubt about the depletion of the ozone layer and the damage that it causes. Ozone (O_3) absorbs ultraviolet (UV) rays from the sun, and without the ozone layer 10 to 30 miles above the planet human life could not exist. The ozone layer is being attacked by the emission of chlorofluorocarbons (CFCs), a chemical group that gasifies at low temperatures. Because of its low gasification point, CFCs are a good refrigerant and insulator and are found in refrigerator and air conditioner coolants and in products such as styrofoam. CFCs are also found in many spray can propellants, halon in fire extinguishers, and industrial solvents. Approximately 771,000 metric tons are spewed into the atmosphere annually. Overall, the ozone layer has been thinned by about 2 percent, with the most dramatic depletion occurring over Antarctica. There a hole has developed with as much as a 70 percent depletion of atmospheric O_3. The hole is increasing, and in 1989 it measured slightly over 10 million square miles, an area larger than the Soviet Union.

Emissions of CFCs create several problems. One is that they add to the greenhouse effect, as noted above. More to the point here, the thinning of the ozone layer increases the penetration of UV rays that cause cancers and other mutations in life forms below. Scientists estimate that each 1 percent decrease in the ozone layer will increase skin cancer, depending on its type, from 1 to 3 percent. The impact that is already having on Americans was noted in chapter 1 (p. 14). In part to test the impact of ozone depletion, an international team of scientists conducted a trans-Antarctic expedition in 1989–90. The members had to keep their skin covered completely at all times, and special clothes were needed because UV rays also attack fibers. "It was like standing under a huge ultraviolet sunlamp for 24 hours a day," Will Seeger, the expedition's leader reported (*HC,* 5/27/90:A6). One group member, Qin Dahe of China, was inadvertently exposed to the sun for a few hours. As a result, according to Seeger, Qin "suffered severe burns. His face swelled. He was nauseated for days." The hole is also beginning to reach populated areas. Australia and New Zealand have measured temporary increases in UV radiation of as much as 20 percent. Light-skinned Australians have the world's highest skin cancer rate, and the country's media broadcasts daily UV readings and alerts to stay indoors

Even at play, we are all threatened by pollution. Getting a tan may also mean getting skin cancer. Swimming is often impossible or dangerous in polluted water, debris washes up on beaches, fishermen catch fish laced with carcinogenic chemicals, and bird-watchers have fewer species to enjoy. The hazy horizon spoils our view of the scenery of the world stage.

during the worst periods. It should also be noted that all life forms can be affected. Scientists are concerned, for example, that UV-ray bombardment could cause mutations in plankton. This marine organism is at the bottom of the food chain, and its reduced production could drastically reduce fish numbers. Plankton also absorbs CO_2, and reduced plankton could increase global warming.

Environmental Protection: The International Response

Like many of the other issues discussed in this chapter, environmental problems have been slowly growing for centuries, have accelerated rapidly in this century, and in some cases reached hypervelocity growth in the last 50 years. Only recently has widespread public and governmental concern been sparked. The result is that programs are just beginning to get under way. Most of the work that has been done has had a national focus, and there have been many advances. In a great part of the developed world, where the problems were most acute and which had the resources to fund programs, water is cleaner, acid rain is being curbed, trees are being planted, toxic wastes are being dealt with better, recycling is under way, and a host of other positive programs have stemmed and sometimes reversed the flood tide of pollution. Because many forms of pollution spread internationally, the national programs have been beneficial.

Importantly, public attitudes have begun to change. A poll in 1989 asked American, British, French, German, and Japanese respondents if they were particularly worried about global warming, ozone layer destruction, deforestation, wildlife destruction, and acid rain. A majority of the citizens of each country except Japan answered that they were significantly concerned (Hastings & Hastings, 1989). The vast majority of each country's respondents believed they were personally careful to avoid polluting, and by majorities ranging from 57 percent in Japan to 74 percent in Great Britain they agreed their government should do more to be involved in the worldwide environment program. A majority in each country also maintained that environmental protection should be given priority over economic expansion.

The difficulty comes when citizens are faced with the real costs of putting these abstract thoughts into action. Choices are sometimes difficult. You cannot at the same time build a hydroelectric dam (providing non–air-polluting energy) on a river and maintain the river's natural state. Environmental protection often also involves high costs. Government spending on the environment among Western European nations increased from $46 to $73 billion between 1987 and 1990 alone, and there are other costs such as sometimes higher product expenses. There are savings too, especially in the long run, but those are often harder to see. Taxpayer resistance to spending will be even greater if and when there is an attempt to amass the funds that need to be spent internationally to help the LDCs simultaneously develop and protect the environment. While professing support for greater international action by their respective governments, for instance, a majority of citizens in each of the five countries thought their tax burdens were already too heavy. Similarly, a November 1990 *CNN/Time* poll found most Americans favoring environmental protection and perceiving themselves as contributing to cleaning up the environment by recycling and other techniques (*Time,* 12/24/90:48). When asked if they would pay $200 in extra taxes to clean up the environment, a laudable 70 percent said yes. That was the limit of the majority's financial commitment, though. When the next question raised the clean-up bill to an extra $500, only 44 percent said yes. Americans also defeated a number of state referendums in November 1990 that would have cost tax dollars, restricted product availability, and taken other measures.

As a result, international progress has been slow, but it has begun. The United Nations has been involved in a number of efforts beginning with the 1972 Conference on the Human Environment in Stockholm. This conference initiated the international dialogue on the environment, and it also led to the establishment of the United Nations Environmental Program (UNEP). Among other things, UNEP sponsored a 1987 conference on protection of the ozone layer at which 46 countries agreed to reduce their CFC production and consumption by 50 percent before the end of the century. That agreement was soon outstripped by the rising scientific evidence of the dangers of CFCs. International conventions in Helsinki (May 1989) and in Geneva (May 1990) resulted in an agreement by 86 countries to phase out CFC production and consumption completely by the year 2000. There was also an agreement in principle to establish a fund to help LDCs eliminate CFCs, but the estimated $400 million a year that is needed initially has not been forthcoming. Without such help, it will be difficult to eliminate CFCs. In fact, the drive to upgrade living standards in many Third World countries presents a major problem. As one researcher put it, "simply allowing every Chinese family to have a refrigerator . . . will swamp" efforts in the developed countries to limit CFCs (*NYT*, 12/18/90:C1).

Progress on dealing with the greenhouse effect has been more limited. The reduction of CFCs will have a positive impact because of their strong role in global warming. The reduction of CO_2 from fossil fuel burning will be more difficult. There is increased recognition of the need to act however, and a UNEP–sponsored World Climate Conference convened in Geneva in October 1990 with the CO_2 problem as a major priority. At that meeting of 130 countries, there was a pledge by most Western European countries, Australia, Japan, and others to stabilize or reduce greenhouse gas emissions by the year 2000. The United States, however, declined to join in because of concern about cost and negative domestic economic impact. Here again, Third World countries also are reluctant to join such pledges without offsetting promises of massive aid because they wish to develop, and they often are economically incapable of instituting expensive energy conservation programs.

There has also been some international response to the problem of international waste dumping and Third World ground pollution. A March 1989 treaty signed by 105 countries in Basel, Switzerland, limits international dumping. International funding agencies, such as the World Bank, are increasingly requiring environmental impact statements as part of loan and grant applications. Also, some national governments are beginning to give environmental foreign aid. In 1989, Japan pledged $2.25 billion to help prevent and clean up pollution in the Third World.

Marine pollution has also been on the international agenda for some time and progress has been made. One of the first multilateral efforts was the International Convention for the Prevention of Pollution from Ships. There are also a number of regional marine conventions: in November 1990, 43 countries, including the world's largest industrial countries, agreed to a global ban on dumping industrial wastes in the oceans by 1995. The countries also agreed not to dispose of nuclear waste in the oceans.

There are many other ideas that are being generated. In a 1989 speech to the UN General Assembly, Austrian foreign minister Alois Mock recommended the creation of a UN environmental police force. Referring to the blue helmets traditionally worn by UN peacekeeping forces, Mock proposed that a new green-helmeted force be created to watch over endangered species, protect the international oceans against pollution, and otherwise act as guardians of the biosphere. It is an idea whose time may not have come, but it is not an idea whose time will surely never be.

After reading this chapter, like those on international law, international organiza-

It is hard to discern the silver lining in the disastrous oil discharge into the Persian Gulf during the 1991 Middle East war. But there was one. People and countries from around the world, irrespective of their views on the war itself, rushed to assist in the containment and cleanup of the viscous oil at sea and on the beaches; volunteers attempted to save wildlife such as this cormorant. International cooperation thus took a small step forward.

tion, arms control, and economic cooperation, it is easy to be discouraged. The problems are immense and complex. Barriers to cooperation are formidable. In many cases, failure to find a solution carries the potential of the direst of consequences. And sometimes when you begin to think you are making progress, as the world has in recent years, a setback occurs. If unintended environmental degradation was not bad enough, 1991 witnessed the sad spectacle of humankind's first calculated attack on the atmosphere. As discussed in chapter 10 (p. 278), there have long been concerns about a nuclear winter caused by the effect of warfare on the environment. The 1991 war in the Middle East showed that conventional war can also bring environmental havoc. Iraq set fire to some oil facilities and others were set ablaze by allied military action. Not only was a huge reservoir of a valuable natural resource wasted, but the conflagration billowed immense amounts of CO_2 into the atmosphere, adding to the thermal blanket forming around the Earth. Even worse, the Iraqis opened oil pipelines and emptied tankers, spewing a black tide of crude petroleum into the Persian Gulf. Within days a 350-square-mile oil slick was strangling the Gulf with an estimated 460 million gallons of petroleum. The Iraqi attempt to create a new Dead Sea in the region added to global CO_2 emissions and was by far the single greatest man-made environmental catastrophe in human history.

Still, the world must and does continue to try to preserve and improve the condition of the Earth and its people. Surely the current level of cooperation, when compared with these stark realities, seems woefully inadequate.

Should we despair? Perhaps not!

The message here is not to adopt the extreme of either unguarded optimism or hopeless pessimism. It is equally unwise to take either the optimistic "it's darkest before the dawn" approach or the pessimistic approach represented by comedian Eddie Murphy's observation that "sometimes it's darkest before the light goes out completely."

Don't sell the early efforts too short. It is only during this century, and really since World War II, that the need to cooperate has penetrated our consciousness and our conscience. The intervening four decades have been a microsecond in human history. In that sense, much has been done.

Still, much remains to be done, and we have so little time to do it. There may, after all, be only a few microseconds left.

Chapter Summary

1. Population is a significant problem facing the world, with the global population having already passed the 5-billion mark. Thus far the international effort has been limited, but the 1984 World Population Conference in Mexico marks the beginning of a greater level of consciousness and cooperation.

2. Food is another, and closely related, problem. There is a need to supply both short-term food aid and long-term developmental assistance to agriculture. A number of international efforts exist in this field, such as the United States Food for Peace program and multilateral programs through United Nations–associated agencies.

3. The health of the world's population is another focus of international effort, the World Health organization being the lead agency. The United Nations Educational, Scientific, and Cultural Organization is the best known among a number of international organizations involved in education.

4. Human rights is another growing area of international concern and is one of the most difficult to work in because violations are usually politically based, so that efforts are often resented and rejected by target countries. The greatest progress has been made in adopting a number of UN declarations, such as the

Universal Declaration of Human Rights, and multilateral treaties that define basic human rights. The enforcement of human rights is much less well developed, but the rising level of awareness and disapproval of violations on a global level is having a positive impact.

5. Yet another problem area is preservation of our natural resources and the environment. Most analysts view this as a serious problem, although there are those who minimize the degree of danger. At this time, efforts at meaningful international cooperation are just beginning.

6. In reviewing the efforts at international cooperation in the areas discussed in this chapter, we return to the question of standards of judgment. It is easy to view the vast extent of the problems facing the globe, to measure the limited effort being made to resolve them, and to dismiss the entire subject of international cooperation as superficial. It is true that not nearly enough is being done. But it is also true that only a very few decades ago nothing was being done. From that zero base, the progress made since World War II is encouraging. The only question is whether or not we will continue to expand our efforts and whether or not we will do enough, soon enough.

Where I did begin, there I shall end.

Shakespeare, *Julius Caesar*

AN EPILOGUE TO THE TEXT/ A PROLOGUE TO THE FUTURE

So here it is some months later, and we are at the end of this book and this course. Finals await, and then, praise be, vacation. That well-deserved break from your academic labors brings you to an implicit point of decision about what to do with this text, the other course readings, and the knowledge you have gained from your instructor. One option is to sell what books you can back to the bookstore and forget the rest. I can remember from my undergraduate days how attractive an idea that sometimes seems.

But then, again, is that really the best option? Probably not. We began our semester's journey with the idea that we are all inescapably part of the world drama. There may be times when we want to shout, "Stop the world, I want to get off," but we cannot. We have also seen that we are both audience and actors in the global play's progress. At the very least, we are all touched by the action in ways that range from the foreign designer jeans that we wear to, potentially, our atomized end.

We can leave it at that, shrug our shoulders, and complain and mumble at the forces that buffet us. But we also can do more than that. We do not have to be just passive victims. We can, if we want and if we try, help write the script. The plot is ongoing and improvisational. The final scene is yet unwritten. We are not even sure when it will occur. It could be well into the far distant future—or it could be tomorrow. This, more than any particular point of information, is the most important message. You are not helpless, and you owe it to yourself and your fellow humans to take an active role in your life and in the world's tomorrows.

The world is beset by great problems. War continues to kill without cessation. A billion-dollar diet industry prospers in many countries of the North due to the fact that many of its citizens are overweight, while in the South, infants and the elderly starve to death in the dry dust. As if localized malnutrition were too slow and selective, we globally attack our environment with the waste products of our progress, and the human population tide threatens to overwhelm the Earth's ability to sustain the people who live on it. Of even more immediate peril, an expanse of nuclear mushroom clouds could instantly terminate our biosphere's more evolutionary decay.

579

To face these problems, we have, at best, a primitive political system. Sovereignty strengthens nationalities but divides the world. Frontier justice is the rule. As in a grade-B western, most of the actors carry guns on their hips and sometimes shoot it out. The law is weak, and the marshals have more authority in theory than in practice.

There are few anymore who really try to defend the system of assertive sovereignty as adequate for the future. Clearly, it is not. What is less certain is what to do next and how to do it. Cooperation, humanitarianism, enlightenment, and other such words provide easy answers, but they are vague goals. Real answers are difficult to come by. They may involve tough choices such as our being asked to give up some things now so that they will not be taken later, be less sovereign, curb our life-style, risk arms control in the hope of avoiding nuclear war, and think of the world in terms of "we."

At every step there will be those who urge caution, who counsel self-preservation first, who see the world as a lifeboat. Maybe they will be right—but probably not. We *have* begun to move toward a more rational order. The last five chapters clearly show this. But they also show how limited and fragile this progress has been. This is where you come in. Your job is to work to make the world the place you want it to be. It is your job to consider the problems, to ponder possible solutions, to reach informed opinions, and to act on your convictions. Think? Yes, of course. But also DO!! That is what is really important.

We began this study with the thought from Shakespeare's *Henry V* that "the world [is] familiar to us and [yet] unknown." My hope is that this text and the course you have just about completed have made the world more familiar, less unknown to you. What you do with what you have learned is now the issue. Will you treat this moment as an end? Or is it a beginning? Heed, if you will, the counsel of Shakespeare's King Lear:

Be governed by your knowledge and proceed.

GLOSSARY

Actors (international) Individuals or organizations that play a direct role in the conduct of world politics. See **Subnational actors**. **33**

Actual power Power that currently exists and that can be utilized. **226**

Adjudication The legal process of deciding an issue through the courts. **481**

Appeasement Trying to satisfy an aggressor by making concessions. See **Munich syndrome**. **94**

Autarky Economic independence from external sources. **359**

Balance of payments A figure that represents the net flow of money into and out of a country due to trade, tourist expenditures, sale of services (such as consulting), foreign aid, profits, and so forth. **390**

Bilateral diplomacy Negotiations between two countries. **324**

Bilateral (foreign) aid Foreign aid given by one country directly to another. **416**

Bipolar system A world political system in which power is primarily held by two international actors. **34**

Bretton Woods system The international monetary system that existed from the end of World War II until the early 1970s; named for an international economic conference held in Bretton Woods, New Hampshire, in 1944. **385**

Bureaucracy The bulk of the state's administrative structure that continues even when leaders change. **124**

Capital needs The requirements of all countries, and LDCs in particular, for money to expand their economies. **405**

Capitalism An economic system based on the private ownership of real property and commercial enterprise, competition for profits, and limited government interference in the marketplace. **175**

Cartel An international agreement among producers of a commodity that attempts to control the production and pricing of that commodity. **422**

Circular error probability (CEP) The radius within which there is a 50 percent chance that a warhead can be delivered accurately. **287**

Codify To write down a law in formal language. **477**

Coercive diplomacy Using threats or force as a diplomatic tactic. **338**

Collective security The original theory behind UN peacekeeping. It holds that aggression against one state is aggression against all and should be defeated by the collective action of all. **455**

Communism A wide-ranging and diverse economic doctrine, with origins in Marxism-Leninism, that has significant political ramifications. **175**

Conference on Security and Cooperation in Europe Series of conferences among 34 NATO, former Soviet bloc, and neutral European countries. Established by 1976 Helsinki Accords. There are plans to establish a small, permanent CSCE headquarters and staff. **527**

Consensual policy Policy based on existing principles that are widely accepted by decisionmakers and followers in a country. **122**

Conventional weapons Nonnuclear arms. **267**

Counterforce targeting Attacking an opponent's military forces, especially nuclear forces. Often associated with first-strike attacks and NUT doctrine. Also has second-strike utility in a limited nuclear war. **283**

Countervalue targeting Attacking an opponent's civilian population, political leadership, and general economic infrastructure. Often associated with massive retaliation and MAD doctrine. **283**

Covert Secret. **302**

Crisis A situation in which decisionmakers are surprised by an event, feel some sense of threat to their values, and believe that they have a limited time in which to respond. The greater the surprise and/or the threat and the shorter the perceived response time, the greater will be the crisis. **341**

Cultural imperialism The attempt to impose your own value system on others, including judging others by how closely they conform to your norms. **188, 204**

Current dollars The value of the dollar in the year for which it is being reported. Sometimes called inflated dollars. Any currency can be expressed in current value. See **Real dollars**. **360**

Dependencia model The belief that the industrialized North has created a neocolonial relationship with the South in which the LDCs are dependent on and disadvantaged by their economic relations with the capitalist industrial countries. **400**

Dependent variable Something that changes in accordance with changes in yet another factor (independent variable). For example, increased gasoline prices (independent variable) may reduce the amount you drive (dependent variable). See **Independent variable**. **29**

Deployment The actual positioning of weapons systems in a combat-ready status. **506**

Deterrence Persuading an opponent not to attack by having enough forces to disable the attack and/or launch a punishing counterattack. **282**

Diplomatic cover Stationing intelligence agents in another country under the guise of diplomatic (and therefore protected) status. **298**

Direct investment Buying stock, real estate, and other assets in another country with the aim of gaining a controlling interest in foreign economic enterprises. Different from portfolio investment, which involves investment solely to gain capital appreciation through market fluctuations. **362**

Disinformation False stories and information planted to embarrass or confuse another country. **299**

Domestic law Law that applies within a state. **477**

East-West Axis The cold-war conflict between the Soviet Union and its allies and the United States and its allies. **20**

Economic orientation The approach used by political scientists who believe that economic forces play a primary role in international relations. They therefore study world political structure and process from the perspective of the control and distribution of economic resources. **29**

Economic theories Beliefs about economic forces and their impact on politics and society. **175**

Elites Those individuals in a political system who exercise disproportionate control of policy either by occupying policy-making positions or by having direct access to and influence over those who do. **134**

Escalation Increasing the level of fighting. **267**

Europe 1992 A term that represents the European Community's decision to eliminate by the end of 1992 all internal barriers (between member countries) to the movement of trade, financial resources, workers, and services (banking, insurance, etc.). **539**

European Community (EC) The Western European regional organization established in 1967 that includes the European Coal and Steel Community (ECSC), the European Economic Community (EEC), and the European Atomic Energy Community (EURATOM). **536**

European Economic Community (EEC) The regional trade and economic organization established in Western Europe by the Treaty of Rome in 1958; also known as the Common Market. **537**

Exchange rate The values of two currencies relative to each other—for example, how many yen equal a dollar or how many lira equal a pound. **384**

Extended deterrence This means using one's forces, particularly nuclear forces, to deter an opponent from conventionally attacking a third party or territory (including colonies) that is distant from one's territorial core. **261**

Free trade The international movement of goods unrestricted by tariffs or nontariff barriers. **368**

Functional relations Relations that include interaction in such usually nonpolitical areas as communication, travel, trade, and finances. **475**

Functionalism International cooperation in specific areas such as communications, trade, travel, health, or environmental protection activity. Often symbolized by the specialized agencies, such as the World Health Organization, associated with the United Nations. **438**

General Agreement on Tariffs and Trade (GATT) The world's primary organization promoting the expansion of free trade. Established in 1947, it has grown to a membership of over 100. **542**

General and complete disarmament (GCD) Total disarmament. **503**

General Assembly The main representative body of the United Nations, composed of all member states. **444**

Government An organization that controls a state. **113**

Gross Domestic Product (GDP) A measure of income within a country that excludes foreign earnings. **360**

Gross National Product (GNP) A measure of the sum of all goods and services produced by a country's nationals, whether they are in the country or abroad. **360**

Group of Seven (G-7) The seven economically largest free market countries: Canada, France, Great Britain, Italy, Japan, the United States, and Germany. **363**

Group of 77 Group of 77 Third World countries that cosponsored the Joint Declaration of Developing Countries in 1963 calling for greater equity in North-South trade. This group has come to include more than 125 members and represents the interests of the less developed countries of the South. **421, 536**

Groupthink How an individual's membership in an organization/decision-making group influences his or her thinking and actions. In particular there are tendencies within a group to think alike, to avoid discordancy, and to ignore ideas or information that threaten to disrupt the consensus. **88**

Hard currency Currencies, such as dollars, marks, francs, and yen, that are acceptable in private channels of international economics. **405**

Hegemony   The domination of one state over another state, a region, or the world. *Hegemonic (adj.)*. **49**

Idealists   Analysts who reject power politics and argue that failure to follow policies based on humanitarianism and international cooperation will result in disaster. **27**

Ideology   A set of related ideas, usually founded on identifiable thinkers and their works, that offers a more or less comprehensive picture of reality. **168**

Incremental decision-making   Also incrementalism. The tendency of decisionmakers to treat existing policy as a given and to follow that policy ("policy inertia") or make only marginal changes in the policy. **88**

Incremental policy   See **Incremental decision-making**. **122**

Independent variable   Something that when it changes affects yet another factor (dependent variable). For example, increased gasoline prices (independent variable) may reduce the amount you drive (dependent variable). See **Dependent variable**. **29**

Individual-level analysis   An analytical approach that emphasizes the role of individuals as either distinct personalities or biological/psychological beings. **30**

Innovative policy   A policy that breaks with the past; that establishes a new direction in a country's general conduct of policy. **122**

Intangible power   Elements of power that are relatively difficult to observe or measure, such as leadership and morale. **233**

Interdependence (economic)   The close interrelationship and mutual dependence of two or more domestic economies on each other. **359**

Intergovernmental organizations (IGOs)   International/transnational actors composed of member countries. **60, 432**

Intermestic   The merger of *inter*national and do*mestic* concerns. **8**

International Court of Justice (ICJ)   The world court, which sits in The Hague with 15 judges and which is associated with the United Nations. **481**

International Monetary Fund (IMF)   The world's primary organization devoted to maintaining monetary stability by helping countries fund balance-of-payments deficits. Established in 1947, it now has 148 members. **406, 545**

Issue areas   Substantive categories of policy that must be considered when evaluating national interest. **122, 215**

Jingoism   An aggressive attitude combined with excessive patriotism. **153**

League of Nations   The first true general international organization. It existed between the end of World War I and the beginning of World War II and was the immediate predecessor of the United Nations. **434**

Least developed countries   Those countries in the poorest of economic circumstances. In this book, this includes those countries with a per capita GNP of less than $400 in 1985 dollars. **397**

Less developed countries (LDCs)   Countries, located mainly in Africa, Asia, and Latin America, with economies that rely heavily on the production of agriculture and raw material and whose per capital GNP and standard of living are substantially below Western standards. **22, 395**

Levels of analysis   Different perspectives (system, state, individual) from which international politics can be analyzed. **30**

Lifeboat ethic   The argument that there are not enough resources to go around and, therefore, the wealthy should not try to aid the weakest countries. **532**

Linkage diplomacy   The practice of considering another country's general international behavior as well as the specifics of the question when deciding whether to reach an agreement on an issue. **341**

MAD (Mutual Assured Destruction)   A situation in which each nuclear superpower has the capability of launching a devastating nuclear second strike even after an enemy has attacked it. The belief that a MAD capacity prevents nuclear war is the basis of deterrence by punishment theory. **280**

Majoritarianism   One voting scheme used in international organizations; based on one vote for each member, with most issues decided by majority vote. **213, 446**

Mass   The non-elite element of a political society. The majority of people who do not occupy policy-making positions and who do not have direct access to those who do. **134**

Messianism   The belief that you are just/holy/good and have a duty/right to save others, even from themselves. **153**

Microstate   A country with a small population that cannot economically survive unaided or that is inherently so militarily weak that it is an inviting target for foreign intervention. **162**

Mirror image   The propensity of countries and people to have similar (good or bad) images of each other. **103**

Monetary relations   The entire scope of international money issues, such as exchange rates, interest rates, loan policies, balance of payments, and regulating institutions (for example, the International Monetary Fund). **384**

Multilateral diplomacy   Negotiations among three or more countries. **324**

Multilateral (foreign) aid   Foreign aid distributed by international organizations such as the United Nations. **416**

Multinational corporations (MNCs)   Private enterprises that have production subsidiaries or branches in more than one country. **375**

Multinational states   Countries in which there are two or more significant nationalities. **157**

Multipolar system   A world political system in which power primarily is held by four or more international actors. **34**

Multistate nationalities   Nations whose members overlap the borders of two or more states. **161**

Munich syndrome   A belief among post–World War II leaders, particularly Americans, that aggression must always be met firmly and that appeasement will only encourage an aggressor. Named for the concessions made to Hitler by Great Britain and France at Munich during the 1938 Czechoslovakian crisis. **94**

Nation   A group of culturally and historically similar people who feel a communal bond and who feel they should govern themselves to at least some degree. **113, 213**

National technical means (NTM)   Satellites, listening stations, and other sophisticated devices used to gather information. **302**

Nationalism   The belief that the nation is the ultimate basis of political loyalty and that nations should have self-governing states. See **Nation-state**. **143**

Nationalization   The process of a country's taking over control of the assets within the country of a foreign-owned multinational corporation. **424**

Nation-state   A politically organized territory that recognizes no higher law; and whose population politically identifies with that entity. See **State**. **38, 142**

Natural rights   The belief that humans have inalienable rights, which existed before societies and which cannot be legitimately denied by society. **183**

Naturalist (school)   Those who believe that law springs from the rights and obligations that humans have by nature. **477**

Negative voting   A voting scheme whereby a single negative vote can block action. See **Veto** for one example. **446**

Neocolonialism   Control of less developed countries (especially in the South) by more developed countries through indirect means, such as economic dominance and coopting the local elite. **400**

New International Economic Order (NIEO)   A term that refers to the goals and demands of the Third World for basic reforms in the international economic system. **422**

Newly industrializing countries (NICs)   Less developed countries whose economies and whose trade now include significant amounts of manufactured products. As a result, these countries have a per capita GNP significantly higher than the average per capita GNP for less developed countries. **22, 404**

Nongovernmental organizations (NGOs or INGOs)   International/transnational organizations with private memberships. **60, 432**

Nonproliferation   A prohibition against the transfer of nuclear weapons, material, or technology from nuclear-capable to non–nuclear-capable countries. **509**

Nontariff barrier   A nonmonetary restriction on trade, such as quotas, technical specifications, or unnecessarily lengthy quarantine and inspection procedures. **366**

North-South Axis   The growing tension between the few economically developed countries (North) and the many economically deprived countries (South). The South is demanding that the North cease economic and political domination and redistribute part of its wealth. **22**

Nuclear freeze   A proposal to halt immediately the development, production, transfer, and deployment of nuclear weapons. **506**

NUT (Nuclear Utilization Theory)   The belief that because nuclear war might occur, countries must be ready to fight, survive, and win a nuclear war. NUT advocates believe this posture will limit the damage if nuclear war occurs and also make nuclear war less likely by creating retaliatory options that are more creditable than massive retaliation. **280**

On-site inspection (OSI)   An arms control verification technique that involves stationing your or a neutral country's personnel in another country to monitor weapons or delivery vehicle manufacturing, testing, deployment, or other aspects of treaty compliance. **523**

Open diplomacy   The public conduct of negotiations and the publication of agreements. **326**

Operational reality   The process by which what is perceived, whether that perception is accurate or not, assumes a level of reality in the mind of the beholder and becomes the basis for making an operational decision (a decision about what to do). **104**

Overt   In the open. **302**

Pacta sunt servanda   Translates as "treaties are to be served/carried out" and means that agreements between states are binding. **477**

Parliamentary diplomacy   Debate and voting in international organizations to settle diplomatic issues. **325**

Peacekeeping   The use of military means by an international organization such as the United Nations to prevent fighting, usually by acting as a buffer between combatants. The international force is neutral between the combatants and must have been invited to be present by at least one of the combatants. See **Collective security**. **456**

Perceived power   The power that others think you have, whether it actually exists or not. **227**

Plenary representative body   An assembly, such as the UN's General Assembly, that consists of all members of the main organization. **444**

Political leadership   Those officials, usually but not always in the executive branch of a government, who are at the center of foreign policy-making and whose tenures are variable and dependent on the political contest for power. **123**

Positivist (school)   Those who believe that law reflects society and the way that people want the society to operate. **477**

Potential power   Power that can be developed in the future, such as untapped natural resources or untrained workers. **226**

Power to defeat   The ability to overcome in a traditional military sense—that is, to overcome enemy armies and capture and hold territory. **264**

Power to hurt   The ability to inflict pain outside the immediate battle area; sometimes called coercive violence. It is often used against civilians and is a particular hallmark of terrorism and nuclear warfare. **264**

Primary products   Agricultural products and raw materials, such as minerals. **400**

Protectionism   The use of tariffs and nontariff barriers to restrict the flow of imports into one's country. **368**

Public diplomacy   A process of creating an overall international image that enhances your ability to achieve diplomatic success. **331**

Real dollars   The value of dollars expressed in terms of a base year. This is determined by taking current value and subtracting the amount of inflation between the base year and the year being reported. Sometimes called uninflated dollars. Any currency can be valued in real terms. See **Current dollars**. **360**

Real power   Power that objectively exists, that can be established as a fact. **227**

Realists   Analysts who believe that countries operate in their own self-interests and that politics is a struggle for power. **26**

Realpolitik   Operating according to the belief that politics is based on the pursuit, possession, and application of power. **42**

Regime   A complex of norms, treaties, international organizations, and transnational activity that orders an area of activity such as the environment or oceans. **60**

Relative power   Power measured in comparison with the power of other international actors. **231**

Research and development (R&D)   The period in weapon system acquisition (research, design, testing, evaluation) prior to deployment. **498**

Role   How an individual's position influences his or her thinking and actions. **87**

SALT I   The Strategic Arms Limitation Treaty signed in 1972. **509**

SALT II   The Strategic Arms Limitation Treaty signed in 1979 but withdrawn by President Carter from the U.S. Senate before ratification in response to the Soviet invasion of Afghanistan. **509**

Scientific school   An approach taken by political scientists who attempt to find recurring patterns and causal relations in international politics. This approach is especially likely to use quantitative methods to study political phenomena. **29**

Secretariat   The administrative organ of the United Nations, headed by the secretary-general. In general, the administrative element of any IGO, headed by a secretary-general. **449**

Security Council   The main peacekeeping organ of the United Nations. The Security Council has 15 members, including 5 permanent members. **445**

Situational power   The power that can be applied, and is reasonable, in a given situation. Not all elements of power can be applied to every situation. **231**

Social Darwinism   A social theory that argues it is proper that stronger races will prosper and will dominate lesser peoples. **174**

Social theories   Theories about the nature of world society and about the roles and the importance of various types of people. **173**

Sovereignty   The most essential characteristic of an international state. The term strongly implies political independence from any higher authority and also suggests at least theoretical equality. **110**

Spaceship Earth   The argument that the fate of all the world's people is inseparably intertwined and that if we do not aid the needy, we are not only derelict in our responsibility but we are also, in the long term, working against our own best interest. **533**

Special Drawing Rights (SDRs)   Reserves held by the International Monetary Fund that the central banks of member countries can draw on to help manage the values of their currencies. SDR value is based on a "market-basket" of currencies and SDRs are acceptable in transactions between central banks. **388**

Sphere of influence   A region that a big power claims is of special importance to its national interest and over which the big power exercises special influence. **203, 267**

Star Wars   The popular name given to the U.S. proposals to develop land- and space-based ballistic missile defense systems. Formally called the Strategic Defense Initiative. **291**

START   Strategic Arms Reduction Talks; the Reagan administration's designation of strategic arms talks with the Soviets. **504**

State   A political actor that has sovereignty and a number of characteristics, including territory, population, organization, and recognition. **109**

State terrorism   Terrorism carried out directly by, or encouraged and funded by, an established government of an international state. **315**

State-level analysis   An analytical approach that emphasizes the actions of states and the internal (domestic) causes of their policies. **30**

Strategic nuclear weapons   Weapons that could be delivered intercontinentally, especially between the United States and the Soviet Union and/or China. **287**

Subjective national interest   The preferred policies and goals of an individual or regime that spring from a particular set of views and predispositions. **201**

Subnational actors   Individuals or organizations that play a direct role in the politics of a country. **123**

Summitry   Diplomatic negotiations between national leaders. **328**

Supranational organization   Organizations that are founded and operate, at least in part, on the idea that international organizations can or should have authority higher than individual states and that those states should be subordinate to the supranational organization. **462**

System-level analysis   An analytical approach that emphasizes the importance of world conditions (economics, technology, power relationships, and so forth) on the actions of states and other international actors. **30, 33**

Tactical nuclear weapons   Relatively low-yield weapons used against enemy military forces on a battlefield. **269**

Tangible power   Elements of power that are relatively easy to observe and measure, such as factories and soldiers. **233**

Targeting   Selecting target options for nuclear weapons. **272**

Tariff   A tax, usually based on percentage of value, that importers must pay on items purchased abroad; also known as an import tax or import duty. **366**

Transnational   Extending beyond the borders of a single country; applied to a political movement, issue, organization, or other phenomenon. **436**

Transnational organizations   Organizations that are not part of any single national government and that perform specialized functions across international boundaries. **60**

Trilateral countries   The United States and Canada, Japan, and the Western European countries. **53**

Tripolar system   A world system that is dominated by three superpowers. In the future the most likely combination is the United States, the Soviet Union, and China. **49**

Unipolar system   Domination of the world by one actor. **49**

Verification   The process of checking on the other side's arms control compliance. **508**

Veto   A negative vote cast in the UN Security Council by one of the five permanent members; has the effect of defeating the issue being voted on. **446**

Weighted voting   A voting scheme that gives some members more votes than others, based on population, wealth, or some other factor. **446**

World Bank   A collective term for the closely linked institutions of the International Bank for Reconstruction and Development, the International Development Association, and the International Finance Corporation. All three, with different foci, make loans to countries for economic development. **546**

World government   The concept of a supranational world authority to which current countries would surrender some or all of their sovereign authority. **437**

Xenophobia   Fear of others, "they-groups." **152**

Zionism   The belief that Jews are a nation and that they should have an independent homeland. **154**

REFERENCES AND BIBLIOGRAPHY

Adelman, Kenneth L. (1986). "The challenge of negotiating by democracies." *Presidential Studies Quarterly, 16,* 200–205.

Aldrich, John H., Sullivan, John L., & Borgida, Eugene. (1989). "Foreign affairs and issue voting: Do presidential candidates 'waltz before a blind audience'?" *American Political Science Review, 83,* 123–42.

Alger, Chadwick F. (1990, April). "U.S. public opinion of the U.N.: A mandate for more creative U.S. participation in the U.N. system?" Paper presented to the International Studies Association convention, Washington, D.C.

Allison, Graham T., Carnesale, Albert, & Nye, Joseph S., Jr. (Eds.). (1985). *Hawks, doves, and owls: An agenda for avoiding nuclear war.* New York: W. W. Norton.

Allyn, Bruce J., Blight, James G., & Welch, David A. (1990). "Essence of revision: Moscow, Havana, and the Cuban missile crisis." *International Security, 14,* 136–72.

Alt, James E., Calvert, Randall L., & Humes, Brian D. (1988). "Reputation and hegemonic stability: A game-theoretic analysis." *American Political Science Review, 82,* 446–66.

Altbach, Phillip G. (Ed.). (1989). *Student political activism: An international reference handbook.* Westport, CT: Greenwood Press.

Ambrose, Stephen E. (1983). *Rise to globalism: American foreign policy since 1938* (3rd ed.). New York: Penguin.

Amnesty International. (1981). *Amnesty international report, 1981.* London.

Anderson, P., & McKeown, T. J. (1987). "Changing aspirations, limited attention, and war." *World Politics, 40,* 1–29.

Archer, Clive. (1983). *International organizations.* London: Allen & Unwin.

Arieli, Yehoshua. (1982). "History as reality shaped by images." In Nissan Oren (Ed.), In *Images and reality in international politics* (pp. 57–69). New York: St. Martin's Press.

Arkin, William M., & Handler, Joshua. (1989). "Naval nuclear accidents: The secret history." *Greenpeace, 14,* 14–18.

Arms Control and Disarmament Agency. *See* U.S. (ACDA).

Armstrong, David. (1989). *The Rise of the international organization.* New York: St. Martin's Press.

Armstrong, J. D. (1977). *Revolutionary diplomacy: Chinese foreign policy and the united front doctrine.* Berkeley: University of California Press.

Armstrong, John A. (1982). *Nations before nationalism.* Chapel Hill: University of North Carolina Press.

Aron, Raymond. (1981). *Peace and war: A theory of international relations.* (Richard Howard & Annette Baker Fox, Trans.). Garden City, NY: Doubleday. (Original work published 1966).

Asher, Herbert B. (1988). *Presidential elections and American politics* (4th ed.). Chicago: Dorsey Press.

Ausland, John C. (1989). "Is the cold war really over?" *Bulletin of Peace Proposals, 20,* 399–404.

Bailey, Thomas A. (1968). *The art of diplomacy.* New York: Appleton-Century-Crofts.

Baker, James. (1989). "Points of mutual advantage: *Perestroika* and American foreign policy." Address to the Foreign Policy Association, New York City, October 16, 1989. Reproduced in U.S. Department of State, Bureau of Public Affairs, *Current Policy* No. 1213.

Baker, Russell, & Peters, Charles. (1979). "The prince and his courtiers." In Charles Peters & Nicholas Leman (Eds.), *Inside the system.* New York: Holt, Rinehart, & Winston.

Balassa, Bela, & assoc. (1971). *The structure of protectionism in developing countries.* Baltimore: Johns Hopkins Press.

Baldwin, David A. (1979). "Power analysis and world politics." *World Politics, 31,* 164.

Baldwin, David A. (1985). *Economic statecraft.* Princeton, NJ: Princeton University Press.

Ball, Desmond. (1985). "Targeting for strategic deterrence." *Adelphi Papers*, No. 185. London: The International Institute for Strategic Studies.

Ball, Desmond, & Toth, Robert C. (1990). "Revising the SIOP: Taking war-fighting to dangerous extremes." *International Security, 14,* 65–92.

Ball, Nicole, & Leitenberg, Milton. (Eds.). (1983). *The structure of the defense industry: An international survey.* New York: St. Martin's Press.

Bandow, Doug. (1989). "What's still wrong with the World Bank?" *Orbis, 34,* 73–89.

Barber, James David. (1985). *Presidential character* (3rd ed.). Englewood Cliffs, NJ: Prentice Hall.

Barilleaux, Ryan J. (1986). "The President, 'intermestic' issues and the risks of policy leadership." *Presidential Studies Quarterly, 15,* 154–76.

Barnet, Richard. (1979). "Human rights implications of corporate food policies." In Ralph Pettman (Ed.), *Moral claims in world affairs*. New York: St. Martin's Press.

Barnet, Richard J., & Muller, Ronald E. (1974). *The global reach: The power of the multinational corporations*. New York: Simon & Schuster.

Barston, Ronald Peter. (1988). *Modern diplomacy*. Essex, U.K.: Longman.

Barzun, Jacques. (1989, March/April) "Is democratic theory for export?" *Society*, pp. 16–23.

Bebler, Anton, & Seroka, Jim. (1990). *Contemporary political systems: Classifications and typologies*. Boulder, CO: Lynne Rienner.

Beck, Emily Morison. (Ed.). (1983). *Bartlett's familiar quotations* (15th ed.). Boston: Little, Brown.

Becker, C. M. (1987). "Economic sanctions against South Africa." *World Politics*, *39*, 203–30.

Beckman, Peter. (1984). *World politics in the twentieth century*. Englewood Cliffs, NJ: Prentice Hall.

Beer, Francis A. (1981). *Peace against war: The ecology of international violence*. San Francisco: W. H. Freeman.

Bennett, A. LeRoy. (1988). *International organization: Principles and issues*. Englewood Cliffs, NJ: Prentice Hall.

Bennett, John C. & Seifert, Harvey. (1977). *U.S. foreign policy and Christian ethics*. Philadelphia: Westminster Press.

Berkowitz, Bruce D. (1985). "Proliferation, deterrence, and the likelihood of nuclear war." *Journal of Conflict Resolution 29*, 112–36.

Berkowitz, Leonard. (1978). "Whatever happened to the frustration-aggression hypothesis?" *American Behavioral Scientist, 21*, 690–701.

Bernholz, Peter. (1985). *The international game of power*. Berlin, West Germany: Mouton Publishers.

Betts, Richard K. (1978). "Analysis, war, and decision: Why intelligence failures are inevitable." *World Politics, 31*, 61–89.

Binkin, Martin. (1985). "Manpower." In George E. Hudson & Joseph Kruzel (Eds.), *American defense annual, 1985-1986*. Lexington, MA: Lexington Books.

Black, Robert, Blank, Stephen, & Hanson, Elizabeth. (1978). *Multinationals in contention: Responses at governmental and international levels*. New York: The Conference Board.

Blake, David H., & Walters, Robert S. (1987). *The politics of global economic relations*. Englewood Cliffs, NJ: Prentice Hall.

Blechman, Barry M., & Kaplan, Stephen. (1978). *Force without war: U.S. armed forces as a political instrument*. Washington, D.C.: Brookings.

Blechman, Barry M., & Kaplan, Stephen. (1979). "U.S. military forces as a political instrument." *Political Science Quarterly, 94*, 193–210.

Blechman, Barry M., & Utgoff, Victor A. (1987). "The macroeconomics of strategic defenses." *International Security, 11*, 33–69.

Blight, James G. (1990). *The shattered crystal ball: Fear and learning in the Cuban missile crisis*. Savage, MD: Rowman & Littlefield.

Bloom, Allan, Hassner, Pierre, Himmelfarb, Gertrude, Kirstol, Irving, Moynihan, Daniel Patrick, & Sestanovich, Stephen.

(1989, Summer). "Individual responses to Fukuyama." *The National Interest* No. 16, 19–34.

Blum, William T. (1971). *Ideologies and attitudes*. Englewood Cliffs, NJ: Prentice Hall.

Bobrow, Davis B., & Hill, Stephen R. (1985). "The determinants of military budgets: The Japanese case." *Conflict Management and Peace Science*, *9*, 1–18.

Bociurkiw, Bohdan R. (1979). *Perceptions: Relations between the United States and the Soviet Union*. Testimony before the U.S. Congress, Senate Committee on Foreign Relations. Washington, D.C.

Bogdan, Corneliu, & Preda, Eugen. (1988). *Spheres of influence*. Social Science Monographs, Boulder. New York: Columbia University Press.

Bohlen, Charles E. (1973). *Witness to history*. New York: Norton.

Borchert, Manfred, & Schinke, Rolf. (Eds.). (1990). *International indebtedness*. London: Routledge.

Borenstein, Morris. (1981). "Issues in East-West trade." In Morris Borenstein & William Zimmerman (Eds.), *East-West economic relations and the future of Europe*. London: Allen & Unwin.

Boserup, Esten. (1981). *Population and technological change*. Chicago: The University of Chicago Press.

Boulding, Kenneth E. (1989). *Three faces of power*. Newbury Park, CA: Sage.

Brady, Nicholas F. (1989). "Dealing with the international debt crisis." *Department of State Bulletin*, May 1989, 53–56. Reprint of a speech delivered on March 10, 1989.

Brecher, Michael. (1972). *The foreign policy system of Israel*. New Haven, CT: Yale University Press.

Brelauer, George W. (1987). "Ideology and learning in Soviet Third World policy." *World Politics*, *39*, 429–48.

Brilmayer, Lea. (1989). *Justifying international acts*. Ithaca, NY: Cornell University Press.

Broad, William J. (1987, June 28). "The secrets of Soviet Star Wars." *The New York Times Magazine*, pp. 24 et seq.

Brown, David. (Ed.). (1987). *The utility of economic sanctions*. New York: St. Martin's Press.

Brown, Lester R., Chandler, William U., Flavin, Christopher, Jacobson, Jodi, Pollock, Cynthia, Postel, Sandra, Starke, Linda & Wolf, Edward C. (1987). *State of the world, 1987*. New York: W. W. Norton.

Brown, Lester R., & Jacobson, Jodi. (1987). "Assessing the future of urbanization." In Lester R. Brown, William U. Chandler, Christopher Flavin, Jodi Jacobson, Cynthia Pollock, Sandra Postel, Linda Starke, & Edward C. Wolf (Eds.), *State of the world, 1987*. New York: W. W. Norton.

Brown, Michael E. (1990). "The case against the B-2." *International Security, 15*, 129–53.

Brown, Seyom. (1987). *The causes and prevention of war*. New York: St. Martin's Press.

Brown, Seyom. (1988). *New forces, old forces, and the future of world politics*. Glenville, IL: Scott, Foresman.

Bryne, Robert. (Ed.). (1985). *The other 637 best things anybody ever said*. New York: Atheneum.

Brzezinski, Zbigniew. (1983). *Power and principle*. New York: Farrar, Straus, Giroux.

Bueno de Mesquita, Bruce, & Lalman, David. (1988). "Empirical support for systemic and dyadic explanations of international conflict." *World Politics, 41,* 1–20.

Bull, Hedley. (1977). *The anarchical society: A study of order in world politics.* New York: Columbia University Press.

Bull, Hedley. (1987). "The balance of power and its present relevance." In William C. Olson (Ed.), *The theory and practice of international relations* (pp. 66–73). Englewood Cliffs, NJ: Prentice Hall.

Bull, Hedley, & Watson, Adam. (1982). *The expansion of international society.* London: Oxford University Press.

Burke, John P., & Greenstein, Fred I. (1989). "Presidential personality and national security leadership: A comparative analysis of Vietnam decision-making." *International Review of Political Science, 10,* 73–92.

Burton, John, Groom, A. J. R., Light, Margot, Mitchell, C. R., & Bennis, J. D. (1985). *Territorial power domains, Southeast Asia and China.* London: Grower.

Butler, William E. (1989). "International law, foreign policy and the Gorbachev style." *Journal of International Affairs, 42,* 363–77.

Canada, Department of External Affairs. (1986). *Annual Report, 1984–1985.* Ottawa: Minister of Supply and Services.

Carnesale, Albert, & Haass, Richard N. (1987). "Conclusions: Weighing the evidence." In Albert Carnesale & Richard N. Haass (Eds.), *Superpower arms control: Lessons learned from experience.* Cambridge, MA: Ballinger.

Carr, Edward H. (1945). *Nationalism and after.* London: Macmillan.

Carr, Fergus. (1982). "The view from the Third World." In William Kincade & Christoph Bertram (Eds.), *Nuclear proliferation in the 1980s.* New York: St. Martin's Press.

Carroll, John E. (1983). *Environmental diplomacy: An examination and a perspective of Canadian–U.S. transboundary environmental relations.* Ann Arbor: University of Michigan Press.

Carter, Ashton B. (1985). "The command and control of nuclear war." *Scientific American, 222* (January), 32–39.

Carter, Jimmy. (1979, January). Speech, December 6, 1978. *Department of State Bulletin.*

Carter, Ralph G. (1987, April). "Assertiveness in congressional foreign policy behavior." Paper presented to the International Studies Association, Washington, D.C.

Carter, Ralph G. (1989). "Morality in the making of foreign policy." In James S. Bowman & Frederick A. Elliston (Eds.), *Ethics, Government, and Public Policy* (pp. 109–23). Westport, CT: Greenwood Press.

Central Intelligence Agency. *See* U.S. (CIA).

Chai, Trong R. (1979). "Chinese policy toward the Third World and the superpowers in the UN General Assembly, 1971–1977: A voting analysis." *International Organization, 33,* 391–403.

Chan, Steve. (1989). "Income inequality among LDCs: A comparative analysis of alternative perspectives." *International Studies Quarterly, 33,* 45–65.

Chen, Lung-chu. (1989). *An introduction to contemporary international law: A policy-oriented perspective.* New Haven, CT: Yale University Press.

Chilcote, Ronald H. (1981). *Theories of comparative politics.* Boulder, CO: Westview Press.

Chirac, Jacques. (1989). "Soviet change and western security." *Strategic Review, 17,* 9–15.

Chittick, William O., & Billingsley, Keith R. (1989, March). "American foreign policy beliefs: The perils of the flatland." Paper presented to the International Studies Association convention, London.

Chiu, Hungdah. (1987). "Chinese views on sources of international law." *Harvard International Law Journal, 28,* 289–307.

Choate, Pat. (1990). *Agents of influence.* New York: Alfred A. Knopf.

Chowdhury, Subrata Roy. (1972). *Genesis of Bangladesh.* New York: Asian Publishing House.

Christensen, Thomas J., & Snyder, Jack. (1990). "Chain gangs and passed bucks: Predicting alliance patterns in multipolarity." *International Organization, 44,* 137–68.

Christopher, Andrew, & Gordievsky, Oleg. (1990). *KGB: The inside story.* New York: HarperCollins. Quotations are taken from excerpts in *Time,* October 22, 1990, pp. 72–82.

CIA. *See* U.S. (CIA).

Clark, Donald L. (1986). "Could be wrong." In Herbert M. Levine (Ed.), *World politics debated* (2nd ed., pp. 407–14). New York: McGraw-Hill.

Clark, Ian. (1989). *The hierarchy of states: Reform and resistance in the international order.* Cambridge, U.K.: Cambridge University Press.

Claude, Inis L., Jr. (1981). "Comment." *International Studies, 25,* 198–202.

Cleaver, Harry. (1989). "Close the IMF, abolish the debt and end development: A class analysis of the international debt crisis." *Capital and Class, 39,* 317–44.

Cleveland, Harlan. (1988, May–June). "The future of international governance." *The Futurist,* pp. 9–12.

Clifford, J. Garry. (1989, December 12). "Remember the Monroe Doctrine?" *Hartford Courant,* p. D15.

Cline, Ray S. (1977). *World power trends and U.S. foreign policy for the 1980s.* Boulder, CO: Westview Press.

Cline, Ray S. (1980). *World power trends and U.S. foreign policy.* Boulder, CO: Westview Press.

Clinton, W. David. (1986). "The national interest: Normative foundations." *The Review of Politics, 48,* 495–519.

Coate, Roger A. (1990). "Changing patterns of conflict: The United States and UNESCO." In Margaret P. Karns & Karen A. Mingst (Eds.), *The United States and multilateral institutions* (pp. 231–60. Boston: Unwin Hyman.

Coate, Roger A., & Puchala, Donald J. (1990). "Global policies and the United Nations system: A current assessment." *Journal of Peace Research, 27,* 127–40.

Cohen, Benjamin J. (1973). *The question of imperialism.* New York: Basic Books.

Cohen, Benjamin J. (1987). "A brief history of international monetary relations." In Jeffry A. Frieden & David A. Lake (Eds.), *International political economy: Perspectives on global power and wealth.* New York: St. Martin's Press.

Cohen, Carol. (1987). "Slick'ems, glick'ems, Christmas trees, and cookie cutters: Nuclear language and how we learned to pat the bomb." *Bulletin of the Atomic Scientists, 43* (June), 17–24.

Cohen, Raymond. (1987). *Theater of power: The art of diplomatic signaling.* Essex, U.K.: Longman.

Cohen, Richard, & Wilson, Peter A. (1988). "Superpowers in decline? Economic performance and national security." *Comparative Strategy, 7,* 99–132.

Cohen, Saul. (1973). *Geography and politics in a world divided* (2nd ed.). New York: Oxford University Press.

Cohen, Sheldon M. (1989). *Arms and judgment: Law, morality, and the conduct of war in the twentieth century.* Boulder, CO: Westview Press.

Coleman, William D. (1984). *The independence movement in Quebec, 1945–1980.* Toronto: The University of Toronto Press.

Committee on International Security and Arms Control, National Academy of Sciences. (1985). *Nuclear arms control: Background and issues.* Washington, D.C.: National Academy Press.

Congress. *See* either U.S. Congress or specific committee name.

Congressional Research Service. (1979). "Diplomacy and negotiation in historical perspective." In *Soviet diplomacy and negotiating behavior* (pp. 11–26). A study prepared for the U.S. Congress, House of Representatives, Committee on Foreign Affairs. Washington, D.C.

Connor, Walter. (1979). "Nation-building or nation-destroying." In Fred A. Sondermann, David S. McLellan, & William C. Olson (Eds.), *The theory and practice of international relations.* Englewood Cliffs, NJ: Prentice Hall.

Council on Environmental Quality, & Department of State. (1980). *The global 2000 report to the president.* Washington, D.C.: U.S. Government Printing Office.

Cowling, Keith, & Sugden, Roger. (1987). *Transnational monopoly capitalism.* Sussex, U.K.: Wheatsheaf Books.

Cropey, Joseph. (1977). *Political philosophy and the issues of politics.* Chicago: University of Chicago Press.

Crzybowski, Kazimierz. (1970). *Soviet public international law.* Leyden, the Netherlands: Sitkjhoff.

Culbertson, John M. (1990). "Workable trade policy for today's economic and political world." *Academy of Political Science, 37,* 151–64.

Cypher, James M. "Military spending, technical change, and economic growth: A disguised form of industrial policy." *Journal of Economic Issues, 21,* 33–57.

Daggett, Stephen, & Husbands, Jo L., with Kaufmann, William W. (1987). *Achieving an affordable defense: A military strategy to guide military spending.* Cambridge, MA: The Committee for National Security.

Dahl, Robert A. (1971). *Polyarchy.* New Haven CT: Yale University Press.

Dallin, Alexander. (1981). "The Domestic sources of Soviet foreign policy." In Seweryn Bialer (Ed.), *The domestic context of Soviet foreign policy.* Boulder, CO: Westview Press.

D'Amato, Anthony. (1990). "The invasion of Panama was a lawful response to tyranny." *American Journal of International Law, 84,* 516–24.

Damrosch, Lori F. (Ed.). (1987). *The International Court of Justice at a crossroads.* Ardsley-on-the-Hudson, New York: Transnational Publishers.

Davies, Richard T. (1990). "Which 'voice' for America? U.S. international broadcasting after the cold war." Typescript of address delivered at the University of Connecticut, October 10, 1990.

de Callierres, Francois. (1919). *Of the manner of negotiating with sovereigns.* Boston: Houghton Mifflin. (Original work published 1716).

Deardorff, Alan V., & Stern, Robert M. (1990). "Options for trade liberalization in the Uruguay Round negotiations." *Academy of Political Science, 37,* 17–27.

DeGrasse, Robert W., Jr. (1987). "Military expansion, economic decline." In William M. Evan and Stephen Hilgartner (Eds.), *The arms race and nuclear war.* Englewood Cliffs, NJ: Prentice Hall.

DeMars, William. (1988, March). "Political uses of nuclear weapons: Nuclear threats and extended deterrence." Paper presented to the International Studies Association, St. Louis, MO.

DeMars, William. (1990, April). "Changing patterns of international and civil war: Revising the conventional facts." Paper presented to the International Studies Association convention, Washington, D.C.

Deutsch, Karl W. (1966). *Nationalism and social communication.* Cambridge, MA: MIT Press.

Deutsch, Karl W. (1978). *The analysis of international relations* (2nd ed.). Englewood Cliffs, NJ: Prentice Hall.

Deutsch, Karl W. (1979). *Tides among nations.* New York: Free Press.

Deutsch, Karl W., Burrell, Sidney A., Kahn, Robert A., Leem, Maurice L., Jr., Lichterman, Martin, Lindgren, Raymond E., Lowenheim, Francis, & Van Wagenen, Richard W. (1957). *Political community and the North Atlantic area.* Princeton, NJ: Princeton University Press.

Devlin, Robert. (1989). *Debt and crisis in Latin America: The supply side of the story.* Princeton, NJ: Princeton University Press.

Dicken, Peter. (1986). *Global shift: Industrial change in a turbulent world.* London: Harper & Row.

DiClerico, Robert E. (1979). *The American president.* Englewood Cliffs, NJ: Prentice Hall.

Diehl, Paul F. (Ed.). (1989). *The politics of international organizations: Patterns and insights.* Chicago: Dorsey Press.

Diehl, Paul F. (1989a). "The conditions for success in peacekeeping operations." In Paul Diehl (Ed.), *The politics of international organizations* (pp. 173–88). Chicago: Dorsey Press.

Diehl, Paul F. (1989b). "A permanent UN peacekeeping force: An evaluation." *Bulletin of Peace Proposals, 20,* 27–36.

Diehl, Paul F. (1990, April). "What are they fighting for?: The importance of issues in international conflict research." Paper presented to the International Studies Association convention, Washington, D.C.

Diehl, Paul F., & Kingston, Jean. (1987). "Messenger or message?: Military buildups and the initiation of conflict." *Journal of Politics, 49,* 801–13.

Dittmer, Lowell. (1987). "The strategic triangle: A critical review." In Ilpyong J. Kim (Ed.), *The strategic triangle: China, the United States, and the Soviet Union* (pp. 29–47). New York: Paragon House.

Dixon, William J. (1983). "Evaluation of weighted voting schemes for the United Nations General Assembly." *International Studies Quarterly, 27,* 295–314.

Dixon, William J. (1986). "Reciprocity in United States–Soviet relations: Multiple symmetry or issue linkage." *American Journal of Political Science, 30,* 421–445.

Dixon, William J. (1989). "The evaluation of weighted voting schemes for the United Nations General Assembly." In Paul Diehl (Ed.), *The politics of international organizations* (pp. 134–51). Chicago: Dorsey Press.

Dobratz, Betty A. (1988). "Foreign policy and economic orientations influencing party preferences in the socialist nation of Greece." *East European Quarterly, 21,* 413–30.

Dodge, Dorothy Rae, & Baird, Duncan H. (1975). *Continuities and discontinuities in political thought.* New York: Wiley.

Donnelly, Jack. (1989). *Universal human rights in theory and practice.* Ithaca, NY: Cornell University Press.

Donnelly, Jack. (1990). "Global policy studies: A skeptical view." *Journal of Peace Research, 27,* 221–30.

Doose, Douglas, Gowland, David, & Hartley, Keith. (Eds.). (1982). *The collaboration of nations: A study of European economic integration.* New York: St. Martin's Press.

Doran, Charles. (1989). "Systemic disequilibrium, foreign policy role, and the power cycle." *Journal of Conflict Resolution, 33,* 371–401.

Dore, Issak I. (1984). *International law and the superpowers.* New Brunswick, NJ: Rutgers University Press.

Dorpalen, Andreas. (1942). *The world of General Haushofer.* New York: Farrar & Rinehart.

Dougherty, James E., & Pfaltzgraff, Robert L., Jr. (1990). *Contending theories of international relations* (3rd ed.). New York: Harper & Row.

Doxey, Margaret. (1989, March). "Constructive internationalism: A continuing theme in Canadian foreign policy." Paper presented to the International Studies Association convention, London.

Draper, Theodore. (1977). "Appeasement and détente." In Steven L. Spiegel (Ed.), *At issue: Politics in the world arena* (2nd ed.). New York: St. Martin's Press.

Dror, Yeheckel. (1973). *Crazy states.* Lexington, MA: D. C. Heath.

Drucker, H. M. (1974). *The political uses of ideology.* New York: Harper & Row.

Duchacek, Ivo D. (1975). *Nations and men* (3rd ed.). Hinsdale, IL: Dryden Press.

Duchacek, Ivo D., Latouche, Daniel, & Stevenson, Garth (Eds.). (1988). *Perforated sovereignties and international relations: Trans-sovereign contracts of subnational governments.* Westport, CT: Greenwood Press.

Dumas, Lloyd J. (Ed.). (1988). "Swords into ploughshares." [Special issue]. *Bulletin of Peace Proposals, 19,* 1–165.

Dunn, Lewis A. (1982). *Controlling the bomb.* New Haven CT: Yale University Press.

Eckhardt, William. (1988, March). "Civilian death in wartime." Paper presented at the International Studies Association, St. Louis, Missouri.

Eckhardt, William. (1990). "Civilizations, empires, and wars." *Journal of Peace Research, 27,* 9–24.

Einhorn, Martin B., Kane, Gordon L., & Nincic, Miroslav. (1984). "Strategic arms control through test constraints." *International Security, 8,* 114–19.

Einhorn, Robert J. (1985). *Negotiating from strength: Leverage in U.S.–Soviet arms control negotiations.* New York: Praeger.

El-Agraa, Ali M. (Ed.). (1980). *The economics of the European Community.* New York: St. Martin's Press.

Epstein, William, & Robles, Alfonzo Garcia. (1984). "UN Disarmament Campaign." *Bulletin of the Atomic Scientists, 40,* (March), 37–39.

Ethridge, Lloyd S. (1978). "Personality effects on American foreign policy, 1898–1968: A test of interpersonal generalization theory." *American Political Science Review, 72,* 434–51.

Euromonitor. (1990). *International marketing data and statistics, 1990.* London: Euromonitor Publications.

Fairbanks, Charles H., Jr., & Shulsky, Abraham. (1987, Summer). "From 'arms control' to arms reductions: The historical experience." *The Washington Quarterly,* 59–72.

Falk, Richard. (1989). *Revitalizing international law.* Ames, IA: Iowa State University Press.

Farer, Tom J. (1990). "Panama: Beyond the charter paradigm." *American Journal of International Law, 84,* 503–15.

Feld, Werner J., & Jordan, Robert S., with Leon Hurwitz. (1988). *International organizations: A comparative approach* (2nd ed.). Westport, CT: Praeger.

Ferencz, Benjamin B. (1983). *Enforcing international law: A way to world peace.* London: Oceana.

Finkelstein, Lawrence S. (1990, April). "The IR of IGOs—another look." Paper presented to the International Studies Association convention, Washington, D.C.

Finkelstein, Lawrence S. (1990a, July). "From collective security to collective defense to . . . ?" Paper presented to the Senior Academics Conference on East-West Security, NATO/Paul Loebe Institute, Berlin.

Fitzgerald, Mary C. (1986). *Marshal Ogarkov on modern war: 1977–1985* (Professional Paper No. 443.10). Alexandria, VA: Center for Naval Analysis.

Forsythe, David P. (Ed.). (1989). *The United Nations in the world political economy.* New York: St. Martin's Press.

Fox, William T. R. (1980, April 17–19). "Human freedom in a world of states." *Proceedings of the 74th Annual Meeting of the American Society of International Law.* Washington, D.C.

Franck, Thomas. (1983). *Human rights in the Third World perspective.* London: Oceana Press.

Franck, Thomas M. (1989). "Soviet initiatives: U.S. responses—new opportunities for reviving the United Nations system." *American Journal of International Law, 83,* 531–43.

Frieden, Jeff. (1987). "Third World indebted industrialization: International finance and state capitalism in Mexico, Brazil, Algeria, and South Korea." In Jeffry A. Frieden & David A. Lake (Eds.), *International political economy: Perspectives on global power and wealth* (pp. 298–317). New York: St. Martin's Press.

Fry, Earl H. (1990, April). "Foreign direct investment in the United States: Public policy options." Paper presented to the International Studies Association convention, Washington, D.C.

Fukuyama, Francis. (1989, Summer). "The end of history?" *National Interest*, No. 16, 3–18.

Fulbright, J. William. (1966). *Arrogance of power*. New York: Random House.

Gabor, Denis, & Colombo, Umberto, with King, Alexander & Galli, Riccardo. (1978). *Beyond the age of waste: A report to the Club of Rome*. New York: Pergamon Press.

Gallup, George H. (1980). *The International Gallup Polls, Public Opinion, 1978*. Wilmington, DE: Scholarly Resources.

Galtung, Johan. (1971). "A structural theory of imperialism." *Journal of Peace Research*, 8, 81–117.

Gasiorowski, Mark J. (1990). "The political regimes project." *Studies in Comparative International Development*, 25, 109–25.

Gastil, Raymond D. (1981). "The comparative survey of freedom." *Freedom at Issue*, 2, 14–20.

Gastil, Raymond D. (1985). "The past, present, and future of democracy." *Journal of International Affairs*, 38, 161–180.

Gastil, Raymond D. (1990). "The comparative survey of freedom: Experiences and suggestions." *Studies in Comparative International Development*, 25, 25–50.

(GATT) General Agreement on Tariffs and Trade. (1983). *International trade, 1982–1983*. Geneva.

(GATT) General Agreement on Tariffs and Trade. (1987). *International trade, 1986–1987*. Geneva.

Geller, Daniel S. (1990). "Nuclear weapons, deterrence, and crisis escalation." *Journal of Conflict Resolution*, 34, 291–310.

General Agreement on Tariffs and Trade. *See* (GATT).

George, Alexander L. (1987). "Ideology and international relations: A conceptual analysis." *The Jerusalem Journal of International Relations*, 9, 1–21.

George, Alexander L., Hall, David, & Simons, William. (1971). *The limits of coercive diplomacy*. Boston: Little, Brown.

Gerner, Deborah J. (1990). *One land, two peoples: The conflict over Palestine*. Boulder, CO: Westview Press.

Gilpin, Robert. (1975). "Three models of the future." *International Organization*, 29, 37–60.

Gilpin, Robert. (1981). *War and change in world politics*. Cambridge, U.K.: Cambridge University Press.

Gilpin, Robert, with Gilpin, Jean M. (1987). *The political economy of international relations*. Princeton, NJ: Princeton University Press.

Glad, Betty. (1989). "Personality, political and group process variables in foreign policy decision making: Jimmy Carter's handling of the Iranian hostage crisis." *International Political Science Review*, 10, 35–61.

Goldschmidt, Arthur, Jr. (1983). *A concise history of the Middle East* (2nd ed.). Boulder, CO: Westview Press.

Goldstein, Donald J. (1988). "Foreign direct investment in the United States and national security policy." *Comparative Strategy*, 7, 143–58.

Goldstein, Joshua S. (1987). "The emperor's new genes: Sociobiology and war." *International Studies Quarterly*, 31, 33–43.

Goldstein, Joshua S. (1988). *Long cycles: Prosperity and war in the modern age*. New Haven, CT: Yale University Press.

Goldstein, Martin E. (1984). *America's foreign policy: Drift or decision*. Wilmington, DE: Scholarly Resources.

Gorbachev, Mikhail S. (1987). *Perestroika: New thinking for our country and the world*. New York: Harper & Row.

Gorbachev, Mikhail S. (1989, July 6). "The international community and change: A common European home." Address delivered to the Council of Europe, Strasbourg, France. Reprinted in *Vital Speeches of the Day, 55,* (September 15, 1989), 706–11.

Graebner, Norman. (Ed.). (1964). *Ideas and diplomacy*. New York: Oxford University Press.

Graham, Thomas W. (1988). "The pattern and importance of public knowledge in the nuclear age." *Journal of Conflict Resolution*, 32, 319–34.

Gray, Colin S. (1982). *Strategic studies and public policy*. Lexington: University of Kentucky Press.

Graybeal, Sidney N. (1986). "Soviet negotiating practice." In Leon Sloss & M. Scott Davis (Eds.), *A game for high stakes: Lessons learned in negotiating with the Soviet Union*. Cambridge, MA: Ballinger.

Gregor, A. James. (1990). "The balance of power conflicts of Eurasia." *Global Affairs*, 5, 45–70.

Gross, Leo. (1986). "Underutilization of the International Court of Justice." *Harvard International Law Journal*, 27, 572–98.

Gross, Thomas F. (1989, September). "Europe 1992: A global fulcrum for European companies." *Management Review, 17,* 21–24.

Gupta, R. S. (1986). "Resolutions of the United Nations General Assembly as a source of international law." *International Studies*, 23, 143–54.

Haas, Ernst B. (1983). "Regime decay: Conflict management and international organizations, 1945–1981." *International Studies*, 37, 189–256.

Hackett, James T. (1990). "The ballistic missile epidemic." *Global Affairs*, 5, 38–57.

Hagan, Joe D. (1987). "Regimes, political oppositions, and the comparative analysis of foreign policy." In Charles F. Hermann, Charles W. Kegley, Jr., & James N. Rosenau (Eds.), *New direction in the study of foreign policy*. Boston: Allen & Unwin.

Hagan, Joe D. (1989). "Domestic political regime changes and Third World voting realignments in the United Nations, 1946–84." *International Organization*, 43, 505–34.

Hagan, Joe D. (1990, April). "Testing a multidimensional model of domestic political regime constraints on foreign policy." Paper presented to the International Studies Association convention, Washington, D.C.

Haggard, Stephen, & Simmons, Beth A. (1987). "Theories of International Regimes." *International Organization*, 41, 497–517.

Hahn, Richard W., & Richards, Kenneth R. (1989). "The internationalization of environmental regulation." *Harvard International Law Journal*, 30, 421–46.

Hahn, Walter F. (1990). "NATO and Germany." *Global Affairs*, 5, 9–18.

Hall, John A., & Ikenberry, G. John. (1989). *The state*. Minneapolis: University of Minnesota Press.

Halliday, Bruce. (1989). "The triangle of population, poverty, resources and environment and its relationship to security." Testimony and written submission to U.S. Congress, House of Representatives, Subcommittee on Natural Resources, Agriculture and Environment of the Committee on Science, Space, and Technology (*Hearings*, February 23, 28, 1989. No. 3. 101 Cong., 1st sess.).

Halperin, Morton H. (1974). *Bureaucratic politics and foreign policy*. Washington, D.C.: Brookings Institution.

Hamilton, Lee. (1982). "Congress and foreign policy." *Presidential Studies Quarterly, 12*, 133–37.

Handl, Gunter. (1980, April 17–19). "The environment: International rights and responsibilities." *Proceedings of the 74th annual meeting of the American Society of International Law*. Washington, D.C.

Hansen, Wendy L. (1990). "The international trade commission and the politics of protectionism." *American Political Science Review, 84*, 21–46.

Harden, Sheila. (1985). *Small is dangerous: Micro states in a macro world*. New York: St. Martin's Press.

Hardin, Garrett. (1968). "The tragedy of the commons." *Science, 162*, 1243–48.

Hardin, Garrett. (1974). "Living in a lifeboat." *Bioscience, 24*, 561–68.

Harkabi, Yehoshataf. (1989). "A policy for the moment of truth." In John T. Rourke (Ed.), *Taking sides: Clashing views on controversial issues in world politics* (2nd ed.) (pp. 78–85). Guilford, CT: Dushkin Publishing Group.

Harris, Geoffrey, Kelly, Mark, & Pranowo. (1988). "Trade-offs between defense and education/health expenditures in developing countries." *Journal of Peace Research, 25*, 165–77.

Hartmann, Frederick. (1962). *The relations of nations* (2nd ed.). New York: Macmillan.

Haslam, Jonathan. (1989). "The UN and the Soviet Union: New thinking?" *International Affairs* (London), *65*, 677–84.

Hastedt, Glenn. (1987, April). "Controlling intelligence: Values and perspectives of administration." Paper presented to the International Studies Association, Washington, D.C.

Hastings, Elizabeth Hann, & Hastings, Philip. K. (1989). *Index to international public opinion, 1988–1989*. Westport, CT: Greenwood Press.

Hawkins, William R. (1985, August 9). "Arms control: Three centuries of failure." *National Review*, 26–32.

Hawkins, William R. (1989, October). "Politics over economics: Thinking about trade and industry." *World and I*, pp. 527–545.

Hawley, Jim. (1987). "The internationalization of capital: Banks, Eurocurrency and the instability of the world monetary system." In Jeffry A. Frieden & David A. Lake (Eds.), *International political economy: Perspectives on global power and wealth* (pp. 269–84). New York: St. Martin's Press.

Hazledine, Tim. (1988). "Review article and comment: Canada–U.S. free trade? Not so elementary, Watson." *Canadian Public Policy, 14*, 204–13.

Henkin, Louis, Hoffmann, Stanley, Kirpatrick, Jeane J., Gerson, Allan, Rogers, William D., & Scheffer, David J.

(1989). *Right v. might: International law and the use of force*. New York: Council on Foreign Relations Press.

Herek, Gregory M., Janis, Irving L., & Huth, Paul. (1987). "Decision-making during international crisis: Is the quality of profess related to the outcome?" *Journal of Conflict Resolution, 31*, 203–36.

Herek, Gregory M., Janis, Irving L., & Huth, Paul. (1989). "Quality of U.S. decision-making during the Cuban missile crisis: Major errors in Welch's reassessment." *Journal of Conflict Resolution, 33*, 446–59.

Hermann, Charles F. (1986). "International crisis as a situational variable." In John Vasquez (Ed.), *Classics of international relations* (pp. 171–81). Englewood Cliffs, NJ: Prentice Hall.

Hermann, Charles F. (1987, April). "Political opposition as potential agents of foreign policy change: Developing a theory." Paper presented to the International Studies Association, Washington, D.C.

Hermann, Margaret G., & Hermann, Charles F. (1989). "Who makes foreign policy decisions and how: An empirical inquiry." *International Studies Quarterly, 33*, 316–88.

Herz, John H. (1959). "The rise and demise of the territorial state." *World Politics, 9*, 473–93.

Herz, John H. (1969). "The territorial state revisited." In James N. Rosenau (Ed.), *International relations and foreign policy*. New York: Free Press.

Herz, John H. (1981). "Political realism revisited." *International Studies Quarterly, 25*, 182–97.

Higgins, Benjamin, & Higgins, Jean Downing. (1979). *Economic development of a small planet*. New York: Norton.

Higgins, Rosalyn. (1987). "Contending systems of world public order and international law: An overview." *The Atlantic Community Quarterly, 25*, 145–59.

Hinckely, Ronald H. (1988). "Public attitudes toward key foreign policy events." *Journal of Conflict Resolution, 32*, 295–318.

Hobsbawm, Eric J. (1990). *Nations and nationalism since 1780: Programme, myth, reality*. Cambridge, U.K.: Cambridge University Press.

Hoffmann, Stanley. (1978). *Decline or renewal? France since the 1930s*. New York: Viking Press.

Hoffmann, Stanley. (1981). *Duties beyond borders: On the limits and possibilities of ethical international politics*. Syracuse, NY: Syracuse University Press.

Hoffmann, Stanley. (1986). "The balance of power." In Herbert Levine (Ed.), *World politics debated* (2nd ed., pp. 90–96). New York: McGraw-Hill.

Hollis, Martin, & Smith, Steve. (1986) "Roles and reasons in foreign policy decision making." *British Journal of Political Science, 26*, 269–86.

Holloway, Steven. (1990). "Forty years of United Nations General Assembly voting." *Canadian Journal of Political Science, 23*, 279–96.

Holm, Hans-Henrik. (1989). "A democratic revolt? Stability and change in Danish security policy 1979–1989." *Cooperation and Conflict, 24*, 179–97.

Holmes, Jack E., & Elder, Robert E. (1989, March). "Prosperity, consensus, and U.S. foreign policy." Paper presented to the International Studies Association convention, London.

Holmes, Robert L. (1989). *On war and morality*. Princeton, NJ: Princeton University Press.

Holsti, K. J. (1977). *International politics: A framework for analysis*. Englewood Cliffs, NJ: Prentice Hall.

Holsti, Ole R. (1962). "The belief system and national images: A case study." *Journal of Conflict Resolution, 6*, 244–52.

Holsti, Ole R., North, Robert C., & Brody, Richard. (1968). "Perceptions and Action in the 1914 crisis." In J. David Singer (Ed.), *Quantitative international politics*, (pp. 123–58). New York: Free Press.

Holsti, Ole R., & Rosenau, James N. (1988). "The domestic and foreign policy beliefs of American leaders." *Journal of Conflict Resolution, 32*, 248–94.

Hoole, Francis W., & Huang, Chi. (1989). "The global conflict pattern." *Journal of Conflict Resolution, 33*, 142–63.

Hough, Jerry F. (Ed.). (1990). Introduction and tables. *Journal of the Soviet nationalities, 1*, 1–13.

Houweling, Henk, & Siccama, Jan G. (1988). "Power transitions as a cause of war." *Journal of Conflict Resolution, 32*, 87–102.

Huddleston, Barbara. (1988, September/October). "Why FAO?" *Society*, pp. 26–31.

Hufbauer, Gary C., & Schott, Jeffery J. (1985). *Economic sanctions reconsidered: History and policy content*. Washington, D.C.: Institute for International Economics.

Hughes, Barry B. (1978). *The domestic context of American foreign policy*. San Francisco: W. H. Freeman.

Huntington, Samuel P. (1989, Fall). "No exit: The errors of endism." *The National Interest*, No. 17, 3–10.

Hurwitz, Jon, & Peffley, Mark. (1987a). "The means and ends of foreign policy as determinants of presidential support." *American Journal of Political Science, 31*, 236–58.

Hurwitz, Jon, & Peffley, Mark. (1987b). "How are [US] foreign policy attitudes structured? A hierarchical model." *American Political Science Review, 87*, 1099–1120.

Huth, Paul K. (1990). "The extended deterrent value of nuclear weapons." *Journal of Conflict Resolution, 34*, 270–90.

Huth, Paul K., & Russett, Bruce. (1990). "Testing deterrence theory: Rigor makes a difference." *World Politics, 42*, 466–501.

Imbeau, Louis M. (1988). "Aid and ideology." *European Journal of Political Research, 16*, 3–28.

(IMF) International Monetary Fund. (1985, February). *International financial statistics*. Washington, D.C.

(IMF) International Monetary Fund. (1987). *Annual report, 1987*. Washington, D.C.

(IMF) International Monetary Fund. (1988, February 22). *IMF survey*. Washington, D.C.

(IMF) International Monetary Fund. (1988, May 2). *IMF survey*. Washington, D.C.

(IMF) International Monetary Fund. (1989). *Governmental Financial Statistics Yearbook (1989)*. Washington, D.C.

(IMF) International Monetary Fund. (1990). *World Economic Outlook, 28* (May, 1990).

(IMF) International Monetary Fund. (1990a). *International Financial Statistics, 43*, (November, 1990).

Independent Commission on Disarmament and Security Issues. (1982). *Common security: A blueprint for survival*. New York: Simon & Schuster.

International Institute for Strategic Studies. (1985). *The military balance, 1985–1986*. London.

International Monetary Fund. *See* (IMF).

Intriligator, Michael, & Brito, Dagobert L. (1984). "Arms races lead to the outbreak of war." *Journal of Conflict Resolution, 28*, 63–84.

Isaak, Robert. (1981). *Individuals and world politics*. Belmont, CA: Duxbury Press.

Islam, Shafiqul. (1989). Testimony before the U.S. House of Representatives, Committee on Banking, Finance and Urban Affairs. *Third World Debt: Public Reaction to the Brady Plan* (*Hearings*, April 15, 1989:61–87).

Ives, Jane H. (Ed.). (1985). *Transnational corporations and the environmental control issues: The export of hazard*. Boston: Routledge & Kegan Paul.

Jacobson, Harold, Reisinger, William, & Mathers, Todd. (1989). "National entanglements in international governmental organizations." In *The Politics of International Organizations* (pp. 68–82). Chicago: Dorsey Press.

Jacobson, Jodi. (1988). "Planning the global family." In Lester Brown et al. (Eds.), *State of the World, 1988* (pp. 231–76). New York: W. W. Norton.

James, Patrick. (1987). "Externalization of conflict: Testing a crisis-based model." *Canadian Journal of Political Science, 20*, 579–98.

James, Patrick. (1988). *Crisis and war*. Montreal: McGill Queen's University Press.

Janis, Irving. (1983). *Groupthink: Psychological studies of policy decisions and fiascoes*. Boston: Houghton Mifflin.

Jensen, Lloyd. (1983). *Explaining foreign policy*. Englewood Cliffs, NJ: Prentice Hall.

Jentleson, Bruce W. (1986). *Pipeline politics: The complex political economy of East-West energy trade*. Ithaca, NY: Cornell University Press.

Jervis, Robert. (1968). "Hypotheses on misperception." *World Politics, 20*, 454–79.

Jervis, Robert. (1976). *Perception and misperception in international politics*. Princeton, NJ: Princeton University Press.

Joffe, Josef. (1987). "Peace and populism: Why the European anti-nuclear movement failed." *International Security, 11*, 3–18.

Johnson, Paul M., & Wells, Robert A. (1986). "Soviet military and civilian resource allocation, 1951–1980." *Journal of Conflict Resolution, 20*, 195–219.

Judge, Anthony J. N. (1978). "International institutions: Diversity, borderline cases, functional substitutes, and possible alternatives." In Paul Taylor & A. J. R. Groom. (Eds.), *International organization: A conceptual approach*. London: Francis Printer.

Kaempfer, William H., Lehman, James A., & Lowenberg, Anton D. (1987). "Divestment, investment sanctions, and disinvestment: An evaluation of anti-apartheid policy instruments." *International Organization, 41*, 456–73.

Kagan, Robert. (1990, Spring). "There to stay: The U.S. and Latin America." *The National Interest*, No. 19, 59–67.

Kahn, Herman. (1968). *On escalation: Metaphors and scenarios* (rev. ed.). Baltimore: Penguin.

Kaiser, Karl, Lever, George, Mertes, Alois & Schulze, Franz-Josef. (1982). "Nuclear weapons and the preservation of peace: A German response to no first use." *Foreign Affairs, 60*, 1157–70.

Kamenka, Eugene. (1976). "Political nationalism—The evolution of the idea." In Eugene Kamenda (Ed.), *Nationalism: The nature and evolution of an idea*. New York: St. Martin's Press.

Kaplan, Fred. (1983). *The wizards of Armageddon: Strategists of the nuclear age*. New York: Simon & Schuster.

Kaplan, Morton A. (1957). *System and process in international politics*. New York: Wiley.

Kaplan, Morton A. (1969). "Variants on six models of the international system." In James Rosenau (Ed.), *International politics and foreign policy* (pp. 291–303.) New York: The Free Press.

Kaplan, Morton A. (1979). *Toward professionalism in international theory*. New York: Free Press.

Karns, Margaret P., & Mingst, Karen A. (1990). *The United States and multilateral institutions*. Boston: Unwin Hyman.

Karp, Aaron. (1988). "The frantic Third World quest for ballistic missiles." *Bulletin of the Atomic Scientists, 44* (June), 14–21.

Karp, Aaron. (1990). "Ballistic missile proliferation." *SIPRI Yearbook 1990* (pp. 369–92). Oxford, U.K.: Oxford University Press.

Kass, Ilana. (1989). "Gorbachev's strategy: Is our perspective in need of restructuring?" *Comparative Strategy, 98*, 181–90.

Kaufmann, Johan. (1989). "The Economic and Social Council and the New International Economic Order." In David P. Forsythe (Ed.), *The United Nations in the world political economy* (pp. 54–68). New York: St. Martin's Press.

Kaysen, Carl. (1990). "Is war obsolete?: A review essay." *International Security, 14*, 42–63.

Kearns, Doris. (1976). *Lyndon Johnson and the American dream*. New York: Harper & Row.

Keeley, James F. (1990). "Toward a Foucauldian analysis of international regimes." *International Organization, 44*, 83–106.

Keeny, Spurgeon M., Jr., & Panofsky, Wolfgang K. H. (1981). "MAD versus NUTS: Can doctrine or weaponry remedy the mutual hostage relationship of the superpowers?" *Foreign Affairs, 60*, 287–304.

Kegley, Charles W., Jr., & Wittkopf, Eugene R. (1987). *American foreign policy: Pattern and process* (3rd ed.). New York: St. Martin's Press.

Kennan, George F. (1984). "The impending food-population crisis." In William C. Olson, David S. McLellan, & Fred A. Sondermann (Eds.), *Theory and Practice of International Relations* (6th ed.). Englewood Cliffs, NJ: Prentice Hall.

Kennan, George F. (1986). "Morality and foreign policy." *Foreign Affairs, 64*, 205–18.

Kennedy, Paul. (1988). *The rise and fall of the great powers*. New York: Random House.

Keohane, Robert O., & Nye, Joseph S. (1977). *Power and interdependence: World politics in transition*. Boston: Little, Brown.

Kerry, Richard J. (1990). *The star-spangled mirror: America's image of itself and the world*. Savage, MD: Rowman & Littlefield.

Killick, Tony. (1984). *The IMF and stabilization: Developing country experiences*. New York: St. Martin's Press.

Kim, Ilpyong J. (Ed.). (1987). *The strategic triangle: China, the United States, and the Soviet Union*. New York: Paragon House Publishers.

Kim, Woosang. (1989). "Power, alliances, and major war, 1816–1975." *Journal of Conflict Resolution, 33*, 255–73.

Kirkpatrick, Jeane J. (1986, June 11). "U.N. votes: Unwelcome mirror." *Hartford Courant*, p. C6.

Kissinger, Henry A. (1964). *A world restored—Europe after Napoleon*. New York: Grosset & Dunlap.

Kissinger, Henry A. (1970). "The just and the possible." In U.S. Congress, Senate Committee on Government Operations, *Negotiation and statecraft: A selection of readings* (91st Cong., 2nd sess).

Kissinger, Henry A. (1979). *The White House years*. Boston: Little, Brown.

Klare, Michael T. (1988). "Secret operatives, clandestine trades: The thriving black market for weapons." *Bulletin of the Atomic Scientists, 44* (April), 16–25.

Klein, Bradley S. (1987, April). "The textual strategies of military strategy: Or, have you read any good defense manuals lately?" Paper presented to the International Studies Association, Washington, D.C.

Kober, Stanley. (1990). "Idealpolitik." *Foreign Policy*, No. 79, 3–24.

Koenig, Louis E. (1975). *The chief executive*. New York: Harcourt Brace Jovanovich.

Kogan, Norman. (1981). *A political history of postwar Italy*. New York: Praeger.

Koistinen, Paul A. C. (1980). *Military-industrial complex: A historical perspective*. New York: Praeger.

Kolko, Jerry. (1989). "Third World development: The strategy debate." In Sheikh R. Ali (Ed.), *Third World at the crossroads* (pp. 13–24). New York: Praeger.

Komisar, Lech. (1990, January–February). "Europe erupts, NATO squirms." *The Bulletin of the Atomic Scientists, 46*, 6–10.

Krasner, Stephen D. (1978). *Defending the national interest*. Princeton, NJ: Princeton University Press.

Krasner, Stephen D. (1982). "Structural causes and regime consequences." *International Organization, 36*, 185–206.

Krasner, Stephen D. (1985). *Structural conflict: The Third World against global liberalism*. Berkeley: University of California Press.

Krasner, Stephen D. (1987). "Comment on trade policy as foreign policy." In Robert M. Stern (Ed.), *U.S. trade policies in a changing world*. Cambridge, MA: The MIT Press.

Kratochwil, Friedrich. (1982). "On the notion of 'interest' in national relations." *International Organization, 36*, 1–22.

Kratochwil, Friedrich, & Ruggle, John Gerard. (1989). "International organizations: The state of the art." In Paul F. Diehl (Ed.), *The politics of international organizations* (pp. 17–27). Chicago: Dorsey Press.

Krause, Keith. (1989, March). "The political economy of the international arms transfer system: The diffusion of military technique via arms transfers." Paper presented to the International Studies Association convention, London.

Krause, Melvyn B. (1983). *Development without aid.* New York: McGraw-Hill.

Krenzler, Horst. (1989). "Toward healthy and open world markets." *Europe,* No. 292, 16–18.

Krenzler, Horst. (1989, December). "Toward healthy and open world markets." *Europe, 15,* 16–17.

Krepon, Michael. (1985). "The political dynamics of verification and compliance debates." In William C. Potter (Ed.), *Verification and arms control* (pp. 135–51). Lexington, MA: Lexington Books.

Krepon, Michael. (1989). "Spying from space." *Foreign Policy, 75,* 92–108.

Kugler, Jacek, & Arbetman, Marina. (1989). "Choosing among measures of power: A review of the empirical record." In Richard J. Stoll and Michael Ward (Eds.), *Power and world politics* (pp. 49–78). Boulder, CO: Lynne Rienner Publishers.

Kurian, George Thomas. (1982). *Encyclopedia of the Third World.* (rev. ed.). New York: Facts on File.

Kurtz, Lester R. (1988). *The nuclear cage: A sociology of the arms race.* Englewood Cliffs, NJ: Prentice Hall

Lackey, Douglas P. (1989). *The ethics of war and peace.* Englewood Cliffs, NJ: Prentice Hall.

Lake, Timothy W. (1989). "On post-war: The significance of symbolic action in war and deterrence." *Alternatives, 14,* 343–62.

Lalman, David. (1988). "Conflict resolution and peace." *American Journal of Political Science, 32,* 590–615.

LaPonce, J. A. (1987). "Language and communication: The rise of the monolingual state." In Claudio Ciioffi-Revella, Richard L. Merritt, & Dina A. Zinnes (Eds.), *Communication and interaction in global politics.* Newbury Park, CA: Sage.

Laqueur, Walter. (1976). *Guerrilla.* Boston: Little, Brown.

Laqueur, Walter. (1978). *The terrorism reader.* Philadelphia: Temple University Press.

Laqueur, Walter. (1987). *The age of terrorism.* Boston: Little, Brown.

Lazlo, Ervin, Baler, Robert, Jr., Einsenberg, Eliot, & Raman, Venkata. (1980). *The Objectives of the New International Economic Order.* New York: Pergamon Press.

Lebovic, James H. (1988). "National interests and U.S. foreign aid: The Carter and Reagan years." *Journal of Peace Research, 25,* 115–35.

Lebow, Richard Ned, & Stein, Janice Gross. (1990). "Deterrence: The elusive dependent variable." *World Politics, 42,* 336–69.

Lefever, Ernest W. (1979). "The trivialization of human rights." In Fred A. Sondermann, David S. McLellan, & William C. Olson (Eds.), *The theory and practice of international relations.* Englewood Cliffs, NJ: Prentice Hall.

Lellouche, Pierre. (1982). "The dilemmas of non-proliferation policy: The supplier countries." In David Carlton & Carlo Schaerf (Eds.), *The arms race in the 1980s.* New York: St. Martin's Press.

LeLoup, Lance T., & Shull, Steven A. (1979). "Congress v. the executive: The two presidencies reconsidered." *Social Science Quarterly, 59,* 704–19.

L'Etang, Hugh. (1970). *The pathology of leadership.* New York: Hawthorne Books.

Leventhal, Paul. (1984). "Getting serious about proliferation." *Bulletin of the Atomic Scientists 40* (March), 7–11.

Levi, Werner. (1979). *Contemporary international law.* Boulder, CO: Westview Press.

Levy, Jack S. (1987). "Declining power and the preventive motivation for war." *World Politics, 40,* 82–107.

Levy, Jack S. (1988, March). "The diversionary theory of war: A critique." Paper presented to the International Studies Association, St. Louis, MO.

Levy, Jack S. (1988b). "Contending theories of war." In Charles W. Kegley, Jr. & Eugene R. Wittkopf (Eds.), *The global agenda: Issues and perspectives.* New York: Random House.

Lichenstein, Charles M. (1986). "China in the U.N.: The case of Kampuchea." *World Affairs, 149,* 21–24.

Licklider, Roy. (1988). "The power of oil: The Arab oil weapon and the Netherlands, the United Kingdom, Canada, Japan, and the United States." *International Studies Quarterly, 32,* 205–26.

Lind, Michael. (1990, Spring). "German fate and allied fears." *The National Interest, 26,* 34–44.

Lindblom, Charles E. (1959). "The science of muddling through." *Public Administration Review, 19,* 79–88.

Lindert, Peter H., & Kindleberger, Charles P. (1982). *International economics* (7th ed.). Homewood, IL: Irwin.

Lister, Frederick. (1989). "Exploiting the recent revival of the United Nations." *International Relations* (London), *9,* 419–38.

Litwak, Robert S. (1987). "Ideology and the conduct of Soviet policy in the Third World." *The Jerusalem Journal of International Relations, 9,* 22–41.

Lock, Harry G. (1985, March). "Vietnam casualty statistics." *Marine Corps Gazette,* pp. 23–25.

Lockhart, Charles. (1979). *Bargaining in international conflict.* New York: Columbia University Press.

Lodge, Juliet. (Ed.). (1983). *Institutions and policies of the European Community.* New York: St. Martin's Press.

Lukashuk, I. I. (1989, July). "The principle of *pacta sunt servanda* and the nature of obligation under international law." *American Journal of International Law, 83,* 513–18.

Lundin, S. J. (1990). "Chemical and biological warfare: Development in 1989." *SIPRI Yearbook 1990* (pp. 107–133). Oxford, U.K.: Oxford University Press.

Lyne, Roderic. (1987). "Making waves: Mr. Gorbachev's public diplomacy, 1985–1986." *International Affairs, 63,* 205–23.

Machiavelli, Niccolò. (1950). *The prince and the discourses.* New York: Random House. (Original work published 1513).

Mackinder, Sir Halford. (1919). *Democratic ideals and reality.* New York: Henry A. Holt.

Magdoff, Harry. (1978). *Imperialism: From the colonial age to the present.* New York: Monthly Review Press.

Major, R. L. (1980). "Recent trends in world trade in manufactures." In R. A. Bachelor, R. L. Major, & A. D. Morgan, *Industrialization and the basis for trade.* Cambridge, U.K.: Cambridge University Press.

Malawer, Stuart S. (1988). "Reagan's law and foreign policy, 1981–1987: The 'Reagan Corollary' of international law." *Harvard Journal of International Law, 29,* 85–110.

Mandela, Nelson. (1990a). "Statement of the deputy president of the African National Congress, Nelson Mandela, at the United Nations: New York, June 22, 1990." Transcript provided to author by the African National Congress liaison office, Washington, D.C.

Mandela, Nelson. (1990b). "Statement of the deputy president of the African National Congress, Nelson Mandela, to the Joint Session of Congress of the United States of America: Washington, D.C., June 26, 1990." Transcript provided to author by the African National Congress liaison office, Washington, D.C.

Manicas, Peter T. (1989). *War and democracy.* Cambridge, MA: Basil Blackwell.

Maning, Bayless. (1979). "The Congress, the executive and intermestic affairs." *Foreign Affairs, 57,* 308–24.

Mansfield, Edward D. (1988). "The distribution of wars over time." *World Politics, 41,* 21–51.

Maoz, Zeev. (1989). "Joining the club of nations: Political development and international conflict, 1816–1876." *International Studies Quarterly, 33,* 199–231.

Maoz, Zeev. (1989a). "Power, capabilities, and paradoxical conflict outcomes." *World Politics, 41,* 239–66.

Maoz, Zeev, & Abdolali, Nasrin. (1989). "Regime type and international conflict, 1816–1976." *Journal of Conflict Resolution, 33,* 3–35.

Marín-Bosch, Miguel. (1987). "How nations vote in the General Assembly of the United Nations." *International Organization, 41,* 705–26.

Marra, Robin F., Ostrom, Charles W., Jr., & Simon, Dennis M. (1989, April). "Foreign policy and the perpetual election." Paper presented to the Internaitonal Studies Association convention, London.

Mastanduno, Michael. (1985). "Strategies of economic containment: U.S. trade relations with the Soviet Union." *World Politics, 37,* 503–31.

Masters, Roger D. (1969). "World politics as a primitive political system." In James N. Rosenau (Ed.), *International politics and foreign policy.* New York: Free Press.

May, Ernest R. (1973). *Lessons of the past.* London: Oxford University Press.

Mayall, James. (1990). *Nationalism and international society.* Cambridge, U.K.: Cambridge University Press.

McColm, R. Bruce, Finn, James, Payne, Douglas W., Ryan, Joseph E., Sussman, Leonard R., & Zarycky, George. (1990). *Freedom in the world: Political rights & civil liberties, 1989–1990.* New York: Freedom House.

McCormick, James. (1989). "International organizations and cooperation among nations. In Paul F. Diehl (Ed.), *The politics of international organizations* (pp. 83–98). Chicago: Dorsey Press.

McCulloch, Rachel. (1990). "The United States–Canada Free Trade Agreement." *Academy of Political Science, 37,* 79–89.

McWhenney, Edward. (1979). *The World Court and the contemporary international law-making system.* Alphen aan den Rijn, the Netherlands: Sijthoff & Noordhoff.

Meadows, Donella H., Meadows, Dennis L., Randers, Jorgen, and Behrens, William W., III. (1974). *The limits to growth.* New York: Universe Books.

Mearsheimer, John J. (1990a, August). "Why we will soon miss the cold war." *The Atlantic Monthly, 266,* 35–50.

Mearsheimer, John J. (1990b). "Back to the future: Instability in Europe after the cold war." *International Security, 15,* 5–56.

Melman, Seymour. (1986). "Limits to military power." *International Security, 11,* 72–88.

Merritt, Richard L., & Zinnes, (1989). "Alternative indexes of national power." In Richard J. Stoll & Michael Ward (Eds.), *Power and World Politics* (pp. 11–28). Boulder, CO: Lynne Rienner Publishers.

Meyer, Stephen M. (1985). "Soviet perspectives on the paths to nuclear war." In Graham T. Allison, Albert Carnesale, & Joseph S. Nye, Jr. (Eds.), *Hawks, doves and owls: An agenda for avoiding nuclear war* (pp. 167–205). New York: W. W. Norton.

Meyer, Stephen M. (1985a). "Verification and risk in arms control." *International Security, 8,* 111–26.

Meyer, Stephen M. (1987). "Soviet nuclear operations." In Ashton B. Carter, John Steinbruner, & Charles A. Zraket (Eds.), *Managing nuclear operations.* Washington, D.C.: Brookings Institution.

Michaelson, Karen. (Ed.). (1981). *And the poor get children: Radical perspective on population dynamics.* New York: Monthly Review Press.

Michalak, Stanley J. (1989). "UNCTAD as an agent of change." In David P. Forsythe (Ed.), *The United Nations in the world political economy* (pp. 69–83). New York: St. Martin's Press.

Miewald, Robert, & Welch, Susan. (1983). "Natural resource scarcity." In Robert Miewald & Susan Welch (Eds.), *Scarce natural resources: The challenge to public policymaking.* Beverly Hills, CA: Sage.

Miller, Abraham H. (Ed.). (1982). *Terrorism, the media, and the law.* Ardsley-on-the-Hudson, New York: Transnational Publishers.

Miller, Lynn H. (1990). *Global order: Values and power in international politics* (2nd ed.). Boulder, CO: Westview Press.

Miller, Steven E. (1984). "Politics over promise: Domestic impediments to arms control." *International Security, 8,* 79–84.

Milner, Helen V. (1989). *Resisting protectionism: Global industries and the politics of international trade.* Princeton, NJ: Princeton University Press.

Mintz, Alex. (1989). "Guns versus butter: A disaggregated analysis." *American Political Science Review, 83,* 1285–96.

Mitchell, Judson. (1983). *Ideology of a superpower: Contemporary Soviet doctrine on international relations.* Stanford, CA: Hoover Institution Press.

Mitrany, David. (1966). *A working peace system.* Chicago: Quadrangle Books.

Modelski, George. (1987). *Long cycles in world politics.* Seattle, WA: University of Washington Press.

Mok, Jin Whyu, & Duval, Robert D. (1988, April). "The choice of illusion: The continuing analysis of defense and social welfare spending trade-off issues." Paper presented to the International Studies Association convention, St. Louis, Missouri.

Moon, Chung-in. (1988). "Complex interdependence and transnational lobbying: South Korea in the United States." *International Studies Quarterly, 32*, 67–90.

Mooney, Peter J. (1982). *The Soviet superpower.* London: Heinemann Educational Books.

Moran, Theodore H. (1990). "The globalization of America's defense industries: Managing the threat of foreign dependence." *International Security, 15*, 57–99.

Morgan, Patrick. (1984). *Theories and approaches to international relations.* New Brunswick, NJ: Transaction Books.

Morgan, T. Clifton. (1990). "Issue linkages in international crisis bargaining." *American Journal of Political Science, 34*, 311–33.

Morgan, T. Clifton, & Campbell, Sally Howard. (1990, April). "Domestic structure, decisional constraints and war: So why Kant democracies fight?" Paper presented to the International Studies Association convention, Washington, D.C.

Morgenthau, Hans W. (1973). *Politics among nations* (5th ed.). New York: Knopf.

Morgenthau, Hans W. (1984). "Human rights and foreign policy." In Kenneth W. Thompson (Ed.), *Moral dimensions of American foreign policy* (pp. 341–48). New Brunswick, NJ: Transaction Books.

Morita, Akio. (1989, May). "Getting the word out." *Speaking of Japan, 9*, 18–21.

Morozov, Gregorii. (1981). "The socialist conception of international organization." In Georges Abi-Saab (Ed.), *The conception of international organization.* Paris: UNESCO.

Morphet, Sally. (1989, March) "The significance and relevance of the Security Council and its resolutions and vetoes." Paper presented to the International Studies Association convention, London.

Morris, Charles R. (1989, October). "The coming global boom." *The Atlantic Monthly, 265*, 51–64.

Morrow, James D. (1988). "Social choice and system structure in world politics." *World Politics, 41*, 75–97.

Morrow, James D. (1989). "A twist of truth: A reexamination of the effects of arms races on the occurrence of war." *Journal of Conflict Resolution, 33*, 500–29.

Motyl, Alexander J. (1989). "Reassessing the Soviet crisis: Big problems, muddling through, business as usual." *Political Science Quarterly, 104*, 269–79.

Mozaffari, Mehdi. (1987). "Authority in Islam: From Muhammad to Khomeini." *International Journal of Politics, 16*, 89–106.

Mueller, John. (1989). *Retreat from doomsday: The obsolescence of major war.* New York: Basic Books.

Müller, Harold. (1990). "Prospects for the fourth review of the Non-Proliferation Treaty." *SIPRI Yearbook 1990* (pp. 553–86). Oxford, U.K.: Oxford University Press.

Mullerson, R. A. (1989). "Sources of international law: New tendencies in Soviet thinking." *American Journal of International Law, 83*, 494–513.

Muncaster, Robert G., & Zinnes, Dina A. (1990). "Structure and hostility in international systems." *Journal of Theoretical Politics, 2*, 31–58.

Murphy, Craig. (1989). "What the Third World wants: An interpretation of the development and meaning of the New International Economic Order ideology." In Paul F. Diehl (Ed.), *The politics of international organizations* (pp. 226–41). Chicago: Dorsey Press.

Murphy, J. Carter. (1979). *The international monetary system: Beyond the first state of reform.* Washington, D.C.: American Enterprise Institute.

Myers, Kenneth A. (Ed.). (1980). *NATO: The next thirty years.* Boulder, CO: Westview Press.

Myers, Robert J. (1989). "The Carnegie poll on values in American foreign policy." *Ethnics & International Affairs, 3*, 297–302.

Nelsen, Harvey W. (1989). *Power and insecurity: Beijing, Moscow, and Washington, 1949–1988.* Boulder, CO: Lynne Rienner Publishers.

Neuberger, Benjamin. (1986). *National self-determination in post-colonial Africa.* Boulder, CO: Lynne Rienner Publishers.

Neuchterlein, Donald E. (1979). "The concept of national interest: A time for new approaches." *Orbis, 23*, 73–94.

Newson, David D. (1987). *Private diplomacy with the Soviet Union.* Lanham, MD: University of America Press.

Nicholson, Harold. (1979). "Transition from the old to the new diplomacy." In Elmer Plischke (Ed.), *Modern diplomacy: The art and the artisans.* Washington, D.C.: American Enterprise Institute.

Nincic, Miroslav. (1983). "Fluctuations in Soviet defense spending." *Journal of Conflict Resolution, 27*, 648–60.

Nincic, Miroslav. (1988). *United States foreign policy: Choices and tradeoffs.* Washington, D.C.: Congressional Quarterly Press.

Niou, Emerson M. S., Ordeshook, Peter C., & Rose, Gregory F. (1989). *The balance of power: Stability in international systems.* Cambridge, U.K.: Cambridge University Press.

Nixon, Richard M. (1978). *RN: The memoirs of Richard Nixon.* New York: Grosset & Dunlap.

Nixon, Richard M. (1980). *The real war.* New York: Warner Books.

Nixon, Richard M. (1985). "Superpower summitry." *Foreign Affairs, 64*, 1–11.

Nixon, Richard M. (1988, March 13). "Dealing with Gorbachev." *New York Times Magazine*, pp. 26–30, 66, 78–79.

Nogee, Joseph L., & Spanier, John. (1988). *Peace impossible—war unlikely: The cold war between the United States and the Soviet Union.* Glenville, IL: Scott, Foresman.

Nossal, Kim Richard. (1989). "International sanctions as international punishment." *International Organization, 43*, 301–22.

Nueman, Stephanie G. (1989). "The arms market: Who's on top?" *Orbis, 33*, 509–30.

Nye, Joseph S., Jr. (1986). *Nuclear ethics.* New York: The Free Press.

Nye, Joseph S., Jr. (1988). "Neorealism and neoliberalism." *World Politics, 40*, 235–51.

Nye, Joseph S., Jr. (1990). "The changing nature of world power." *Political Science Quarterly, 105*, 177–92.

O'Brien, William V. (1981). *The conduct of just and limited war.* New York: Praeger.

Officer, Lawrence H. (1990). "The International Monetary Fund." *Academy of Political Science, 37,* 28–36.

O'Leary, Greg. (1980). *The shaping of Chinese foreign policy.* New York: St. Martin's Press.

Oliver, Roland, & Atmore, Anthony. (1981). *The African middle ages, 1400–1800.* Cambridge, U.K.: Cambridge University Press.

Olmer, Lionel H. (1989). "Statement on EC 1992 and the requirement for U.S. industry and government partnership." *Europe 1992.* Hearings before the U.S. Congress, House of Representatives, Subcommittee on Trade of the Committee on Ways and Means. March 20, 1989: 128–35.

Olsen, Edward. (1987). "A case for strategic 'protectionism.' " *Strategic Review, 15*(4), 63–69.

Oneal, John R. (1988). "The rationality of decision-making during international crises." *Polity, 20,* 598–622.

Oren, Ido. (1990). "The war proneness of alliances." *Journal of Conflict Resolution, 34,* 208–33.

Orme, John. (1987). Deterrence failures: A second look. *International Security, 11,* 97–124.

Ostrom, Charles W., & Aldrich, H. J. (1978). "The relationship between size and stability in the major power international system." *American Journal of Political Science, 22,* 743–71.

Ostrom, Charles W., & Marra, Robin F. (1986). "U.S. defense spending and the Soviet estimate." *American Political Science Review, 60,* 821–42.

Paige, Glenn D. (1958). *The Korean decision, June 24–30, 1950.* New York: The Free Press.

Paige, Glenn D. (1972). "Comparative case analysis of crises decisions: Korea and Cuba." In Charles F. Hermann (Ed.), *International crises: Insights from behavioral research* (pp. 41–55). New York: The Free Press.

Panofsky, Wolfgang K. H. (1986). "Arms control: Necessary process." *Bulletin of the Atomic Scientists, 42* (March), 35–38.

Papp, Daniel S. (1990, July). "Changes in Soviet thinking on security and military strategy: Their implications for NATO." Paper presented to the Senior Academics Conference on East-West Security, NATO/Paul Loebe Institute, Berlin.

Paterson, Thomas G. (Ed.). (1989). *Major problems in American foreign policy, Volume I: To 1914* (3rd ed.). Lexington, MA: D. C. Heath.

Paterson, Thomas G., & Brophy, William J. (1986). "October missiles and November election: The Cuban missile crisis and American politics." *Journal of American History, 73,* 87–119.

Paterson, Thomas G., Clifford, J. Gary, & Hagan, Kenneth J. (1983). *American foreign policy: A history, Vol. II: Since 1900.* Lexington, MA: D. C. Heath.

Paxton, John. (Ed.). (1990). *The statesman's year-book, 1989–1990.* New York: St. Martin's Press. (Published annually).

Peebles, Curtis. (1983). *Battle for space.* New York: Beaufort Books.

Pentland, Charles. (1989). "International organizations and their roles." In Paul F. Diehl (Ed.), *The politics of international organizations* (pp. 5–14). Chicago: Dorsey Press.

Pepes, Daniel. (1984). "Understanding Islam in politics." *Middle East Review, 16,* 3–15.

Peretz, Don. (1990). *Intifada: The Palestinian uprising.* Boulder, CO: Westview Press.

Perkins, Ray, Jr. (1991). *The ABCs of the Soviet-American nuclear arms race.* Pacific Grove, CA: Brooks/Cole.

Perry, Clive. (1968). "The function of law in the international community." In Max Sorensen (Ed.), *Manual of public international law.* New York: St. Martin's Press.

Petraeus, David H. (1989). "Military influence and the post-Vietnam use of force." *Armed Forces and Society, 15,* 489–506.

Pettman, Jan. (1979). "Race, conflict and liberation in Africa." In Jan Pettman (Ed.), *Moral claims in world affairs* (pp. 131–46). New York: St. Martin's Press.

Pickles, Dorothy. (1968). "French foreign policy." In F. S. Northedge (Ed.), *The foreign policy of the powers.* New York: Praeger.

Pilat, Joseph F., & Pendley, Robert E. (Eds.). (1990). *Beyond 1995: The future of the NPT regime.* New York: Plenum Press.

Pilon, Juliana Geran. (1988, September/October). "Becoming part of the problem." *Society,* pp. 4–11.

Piscatori, James. (1984). *Islam in a world of nation-states.* New York: Cambridge University Press.

Plischke, Elmer. (1979). "The new diplomacy." In Elmer Plischke (Ed.), *Modern diplomacy: The art and the artisans.* Washington, D.C.: American Enterprise Institute.

Pollins, Brian M. (1990). "Does trade still follow the flag?" *American Political Science Review, 83,* 465–80.

Pomfret, Richard. (1989). "Ten years of direct foreign investment in China." *Asian Perspective, 13,* 35–53.

Preston, Samuel H. (1990). Preface to *world population: Approaching the year 2000.* In *the Annals of the American Academy of Political and Social Science, 510,* 1–12.

Putnam, Robert D. (1988). "Diplomacy and domestic politics: The logic of two-level games." *International Organization, 42,* 427–60.

Ramati, Yohanan. (1989, April). "A PLO state and Israel's security." *Midstream, 35,* 3–6.

Rappaport, David C. (1988). "Messianic sanctions for terror." *Comparative Politics, 20,* 195–214.

Rasler, Karen A., & Thompson, William R. (1983). "Global war, public debts, and the long cycle." *World Politics, 25,* 489–516.

Rasler, Karen A., & Thompson, William R. (1988). "Defense burdens, capital formation, and economic growth: The systemic leader case." *Journal of Conflict Resolution, 32,* 61–86.

Rathjens, George W., & Reed, Laura. (1986). "Neither MAD nor starstruck—and doubts, too, about arms control." Unpublished paper, Defense and Arms Control Studies Program, MIT.

Rattinger, Hans. (1990, April). "Foreign policy vs. domestic issues as determinants of voting behavior in the 1988 presidential election." Paper presented to the International Studies Association convention, Washington, D.C.

Ray, James Lee. (1989). "The abolition of slavery and the end of international war." *International Organization, 43,* 405–40.

Reagan, Ronald. (1984, May). "A historic opportunity for the U.S. and China." Speech to Chinese Leaders, Beijing, China, April 27, 1984. In *Realism, strength, negotiation: Key foreign policy statements of the Reagan administration.* Washington, D.C.: Bureau of Public Affairs, U.S. Department of State.

Reagan, Ronald W. (1990). *An American life.* New York: Simon & Schuster. The quotes herein are from excerpts published in *Time* magazine in its editions of November 5, 1990 (pp. 60–75) and November 12, 1990 (pp. 64–79).

Reich, Robert B. (1983). "Beyond free trade." *Foreign Affairs, 61*, 77–92.

Reilly, John E. (Ed.). (1987). *American public opinion and U.S. foreign policy 1987.* Chicago: Chicago Council on Foreign Relations.

Reisman, W. Michael. (1989). "The Arafat visa affair: Exceeding the bounds of host state discretion." *American Journal of International Law, 83*, 519–26.

Reiss, Mitchell. (1988). *Without the bomb: The politics of nuclear nonproliferation.* New York: Columbia University Press.

Rejai, Mostafa, & Enloe, Cynthia H. (1979). "Nation-states and state nations." In Fred A. Sondermann, David S. McLellan, & William C. Olson (Eds.), *The theory and practice of international relations.* Englewood Cliffs, NJ: Prentice Hall.

Remmer, Karen L. (1986). "The politics of economic stabilization: IMF standby programs in Latin America, 1954–1984." *Comparative Politics, 19*, 1–24.

Remmer, Karen L. (1990). "Democracy and economic crisis: The Latin American experience." *World Politics, 42*, 315–335.

Renan, Ernest. (1964). "Qu'est-ce qu'une Nation?." In Louis L. Snyder (Ed.), *The dynamics of nationalism.* New York: D. Van Norstrand.

Renninger, John P. (Ed.). (1989). *The future role of the United Nations in an interdependent world.* Dordrecht, the Netherlands: Marinus Nijhoff.

Renteln, Allison Dundes. (1990). *International human rights: Universalism versus relativism.* Newbury Park, CA: Sage Publications.

Repetto, Robert. (1979). *Economic equality and fertility in developing countries.* Baltimore, MD: Johns Hopkins University Press.

Riccards, Michael P. (1977). "The presidency in sickness and health." *Presidential Studies Quarterly, 7*, 223–31.

Rice, Donald. (1990). "The manned bomber and strategic deterrence: The U.S. Air Force perspective." *International Security, 15*, 100–128.

Richardson, J. L. (1988). "New perspectives on appeasement: Some implications for international relations." *World Politics, 40*, 289–316.

Riddell, Roger C. (1987). *Foreign aid reconsidered.* Baltimore: The Johns Hopkins University Press.

Riggs, Fred W. (1986). "What is ethnic? What is national? Let's turn the tables." *Canadian Review of Studies in Nationalism, 13*, 111–23.

Riggs, Robert E., & Plano, Jack C. (1988). *The United Nations: International organization and world politics.* Chicago: Dorsey Press.

Risse-Kappen, Thomas. (1990, April). "Public opinion, domestic structure, and security policy in liberal democracies: France, Japan, West Germany, and the United States." Paper presented to the International Studies Association convention, Washington, D.C.

Rivlin, Benjamin. (1988). "Changing perspectives on internationalism at the United Nations: The impact of the ideological factor on the Arab-Israeli dispute." *The Jerusalem Journal of International Relations, 10*, 1–11.

Robinson, Joan. (1987). "Trade in primary commodities." In Jeffry A. Freiden and David A. Lake (Eds.), *International Political Economy.* New York: St. Martin's Press.

Robinson, Thomas W. (1969). "National interests." In James N. Rosenau (Ed.), *International politics and foreign policy* (rev. ed., pp. 117–89). New York: Free Press.

Robinson, Thomas W. (1987). "On the further evolution of the strategic triangle." In Ilpyong J. Kim (Ed.), *The strategic triangle: China, the United States, and the Soviet Union.* New York: Paragon House Publishers.

Robock, Alan. (1989). "New models confirm nuclear winter." *The Bulletin of the Atomic Scientists, 44*, 32–35.

Roeder, Philip G. (1987, April). "The two tiers of Soviet foreign policy-making." Paper presented to the International Studies Association, Washington, D.C.

Rogers, Bernard W. (1987, July 14). "Why compromise our deterrent strength in Europe?" *New York Times*, p. A18.

Rogers, J. Phillip. (1987, April). "The crisis bargaining code model: A cognitive schema approach to crisis decision-making." Paper presented to the International Studies Association, Washington, D.C.

Roney, John C. (1982). "Grain embargo as diplomatic lever: A case study of the U.S.-Soviet embargo of 1980–81." In U.S. Congress, Joint Economic Committee, *Soviet Economy in the 1980s*, Part II (97th Cong., 2nd sess.).

Roosa, Robert V., Gutowski, Armin, & Matsuka, Michiya. (1982). *East-West trade at the crossroads.* New York: New York University Press.

Root, Franklin R. (1973). *International trade and investment* (3rd ed.). Cincinnati: South-Western Publishing.

Rose, Richard. (1990). "Is Europe a community?" In *World Politics 90/91* (pp. 58–60), Annual Editions series. Guilford, CT: Dushkin Publishing Group.

Rosecrance, Richard N. (1963). *Action and reaction in world politics.* Boston: Little, Brown.

Rosecrance, Richard N. (1987). "Long cycle and international relations." *International Relations, 41*, 291–95.

Rosenau, James N. (1966). "Pre-theories and theories of foreign policy." In R. Barry Farrell (Ed.), *Approaches to comparative and international politics* (pp. 27–93). Evanston, IL: Northwestern University Press.

Rosenau, James N. (1971). *The scientific study of foreign policy.* New York: Free Press.

Rostow, Walt W. (1978). *The world economy.* Austin: The University of Texas Press.

Rourke, John T. (1971). "National interest: Toward an operational definition." Unpublished paper, Storrs, CT.

Rourke, John T. (1979). "The relationship between voting in the United Nations General Assembly and the International Court of Justice." *International Review of History and Political Science, 16*, 318–27.

Rourke, John T. (1983). *Congress and the presidency in U.S. foreign policymaking: A study of interaction and influence, 1945–1982.* Boulder, CO: Westview Press.

Rourke, John T. (Ed.). (1987). *Taking sides: Clashing views on controversial issues in world politics.* Guilford, CT: Dushkin Publishing Group.

Rourke, John T. (1987a). "Perceptions, the two presidencies thesis, and the Reagan administration." Paper presented to the Northeast Political Science Association, Philadelphia, PA, November, 1987.

Rourke, John T. (1989). *The United States, the Soviet Union, and China.* Chicago: Dorsey Press.

Rourke, John T. (1990). *Making foreign policy: United States, Soviet Union, China.* Pacific Grove, CA: Brooks/Cole.

Rubin, Seymour J., & Graham, Thomas R. (1982). *Environment and trade.* Totowa, NJ: Allanheld, Osmun, & Co.

Rummel, R. J. (1963). "Dimensions of conflict behavior within states and between nations." *General Systems Yearbook,* Vol. 8.

Rummel, R. J. (1976). *The conflict helix.* Vol. 2 of *Understanding conflict and war.* Beverly Hills, CA: Sage.

Rummel, R. J. (1989, November/December). "The politics of cold blood." *Society,* pp. 32–40.

Russett, Bruce M., & Hansen, Elizabeth C. (1975). *Interest and ideology: The foreign policy beliefs of American businessmen.* San Francisco: W. H. Freeman.

Russett, Bruce M., & Starr, Richard. (1981). *World politics: A menu for choice* (2nd ed.). New York: W. H. Freeman & Company.

Sadler, Todd, & Scott, John L. (1987). "Terrorist success in hostage-taking incidents." *Journal of Conflict Resolution, 31,* 35–53.

Salvatore, Dominick. (1987). *The new protectionism: Threat to world welfare.* Amsterdam: North-Holland.

Sanders, David, Ward, Hugh, & Marsh, David, with Fletcher, Tony. (1987). "Government popularity and the Falklands war: A reassessment." *British Journal of Political Science, 17,* 281–313.

Sanford, Jonathan E. (1983). *U.S. foreign policy and multilateral development banks.* Boulder, CO: Westview Press.

Sargeant, Lyman Tower. (1990). *Contemporary political ideologies: A comparative analysis* (8th ed.). Pacific Grove, CA: Brooks/Cole.

Scarborough, Grace Iusi. (1988). "Polarity, power, and risk in international disputes." *Journal of Conflict Resolution, 32,* 511–33.

Schaetzel, J. Robert, & Malgren, H. B. (1980). "Talking heads." *Foreign Policy,* No. 39, 130–42.

Schear, James A. (1985). "Arms control treaty compliance: Buildup to a breakdown." *International Security, 10,* 141–82.

Scheer, Robert. (1982). *With enough shovels.* New York: Random House.

Schelling, Thomas C. (1966). *Arms and influence.* New Haven, Ct: Yale Unversity Press.

Schlesinger, Arthur M., Jr. (1967). *A thousand days: John F. Kennedy in the White House.* Greenwich, CT: Fawcett Publications.

Schlesinger, Arthur M., Jr. (1973). "Morality and international politics." In Frederick Hartmann (Ed.), *Moral claims in world affairs* (4th ed.). New York: Macmillan.

Schmidt, Helmut. (1987, April 29). "If the missiles go, peace may stay." *New York Times,* p. A16.

Schroeer, Dietrich. (1984). *Science, technology, and the arms race.* New York: John Wiley & Sons.

Schuman, Frederick L. (1969). *International politics* (4th ed.). New York: McGraw-Hill. (Original work published 1933).

Schwartz, Frederick A. O. (1965). *Nigeria: The tribes, the nation, or the race—Problems of independence.* Cambridge, MA: MIT Press.

Scolnick, Joseph M. (1988). Letter to the author, April 22, 1988.

Scribner, Richard A., Ralston, Theodore J., & Metz, William D. (1985). *The verification challenge.* Boston: Birkhäuser.

Sederberg, Peter C. (1989). *Terrorist myths: Illusion, rhetoric, and reality.* Englewood Cliffs, NJ: Prentice Hall.

Sefan, Charles G. (1987). "The ups and downs of summitry." *Foreign Service Journal, 64*(10), 29–31.

Segal, Aaron. (1990). "Managing the world economy." *International Political Science Review, 11,* 361–69.

Segal, Gerald. (1989). "China, the Pacific, and the balance of power." *Jerusalem Journal of International Relations, 11,* 121–38.

Segal, Ronald. (1979). *Leon Trotsky.* New York: Pantheon Books.

Seldes, George H. (1970). *Sawdust caesar: The untold story of Mussolini and Fascism.* New York: AMS Press. (Original work published 1935).

Sensi, Luigi. (1988, April). "Superpower interventions in civil war, 1945–1987." Paper presented to the International Studies Association, St. Louis, MO.

Servan-Schreiber, Jean-Jacques. (1968). *The American challenge.* New York: Atheneum.

Shafer, Boyd C. (1972). *The faces of nationalism.* New York: Harcourt Brace Jovanovich.

Shafer, D. Michael (1990). *Deadly paradigms: The failure of U.S. counterinsurgency policy.* Princeton, NJ: Princeton University Press.

Shakhnazarov, Goergi. (1989). " 'Questions of theory': The world community is amenable to government." *Alternatives, 14,* 245–57.

Shambaugh, David L. (1988). "Anti-Americanism in China." *The Annals of the American Academy of Political and Social Science, 497,* 142–56.

Shapiro, Robert T., & Page, Benjamin I. (1988). "Foreign policy and the rational public." *Journal of Conflict Resolution, 32,* 211–47.

Shaw, R. Paul, & Wong, Yuwa. (1987). "Ethnic mobilization and the seeds of warfare: An evolutionary perspective." *International Studies Quarterly, 31,* 5–31.

Shelley, Louise L. (1989). "Human rights as an international issue." *Annals of the American Academy of Political and Social Science, 506,* 42–56.

Shepard, Graham H. (1988). "Personality effects on American foreign policy, 1969–84: A second test of interpersonal generalization theory." *International Studies Quarterly, 32,* 91–123.

Shepard, William E. (1987). "Islam and ideology: Towards a typology." *International Journal of Middle East Studies, 19,* 307–36.

Sherill, Robert. (1979). *Why they call it politics.* New York: Harcourt Brace Jovanovich.

Shestack, Jerome J. (1989). "Human rights, the national interest, and U.S. foreign policy." *Annals of the American Academy of Political and Social Science, 506,* 17–29.

Shevchenko, Arkady. (1985). *Breaking with Moscow.* New York: Alfred A. Knopf.

Shlapentokh, Vladimir. (1988). "The changeable Soviet image of America." *The Annals of the American Academy of Political and Social Science, 497,* 157–71.

Shue, Henry (Ed.). (1989). *Nuclear deterrence and moral restraint.* Cambridge, U.K.: Cambridge University Press.

Shultz, George. (1985, December). "Morality and realism in American policy." *Department of State Bulletin.*

Sigelman, Lee. (1979). "A reassessment of the two presidencies thesis." *Journal of Politics, 41,* 1197–1208.

Simes, Dimitri K. "Gorbachev: A new foreign policy?" *Foreign Affairs, 65,* 477–502.

Simon, Herbert A. (1959). *Administrative behavior.* New York: Macmillian.

Simon, Julian. (1983, August). "Life is getting better, not worse." *The Futurist,* pp. 14–18.

Simonds, Frank H. (1939). *The great power in world politics.* New York: American Book Company.

Simowitz, Roslyn L. (1983). *The logical consistency and soundness of the balance of power theory.* Monograph Series in World Affairs, Vol. 19 (Book 3). Denver: Graduate School, The University of Denver.

Simpson, James B. (1988). *Simpson's contemporary quotations.* Boston: Houghton Mifflin.

Singer, J. David. (1969). "The level-of-analysis problem." In James N. Rosenau (Ed.), *International poltics and foreign policy.* New York: Free Press.

Singh, Nagendra. (1989). *The role and record of the International Court of Justice.* Dordrecht, the Netherlands: Martinus Nijhoff.

(SIPRI) Stockholm International Peace Research Institute. (1987, 1990). *SIPRI Yearbook* (annual). Oxford, U.K.: Oxford University Press.

Sivard, Ruth Leger. (1986). *World military and social expenditures.* Washington, D.C.: World Priorities. (Published annually).

Siverson, Randolph M., & Emmons, Juliann. (1990, April). "Birds of a feather: Democratic political systems and alliance choices in the twentieth century." Paper presented to the International Studies Association convention, Washington, D.C.

Siverson, Randolph M., & Starr, Harvey. (1989). "Opportunity, willingness, and the diffusion of war." *American Political Science Review, 84,* 47–68.

Siverson, Randolph M., & Sullivan, Michael. (1984). "A new examination of an old problem." *Journal of Conflict Management and Peace Science, 8,* 1–13.

Sloan, Robert D. (1988). "The Third World debt crisis: Where we have been and where we are going." *The Washington Quarterly, 11*(1), 103–17.

Small, Melvin. (1988). *Johnson, Nixon, and the doves.* New Brunswick, NJ: Rutgers University Press.

Smith, Anthony D. S. (1971). *Theories of nationalism.* London: Duckworth.

Smith, Michael Joseph. (1986). *Realist thought from Weber to Kissinger.* Baton Rouge: Louisiana State University Press.

Smith, Steve. (1984). "Groupthink and the hostage rescue mission." *British Journal of Political Science, 15,* 117–26.

Smith, Steve. (1985). "Policy preferences and bureaucratic position: The case of the American hostage rescue mission." *International Affairs* (London), *61,* 9–26.

Snidal, Duncan. (1988). "IGOs, regimes, and cooperation: Challenges for international relations theory." In Margaret P. Karns & Karen A. Mingst (Eds.). *The United States and multilateral institutions* (pp. 123–46). Boston: Unwin Hyman.

Snider, Lewis W., & Beringer, Julia. (1990, April). "Does defense spending begger welfare: A cross-sectional poll time series analysis of 18 industrial democracies." Paper presented to the International Studies Association convention, Washington, D.C.

Snow, Donald M. (1980). "Lasers, charged-particle beams, and the strategic future." *Political Science Quarterly, 95,* 227–94.

Snow, Donald M. (1987). *National security: Enduring problems of U.S. defense policy.* New York: St. Martin's Press.

Snyder, Jack. (1990). "Averting anarchy in the new Europe." *International Security, 14,* 5–41.

Snyder, Louis L. (1964). *Dynamics of nationalism.* New York: D. Van Norstrand.

Snyder, Louis L. (1977). *Varieties of nationalism.* Hinsdale, IL: Dryden Press.

Snyder, Louis L. (1990). *Encyclopedia of nationalism.* New York: Paragon House.

Sondermann, Fred A. (1977). "The concept of national interest." *Orbis, 21,* 121–34.

Spanier, John, & Uslander, Eric M. (1985). *American foreign policy making and the democratic dilemmas* (4th ed.). New York: Holt, Rinehart, & Winston.

Spector, Leonard S. (1987). *Going nuclear.* Cambridge, MA: Ballinger.

Spector, Leonard S., with Smith, Jacqueline R. (1990). *Nuclear ambitions: The spread of nuclear weapons 1989–1990.* Boulder, CO: Westview Press.

Spero, Jane Edelman. (1985). *The politics of international economic relations* (3rd ed.). New York: St. Martin's Press.

Spykman, Nicholas. (1944). *Geography of peace.* New York: Harcourt, Brace.

Ståhlberg, Krister. (1987). "Public opinion in Finnish foreign policy." *Yearbook of Finnish foreign policy, 1987* (pp. 17–25). Helsinki: Finnish Political Science Association.

Starr, Harvey. (1984). *Henry Kissinger: Perceptions of international politics.* Lexington: The University of Kentucky Press.

Stavrianos, L. S. (1981). *Global rift: The Third World comes of age.* New York: William Morrow.

Stefan, Charles. (1987). "The ups and downs of summitry." *Foreign Service Journal* (U.S.), *64*(10), 29–31.

Stein, Arthur. (1976). "Conflict and cohesion: A review of the literature." *Journal of Conflict Resolution, 29,* 143–72.

Sterling, Richard W. (1974). *Macropolitics: Foreign relations in a global society*. New York: Knopf.

Steward, Frances, & Sengupta, Arjun. (1982). *International financial cooperation*. Boulder, CO: Westview Press.

Stewart, Phillip D., Hermann, Margaret, & Hermann, Charles F. (1989). "Modeling the 1973 Soviet decision to support Egypt." *American Political Science Review, 83*, 35–60.

Stockholm International Peace Research Institute. *See* (SIPRI).

Stoessinger, John G. (1965). *The United Nations and the superpowers*. New York: Random House.

Stoessinger, John G. (1979). *Crusaders and pragmatists: Movers of American foreign policy*. New York: Norton.

Stoll, Richard J. (1987). "The sound of guns: Is there a congressional rally effect after U.S. military action?" *American Politics Quarterly, 15*, 223–37.

Stoll, Richard J., & Ward, Michael D. (Eds.). (1989). *Power in world politics*. Boulder, CO: Lynne Rienner Publishers.

Strange, Susan. (1989). "*Cave hic dragones*: A critique of regime analysis." In Paul F. Diehl (Ed.), *The politics of international organizations* (pp. 51–65). Chicago: Dorsey Press.

Stremlau, John M. (1977). *The international politics of the Nigerian Civil War, 1967–1970*. Princeton, NJ: Princeton University Press.

Subrahmanyam, K. (1986). "Regional conflicts and nuclear fears." In Herbert M. Levine & David Carlton (Eds.), *The nuclear arms race debated* (pp. 344–49). New York: McGraw-Hill.

Suganami, Hidemi. (1989). *The domestic analogy and world order proposals*. New York: Cambridge University Press.

Sukovic, Olga. (1982). "Non-proliferation and developing countries." In David Carlton & Carlo Schaerf (Eds.), *The arms race in the 1980s*. New York: St. Martin's Press.

Sullivan, John D. (1964). "International alliances." In Michael Haas (Ed.), *International systems*. New York: Chandler.

Symmons-Symonolewicz, Konstantin. (1985). "The concept of nationhood: Toward a theoretical clarification." *Canadian Review of Studies in Nationalism, 12*, 215–22.

Taber, Charles S. (1989). "Power capability indexes in the Third World." In Richard J. Stoll & Martin D. Ward, *Power in world politics*. (pp. 29–48). Boulder, CO: Lynne Rienner Publishers.

Taylor, Paul. (1978). "Confederalism: The case of the European Communities." In Paul Taylor & A. J. R. Groom (Eds.), *International organization: A conceptual approach*. London: Francis Printer.

Tétreault, Mary Ann. (1988). "Regimes and liberal world orders." *Alternatives, 13*, 5–26.

Thakur, Ramesh. (1987). "International peacekeeping, U.N. authority, and U.S. power alternatives." *Alternatives, 12*, 461–92.

Thayer, Nathaniel B., & Weiss, Stephen E. (1987). "Japan: The changing logic of a former minor power." In Hans Binnendijk (Ed.), *National negotiating styles*. A study by the Center for the Study of Foreign Affairs. Washington, D.C.: Foreign Service Institute, U.S. Department of State.

Thee, Mark. (1987). "Military technology, arms control, and human development." *Bulletin of Peace Proposals, 18*, 1–11.

Thompson, James C. Jr., (1989). "Historical legacies and bureaucratic procedures." In Thomas G. Paterson (Ed.), *Major problems in American foreign policy* (Vol. II, pp. 589–98). Lexington, MA: D. C. Heath.

Thompson, Janice E. (1990). "State practices, international norms, and the decline of mercenarism." *International Studies Quarterly, 34*, 23–47.

Thompson, Kenneth W. (1966). *Moral issues and statecraft*. Baton Rouge: Louisiana State University Press.

Thompson, Kenneth W. (1984). "The ethical dimensions of diplomacy." *Review of Politics, 46*, 379–92.

Thompson, William R. (1986). "Polarity, the long cycle, and global power warfare." *Journal of Conflict Resolution, 30*, 587–615.

Thompson, William R. (1988). *On global war: Historical structural approaches to world politics*. Columbia, SC: University of South Carolina Press.

Thompson, William R. (1990). "Long waves, technological innovation, and relative decline." *International Organization, 44*, 201–34.

Throdarson, B. (1972). *Trudeau and foreign policy*. Toronto, Canada: Oxford University Press.

Tomasevski, Katarina. (1989). *Development aid and human rights*. New York: St. Martin's Press.

Tunkin, Gregory I. (1974). *Theory of international law* (W. E. Butler, Trans.). Cambridge, MA: Harvard University Press.

Turco, R. P., Toon, O. B., Ackerman, T. P., Pollack, J.B., & Sagan, C. (1990). "Climate and smoke: An appraisal of nuclear winter." *Science, 247*, 166–74.

Turner, James A. (1990). "Power and economic data booklet." Unpublished manuscript generously supplied by the author. Colorado Springs, CO.

Turner, Robert F. (1988). "International law, the use of force, and reciprocity: A comment on Professor Higgins' overview." *The Atlantic Community Quarterly, 25*, 160–74.

Tussell, Javier. (1988). "The transition to democracy and Spain's membership in NATO." In Frederico G. Gil & Joseph S. Tulchin (Eds.), *Spain's entry into NATO: Conflicting political and strategic perspectives* (pp. 218–46). Boulder, CO: Lynne Rienner Publishers.

Ulam, Adam. (1979). *The unfinished revolution: Marxism and communism in the modern world*. Boulder, Co: Westview Press.

(UN) United Nations. (1986). *Demographic Yearbook, 1985*. New York.

(UN) United Nations. (1987). *World Economic Survey, 1987*. New York.

(UN) United Nations. (1988). *Monthly Bulletin of Statistics* (1988, May). New York.

(UN) United Nations. (1990a). *Demographic yearbook, 1988*.

(UN) United Nations. (1990b). UN Statistical Office, *Monthly Bulletin of Statistics, 44* (August 1990).

(UN) United Nations. (1990c). UN Statistical Office, *Monthly Bulletin of Statistics 44* (October 1990).

(UN) United Nations. (1990d). *World economic survey, 1990*.

(UN) United Nations. (1990e). *The blue helmets: A review of United Nations peace-keeping*.

(UN, FAO) United Nations Food and Agricultural Organization. (1989). *Yearbook, 1988*. New York.

(UNCTAD) United Nations Conference on Trade and Development. (1990). *Handbook of international trade and development statistics, 1989*.

(UNIDO) United Nations Industrial Development Organization. (1989). *Industry and development: Global report 1989/90.* Vienna.

Union of International Associations. (1990). *Yearbook of international organizations 1990/91.* Volume 2. New York: K. G. Saur München.

United Nations. *See* (UN).

Untawale, Mukund G. (1990). "Global environmental degradation and international organizations." *International Political Science Review, 11,* 371–83.

U.S. (ACDA) Arms Control and Disarmament Agency. (1987, April). *World Military Expenditures and Arms Transfers, 1986* (ACDA Publication No. 127). Washington, D.C.

U.S. (ACDA) Arms Control and Disarmament Agency. (1988, January 3). *Arms Control Update* (No. 3). Washington, D.C.

U.S. Advisory Commission on Public Diplomacy. (1986). *1986 report.* Washington, D.C.

U.S. (AID) Agency for International Development. (1987). *Highlights, 4*(3), 1. Washington, D.C.

U.S. (AID) U.S. Agency for International Development. (1990). *Development and the national interest.* Washington, D.C.

U.S. Bureau of Mines. (1990). *Mineral commodity summaries 1990.*

U.S. (CIA) Central Intelligence Agency. (1986, September). *The Soviet weapons industry: An overview* (DI 86–10016). Washington, D.C.

U.S. (CIA) Central Intelligence Agency. (1989). *Handbook of economic statistics, 1989.* Washington, D.C.

U.S. Congress, Senate Committee on Armed Services. (1980). *Recent false alerts from the nation's missile attack warning system* (Report, 96th Cong., 2nd sess). Washington, D.C.

U.S. Council on Environmental Quality, & U.S. Department of State. (1980). *The global 2000 report to the president.* Washington, D.C.

U.S. Department of Commerce. (1990). *Statistical abstract of the United States, 1990.*

U.S. Department of Commerce. (1990a). *Survey of current business, 70* (September 1990).

U.S. Department of Defense. (1983). *Annual Report to Congress, Fiscal Year 1983.* Washington, D.C.

U.S. Department of Defense. (1987). *Soviet Military Power, 1987.* Washington, D.C.

U.S. Department of Energy. (1989). *Annual Energy Review 1989.*

U.S. Department of State. (1979). *SALT II and American security.* Washington, D.C.

U.S. Department of State. (1984). *Realism, strength, negotiation: Foreign policy statements of the Reagan administration.* Washington, D.C.

U.S. Department of State. (1985). *Atlas of United States foreign relations* (2nd ed.). Washington, D.C.

U.S. Department of State. (1985a). *Patterns of Global Terrorism: 1985.* Washington, D.C.

U.S. Department of State. (1988). *United States contributions to international organizations, FY 1988.* 37th Annual Report to Congress.

U.S. Department of State. (1990). *Patterns of global terrorism.* Washington, D.C.

U.S. Department of State. (1990a, March 11). *Report to the Congress on voting practices in the United Nations, 1989.*

U.S. Department of State. (1990b). "America's stand against aggression." Address of George Bush to Veterans of Foreign Wars, August 20, 1990. *Current Policy* (Bulletin), No. 1294.

U.S. General Accounting Office. (1986, August). *Export Controls: Assessment of the Commerce Department's Foreign Policy Report to Congress* (GAO/NSIAD-86-172). Washington, D.C.

U.S. House Committee on Foreign Affairs. (1979). *Soviet diplomacy and negotiating behavior.* A study prepared by the Congressional Research Service, Washington, D.C.

U.S. House Committee on Ways and Means. (1985). *Trade emergency and export promotion act.* Testimony of Clayton Yeutter, U.S. Trade Representative (99th Cong., 1st sess). Washington, D.C.

U.S. Office of Technology Assessment. (1979). *The effects of nuclear war.* Washington, D.C.

U.S. President. (1990). *Economic report of the president.* Transmitted to the Congress February, 1990.

U.S. President's Commission on Industrial Competitiveness. (1985). *Global competition: The new reality* (Vol. I). The Report of the President's Commission on Industrial Competitiveness. Washington, D.C.

U.S. Senate Foreign Relations Committee. (1983). *The premises of East-West commercial relations* (Workshop, 98th Cong., 1st sess).

Valenta, Jiri. (1979). *Soviet intervention in Czechoslovakia, 1968.* Baltimore: The Johns Hopkins University Press.

Vance, Cyrus. (1983). *Hard choices.* New York: Simon & Schuster.

Vance, Cyrus. (1986). "The human rights imperative." *Foreign Policy, 63,* 3–18.

Vasquez, John A. (1987). "The steps to war: Toward a scientific explanation of correlates of war findings." *World Politics, 40,* 108–45.

Vernon, Raymond. (Ed.). (1970). *The technology factors in international trade.* New York: National Bureau of Economic Research.

Vernon, Raymond. (1990). "European Community 1992: Can the U.S. negotiate trade equality?" *American national interest: Virtue and power in foreign policy.* Westport, CT: Praeger.

Waldheim, Kurt. (1984). "The United Nations: The tarnished image." *Foreign Affairs, 63,* 93–107.

Waldron, Arthur N. (1985). "Theories of nationalism and historical explanation." *World Politics, 37,* 416–41.

Waler, William, & Lonnroth, Mans. (1984). "Proliferation and nuclear trade." *Bulletin of the Atomic Scientists, 40* (April), 29–33.

Walker, Stephen G. (1987). "Role theory and the origins of foreign policy." In Charles F. Hermann, Charles W. Kegley, Jr., & James N. Rosenau (Eds.), *New directions in the study of foreign policy* (pp. 269–84). Boston: Allen & Unwin.

Wallerstein, Immanuel. (1976). *The modern world system.* New York: Academic Press.

Waltz, Kenneth N. (1959). *Man, the state, and war.* New York: Columbia University Press.

Wang, Kevin, & Ray, James Lee. (1990, April). "The initiation and outcome of international wars involving great powers, 1495–1985." Paper presented to the International Studies Association convention, Washington, D.C.

Watson, William G. (1988). "The case of the disputed benefit: A reply to Tim Hazledine." *Canadian Public Policy, 14*, 214–21.

Wayman, Frank Whelon. (1989, April). "Power shifts and war." Paper presented to the International Studies Association convention, London.

Weinstein, Edwin A. (1981). *Woodrow Wilson: A medical and psychological biography.* Princeton, NJ: Princeton University Press.

Weisbrodt, David. (1987). "Humanitarian law in armed conflict: The role of international nongovernmental organizations." *Journal of Peace Research, 24*, 297–306.

Weiss, Thomas G. (1982). "International bureaucracy: Myth and reality of the international civil service." *International Affairs, 58*, 286–306.

Weiss, Thomas G. (1986). *Multilateral development diplomacy in UNCTAD.* New York: St. Martin's Press.

Weiss, Thomas G., & Kessler, Meryl. (1990, Summer). "Moscow's U.N. policy." *Foreign Affairs,* No. 79, 94–112.

Welch, David A. (1989). "Crisis decision making reconsidered." *Journal of Conflict Resolution, 33,* 430–45.

Wesson, Robert. (1990). *International relations in transition.* Englewood Cliffs, NJ: Prentice Hall.

White, Ralph K. (1971). "Propaganda: Morally questionable and morally unquestionable techniques." *Annals of the American Academy of Political and Social Science,* No. 398, 26–35.

Whitehead, John C. (1987, December). "Third World dilemma: More debt or more equity." *Department of State Bulletin,* pp. 54–56.

Wiarda, Howard J. (1990). *Foreign policy without illusion.* Glenview, IL: Scott, Foresman/Little, Brown.

Wight, Martin. (1987a). "Powers: A philosophical and historical perspective." In William C. Olson (Ed.), *The theory and practice of international relations* (7th ed., pp. 17–21). Englewood Cliffs, NJ: Prentice Hall.

Wight, Martin. (1987b). "Nine variations of the balance of power." In William C. Olson (Ed.), *The theory and practice of international relations* (7th ed.). Englewood Cliffs, NJ: Prentice Hall.

Wildavsky, Aaron. (1966). The two presidencies. *Trans-Action, 4,* 7–14.

Wilkenfield, Jonathan. (1976). "Domestic and foreign conflict behavior of nations." In William D. Coplin & Charles W. Kegley, Jr. (Eds.), *Analyzing international relations.* New York: Praeger.

Wilkinfield, Jonathan, & Brecher, Michael. (1984). "International crises, 1945–1975: The UN dimension." *International Studies Quarterly, 28,* 45–62.

Wilkenfield, Jonathan, & Zinnes, Dina. (1971). "An analysis of conflict behavior." In Wolfram F. Hanrieder (Ed.), *Comparative Foreign policy.* New York: McKay.

Williams, Douglas. (1987). *The specialized agencies and the United Nations: The system in crisis.* New York: St. Martin's Press.

Williams, Phil. (1976). *Crisis management.* New York: Wiley.

Wilson, Heather A. (1988). *International law and the use of force by national liberation movements.* Oxford, U.K.: Clarendon Press.

Wise, Kenneth L. (1990, July). "The future role of alliances: Balance, coalition, good feelings, or geostrategy?" Paper presented to the Senior Academics Conference on East-West Security, NATO/Paul Loebe Institute, Berlin.

Wittkopf, Eugene R. (1987). "Elites and masses: Another look at attitudes toward America's world role." *International Studies Quarterly, 31,* 131–60.

Wolfers, Arnold. (1969). "The pole of power and the pole of indifference." In James N. Rosenau (Ed.), *International relations and foreign policy.* New York: Free Press.

Woodward, Bob. (1987). *Veil: The secret wars of the CIA, 1981–1987.* New York: Simon & Schuster.

World Almanac & Book of Facts, 1988. New York: Pharos Books.

World Almanac & Book of Facts, 1990. New York: Pharos Books.

World Bank. (1989). Social indicators of development, 1989. Baltimore, MD.: The Johns Hopkins University Press.

World Bank. (1989). *World Development Report, 1989.* New York: Oxford University Press.

World Bank. (1990a). *1988–1989 world debt tables.* Washington, D.C.: World Bank.

World Bank. (1990b). *World tables* (1989–1990 Ed.) Baltimore, MD: Johns Hopkins University Press.

World Resources Institute and International Institute for Environmental Development. (1986). *World Resources, 1986.* New York: Basic Books.

Yankelovich, Daniel, & Doble, John. (1984). "The public mood: Nuclear weapons and the U.S.S.R." *Foreign Affairs, 63,* 38–51.

Yergin, Daniel. (1977). *The shattered peace.* Boston: Houghton Mifflin.

Young, Oren R. (1989). *International cooperation: Building regimes for natural resources and the environment.* Ithaca, NY: Cornell University Press.

Young, Oren R. (1989a). "International regimes: Problems of concept formation." In Paul F. Diehl (Ed.), *The politics of international organizations* (pp. 28–50). Chicago: Dorsey Press.

"Z." (1989). "To the Stalin mausoleum." *Daedaleus,* 295–340.

Zacher, Mark W. (1990). "Toward a theory of international regimes." *Journal of International Affairs, 44,* 139–58.

Zartman, I. William, & Berman, Maureen. (1982). *The practical negotiation.* New Haven, CT: Yale University Press.

Zeigler, Andrew H., Jr. (1987). "The structure of Western European attitudes toward Atlantic co-operation." *British Journal of Political Science, 17,* 457–77.

Ziegler, Charles E. (1988, March). "Political adaptation in Soviet foreign policy: Linkages to domestic politics." Paper presented to the International Studies Association convention, St. Louis, MO.

Zuk, Gary, & Woodbury, Nancy R. (1986). "U.S. defense spending electoral cycles, and Soviet-American relations." *Journal of Conflict Resolution, 30,* 45–68.

Zur, Ofer. (1987). "The psychohistory of warfare: The co-evolution of culture, psyche, and enemy." *Journal of Peace Research, 24,* 125–34.

And in such indexes, although small pricks
To their subsequent volumes, there is seen
The baby figure of the giant mass
Of things to come. . . .
Shakespeare, *Troilus and Cressida*

INDEX

Boldface terms are glossary terms. **Boldface** page numbers refer to the pages in which the terms are defined. Number preceded by T indicates table.

STAFF

Editor   John S. L. Holland
Copy Editor   Robert Mill
Production Manager   Brenda S. Filley
Art Editor   Pamela Carley Petersen
Designers   Harry Rinehart and Charles Vitelli
Typesetting Supervisor Libra Ann Cusack
Typesetter   Juliana Arbo
Editorial Assistant   Diane Barker
Systems Manager   Richard Tietjen
Graphic Assistant   Tom Goddard
Photo Research   Wendy Connal